Jerzy Sołdek, Jerzy Pejaś (Ed.)

ADVANCED COMPUTER SYSTEMS

Eighth International Conference, ACS '2001
Mielno, Poland
October 17-19, 2001
Proceedings

SPRINGER SCIENCE+BUSINEDD MEDIA, LLC

Library of Congress Cataloging-in-Publication Data

A C.I.P. Catalogue record for this book is available
from the Library of Congress.
ISBN 978-1-4613-4635-7   ISBN 978-1-4419-8530-9 (eBook)
DOI 10.1007/978-1-4419-8530-9

Copyright © 2002 by Springer Science+Business Media New York
Originally published by Kluwer Academic Publishers in 2002
Softcover reprint of the hardcover 1st edition 2002
All rights reserved. No part of this publication may be reproduced, stored in a
retrieval system or transmitted in any form or by any means, mechanical, photo-
copying, recording, or otherwise, without the prior written permission of the
publisher, Kluwer Academic Publishers, 101 Philip Drive, Assinippi Park, Norwell,
Massachusetts 02061

Printed on acid-free paper.

ADVANCED COMPUTER SYSTEMS

THE KLUWER INTERNATIONAL SERIES
IN ENGINEERING AND COMPUTER SCIENCE

Table of Contents

Chapter 1
Methods of Artificial Intelligence

Chapter 2
Intelligent Agents and Distributed Activities

Chapter 3
Distributed Production Networks and Modelling Complex Systems

Chapter 4
Computer Graphics and Pattern Recognition

Chapter 5
Computer Security and Safety

Chapter 6
Logic Synthesis and Simulation

Preface

The main aim of Advanced Computer Systems Conference (ACS), organized for the eighth time, is the presentation of the advanced changes and exchange of the experience in the whole field of computer science and engineering. From the first time this conference acts as an international forum for researches and practitioners from academia and industry with a forum to report on the latest developments in advanced computer systems and their applications within the telecommunications and networking, computational intelligence, data visualisation, interactive and collaborative computing, industrial systems, IT security and safety.

This forum is the result of the creative durable cooperation of the following universities and research organizations:

- Faculty of Computer Science and Information Systems, Technical University of Szczecin (Poland),
- University of Technology Troyes (France),
- Ecole Centrale de Lyon (France),
- Albert-Ludwigs University (Germany),
- Belarussian Academy of Sciences (Belarus),
- Electrotechnical University of Sankt Petersburg (Russia),
- Polish Academy of Sciences (Poland),
- State University of Informatics and Radioelectronics (Belarus),
- Saint Francis Xavier University (Canada),
- University of Goettingen (Germany),
- Warsaw University of Technology (Poland),
- STAR- Specialized Training in Aeronautics Research (Merignac, Bordeaux – France).

This book contains the selected papers from ACS'2001 Conference. There were chosen 39 "advanced solutions" between all 81 papers created to Conference. Those 39 papers are organized in six topics.

The topic on methods of artificial intelligence (chapter 1) contains 8 papers providing a discussion of: fuzzy expert systems, covariance matrix, genetic algorithms, neural networks, solutions of integer optimization and visualization of multivariate data. These elements were treated as the basis for economic and engineering applications.

Next important topic is application of intelligent agents in distributed activities (chapter 2). There are presented 7 papers describing mechanisms that address inter-agent negotiations, user interface for distributing algorithm, distributed computing, intelligent tutoring system, shared virtual environment, work flow model at distributed intelligent production and knowledge sharing system.

Chapter 3 *"Distributed production network and modeling of complex systems"* contains 6 papers concerning production at technological process with probability, temporal data presentation, e-business and other problems.

The problems of the computer graphics and pattern recognition are presented in chapter 4. This chapter describes new approaches to the techniques of image synthesis and face recognition.

Chapter 5 *"Computer security and safety"* contains 8 papers concerning cryptanalysis of DES cryptographic algorithm, logic of authentication, authentication in distributed supervisory and control systems, authentication protocols with Petri nets, algorithms for sharing a key, distributed password, generating bent functions and collaborative risk management.

In chapter 6 are presented papers concerning logic synthesis and simulation. These papers discuss some problems of multi-value logic (MVL) design, the model-checking tool support available for MVL, digital circuit design and the code parallelism paradigm.

Many people deserve thanks for their contributions to the success of ACS'2001. Jerzy Pejaś and Imed El Fray were responsible for the general arrangements, and the smooth operation of the conference was due to them. Thanks are due to the members of the program committee for their efforts in evaluating the submissions and selecting the program, and of course to the authors and our special guests, Prof. Gisella Facchinetti, Dr Peer Johannsen, Prof. Marian Srebrny and Prof. Karol Myszkowski, without whose contributions there could be no conference.

All papers of ACS'2001 Conference are issued also as conference proceedings by INFORMA Szczecin (Poland). The list of all papers is available on http://acs.wi.ps.pl, as well as variety of other related material.

Szczecin, October 2001   Jerzy Sołdek
                                          Dean of Faculty of Computer Science
                                          and Information Systems

PROGRAM COMMITTEE

J. Sołdek	*Poland*
S. Ablameyko	*Belarus*
R. Drechsler	*Germany*
M. Adamski	*Poland*
A. Bartkowiak	*Poland*
W. Bielecki	*Poland*
W. Burakowski	*Poland*
Ch. Chu	*France*
Z. Czech	*Poland*
A. Dolgui	*France*
N. Enlund	*Sweden*
R. French	*USA*
J. Górski	*Poland*
A. Javor	*Hungary*
G. Kuchariew	*Poland*
E. Kuriata	*Poland*
C. Moraga	*Germany*
K. Myszkowski	*Germany*
W. Pedrycz	*Canada*
A. Piegat	*Poland*
O. Popov	*Poland*
D. Puzankov	*Russia*
W. Rucinski	*Poland*
R. Sadykhov	*Belarus*
V. Shmerko	*Poland*
B. Sovetov	*Russia*
M. Srebrny	*Poland*
R. Stankovic	*Yugoslavia*
J. Stoklosa	*Poland*
W. Swinarski	*USA*
A. Verlan	*Ukraine*
J. Weglarz	*Poland*
S. Yanushkievitch	*Poland*
O. Zaikin	*Poland*

GENERAL CHAIRS

J. Pejaś	*Poland*
I. El Fray	*Poland*
M. Fiodorov	*Poland*

Advanced Computer Systems '2001 was organized by: Technical University of Szczecin (Poland), Albert-Ludwigs-University (Germany), University of Technology of Troyes (France) and was held in cooperation with:Belarussian Academy of Sciences (Belarus), Electrotechnical University of Sankt Petersburg (Russia), Polish Academy of Sciences (Poland), State University of Informatics and Radioelectronics (Belarus), University of Goettingen (Germany), Ukrainian Academy of Sciences (Ukraine), Warsaw University of Technology (Poland).

Chapter 1

Methods of Artificial Intelligence

Fuzzy Expert Systems: Economic and Financial Applications

GISELLA FACCHINETTI

Faculty of Economics-University of Modena and Reggio Emilia,
Via Berengario 51-41100 MODENA Italy, e-mail: fachinetti@unimo.it

Resorting to mathematical modelling is very often the way to explain real world phenomena under investigation. However, in some case, the phenomenon complexity is so hard that building a mathematical model is an impossible or very difficult task. In those cases, some heuristic approaches can be used to deal both with missing information and the complexity. Moreover, some lack of knowledge exists and then the phenomenon cannot be deeply described with traditional quantitative tools, then only an incomplete model can be developed.

It turns out that sometimes traditional mathematical and statistical models are not able to precisely emulate the phenomena under investigation. In those situations, the Artificial Intelligence approach can provide tools for understand and treat with complex or incomplete phenomena. It is remarkable that in those cases Artificial Intelligence enjoyed many successes, most of which are due to Expert Systems. An Expert System incorporates the reasoning of human experts in a particular domain, and combines it with the computer processing and memory capacities.

The most important characteristics of an Expert System are: (Schneider and others 1996)

1. user-friendliness
   Since the user is not necessarily familiar with the inner operations of the system, it should be easy to use and its functionality should be self-explanatory.
2. learning capacities from past experience.
   As with human experts, the ability to learn means that the expert system is able to reach similar solution faster when the same problem is presented more than once. It is possible to divide learning in three types: learning from examples, learning by analogy, learning by skill refinement
3. self-explaining performances
   Similarly to human experts, it should be able to explain its reasoning process and answer questions about the inference procedure. This is an important feature since it is the only way to make the user confident that the decision-making mechanism is, at least, complementary if not superior to his own decision-making process.

4. performance in real time response
    Often, it is required to perform under time constraints. Many "real world" applications require real-time response. In some cases this will mean finding " a good solution" and not necessarily the optimal one.

It is now realised that uncertainty is not only embedded in human knowledge, but allowing some degree of uncertainty in a complex system model is perhaps the most significant way of simplifying and treat with it. The knowledge base of an expert system is a repository of human knowledge. Since much of human knowledge is imprecise in nature, the knowledge base usually consists of a collection of rules and facts, most of which are neither totally certain, nor totally consistent. The uncertainty of information in the knowledge base induces some uncertainty in the validity of the drawn conclusions.

The here proposed point of view is that conventional approaches to the management of uncertainty in expert system are intrinsically inadequate. The main reason consists on observing that that much of the uncertainty in such system is possibilistic rather than probabilistic.

There are several fundamentally different types of uncertainty. However, the sources of uncertainty can be divided in two main categories:

*   Uncertainties in the knowledge base
*   Uncertainties in the information provided by the user (the data)

The various types of uncertainty can be properly characterised and investigated within the framework of Fuzzy Set Theory. Fuzzy Set Theory was originally proposed by Lofti Zadeh as a quantitative tool to represent uncertainty and to formalise qualitative concepts with no precise definition.

Thus, the ability to operate in uncertain and unknown environments is an essential components of any intelligent system. It reflects the fact that many applications involve human expertise and knowledge which are invariably imprecise, incomplete or not totally reliable. Therefore, the intelligent systems must combine knowledge-based techniques for gathering and processing information and uncertain environments. Often, the data and the knowledge about the problem domain are fuzzy or incomplete, so an expert system has to work in conditions of uncertainty. Therefore, fuzzy inference procedure are becoming crucial for the managing uncertainty process. Fuzzy Set Theory provides a systematic framework to deal with fuzzy quantifiers with different types of uncertainty.

For these reasons, we have decide to use Fuzzy Expert Systems to treat complex problem in Economic and Financial environment.

The essential steps for a fuzzy system design (Kasabov, 1996; von Altrock, 1997) are: (i)identification of the problem and the selection of the type of fuzzy system that best suits the characteristics of the problem, (ii)definition of the input and output variables, their fuzzy values, and their membership function (fuzzification of input and output), (iii)construction of blocks of control rules and the translation of the latter into a fuzzy relation, (iv)treatment of any input information to select the fuzzy inference method, (v)translation of the fuzzy output into a crisp (numerical) value (defuzzification methods).

The fuzzification and the construction of blocks of fuzzy rules are the main problem in building a fuzzy expert system. These two steps could be obtained in different ways.
1. One approach is the interview with experts on the problem.
2. Another is the use of the methods of machine-learning, neural networks and genetic algorithms to determine membership functions and fuzzy rules.

The two approaches are quite different. The first does not use the past history of the problem and lets a real contact with the experts, which may permit all the experience matured in years of work in that field to enter into the study. The second is based only on the past data and transfers the same structure of the past to the future. We have liked better the first approach for different motivations in the several fields of application.

We have used fuzzy expert systems for these problems.
- Efficiency evaluation of services: teaching activity in University
- Definition of "Industrial District"
- Detection of insurance fraud
- Evaluation of strategic investments
- Firm creditworthiness evaluation in bank lending

In the following we present a summary of the results obtained with this techniques.

Efficiency evaluation of services: teaching activity in University

The problem of evaluation is current in many different situations: the social politics evaluation, the labour politics evaluation, the efficiency of public services evaluation toward citizens or private undertaking service toward customers, etc.

The evaluation of research and teaching activities, in the university, is established by the Law no. 370 (of 19/10/1999, Official Gazette, General Series, no. 252 of 26/10/1999): the defaulting administrations will be excluded from some grants. The Ministry of University and Scientific and Technological Research (MURST) recently founded an Observatory (now, a Committee) for the University System Evaluation, which proposed a course-evaluation questionnaire with items using a four-point Likert scale: ①*Definitely no*, ②*No rather than yes*, ③*Yes rather than no*, ④*Definitely yes* (MURST scale). They also suggested using means and variances to analyze data, translating the categories (or labels) into a *decimal scale* as follows: ①=2, ②=5, ③=7, ④=10. The University of Modena and Reggio Emilia adopted a set of categorical alternatives like: ①*Very insufficient*, ②*Insufficient*, ③*Sufficient*, ④*Good*, ⑤*Very good* (mark scale) because it seemed more suited to the evaluation procedure as it is fairly similar to the score system used at the previous school levels. The score of each item could be translated into a decimal scale by multiplying by two the numerical label of the category. The paper presents a fuzzy system to evaluate teaching activity showing that it overcomes the dispute about the middle position of a Likert scale and it is more flexible to handle data and replays to different problems congenital with the classic approach like that: (1)the evaluation of a single item or domain is conventionally made by an average of the numerical label or the corresponding decimal scale values, (2)the items included in a domain have the same importance.

The categories of the adopted scales were labeled by linguistic terms and their translation into the corresponding numeric values could be completely arbitrary. To remedy this problem we have proposed a questionnaire to the students in which they attribute a crisp number to every linguistic term. The analysis of these results enabled us to carry out the fuzzification of the inputs.

The use of an expert system lets the possibility to put the single inputs at the different level of importance through their position in the decision tree and the rule-blocks, where the place of entry and the combinations of the alternatives indicate the most important variables.

The questionnaire provided by the local Committee for Technical Evaluation had five Sections for a total of twenty-four items. **Section I**, *lecture room and resource room*, contained three items: (1)Adequacy of the Lecture Room, ALR, (2)Adequacy of the Resource Room, ARR, (3)Adequacy of the Resource Equipment, ARE. **Section II**, *work load and teaching organization*, enclosed four items: (4)Adequacy of the Work Load requested, AWL, (5)Adequacy of the Work Load requested by other Current Courses, AWLCC, (6)Adequacy of the Scheduling for other Current Courses, ASCC, (7)Adequacy of Exam Scheduling for other Current Courses, AESCC. **Section III**, *lectures*, included eight items: (8)Correspondence between Actual and Planned lectures, CAP, (9)Correspondence of the number and duration of the Lectures with respect to Official Schedule, CLOS, (10)Adequacy of the Teaching Materials —course books, handouts, *etc.*— , ATM, (11)Notification of the Form and rules of the Exams, NFE, (12)In-depth Study of the Lectures subjects, ISL, (13)Clarity of the Teacher's Presentations, CTP, (14)Motivation and Interests aroused by Teacher, MIT, (15)Teacher Availability during Office hours, TAO. The item (16) was discarded because it asked just a global evaluation of the lecture domain and it was judged as redundant. **Section IV**, *teaching-support*, presented four items: (17)Usefulness of Teaching-Support Activities — seminars, workshops, *etc.*— , UTS, (18)Adequacy of the Teaching-Support difficulty Level, ATS, (19)Completeness of the Answers given by Tutors, CAT, (20)Correspondence of the number and duration of the Tutors' Lectures with respect to official Schedule, CTLS. **Section V**, *further information*, (21)Level of Background Knowledge of the subject, LBK, (22)Level of Interest in the Subject matter, LIS, (23)Level of Overall Satisfaction of the course, LOS, (24)Attendance and Study planned (by students) to pass the Exam at the first time, ASE.

The evaluation of a single item or domain is conventionally made by an average of the numerical label or the corresponding decimal scale values. The items included in a domain have the same importance, while it is easy to note that there are variables indicating the efficiency of the course better than others. The categories of the adopted scales were labeled by linguistic terms and their translation into the corresponding numeric values could be completely arbitrary. Furthermore, there was the controversy about the middle position. An interesting solution is given by a fuzzy expert system to generate the evaluation of a single item or specific domain. In fact, the fuzzy set theory represents an ideal tool to handle this kind of data, as it was originally proposed as a means to represent the indeterminacy and to formalize qualitative concepts that generally have no precise boundaries. An expert system lets the possibility to use the single inputs at the different level of importance through the decision tree and the rule-blocks, where the place of entry and the combinations of the alternatives indicate the most important variables.

The fuzzy expert system had 23 inputs (or items) and it produces many different outputs: see Figure 1, where the final evaluation of the total decision tree is most important, but many other partial outcomes are yielded as pieces of branches (intermediate outputs) till to the translation of a single fuzzy variable in a crisp value obtained in a new way. These partial outcomes are interesting for a teacher and the local Committee to have an evaluation not only for a course as a global entity, but also for a group of variables —such as lectures, logistics, teaching-support— and a single item —such as ALR, AWL, CAP, CTP—. The production of a crisp value for a single fuzzy variable represents a new procedure with the respect to the usual application of a fuzzy expert system, which needs at least two inputs to be able to work.

The complete system was reported in Figure 1. Its structure consisted of several fuzzy modules linked together step by step and the input variables were introduced at a different level of importance, depending on the distance of the input node from the last output node (Evaluation in Figure 1) along the decision tree: the weight increases as this distance decreases. Each single aggregation produced intermediate variables that had a particular meaning.

The fuzzification of input variables, (*ii*), was carried out by using the answers collected by the corresponding questionnaire [5] using a mark scale. For example, LIS had alternatives: ①*Very insufficient*, ②*Insufficient*, ③*Sufficient*, ④*Good*, and ⑤*Very good*. The students numerically evaluated these labels on a decimal scale. The scores collected for each term of each question were analyzed in order to identify the form, peak, and amplitude of the corresponding fuzzy number. The relative frequency distributions had been normalized at one to be comparable and to derive the membership function of the relative linguistic attributes. Almost all the terms were represented by piece-linear functions. Figure 2, as an example, illustrates the fuzzification for this variable.

The rule-blocks, (*iii*), were set up through the experts' opinions, *i.e.*, the experience of teachers and students. The aggregation operator, selected for the precondition (*iv*), was the MIN Operator. The resulting linguistic output of each module (intermediate inputs) was also the (linguistic) input of the next module. Its function permitted, therefore, the connection between the rule-blocks. Defuzzification, (*v*), was carried out for each respondent after having inserted the data in the system. The crisp value, corresponding to the best representation of the fuzzy value of the linguistic output, was obtained by the method of the "Center of Area" (CoA).

To have information about the domains, the partial outputs were produced with respect to single items and groups of variable. For example, see Figure 1, the aggregation {21, 22, 23} generated a partial output which may be considered as a new variable, which was termed Tendency (TEND). Following this idea, 7 new systems were built up which produce the first partial outputs, and so on till the end of the tree. The newness was the fuzzy output for a single input variable. For example, the input variable {22} contained information about the level of student interest for the matter. Each student selected an option having an integer decimal value, above-mentioned. The crisp value of the single fuzzy input was determined by the abscissa of the center of gravity of the figure obtained as it follows: the fuzzy representation of each input crisp value, attributable by a student in an answer, produces always a new figure built by the union of the two linguistic attributes that the crisp value fires, cut at the level of activation of the single attributes. This is a fuzzy set not normalized but for which is possible to calculate the center of gravity, see Figure 3.

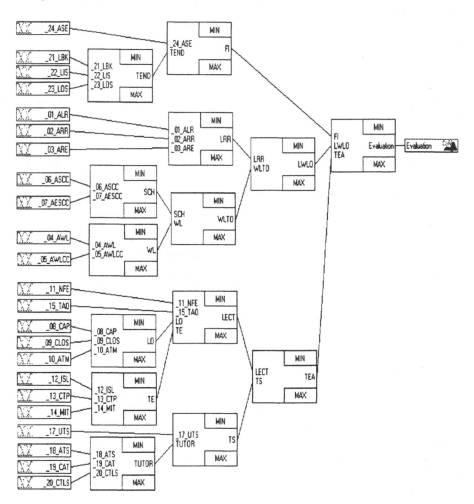

Fig. 1. Fuzzy inference system for teacher and course evaluation

The last figure shows that, to the student replays "Insufficient", the crisp value is translated in "four", while the fuzzy translation is 3.178. This fact is due to the students replays to the values attributed to the different linguistic terms.

Following this way we have the 23 single " fuzzy average values" to compare with the single "crisp average value".

We present the results of the analysis made by the two models on the students replays at the end of the first semester in the Faculty of Economics of Modena and Reggio Emilia.

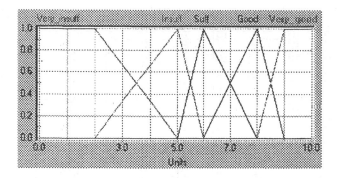

Fig. 2. Fuzzification of the LIS variable

A fuzzy inferential system easily overcomes the dispute four/five-point Likert scale. However, the fuzzy approach offered the possibility of the mark scale to use values more flexible and proximate to those the students really wanted to attribute to them.

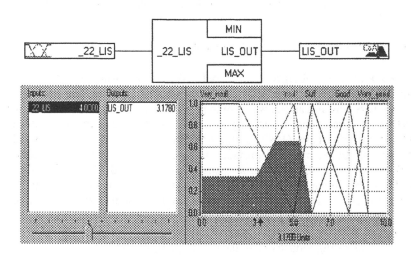

Fig. 3. Block of LIS output variable

The rule-blocks set up accounted for links between the inputs and the importance that teachers and students attributed to the single input (item), although this is a critical step, as it is affected by an extremely subjective point of view.

Moreover, a new target was examined: the transformation of a single label value, corresponding to the student answers, into a single crisp (fuzzy) value. The suggested procedure uses a fuzzy expert system technique with only one input to obtain a crisp translation of the single fuzzy number and the evaluation of a single concept was given by an average (mean) of these values, *i.e.*, a "fuzzy average of fuzzy numbers" which requires further in-depth. There are a lot of definitions of Fuzzy average value, like those introduced by Dubois-Prade and Campos- Gonzales for ranking fuzzy numbers, either dependent from additive measure or fuzzy measure using Choquet integral. The use of these definitions will carry out interesting results in the future.

ALR	ATM	AVL	CAR	CTF	LIB	TAO	UTB	Average	FUZZY AVERAGE
8	8	8	10	10	6	10	4	7,75	6,88
10	8	10	4	10	8	8	2	7,50	8,12
10	8	10	8	10	10	8	6	8,75	10,00
8	8	10	8	8	6	6	6	7,50	8,13
8	8	10	8	10	8	8	2	7,75	8,12
8	8	8	8	8	6	6	6	7,25	8,13
8	8	10	6	10	8	8	8	8,25	9,37
8	8	8	8	8	8	8	4	7,25	8,13
8	8	6	6	8	6	6	10	7,00	6,87
6	6	6	6	8	4	6	4	5,75	3,91
8	6	8	6	6	6	10	6	7,00	6,87
8	6	10	8	10	8	6	4	7,50	6,25
10	8	8	8	8	6	6	4	7,25	6,88
10	10	10	10	10	6	6	4	8,25	7,50
10	8	10	6	10	8	8	6	8,25	9,37
8	8	6	6	10	6	8	6	7,25	8,12
2	2	4	2	6	2	10	6	4,25	2,50
8	10	2	8	8	6	10	4	6,75	6,25
10	6	10	8	8	10	10	8	8,75	9,37
6	6	8	8	4	2	6	4	5,50	2,50
8	8	10	10	8	6	10	10	8,75	9,37
8	6	8	6	8	8	10	6	7,50	7,50
10	6	8	6	10	8	6	8	7,75	8,75
6	6	6	2	6	4	6	4	5,00	2,50
2	2	2	2	2	2	2	2	2,00	0,00
6	6	6	4	4	4	6	10	5,75	3,12
8	6	8	8	10	6	6	10	7,75	8,12
8	8	8	6	6	8	10	10	8,00	10,00
Average (825 cases)								7,29	7,07

Tab. 1. Evaluation of the eight items for a Mathematics course, means, and fuzzy responses

Definition of "Fuzzy Industrial District"

Pyke and Sengenberger (1990) defined an industrial district as a "local productive system, characterized by a large number of firms that are involved at various stages, and in various ways, in the production of a homogeneous product. A significant feature is that a very high proportion of these firms are small or very small". Brusco and Paba (1997) building on Istat (1995) have recently developed a mathematical algorithm which provides an estimate of the number and quantitative importance of the Italian industrial districts in the period 1951-1991. The spatial units of observation are the 955 "local labor systems", defined for the year 1981 (see Istat-Irpet (1986)). This algorithm is based on four distinct indexes that must be greater than one. Indicating the total employment in the nation with L, the local labor system with the subscript j, each manufacturing sector with the subscript i, the whole manufacturing industry with the subscript m, we get:

$$\frac{L_{jm}}{L_j} \Big/ \frac{L_m}{L} > 1 \text{ [share of manufacturing]} \tag{1}$$

$$\frac{L_{jm,small}}{L_{jm}} \Big/ \frac{L_{m,small}}{L_m} > 1 \text{ [small firm condition]} \tag{2}$$

where the subscript small indicates employment in firms with less than 100 employees and L_m is total manufacturing employment in the nation.

For at least one sector i :

$$\frac{L_{ji}}{L_{jm}} \bigg/ \frac{L_i}{L_m} > 1 \quad \text{[specialization index]} \tag{3}$$

where L_i is the total national employment in the sector i.

For at least one sector i for which the index defined in 3 is satisfied, it is required that:

$$\frac{L_{ji,small}}{L_{ji}} \bigg/ \frac{L_{i,small}}{L_i} > 1 \quad \text{[small firms in the specialized sector]} \tag{4}$$

All the indexes are calculated with respect to national averages. If a local system satisfies conditions (1) and (2) and, for at least one sector i, conditions 3 and 4 are also satisfied, the local system is called «industrial district» and the sectors i, for which conditions (3) and (4) are satisfied, are called «specialization» of the district. One district may have more than one specialization. The sector with the highest index (3) is called the «dominant sector» and it is usually identifies the district. Unfortunately this algorithm is too restrictive and rules out some important and well-known small-firms, specialised local industries. This, for example, is the case of the textile district of Biella, a small town in which 850 firms and 12,000 employees work in the textile sector.

Looking at this problem we have noticed that the economists speak of "medium-sized companies", "high leveraged companies", "low level of employment", and use all these adjectives as useful approximations to classify objects. For example, the first condition of the crisp algorithm is

$$\frac{L_{jm}}{L_j} \bigg/ \frac{L_m}{L} > 1 \tag{1}$$

This is a crisp mathematical translation of the following linguistic expression: "The share of manufacturing employment over total employment in the local labour system j has to be *greater than* the share of manufacturing employment over total employment at country level". What do we mean by *greater than*? The crisp definition has translated this linguistic statement in "the ratio is greater than 1", treating in the same way quotient results like 1.5, 4, 10.7, and considering in a really different way a result like 0,9999. The Boolean translation of the linguistic statement *greater than* does not allow us to distinguish between different values of the index, except at the boundary. But, in economic terms, is it reasonable to consider a local labour system with a value of 0.9999 so different from one that shows for the same index the value of 1,0001? This problem has been at the base of our idea to apply a fuzzy logic approach to the definition of industrial districts.

At the beginning, we develop a Fuzzy Expert System that translates the crisp algorithm. As the crisp approach does not discriminate between a district with few employees and a district employing a relevant share of workers in a specific sector, the simple fuzzification of the four indexes provides a ranking in which industrial districts with a small number of workers may be ranked in a better position than districts that are much more important in terms of employment (Bruni-Facchinetti-Paba (1999). To avoid this and to provide a ranking which has a clear economic interpretation, we add three new variables. For each manufacturing sector, these are (i) the share of employment in firms with less than 200 employees, (Empl <200), (ii) the share of employees in the local system over total national employment in the sector (Empl-perc (iii) the absolute number of employees in the local system (Employees).

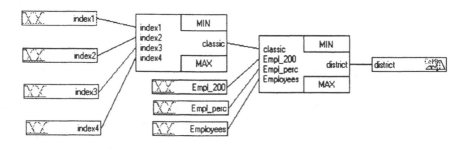

Figure 3

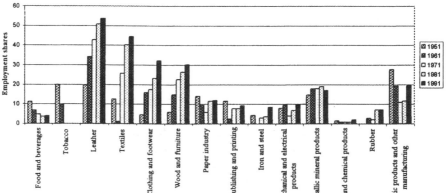

For the fuzzification of the new variables we consider that the literature defines an industrial district with reference to the geographical space rather than to a specific sector (see Becattini (1990)). For example, when we speak of the industrial district of Prato we include in the definition not only the textile industry, for which all the indexes are easily satisfied, but also the employment in all the other manufacturing sectors even if for some of them the indexes are less than one. Clearly, Prato is not a problem, because the textile sector is predominant in the local economy, and this is consistent with Marshall's idea of an industrial district (1980) , who emphasised the local predominance of a specific industry. In his own words, that industry must be so important that its "secrets are in the air". But this is not always the case. In Brusco and Paba (1997), a local system may be an industrial district even if its most important specialized sector accounts for a negligible share of local employment. This is clearly unsatisfactory and in contrast with the Marshallian approach.

So we decided to take into account the relative weight in terms of employment of the sectors that satisfy our fuzzy algorithm for each local system. We than label "industrial districts" only the local systems for which the sum of employment shares of the above sectors is bigger than 0,25. In other words, we require that more than a quarter of total manufacturing employment of a local system be employed in sectors that share the characteristics of the district.

Using the census database, we are now able to estimate the relative importance of industrial districts in the Italian industry for the period 1951-1991. Although the number and types of the local systems included is different, in Table 2, we see the aggregate results in terms of employment that are quite similar to those obtained by Brusco-Paba, but only for the last three census years. They differ significantly in 1951 and 1961, where the fuzzy estimates are respectively 7 and 11 percentage points higher. Notice, however, that even when the estimates are similar, the list of districts can be quite different. The set of fuzzy districts includes not only all the important crisp districts, but it also includes important small-firm, specialized local systems excluded by the crisp approach Figure 4 shows the behaviour of the employment shares for each manufacturing sector.

Table 2. Employment in industrial districts over total manufacturing employment	1951	1961	1971	1981	1991
Fuzzy districts	0.176	0.248	0.191	0.270	0.319
Brusco-Paba districts	0.103	0.136	0.201	0.259	0.317

In comparison to the crisp approach prevailing in the literature, the application of a fuzzy algorithm to the empirical quantification of industrial districts presents two main advantages. First, its allows the inclusion of some important districts which are usually ruled out by the rigid rules of the crisp algorithm. This makes the estimates of importance of this system of production more reliable than the existing ones. Second, it provides a ranking of the districts according to their quantitative importance and to their adherence to the characteristics emphasized in the literature. This ranking not only improves our knowledge of this type of industrial organization but it is crucial for the analysis of the dynamic behavior of industrial districts over time, which is the subject of our future work. The ranking may also be used for industrial policy purposes.

In several important meetings some economists suggests that should be very important to introduce the definition of "super-district" and experts of the research sector have appreciated our approach which goes in the correct direction.

Evaluation of insurance fraud

We have faced the problem of the evaluation that insurance has to do when has to replay to a claim for damage in the field of motor insurance. Unfortunately, till now, the willingness of companies to disclose system details about fraud detection systems is very low. In the field of motor insurance, most fraud is not perpetrated by professional criminals but rather by otherwise law-abiding individuals with many different motives for their behaviour. The deregulation of insurance prices has produced competition between the companies, not only in the price of the policy, but even in the proof of efficiency that the company shows at the moment of the accident winding-up. This second point produces in the company a decision dilemma. From one side the customer requests to be paid off in a short time, and to reduce the bureaucracy for the case excursus' examination, from the other side the rapid pay off do not let the company to make the controls considered useful for the identifications of possible frauds. The velocity in the winding-up and the certainty not to pay fraudulent claims are, clearly, two antithetic choices. Thus, insurance companies are interested to implement a fraud detection decision system that looks at multiple factors in every insurance claim and lets, in real time, to divide the accidents in two classes: the sure ones and the risky ones. The first ones may be paid immediately and the second ones have the necessity of a manual review. In this paper we propose a fuzzy logic system that produces a degree of fraud risk. The experts of four of the most important Italian insurance have determined the input thirteen variables.

The fuzzification of the linguistic variables and the building of the rule blocks are the mathematical transaction of the experts' decisions.

The degree of fraud risk is computed by the fuzzy logic system as a number between zero and one. ZERO indicates that an insurance claim was evaluated as totally non-fraudulent, while ONE indicates a very high fraud risk. The fuzzy logic system tests the client-event data and produce a degree of fraud risk. This value is compared to a threshold value pre-determined by insurance. If the result is lower than the threshold, the claim is immediately paid out to the customer. If the result is higher than the threshold, the claim is passed on to a claims auditor. The claims auditor will then manually review the claim and make the final decisions on what further steps are to be taken. Unsuspicious claims can thus be settled automatically, even by non-expert call centre operators. Claim auditors can then spend more time with the potentially fraudulent claims. The data, over 400, are all relative to the city of Modena. This system, even if so simple, produces very good results. (1) All the cases not paid by insurance, because connected with fraudulent claims, have been identified. (2) The output offers a rating of risky situations, useful to speed up the decision. (3) The threshold value is pre-determined by insurance and it depends from the policy that the company has decided to apply in that market.

Potential applications of intelligent decision systems for insurance lie in the areas of workflow control, fraud and abuse detection, quality assurance, and premium pricing. We think that, for insurance company, it is surely useful to have expedites insurance claim processing for the identification of unsuspicious claims. Such claims are settled automatically with lower operational costs. Fraud is detected with consistent quality and human fraud auditors are supported with their work.

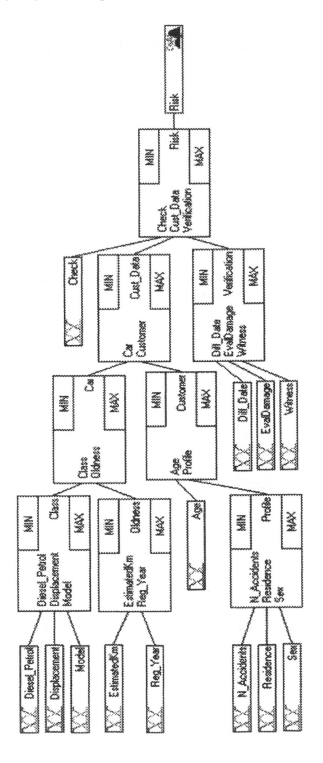

Variable Name	Variable Explanation	Term Names
Age	Age	young, middle_aged, elderly
Check	The expert's opinion	negative, positive
Diesel_Petrol	Fuel	Diesel, Petrol
Diff_Date	Difference of date between accident and declaration	low, medium, high
Displacement	Piston displacement	low, medium, high
EstimatedKm	Estimated Km	low, medium, high
EvalDamage	Evaluation of damage	low, medium, high
Model	Car type	LR_or_SW, Sporting, Sedan
N_Accidents	Number of accidents in the last year	low, medium, high
Reg_Year	Resistration's year of the car	low, medium, high
Residence	Residence	cl_1, cl_2, cl_3, cl_4, cl_5
Sex	Sex	female, male
Witness	Number of witnesses	low, medium, high
Risk	Final evaluation of risk	very_low, low, medium_low, medium, medium_high, high, very_high
Car	Car	low, medium_low, medium_high, high
Class	Class of the car	low, medium, high
Cust_Data	Customer data	very_low, low, medium, high, very_high
Customer	Customer	low, medium_low, medium_high, high
Oldness	Oldness	low, medium, high
Profile	Profile	low, medium, high
Verification	Information and data verification	low, medium, high

Evaluation of strategic investments

Investment evaluation is one of the major issues in the field of economic decisions. Financial mathematics and theory of finance provide several tools for appraising an investment. Unfortunately, they fit well only in exceptional cases and hardly ever can be applied for solving a strategic investment decision process. In particular, financial mathematics and theory of finance offer tools which are formally complex and yet based on rather simplistic assumptions: On the other side, business economics does not provide models, but just schemata informally sketched, where some variables are shown but nothing is said about the way they are connected (or must be connected) to reach the final decision. This paper shows how to describe a strategic investment by means of a fuzzy expert system, which is capable of replicating the cognitive processes of the decision-maker and then automatically reach the same solution. The model presented is readily applicable and understandable by any manager and practitioner. We have replicated a real-life decision process, solved by the experts of Florim S.p.a., an important italian ceramic tile firm. As we will see, the model is a good replication of the way of reasoning of Florim's experts, since our model automatically provides a solution, which, on the ground of the same data available to the expert, is consistent with the decision taken by Florim. Florim had the opportunity of acquiring 25% of the shares of a firm producing ceramic tiles, located in the USA. Alongside this project Florim had the following options: an option (not the obligation) to develop the investment by buying another 26% percent in the future, an option to abandon the project selling back the shares (this was contractually stipulated), and an implicit option of expanding the scale of production by construction of new plants (this is due to the fact that the firm is located in a wide area only part of which is currently destined to production). Firstly, we have interviewed the experts and drawn the variables which, implicitly and explicitly, were considered fundamental in order to reach the decision. We have 17 variables, which we call value drivers. We have connected the value drivers by means of a modular approach and using fuzzy logic: the set of the value drivers is divided in subsets of drivers which are grouped together and contribute to determine a new variable, by means of "rule blocks" which are the core of our expert system. For example, consider the variable *(CompPower)* which depends on the three variables *(MarketShare), (ProdCap), (Technology)*. Each of the latter is made to take on 3 possible linguistic values: Low, Medium, High. So we have a rule block of $3 \cdot 3 \cdot 3 = 27$ rules for this variable. Some of these are, for example:

IF *(MarketShare)* is Low **AND** *(ProdCap)* is Low
AND *(Techn.)* is Low **THEN** *(CompPower)* is Low
IF *(MarketShare)* is High **AND** *(ProdCap)* is High
AND *(Techn.)* is High **THEN** *(CompPower)* is High
IF *(MarketShare)* is Low **AND** *(ProdCap)* is Medium
AND *(Techn)* is High **THEN** *(CompPower)* is Medium
Drivers:
(AbOpt_EP)=Abandonment Option Exercise Price,
(ExpOpt_EP)=Expansion Option Exercise Price,
(Landsize)=Land Size,
(CostReduct)=Cost Reduction,
(Differentiation)=Differentiation,
(MarketGrow)=Market Growth,
(GrowOpt_EP)=Growth Option Exercise Price,
(Risk)=Risk, *(MarketShare)*=Market Share,
(ProdCap)=Production Capacity,
(Technology)=Technology,
(DistrChUSA)=Distribution channels in USA,
(Synergies)=Synergies,
(InvCost)=Investment Cost,
(Manager)=Management abilities and skills
(MarketKnow)=Market-Knowledge,
(StratConsist)=Strategic Consistency
Other variables:
(ExpValue_D)=Expected Value Demand,
(CompPower)=Competitive Power,
(SynergPower)=Synergic Power,
(CorpEval)= Corporate Evaluation,
(QualitAn)=Qualitative Analysis,

(AbOpt)=Abandonment Option,
(ExpOpt)=Expansion Option,
(GrowOpt)=Growth Option,
(StratAttract)=Project's Strategic Attractivity,
(ImplOpt)=Implicit Options,
(InvProp)=Propensity to invest,
(InvValue)=Investment Value

The variables generated in this way are in turn gathered in groups which give rise to new variables through use of other rule blocks. The process goes on until the final output *(InvValue)* is reached. We could then consider the model as a composed function: we go from the independent variables to other variables, which in turn determine other variables and so on until a single final variable is reached (the investment value). Once we have fixed the value of the drivers (crisp values), the system fuzzifies them and via the rule blocks reaches the final output: The linguistic value of the final output is then defuzzified and a 'crisp' number is provided by the system. All rules and all value drivers, as well as the schema, have been found with the help of Florim's managers, so the model is the actual representation of their cognitive process. Our expert system, with the value fixed by Florim's managers, provides the solution *(InvValue)*=0.9, where *(InvValue)* could take on values in the interval [0,1]. This means that the undertaking of the investment is certainly suggested. The experts confirmed us that the value of investment has been deemed very high and that 0.9 is consistent with their informal estimate. The fuzzy expert system this work proposes seems to overwhelm most of the drawbacks found in the models existing in the literature, in particular as regards its actual implementation. Actually, there aren't models in the literature capable of realistically representing a capital budgeting decision process, in particular a strategic investment, where many different variables are at work in the decision maker's mind in a nontrivial way. Among other things, our model is capable of considering qualitative variables, such as *(StratConsist), (Differentiation), (Manager)* etc, which is an impossible task for 'crisp' mathematics. The drawbacks of both disciplines (finance and business economics) can be reversed by looking at the other side of the medal: finance suggests us that we do need models, business economics suggests us that reality cannot be described with mathematical models (complex in their application and simplified in their assumptions).

This model seems to meet both requirements, at least at a certain extent, by formally modeling a situation with no use of simplistic assumptions and no mathematical technicalities. We think this approach could be appealing for managers, practitioners, analysts for it is easy to understand and easy to implement, it does not require advanced knowledge of mathematics and does not make any particular assumption on the variables affecting the value of the option. The solution derives from logical implications (the ``if-then'' rules) not from complex differential equations. Implications are our natural cognitive tools, so anyone can understand them and construct them. At the same time we have a methodology which is actually a formal model, automatically giving us the solution. Fuzzy logic is in this sense a superb tool of describing strategic investments, since the complexity of real-life situations is handled through ``vague'' variables and ``vague'' interactions, which better replicate human mind as well as economic phenomena.

We think that there is need for models, as theory of finance suggests us, but, as business economics suggests us, we must try to remove all possible obstacles to creating *realistic* decision models for strategic investments. They may be less precise but are more readily implementable and may become the decision-making frameworks employed in practice.

Firm creditworthiness evaluation in lending credit

Credit scoring systems are useful for screening and for creditworthiness assessment; they can also play a positive role in marketing, market research, product promotion and new customer acquisition. In these activities, credit scoring systems are important for decision-making and for supporting bank personnel in their subjective evaluations.

The applications of credit scoring models have gradually moved towards commercial customer management and marketing but the main *stages* in traditional banking are: pre-contractual lending screening (*application scoring*) and post contractual monitoring (*behavioural scoring*). In particular, monitoring includes the assessment of the whole financial situation of the firm, the loan adequacy, the analysis of temporary financial stress and its specific determinants. In other organizational bank areas, credit scoring systems could be used for marketing purposes (*customer scoring*) and for supporting commercial activities.

Credit scoring systems use statistical and mathematical techniques in order to process and compute a lot of customer financial and social information. The problem is to optimise the trade-off between proved and objective data and the flexibility of the system. For these systems have to attribute a score to every applicant or borrower that reflects the synthetic final assessment (judgement) and ranks them in terms of risk. This assessment is on the basis of an algorithm that gives a grade to every item of information and their particular combinations.

Credit rating techniques and credit scoring systems were born in the 1950s. By the end of the '60s, a new era of credit scoring system started with Altman's model (1968), named Z-score model. The model appeared very distant from traditional models, based on simple balance sheet analysis. (Beaver 1967, Foster 1986). The main difference was the use of discriminant analysis in order to construct a function, called Z-score, based on five financial statement ratios regarding both financial and market ratios.

There are many credit scoring systems in academic and business literature. The most important difference among them is their specific mathematical or statistical technique used in processing and computing all the economic, financial and social information. In fact, most of the existing models make use of standard statistical techniques in order to evaluate the insolvency probability on the basis of historical economical, financial and relationship data and the performance of previously made loans. The real difference is the underlying linear model with a different default probability distribution function.

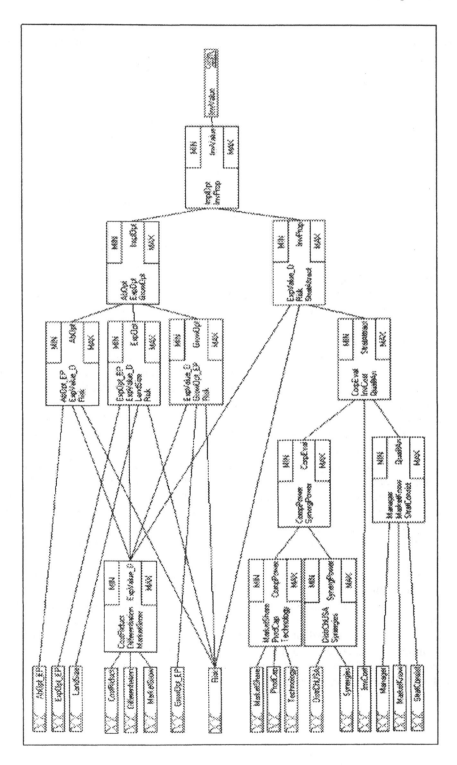

The useful role of credit scoring in lending has stimulated the research, improving its forecasting capability and early-warning timing. Moreover, information technology, artificial intelligence and expert systems can process more information, so credit scoring has achieved an appreciable degree of flexibility and a greater chance of application. In fact, the newer systems try to use different techniques, including option pricing theory and neural network. (AA.VV. 1995, Altman-Saunders 1997, Gulden-Rosignoli-Salcioli 1994).

Why do banks and firms not use credit-scoring systems? Probably, in order to adopt a credit scoring system, both forecasting precision and the timing of the assessment are important. For a long time, these models were often weak as early-warning devices and were useless for managing lending and borrowers.

Now, the situation is changing. There is a wider diffusion of this management instrument, both for corporate and private borrower targets. In fact, banks are getting used to managing retail and consumer lending, especially credit cards, by credit scoring systems. In many cases banks start managing small firm credit risk by the help of credit scoring systems and the results are really encouraging. In fact, some early researches pointed out that credit scoring systems reduce credit rationing in low and moderate-income areas and improve lending towards firms located in non-branched areas.

Our analysis is based on a sample 1283 loans granted by an Italian local bank during the first semester of 1998. For each of them, the following fourteen 1997 financial statement ratios were available:

FinExpCharge Financial expense charge = Net Interest expense/Net sales;

Cprof_Sales Current profitability on sales = Earning before taxes and non recurrent items/ Net sales;

Return_Sales Return on sales = Operating Income / Net sales;

AV_NetSales Annual Increase (decrease) in Net sales (%);

AV_OpInc Annual Increase (decrease) in operating income (%);

CurrentR Current ratio = Current assets/current liabilities;

AcidTestR Acid test ratio = (Cash + cash equivalents + marketable securities + account receivable) / Current liabilities;

AccRec Accounts receivable collection period= Accounts receivable / Average daily sales;

AV_AccRec Annual Increase (decrease) in Accounts receivable collection period (%);

DSinInv Days' sales in Inventory = Daily inventory / Average daily sales;

AV_DSinInv Annual Increase (decrease) in days' sales in Inventory (%);

FinLevR Financial leverage ratio = Total asset / Equity capital;

AV_FinLevR Annual Increase (decrease) in Financial leverage ratio (%);

PandE_Cover Plant and equipment Coverage = Plant and equipment (net)/ Equity capital.

In this sample 51 positions became bad loans by the end of March 2000.

The local bank computes a credit score based on different inputs: financial statement data, credit bureau information, and relationship banking information and business cycle analysis. The final evaluation is a weighted average of each area score. With reference to the financial statement data, the area score comes from a weighted average of grades attributed to the fourteen above-mentioned ratios; the single grade is a function of the borrower's ratio with respect to the corresponding business sector ratio.

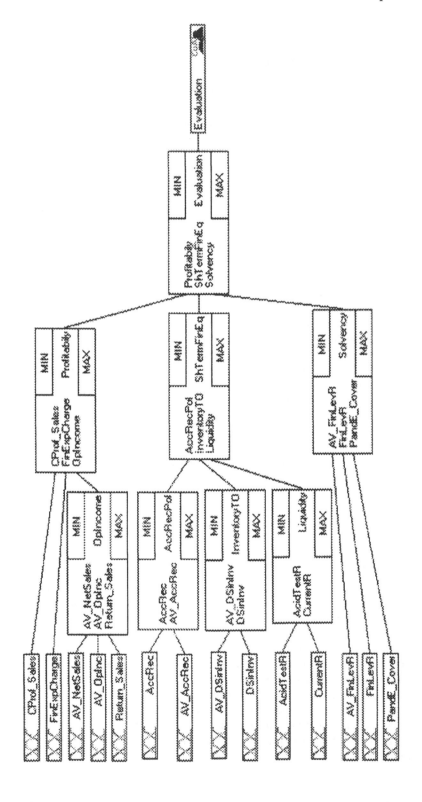

The results from our fuzzy expert system will be compared with the bank's financial statement score only.

In order to compare the classical and the fuzzy approach, we present the two tables and two indexes of discriminant power of the models as Maximum Spread and Span Area. In Tab.1 we present the results of the bank score (FV98-B), in Tab.2 the fuzzy system results. Both in Tab.1 and in Tab.2 the first column shows the "Score" value, the "Good Customers" and the "Bad Customers". The "Score" column gives a creditworthiness evaluation and proposes different levels of scoring threshold beneath which the bank decides to refuse requests. The "Good Customers" column proposes the cumulated percentage of Good. The same happens for the Bad column. The Maximum Spread measures the maximum distance between the cumulated distributions of the "Good" and the "Bad" Customers. The higher this value, the higher is the model's discriminant power. The Span Area is the area between the same distributions. Even in this case higher values correspond to higher discriminant capacity of the model.

The bank score produces a Maximum Spread of 66.1 and a Span Area of 17.2.

The fuzzy score produces a Maximum Spread of 86.8 and a Span Area of 45.6..

The results obtained show that a fuzzy expert system offers a better measurement of the discriminant power of the model. Creditworthiness evaluation in bank lending is a complex problem that involves a lot of variables that, often, lack a precise range of variability. When we are faced with imprecision and insufficient information, the use of simple statistical instruments is not sufficient to have a significant replay. Fuzzy logic is born exactly to deal with these types of problems. We think that the combination of the strong structure of a fuzzy system with the background knowledge of the decision-makers is a correct way to obtain good results

FV98-B

FV98-B		
Score	Good	Bad
0,0	0,00	0,00
0,5	0,00	0,00
1,0	0,00	0,00
1,5	0,00	0,00
2,0	0,00	0,00
2,5	0,00	0,00
3,0	0,00	1,96
3,5	0,00	1,96
4,0	0,00	9,80
4,5	0,70	29,41
5,0	2,65	52,94
5,5	8,96	70,59
6,0	19,10	84,31
6,5	35,07	94,12
7,0	57,13	98,04
7,5	78,57	100,00
8,0	93,61	100,00
8,5	99,30	100,00
9,0	100,00	100,00
9,5	100,00	100,00
10,0	100,00	100,00

max h = 66,1

area = 17,2%

Good ⁓ Bad

FUZZY

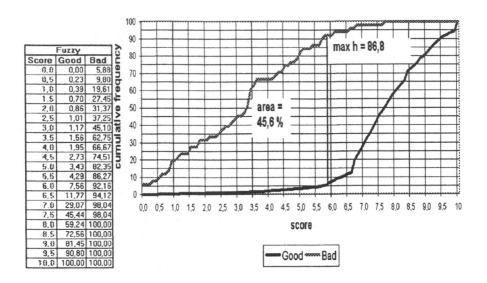

Fuzzy Score	Good	Bad
0.0	0.00	5.88
0.5	0.23	9.80
1.0	0.39	19.61
1.5	0.70	27.45
2.0	0.86	31.37
2.5	1.01	37.25
3.0	1.17	45.10
3.5	1.56	62.75
4.0	1.95	66.67
4.5	2.73	74.51
5.0	3.43	82.35
5.5	4.29	86.27
6.0	7.56	92.16
6.5	11.77	94.12
7.0	29.07	98.04
7.5	45.44	98.04
8.0	59.24	100.00
8.5	72.56	100.00
9.0	81.45	100.00
9.5	90.80	100.00
10.0	100.00	100.00

max h = 86,8

area = 45,6 %

Good ~~~ Bad

Reference

Altman, E.I. (1968). "Financial ratios, discriminant analysis and the prediction of corporate bankruptcy" The Journal of Finance 23, 589-609.

Altman E.I, Saunders A., (1997), *"Credit risk Measurement: developments over the last 20 years"*, in Journal of Banking and Finance.

Bandermer H., Gottwald S. (1996) *Fuzzy sets, fuzzy logic fuzzy methods*. John Wiley & Sons New York.

Beaver W, (1967), "Financial Ratios as Predictors of Failure" in *Journal of Accounting Research*.

Becattini G., *The Marshallian industrial district as a socio-economic notion*, in Pyke F., Becattini G., G.Bojadziev, M.Bojadziev (1997). *Fuzzy Logic for Business, Finance and Management*, World Scientific Publishing co, Singapore.

Bruni S.-Facchinetti G.- Paba S.: (1999) *"A Fuzzy Classification for the Definition of Industrial District"* Proceedings of the 11th Italian Workshop on Neural Nets, Vietri-99. 408-413 Springer Press.

Bruni S.-Facchinetti G.-Paba S.: (1999) *"A Fuzzy Algorithm for a Defintion of Industrial District"* Advances in Fuzzy Systems and Intelligent Technologies, F. Masulli, R. Parenti, G. Pasi, Ed.s, 49-55 Shaker Publishing (NL).

Brusco S., Paba S. (1997) Per una storia dei distretti industriali italiani dal secondo dopoguerra agli anni novanta, in Storia del capitalismo italiano Barca F. Donzelli eds,. 265-333

Chiandotto, B. and M.M. Gola (1999*). Questionario di base da utilizzare per l'attuazione di un programma per la valutazione della didattica da parte degli studenti*, internet site of the murst,: http://www.murst.it/osservatorio/attivnuc.htm.

Dixit, A. and Pindyck, R., 1994. *Investment under Uncertainty*, Princeton NJ, Princeton University Press.

Facchinetti G.-Ghiselli Ricci R.-Muzzioli S.: (1998) *"Note on ranking fuzzy triangular numbers"*. International Journal of Intelligent Systems. Vol.13, 613-622 John Willey & Sons, Inc.

Facchinetti G.-Ghiselli Ricci R.: (1999) *"A class of ranking functions for triangular fuzzy numbers"*. Presented at NEU'99, Venezia 6-7 maggio 1999. Published on Economics & Complexity. 2000

Facchinetti G.-Mastroleo G.-Paba S.: (2000) *"A fuzzy approach to the geography of industrial districts"*; "Proceedings of the 2000 ACM Symposium on Applied Computing" Carrol J., Damiani E., Haddam H., Oppenheim D. Editors. ISBN: 1-58113-239-5, Vol.1 514-518.

Facchinetti G.-Bordoni S.-Mastroleo G.: (2000) *Bank Creditworthiness using Fuzzy Systems: A Comparison with a Classical Analysis Technique*. In Risk Assesment and Management in Technology, Environment and Finance. Da Ruan, Fedrizzi M. e Kacprzyk J. Editors. Springer Verlag Press. Published in Fuzzy Applications and Library http:/www.fuzzytech.com.

Lalla M.-Facchinetti G.: (2000). *Inferential fuzzy system for rating istruction*. Economics & Complexity. Vol.2, n.3, pp.31-56.

Facchinetti G.-Mastroleo G.-Paba S.: (2000). *A Fuzzy Approach for the Empirical Identification of Industrial Districts*. on the web page Fuzzy Applications and Library http:/www.fuzzytech.com.

Facchinetti G.-Mastroleo G.: (2000).*A fuzzy approach for granting personal credit*. Proceedings of Third Spanish-Italian Meeting on Financial Mathematics. Bilbao 27-30 Aprile 2000

Magni C.- Facchinetti G.-Mastroleo **G.**. *A Proposal for Modelling Real Options through Fuzzy Expert Systems"* on Proceedings ACM SAC 2001 Las Vegas 11-13 Marzo 2001..

Facchinetti G.- Magni C.- Mastroleo M- Vignola V. *An application of fuzzy expert systems to strategic investments: The case of Florim S.p.a.* In proceedings of Soft Computing And Intelligent System (SOCO 2001) June 26-29 Paisley Scotland (UK)

Facchinetti G.- Magni C.- Mastroleo M- Vignola V. *Valuing strategic investment with a fuzzy expert system: an italian case*. In proceedings of International Fuzzy System Association Fuzzyness And Soft Computing In The New Millenium (*IFSA* 2001), July 25-28 Vancouver Canada.

Facchinetti G.-Cosma S.-Mastroleo G.–Ferretti R *A fuzzy credit rating approach for small firm creditworthiness evaluation in bank lending. An Italian case.* In proceedings of The second International ICSC Congress on Computational Intelligence: Methods & Applications (CIMA 2001) Bangor, U.K., June 19-22, 2001.

Foster, G. (1986), *Financial statement analysis* Englewood Cliffs

Golden R, Rosignoli C, Salcioli G, (1994), L'adozione di sistemi basati sulla conoscenza nell'area fidi degli enti creditizi. In Il Risparmio, n.2.

Hand, D.J. and M.J. Crowder (1996). *Practical Longitudinal Data Analysis*. Chapman & Hall, London Istat . (1995) *Rapporto annuale . La situazione del Paese nel 1955*, Roma, Istat,1996.

Istat-Irpet. (1986) *I mercati del lavoro in Italia*, in Quaderni di Discussione, (Istat, Roma).

Lalla M.-Facchinetti G.: (2000). *Scala di voto ed insiemi sfocati per valutare la didattica"* in Proc. Of Ingegnerizzazione del processo di produzione dei dati statistici" Firenze 9 Aprile 1999

Lalla M.-Facchinetti G- Mastroleo G. (2001) *Evaluation of Teaching Activity through a Fuzzy System*. In Proceedings. of Wirn 2001 Vietri May 18-21-2001 Springer Verlag

Lalla M.-Facchinetti G- Mastroleo G. (2001) *A fuzzy expert system for the evaluation of University efficiency: the teaching activity*. In Proceddings of IFAC Symposium on modelling and Control of Economic Systems Klagenfurt September 6-8. 2001

Lander, D.M. and Pinches, G.E., 1998. *Challenges to the Practical Implementation of Modeling and Valuing Real Options*, The Quarterly Review of Economics and Finance, vol.38, Special Issue, 537-567.

Magni, C.A., 1998. Aspetti quantitativi e qualitativi nella valutazione di un'opzione di investimento, Finanza, Marketing e Produzione, 3, 123-149.

Marshall A., (1980) Principles of Economics, Macmillan, London

Micalizzi, A. and Trigeorgis, L., 1999. *Real Options Applications*, Proceedings of the first Milan international workshop on Real Options, EGEA.

Kasabov N.K. (1996) Foundations of Neural Networks, Fuzzy Systems, and Knoledge Engineering. MIT Press.

Porter, M.E., 1980. *Competitive Strategy*, The Free Press.

Pyke F., Beccattini G. Sengenbergher (1990.) W., *Industrial Districts and inter-firm co-operation in Italy*, International Institute for Labour Studies, Geneva,

Ray, J.J. (1990). *Acquiescence and Problems with Forced-choice Scales*. Journal of Social Psychology, 130 (3), pp. 397-399.

Sengenberger W. (Eds), *Industrial districts and inter-firm cooperation in Italy*, Geneva, International Institute for Labour Studies, 1990.

Schuman H., Presser S. (1996). *Questions and Answers in Attitude Surveys: Experiments* on Question Form, Wording, and Context; Sage Publications, Thousand Oaks, CA.

von Altrock C. (1997). Fuzzy Logic and neurofuzzy applications in business and finance. Prentice Hall.

Backprojection of data vectors using a given covariance matrix

ANNA BARTKOWIAK, KRYSTYNA ZIĘTAK
Institute of Computer Science, University of Wrocław, Poland,
e-mail: {aba,zietak}@ii.uni.wroc.pl

Abstract: Very often analyzed data are contaminated with outliers which are due to some erroneous recording. After sorting out the suspected erroneous observations and coming to the conclusion that they are really erroneous, we would like to adjust them to the proper values.

In the paper we propose two methods (called *Plug-in* and *Procrustes*) which – taking into account the interdependencies between the variables provided in a robust covariance matrix S^* – permit to reconstruct the data matrix in such a way, that its covariance matrix is exactly equal to the given robust covariance matrix S^*. We call this process *backprojection* through the robust covariance matrix. The proposed method of backprojection is shown on four benchmark data sets.

Key words: Outliers, Robust covariance matrix, QR-factorization, Visualization of multivariate data

1.   INTRODUCING THE PROBLEM

The covariance or correlation matrices calculated from the observed data are the starting point for many multivariate analyses, a.o., for dimensionality reduction by principal components, graphical displays by biplots, canonical discriminant analysis, regression analysis etc.

It is well known that the gathered observations contain often some big measurement or data processing errors, which may influence the covariances calculated from such data, and in turn distort seriously further statistical analyses for that data.

To account for such situations some robust methods of estimating the covariance matrices has been proposed. Speaking generally, these methods aim at evaluating the covariances in such a way that truly only the proper uncontaminated part of the data is taken into account while the outlying observations are given less weight.

There are known several methods for an efficient construction of robust covariance matrices [4, 3]. In the following we will use the method developed by Rocke and Woodruff [10], which appears to us as being stabile and trustworthy [2].

We will consider the following problem: Suppose, we have a data matrix X suspected to be contaminated with outliers which are due to measurement errors. Suppose further, we have a covariance matrix S^* estimated in a robust way. Using the information contained in S^* we want to construct such a (adjusted) data matrix X^*, that the covariance matrix computed from X^* is exactly equal to S^*. We expect that in the constructed data matrix X^* the data vectors accounted formerly as outliers will be now adjusted to be concordant with the overall 'true' interdependence structure of the data.

In Section 2 we propose two algorithms for constructing a data matrix X^* with the properties described above. In Section 3 we consider four benchmark data known to contain outliers and show for them the reconstructed by our methods data matrices X^*. Section 5 contains some discussion on the proposed methods and the obtained results.

2.   METHODS

2.1   Denotations

Let X of size $n \times p$ denote a data matrix containing n rows and p columns. Each row, x_i ($i = 1, \ldots, n$) may be considered as a data vector, containing observations of p variables gathered for one (the i-th) individual.

Let $\widetilde{X}$ be the corresponding centered data matrix (for centering we may use the means or medians of subsequent variables). Then the covariance matrix S corresponding to X may be computed from $\widetilde{X}$ as $S = (1/n)\widetilde{X}^T \widetilde{X}$ (for small n often the factor $1/(n-1)$ instead of the factor $1/n$ is used).

It may happen that the data given in the matrix X contain some outliers, which may influence heavily the computed covariances. To avoid it, the covariances may be estimated in a robust way.

Suppose, we got a robust covariance matrix S^* which is of order p and of full rank. Being a covariance matrix it is symmetric. Being of full rank it is nonsingular, i.e. positive definite.

Our goal is the construction of a matrix $\widetilde{X}^*$ of size $n \times p$ such that the newly constructed matrix has the same covariance matrix as the given matrix S^*, i.e. that:

$$(1/n)(\widetilde{X}^*)^T \widetilde{X}^* = S^*. \tag{1}$$

For the reconstruction of the data matrix $\widetilde{X}^*$ with the property stated in eq. (1) we propose here two methods called by us *the Plug-in method* and *the Procrustes method*. From these methods we will obtain reconstructed centered data matrices denoted $\widetilde{X}_1^*$ and $\widetilde{X}_2^*$. Adding to them the centering vector we will obtain the reconstructed data matrices X_1^* and X_2^* expressed in the same scale as the original data matrix X.

Now we will describe briefly the proposed 2 methods. Both of them use the following two basic paradigms from numerical algebra:

Paradigm on Cholesky factorization of the matrix S^*. For a nonsingular Gramian matrix S^* there exists an unique upper triangular matrix R^* of order p, with all diagonal elements positive, such that

$$S^* = (1/n)(R^*)^T R^* . \tag{2}$$

The matrix R^* constitutes the Cholesky factor of the matrix nS^* (see, e.g. [7], p. 141).

Paradigm on QR factorization of the matrix $\widetilde{X}^*$. Suppose that the sought matrix $\widetilde{X}^*$ satisfies (1). Then the matrix $\widetilde{X}^*$ has to have the following QR factorization (for the definition and the computation of the QR factorization see, for example, Golub and Van Loan [7], pp. 211–212):

$$\widetilde{X}^* = Q \begin{bmatrix} R^* \\ 0 \end{bmatrix}, \quad Q - \text{orthogonal}, \tag{3}$$

where R^* is the Cholesky factor of nS^* (see eq. (2)). Let us notice, that taking into account the property (3) of the sought matrix $\widetilde{X}^*$, our task has reduced to find a proper Q.

As a measure of the distance between the matrices $\widetilde{X}^*$ and $\widetilde{X}$ we will take the Frobenius norm of the matrix D defined as the difference between the constructed and the observed data matrices: $D = \widetilde{X}^* - \widetilde{X}$.

Let us remind that for a matrix $A = [a_{ij}]$ its Frobenius norm $\|A\|_F$ is defined as

$$\|A\|_F = (trace(A^T A))^{1/2} = \left(\sum_{i,j} |a_{ij}|^2 \right)^{1/2} . \tag{4}$$

Let us notice that the Frobenius norm of a matrix A is the same as that of A^T.

2.2 Method I: Plug-in

Let $\tilde{X}$ of size $n \times p$ be the centered matrix of full rank, obtained from data suspected to contain outliers.

Similarly as for $\tilde{X}^*$, we may compute also the QR factorization of $\tilde{X}$ – compare (3) – obtaining:

$$\tilde{X} = \tilde{Q} \begin{bmatrix} \tilde{R} \\ 0 \end{bmatrix}, \quad \tilde{Q} - \text{orthogonal}, \tag{5}$$

where $\tilde{R}$ is upper triangular with all diagonal elements positive. It is known that the columns of $\tilde{Q}$ form the orthonormal base for the linear subspace range $(\tilde{X})$ spanned by columns of $\tilde{X}$ (see Golub and Van Loan [7], pp. 233–234).

In our proposed *Plug-in* method we substitute into (3) as Q the base matrix $\tilde{Q}$ from (5). This results in the matrix $\tilde{X}_1^*$ defined as follows:

$$\tilde{X}_1^* = \tilde{Q} \begin{bmatrix} R^* \\ 0 \end{bmatrix}, \tag{6}$$

where R^* is taken from eq. (2) and $\tilde{Q}$ from eq. (5).

Obviously $\tilde{X}_1^*$ satisfies (1), moreover it is an approximation of $\tilde{X}$. Let us notice that the linear subspaces spanned by the columns of $\tilde{X}_1^*$ and $\tilde{X}$ are the same.

The distance (closeness) between $\tilde{X}_1^*$ and $\tilde{X}$ is measured by

$$\delta_1 = ||\tilde{X}_1^* - \tilde{X}||_F = ||R^* - \tilde{R}||_F. \tag{7}$$

2.3 Method II: Procrustes transformation

Let A and B be two given $n \times p$, $(p < n)$ real matrices. In the classical orthogonal Procrustes problem encountered firstly in factor analysis – see, e.g., Cattell and Khanna [5], Schönemann [12] – A and B were denoting matrices of factor loadings, derived – say – from two experiments or two groups of data. Since the factor loadings are usually determined up to an orthogonal factor (orthogonal rotation), the problem was to find such a rotation matrix Q which applied to one of these matrices, say B, would bring it as near as possible to the other matrix, in our case A.

Of course the 'nearness' should be specified in terms of a mathematical criterion imposed on the matrix A and the derived by the orthogonal transformation matrix $B_{transf} = BQ$.

Usually the least squares criterion is used and the problem, called the *Procrustes problem*, is formulated as the minimization problem introduced below:

Let O_p denote the set of all orthogonal matrices of order p. We want to find $\hat{Q} \in O_p$ for which the following minimum is attained

$$\min_{Q \in O_p} \| A - BQ \|_F .$$ (8)

The solution of the Procrustes problem given by eq. (8) above can be obtained by means of the singular value decomposition (the SVD) of the matrix $C = B^T A$ (for the definition and properties of the SVD see for example Golub and Van Loan [7], pp. 427–430). Let C have the following SVD

$$C = U_c \Sigma_c V_c^T, \quad U_c, V_c \in O_p, \quad \Sigma_c = diag(\sigma_j),$$ (9)

where σ_j $(j = 1, \ldots, p)$ are the singular values of C. It is well known that

$$\hat{Q} = U_c V_c^T$$ (10)

is the minimizer of (8). If C has full rank then the minimizer of (8) is unique.

We now apply the concept of the orthogonal Procrustes problem to chose an orthogonal matrix Q in (3). For this purpose we consider the following problem: Find $Q^* \in O_n$, for which the following minimum is attained:

$$\min_{Q \in O_n} \left\| \tilde{X} - Q \begin{bmatrix} R^* \\ 0 \end{bmatrix} \right\|_F .$$ (11)

It is the Procrustes problem (8) with $A = \tilde{X}^T$, $B = [(R^*)^T, 0]$ and Q^T instead of Q, because Frobenius norms of a matrix and its transpose are the same.

We solve this problem similarly as the previous one formulated in eq. (8). We compute the matrix C which is now defined as

$$C = B^T A = \begin{bmatrix} R^* \tilde{X}^T \\ 0 \end{bmatrix},$$ (12)

seek for its SVD decomposition (see (9)), and find the solution as $Q^* = (\hat{Q})^T = V_c U_c^T$, where $\hat{Q}$ is determined in (10).

Substituting into (3) $Q = Q^*$ we obtain:

$$\widetilde{X}_2^* = Q^* \begin{bmatrix} R^* \\ 0 \end{bmatrix}.$$ (13)

This is our second proposal for constructing a data matrix $\widetilde{X}^*$ having the desired property (1).

The matrix $\widetilde{X}_2^*$ obtained by solving of the appropriate Procrustes problem is closer – in the meaning of the Frobenius norm defined in eq. (4) – to $\widetilde{X}$ than the matrix $\widetilde{X}_1^*$ computed by using eq. (6). We have

$$\delta_2 = \| \widetilde{X}_2^* - \widetilde{X} \|_F \leq \delta_1 = \| \widetilde{X}_1^* - \widetilde{X} \|_F .$$ (14)

3.   EXAMPLES OF APPLICATION

We will illustrate the behaviour of the proposed methods by considering 4 data sets used by statisticians as benchmarks for detecting outliers. A comprehensive review of these and other data sets, also of methods for detecting outliers, may be found in Bartkowiak & Zdziarek [2]. Relatively up-to-date information on algorithms for identifying outliers may be found in Billor, Hadi and Velleman [4]. For our analysis we have calculated the robust covariance matrices using the algorithm proposed by Rocke and Woodruff [10] using the software (in C+) obtained from the authors.

For each data set given as the data matrix X of size $n \times p$ – by applying our two proposals – we obtain two reconstructed matrices which will be denoted as X_1^* and X_2^*. The centering was done using medians of the variables observed in X.

Our next task is to visualize graphically how much the reconstructed data matrices X_1^* and X_2^* differ from the original (contaminated) data matrix X. We have chosen for that purpose the technique called *parallel coordinate plot* [14]. The method plots individual data vectors as line segments connected at vertical spikes denoting axes for subsequent variables (the spikes are invisible in our plots). We have used for our computations the function *parallel-plot* implemented in XLispStat [13]. Thanks to interactive graphics possible when using XLispStat we were able easily to select and mark with different colour indicated data vectors, in our case those data vectors, about which we know that they are outliers. In subsequent plots black line segments represent the known outliers and cyan (light gray) colour indicates the remaining data vectors. The plots are bordered by yellow (very light gray) segments indicating the *min* and *max* value of each variable as observed in the original (contaminated) data set.

3.1 The Kass data

The Kass data are synthetic data described in the paper by Hawkins, Bradu and Kass [8], in which also the source of the data may be found. The data were considered by the authors of that paper in the context of a regression analysis. There are 14 outliers; 10 of them (*no.'s* 1–10) are bad leverage points and 4 of them (*no.'s* 11–14) are good leverage points. The remaining data vectors (*no.'s* 15–75) represent a homogeneous data cloud and constitute the 'clean' part of the data.

Parallel coordinate plots for that data set are shown in *Figure 1*.

The outstanding nature of the 14 outliers is strikingly obvious. What concerns the reconstructed data vectors *no.* 1–10 it can be seen that they belong to the area covered by the 'clean' part of the data. What concerns the bad leverage points *no.* 11–14 it can be seen that they have changed also their position dramatically, none the less they exhibit still a small heterogeneity as compared with the 'clean' part of the data, which can be seen especially in the middle plot.

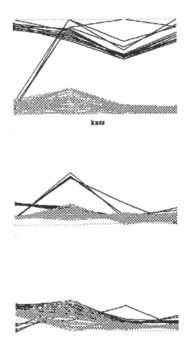

Fig. 1. Parallel coordinate plots for the Kass data; $\delta_1 = 140.03$, $\delta_2 = 132.38$

Explanations. Upper exhibits show original data, middle – backprojection by the *Plug-in* method, bottom – backprojection by the *Procrustes* method.

Outliers are marked by *black* and remaining data by *cyan* line segments. Nearly horizontal yellow lines at the top and bottom of each plot show artificial data vectors with variable values representing the maximum and minimum of subsequent variables attained in the original, contaminated data set.

Take notice, how the line segments representing the outliers with atypical structure clearly visible in top exhibits became – in the middle and bottom exhibits – more concordant with the interdependence structure of the remaining data vectors.

Distances δ_1 and δ_2 of the backprojected and the original data are defined in eq. (7) and eq. (14)

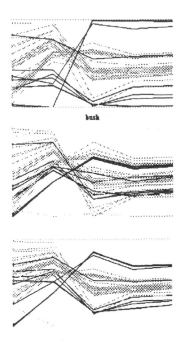

Fig. 2. Parallel coordinate plots for the Bushfire data; δ_1=817.76, δ_2=431.77

3.2   The Bushfire data

The considered bushfire data contain some satellite observations on $p = 5$ frequency bands, corresponding to each of $n = 38$ pixels and were recorded by N.A. Campbell from CSIRO with the aim to locate bushfire scars. The source of the data may be found in [9]. It is known that the data contain two sets of outliers:

the set $S5 = \{7, 8, 9, 10, 11\}$;
the set $S7 = \{32, 33, \ldots, 38\}$.

The remaining data vectors constitute the 'clean' part of the data and are relatively homogeneous. It is known that the set $S7$ is masked by the set $S5$ and for that reason it is difficult to detect when using traditional methods.

The parallel coordinate plots for that data set are shown in Figure 2. Again, one may note here the outstanding position of the data vectors belonging to the sets $S5$ and $S7$. The reconstructed data vectors are relatively much more concordant with the 'clean' part of the data – as compared to their position in the original data cloud.

3.3   The Milk Container data

The considered milk container data consist of 8 measurements carried out on 86 samples of milk taken from milk containers. One sample is duplicate, another one seems to contain a big error, probably a wrong digit. We have removed the duplicate sample, thus we have taken for our analysis only $n = 85$ samples. The data contains about 17 samples which may be considered as outliers, some of them are masked by others. The earliest reference to the data is in the paper by Daudin, Duby and Trécourt [6], later the data have been analyzed by many authors, a.o. by Atkinson [1], Rocke and Woodruff [10] and Bartkowiak and Zdziarek [2].

Parallel coordinate plots for the original and backprojected data are shown in *Figure 3*. Again one may notice the adjustment of the outliers and their shift toward the cloud constituting the central part of the data.

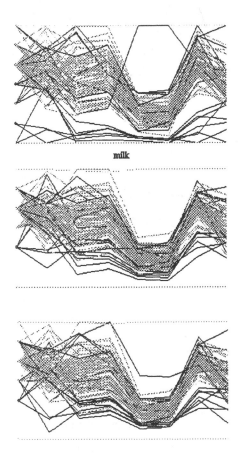

Fig. 3. Parallel coordinate plots for the Milk Container data; δ_1=21.99, δ_2=17.59.
Explanations: as under Fig. 1

3.4   The Modified Wood Gravity data

The modified wood gravity data consist of $n = 20$ data vectors, each containing $p = 6$ observations. The source of the data may be found in Rousseeuw and Leroy [11].

The data are part of real observations; however the data vectors *no*. 4, 6, 8, 19 contain specially implanted errors making these data vectors appear as outliers.

The parallel coordinate plots exhibiting the contaminated data matrix X and the backprojected matrices X_1^* and X_2^* are shown in *Figure 4*.

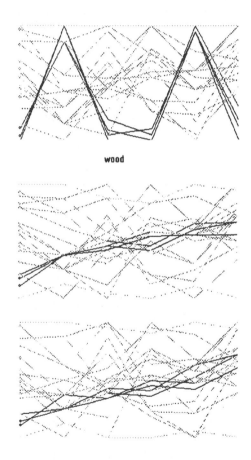

wood

Fig. 4. Parallel coordinate plots for the Modified Wood data; $\delta_1 = 0.4088$, $\delta_2 = 0.3809$.
Explanations: as under Fig. 1

Looking at that figure one may observe again clearly the outstanding structure of the four implanted outliers and the adjustments introduced during the backprojection: the atypical structure of the 4 outliers visible in the upper exhibit is clearly reduced.

4. DISCUSSION

In all 4 examples we have seen clearly that after backprojection the outstandingness and atypicalness of the outliers has diminished and the respective data vectors have been brought nearer to the area covered by the 'clean' part of the data set.

However one has to be careful.

The backprojection shows data vectors as they should appear accordingly to the overall internal structure of the data. If the outliers were due errors in measurements, then the proposed backprojection corrects to some extent these errors. Such procedure might be proper, e.g., in laboratory environments for some blood tests, when *post hoc* it was stated, that at some day the calibration of one device was not proper. The best thing would then be to repeat the measurements, but when the patients are no more available, then their readings could be adjusted by backprojection.

On the other hand, a data vector identified as outlier might contain true, really observed values – due to an atypical individual belonging to different population as the other individuals. In such case the backprojection for that individual would falsify his/her findings and should not be taken into account.

In some cases the proposed method could serve as a tool for indicating suspected outliers. Some methods for calculating robust covariance matrices yield in the same run also the list of suspected outliers (e.g. the algorithm by Rocke and Woodruff [10] has this property). Some other methods do not do it (e.g. the DSD algorithm [3] does not have that property). When performing our backprojection for the benchmark data sets it was observed that the biggest changes (i.e. displacements of the data vectors in the original and backprojected data matrices) have occurred for the (known) outliers.

What concerns the computational methods, we have used only standard algorithms. When analyzing larger data sets (performing data mining) possibly some other algorithms would be more effective. In particular, the Q^* factor for the optimal Procrustes method yielding the matrix appearing in (13) could be computed seemingly more effectively using the polar decomposition (see e.g. [15]) of the appropriate matrix C appearing in (12). Also, more could be said on the conditions of the uniqueness or non uniqueness of solutions of (8) and (11).

We are also not specially happy using the Frobenius norm (4) as the measure of closeness of the original and the reconstructed data matrices (see (7) and (14)). We feel that in our problem this measure should be defined in a different way.

Work on these topics is in progress and will be presented elsewhere.

5. REFERENCES

[1] Atkinson A.C. 1994. 'Fast very robust methods for the detection of multiple outliers'. *JASA* 89, pp. 1329–1339.
[2] Bartkowiak A., Zdziarek J. 2001. 'Identifying outliers – a comparative review of 7 methods applied to 7 benchmark data sets'. Manuscript pp. 1–16.

[3] Bartkowiak A., Ziętak K. 2000. 'Correcting possible non-positiveness of a covariance matrix estimated elementwise in a robust way.' In: J. Sołdek, J. Pejaś (Eds), Advanced Computer Systems, ACS'2000, Proceedings, October 2000, Fac. of Computer Science & Information Systems, Technical University of Szczecin, pp. 91–96.

[4] Billor N., Hadi A.S., Velleman P.F. 2000. 'BACON, blocked adaptive computationally efficient outlier nominator.' Computational Statistics & Data Analysis 34, 279–298.

[5] Cattell R.B., Khanna D.K. 1977. 'Principles and procedures for unique factor rotation in factor analysis.' In: K. Enslein, A. Ralston and H.S. Wilf (Eds), Mathematical Methods for Digital Computers, Vol. 3: Statistical Methods for Digital Computers. Wiley, New York, 166–202.

[6] Daudin J.J., Duby C., Trécourt P. 1988. 'Stability of principal component analysis studied by the bootstrap method.' Statistics 19, 241–258.

[7] Golub G.H., Van Loan Ch.F. Matrix Computations. The Johns Hopkins Univ. Press, Baltimore, 1991.

[8] Hawkins D.M., Bradu D., Kass G.V. 1984. 'Location of several outliers in multiple regression using elemental subsets'. Technometrics 26, 197–208.

[9] Maronna R.A. and Yohai V.J. 1995. 'The behaviour of the Stahel-Donoho robust multivariate estimator.' *JASA* 90, 330–341.

[10] Rocke D., Woodruff D.L. 1996. 'Identification of outliers in multivariate data'. *JASA* 91, no 435, pp. 1047–1061.

[11] Rousseeuw P.J., Leroy A. Robust Regression and outliers detection. Wiley, New York, 1987.

[12] Schönemann P.H. 1966. 'The generalized solution of the orthogonal Procrustes problem'. Psychometrika 31, 1–16.

[13] Tierney L. LISP-STAT, an Object-Oriented Environment for Statistical Computing and Dynamics Graphics. Wiley New York 1987.

[14] Wegman E.J. 1990. 'Hyperdimensional data analysis using parallel coordinates'. *JASA* 85, pp. 664–675.

[15] Zieliński P., Ziętak K. 1995. 'The polar decomposition – properties, applications and algorithms.' Annals of Polish Math. Soc. 38, 23–49.

Peculiarities of Genetic Algorithm Usage When Synthesizing Neural and Fuzzy Regulators

BURAKOV M. V., KONOVALOV A. S.
State University of Aerospace Instrumentation (GUAP)
St.-Petersburg, Russia, bmv@acts.aanet.ru

Abstract: The paper considers the peculiarities of the genetic algorithm usage when adjusting the neural and fuzzy controllers to control the dynamic objects. Main attention is paid to the matters concerning formation of fitness function, whose computation is the key moment in the genetic algorithm operation. The joint use of the fitness qualitative and quantitative assessments is suggested. For this purpose notions of fuzzy trajectory and fuzzy fitness are introduced. The examples of computer simulation are shown.

Key words: Genetic algorithm, neural control, fitness function

1. INTRODUCTION

Genetic algorithm (GA) takes a specific place among the vast range of optimization techniques since it is a generalization of random search methods and it may be used for searching the global minimum in multi-extreme problems. However, in spite of the impressive capability of the state-of-the-art computing engineering, the search space and local extremum number in real problems may be too high for the GA effective usage. In particular, it concerns the problems of neural and fuzzy controller parameters adjustment. Here, a specific problem occurs related to the solution qualitative assessment that is provided by one or another variant of controller parameters. It is necessary to compare the desired and real transients when introducing the controller into the feedback circuit. This problem becomes especially complicated for the multiconnection objects where it becomes similar to pattern recognition problems. As it is known, in case of pattern recognition the use of quantitative assessments only does not always result in success. Here, the use of qualitative assessments is also required. The theory of fuzzy sets ([1] and others) may be an effective tool for the qualitative assessment construction.

2.   GENETIC ALGORITHM

The use of the GA supposes the parameters coding. Usually, the parameters, by which the search is conducted, are coded by means of a chromosome – binary code whose length depends on the number of parameters. Separate chromosome components are called the genes. Then, the GA assumes a chain of actions:

1.   Initialization of population of N chromosomes. Each chromosome is an alternative for the problem solution. Initially, the chromosomes get random values.
2.   Chromosome fitness assessment. Each chromosome is assessed by means of fitness function, which shows the extent of correspondence between the solution provided by this chromosome and the target variant.
3.   Copying. At this phase the population modernization takes place, in the course of which every chromosome is reproduced in increased or decreased number according to its relative fitness.
4.   Crossover. This genetic operator groups chromosomes in pairs and exchanges their genes beginning from some random position.
5.   Mutation. This operation is a random change of a small number of the chromosome genes.
6.   A check takes place, whether a satisfactory quality of solution is achieved. In case of negative answer, the return to Item 2 occurs. In case of positive answer, the algorithm operation is terminated.

Here, it is important to note that in case of unsuccessful initial distribution of chromosomes, one can occur in the vicinity of the global minimum only due to mutations. This process may be very slow when the chromosome length is large and the population size is considerable. That's why the above-described algorithm must be modified by introduction of the new item:

2': Population fitness assessment. The qualitative fitness assessments are computed. If none of the population chromosomes corresponds qualitatively to the conception about correct solution, the return to Item 1 takes place.

With account of this supplement the GA may be described as follows (Fig. 1):

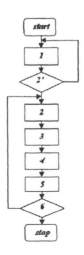

Fig. 1

3. LEARNING OF NEURAL AND FUZZY CONTROLLERS BY MEANS OF THE GA

Genetic algorithm is an effective means for the neural and fuzzy controllers learning in those cases, when sufficiently adequate and high-speed simulation model of object may be used.

Here, the control law is synthesized as a result of multiple experiments with the model in the course of which the controller parameters are being corrected (Fig. 2).

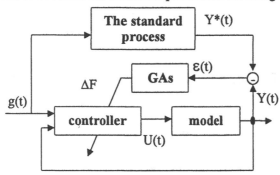

Fig 2.

Usually the values of synaptic weights of neural net, and more seldom, the parameters of neural activation functions are corrected for the neural controller (e.g. [2]).

For the fuzzy controller the numbers of the linguistic variable (LV) terms which are included in the control rules, LV terms parameters, as well as the total number of rules and each rule contribution into the control signal forming may be corrected ([3-5] and others).

In both cases the controller parameters are encoded by the chromosome, consisting of a bit chain, whose length corresponds to the power of the Cartesian product of parameter value sets. Sub-optimal solution, corresponding to the desired behavior of the controller, is sought within the population – sufficiently large set of chromosomes. The GA operation takes place in compliance with Fig. 1.

The specificity of designing controllers by means of the GA lies in the fact that the relative fitness function selection in many respects defines the efficiency of the learning process (especially it refers to multi-dimensional objects). If the relative fitness function inadequately characterizes each of the chromosomes, the learning process may become protracted, may go in cycles or stop. This is especially apparent for large lengths of chromosomes when the search area turns out to be very large.

When constructing the chromosome relative fitness function, it is necessary to compare the real and desired processes. Let y^* be a reference process and y_1 and y_2 be implementations obtained at various parameters of controller, which are encoded by chromosomes 1 and 2 (Fig. 3).

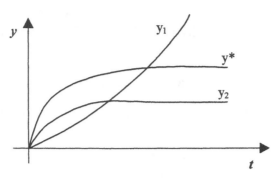

Fig. 3

For comparison of these variants one can use the qualitative criteria. For example:

$$J = \frac{1}{\sum\limits_{i=1}^{N}\left|y_i^* - y_i^k\right|};\qquad k = \overline{1,2};\qquad\qquad (1)$$

Here, N – the number of time moments being considered.

It is obvious, in compliance with criterion (1), $J_1 \approx J_2$, though y_1 – a curve does not correspond quantitatively with the reference process. If chromosomes 1 and 2 simultaneously are present in the population, the GA operation will continue successfully. The descendants of chromosome 2 which qualitatively correspond with the desired process, gradually will get higher assessments and will allow to obtain the problem solution.

The case is much worse when all chromosomes in the population provide the 1-type processes. In this case the GA operation on the basis of fitness assessment (1) will cause roaming in the vicinity of the local extremum and probability to fall in the vicinity of the global extremum at the expense of mutations at large chromosomes length will be very low.

This problem is even more a factor for the objects having m outputs, where actually, it is necessary to make decision on the degree of proximity of the reference pattern specified by a set of parametric functions and the real pattern also specified by a set of functions. Here, equation (1) must be as follows:

$$J = \frac{1}{\sum\limits_{j=1}^{m}\sum\limits_{i=1}^{n}k_j \cdot \left|y_i^j - (y_i^j)^*\right|}\qquad\qquad (2)$$

where k_j – a scale factor.

As multiple studies in the field of pattern recognition ([6] and others) evidence show, for these purposes it is not sufficient to use quantitative assessments such as (1). For adequate comparison of variants it is necessary to complete the calculation of the distance functions by the estimation of structure correspondence in the problem solution variants being compared. The structures estimation requires the qualitative assessments to be made and in this case the use of the fuzzy mathematics apparatus may be effective.

4. CONSTRUCTION OF FUZZY FITNESS ASSESSMENTS

The fuzzy fitness assessments, which are necessary for the block 2' operation (Fig. 1), are constructed in compliance with the following algorithm.

Let the process implementation $Y(t)$ be obtained at some parameters of the controller. It is required to estimate its similarity to the familiar desired process $Y^*(t)$.

Let us consider $y_i(t)$ be the i-th component of $Y(t)$ vector at discrete times t_j whose number must be sufficient for an adequate estimation of the process (Fig. 4).

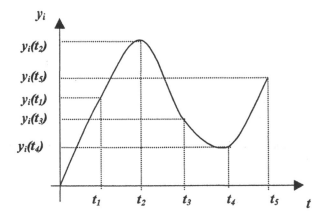

Fig. 4

Each meaning of $y_i(t_j)$ is transformed into a fuzzy number. In this case $y_i(t_j)$ is considered as the center of the triangular membership function (Fig. 5).

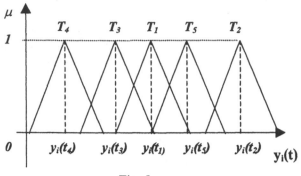

Fig. 5

The set of such fuzzy values may be considered as T_i terms of the linguistic variable (LV) with the name corresponding to $y_i(t)$:

$$\widetilde{Y}_i = \{T_1^i, T_2^i, \ldots T_n^i\}$$

The set of m linguistic variables (where m is dimension of $Y(t)$ vector) may be named as a fuzzy trajectory:

$$\widetilde{TR} = \{L_1, L_2, \ldots L_m\}$$

Similarly, the reference fuzzy trajectory may be constructed:

$$\widetilde{TR}^* = \{L_1^*, L_2^*, \ldots L_m^*\}$$

For computing the distance apart fuzzy trajectories the equation may be suggested as follows:

$$\rho(\widetilde{TR}, \widetilde{TR}^*) = 1 - \min_i \left(\min_j \left(\mu_j^i \left(T_j^i, (T_j^i)^*\right)\right)\right),$$

$$i = \overline{1, m}; \qquad j = \overline{1, n}.$$

In this equation the μ_j^i describes the likeness of j-th terms of reference and real trajectories' i-th LV (Fig. 6):

$$\mu_j = \begin{cases} 1 - \dfrac{|X|}{D}, & |X| \le D \\[2mm] 0, & |X| > D \end{cases}$$

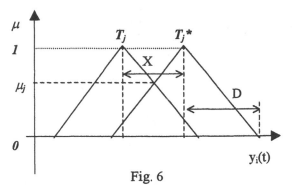

Fig. 6

Thus, the distance apart fuzzy trajectories varies from 0 to 1. The "0" value means the full likeness of trajectories, and the "1" value – full difference. In accord with Fig. 6 the "D"-parameter allows to vary the sensitivity of the introduced distance function. The more D, the less trajectories will be at maximum distance from reference trajectory.

5. SIMULATION RESULTS

The described fuzzy distance computation criterion has been testing as applied to the adjustment problem by means of the GA of fuzzy and neural controllers for the purpose of the inverse pendulum control. This well-known problem is described, for example, in [7]. Here, the object has two controlled variables – the pendulum angle of inclination and the distance from the reference point.

Fig. 7 and 8 show two process implementations (*a* and *b*), obtained at various controller parameters (chromosomes), and the reference trajectory (*x*).

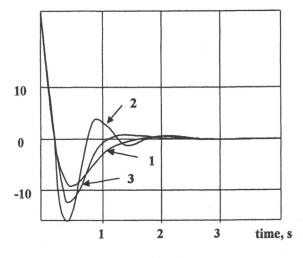

Fig. 7

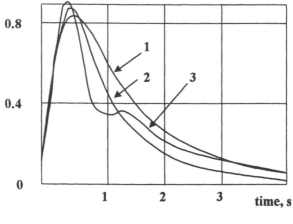

Fig. 8

Table 1 shows the assessments of these variants according to two criteria.

variant	J	ρ
2	0.19	0
3	0.16	0.33

Table 1

It is apparent that variants are close according to the first of the criteria and dissimilar according to the second criterion. The use of the ρ-criterion in this situation allows to choose in favour of the b-variant, though it is somewhat worse according to the J-criterion. This choice allows to get the minimum error when adjusting controller.

Initially, when starting the GA, one can use high values of the D-parameter (see Fig. 6), that allows by means of the ρ-criterion to perform repeatedly the population random initialization in those cases when $\rho = 1$ for all of the chromosomes (restriction 2' at Fig. 1). After that, when population falls into vicinity of global optimum, the D value may be decreased gradually, in order to make the GA to search for more and more precise solution of the problem.

6.   CONCLUSION

The paper presents the variant of the relative fitness function construction for neural and fuzzy controller learning. For this purpose the concept of fuzzy distance between the reference and real trajectories of the controlled object is introduced. The calculation of the fuzzy distance allows to reveal and discard those chromosomes which deliberately do not meet the requirements for the transient process, quality though may have quite good values of the relative fitness functions constructed on the basis of quantitative assessments, only.

The construction of the fuzzy distance is based on substitution of each output coordinate range of the object for a set of fuzzy numbers which may be treated as values (terms) of corresponding linguistic variables (LV) at various time moments. The set of all LVs constructed in such way forms the fuzzy trajectory of an object. The comparison of the object fuzzy trajectory obtained for particular chromosome and the reference fuzzy trajectory may be performed according to the fuzzy mathematics laws.

The paper presents examples, confirming the practical significance of the proposed approach for the effective usage of the GA when synthesizing the controllers which implement the dynamic objects control.

7. REFERENCES

[1] Zadeh L.A. The Concept of a Linguistic Variable and Its Application to Approximate Reasoning, Information Sciences, Part 1, 8 (1975), 199-249; Part 2, 8 (1975), 301-357; Part 3 8 (1975), 43-80.
[2] Burakov M., Konovalov A. Development of dynamic object's neural controller by means of decomposition // Intern. Conf. Of Advanced Computer systems "ACS'2000", 23-25 October 2000, Szchecin, Poland, pp.307-311.
[3] Sinn-Cheng Lin, Yung-Yaw Chen. Design of self-learning fuzzy sliding mode controllers based on genetic algorithms // Fuzzy sets and systems, 86 (1997) pp. 139-153.
[4] F. Herrera, M. Losano, J.L. Verdegay. A learning process for fuzzy control rules using genetic algorithms // Fuzzy sets and systems, 100 (1998) pp. 143-158.
[5] H.B. Gurocak, A genetic-algorithm-based method for tuning fuzzy logic controllers // Fuzzy sets and systems 108 (1999) pp. 39-47.
[6] R.O. Duda, P.E. Hart. Pattern classification and scene analysis. New York, 1973.

Application of the Probabilistic RBF Neural Network in Multidimensional Classification Problems

MARCIN PLUCIŃSKI

Faculty of Computer Science and Information Systems, Technical University of Szczecin, ul.Żołnierska 49, PL-71210 Szczecin, e-mail: marcin.plucinski@wi.ps.pl

Abstract: Neural network is an universal classifier and with the proper choosing of its architecture it can solve any, even very complicated, classification task. The main problem in neural network applications lies in the fact, that their learning process is complicated and time-consuming. It concerns especially multidimensional tasks for which neural network architecture is very extended. The probabilistic RBF neural network does not possess all of the mentioned disadvantages. It has only one coefficient to tune so its learning is very easy and much faster than a feedforward multilayer network.
The paper describes some experiments with the probabilistic RBF neural network used in multidimensional classification problems.

Key words: RBF neural network, probabilistic neural network, classification

1. INTRODUCTION

Neural networks are often used in classification – it is one of their most popular applications. Neural network is an universal classifier and with the proper choosing of its architecture it can solve any, even very complicated, classification task. The main problem in neural network applications lies in the fact that their learning process is complicated and time-consuming. It concerns especially multidimensional tasks, for which neural network architecture is very extended.

As an example we can take into account the feedforward network with one hidden layer and output layer. We want to create a classifier with 100 inputs, so we assume that there we have 20 neurons in the hidden layer and one in the output layer. Next we assume that all inputs are connected with all neurons in the hidden layer, which are next connected with the output layer. In result we obtain the network with $20\cdot20+20$ connections and it means that we have 420 weights to find.

Learning process of such network may be very difficult and very long. It should be repeated many times with many different start weight values and to obtain properly working network sufficiently large data set should be prepared.

The probabilistic RBF neural network does not posses all of the mentioned above disadvantages. It has only **one** coefficient to tune so its learning is very easy and much faster than the feedforward multilayer network. One of the probabilistic network faults is that it has very strong tendency for overfitting, so tuning of its coefficient **must be** realised with the usage of test data or crossvalidation techniques.

2.   PROBABILISTIC RBF NEURAL NETWORK

The probabilistic RBF neural network [2, 3] works with data set (file) which acts as a learning set for the feedforward neural network. Let's assume that classified sample $\mathbf{X}_i$ is described by the certain set of inputs (attributes). The classification result depends on input values x_{ij}. The data set is defined by samples with the known membership to the class and it can take a form (1):

$$
\begin{matrix}
x_{11} & x_{12} & \cdots & x_{1j} & \cdots & x_{1p} & c_1 \\
x_{21} & x_{22} & \cdots & x_{2j} & \cdots & x_{2p} & c_2 \\
\vdots & \vdots & & \vdots & & \vdots & \vdots \\
x_{i1} & x_{i2} & \cdots & x_{ij} & \cdots & x_{ip} & c_i \\
\vdots & \vdots & & \vdots & & \vdots & \vdots \\
x_{m1} & x_{m2} & \cdots & x_{mj} & \cdots & x_{mp} & c_m
\end{matrix}
\tag{1}
$$

where:
$\mathbf{X}_i = [x_{i1}, x_{i2}, \dots, x_{ip}]$ – the sample i,
x_{ij} – the value of input j for sample i,
c_i – the class which the sample i belongs to,
q – the number of classes,
m – the number of samples,
p – the number of inputs,
$i = 1, \dots, m$,
$j = 1, \dots, p$,
$k = 1, \dots, q$.

The quality of classification first of all depends on taken tuning coefficient but also on size of the data set, inputs taken into account and their normalisation method. The structure of the probabilistic RBF neural network is presented in Fig. 1.

Function $g_k(\mathbf{X})$ is the estimate of the probability density function for the class k. Such estimate can be calculated from:

$$g_k(\mathbf{X}) = \frac{1}{n_k \cdot \sigma} \sum_{i=1}^{n_k} W\left(\frac{\mathbf{X} - \mathbf{X}_i^{(k)}}{\sigma}\right) \tag{2}$$

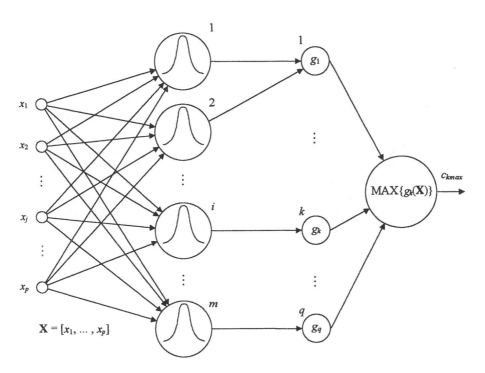

Figure 1. Symbolic scheme of the probabilistic RBF neural network

The Gauss function is often used as a *W* function, so the estimate takes the form:

$$g_k(\mathbf{X}) = \frac{1}{n_k \cdot \sigma^p \cdot (2\pi)^{p/2}} \sum_{i=1}^{n_k} \exp\left(\frac{-\sum_{j=1}^{p}\left(x_j - x_{ij}^{(k)}\right)^2}{2\sigma^2}\right) \tag{3}$$

where:
n_k – number of classes classified to the class k,
$x_{ij}^{(k)}$ – samples from the data set classified to the class k,
σ – coefficient defining the action range of the Gauss function.

Function (3) can be simplified for the classification purpose. If we assume the same value of σ for all classes, then the formula (4) can be used:

$$\tilde{g}_k(\mathbf{X}) = \frac{1}{n_k} \sum_{i=1}^{n_k} \exp\left(\frac{-\sum_{j=1}^{p}\left(x_j - x_{ij}^{(k)}\right)^2}{(p\sigma)^2}\right) =$$

$$= \frac{1}{n_k} \sum_{i=1}^{n_k} \exp\left(-c\sum_{j=1}^{p}\left(x_j - x_{ij}^{(k)}\right)^2\right),$$

(4)

where: c – tuning coefficient which must be found. As a classification result, the network returns the class for which the value of $\tilde{g}_k(\mathbf{X})$ function is maximum.

The values of inputs x_{ij} usually change in the certain limited domains and for various inputs their limits can be quite different. That's why inputs need normalisation before processing by the probabilistic RBF neural network. The normalisation of value x, which varies in the interval [x_{min}, x_{max}], consists in reducing it by appropriate scaling to the normalised interval, for example [0,1]. The network with normalised interval works better and what is important, it is much easier to find its tuning coefficient c. The essence of the normalisation of input signals is represented in Fig. 2.

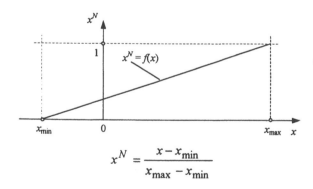

$$x^N = \frac{x - x_{min}}{x_{max} - x_{min}}$$

Fig. 2. Normalisation of input signals [4]

The selection of the tuning coefficient c must be done with a special care. When we choose large enough value of c, the network can correctly classify all samples from the data set, so the overfitting of the network is very easy. In practice, the test file must be created from the data file and as the final value of c we must choose the largest of found values (there is often a number of such values) which assures the minimum classification error of the test file.

If the main data set is small, we can not exclude from it a part of samples to create the test set. Accidentally, some important sample could be excluded and the classifier would work wrong. In such situation a crossvalidation methods can be used. One of the most popular method is the "leave one out" method. It consists in leaving one sample from the data set and then in classifying it. Such step must be repeated for all samples and the classification error can be calculated as:

$$e_{cv} = \frac{r_{cv}}{m} \qquad\qquad\qquad (5)$$

where: r_{cv} – the number of wrong classified samples. Similarly as above, we choose the largest of found c values which assures the minimum classification error e_{cv}.

3. EXPERIMENTS

3.1 Detection of molecular subunits

An experiment will consist in detection of specific molecular subunits (substructures, chemical groups) from their infrared spectra. In the presented classification problem there is 140 inputs which corresponds to the coded part of the infrared spectra of about 1500 different chemical substances. The output takes the value 1 or 0 if the examined molecular subunit is present in the substance or not.

The experiment will be divided into 3 parts:
1. detection of the amine ($-NH_2$) substructure,
2. detection of the carboxylic ($-COOH$) substructure,
3. detection of the metylic substructure.

As in the data files, prepared for each substructure, each sample represents the certain compound; it is not possible to create test files. We must decide for leave-one-out-crossvalidation method, which assures the optimal value of the tuning coefficient c.

The number of wrong classified samples in crossvalidation process with respect to the coefficient c is presented in Fig. 3.

As it can be seen in Fig. 3 the error r_{cv} as a function of the tuning coefficient c has some local minima. For certain classification problems an amount of minima could be quite large, so finding an optimum value of c must be done with a special care. The best value of c is the largest from values for which the crossvalidation error e_{cv} (or r_{cv}) is minimum. It is the largest because for this value the data file classification error e_{data} (or r_{data}) has the least value.

Table 1 presents the results of learning of the RBF probability neural network. We can see that results of classifying (detecting chemical subunits) are very good. Almost all samples (1 wrong) were classified correctly in the data file and what is more important the crossvalidation error wasn't larger than about 25%.

a)

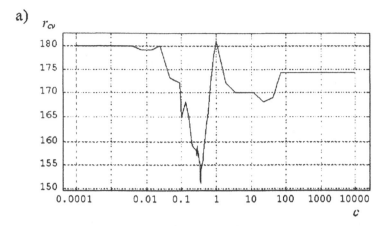

b)

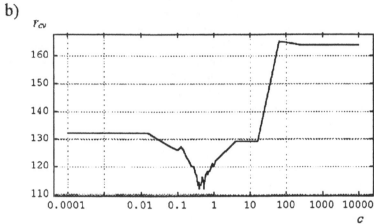

c)

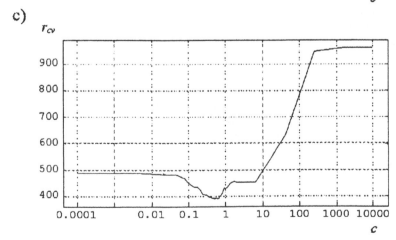

Fig. 3. Number of wrong classified samples in crossvalidation process with respect to the coefficient *c* (a) amine, b) carboxylic, c) metylic substructure)

Substruc-ture	Best c value	e_{cv} %	r_{cv}	e_{data} %	r_{data}
amine	0.3458	0	0	10.06	151
carboxylic	0.5244	0.07	1	7.47	112
metylic	0.5743	0	0	25.9	389

Tab. 1. Results of learning of the RBF probability neural network

Experiments with the same data used for learning an expert system are described in [1]. The data error e_{data} of the created system was about 10%, so the RBF probability neural network works more exact and its tuning is easier.

3.2 Detection of a credit card approval[*]

In the experiment we will predict the approval or non-approval of a credit card to a customer [5]. Each sample represents real data used by bank with 51 inputs which are continuous, nominal with small numbers of values and nominal with larger numbers of values, and the output which describes whether the bank granted the credit card (1) or not (0). The whole data set includes 690 examples.

As in the previous example, the best value of tuning coefficient c will be found with the leave one out crossvalidation method. The number of wrong classified samples in crossvalidation process with respect to the coefficient c is presented in Fig. 4.

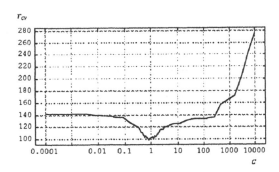

Fig. 4. Number of wrong classified samples in crossvalidation process with respect to the coefficient c in detection of a credit card approval

Table 2 presents the results of learning of the RBF probability neural network. The crossvalidation error in this case was about 14% and the data file classification error was about 18%. This results are comparable to results obtained for different feedforward multilayer network architectures described in [5].

---

[*] Data taken from PROBEN1 – a collection of problems for neural network learning in the realm of pattern classification and function approximation. The PROBEN1 benchmark set is available for anonymous FTP from the Neural Bench archive at Carnegie Mellon University: `ftp.cs.cmu.edu`, directory: `afs/cs/project/connect/bench/contrib/prechelt`, file: `proben1.tar.gz`.

Experiment	Best c value	e_{cv} %	r_{cv}	e_{data} %	r_{data}
credit card	0.8136	14.35	99	8.84	61
heart disease	1.2228	17.28	158	10.00	92

Tab. 2. Results of learning of the RBF probability neural network

3.3   **Prediction of a heart disease***

In the last experiment we will predict the heart disease [5]. The decision is made based on personal data such as: age, sex, smoking habits, subjective patient pain descriptions, and results of various medical examinations such as blood pressure and electro-cardiogram results. Each sample has 35 inputs, 1 output and the whole data set consists of 920 samples.

The number of wrong classified samples in crossvalidation process with respect to the coefficient c is presented in Fig. 5 and the results of the network learning are presented in Table 2.

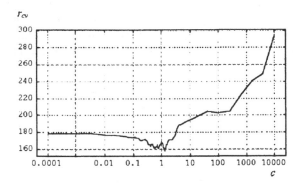

Fig. 5. Number of wrong classified samples in crossvalidation process with respect to the coefficient c in prediction of heart disease

The results obtained for the RBF probability neural network are better (about 2%) than the results obtained for different feedforward multilayer neural network architectures described in [5].

4.   CONCLUSION

The described experiments prove that the RBF probability neural network is a very effective classification tool. The classification quality of the RBF probability neural network is usually better or comparable to other classification techniques. Its learning is fast and easy so it can be a good alternative for "classic" feedforward multilayer neural networks.

5. REFERENCES

[1] Dębska B., Guzowska-Świder B.: SCANKEE – computer system for interpretation of infrared spectra, Journal of Molecular Structure 511-512, 1999, pp. 167-171

[2] Kim M.W., Arozullah M.: Generalized probabilistic neural network based classi-fiers, International Joint Conference on Neural Networks, Baltimore, 1992

[3] Masters T.: Sieci neuronowe w praktyce –programowanie w języku C++, Wydawnictwa Naukowo Techniczne, Warszawa, 1996

[4] Piegat A.: Fuzzy modeling and control, Physica-Verlag, Heidelberg, 2001

[5] Prechelt L.: PROBEN1 – A set of neural network benchmark problems and bench-marking rules, Technical Report, 1994

Visual Solution of Integer Optimization Problems

VLADIMIR MOISEEV

Faculty of Computer Science & Information Systems, Technical University of Szczecin, 49, Zolnierska st., 71-210 Szczecin, Poland, e-mail: vmoisseev@wi.ps.pl

Abstract: There is an objective contradiction between the allowable amount of computer researches and the feasibility of getting the optimal result in mathematical integer programming problems. The visual technique is proposed to settle this contradiction by means of the direct user participation in computer researches. The user determines the computer research amount indispensable and sufficient to obtain a quasi-optimal solution with the aid of a new graphic characteristic (the genealogy of integer solutions syndrome). The technique is based on stochastic multilevel investigation of integer solutions. It may be applied to linear and nonlinear integer as well as to combined (partially integer) problems of mathematical programming.

Key words: Visual techniques, computational optimization, integer programming, interactive search, optimal solutions

1. INTRODUCTION

Many important optimization problems of economics, management and design are formalized in terms of mathematical integer (discrete) programming. The traditional approach to computer solution of integer optimization problems [1,2] is based on utilizing the offline mode. In many cases, however, interactive visual solution of optimization problems in the online mode is more effectual. In interactive visual models of online type the borders between the problem formulation, its solution and the result interpretation disappear.

In the present paper the visual technique for graphic solution of integer optimization problems on the basis of stochastic investigation of integer solutions is proposed. The information support of the visual technique is provided by a graphic characteristics - the syndrome of integer solutions.

The special features of the visual technique are the following.

- The direct participation in the process of solving an integer problem on a computer optimization model is provided for the user of this model. Analyzing the syndrome genealogy the user selects the range of investigating integer solutions in the neighbourhood of the optimal real solution and determines the amount of computer research.

- As integer solutions searching is based on the random search procedure, the technique does not guarantee finding the accurate solution for an integer optimization problem. The solution found is always a strictly integer one, but in the general case there may be other integer solutions characterized by a lesser objective function value.
- The technique may be applied to both completely integer (linear and nonlinear) and combined (partially integer) problems of mathematical programming.
- The visual technique makes it possible to detect the contradictoriness of a computer model when there are no allowed integer solutions. In this case the visualization of integer solutions syndrome remains blocked during the entire computer search.

2.   MATHEMATICAL PROBLEM FORMULATION

The integer programming problem is formulated in the following way. To minimize the objective function

$$F = F(x_1, x_2, ..., x_n) \tag{1}$$

under functional constraints

$$H_j = H_j(x_1, x_2, ..., x_n) \leq 0, \ j = \overline{1, m} \tag{2}$$

and non-negative integer variables, i.e.

$$x_i \geq 0, \ i = \overline{1, n}, \tag{3}$$

$$x_1, x_2, ..., x_n \ \text{are integers} \tag{4}$$

The objective function (1) and the constraints (2) may be both linear and nonlinear.

3.   SOLUTION PHASES

In the general case the integer programming problem (1)-(4) is solved in the interactive mode on the basis of the following three phase procedure.

3.1 To obtain and analyze the optimal real solution

The optimal real solution $x_i^{(real)}, i = \overline{1,n}$ is the solution for the original problem without considering the integer requirement. To obtain the visual solution use is made of the interactive graphic models proposed in [3]. In the general case the solution $x_i^{(real)}, i = \overline{1,n}$ does not satisfy integer conditions, therefore it cannot be considered to be definitive. In a special case, however, this solution may turn out to be integer.

3.2 To determine and analyze the basic integer solution

The basic integer solution $x_i^{(bas)}, i = \overline{1,n}$ is the allowed integer solution in the neighbourhood of point $x_i^{(real)}, i = \overline{1,n}$, which is the basis for comparing it with the subsequent allowed integer solution. The basic solution may also be regarded as the final integer problem solution (if there is no subsequent allowed integer solution).

3.3 To search for the quasi-optimal solution

The quasi-optimal solution $x_i = x_i^{(qopt)}, i = \overline{1,n}$ is the allowed integer solution which is characterized by the lesser or equal objective function value as compared with the basic solution $x_i^{(bas)}, i = \overline{1,n}$.

4. FINDING INTEGER SOLUTIONS

The integer solutions under investigation $x_i^{(int)}(\eta), i = \overline{1,n}$ are chosen by means of iteration procedure in the following way:

$$
\left.
\begin{aligned}
&x_i^{(int)}(\eta) = \text{round}\{x_i^{(real)} + \chi_i[r_1(k), r_2(k)]\}, \\
&\chi_i[r_1(k), r_2(k)] = \text{sign}(\xi - 0.5) \cdot \{r_1(k) + \\
&+ \chi_i \cdot [r_2(k) - r_1(k)]\}
\end{aligned}
\right\} \tag{5}
$$

under the conditions

$$
F[x_1^{(int)}(\eta), x_2^{(int)}(\eta), ..., x_n^{(int)}(\eta)] > F^{(real)}, \tag{6}
$$

$$
H_j[x_1^{(int)}(\eta), x_2^{(int)}(\eta), ..., x_n^{(int)}(\eta)] \le 0, \tag{7}
$$

$$
j = \overline{1, m}.
$$

Here:

- $\eta = 1, 2,...$ is an integer solution number;

- round{...} is a roundoff function to the nearest integer;

- $\chi_i[r_1(k), r_2(k)]$ are random numbers with uniform distribution within

$$\pm[\frac{r_1(k) + r_2(k)}{2} \mp \frac{r_1(k) - r_2(k)}{2}], \quad r_1(k) \geq 0, \quad r_2(k) > 0, \quad r_1(k) < r_2(k)$$

(figure 1);

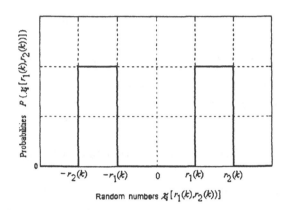

Fig. 1. The law of probabilities distribution of random numbers $\chi_i[r_1(k), r_2(k)]$.
At $r_1(k) = 0$ the random numbers are uniformly distributed within $\pm r_2(k)$

- ξ, χ_i are continuous random numbers distributed by the uniform law within [0,1];

- the parameter k=1,2,... characterizes the level of investigating integer solutions. At the first level (k=1) $r_1(k)$= 0, $r_2(k)$> 0. The subsequent levels (k>1) are defined at $r_1(k)$= $r_2(k-1)$, $r_2(k)$> $r_2(k-1)$. At all the levels (k=1,2,...) the values of $r_2(k)$ are chosen heuristically.

Each integer solution is defined in terms of relations (5)-(7) by means of the iteration procedure (figure 2). According to this procedure the conditions (7) are verified only in case the condition (6) is fulfilled.

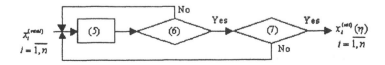

Fig. 2. Iteration procedure for defining integer solutions

5. FINDING BASIC AND QUASI-OPTIMAL SOLUTIONS

The first integer solution $x_i^{(bas)} = x_i^{(int)}(1)$, $i = \overline{1,n}$ obtained according to (5)-(7) at $r_1(k) = 0, r_2(k) > 0$, $k=1$ is the basic solution. Since there are no other integer solutions on the given search phase, the basic solution is regarded as the first approximation to the quasi-optimal solution sought, i.e.

$$x_i^{(qopt)} = x_i^{(bas)}, i = \overline{1,n},$$
$$F^{(qopt)} = F^{(bas)} = F[x_1^{(bas)}, x_2^{(bas)}, ..., x_n^{(bas)}].$$

Subsequent integer solutions (at $\eta > 1$) are defined according to (5)-(7) at $r_1(k) \geq 0$, $r_2(k) > r_1(k)$, $k \geq 1$ and under the additional condition

$$F[x_1^{(int)}(\eta), x_2^{(int)}(\eta), ..., x_n^{(int)}(\eta)] < F^{(qopt)} \tag{8}$$

Each of these solutions is regarded as another approximation to the quasi-optimal solution sought. Therefore it is assumed

$$x_i^{(qopt)} = x_i^{(int)}(\eta), i = \overline{1,n},$$
$$F^{(qopt)} = F[x_1^{(int)}(\eta), x_2^{(int)}(\eta), ..., x_n^{(int)}(\eta)].$$

The iteration procedure for choosing quasi-optimal solutions is presented in figure 3.

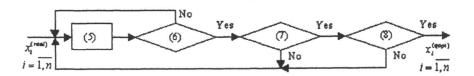

Fig. 3. Iteration procedure for defining quasi-optimal solutions

The example of defining the quasi-optimal integer solution for a problem with two variables and two linear constraints is presented in figure 4.

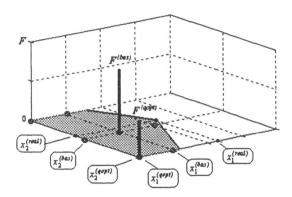

Fig. 4. The example of quasi-optimal integer solution $x_1^{(\text{qopt})}, x_2^{(\text{qopt})}$. This solution has a lesser objective function F value as compared with the basic solution $x_1^{(\text{bas})}, x_2^{(\text{bas})}$

6. VISUAL SUPPORT

The information support of visual integer programming procedure is provided by a graphic characteristic - the syndrome of integer solutions [3, 4]. The syndrome is a non-descending function of the form

$$S_y(\eta) = -\text{abs}(F^{(\text{qopt})} - F^{(\text{real})}),$$
$$\eta = 1,2,..,\eta_c.$$

Here η_c is the current number of an integer solution.

The first syndrome point characterizes the basic solution (defined according to figure 2) and the subsequent points characterize quasi-optimal solutions (defined according to figure 3).

7. MAKING DECISIONS
BY THE SYNDROME GENEALOGY

The genealogy of integer solutions syndrome is a vector of numerical syndrome values accumulated by the current moment of computer research into the problem (1)-(4), i.e.

$$\mathbf{S_y}(\eta_c) = [S_y(1), S_y(2),...,S_y(\eta_c)].$$

By the genealogy graph of the syndrome $\mathbf{S_y}(\eta_c)$ the user may:

-   choose the areas for investigating integer solutions;
-   make decisions about continuation or discontinuation of the computer search.

To take the appropriate decisions the user employs the basic concepts of a *steady-state* and a *saturated* syndrome.

Def. 1. A steady-state syndrome is the constant value $S_y(\eta) = \text{const}$ which remains for a considerable number of integer solutions $\eta \leq \eta_c$.

Def. 2. A syndrome is saturated if the constant value $S_y(\eta) = \text{const}$ remains at the two neighbouring levels of investigating integer solutions.

Allowing for the syndrome features specified the following heuristic decisions may be taken.

7.1 The decision to continue searching at the assigned level

If the syndrome is not steady-state at the assigned level of investigation k, i.e. there is no constant value $S_y(\eta)$ in the syndrome $S_y(\eta) = \text{const}, \eta \leq \eta_c$ genealogy (figure 5), then it is necessary:

-   to retain the investigation parameters $r_1(k), r_2(k)$;
-   to continue searching for a new quasi-optimal solution.

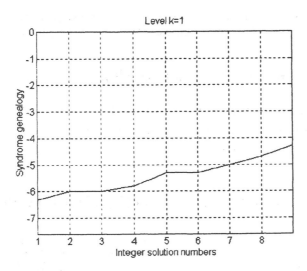

Fig. 5. The genealogy example of nonsteady-state syndrome $S_y = S_y(\eta)$ for the investigation level k=1 [it is reasonable to continue searching by the same parameters $r_1(k), r_2(k)$]

7.2   The decision to continue searching at the next level

If the syndrome is steady-state and not saturated at the assigned level of investigation k (figure 6), it is reasonable to proceed to the next level of investigating integer solutions $k+1$. For this to be done it is necessary:

–   to assume $r_1(k+1) = r_2(k)$, $r_2(k+1) > r_2(k)$;

–   to continue searching.

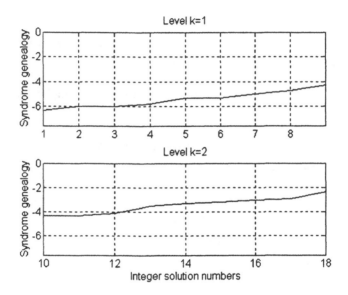

Fig. 6. The genealogy example of steady-state and non-saturated syndrome $S_y = S_y(\eta)$ for the investigation level $k=1$ [it is reasonable to continue searching at the next level $k=2$]

7.3   The decision to cease searching

If the syndrome is saturated at the assigned level of investigation k (figure 7), the search may be ceased. In this case $x_i = x_i^{(qopt)}$, $i = \overline{1,n}$, $F = F^{(qopt)}$ will be the solution for the problem (1)-(4).

8.   THE EXAMPLE OF VISUAL SOLUTION

The above considered interactive technique for solving integer optimization problems on the basis of the stochastic investigation of integer points is illustrated by the example of an integer problem for linear programming (further we shall term it the problem **IP-221**).

The external model IP-221. It is required to find the integer solution minimizing the objective function

$$F = -0,8x_1 - x_2 = \min \tag{9}$$

under the constraints

$$H_1 = 0,2x_1 + 0,8x_2 - 4,5 \le 0, \tag{10}$$
$$H_2 = 0,67x_1 + 0,33x_2 - 3,94 \le 0 \tag{11}$$

and boundary conditions

$$x_1 \ge 0, x_2 \ge 0. \tag{12}$$

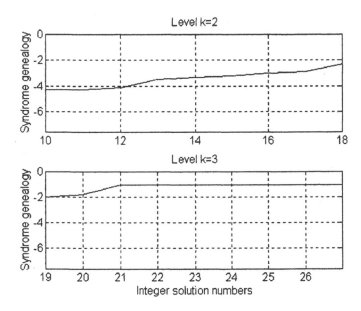

Fig. 7. The genealogy example of saturated syndrome $S_y = S_y(\eta)$ for the investigation levels $k=2,3$

The additional conditions for the problem consist in that the variables must be integers, i.e.

$$x_1, x_2 \text{ are integers} . \tag{13}$$

The geometrical interpretation of the problem (9)-(13) is presented in figure 8.

The internal model IP-221 (phase 1). We shall organize searching for the optimal real solution on the basis of the gradient differential equation system. For the problem under consideration (9)-(13) this equation system assumes the following form [3]

$$\frac{dx_1^*}{dt} = -\frac{\Delta}{\tau}\cdot(-0,8) - \frac{1}{\tau}(\mu_1 x_1 +$$
$$+ 0,2\lambda_1 H_1 + 0,67\lambda_2 H_2), \tag{14}$$

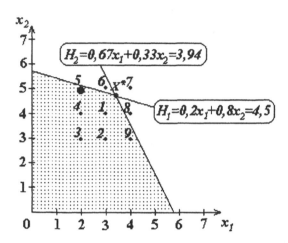

Fig. 8. Geometrical interpretation of the linear integer programming problem **IP-221**. The optimal real solution is at point X^*, where $x_1 \approx 3,5$, $x_2 \approx 4.7$, $F \approx -7,6$. The optimal integer solution corresponds to point *5* with coordinates $x_1 = 2, x_2 = 5$ ($F = -6,6$)

$$\frac{dx_2^*}{dt} = -\frac{\Delta}{\tau}\cdot(-1) - \frac{1}{\tau}(\mu_2 x_2 +$$
$$+ 0,8\lambda_1 H_1 + 0,33\lambda_2 H_2), \tag{15}$$

$$max = \mathbf{max}(|\frac{dx_1^*}{dt}|,|\frac{dx_2^*}{dt}|), \tag{16}$$

$$\frac{dx_1}{dt} = \frac{\Delta}{max\cdot\tau}\cdot\frac{dx_1^*}{dt}, \tag{17}$$

$$\frac{dx_2}{dt} = \frac{\Delta}{max\cdot\tau}\cdot\frac{dx_2^*}{dt}. \tag{18}$$

The model (14)-(18) parameters are the following.
- The parameter Δ restricting sizes of coordinate movements for a search point in one iteration.
- The numerical integration step τ of differential equations.
- Logical variables $\mu_i, i = 1,2$ and $\lambda_j, j = 1,2$ defined as $\mu_i = 0$ at $x_i \geq 0$, $\mu_i = 1$ at $x_i < 0$ and $\lambda_j = 0$ at $H_j \leq 0$ and $\lambda_j = 1$ at $H_j > 0$.

The search procedure for the optimal real solution (phase 1). On the first phase the problem (9)-(12) is solved without considering the integer requirement (13). With the internal model (14)-(18) at $\Delta = \tau = 0.01$ being employed, the starting search point may be arbitrary, and the real solution obtained as a result of search corresponds to point X^* in figure 9.

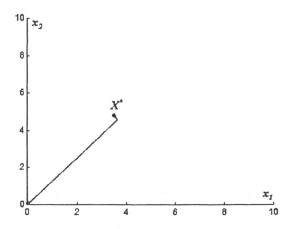

Fig. 9. The solution X^* search path for the problem (9)-(12), with the starting position
$$x_1 = 0, x_2 = 0$$

Figure 9 shows the computer search path of the solution X^* on the model (14)-(18), the start being at the beginning of coordinates. For the problems of an arbitrary dimension the similar path cannot be presented in the visual graphic form. In this case the point X^* search termination on the model may be determined, for example, by the phasogram graph $\Phi(t) \to 0$ [3].

A phasogram for the problem under consideration is presented in figure 10. The zero value of $\Phi(t)$ testifies that the solution has been found. The coordinates of a point are integers (see figures 8, 9), therefore solving the problem must be continued.

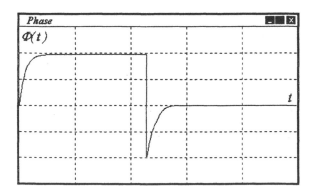

Fig. 10. The phasogram of the problem (9)-(12) solution

The search procedure for the basic solution (phase 2). The result of searching for the basic solution is presented in figure 11.

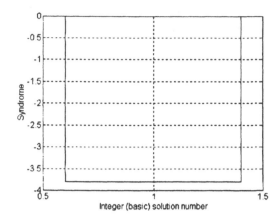

Fig. 11. Basic solution syndrome for the problem (9)-(13) [by the parameters
$$r_1(1) = 0, r_2(1) = 3]$$

The search procedure for the quasi-optimal solution (phase 3). On the third phase the multistep procedure of stochastic investigation of the integer solutions in the neighbourhood of the real point X^* is carried out. The process of searching for the quasi-optimal solution is presented in figures 12, 13.

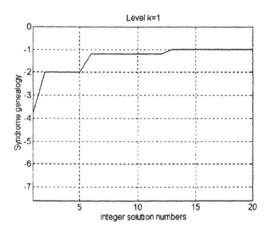

Fig. 12. The syndrome genealogy of integer solutions when solving the problem (9)-(13) for the investigation level $k=1$ [by the parameters $r_1(1) = 0, r_2(1) = 3$]. The syndrome saturation is the ground for thinking that the integer solution will not further improve

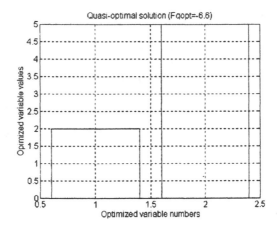

Fig. 13. The quasi-optimal solution for the problem (9)-(13). The quasi-optimal solution obtained is simultaneously a strictly optimal solution (see figure 8)

9. CONCLUSION

The visual technique for integer programming based on random search is characterized by the following special features.

1. The technique ensures finding sequentially the quasi-optimal integer solutions, with convergence of the solutions toward the optimal solution sought being visually presented.

2. Random search is carried out in interactive mode on the basis of multilevel iteration procedure.

3. The technique provides the feasibility of solving integer optimization problems with the use of a graphic characteristic – the syndrome of integer solutions.

4. The direct participation in the process of solving an integer problem on a computer model is provided for the user of this model. Analyzing the syndrome genealogy the user selects the range of investigating integer solutions in the neighbourhood of the optimal real solution and determines the amount of computer research.

5. Both linear and nonlinear problems of integer programming are solved by means of the visual interactive technique.

6. The technique may be applied to both completely integer and combined (partially integer) problems of mathematical programming.

7. The interactive technique makes it possible to detect the contradictoriness of a computer model when there are no allowed integer solutions. In this case the visualization of integer solutions syndrome remains blocked during the entire computer search.

10.   REFERENCES

[1] Using MATLAB, version 5, The Math Works, Inc.

[2] R. Gebhardt. *Excel 97*, Schnellubersicht, Markt&Technik, 1997.

[3] Moiseev V. *Interactive Optimization with Graphic Support*, Informa, Szczecin, Poland, 2000, ISBN 83-87362-26-3.

[4] Moiseev V. *The Interactive Technique of Integer Programming on the Basis of Random Search with the Graphic Support*. Proceedings of the International Workshop on Discrete Optimization Methods in Scheduling and Computer-aided Design, Minsk, Belarus, 2000, P. 155-158.

Two methods of robust estimation of a covariance matrix – a practice study for some liver data

JOANNA ZDZIAREK
Institute of Computer Science, University of Wroclaw

Abstract: We consider two methods of computing robust covariance matrices: the hybrid method proposed by Rocke and Woodruff (1996) and the Fast-MCD method proposed by Rousseeuw and van Driessen (1999). We compare the obtained robust covariance matrices both analytically and graphically. The evaluations are done using some medical data. The comparison of the obtained matrices for these data shows, that the two robust methods give systematically slightly differing results, in particular: The MCD method points to more outliers than the Hybrid method proposed by Rocke and Woodruff.

Key words: Covariance matrix, Outliers, Mahalanobis distances, Robust estimation.

1. INTRODUCTION

In the paper we compare 2 methods for computing robust covariance matrices. The covariance matrix is important in calculations concerned with many statistical data analysis techniques such as regression, forecast, hypothesis testing and dimensionality reduction, so it is very important to obtain a good estimate of covariance matrix from the data we have.

We have taken comparison for our two methods of computing robust covariance matrices: the hybrid method proposed by Rocke and Woodruff [5] and the Fast-MCD method proposed by Rousseeuw and van Driessen [6]. There are of course other methods, but these are relatively new and based on different approach.

In Section 2 we present shortly the two considered robust methods. These methods are applied to some real data, the BUPA liver disorders data, which are described in Section 3. The obtained robust covariance matrices and their comparison is shown in Section 4. Our comparison is based on an analytical test and on two methods of graphical visualisation of the obtained matrices.

In Section 5 we check also outliers in the data set, because a big number of outliers may distort estimate of covariance matrix, and that is why we need robust methods.

2.   METHODS FOR ESTIMATING
COVARIANCE MATRICES

Let X be an $n \times p$ array representing a random sample of size n from a p-dimensional population. Each row of that table denoted as $\underline{x}_i = (x_{i1}, \ldots, x_{ip}), (i = 1, \ldots, n)$, may be viewed as a data vector containing observations for the ith individual or alternatively as a data point belonging to the p-dimensional variables space R^p.

We will consider 3 methods for evaluating a covariance matrix: the usual, used in standard textbooks and two robust methods.

2.1   Usual sample covariance matrix

The usual sample covariance matrix

$$S = [s_{ij}] \tag{1}$$

is defined by its elements

$$s_{ij} = \frac{1}{n} \sum_{k=1}^{n} (x_{ik} - c_i)(x_{jk} - c_j), \ i, j = 1, \ldots, p,$$

where

$$c_j = \frac{1}{n} \sum_{i=1}^{n} x_{ij}. \tag{2}$$

The matrix (1) is an estimate of the population covariance matrix Σ, from which the data vectors $\underline{x}_1, \ldots, \underline{x}_n$ were sampled.

2.2   A robust method using rescaled shape estimators –'Rocke'

This method yields a robust estimate of covariance matrix. It is a hybrid method using rescaled shape estimators by Rocke. The method works in two stages called *phases* and is described in [5], see also [4].

In *phase I* we estimate a robust location and shape of the data. Shape of the data is defined as $S/|S|^{1/p}$ with S denoting the covariance matrix of considered data.

In *phase II* we scale the shape estimate so that it can be used to suggest which points are far enough from the location estimate to be considered possible outliers.

Speaking a little more in detail we may describe the algorithm as follows.

In *phase I* we perform a hybrid estimation with roughly T seconds allowed (large T).

1) We partition the data into $[n\gamma(p)]$ cells where $\gamma(p)$ is a function determining the size of partition.
2) Repeat for each partition j:
♦ For each cell spend $T[n\gamma(p)]$ seconds on a search for the MCD (Minimum Covariance Determinant)
♦ Use the found MCD for a point sequential addition similarly as in [1]
♦ Apply to the result a translated biweight M estimation [4] using the entire sample of size n. This yields estimates $\hat{\mu}, \hat{\Sigma}$ of location and shape.

3) Select the index j_0 for which $\left|\hat{\Sigma}_{j_0}\right|$ is the least and set $\hat{\mu} = \hat{\mu}_{j_0}$ and $\hat{\Sigma} = \hat{\Sigma}_{j_0}$

In Phase II we perform scaling and outlier determination.

On entry to this phase we have data consisting of n points in dimension p and estimates of $\hat{\mu}, \hat{\Sigma}$ obtained at the end of *phase I*.

The shape matrix of the data is standardized in such way that the hth order statistics is equal to $\sqrt{\chi^2_{p;hn}}$ with $h = (n + p + 1)/2$.

Perform the following 3 steps:

1) Determine by simulation a cutoff point $L_{\alpha 1}$ such that when multivariate normal samples of size n in dimension p are submitted to the phase I process a fraction α_1 of the points on the average lie beyond $L_{\alpha 1}$.
2) Determine a new shape matrix based on the covariance matrix of all points whose distance at the first step is less than $L_{\alpha 1}$. The new location estimator is the mean of those points.
3) Reject as outliers any points whos distance evaluated using the revised location and shape is larger than $\chi^2_{p;1-\alpha 2}$ (usually $\alpha 1 = \alpha 2 = 0.01$; smaller numbers may be used at the cost of more simulation time – if one wishes to reject fewer good points).

2.3 A robust method called 'Fast-MCD'

The algorithm was proposed by Rousseeuw and van Driessen [6]. The authors claim, that this estimator yields a highly robust estimator of multivariate location and scale. It may be applied to very large data sets.

The basic element of the algorithm consists of so-called C-steps which stand for 'concentration' steps. The correspondent theorem reads:

Theorem: Let $\underline{x}_1, \ldots, \underline{x}_n$ be n vectors containing p-variate observations each. Let H_1 be a subset of size h of the indices $\{1, \ldots, n\}$.

Let c_1 and S_1 be the mean and covariance matrix calculated from the data vectors with indices i belonging to H_1.

Let $D_1(i;c_1,S_1)$, $i=1, \ldots, n$ denote the Mahalanobis distances (3) evaluated using the location c_1 and covariance matrix S_1.

Order these distances into ascending sequence, and define the subset H_2 as subset of those indices $i_1, \ldots, i_h$,

$$D_1(i_1) \le D_1(i_2) \le \cdots D_1(i_h) \le D_1(i_{h+1}) \le D_1(i_n) \qquad \text{for which the}$$

Mahalanobis distances – calculated using estimates c_1, S_1 – are smallest. Thus: $H_2 = \{i_1, \ldots, i_h\}$. Compute c_2 and S_2 basing only on the subset H_2. Then it holds: $\det(S_2) \le \det(S_1)$.

It is said that the subset H_2 is more concentrated then H_1.

The proposed Fast-MCD (Minimum Covariance Determinant) algorithm makes many restarts determining sets H_1. Then it iterates descending from the determined sets H_1 to the respective more concentrated sets H_2.

The obtained estimates are affine equivariant, which means that – when the data are translated or subjected to a linear transformation – the resulting best estimates (c_b, S_b) will transform accordingly.

In final step, to obtain consistency with data coming from a multinormal distribution, an adjusting coefficient is applied to S_b; as a result we obtain S_{MCD}, the MCD estimate of S. Next a one-step reweighted estimate is computed with weight put to 0 for data vectors with distances surpassing a cutoff established by use of a corresponding quantile of a χ_p^2 distribution:

$$W_i = \begin{cases} 1, & \text{if } D(i; c_{MCD}, S_{MCD}) \le \sqrt{\chi_{p;1-\alpha/2}^2} \\ 0, & \text{otherwise.} \end{cases}$$

3.   DATA

We consider the BUPA liver disorders data recorded and donated to the Irvine data repository by the BUPA Medical Research LTD.

The data contains 5 blood tests:
1.   mean corpuscular volume
2.   alkaline phosphotase
3.   alamine aminotransferase
4.   aspartate aminotransferase
5.   gamma-glutamyl transpeptidase

and one additional variable 'drinks' indicating the number of half-pint equivalents of alcoholic beverages drunk per day.

The entire data set contains observations (data vectors) for n=345 patients; but 4 from them were duplicates, which were an impediment for the Rocke method – thus we removed them. The remaining data were subdivided into 4 subgroups (n_1=117, n_2=51, n_3=88 and n_4=85) depending on the amount of the drinks taken each day ('drinks' 0 or 0.5; 1 or 2; 3 4 5; more than 5).

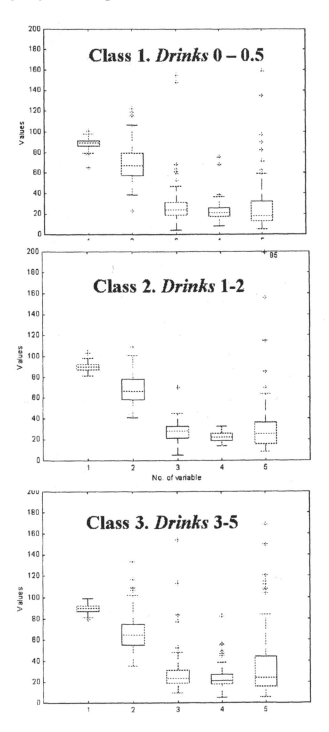

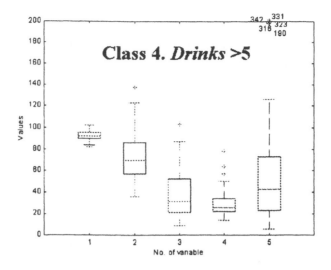

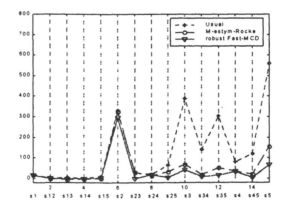

Fig. 1. Boxplots of 5 variables for 4 'drink' classes,
* denotes points out of range in scale of the plotes

In *Fig. 1* we present boxplots of 5 variables.

The boxplots were drawn separately for each *'drink'* class. We took care to make the vertical scale in all 4 plots the same. It was set to be in the range [0, 200].

Looking at *Fig. 1* one may see that the values of the variables 2-5 have a big spread. In class 2 the observation 85 with value 297 was out of the set range; so were in class 4 the observations 190 (value 201), 316, 323, 342 (value 203) and 331 (value 225). The out of range points are specially marked.

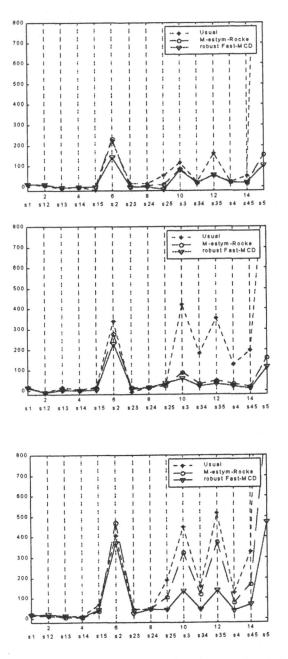

Fig. 2. 'Value plots' for 4 classes, from top to bottom: class 1, 2, 3, 4

4. A COMPARISON OF THE MATRICES OBTAINED BY THE THREE METHODS

For each data set (class of drinks) we computed 3 covariance matrices:
- the usual one defined by formula (1),
- the robust one by the 'Rocke' method described in subsection 2.2,
- the robust one using the Fast-MCD algorithm described in subsection 2.3.

Taking the upper triangle of each covariance matrix we may write down its values as s1, s12, s13, s14,s15, s2, s23, ...,s5, where the symbols s1,...,s5 stand for the variances and sij, i<j, for the covariances between the i-th and j-th variable.

The magnitudes of subsequent elements s1, s12, ..., s5 are visualized – in the form of index plots – in *Fig. 2*. We call these plots 'value plots' of the matrices. Covariance matrices estimated by the usual method have the biggest values especially variances. The Rocke and Fast-MCD robust methods gave us similar matrices. Especially in class 2 and 3 robust matrices are almost equal.

Statistical test for equality of covariance matrices was computed after [3] and is based on the statistic $T \cdot C$ (T and C defined below). TC has approximately, for big n_i, the χ^2-distribution with df=p(p+1)/2=15 degrees of freedom, the critical value equal to $\chi^2_{15;0.05}=24,99$.

$$T = \left(\sum_{i=1}^{p} (n_i - 1) \right) \log \det S - \sum_{i=1}^{p} (n_i - 1) \log \det S_i$$

$$C = 1 - \frac{2p^2 + 3p - 1}{18(p+1)} \left[\sum_{i=1}^{p} \frac{1}{n_i - 1} - \frac{1}{\sum_{i=1}^{p} n_i - 1} \right]$$

where S_i is a sample covariance matrix obtained by considered methods and

$$S = \sum_{i=1}^{p} (n_i - 1)S_i \bigg/ \sum_{i=1}^{p} (n_i - 1).$$

We test the hypothesis if each 2 of obtained matrices in each class are equal. In *Table 1.* we present the results:

It follows that only in class 2 and 3 we can not reject the hypothesis, that the matrices from the Rocke and Fast-MCD methods are equal. Matrices estimated by usual method are very much different from robust ones.

Let us now make a comparison of correlation matrices. A correlation coefficient is defined as

$$rij = sij \cdot si^{-\frac{1}{2}} \cdot sj^{-\frac{1}{2}}, \tag{3}$$

where s*ij* denotes covariance between i*th* and j*th* variable, and s*i* variances of i*th* variable.

Class	Values of statistic *TC*		
	Compared methods		
	Rocke-Fast	Usual-Rocke	Usual-Fast
1	27,61***	115,92**	200,88***
2	11,85	76,70**	113,72***
3	16,34	124,49**	190,30***
4	38,98***	51,20**	132,65***

Tab. 1. Results of testing equality of covariance matrices

In *Fig. 3a, 3b.* we present a new graphical method to visualize matrices correlation. We call such plots as radial plots. Values of correlation coefficients belong to the interval [-1, 1] – it is on the radius of the circle. On the circle we have correlation coefficients in succession.

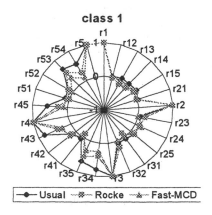

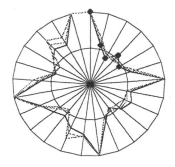

Fig. 3a. Radial plots of correlation matrices for class 1 and 2

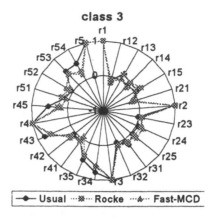

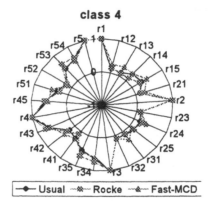

Fig. 3b. Radial plots of correlation matrices for class 3 and 4

We can in these plots compare values of correlation matrices obtained by 3 considered methods. In class 1 the biggest differences are for r35, r45 and r34. In class 2 and 3 there is no big difference between values of the Rocke and Fast-MCD estimate of correlation coefficients. In class 4 the biggest differences are for correlation with first variable of our data (r1j, for j=2..5).

5.   OUTLIERS DETECTED BY
       THE THREE METHODS

In case when the data set is contaminated with outliers, the usual estimate S of the covariance matrix may be heavily biased. To alleviate this, we use robust estimators.

The aim of the robust methods is to find an estimate of the covariance matrix which is proper for the main part of the data cloud. Data vectors located far from the centre are given less weight.

Most of the analytical methods for calculating a robust covariance matrix use the Mahalanobis distance for judging whether the data points are far away from the centre of the data cloud. Let c and S denote the centre (location) and the covariance matrix of the data. The Mahalanobis distance of the ith data point (for $i=1 \ldots n$) relatively to the centre c with metric established by the inverse of the covariance matrix S is defined as

$$D_i(c, S) = \sqrt{(x_i - c)S^{-1}(x_i - c)^T}, \qquad (4)$$

Points, for which the corresponding D_i^2 value exceeds the cutoff determined as $\chi^2_{5,0.01}=15.086$, are considered as outliers.

class	method	Outliers	
		k	Maximal items
1	Usual	5	36 233 205 224 20
1	Rocke	12	36 233 205 224 53 25
	Fast-MCD	23	233 36 205 25 53 235
2	Usual	2	85 261
2	Rocke	5	85 77 252 261 250
	Fast-MCD	13	85 77 252 250 265 81
3	Usual	5	300 134 115 111 286
3	Rocke	18	300 115 134 294 111 139
	Fast-MCD	25	300 115 134 294 307 111
4	Usual	3	323 331 186
4	Rocke	8	323 331 186 190 342 316
	Fast-MCD	24	323 331 190 179 342 316

Tab. 2. Number of outliers (k) in groups 1–4 identified by the considered methods. Also the numeros (#–es) of the largest (max 6) outliers are listed

To find outliers in our data we will evaluate the D_i^2 values substituting into (4) three different estimates of c and S:
- the usual mean and sample covariance matrix defined by (2) and (1).
- Robust mean and covariance matrix estimate obtained from the Rocke algorithm.
- Robust mean and covariance estimate obtained from the Fast-MCD algorithm.
  We will look at the biggest outliers detected by 3 considered methods.

In *Table 2* we show the numbers (k) of outliers detected by each method and also, which data vectors (items) these are. This comparison shows that the biggest outliers are repeated in results obtained by all three methods. Generally we state, that:
- The 'Rocke' method points to more outliers as the 'usual' method;
- The 'Fast-MCD' algorithm points to more outliers as found by the 'Rocke' method.

This is in agreement with our former results reported in the paper [2].

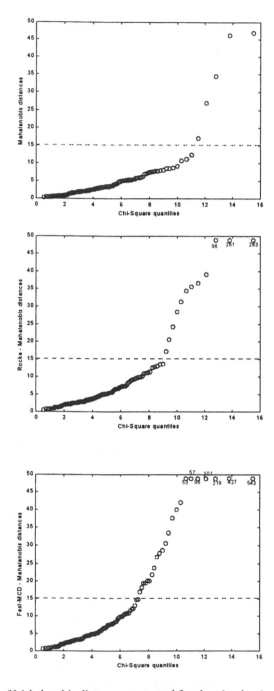

Fig. 4. Q-Q plots of Mahalanobis distances computed for class 1 using 3 considered methods; top: usual, middle: Rocke, bottom: Fast- MCD.
Some points are out of range of the plot

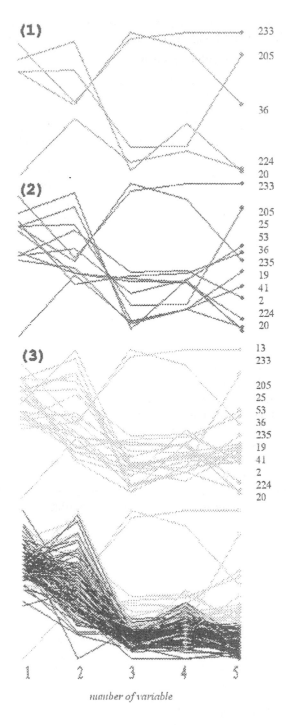

Fig. 5. Parallel-coordinate-plots for class 1. Plots (1), (2), (3) represents only outliers, bottom: all data vectors from class 1

To see the outliers we construct so called Q-Q plots shown in *Fig. 4*. The horizontal variable denotes chi-square quantiles and the vertical variable – the sorted Mahalanobis distances. The cutoff point is $\chi^2_{5;0.01} = 15.086$. We took care to make the vertical scale in all 3 plots the same. It was set to be in the range [0, 50]. We specially marked the observations (with their Mahalanobis distances) which were out of the range of the plot: three in the Rocke method (36, 233, 205) and seven in the Fast-MCD method (233, 36, 205, 25, 53, 235, 41). This were the biggest outliers.

Another plot where we can see original data set is the parallel-coordinate-plot [7]. On the first axis we have the number of variable, on the second are scaled values. In *Fig.5* we see parallel-coordinate-plots for class 1. On top we have observations detected as outliers by usual method, in the 2nd picture – detected by the Rocke method, 3rd by the Fast-MCD method and bottom: all observations from class 1. At the 1st -3rd plots there are marked items of data vectors (at 3rd –not all because of lack of space).

6. DISCUSSION-CONCLUDING REMARKS

Taking into account some real medical data subdivided into 4 classes and known as containing outliers we have investigated the behaviour of two robust estimators of a covariance matrix – when applied to these data. Both methods, i.e. the 'Rocke' method and 'Fast-MCD' method are computationally feasible, work fine and yield fairly similar estimates of the covariances. This can be visualized using value-plots of the derived covariance matrices, also by drawing radial plots of the corresponding correlation matrices. However formal statistical test indicate for a statistical difference between the matrices obtained by the two methods.

The major outliers hidden in the data were properly identified by both methods; however, we have noticed that the 'Fast-MCD' method has pointed to much more outliers as the 'Rocke' method.

After finding the suspected outliers one should always verify them in an independent way, e.g. graphically, by using parallel-coordinate-plots.

7. REFERENCES

[1] Atkinson, A.C. 'Stalactite plots and robust estimation for the detection of multivariate outliers'. *New Directions in Statistical Data Analysis and Robustness*, Eds. S. Morgenthaler, E. Ronchetti, and W.A. Stahel. 1993.

[2] Bartkowiak A., Zdziarek J. 2001. 'Identifying outliers - a comparative review of 7 methods applied to 7 benchmark data sets'. Manuscript pp. 1-16.

[3] Box G.E.P. 1949. 'A general Distribution Theory or a Class of Likelihood Criteria', *Biometrika* 36, pp 317-346.

[4] Rocke D.M. 1996. 'Robustness properties of S-estimators of Multivariate Location and Shape in High Dimension'. *Annals of Statistics* 24, pp 1327-1345.

[5] Rocke D., Woodruff D.L. 1996. 'Identification of outliers in multivariate data'. *JASA* 91, no 435, pp 1047-1061.

[6] Rousseeuw P.J., van Driessen K. 1999. 'A fast algorithm for the minimum covariance determinant estimator'. *Technometrics* 41, pp 212-223.

[7] Wegman E. J. 1990. 'Hyperdimensional data analysis using parallel coordinates'. *JASA* 85, pp. 664-675.

Visualisation of multivariate data using parallel coordinate plots and Kohonen's SOM's. Which is better?

ADAM SZUSTALEWICZ
Institute of Computer Science, University of Wroclaw

Abstract: Parallel coordinate plot is a convenient method for presenting a set of multivariate data points in simple two-dimensional form. Each data point is represented by a horizontal segment line connecting vertical axes corresponding to subsequent variables. Another very convenient method for representing multivariate data is their visualisation by use of self-organizing maps. Both methods were applied for visualisation of the differences between two sets of data representing randomly distorted letters printed in different fonts. Each letter was characterized by 16 statistical features.
We wanted to observe how much differ the positions occupied by samples of these letters when viewed in sixteen-dimensional feature space. We will show the plots visualising the locations of the pairs of letters: *I&W* and *F&J*. We came to conclusion that the introduced visualisation methods complement each other.

Key words: Multidimensional visualisation, Visual data exploration, Feature space, Identification of randomly distorted characters, Parallel coordinates, Artificial neural network, Multivariate data analysis

1. INTRODUCTION

Growing variety of considered data forces users to look for better visualisation methods. We consider two sets of data containing a large number of 16-dimensional integer vectors describing two different capital letters. The objective is to reveal similarities and dissimilarities between two classes consisting of vectors representing the letters: *I&W* in the first data set and *F&J* in the second appropriately. We use for that purpose *parallel coordinate plots* and *self-organizing maps* (Kohonen 1995). The first method presents a set of multivariate data vectors in simple two-dimensional form. Each data point is represented by a horizontal segment line connecting vertical axes corresponding to subsequent variables. The second method is a specific method of neural networks, where the neurons are located in a rectangular two-dimensional grid, called *map*. The neurons have so called codebook vectors, which – during the process of training – adapt themselves to reflect the position and density of data points in R^{16}. We present shortly both methods in Section 3.

2.   DATA

The data were created by D. J. Slate [5] and published in the internet at the address [6]. The objective was to identify each of a large number of black-and-white rectangular pixel displays as one of the 26 capital letters from the English alphabet. The character images were based on 20 different fonts and each letter within these 20 fonts was randomly distorted to produce a file of 20,000 unique rasters. Each raster was converted into $p=16$ primitive numerical attributes (statistical moments and edge counts):

1.   *x-box*   horizontal position of box,
2.   *y-box*   vertical position of box,
3.   *width*   width of box,
4.   *high*   height of box,
5.   *onpix*   total # on pixels,
6.   *x-bar*   mean x of on pixels in box,
7.   *y-bar*   mean y of on pixels in box,
8.   *x2bar*   mean x variance,
9.   *y2bar*   mean y variance,
10. *xybar*   mean x y correlation,
11. *x2ybr*   mean of x * x * y,
12. *xy2br*   mean of x * y * y,
13. *x-ege*   mean edge count left to right,
14. *xegvy*   correlation of x-ege with y,
15. *y-ege*   mean edge count bottom to top,
16. *yegvx*   correlation of y-ege with x.

The values of these attributes were next transformed to the integers from the interval [0, 15]. Thus each letter is represented by a data vector containing $p=16$ components, called in the following features or variables. In our analysis we will look for the statistical differences between the letters *I&W* (with counts $nI=755$, $nW=752$ in the first analysis) and between the letters *F&J* (with counts $nF=775$, $nJ=747$ in the second).

It can be expected that the letters *I&W* should be more differentiated than the letters *F&J*.

3. TWO METHODS FOR VISUALISATION OF MULTIVARIATE DATA

The first method is based on a multidimensional system of parallel coordinates – a one-to-one mapping between subsets of Euclidean space R^p and subsets of R^2 (see [3], [4], [7]).

The second method is one of the most popular neural network models for the analysis and visualisation of high-dimensional data (see [8]).

We will now introduce shortly both methods.

3.1 Parallel Coordinate Plots

The parallel coordinate plots were introduced in 1981 by A. Inselberg in [1] and then in [2], as a new way to represent multi-dimensional information. In the traditional Cartesian coordinates, all axes are mutually perpendicular, so we can visualise their projections onto two- or three-dimensional space only. For 16-dimensional data vectors it yields a very poor effect.

In parallel coordinates, all axes are parallel each other, usually vertical and equally spaced. For each point the value of subsequent variables are placed in the corresponding lines (axes). The marked values are linked by horizontal segment line intersecting the vertical axes. Thus, a p-dimensional data vector (point) is drawn in the form of horizontal segment line intersecting the vertical axes.

The result is a graph of line segments connected between axes, see Figure 1. Such plot makes possible to discover some positive or negative correlations between data variables: segments of lines with a similar slope can indicate that their data records correlate positively; if the lines converge to a single point between variables, then negative correlation is graphed.

It is convenient to permute selected axes in order to reveal hidden correlations between the responsible data variables.

Clustering can be notice very easy as well – if a group of lines started from one axis is grouped continuously on adjacent axes. Selection of adequate variables can be done conveniently by permutation of appropriate axes as well.

An isolated segment line lying outside of the main bulb of data lines is visible easily in the parallel coordinate plots plane as well and can be identified as outlier.

3.2 Self-Organizing Map

The Self-Organizing Map (SOM) – a neural network algorithm is based on unsupervised learning, which means that the training is entirely data-driven and that no *a priori* information about the input data is required.

SOM consists of neurons which are organized in the form of a regular, typically 2-dimensional grid. The number of neurons may vary from a few dozen up to several thousands. Each neuron is represented by a p-dimensional weight vector, where p is equal to the dimension of the input vectors. The SOM algorithm performs a topology preserving mapping from the high-dimensional input space to the map units so, that the relative distances between data points are preserved. Data points lying near each other in the input space are mapped to nearby map units of the SOM. Thus, the SOM can serve as a clustering tool of high-dimensional data.

A SOM is trained iteratively. In each training step one data vector is presented and the distance between it and each weight vector of the SOM is calculated using some distance measure, e.g. Euclidean distance. The neuron whose codebook vector is closest to the presented data vector is the *winner*. After finding the winner, the codebook vectors of the winner and of its topological neighbours are updated by moving them towards the presented data vector. This means that the codebook vectors tend to drift there where the data set is dense, while only a few of them stay there where data is sparsely located.

In the training phase the neighbourhood function can be either bubble or gaussian and the learning coefficient can be selected to decrease either linearly or proportionally to the inverse of time.

The map visualization can be obtained by presenting the distribution of the map units in the form of cells. Each cell is marked in colours responding to the classes of input vectors. The area of the coloured parts of cell is proportional to the number of total winnings of the map unit with respect to the considered classes. Coloured parts are drawn in size order from largest to smallest and this insures that all colours ought to be visible, see Figure 2.

4.   DATA ANALYSIS

4.1   I & W Data Set

The set of 16-dimensional data points contains two different classes of elements: I and W. The first class consists of nI=755 vectors identified as letter I, the second consists of nW=752 vectors responding to the letter W.

Analysis by parallel coordinate plots

Let us look at the Figure 1. It contains two plots. Each plot is drawn from the entire set of all the 1507 considered data vectors. Vectors corresponding to the I character are drawn in red (darker in the grey scale) and those to W – in green (lighter in the grey scale).

In the top plot as first were drawn the W vectors and next, on the top of them the I vectors. In the bottom plot the order of drawing was reversed.

The axes have been permuted so that the features (variables) with extremely different values for different classes are grouped together. The indices of the variables are drawn below each plot.

For some variables (e.g. 2, 4) the intervals containing the values of these variables are practically the same for both classes. For such variables we see in the upper plot red colour and in the bottom plot green colour only.

This means, that these variables have no discriminative power (among the considered classes).

We look for such variables which take values from non overlapping intervals. The more the intervals are non overlapping, the greater is the discriminative power of that variable.

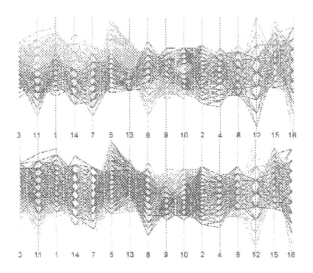

Fig. 1. Parallel coordinate plots for classes I&W.
Top – elements of class I are drawn over class W.
Bottom – elements of W are drawn over class I.

What concerns the discrimination between the letters *I* and *W*, we can state – looking at Fig. 1 – that the most discriminative variables are: 11, 13, 9, 6, 10, 3, 14, 5, 1, 8.

We will see later that really, analysis based on the indicated 10 discriminative variables has the same discriminative power as all the 16 variables.

Constructing a Kohonen's map

First of all we will apply the SOM algorithm to the entire data set containing the letters *I* and *W*. The SOM constructed from these data is shown in Fig. 2.

Looking at that Figure one can see that the cells containing the letters *I* and *W* are clearly split.

It is easy to notice almost a linear "border" –formed by empty clusters – splitting the map into two separated parts. One may notice that only two cells (located in the 6 and 7 rows left) contain vectors belonging to both classes.

Such a simple structure of the obtained Kohonen's map suggests that it might be successful to make a correct classification of all data points with help of the simplest neural network.

Experiments with neural network confirmed our suppositions. It is also possible to obtain quite similar map using a much smaller number of variables

Experiments with neural network

We constructed a feedforward net with one neuron only in one hidden layer, with 16 inputs and one linear output. As a minimization algorithm we used Matlab's procedure realizing the Scaled Conjugate Gradient Method. Really, in 100% of runs we obtained 100% classification effectiveness.

Letters I & W

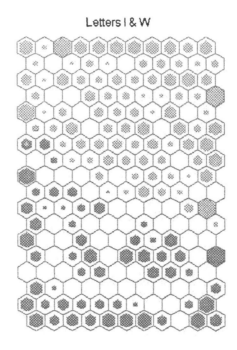

Fig. 2. Kohonen's map for 16-dimensional I&W

Next we repeated calculations taking only 6 most discriminative variables found from the analysis of the parallel coordinate plots. The variables were: 11, 14, 5, 13, 6, 9. The same net with 6 inputs now obtained also 100% classification effectiveness in 100% of runs. In other trial we have reduced the number of variables to four: 11, 13, 6, 9. Again, using the network with one hidden neuron, we obtained 100% classification effectiveness.

The Kohonen's map constructed for the quoted four variables is presented in Fig. 3.

We can say, that for the data set I&W reduction of the data dimension with such a heuristic method succeeded very well decreasing the number of variables needed for classification from 16 to 4.

4.2   F & J Data Set

Let us consider now the second set of data points which consists of two classes F and J containing nF=775 and nJ=747 elements respectively.

Analysis by parallel coordinate plots

Intuitively, the letters *F* and *J* are not as differentiated as *I* and *W* from the previous chapter. Parallel coordinate plots in Figure 4 and the map of Kohonen for all 16 features in Figure 5 confirm this intuition.

Letters I & W

Fig. 3. Kohonen's map for 4-dimensional I&W

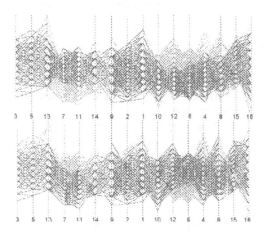

Fig. 4. Parallel coordinate plots for classes F&J.
Top – elements of class F are drawn over class J.
Bottom – elements of J are drawn under class F.

As we see in the bottom plot of Figure 4 – the visible segments in red (dark) color are not so distinct as previously.

Constructing a Kohonen's map

The Kohonen's map in Figure 5 shows also that cells containing *I* and *W* letters are not so differentiated as previously. We see that both classes F and J infiltrate mutually in some part.

Letters F & J

Fig. 5. Kohonen's map for 16-dimensional F&J

Principal components plot

In this situation (not a clear discrimination between the two classes F and J) we have make another plot using first two principal components calculated also from the entire data set. It is shown in Fig. 6.

Red (dark) symbols '*' denote the *F* and green (light) symbols 'o' denote the *J* elements. We see that projections of both classes onto this plane also partially overlap each other.

Experiments with neural network

Experiments with training neural network in order to classify elements of different classes succeeded with 100% efficiency (for 16 inputs) only after we used a net with 9 neurons in one hidden layer and removed four selected individuals from the considered data set.

We have repeated the analysis using smaller number of variables. We have found twelve variables (3, 5, 13, 7, 11, 14, 10, 12, 6, 4, 8, 15) which gave the following result:

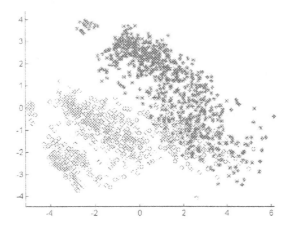

Fig. 6. The plane of the first two principal components for the data set F&J

In 80% of runs using 9 hidden neurons and removing 4 data points we observed a 100% effectiveness of classification.

In Figure 7 we show Kohonen's map obtained from 12 variables. This map shows again some cells containing elements from both classes. This map seems to show a better differentiation between the classes as the former one (compare Fig. 5) based on all 16 features.

Fig. 7. Kohonen's map for 12-dimensional F&J

5. REFERENCES

[1] Inselberg A., N-dimensional graphics, part I – lines and hyperplanes. Technical Report G320-2711, IBM Los Angeles Scientific Center, IBM Scientific Center, 9045 Lincoln Boulevard, Los Angeles (CA), 900435, 1981.

[2] Inselberg A., *The plane with parallel coordinates*, The Visual Computer 1, 69-91, 1985.

[3] Inselberg A., Dimsdale B., *Multidimensional lines i: Representation*, SIAM J. of Appl. Math. 54.2, 559-577, 1994.

[4] Inselberg A., Dimsdale B., *Multidimensional lines ii: Proximity and applications*, SIAM J. of Appl. Math. 54.2, 578-596, 1994.

[5] Frey P. W., Slate D. J., *Letter recognition using Holland-style adaptive classifiers*, Machine Learning 6.2, 1991.

[6] http://www.ics.uci.edu/pub/machine-learning-databases/letter-recognition

[7] http://www.che.ufl.edu/visualize/THESIS/gen.html, Overview of parallel coordinates.

[8] Kohonen T. *Self-Organizing Maps*, Springer Series in Information Sciences 30, Springer, Berlin, 1995.

Application of semantic analysis of Polish speech for purpose of automatic gender identification

MICHAŁ PAŁCZYŃSKI, PIOTR PECHMANN
Technical University of Szczecin, Faculty of Computer Science and Information Systems
ul. Żołnierska 49   71-210 Szczecin, Poland, tel.: +4891 4495561
e-mail: mpalczynski@wi.ps.pl

Abstract: In this paper authors propose to use some elements of the semantic analysis of Polish utterances in order to improve the accuracy of automatic gender identification process. In Polish language for many grammatical units exists a gender as a grammatical parameter. This feature can be useful for determining the gender of a speaker. Authors consider various concepts of combining the result of semantic analysis with the basic signal-based automatic gender identification algorithm

Key words: speaker recognition, gender identification, biometrics, Polish language, semantic analysis, text processing

1.   INTRODUCTION

Human voice is one of the most suitable biometrics for identifying persons because of its great distinguishing power and the simplicity of data collecting. Identifying people by their voices can be useful for purposes like [1]:
−   access control to buildings,
−   information systems,
−   financial transactions (especially over the telephone),
−   crime detection,
−   entertainment,
−   collecting data from audio sources

There are many problems dealt with creating the system of speaker recognition of a good quality. Although many systems successfully work, the research on improving their accuracy still goes on. It's also possible to recognize some characteristics of the speaker instead of his/her identity [5], for example: gender, age (child, adult, older), emotional state, speech defects or spoken language. Unlike the speaker's identification, determining these features for a specific speaker doesn't require training data from this speaker. In other words, once created and trained system should recognize properly anybody's characteristics, even regardless the spoken language.

In this paper, we devote our attention to gender identification. This feature can be used in a few ways:

- information about speaker's sex is needed for some reason, for example for limiting access to some building or service for persons of the appropriate gender or in police work;
- performance of speech recognition systems increase if the gender of a speaker is known, because more adequate speech model can be used [1,2,5];
- in speaker's identification, determining the gender allows limiting the database to entries with the matching gender field (if the database contains such information). This technique, named gender gate [4], reduces computation time and increases system performance.

There is wide range of methods of identifying the gender of a speaker. Most of them use acoustic features of voice, first of all the pitch (F0) estimation and spectral envelope. This approach enables creating language-independent systems [3]. Other algorithms try to recognize speech using male and female speaker independent models. Better recognition score determines the gender of a speaker. Other methods combine several features [5,6].

Today's gender identification systems can achieve accuracy 99% for utterances 2 seconds long [5]. Although this is very good result, it's still below 100%. It means that for a large number of speakers there are some people, whose sex will be not identified correctly. There is still need to improve the accuracy of gender identification methods, especially in applications, where recognition is crucial, or where poor quality of a signal results in decrease of the system performance. For example, gender-gated speaker identification will reject the claimant just because his gender is wrong identified. Also police work requires the best possible accuracy.

Traditional techniques are much less effective for recognizing the sex of children, because boy's and girl's voices are much more similar to each other than voices of adults. Analysis of a text can bring additional information increasing the accuracy of identification.

2.   THE IDEA OF THE METHOD

Most existing systems are based on acoustic features of voice. We propose to improve system performance using the contents of the analysed utterance. There are elements of spoken text, which can help to determine the gender of a speaker. In particular, Polish language can give such information on both syntactic and semantic levels. Next chapter will describe it more precisely.

The presented approach can be applied for many other languages but not for every one. Especially for English the method is not suitable because of lack of the gender parameter. However, for each language, the individual algorithm of text analysis has to be developed.

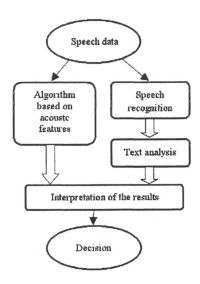

Fig. 1. Block diagram of the presented method

There are some limitations of the presented approach:
- the utterance has to be long enough to content enough text (for example 10s or more, while systems based only on acoustic features need about 1s of speech);
- speakers have to speak spontaneously, so text-dependent gender identification as the basic system will be inappropriate for this method;
- the whole system will not be language-independent even if the basic method is, because the speech recognition has to be done.

In the proposed method, after the basic algorithm (using acoustic features) stops, speech recognition and text analysis proceeds. Then results of both methods are combined into one total result, which is the basis for decision making (Fig. 1). When the basic method use speech recognition scores to determine the gender, text is already recognized and its analysis can start at once (Fig. 2).

3. SEMANTIC ANALYSIS

The goal of the analysis is to extract the information about speaker's gender from the text. There are two kinds of elements, which can be useful for that purpose.

3.1 Grammatical information

The principal element for determining the gender of a speaker, is the grammatical gender of words. Table 1 shows Polish grammatical units, for which the gender is specified [7]. If the word of the specified gender relates to the person who speaks, it identifies his or her gender. In other words, recognition can succeed when the speaker tells something about himself.

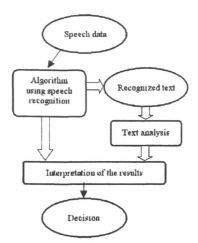

Fig. 2. Modification of the proposed method, when the basic gender identification algorithm uses speech recognition.

Note, that the gender of plural can be ambiguous, because the masculine can be used for the group of masculine objects or mixed – masculine and feminine, while the feminine - either for group of feminine or impersonal objects.

At the beginning of the algorithm, syntactic analysis has to be made in order to determine grammatical parameters of all words including gender and the relations between words. Next, semantic analysis starts discovering if any of words of the known gender relate to the speaker. The final effect is the list of words determining the gender of speaking person, and the values of this parameter.

Grammatical unit	singular			plural	
	masculine	feminine	neuter	masculine	feminine
noun	*mężczyzna*	*kobieta*	*dziecko*	*mężczyźni*	*kobiety*
verb in past tense	*robiłem*	*robiłam*	-	*robiliśmy*	*robiłyśmy*
verb in future tense*)	*będę robił* *będę robić*	*będę robiła* *będę robić*	*będę robiło* *będę robić*	*będziemy robili* *będziemy robić*	*będziemy robiły* *będziemy robić*
adjective	*ładny*	*ładna*	*ładne*	*ładni*	*ładne*
demonstrative pronoun	*ten*	*ta*	*to*	*ci*	*te*
relative pronoun	*który*	*która*	*które*	*którzy*	*które*
interrogative pronoun	*jaki*	*jaka*	*jakie*	*jacy*	*jakie*
possessive pronoun	*mój*	*moja*	*moje*	*moi*	*moje*
ordinal number	*pierwszy*	*pierwsza*	*pierwsze*	*pierwsi*	*pierwsze*
adjectival participle	*idący* *widziany***)	*idąca* *widziana*	*idące* *widziane*	*idący* *widziani*	*idące* *widziane*

*) The second form including infinite (*robić*) doesn't specify the gender.
**) Active and passive forms

Tab. 1. Examples of Polish grammatical units for which the gender is specified

3.2   The contents of the text

The second element of semantic analysis, much more difficult to find is searching spoken utterance for contents typical of specific sex. For example it's almost certain that the sentence:

Jestem w ciąży. (I'm pregnant.)

was spoken by a woman, while:

Idę pograć w piłkę. (I'm going to play football.)

probably spoken a man (or boy). You can imagine a certain, probably not very large, number of such messages. Finding them in the text is barely probable but the goal of the method is to extract maximum information about the speaker's gender.

Again, characteristic words of each searched message should be found in the text. Then semantic analysis should determine if it relates to the speaker. The result is the list of the found phrase characteristics for the specific gender.

3.3   Interpretation of the results of the semantic analysis

Since the text is searched for the specific elements, the result can be defined as a number and type of elements indicating speaker's gender. System has to check consistence of this data, because the text analysed can contain contradictory information. It can happen because of errors at speech recognition or speaker's mistakes or even mimicry. In this case, the algorithm can either give no result or identify the gender, for which more elements were found. Probably the best way would be estimating degree of consistence and making the decision if it exceeds any bias value. A good estimation could be a number of elements corresponding to more numerous represented gender divided by total number of elements.

The other problem requiring a judgement is the total number of the found elements indicating the gender related to the length of the utterance. Making the decision based on one or two words, possibly wrongly recognized, is strongly uncertain. On the other hand, 10 second long utterance can consist of 20-30 words. Taking into consideration, that words indicating the gender of a speaker are only small part of valid speech, the probability of finding them in so small fragment is very low. There are two conclusions possible at this point. First, for short utterances every found element, although uncertain, is valuable for determining the gender. Second, the method is more suitable for long utterances, where measures of certainty can be obtained, for example a number of found elements divided by the total number of words. Again, if this value doesn't exceed some bias, no decision will be made.

3.4   Combining the results of two working methods

Possibly, the most important problem of the interpretation of the results is how to combine them with those of the basic method, especially when they don't match.

There is no doubt that acoustic features give much more certain classifications, but for some voices difference between male and female models is very little and then result of semantic analysis could be useful for making the final decision. It's also possible to do the spoken text analysis in such cases, only. At last, combining the results requires use of appropriate weighting coefficients, because certainty of the methods is different.

For some applications, presentation of both results could be suitable. In such a case, the result would consist of two values: gender identified using acoustic features and gender obtained by text analysis, possibly supplemented by recognition scores.

4.   DISCUSSION

The primary disadvantage of the proposed method is a number of limitations, so it cannot be used for many applications. The most important limitations are:
- the method is suitable only if the acoustic-based algorithm is text-independent;
- the algorithm is language-dependent;
- linguistic features are easy to mimic, therefore speaker being identified shouldn't realize that words are analysed;
- long utterances are required for effective text analysis.

Performance of the method is uncertain - even for very long utterances, finding no information about the gender of a speaker is possible.

The other disadvantage is an increase in computation time caused by necessity of speech recognition, although when the basic method uses speech recognition in order to determine matching acoustic model, the recognized text can be used for semantic analysis.

In spite of all limitations, the method can increase probability of correct gender identification; in other words, it can increase the accuracy of recognition. For applications demanding the best possible accuracy regardless computation time, the method can have valuable solution.

5.   FURTHER RESEARCH

The primary task, which should be done, is to develop the algorithm of speaker's identification using semantic analysis of Polish speech. The first stage, the syntactic analysis, is almost completely solved problem, now [8]. However, the research in semantic analysis still goes on. Especially, finding the information about the speaker in the contents of an utterance is a very difficult problem.

After the algorithm is developed, the problem of interpretation of the results should be solved. The bias values and weighting coefficients, mentioned in chapters 3.3 and 3.4, should be determined either theoretically or experimentally.

Next, the algorithm should be implemented and put together with the selected acoustic based method.

Then testing has to proceed, first using the data of a good quality, then using noisy speech. Several acoustic-based methods have to be tested.

The results have to demonstrate, how much the method increases the accuracy of gender identification. The conditions of effective work of the algorithm should also be determined.

6. REFERENCES

[1] O'Shaughnessy D. - *Speech Communications, Human and machine*, IEEE Press 2000. ISBN 0-7803-3449-3;

[2] Rabiner L., Juang B. - *Fundamentals of speech recognition*, Prentice-Hall PTR 1993. ISBN 0-13-015157-2;

[3] Slomka S., Sridharan S. - *Automatic gender identification optimised for language independence*, TENCON '97. IEEE Region 10 Annual Conference. Speech and Image Technologies for Computing and Telecommunications, Proceedings of IEEE p.145 - 148 vol.1 2-4 Dec. 1997 ISBN: 0-7803-4365-4;

[4] Barger P., Slomka S., Castellano P. and Sridharan S., *Gender gates for automatic speaker recognition*, Proceedings of the Sixth Australian International Conference on Speech Science and Technology (SST-96), p. 19-24, December 1996

[5] Gauvain J., Lamel L. - *Identification of Non-Linguistic Speech Features*, Proceedings of ARPA Workshop on Human Language Technology, pages 96-101, March 1993 http://citeseer.nj.nec.com/gauvain93identification.html;

[6] Parris E.S., Carey M.J. - *Language independent gender identification*, Proceedings of ICASSP-96, p. 685-688, vol. 2, ISBN: 0-7803-3192-3

[7] Bąk P.- *Gramatyka Języka Polskiego*, Wiedza Powszechna, Warszawa, 1984;

[8] Pechmann P. - *Syntactic Analysis of Sentences in Polish Language Using the Syntax Matrix Matching Method* - Proceedings of ACS '2000 International Conference, Wydział Informatyki Politechniki Szczecińskiej, Szczecin 2000

Chapter 2

Intelligent Agents and Distributed Activities

Agent Based Freight Distrbution System
-Inter-agent Negotiation-

NAGASE AKIHIRO, KOBAYASHI SHIN-YA, YAMDA HIROYUKI
Faculty of Engineering, Ehime University

Abstract: Freight distribution system carries packages by transportation, i.e. track, train and airplane. The freight distribution system must carry the packages before deadline, and maximize the number of the packages carried before deadline even if there are packages behind the deadline. In the present freight distribution system, a transport path of the package is fixed, and the adaptability for failure and traffic fluctuation is low. We propose a method that makes the package an agent by giving it intelligent function. In this system, the package itself chooses the route, and the competition on the transportation is dispelled by the negotiation between packages. In this paper, we evaluate the method.

Key words: Freight Distribution system, Negotiation, Agent

1. INTRODUCTION

In the current freight distribution system, transport paths of packages depend on their destinations and deadlines. It is difficult to calculate a number of packages that are put into a depot by customers per day and transportation needs load margin to deal with fluctuation of a number of packages, therefore loading ratio is low. Reducing load margin to raise loading ratio lowers the adaptability for load fluctuation and makes transportation unable to deal with a number of packages increase, in consequence some packages arrive at their destinations after their deadlines. Since each package in a depot has different destination and deadline, it is hard to schedule distribution plan meeting the demands of all packages. Therefore we propose the method that makes the package an agent by giving it intelligent function in the frameworks of the given problem, and the package itself decides a distribution route. The agent decides a suitable distribution route using estimate time and connection information between depots. If the agent considers being not able to arrive at its destination before its deadline, it tries to improve the situation by interaction between agents.

2.   FREIGHT DISTRIBUTION SYSTEM

The freight distribution system consists of transportation, depots and packages. The freight distribution system must ship the packages to their destinations before the deadline, and maximize the number of the packages shipped before deadline even if there are some packages behind the deadline.

The package is received from a customer in the depot and then shipped to its destination before its dedline. The package has the following characteristics:

- Origin

  The depot where the package is received from customer.

- Destination

  The depot where the package must be sent finally.

- Receiving Time

  The time when the package was received from customer.

- Deadline

  The time before which the package must arrive at its destination.

- Capacity

  Weight and volume of the package.

  The transportation carries packages loaded between two depots. The transportation is considered to be a track, train, airplane and so on. The transportation has the following characteristics:

- Travel Time

  The time that the transportation spends moving between two depots.

  However, the travel time is not always equal to real movement time.

- Shipping Time

  The time that transportation leaves a depot to carry packages.

- Maximum Capacity

  Maximum weight and volume that the transportation can carry.

  The depot has the following roles:

- Storage of Packages

  Packages stay in the depot temporarily.

- Connection of Transportation

  Place where the transportation leaves and arrives, and packages are loaded and unloaded in the depot.

3.   MODEL USING AGENTS

In this research we use an agent technology to achieve the goal of the freight distribution system. Therefore we propose a model that the agent loaded on a facility moves on generic network that consists of nodes and arcs. In this model, each agent searches for a suitable route on the network and it moves to its destination. When competition occurs, the agent will resolve it by the inter-agent negotiation.

We apply this model to the freight distribution system and the package itself chooses the distribution route and resolves competition. And agent is called MO (Mobile Object) in this research.

The node corresponds to the depot in the freight distribution system. The node has the network topology and shipping time schedule of the facility. The arc indicates a connection between two depots. If there is a transportation that moves between two depots directly, two nodes corresponded to these depots are connected by the arc. The facility corresponds to the transportation in the freight distribution system. The facility has a capacity function and a delay value that indicates the travel time. The capacity function has an impulse at the shipping time of the transportation, and this impulse amplitude indicates the maximum capacity of the transportation. The MO corresponds to the package in the freight distribution system. MO has a size, a time putting it into the network and a shipping deadline. Since MO cannot move itself between nodes, it moves being loaded on the facility.

4. MOVEMENT METHOD OF MO

The movement method of MO consists of a path selection using relay points and a negotiation.

The path selection using relay points is that MO sets relay points on the network and then searches for a path from a current node to a neighbour relay point. That is, the method does not search for a path directly from the source node to the destination node but repeats searching for a neighbour destination. Consequently, information amount of each node and calculated amount of the path selection are saved.

The aim of the negotiation is to reduce the MO that arrives before its deadline. If a competition within the facility queue occurs, the MO performs the negotiation to shorten a waiting time at a node by changing the position in the queue. The MO that tends to arrive before its deadline negotiates with other MO that leaves earlier. If the negotiation is a success, the possibility to arrive before deadline becomes high by shortening a waiting time at a node. If the MO which negotiates with another MO accepts the negotiation results within its time margin, then it is not late for the deadline if it accepts the negotiation results. Therefore a number of the MOs that arrives before the deadline increases by the negotiation without increasing a number of the facilities.

Figure.1 shows the behaviour of the MO, when the MO arrives at a node. The MO uses the value, a room degree R, described in section 6.1, that digitalizes its time margin. The details of such behaviour are the following:

1. Negotiation Judgment
   When the MO lines up, it calculates the room degree R assumed to line up in the tail.
   If $R < 1$, it performs "Negotiation". If $R \geq 1$, it does not perform "Negotiation", and it lines up in the tail.
2. Negotiation
   The MO performs "Negotiation" to line up ahead as far as possible. If $R < 1$ after "Negotiation", the MOs reserves current position and performs "Renegotiation". The details of "negotiation" are described in section 6.

3. Path Reselection

    The MO chooses the path from current node to its destination node by the path selection method that is described in section 5.

4. Renegotiation Judgment

    If the queue selected at "Path Reselection" is the same as the queue when the MO performs "Renegotiation", the MO lines up the position reserved at "Negotiation". If these queues are different, the MO performs "Renegotiation".

5. Renegotiation

    Renegotiation" is the same as "Negotiation".

6. Queue Selection

    If the MO can line up the position when $R < 1$, it lines up this position. If not, the MO lines up the position such that the MO arrives at destination earlier. The reserved position in the queue which the MO does not take is cancelled.

7. Standby

    The MO that lines up stands by.

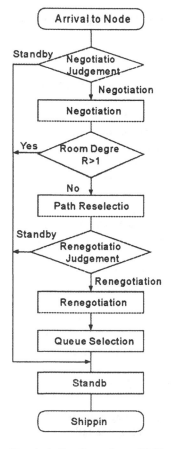

Fig. 1. Action Procedure of MO

If one MO receives the negotiation from the other MO, it judges whether it accepts the negotiation.

5. PATH SELECTION USING RELAY POINTS

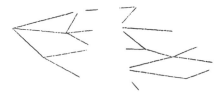

Fig. 2. Relay points and Area

Elements used for the path selection using relay points are described as follows.
1. Area
   The whole network is divided into partial networks, and the partial network is an area.
2. Relay point
   The relay point is the node that represents the area. One area has one relay point, and there must be two or more relay points in the whole network. Each node has the node connection information in the area which it belongs and adjoins to.
3. Link
   If there is a connection between an arbitrary node which belongs to the area A and an arbitrary node belonging to the area B, then there is a link between the area A and the area B. And the link has a weight that indicates an estimate time between two relay points.
4. Relay point network
   The relay point network is a virtual network which connects relay points by a link.

5.1 Procedure of path selection

First, the MO that performs the path selection must get a series of the relay points called "relay point series". The MO uses this series as a target node in the path selection. The relay point series is obtained by performing the shortest path search on the relay point network from a relay point that includes a current node to a relay point that includes the target node. And, the relay point of the area that includes the current and destination node is excluded from the relay point series, since it is a circuitous one.

Second, the MO searches for a shortest path from the current node to the node that is in the top of the relay point series. An estimate time between two nodes is used as a weight of arc. And a range of search is in the area including the current node and the target node.

When one of the following conditions is fulfilled, the MO changes the current target node to the next relay point in the relay point series.

• When the MO moves into the area including the current target node.

• When the MO performs the path reselection.

Thereby, the MO selects the suitable path from the source node to the destination node.

6.   NEGOTIATION

6.1   Room degree

The MO uses the room degree that indicates its time margin to judge whether it accepts the negotiation and performs the negotiation. The room degree is denoted as R and $R > 0$. If $R \geq 1$, the MO considers it to have a time margin. The room degree R is defined the as follows.

$$
\begin{cases}
\dfrac{T_{rem}}{\widetilde{T}_{est}} & (T_{rem} > 0) \\
0 & (T_{rem} \leq 0)
\end{cases}
$$

T_{rem} is the remained time before the deadline and T_{est} is an estimate time from the current node to the destination one. And, the estimate time T_{est} along the path $P = (e_1, e_2, \cdots, e_k)$ is calculated by the following equations:

$$
\widetilde{T}_{est} = \sum_{t=1}^{k} (d_i + \widetilde{w}_i),
$$

$$
\widetilde{w}_i = (n-1)\widetilde{I}_i + \sum \left(\frac{I_i^2}{2T_i} \right)
$$

d_i : The movement time on the arc e_i.

$\widetilde{w}_i$: The estimate waiting time on the arc e_i.

T_i : The period the facility is on the arc e_i.

I_i : The departure interval time the facility is on the arc e_i.

$\widetilde{I}_i$: The mean of I_i.

where n indicates that the MO is shipped by the n-th leaving facility from now on.

6.2 Procedure of Negotiation

The MO divides the queue that it lines up in every same facility, and negotiates with all MOs in this divided groups. That is, the MO repeats selection of the facility and the negotiation as indicated in figure 3. The details of the procedure is the following.
1. Choice of Facility
   The MO negotiates with the facility which leaves earlier. If the negotiation is rejected by all the facilities leaving earlier or accepted by in the facility leaving the earliest, the MO finishes the negotiation without shortening the waiting time in the queue.
2. Negotiation with the MO in the queue
   The MO asks all the MOs which take the facility selected by it for changing the position in the queue. Here, let M_{rem} be the value subtracted from its size capacity margin of the facility that it chooses. If M_{rem} is equal to the sum of the negotiations accepted or more, then the MO performs "Choice of Exchanging the Position", if not, the MO returns to the "Choice of facility".
3. Choice of Exchanging the Position
   The MO chooses the MOs that exchange the positions in the queue from all the MOs that accept the negotiation so that the sum of the size of the MOs that exchange the position which is larger then its size and the size is as small as possible. This is for the sake of increasing efficiency of the shipping.
4. Judgment of the negotiation continuation
   The MO which finished the exchange of the position in the queue calculates the room degree R_f in the position f after exchange, if $R_f < 1$, performs "Choice of facility" to continue the negotiation. It occurs so for the reason the MO that rejects the negotiation before may accept changing the position.

When the MO receives the negotiation, it calculates the room degree R_f after exchanging the position, and if $R_f < 1$, it exchanges the position in the queue.

7. SIMULATION EVALUATION

In order to present effectiveness of our method, we evaluate it by computer simulation.

7.1 Simulation condition

- Network
  The 1,000 nodes are arranged in plane of 500×500 [unit length]. However, there is a constraint that straight distance between arbitrary nodes is more than 10[unit length]. And, an arc of a node connects two nodes that have no connection with the node to a short straight distance order.

100 relay points are selected at random for straight distance between arbitrary relay points which are more than 60[unit length] in all the nodes. The area of few hop orders from the relay point includes the nodes and the number of nodes in one area is less than 40.

- Facility

  Let the departure interval be 20[unit time]. Since it is thought that the travel time and capacity are proportional to the straight distance between nodes, let these values be half of the straight distance.

- Put method

  100 nodes are selected at random from all nodes, and the source node and destination node is selected at random from these nodes.

  Since the deadline is proportional to the straight distance between nodes and thought to be random to some extent, let the deadline be $(\text{straight distance}) \times 2 + (0 \sim 50)$.

- Others

  The connection information between nodes is updated every 50[unit time].

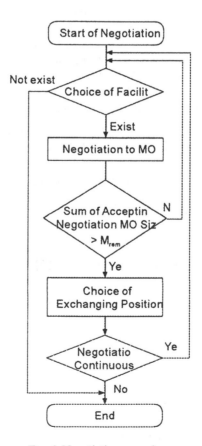

Fig. 3. Negotiation procedure

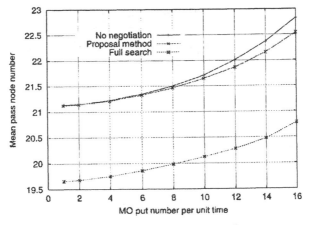

Fig. 4. Mean Number of Pass Node

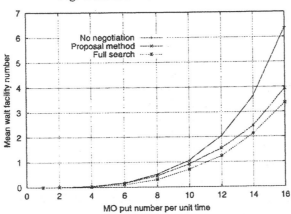

Fig. 5. Mean Number of Wait Facility

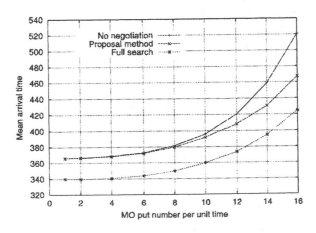

Fig. 6. Mean Arrival time

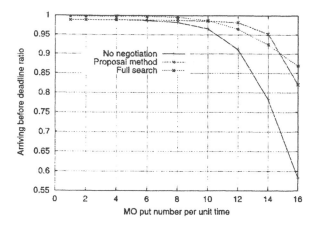

Fig. 7. Arriving before Deadline Ratio

7.2 Result

- Mean Number of Pass Node
  Figure 4 shows the mean number of pass nodes at varying the number of putting MO to the network per unit time. The proposal method achieves small improvement from the no negotiation. Since the negotiation is the exchange of the position in the queue, mean number of pass nodes should not change.
  However, the load was distributed by the negotiation and since taking the path that bypasses the high load node decreased, it is thought that the number of pass node decreased.

- Mean Number of Waiting Facilities
  Figure 5 shows the mean number of waiting facilities at varying the number of putting MO to the network per unit time.
  The proposal method achieves improvement from no negotiation at all loads. As with number of pass node, since the load was distributed, it is thought that the vacant facility is reduced.

- Mean Arrival Time
  Figure 6 shows the mean number of wait facility at varying the number of putting MO to the network per unit time.
  The proposal method achieves improvement from no negotiation at all load. And the improvement grows as increases the load. Since the number of pass node and waiting facilities were reduced by the negotiation, it is thought that the arrival time was shortened.

- Arriving before Deadline Ratio
  Since the proposal method achieves improvement in the mean number of pass node, the mean number of waiting facilities and the mean arrival time, the arriving before deadline ratio is improved greatly from no negotiation. Especially, the proposal method is better than the full-search at the load which is from 12 to 14.
  The proposal method is worth than full-search for the mean arrival time, however it is thought that the effect of negotiation is large in the case of high load.

8. CONCLUSION

In this paper, we proposed the method that makes a package be an agent by giving it an intelligent function for the inter-agent negotiation and choosing the distribution route. And we showed that it achieves reduction in the number of packages that arrive behind deadline by simulation. Especially, it may be better than the full-search.

We will study evaluation at performing the negotiation between three or more agents and characterization of agents.

9. REFERENCES

[1] A. Nagase, S. Kobayashi, H. Yamada, Dynamic Flow Control with Mobile Agents (In Japanese), IPSJ Symposium Series, Vol.2000, 2000, 139-144

Improvement of The User Interface for Autonomous Load Distributing Algorithm

SHUNSUKE KUHARA, SHIN-YA KOBAYASHI

Department of Computer Science, Ehime University

Abstract: In this paper, we improve the User Interface of Autonomous Load Distribution Algorithm which we have designed before. The previous interface is a trial that enables implicit load distribution. However, the previous interface can not handle the modified task. In other words, it distributes the task that becomes unsuitable for distribution after modification. To solve the problem, we propose the additional function to the previous user interface and implement the improved user interface.

Key words: User Interface

1. INTRODUCTION

With the widespread use of Ethernet and FDDI networking techniques, and the advent of cheap computers for workstations, we can find a user environment in which a large number of computers under the same control are mutually connected by a network in laboratories of universities and offices of enterprises. Such systems are named "multi-computer systems" in this paper. In multi-computer systems, network information service (NIS) or network file system (NFS) has been used mostly in which all users can access the same computer and every user can access all the computers simultaneously.

For efficient utilization of system resources and fast processing of tasks input by users in a multi-computer system, we have to take into account the processing power and load conditions of each computer for properly selecting the task-executing computer. However, tasks from users are introduced randomly and the size of the task or the computer where it will be input cannot be predicted in advance. Thus, for proper load distribution, we should know the load condition for each computer dynamically; but this is very difficult for the users. Instead of having the user selected the task-executing computer, a method for load distribution in which the computers determine the suitable task-executing computer by mutual negotiation among themselves is highly desirable.

For these types of load distribution various types of protocols for communication and negotiation among computers have been proposed. We have also proposed the Autonomous Load Distribution Algorithm as a load distribution protocol. This algorithm is that the node where the task execution is required by the user negotiates with the other nodes by one-to-one communication.

So far, we have implemented the Autonomous Load Distribution Algorithm and some other load distribution algorithm (e.g. sender-initiated algorithm, receiver-initiated algorithms, and combinations of both types), and performed evaluation under some conditions. According to the evaluation result, the Autonomous Load Distribution Algorithm is more effective among them in most cases. Hence, we have designed the user interface of the algorithm for practical use and implemented it. The user interface was designed so that a user can distribute a task without making the user conscious of task distribution. This was realized using "alias function". When a user wants a task to be distributed repeatedly, the command of the task is registered by 'alias'. After registered, when the user execute the alias, the task is distributed automatically.

However, in the case that the task for the alias gets modified and it becomes inadequate to be distributed, the modified task will be distributed when a user executes the alias. This is because the alias remains registered despite of the modification of the task. If the modified task is distributed, a user may receive the incorrect or undesirable task response. Even if a user receives the response of a task faster by using a load distribution function, if the response is incorrect or undesirable, the load distribution function is no longer effective.

To meet this problem, modification of task for an alias must be detected. In this paper, we propose modification detection algorithm and implements it. By appending this function to the previous user interface, users can use the Autonomous Load Distribution Algorithm reliably.

2. AUTONOMOUS LOAD DISTRIBUTION ALGORITHM

Here we describe the Autonomous Load Distribution Algorithm. In the algorithm the node to which a task is submitted by the user, requests task execution using one-to-one communication with the other nodes and waits for a yes or no reply. The algorithm has the following characteristics.

– Each node makes decision locally and independently of others. (distributed management)
– Each node knows only a part of the world , not overall. (incomplete information).
– It uses one-to-one communication (nonbroadcast type).

These characteristics can be easily realized in multi-computer systems.

The procedure for negotiation among the nodes for the task-execution request and its reply can be separated into the request decision and the reply decision, based on whether the task is asked to other nodes or is executed at the node itself, and whether the request can be accepted or not. Below, we explain the management of information required for these decisions, and also the procedures for request decision and reply decision.

2.1 Request Decision Procedure

A request decision is done by the node at which the task is introduced or a node which has accepted the request during negotiation. This procedure consists of two processes making a list of candidates and request message transmission.

2.1.1 Making a list of candidates

The expected time to process the task at each node is estimated and a list of candidates is made. The candidates list is used for determining the order of request. In estimating expected time, Node Information which consists of Hardware Information (node name, processing power, communication channel characteristics) and Load Information (total number of processes at the node) is used.

2.1.2 Request message transmission

After making a candidates list, the node that has a task to be done requests the top of the candidates list to execute the task. If the top node is itself, then the node executes the task by itself. If not, then a request is sent to the top node. The request message transmitted to the requested node contains information about the task submitted, the expected time for the requesting node, and Node Information (route node information) of the nodes participating in negotiation.

The reply message for the request is received. The reply message contains Accept/Reject and Node Information of the requested node. When the request is rejected then the top candidate on the list is removed and the next request message is sent to the new top node. If it is accepted then the requested node becomes a new requesting node and performs a request decision.

The Node Information included in the reply message is used to refresh the local information database of the self-node.

2.2 Reply decision Procedure

The node which is requested task execution, the requested node performs a reply decision for the request. The node estimates the processing time for the requested task at the self-node, and then if it is shorter than the expected time of the requesting node, it is accepted and a request decision for the accepted task is done recursively. If not, then the request is rejected.

2.3   Management of local information database

In the Autonomous Load Distribution Algorithm, Node Information about other nodes is obtained by transmitting the route information, containing information on the nodes participating in negotiation, to all the negotiating nodes. The information obtained during negotiation is kept in the local information database. Thus, initially, information on all the nodes in the system is not required, and information on unknown nodes can be indirectly obtained during negotiation.

However, by repeating the negotiation, the information in the database increases. If any time elapses after getting the information on load conditions, reliability is then degraded. Thus, we have to discard unnecessary information. In the Autonomous Load Distribution Algorithm, we determine the long-term reliability validity interval for Hardware Information such as processing speed and the short-term reliability validity interval for Load Information such as load condition, and the information exceeding these intervals is discarded.

3.   USER INTERFACE

For the purpose of using Autonomous Load Distribution Algorithm practicaly, we must design user interface of the algorithm. In the design of it, first of all, we considered the following 2 points;

a)   What does user have to do when using Autonomous Load Distribution Algorithm?

b)   Does user always have to explicitly conscious of task distribution?

a) was considered as the following. There are some tasks which must not be distributed since their result depends on the node to which they are submitted. Moreover, the task selected as an object of load distribution is different among users. Hence, it is necessary to distinguish between a task which is allowed to be distributed and a task which must not be distributed. This distinction is very difficult for computer since a task must be analysed semantically. Therefore, it is necessary to have a user distinguish it.

Speaking about b), it is considered that the user's demand is categorized to two types. One is explicit direction to distribute a task and the other is implicit direction.

We have designed user interface taking these points into consideration. In the following section, we describe the mechanism of the user interface.

3.1   User Interface of the Former Implement

In the former implement, we designed the command "aldcom" to direct task distribution explicitly and to distinguish a task. By using this command, user can distribute a task intentionally. By executing aldcom with a command of the task that will be distributed as the argument (here we assume the command task), the task can be distributed;

[example: aldcom task]

Implicit direction of task distribution is realized using 'alias function of shell (e.g. bash, csh)'. The mechanism is described as below: When user wants a task to be distributed permanently, the user registers the task by 'alias' as following.

[example: `alias task='aldcom task'`]

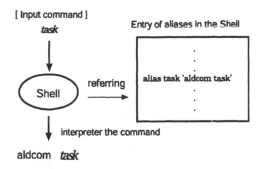

Fig. 1. Mechanism of Implicit Direction

After registering, user executes the alias (`task`), and then the shell replaces the alias with the original command (`aldcom task`) referring the entry of aliases in the shell as in *Figure 1*. Thus, user can direct task distribution implicitly. However, the aliases registered in the shell are valid only while user is logged in the system. Hence, the aliases disappear from the shell after a user has logged out. That is, user can only make an implicit direction temporarily. To make the aliases valid permanently, we prepared the special file. By writing the alias into the file when registering an alias and then executing the file automatically when a user logs in the system again, the alias gets valid permanently.

However, It is annoying for a user to register an alias and to write the alias into the special file for the implicit direction. To make these procedures done more easily, we designed some special command as below.
- aldadd (to register an alias permanently)
- alddel (to cancel an alias registered permanently)
- ald (to register an alias temporarily)
- unald (to cancel an alias registered temporarily)

3.2 Problem of The User Interface with Alias

In the user interface there is a following problem: Even if the task for an alias gets modified, the modification has no influence on the alias and it remains valid in the shell. After the modification by executing the alias the modified task will be distributed. In the case the modified task is inadequate to be distributed, the taskresult becomes incorrect or undesirable. This problem is called "inconsistency between name and reality on the distributed task". Moreover, even if the modified task is adequate to be distributed, unless the user recognizes the modification, the problem as described above may occur later.

4.   IMPROVEMENT OF THE USER INTERFACE

For more reliable user interface, in this paper we proposed a mechanism to solve the above problem. This mechanism notifies the user that a registered task is modified, and then the user can decide either to retain the alias in the shell or to remove the alias from the shell. To implement the mechanism, we have to target the following 2 points.
– When modification detection procedure starts?
– How to detect modification?
We discuss these in the following section.

4.1   When Modification Detection Procedure starts?

We can consider the following 3 instants when detection initiates.
a)   Just before the execution of a command that can modify a task potentially.
b)   Just after the execution of any command
c)   Just before the execution of alias which directs task distribution implicitly.

Each case has the advantage as described below, respectively. In the case of a) a user can decide either to retain the alias in the shell or remove the alias from the shell before the task for an alias gets modified. In the case of b), since user decides it just after the task for an alias has got modified, user can make the decision more easily and correctly. In the case of c), since a modification detection procedure is performed only when each alias is executed, the overhead caused by the procedure is smaller than that of the procedure in the case a) and in the case b).

However, we can't decide a) as the instant of modification detection, since it is impossible to specify commands that can modify a task potentially. Hence, we have to select b) or c) as the instant of modification detection.

In the case of c), since user does not always execute the alias just after the modification has occurred, user may forget that what is content of the modification due to passage of time from the modification to the next execution of the alias. If user can't remember the content of the modification, user may decide either to retain the alias or remove it incorrectly. From the reason, case c) is less reliable than case b). Thus, we think of b) as the best.

The system must trap the instant when a process terminates so that user can make decision just after the execution of any command. Trapping the instant is easy with SIGCHLD signal. The signal is one of UNIX fundamental signals. The signal is sent to the parent process when a child process terminates. The mechanism is shown in *Figure 2*.

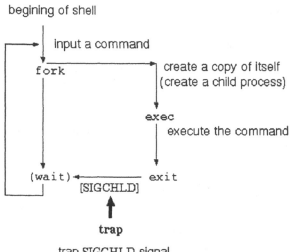

begining of shell

Fig. 2. Trapping of SIGCHLD signal

4.2   How to Detect Modification

In this section, we describe how to detect the modification of task. To detect the modification, we use a time stamp when the task is modified.

When the command for a task gets aliased for implicit direction of task distribution, user records the time stamp of the latest task modification. After that, if a command is executed, the time stamp of task for the alias is gained, and then it is compared with the recorded time. It is decided that if they are equal, no modification has been detected, if not, modification has been detected.

To realize it, a special file is set for recording the time stamp of the latest task modification. Moreover, we improve the commands that we have developed for registration of alias so that the procedure for recording the time stamp of the latest task modification is performed automatically.

When the modification is detected by this modification detection procedure, the process performing this procedure informs the user of the fact and inquires the user whether the alias is retained in the shell or it is removed from the shell. If user selects the former, the time stamp in the special file is refreshed with the time stamp of the latest task modification. If not, the alias is removed from the shell and the time stamp in the file is also removed from the file automatically.

After this procedure, the original shell procedure is restarted. The modification detection algorithm is shown in *Figure 3*.

begining of shell

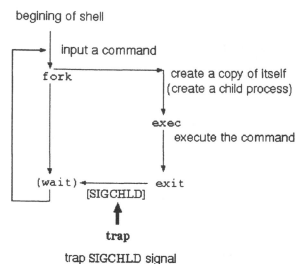

trap SIGCHLD signal

Fig. 2. Trapping of SIGCHLD signal

5. CONCLUSION

In this paper we improved the user interface which has developed before.

The previous user interface used the "alias function of shell" for the implicit direction of task distribution. Hence, Inconsistency between name and reality of the target task can occur. To solve the problem, we proposed the algorithm that when a task for an alias gets modified, the user is informed the modification, and then it makes the user decide either to retain the alias in the shell or to remove the alias from the shell.

To implement the mechanism, at first, we decided the instant which any command is finished as the instant of modification detection. Next, we decided that the modification of a task is detected by watching the change of the time stamp of the latest task modification.

By appending the modification detection function to the previous user interface, user can utilize the Autonomous Load Distribution Algorithm more reliably.

In this improved user interface, there is a following problem: the overhead caused by the modification detection procedure increases with the number of the registered aliases. We will research the solution of it in the future.

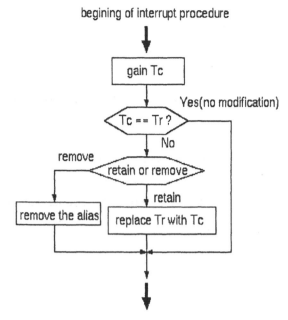

begining of interrupt procedure

Fig. 3. Algorithm of Modification Detection

Tr: the time stamp of the latest task's modification when a command gets aliased
Tc: the time stamp of the latest task's modification at present

end of interrupt procedure, restart the shell

6. REFERENCES

N.G.Shivaratri, P.Krueger, and M.Singhal.
"Load distributing for locally distributed systems."
IEEE Computer 25, No12(p.33-44) (Dec.1992)
L.Letizia and Z.Franco
"Diffusive Balancing Policies for Dynamic Applications."
IEEE Concurrency, January-March 1999 (pp.22-31)
T.Ogawa, S.Kobayashi, H.Kimura, and T.Takebe.
"Evaluation of Autonomous Load Distribution Method." (in Japanese)
TECHNICAL REPORT OF IEICE, vol.93, No436, CPSY 93-51(pp.47-54), Jan.1994
T.Ogawa and S.Kobayashi.
"Evaluation of Load Distribution Method Based on Internode Negotiations." (in Japanese)
IPSJ SIG Notes, vol.94, No.65, 94-PRG-18-10 (pp73-80), July 1994
S.Kobayashi, H.Kimura, and T.Takebe.
"A Load distribution Method for Multicomputer System Based on Inter Computer

Negotiation."

Proceeding of 1993 Joint Technical Conference on Circuits/System, pp.(1993.7)

S.Kobayashi, T.Ogawa, and T.Watanabe

"Autonomous Load Distributing for Multi-Computer Systems." (in Japanese)

IEICE(D-I), vol.J79-D-I, No.11(pp.903-905), November 1996

Y.Tanaka and S.Kobayashi.

"Implementation and Evaluation of Autonomous Load Distribution Method based on Cooperation." (in Japanese)

IPSJ DiCoMo(7) (pp.37-42), July 1997

S.Miyazaki and S.Kobayashi

"User Interface Implementation of Autonomous Load Distribution." (in Japanese)

IPSJ, Symposium Series vol.99, No.7 (pp.465-470)

S.Miyazaki and S.Kobayashi

"Improvement of Autonomous Load Distribution Algorithm with Receiver-Initiated Mechanism." (in Japanese)

IPSJ SIG Notes, 2001-DPS-102 (pp.139-144)

The ROLCoDE framework used in a computational distributed calculation

RUI MANUEL COELHO
Escola Superior de Tecnologia, Instituto Politécnico de Castelo Branco,
Av. do Empresário, 6000 Castelo Branco, Portugal, e-mail: rcoelho@est.ipcb.pt

Abstract: In this paper it is presented the functionality of the distributed calculation in the *ROLCoDE* framework (Online Re-configurable Controller on Distributed Environment). This way it becomes possible to take advantage of the existent computational capacity, as well as, to increase the safety and the functionality of the system. A dynamic equation of state variables was used in the discreet system of the simulator example of the inverse pendulum. For such, it is considered the parameter M (mass of the car) as a dependent variable in the time. The diagrams of tasks and sub-tasks of the process simulator were elaborated in the *ROLCoDE* framework. In the first experiment the results were obtained with just a single processor through the development of a series, with the variable of the iterations to take values every time larger in order to obtain a more rigorous calculation increasing the computational capacity of the system. In a second experiment the results were obtained with two processors. For that, the used previously equation was subdivided in two equations, with the purpose of dividing the calculation for two processors. Finally, the two results were compared, for that, it a polynomial approach of degree three on the results obtained in both experiments took place. It was concluded that the *ROLCoDE* framework could use the computational capacity available in the distributed system in that it is inserted.

Key words: distributed environment, simulation, computational capacity

1.   INTRODUCTION

The ROLCoDE (*Online Re-configurable Controller on Distributed Environment*) framework was firstly presented as a prototype for an online re-configurable computing system (task-based), running over a distributed environment. The main purpose is to widen the possibilities for online re-configuration of software-based controllers, this prototype implements a way to refine the computations without interrupting an overall process of control [1].

This framework allows the user to make simulation processes and also to control them. It is a model-based framework and it allows some flexibility at the user and at the construction level, there is the possibility of a dynamic evolution of this framework along the time. ROLCoDE framework uses a distributed environment, a parallel processing, an object orientated programming (OOP), and a modular system characteristic [2].

The ROLCoDE framework was applied to the study of discrete and continuous simulation through the implementation of the continuous equations of a system, with the discrete and continuous simulation [3].

It is intended with this article to present the functionalities of the distributed calculation in a distributed environment, so that it makes possible to obtain party of the computational capacity, safety and functionality of the system.

One of the objectives of the choice of a distributed environment is taking advantage of the computational capacity that exists. In this paper it is intended to justify the need of the use of that same capacity, for such, the parameter M (mass of the car) of the inverse pendulum example is considered as a dependent variable in time.

2.   DISTRIBUTED CHARACTERISTIC

The distribution takes us to the parallel processing; on the data it must be exchanged between processes. There are some paradigms for this. We are interested in one of them: message passing (MP), which is common to two great systems: Massively Parallel Processing and Distributed Computing. In this last one we have a set of computers connected by a network used to solve a series of problems, which appear when one wants to have a good: performance, reliability and functional requirements [4].

A computer network gets connected to a quite big variety of computers, whose geographical location is dispersed. This system type where we find a diversity of machines and operative systems we call it as a distributed heterogeneous environment.

At the level of the distributed processing, the process is the unit base of parallelism. However, we will consider the task constituted by a group of sub-tasks, which communicate with each other to reach a final result [7]. This sub-task is the process in a distributed environment.

In the parallel simulation using a great number of processors, it is necessary to use synchronization among them [8].

Two great types of primitive communication exist in parallel computation, the blocking and nonblocking [11]. After using a blocking primitive, the process should block and wait until it receives an indication or query for the destination process. These two communication types are realized using the MP paradigm.

The delay of the messages depends on: configuration system, distribution of the destination messages, message length, interconnection network, routing algorithm used [7]. This delay can cause different behavior for the same system.

Some architectures are called architectures of PM because they support this model in hardware, although it is more used in the software of operation system and of communication network [12].

The libraries of PM can be of the specific given architecture, but they can also be generic including a great group of architectures. In this case, it is possible to execute processes on heterogeneous platforms. Some examples of these existent libraries are [6]: *PVM* [9], *MPI, p4, CHIMP, NX, EUI, Express.*

3. THE EXAMPLE

For this presentation we consider the inverse pendulum problem. In this problem the inverted pendulum is mounted on a motor-driven car. The objective of the control action is to keep the space booster in a vertical position. The inveree pendulum is unstable; we only considered two dimensions for the problem.

There is a control force *u* applied to the car to stabilize the system.

We assume that the mass of the car is *M*=7kg, the mass of the pendulum *m*=2kg, length of the pendulum is 2 m, and we consider that the period of time for the pendulum system is T_s = 0.05 sec. We choose a damping ratio ζ=0.5 and an undamped natural frequency w_n=2. Then the desired closed-loop poles at:

$$\mu_1 = -1 + j\sqrt{3}$$
$$\mu_2 = -1 - j\sqrt{3}$$
$$\mu_3 = -5$$
$$\mu_4 = -5$$

3.1 The distributed environment

Now, we intend to construct a simulation system of the inverse pendulum problem and test some control processes. The *ROLCoDE* framework allows to use a distributed environment. We can take advantage of the distributed environment existing in our working place to build a system of control and simulation.

However it is necessary to test the efficiency of this distributed system. In this section we will demonstrate that with *ROLCoDE* framework it is possible to realize performance tests of the available distributed system taking the respective conclusions related with its use.

The *ROLCoDE* uses the PVM environment. This way, it is possible to use distributed heterogeneous environment.

3.2 Mathematical equations

As it was mentioned in the previous subsection, we now intend to effectuate some tests of the network efficiency in order that we will be able to implement a system of control and simulation of the example presented (the inverse pendulum). In this example, the parameter M (car mass) is variable in time.

So we have the equation of states for the continuous system of the inverse pendulum problem [10]:

$$dx(t)/dt = x'(t) = A\ x(t) + B\ u(t) \tag{1}$$

Being $x(t)$ the states vector (with n $\times$ 1 column, for a system with n states), $u(t)$ is the vector of entries or control (p $\times$ 1 column for a system with p entries). A, B are matrices of constant coefficients which relate the output in a determined instant with the system states and the combinations of the entries.

The implementation of this system in the *ROLCoDE* environment requires the conversion of the equations from the continuous system into a discrete system, which means that it is necessary to convert the matrices A and B of the continuous system into the matrices G and H of the following discreet equation [5]:

$$x[k+1] = G\ x[k] + H\ u[k] \tag{2}$$

where: k=0,1,2,...,n

That is, the following state of the system $x[k+1]$ is related with the previous state $x[k]$ and the control entries of the system $u[k]$ through matrices G and H. These matrices are obtained using the method of ZOH[1].

$$G = e^{AT_s} \tag{3}$$

$$H = \int_0^{T_s} e^{A\eta} d\eta B \tag{4}$$

Being $T_s = 0.05$ sec the time period (sampling interval), as it was referred previously, we develop the former equations in the following:

$$G = I + AT\ \Psi \tag{5}$$
$$H = \Psi TB \tag{6}$$

Taking into consideration that I is the identity matrix for Ψ, then we have:

$$\Psi = I + \sum_{n=2}^{\infty} \frac{A^{n-1}T^{n-1}}{n!} \tag{7}$$

For the series with the finite number of elements, N > 1, we have

$$\Psi \approx I + \frac{AT}{2!} + \frac{A^2T^2}{3!} + ... + \frac{A^{N-1}T^{N-1}}{N!} \tag{8}$$

---

[1] Zero-order hold on the inputs

3.3 Experimental results with 1 processor

The equation (8) is a series of N values, if we want a value of Ψ each time more rigorous, than N takes each time bigger values. This calculation process places us in the presence of a quite heavy computational cargo with the successive growing of N.

It will be a good example where one can apply some computational capacity to the existing distributed environment and proceed with its analysis.

For that, one has begun by making the calculation of this equation (8) in one single processor; proceeding by increasing successively the value of N. For each one of the N values, one has proceeded with the measuring between the beginning and he end of the making of the Ψ value calculation, for a given value of the M.

These results can be analyzed in the graphic in Figure 1, we can see that a continuity in the obtained results does not exist in the function used to obtain the machine actual time.

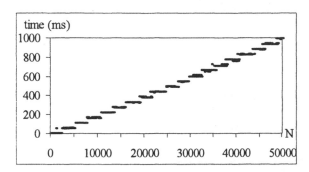

Fig. 1. One processor

We also verified that a relation of proportionality exists between the time spent in the calculation of the expression and the increasing of the N value, in the same expression.

3.4 Experimental results with 2 processors

Now we are going to subdivide the equation (8) into two others, so we can divide the calculation by two processors.

This way we obtain equation (9), with the factor Ω being given by the equation (10), with the value of $P = N/2$ if N even or $P = (N+1)/2$ if N odd.

$$\Psi \approx \left(I + \sum_{n=2}^{P} \frac{A^{n-1}T^{n-1}}{n!} \right) + \frac{A^{P}T^{P}}{(P+1)!}\Omega \tag{9}$$

$$\Omega = I + \frac{AT}{(P+2)} + \frac{A^{2}T^{2}}{(P+3)(P+2)} + \dots + \frac{A^{(N-P)-1}T^{(N-P)-1}}{\prod_{m=2}^{N-P}(P+m)} \tag{10}$$

We placed the calculation of Ω in one processor and the calculation Ψ in another one, knowing that this last calculation will have to receive the values of Ω from the other processor; however, this one has already made practically all of its calculation.

We also verified that the computational capacity between the two processors is practically identical. So we obtain the graphic results of these two processors in figure 2.

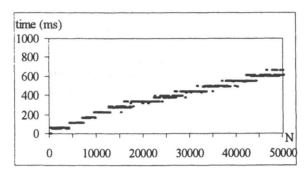

Fig. 2. Two processors

In contrary to the previous graphic, here does not exist proportionality between the time spent and the value of N, what does exist is a decreasing of the time spent with the successive increasing of N.

3.5 Study of the results

In order to compare results, we are going to substitute these same results obtained in each one of the previous graphics for a third-order polynomial. This way we obtain the graphics in figure 3.

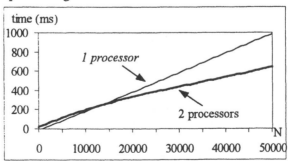

Fig. 3. Comparison of results

In it we verify that the temporal efficiency of calculation is better with one single processor, for values of N inferiors to N_c ($12000 < N_c < 15000$) up to intersection of the two curves.

This fact has to do with the delays introduced in the communications between the two calculation modules which become significative for $N < N_c$

For values of N superiors to the value of N_c, the temporal efficiency of calculation is bigger, when we have two processors making the calculations. That efficiency increases with the growing of the N value.

For the presented simulation of the inverse pendulum, with $T_s = 0.05$ sec, under parameter variable M in time and the considered conditions for this example, we can conclude that we have more computational efficiency with just one processor for the same number of the iterations (N).

4. CONCLUSIONS

We performed two experiments to test computational capacity of the system which mathematical model is presented by the equation (7). In the first experiment just one processor was used, in the second experiment the same mathematical model was calculated, but using two processors.

The figures 1 and 2 present, respectively, efficiency obtained in each experience and the comparison of both experiences in the figure 3. We can observe that for simple calculations with an inferior number of iterations Nc (point of intersection of the two curves) it compensates the use of a single processor. For a superior number of iterations Nc, compensates the use of parallelism (in this case two processors). For calculations of little complexity that needs a reduced number of iterations; it compensates the use of just one processor. For more complex calculations and more iterations the use of more processors becomes advantageous because it improves the efficiency of the calculation of the system.

As a future work, the current PVM environment could be substituted for the MPI environment, once this contemplates a larger number of interfaces of functions beneficial for *ROLCoDE* in this case, namely in the best use of the parallel and distributed programming, as well as new methods of implementation of control and simulation tasks.

5. REFERENCES

[1] R. Coelho, P. Pimenta, "ROLCoDE – On line reconfigurable controller on distributed environment", *In Proceedings of the 6th Advanced Computers System (ACS'99)*, Szczecin, Poland, pp. 329-336, Nov. 1999

[2] R. M. Coelho, *"A modular framework for control and simulations of the processes"*, In Proceedings of the ProSim2000 Workshop, Software Process Simulation Modelling, The Imperial College of Science, Technology and Medicine, London, UK, July 2000

[3] R. M. Coelho, *"The ROLCoDE framework applied to the study of discrete and continuous simulation"*, In Proceedings of the 7th Advanced Computers System (ACS'2000), Technical University of Szczecin, Faculty of Computer Science & Information Systems, Szczecin, Poland, pp. 83-90, October 2000

[4] K. Arvind, K. Ramamritham, J. Stankovic, "A local area network architecture for communication in distributed real-time systems", *J. Real-Time Systems*, Vol.3, No.2, pp. 115-147, May 1991

[5] G. Franklin, J. Powell, M. Workman, "Digital control of dynamic systems", *third edition*, Addison-Wesley, 1998

[6] A. Geist, A. Beguelin, J. Dongarra, W. Jiang, R. Manchek, V. Sunderam, "PVM: a users' guide and tutorial for networked parallel computing", *MIT Press*, 1994

[7] J. Kim, K. Shin, "Execution time analysis of communicating tasks in distributed systems", *IEEE Transactions on Computers*, Vol.45, No.5, pp. 572-579, May 1996

[8] E. Naroska, U. Schwiegelshohn, "Conservative parallel simulation of a large number of processes", *Simulation*, Vol.72, No.3, pp. 150-162, Mar. 1999

[9] PVM Home page, "http://www.epm.ornl.gov/pvm/pvm_home.html", *Oak Ridge National Laboratory*, Apr. 1999

[10] K. Ogata "Modern control engineering", *third edition, Prentice-Hall*, 1997

[11] D. Peng, K. Shin, "Modeling of concurrent task execution in a distributed system for real-time control", *IEEE Trans. Computer*, Vol.36, No.4, pp. 500-516, Apr 1987

[12] G. Wilson, "A glossary of parallel computing terminology", IEEE parallel and distributed technology: systems and applications, 1(1), pp. 52-67, Feb. 1993

Some Tasks of Intelligent Tutoring Systems Design for Civil Aviation Pilots

OREST POPOV[1], ROGER LALANNE[2], GUY GOUARDERES[3], ANTON MINKO[2], ALEXANDER TRETYAKOV[2]

[1] *Faculty of Computer Science & Information Systems, Technical University of Szczecin, Żołnierska Street 49, 71-210 Szczecin, Poland, e-mail: popov@wi.ps.pl*
[2] *STAR, Institut de Maintenance Aeronautique, Rue Marcel Issartier, 33700 Merignac, France, e-mail: roger.lalanne@star-ima.com, anton.minko@star-ima.com, alexandre.tretyakov@star-ima.com;*
[3] *Equipe MISIM-Laboratoire d'Informatique Appliquée - IUT de Bayonne, 64100 Bayonne,France, e-mail: Guy.Gouarderes@iutbay.univ-pau.fr*

Abstract: This article aims to consider the essential problems related to the design of innovative intelligent tutoring systems based on multi-agent technologies. Amongst others, these are:
- problems of elaboration of structure for such systems and of algorithms of agents behaviour,
- problems of creation of training object's models and their verification,
- problems of organisation of structural and functional relations between all elements of training system.
All these problems are considered in the framework of application to intelligent tutoring systems for civil aviation pilots.

Key words: Simulation, Intelligent Tutoring System, MutiAgent System, CBT, Quantitative evaluation

1.   INTRODUCTION

Any concept of the training process supposes the presence of four interacting components: trainee - instructor - simulation system - executed procedures (see Fig.1, a). It is obvious that the role of instructor is paramount, because the instructor is the person who plans the training session and chooses the appropriate pedagogical strategies in order to ensure the best quality of training. But the main task of automation of tutoring process consists in the instructor function simplification by liberating him from routine actions. Therefore, the ITS must interact with all forenamed components (Fig. 1, b).

Training systems are used widely to train a staff of civil aviation to flight on aircraft and to execute the procedures of control. Such systems are usually complex systems. The cost of these systems is rather high, but many tasks of training in aviation can be solved on the base of more simple systems. These training systems are realized only using personal computers and corresponding software.

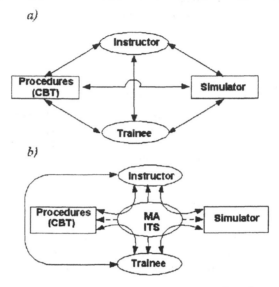

Fig. 1. Actors of aeronautical training: a – classical scheme, b – scheme with MA ITS.

The basic components of such system are actually simulators, which simulate behaviour of the aircraft and its systems in real time, and intelligent training system (ITS) based on Multi-Agent technologies, which assist to a trainee during performance of tasks [5, 7, 11].

2. THE STRUCTURE OF THE TUTORING PROCESS

The analysis of a training process allows presenting it as the structure, which is shown in Fig.2 [11].

It is impossible to clear up main and minor elements because the loss of any of them destroys the system.

All main blocks in this system can be classified in two groups:

The first group are agents:

– detectors of mistakes, qualifiers, assistant, pedagogue.

The second group are blocks, which it is possible to name as analytical:

– the block of modeling of behavior of the plane and systems,
– the block of evaluations of the trainee's actions.

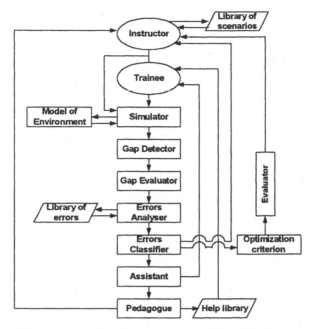

Fig. 2. The structure of training process in intelligent tutoring system

Then, the block of evaluations can be presented as the structure, which is shown in Fig.3.

The development of such system should base on the analysis of each action of the trainee and algorithms of behavior of all elements of a system.

It is necessary to develop specifications of all actions and mistakes of the trainee.

Then, it is necessary to develop (in contact with the expert) rating norms of these actions. For example, for a stage of takeoff preparation and then the takeoff itself these evaluations can have the form shown in table 1 [7].

Such quantitative estimations can form the basis for development of algorithms of the intelligent training system.

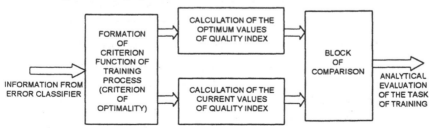

Fig. 3. The structure of the block of evaluations

Parameters	The nominal values	The norms of limiting deviations (evaluations in numbers from 2 to 5)		
		3	4	5
Deviations from the axis of the runway, m	0	5	3	2
Instrumental speed, km/h	230	15	10	5
Angle of pitch, degrees	13	3	2	1

Tab. 1. The norms of limiting pilot's errors at the aircraft takeoff (approximately)

And it is completely clear that the work of all training systems should be based on modelling of flight dynamics and behaviour of aircraft systems. For this reason the behaviour of the dynamic model of the plane should exactly correspond to behaviour of the real aircraft.

We will consider step by step (in rectangular axis system) some deviations of the aircraft taking into account three co-ordinates. Let's set small deviations from the following angles: pitch, yaw, roll from the initial position of the aircraft in space. Changing each co-ordinate, named above, a pilot – expert will be giving quantitative evaluations of the learner's action. If the aircraft is well controlled at the changing one of the angles, a trainee receives positive evaluation (5 or 4, according to the evaluation scale from 2 (the worst) to 5 (the best)). On the other hand, evaluation is negative.

By the way of setting different angles, it is possible to design matrix of quantitative measures of the trainee's action. Quantitative measure of each manoeuvre will afford to receive digital information about possible angles: yaw, roll, pitch.

	yaw	pitch	roll	yaw	pitch	roll	yaw	pitch	roll	yaw	pitch	roll
Value, °	0	15	0	1	0	5	2	0	0	0	5	90
Rating		5			5			5			1	
Value, °	0	15	5	1	0	10	2	0	5	0	5	60
Rating		5			5			5			3	
Value, °	0	15	10	1	0	15	2	0	10	0	15	60
Rating		4			5			5			2	
Value, °	0	15	15	1	5	0	2	0	15	0	15	45
Rating		4			5			5			5	
Value, °	0	10	15	1	5	5	2	5	5	0	20	45
Rating		5			5			5			3	
Value, °	0	5	15	1	5	10	2	10	15	0	20	60
Rating		4			5			5			3	
Value, °	0	5	10	1	5	15	2	10	90	0	20	90
Rating		5			5			1			2	
Value, °	0	0	10	1	10	5	2	15	30	0	0	45
Rating		5			4			4			4	
Value, °	0	0	15	1	15	15	2	15	45	0	0	30
Rating		5			3			3			5	

Tab. 2. Quantitative evaluations of the trainee's actions (approximately)

Approximate character of such evaluations is presented in Table 2. Digital information we have received can be used for formation of the knowledge base for the Tutoring MultiAgent System. In fact, process of the formation of Agents knowledge about pilot training is more complex and difficult, as since, the flight has been characterised by more wide range of the quantitative variables. Therefore, instead of three-dimensional matrix, shown in Table 2, multidimensional presenting of the possible evaluations of the pilot actions must be used in the common problem of the agent training.

Designing of such multidimensional matrices is not a trivial task as for designers of MultiAgent Systems, so for pilots – experts.

3. THE PROBLEM OF FLIGHT DYNAMICS MODELING

The modelling of the plane motion always bases on using of the dynamic equations, which originate from the Newton's laws of mechanics. If to consider the aircraft as a solid body, the spatial movement of the plane can be described by the system of the differential equations of the twelfth order [1, 2, 3]:

$$
\begin{cases}
m(\dot{U} + QW - RV) = X - mg\sin\Theta \\
m(\dot{V} - PW + RU) = Y - mg\cos\Theta\sin\Phi \\
m(\dot{W} - QU + PV) = Z - mg\cos\Theta\cos\Phi \\
A\dot{P} + (C - B)QR - E(\dot{R} + PQ) = L \\
B\dot{Q} + (A - C)PR + E(P^2 - R^2) = M \\
C\dot{R} + (B - A)PQ - E(\dot{P} - QR) = N
\end{cases}
\tag{1}
$$

$$
\begin{pmatrix} P \\ Q \\ R \end{pmatrix} =
\begin{pmatrix}
1 & 0 & -\sin\Theta \\
0 & \cos\Phi & \cos\Theta\sin\Phi \\
0 & -\sin\Phi & \cos\Theta\cos\Phi
\end{pmatrix}
\begin{pmatrix} \dot{\Phi} \\ \dot{\Theta} \\ \dot{\Psi} \end{pmatrix}
\tag{2}
$$

The standard designations accepted in tasks of flight dynamics are hereinafter used. For example, at the equations (1)-(2) the designations are used:

X, Y, Z - components of a main vector of aerodynamic forces, M, N, L - moments of aerodynamic forces, U, V, W - components of speed, P, Q, R - components of rotary speed, I_X, I_Y, I_Z - moments of inertia, D, E, F - centrifugal moments of inertia, Φ, θ, Ψ - Euler's angles (angles of yaw, of pitch and of roll, accordingly).

For determination of the aircraft position and its orientation some various coordinates systems are used.

The main difficulty in work with the dynamics equations is in their non-linear nature. It is caused by nonlinear character of connections in the equations both by nature of aerodynamic forces and moments:

$$
X = \frac{1}{2}\rho S V^2 C_X \quad (X, Y, Z)
$$

$$
L = \frac{1}{2}\rho S b V^2 C_L \quad (L, M, N)
\tag{3}
$$

The dependencies of coefficients of aerodynamic forces C_x, C_y, C_z and moments C_l, C_m, C_n from parameters of motion also have complex non-linear character.

Various transformations of models (well known for experts) are possible. For example, decomposition of spatial aircraft motion into separate kinds of flat motions: longitudinal and lateral motions.

The differential equations of the plane's longitudinal motion:

$$\begin{cases} m(\dot{U} + QW) = X(\alpha, \Theta, \delta_H, \delta_T) - mg \sin \Theta \\ m(\dot{W} - QW) = Z(\alpha, \Theta, \delta_H, \delta_T) - mg \cos \Theta \\ B\dot{Q} = M(\alpha, \dot{\alpha}, Q, \delta_H, \delta_T) \end{cases}$$

The differential equations of the plane's lateral motion:

$$\begin{cases} m(\dot{V} - PW + RU) = Y(\beta, \Theta, \Phi, P, R, \delta_L, \delta_K) \\ \qquad\qquad\qquad - mg \cos \Theta \sin \Phi \\ A\dot{P} = L(\beta, P, R, \delta_L, \delta_K) \\ C\dot{R} = N(\beta, P, R, \delta_L, \delta_K) \end{cases}$$

Other transformations of models are possible also. But in any case the process of creation of dynamic models is the difficult process. **Because it is known, that any model even developed very carefully, is not similar to the original. Its debugging (according to the remarks of the pilot-expert) is required.**

And here again we have difficulty. There are no regular mathematical methods, which allow purposefully modifying the nonlinear dynamics model. It is always a difficult process of tests and mistakes. However, designers of tutoring systems should create model of the aircraft not only of a single type. Because the main aim of such projects is creation of universal system of training, which is invariant to the type of the aircraft. The structure of training system should not be depending on characteristics of a concrete aircraft. And the structure of the plane's model should be universal, too. This structure of a model should suppose reconstruction (reconfiguration). The special methods are necessary for this aim. And such methods we develop and propose. Two main ideas are the basis for these methods.

The first main idea is a representation of dynamic process by a set of linear models dependent on the vector of aircraft state. The appropriate illustration is shown in Fig. 4.

An advantage of such approach is the presence of regular mathematical methods for a model correction under remarks of experts (on the base of analysis of the eigenvalues problem) [6, 9, 10].

The second main idea is the use of identification methods for construction and reconstruction of models set.

The contents of a task of identification is the construction of a mathematical model of a process on the base of experimental observations of input and output vectors of this process. The general structure of such task is shown in Fig.5

An advantage of such approach is an opportunity of construction and correction of mathematical models on the data of flight tests. The main mathematical ideas at this approach are the use of an eigenvalues problem and singular value decomposition of the appropriate matrices [8, 9, 10]. Next the design and further reconstruction of object's mathematical models are made on this basis.

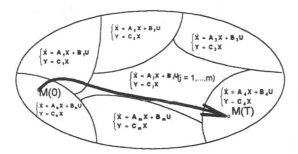

Fig. 4. Representation of dynamic process by set of linear models

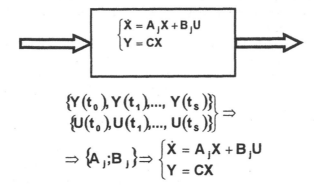

Fig. 5. Using of identification methods for construction of models set

The sequence of this work is:
- Development of the program breadboards in package MathCAD,
- Carrying of these results into package Matlab-Simulink and language C++ for realisation in the appropriate operating system.

The stages of these works and their interrelation are shown in Fig. 6.

The above-stated approach to construction of flight dynamics models allows to receive a set of reconfigurable models. In turn, it allows to make the debugging of a tutoring system and adapt it to tasks of training on different types of planes.

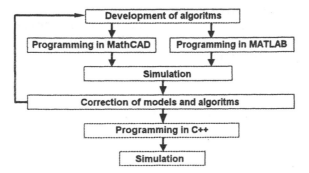

Fig. 6. Stages of algorithm development and software implementation

4.   MULTI-AGENTS SYSTEMS (MAS) IN AERONAUTICAL TRAINING

MAS concept is issued from the classical Artificial Intelligence [4, 5]. Instead of heavyweight monolithic experts systems, MAS proposes to distribute knowledge amongst several entities, called agents. MAS also favours such concepts as co-operation, collaboration, negotiation, and concurrency of agents.

The MAS, which we use, is based on the ASITS architecture [12].

There are several agents in the MAS presented in Fig.2:

Gap Detector is a simple (reactive) agent, which compares the input expected by the system according to the procedure, with the real input coming from the trainee; if there is a difference (which means that an error is committed by the trainee), this agent contacts Gauge agent

Gauge is the agent that measures the value of the difference between the real and expected inputs, and gathers some information about the context of the error (additional parameters which help to determine the origin of the error)

Error analyser is the agent (adaptive) that performs (with the help of Error Classifier) the analysis of the error; the reasoning of this agent is based on pattern matching and diagnostic of the known error type contained in the Library of Errors.

After receiving information about the error committed by Error Analyser, Pedagogical Agent takes the decision about the corrective action (help message, stop simulation, pause simulation) to apply to the trainee; Pedagogical Agent has also several teaching strategies, from which it chooses the most appropriate strategy and applies this strategy to the trainee.

The session of training is composed of three parts: briefing, simulation, debriefing.

Briefing consists in identification of the trainee, with further application of the exercise to perform by the trainee. During this phase only Pedagogical Agent is active, while all other agents are "sleeping". The task of Pedagogical Agents consists in proposing the needed exercise to the trainee.

After understanding the exercise the trainee comes into simulation phase. During this phase functioning of the MA ITS is identical to Fig.2. All interactions of the trainee with the simulator are compared to expectations (given in procedures), and corrective actions are taken by the ITS when needed in order to help the trainee. All interactions are registered by agents.

After the end of the exercise the debriefing phase consists in an overall evaluation presented to the trainee by the ITS. All errors are shown in the evaluation list, a global appreciation is supplied.

5.   MULTI-FACTORIAL EVALUATION OF THE TRAINEE

The major interest of the MA ITS consists in its ability to perform a complex evaluation of the trainee based only on interactions between the trainee and the simulator. In aeronautics there are many situations where the decision taken by the pilot requires a complex simultaneous analysis of multiple interrelated parameters (see Table 2). For example, when it a question of orientation in the air, the pilot operates with three angles - bank, pitch and yaw (supposing that other parameters are constant). It is easy to show that, for example, the roll at 15° allows the pilot to control the plane with more freedom than the pitch at 45° (evaluations presented in Table 2 demonstrate this). The implementation of such analysis tables is done with the help of instructors and varies from one aircraft to another. Such multidimensional tables of dependencies between different parameters allow the designers of MA ITS to give to agents a high level of intelligence; this intelligence being close, by its nature, to the reasoning performed by human instructors.

6. CONCLUSION

In the present work the basic tasks of development of intelligent training systems are shown. The interrelations between components of this problem and ways of organization of their interaction are determined. The way of application of these systems for training of the civil aircraft pilots is shown.

This work is being realised in the framework of ASIMIL project financed by the European Commission within the 5th Framework R&D Program. The project includes 11 partners from 6 countries. The objective of the project is to design and to develop a new kind of training environments in aviation including such components as simulation, intelligent agents, virtual reality. The present work shows one of the directions of the named international project.

7. REFERENCES

[1] BJUSHGENS G.S., STUDNEV R.V., (1983) *Aircraft Dynamics. Spatial Motion*, Moscow, Mashinostroenie (in Russian)

[2] BOGACHEVA N., GUSIEV S., POPOV O., ZHUKOV A., (2000) *Mathematical Model Of Aircraft Simulator* – Proc. Of the 7th International Conference on Advanced Computer Systems ACS'2000, Szczecin, Poland

[3] ETKIN B., (1964) *Dynamics of Flight. Stability and Control*. New York, John Wiley & Sons

[4] FRASSON C., MARTIN L., GOUARDÉRES G., AIMEUR E., (1998) *LANCA: a distance Learning Architecture based on Networked Cognitive Agents* – Proc. of the 4th International Conference on Intelligent Tutoring Systems ITS'98, San Antonio, USA

[5] GOUARDÉRES G., MINKO A., RICHARD L., (2000) *Simulation and Multi-Agent Environment for Aircraft Maintenance Learning* - Proc. of the 7th International Conference on Advanced Computer Systems ACS'2000, Szczecin, Poland

[6] HORN R.A., JOHNSON C.R. (1986) *Matrix Analysis*. Cambridge, Cambridge University Press

[7] KRASOVSKY A.A., (1995) *Bases of the Aircraft Simulators Theory*. Moscow, Mashinostroenie (in Russian)

[8] POPOV O.S., GUSIEV S.A. (1998) *On Analysis of Mathematical Models Dimension and Informative Value of Processes at the Identification and Control problems*. Proc. of the Workshop on European Scientific and Industrial Collaboration WESIC'98 „Advanced Technologies in Manufacturing", Girona, Spain

[9] POPOV O.S., TRETIAKOV A.V. (1998) *On Analysis of Structural Qualities of Dynamic Systems*. Proc. of the 9th International Symposium SMC'98 „System, Modelling, Control", Zakopane, Poland

[10] POPOV O.S., TRETIAKOV A.V. (1999) *Quantitative Measures of Systems Structural Qualities in Control, Management and Identification Problems*. Proc. Of the Workshop on European Scientific and Industrial Collaboration WESIC'99 „Advanced Technologies in Manufacturing", Newport, UK

[11] POPOV O., LALANNE R., GOUARDÈRES G., MINKO A., TRETYAKOV A. (2001) *The Structure of Multi-Agent Learning System and its Applicatioi in Aeronautical Training*. Proc. of the 10th International Symposium SMC'01 „System, Modelling, Control", Zakopane, Poland

[12] C. FRASSON, T.MENGELLE, E.AIMEUR, G.GOUARERES (1996) "An actor-based architecture for intelligent tutroing systems", International Conference on ITS, Montréal-96.

Presence Production in a Distributed Shared Virtual Environment for Exploring Mathematics

CLAUS J. S. KNUDSEN[1], AMBJORN NAEVE[2]
*[1]Division of Media Technology and Graphic Arts, Dept. of Numerical Analysis,
and Computing Science (NADA), Royal Institute of Technology (KTH),
Drottning Kristinas v.47 D, SE-100 44 Stockholm, Sweden
(Tel: +46-8-790 6376; Fax: +46-8-791 8793; E-mail: clausk@gt.kth.se)
[2]Centre for user-oriented IT Design (CID), Dept. of Numerical Analysis,and Computing
Science (NADA), Royal Institute of Technology (KTH), 10044 Stockholm, Sweden
(Tel: +46-8-790 6896; Fax: +46-8-10 24 77; E-mail:amb@nada.kth.se)*

Abstract: It is well known that the current state of mathematics education is problematic in many countries. The Interactive Learning Environments group at CID (Centre for user-oriented IT Design) at the Royal Institute of Technology (KTH) has developed an avatar-based shared virtual environment called *CyberMath*, aimed at improving this situation by allowing interaction with mathematical content in new and exciting ways. CyberMath is suitable for exploring and teaching mathematics in situations where both the teacher and the students are co-present and physically separated. In this virtual reality environment the participants are represented by avatars. The space concept in virtual environments is different from that of any known physical space. Yet people seem to perceive, for example, chat rooms and bulletin board systems as places. Still, avatars have limited possibilities for non-verbal expressions, such as body language, which are important in order to improve the communication quality. To investigate the importance of human-to-human expression and eye-contact between actors in the CyberMath environment, a test lecture in mathematics was carried out between students at Uppsala University and a lecturer at the Royal Institute of Technology (KTH) in Stockholm. The Media Environment group at the KTH Learning Lab was responsible for the production of a sense of presence involving the lecturer and the students, using distance technology such as networked two-way television systems and interactive storytelling. Empirical material was collected from recordings of 5 video sources and through a questionnaire given to the participants in the test. The main goal of the study was to investigate whether students at a distance could adapt to a combination of different shared virtual environments. It was found that presence production mediated as two-way television is a good way to build trust and to enhance non-verbal communication between the actors. The students treated the avatars on the computer screen and the lecturer on the display in front of them as real persons. In the same way, they treated the virtual reality space and the space distributed through two-way television as real spaces.

Key words: Virtual environment, interactive learning, virtual reality, mathematics, non-verbal expression

1.   INTRODUCTION

1.1   The virtual lecture

At the Centre for user-oriented IT Design (CID) [17] an avatar-based 3D learning environment called CyberMath [7], [8], [9] has been developed for the interactive exploration of mathematics. This paper focuses on an assessment study of a learning experience in CyberMath carried out between Uppsala University and the Royal Institute of Technology, both universities partners in the Swedish Learning Lab [20] financed by the Wallenberg foundation [21]. The study connected two tracks of the organized research activity within SweLL called, CVEL (3D communication and visualization environments for learning) [6] and DILS (Distributed Interactive Learning Spaces).

On 5th of October 2000, a preliminary assessment study was performed within the course "Interactive Graphical Systems", organized by Stefan Seipel at DIS [30] in Uppsala. As a preparation for this study, the CyberMath system was installed at the DIS computer lab in Uppsala, and at CID/KTH in Stockholm. It was used by 12 students from the above mentioned course.

These students were divided into 2 groups, and each of these groups were split into 3 subgroups of 2 persons each. The average age of the participants was 23.5 years. They all claimed that they work with computers on a daily basis. Ambjörn Naeve from CID/KTH held a virtual lecture on "generalized cylinders" [2]. He was physically located in Stockholm, while in Uppsala three subgroups at a time were using the 3D computer graphics display to attend the lecture in the Cybermath environment.

Voice communication was provided through Cybermath as well as visual communication amongst the participants using their respective avatars. In addition to the pure avatar-based communication, an "augmented reality interface" was provided by Claus Knudsen, in order to produce a sense of presence and reality [12] between the teachers and the students [13], [14].

The lecture, which took approximately 30 minutes, was performed twice (once for each group). The entire experimental lecture was video-recorded for documentation.

Prior to this virtual lecture, the same topic was taught in the form of a conventional lecture by Ambjørn Naeve given in Uppsala to the rest of the students of the course, (20 students).

1.2   The main goal of the study

The main goal of the study described in this paper was to investigate whether students at a distance could adapt to a combination of two shared virtual environments.

The virtual test lecture was focusing on the following research questions.

- How can a feeling of presence be achieved by technical and narrative means in a distributed learning experience?

- Will an increased feeling of presence and reality increase motivation and improve the learning results?

The second goal was to deliver a proof-of-concept for the effective usage of the CyberMath system in the context of lecturing on the topic of generalized cylinders [2]. This evaluation is described in [6].

2.   METHODS

After the test lecture, the 12 participants were given a questionnaire to fill in and return. This questionnaire served as a tool for the educational evaluation and assessment.

2.1   Methods for telepresence analysis

To measure the experienced degree of presence is not easy. Many factors like the installation characteristics, individual preconditions, sensory environment and content characteristics influence the degree of mental attention [12]. The human factor is essential. According to Sheridan [10], presence is a subjective sensation or mental manifestation that is not easily amenable to objective physiological definitions and measurements. He indicates that "subjective report is the essential basic measurement".

Witmer and Singer have carried out research on the measuring of presence in virtual environments. They have presented a Presence Questionnaire in the MIT Presence Journal [11]. In addition to this, they have developed an immersive tendencies questionnaire in order to measure differences in the tendencies of individuals to experience presence. The term "immersive" often refers to certain types of sensory reproduction systems used in VR and telepresence, where the users actually become part of the experience - which causes exclusion of their immediate reality - as opposed to being a mere observe. For example, a person using a head mounted display or CAVE [27] system would be immersed in the experience, whereas a person viewing a remote location on a simple computer monitor would not.

In this paper a subjective report method has been used for telepresence [29] analysis of the empirical video-recorded material.

3.   THE TEST INSTALLATION COMPONENTS

The virtual components of the test lecture consisted of the CyberMath system and an eye-to-eye telepresence production system bridging the physical distance between the teacher and the students, see Figure 1.

The three spaces involved had both physical and virtual cameras operating from subjective and objective points of view depending on positions and functions. The students operating in CyberMath could choose between an objective point of view, looking over the shoulder of their avatars or a subjective point of view, looking through the eyes of their own avatar. The cameras for the telepresence production were positioned to achieve a subjective point of view for the participants. Two cameras, with an objective point of view, were used for documentation, one in Uppsala and one in Stockholm. In addition to this, the other video sources were also recorded. The recorded material was used for analyses and edited for a documentary.

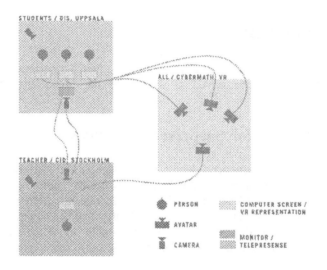

Fig. 1. Connectivity diagram for the virtual lecture and documentation

3.1   The CyberMath environment

The CyberMath system is built on top of DIVE [28], which has the ability to display interactive three-dimensional graphics as well as to distribute live audio between standard desktop PCs. It also supports a number of other hardware configurations, ranging from head-mounted displays to CAVE environments. It is possible to allow different users to access the same virtual environment from workstations with different hardware configurations. In the CyberMath environment avatars can gather and share their experience of mathematical objects. When a person points to an object, a red beam running from his avatar to the object appears on the screens of all the other participators and when the person manipulates the object in some way, the result is directly distributed and therefore visible to all participators. Since the sound is distributed as well, a person can point, act and talk - much as she would do in real reality – as if the mathematical objects were hanging there in front of her. Hence a mathematics teacher is provided with a tool that integrates the best of both the virtual and the real world. Virtual (mathematical) objects can be shared, manipulated and discussed in a realistic way.

The spatial architecture of CyberMath [19] consists of a number of different exhibition halls, each of which contains a collection of mathematical installations expressing a common theme. Each wall is equipped with a projection system, where traditional OH material can be presented. At the same time the avatars are free to move around and study the mathematical objects in practice.

So far, four exhibition halls have been completed. Three of these are filled with content concerning the differential geometry of curves and surfaces [1], [2]. The fourth exhibition hall is devoted to the dynamic exploration of mathematical transformations. Here an arbitrary transformation (from $\mathbf{R}^3$ to $\mathbf{R}^3$) can be specified and the effects of this transformation can be studied interactively by manipulating different objects in the domain and observing what happens in the image.

The animations are controlled through an interface which enables starting and stopping as well as changing between displaying the animations in rendered or wire frame mode.

Fig. 2. CyberMath, the generalized cylinders exhibit, where the distributed lecture was held.

3.2   Augmented reality interface

The two physical spaces in Uppsala and Stockholm were connected by a telepresence system using two-way video on a simple H. 261 protocol with a 128 kbps dialled up ISDN line. The CyberMath system provided communication through the Internet.

In Uppsala, 3 workstations were placed side by side with 2 students at each station. The incoming video was back-projected on a video-wall mounted 2 metres in front of the students. The video projection was adjusted in size and position to optimise the sense of presence of the teacher sitting in front of the students meeting them face-to-face. The students should experience the teacher as sitting in front of his own workstation, at the same level as the students, meeting their eyes when looking up. Because of this, the teacher in Stockholm was produced with a black background in order to achieve a video signal level just beneath the video black level, so that only the body of the teacher would appear on the screen in Uppsala. An advantage caused by isolating the body of the teacher was the reduction of distractions on the incoming video in Uppsala. Another advantage was that the H.261 MPEG compression could work with just the changes in the picture from the movement of the teacher. A remote-controlled camera was placed as low as possible in front of the back-projected screen in Uppsala, representing the eyes of the teacher. The camera was pre-programmed to 3 positions, each one framing a two-shot student group sitting in front of their workstation. It was important to position the camera as close as possible to the position of the projected eyes of the teacher in order to achieve an eye-to-eye contact. Moderate lighting was used in order to achieve better quality of the outgoing video signal from Uppsala.

Fig. 3. Students and the virtual teacher in Uppsala

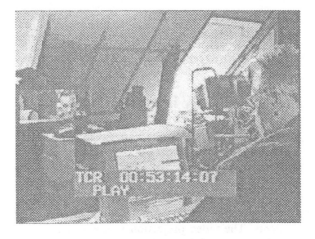

Fig. 4. The studio of the teacher in Stockholm

In Stockholm the teacher was sitting 3 metres in front of a 28` TV monitor with the computer just in front of him. The camera was positioned in the lower part of the video monitor screen in order to achieve eye-to-eye contact.

4. RESULTS

4.1 Vital requirements

Our results indicate that in order to establish verbal communication, face-to-face contact is a vital requirement in virtual environments when individual personal appearance is restricted to avatar representations. To be talked to by a third person who is not included in ones visual frame seems to be particularly annoying when many participants share the same virtual space. We have found that manual self-locomotion in virtual environments for the purpose of initiating a verbal contact appears to be difficult. One reason for this might be that it takes quite some time to navigate towards an intended dialogue partner, and while doing so, the target avatar is quite liable to shift its location.

4.2 Subjective telepresence- observations in Uppsala

The position of the projector for the telepresence production in Uppsala was derived from the calibrated position, which resulted in a reduced sense of eye-to-eye contact between the participants. The Uppsala projection was approximately 20-25 cm off, up to the right, compared with the calibrated position. Optimal eye contact is essential for the feeling of presence between the participants, and the calibrated position must be fixed in future test-installations. The light sources are also important for the quality of the video and should have fixed colour temperature and be adjustable both in direction and level.

4.3 Subjective observations in KTH, Stockholm

The image format of the students appearing on the screen in Stockholm was too small and should be enlarged in future test-installations in order to achieve a better sense of presence and reality. The remote-control of the far-end camera should be made much easier for the teacher to handle during the lecture, so that adjustments can be made in a more intuitive way. The lighting of the teacher in Stockholm should be improved in order to achieve better picture quality.

Moreover, the telepresence system should have provided a connection on the Internet using the H. 323 protocol in order to achieve a more flexible use of the data networks.

4.4   The planned lecture

The teacher introduced himself in a dialogue using the telepresence system in order to build trust between the participants of the learning experience.

While acting in the CyberMath system, telepresence was used for confirmation of understanding by eye-to-eye contact between the teacher and individual students. Often the students replied by just nodding their heads for a yes or shaking them for a no.

The telepresence experience of the first lecture influenced the teacher in strengthening the initial trust-building process of the second lecture. Whereas the students of the first lecture were only identified by their group (1, 2, 3), the students of the second lecture were invited to introduce themselves by their individual names. These names were then recorded by the teacher on a map that related them to their virtual space positions in Uppsala. This enabled the teacher to personalize the lecture by establishing communication with the students on a first name basis, which resulted in an easier dialogue and more active participation (= questions) from the students.

4.5   The Informal Lecture

After the planned lecture something interesting happened which we had not prepared for in our experiment. The students discovered how to take the heads off their avatars, which produced roaring laughter and established a relaxed and informal atmosphere.

The participants then started to mingle and this turned the formal lecture mode into a social interaction mode. When the students were relieved of their learning roles, they became much more talkative and dared to express themselves verbally in a way that they did not do before. During the formal lecture, the students were repeatedly asked if they had any questions, but they did not come up with any questions at all. But during the spontaneous conversation, several questions came up, including one that was not related to the original lecture, but concerned an installation in another part of the exhibition hall. This triggered an improvised lecture on the topic of solar energy.

This event clearly showed the importance of informal social interaction as a means of establishing trust and supporting quality of communication in virtual learning environments.

5.   CONCLUSIONS AND FUTURE WORK

In our study we found that presence production on the two-way television provides an effective way to build trust and to enhance non-verbal communication between the participators in a distributed learning experience. The students treated the avatars on the computer screen and the lecturer on the display in front of them as real persons [16]. In the same way, they treated the virtual reality space and the space distributed through two-way television as real spaces.

From the perspective of the teacher, the pre-positioning of the camera and the name-position map provided the technological support for communicating with the students. Although they were useful, they can both be substantially improved.

The pre-positioning system was locked into three fixed views, which limited the intuitive dialogue process. The discontinuity inherent in jumping between these three positions resulted in the teacher losing part of his spatial orientation with regard to the physical learning space in Uppsala. Moreover, the organization of this space made it impossible to capture the overall presence of all of the students within a single frame, which added to this spatial confusion.

The name-position map made it necessary for the teacher to look down every time he needed to remind himself of a student's name. This resulted in a certain loss of contact, which reduced the transparency of the underlying presence technology and made it harder to maintain the intensity of the non-verbal communication.

In order to improve the presence production in virtual environments, the following improvements should be made:

- Fixed colour temperature on all light sources.
- Better quality routines for the calibration of camera and projectors.
- Development of eye-to-eye applications.
- Development of an intuitive transparent human computer interface for remote control of the far end cameras
- Development of a HUD (head up display) system that supports personalization by superimposing the names on the corresponding images of the students
- Designing a spatial configuration that supports these types of learning experiences that integrate both the physical and the non- physical environment.

6. ACKNOWLEDGEMENTS

Several people have contributed to the experiment reported in this paper. Gustav Taxén has created the CyberMath environment. The mathematical installations (objects and animations) have been created by Ambjörn Naeve in Mathematica® and translated into DIVE by Gustav Taxén. Olle Sundblad has handled the complexity of DIVE, especially the networking aspects. Bosse Westerlund drew the connectivity diagram (Figure 1), and Sinna Lindqvist handled the video camera in Uppsala. The Advanced Media Technology Laboratory [25] hosted the experiment at KTH in Stockholm and DIS [30] did the same in Uppsala. Many thanks to you all!

7.   REFERENCES

7.1   Papers

[1] Naeve, A., *Focal Shape Geometry of Surfaces in Euclidean Space*, CVAP-130, TRITA-NA-P9319, Dissertation, Department of Numerical Analysis and Computing Science, KTH, Stockholm, 1993.

[2] Naeve., A & Eklundh, J.O., *Representing Generalized Cylinders*, Proceedings of the Europe-China Workshop on Geometrical Modeling and Invariants for Computer Vision, pp. 63-70, Xi'an April 27-29, 1995. Published by Xidian University Press, Xi'an, China, 1995.

[3] Naeve, A., *The Garden of Knowledge as a Knowledge Manifold - A Conceptual Framework for Computer Supported Subjective Education*, CID-17, TRITA-NA-D9708, Department of Numerical Analysis and Computing Science, KTH, Stockholm, 1997, http://cid.nada.kth.se/sv/pdf/cid_17.pdf.

[4] Naeve, A., *Conceptual Navigation and Multiple Scale Narration in a Knowledge Manifold*, CID-52, TRITA-NA-D9910, Department of Numerical Analysis and Computing Science, KTH, 1999. http://cid.nada.kth.se/sv/pdf/cid_52.pdf.

[5] Naeve, A., *The Work of Ambjörn Naeve within the Field of Mathematics Educational Reform*, CID-110, TRITA-NA-D0104, KTH, Stockholm, 2001, www.amt.kth.se/projekt/matemagi/mathemathics_educational_reform.doc

[6] Naeve, A. & Seipel, S., *APE track C, Progress Report*, July-Dec. 2000, available from SweLL[20].

[7] Taxén G. & Naeve, A., *CyberMath - A Shared 3D Virtual Environment for Exploring Mathematics*, presented within Course-31, Geometric Algebra - new foundations, new insights, Siggraph2000, New Orleans July 2000.

[8] Taxén G. & Naeve, A., *CyberMath - A Shared 3D Virtual Environment for Exploring Mathematics*, CID/KTH, 2000, the 20:th ICDE world conference on distance education and e-learning, Düsseldorf, April 1-5, 2001, on Compact Disc.

[9] Taxén G. & Naeve, A., *CyberMath - Exploring Open Issues in VR-based Learning*, SIGGRAPH 2001 Educators Program, In SIGGRAPH 2001 Conference Abstracts and Applications, pp. 49-51.

[10] Sheridan, T. B. (1992). *Musings on Telepresence and Virtual presence*. Presence: Teleoperators and Virtual Environments, 1(1), p120-125.

[11] MIT Presence Journal Volume 7, Number 3 · June 1998, *Measuring presence in virtual environments*, A Presence Questionnaire by Bob G. Witmer and Michael J. Singer.

[12] Enlund, N., *The Production of Presence - Distance techniques in Education, Publishing and Art*, ACS'2000 Proceedings, Szczecin, 2000, pp. 44-49.

[13] Handberg, L., Knudsen C., Sponberg H., *New Learning modes in the production of presence – distance techniques for education*, Proceedings of the 20th World Conference on Open Learning and Distance Education, ICDE01, Düsseldorf, 2001, on Compact Disc.

[14] Knudsen, C., *Interaction between musicians and audience in a learning process on the Internet*, ISTEP 2000 Proceedings, Kosice, 2000, pp. 159-164.

[15] Wann, J., & Mon-Williams, M., *What does virtual reality NEED? Human factors issues in the design of three-dimensional computer environments*, International Journal of Human-Computer Studies, 44, 1996, pp. 829–847.

[16] Reeves, B., Nass, C., *The media equation*, Cambridge University Press, New York, 1996.

7.2   Relevant web sites

[17] CID, Center for user oriented IT design URL: http://www.nada.kth.se/cid/

[18] CID/Interactive Learning Environments: http://cid.nada.kth.se/il

[19] CyberMath www.nada.kth.se/~gustavt/cybermath

[20] SweLL (Swedish Learning Lab): www.swedishlearninglab.org

[21] WGLN (Wallenberg Global Learning Network): www.wgln.org

[22] PADLR (Personalized Access to Distributed Learning Repositories) proposal to WGLN, Granted March 2001: www.learninglab.de/pdf/L3S_padlr_17.pdf

[23] ICDE-2001: www.fermuni-hagen.de/ICDE/D-2001

[24] The synchronous virtual space installation, URL: http://www.rl.kth.se/epresence/

[25] The Advanced Media Technology Lab., URL: http://www.amt.kth.se

[26] Royal Institute of Technology, URL: http://www.kth.se

[27] KTH, the PDC CUBE, URL: http://www.pdc.kth/se/projects/vr-cube/

[28] DIVE, Swedish Institute of Computer Science, www.sics.se/dive

[29] Transparent Telepresence Research Group (TTRG), URL: http://telepresence.dmem.strath.ac.uk/index.htm

[30] DIS (Department of Information Science), Uppsala University, www.dis.uu.se

Basic workflow model at distributed intelligent production and its verification

OLEG ZAIKIN, PRZEMYSLAW KORYTKOWSKI
Technical University of Szczecin, Faculty of Computer Science and Information Technology
Zolnierska 49, 71-210, Szczecin, Poland, e-mail: ozaikine@wi.ps.pl

Abstract: The development of an integrated analytical and simulation approach to solve the problem of the resource assignment in the distributed intelligence production is examined in the paper. The task of resource assignment is formulated as definition of parameters of multi-server queuing system. The analytical method of performance evaluation based on the mean value analysis is designed. Verification and validation of proposed method are conducted using simulation.

Key words: distributed intelligent production, queuing systems, simulation

1.   INTRODUCTION

In today's High-Tec and information-age society, sharing of resources and hence waiting in queues is a common phenomenon that occurs in every area of life: manufacturing, communication and education. It is more relevant in logistics, distributed publishing and electronic production, corporate telecommunication networks and distance learning. In spite of different physical content research of these systems requires stochastic approach and optimization methods based on queuing modeling and simulation. It means that general class of distributed intelligent production (DIP) can be introduced and a general mathematical model has to be designed. (Zaikin et al.1999).

The following features are essential for basic workflow model for DIP.

1. We examine distributed production network (DPN) as an oriented graph. Vertices of the graph are processing nodes (PN) and arcs of the graph are communication channels connecting them. Each PN includes a set of uniform manufacturing units operating in parallel. Such structure permits to realize the production process for many products simultaneously.

2. Workflow (WF) arriving at some PN can be deemed as a stream of customer demands for production of one or several kinds of products. At the multi-product production each input stream of demands corresponds to some kind of a product. We consider that all streams of demands arriving at PN are stationary and sequential. The first feature means that parameters of each stream are persistent in time, and the second one means that only one customer demand can appear simultaneously.

3. Each stream of customer demands has its own distribution law of arrivals and servicing time. We examine three basic kinds of distribution:

    −   M- the Marcovian distribution (which implies the Poisson process for arrivals and exponential distribution for servicing time),
    −   Deterministic distribution − fixed time of arrivals and fixed servicing time,
    −   G - General probability distribution for arrival and servicing.

4. Each PN can be represented as multi-server queuing system which includes the following components:

    −   the stream of arriving customer demands;
    −   the number of servers operating in parallel;
    −   an input buffer (IB) of some capacity.

Moreover there is a common unlimited buffer for all processing nodes in DPN. When all servers at some PN are busy, the customer demands are waiting at the input buffer. While input buffer is overflowed, customer demands go to common buffer and in fixed time interval (so called repeating time) returns for servicing.

2.   ANALYTICAL QUEUING MODEL

Using the features (1)-(4), mentioned above, we can formulate the following optimization problem for an isolated PN of DPN:

1. Given:
a) the structure of DPN;
b) a set of parameters of the given PN;
c) a set of streams of customer demands arriving at the PN, and parameters of streams;
2. Determine the number of servers and buffer capacity at the PN.
3. Provide a minimum of a criterion function for a period of optimization.
4. There are two components of a criterion function for an isolated PN:
a) total processing (flow) time for all customer demands, arriving at the given PN;
b) total costs of servers utilization at given PN.

The first component defines the total quality of job servicing, the second one defines the total costs of service and idle time.

In fig.1 the structure of the multi-server queuing system being a kind of G/D/N/S according the Kendall notation is represented. As follows from the problem statement such kind of the queuing system can be the basic one for distributed production network analysis.

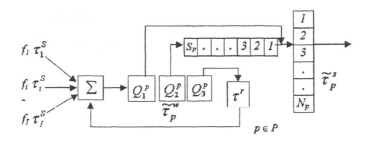

Fig. 1. Structure of the multi-server queuing system

In general case an incoming job goes to any free server for servicing. If all servers are busy, the job goes to a waiting queue. The capacity of the input buffer for the waiting queue is limited. If the input buffer is overflowed, the incoming job goes to the unlimited central buffer and in fixed time interval (so called repeating time) returns for servicing. Obviously, that there can be several numbers of repeating times of a job.

The following notation is accepted in *Figure 1*

$f_i, i = \overline{1, I_p}$ is a set of streams, arriving at PN $p \in P$,

N_P is a number of uniform servers operating in parallel,

S_p is the capacity of the input buffer for the waiting queue,

τ_i^s is a fixed servicing time of a job from FP f_i ,

$\widetilde{\tau}^w$ is an average waiting time for a job,

$\tau_i^r = \tau^r$ is the fixed waiting time for a job in the common buffer. Suppose that $\tau^r \gg \tau_i^s$.

Q_1^P is the probability that arriving job goes for servicing directly (there is an idle server at a moment),

Q_2^P is the probability that arriving job goes to the waiting queue (all servers are busy),

Q_3^P is the probability that arriving job goes to the central buffer (all servers are busy and the input buffer is overflowed at a moment),

In general case the formulated task has not an analytical solution for the represented multi-server queuing system. However, primary evaluation can be obtained on the base of queuing theory (Kleinrock, 1975; Chee Hock, 1997) using following admissions.

1. The total input stream can be modeled as the Markovian one, if the correlation between different streams arriving at the queuing system is not present, i.e. an averaging job will assume a new exponential length. It was shown in (Kleinrock, 1988) that merging several streams at the input of the queuing

system as shown in fig.1 has an effect similar to restoring the independence of inter-arrival times and job servicing time.

Therefore using the Kleinrock independence approximation and assuming a Poisson total arriving stream, we have

$$\Lambda^P = \sum_{i \in I} \lambda_i, \quad \widetilde{\mu}^P = \frac{\sum_{i \in I} \lambda_i}{\sum_{i \in I} \lambda_i \tau_i^s}, \quad \widetilde{\tau}_S^P = \frac{1}{\widetilde{\mu}^P}$$

where Λ^P is a total rate of arrival, $\widetilde{\mu}^P$ and $\widetilde{\tau}_S^P$ is average servicing rate and time, correspondingly.

2. The probability of servicing for incoming job Q_1^P can be defined from the following reasoning: the queuing system (QS) which comprises N parallel servers and an infinite input buffer, can be deemed as the Erlang delay system {M/M/N} according to the Kendall notation.

    The probability of delay Q_D^P for this kind of QS is defined from the following expression

$$Q_D^P = Q_0^P \frac{(a_P)^{N_P}}{N_P!(1 - \rho_P)}, \text{ where }$$

$$Q_0^P = \left[\sum_{k=0}^{N-1} \frac{(a_P)^k}{k!} + \frac{(a_P)^N}{N_P!(1 - \rho_P)} \right]^{-1} \text{ - is}$$

the probability of idle state of QS, $a_P = \dfrac{\Lambda^P}{\widetilde{\mu}^P}$, $\rho_P = \dfrac{\Lambda^P}{N_P \widetilde{\mu}^P}$ are traffic intensity

and utilisation of PN 'p', correspondingly.

It is obvious that the probability Q_1^P is the following $Q_1^P = 1 - Q_D^P$

3. The probability of repeating incoming job Q_3^P because of buffer overflow can be deemed as the probability of blocking for the M/M/N/m queuing system. It can be defined from the formula

$$Q_3^P = Q_{bl} = \frac{(1 - \rho_P)(\rho_P)^s}{1 - (\rho_P)^{s+1}}$$

4. The probability of going to waiting queue for incoming job Q_2^P (all the servers are busy) can be defined from the condition of normalization

$$Q_2^P = 1 - Q_1^P - Q_3^P$$

Therefore the average time $\tilde{\tau}^P$ an incoming job spends at PN 'p' can be defined as follows

$$\tilde{\tau}^P = [\tilde{\tau}_S^P Q_1^P + (\tilde{\tau}_W^P + \tilde{\tau}_S^P)Q_2^P + \tau_R^P Q_3^P)\frac{1}{1-Q_3^P} \tag{1}$$

Here $\tilde{\tau}_W^P$ can be defined from the following formula for the M/M/1/m queuing system

$$\tilde{\tau}_W^P = \frac{\rho^P}{\mu_\Sigma^P - \Lambda_\Sigma^P} - \frac{m^P(\rho^P)^{S+1}}{\mu_\Sigma^P - \Lambda_\Sigma^P(\rho^P)^{S+1}} \tag{2}$$

As it is shown from formulas (1) and (2) the average flow time $\tilde{\tau}^P$ depends on three variables: server utilization ρ^P and buffer capacity S. These dependencies, represented in Figure 3 and 4, allow to define parameters of the PN, providing the given average servicing time of arriving jobs at the PN.

3. VALIDATION OF MODEL THROUGH SIMULATION

More possibilities for the analysis of distributed production network and making of optimal decision are provided by the simulation model (Azadivar and Lee,1988; Guariso, 1996) which does not have any restrictions for dimension, kind of arrival pattern, discipline and time of servicing. The objective of the given simulation experiment is verification of the proposed in p. II analytical model and its using as a low bound for performance optimization of DPN.

To compose the simulation model the program ARENA will be applied, which is the integrated environment for stochastic processes with a simple and efficient programming language. An additional advantage of ARENA is advanced tools for data visualization (Kelton, 1997).

The simulation model was constructed under the following conditions:
1. QN consists of one processing node, as it is shown in fig. 1. It corresponds to the multi-channel queuing system with one kind of a server. All the servers operating in parallel have the same productivity and maintenance cost.
2. A set of arriving streams with different parameters (distribution, rate of arrival and variation) enters the queuing system.
3. Several simulation experiments were conducted for the following kinds of arriving streams:
a) Exponential distribution law of jobs arrivals and exponential distribution law of servicing time;

b) The Poisson distribution law of jobs arrivals and the Poisson distribution of servicing time;
c) Deterministic arrivals of jobs and deterministic servicing time;
d) The Erlang distribution of jobs arrivals and normal distribution of servicing time;
e) Mixed distribution of jobs arrivals and mixed distribution of servicing time.
4. The capacity of the input buffer is limited. However, with buffer overflow the rejected jobs don't leave system, but restart for servicing with interval $\tau_R = 0.5$ *tu.*
5. Discipline of servicing is 'First come-First served'.
6. The observation period is *1000 tu*. It ensures the truth of a simulation trial. Provided simulation experiments shown that simulation which lasts longer than *10 tu* is stationary. The warm-up interval is *10 tu*.

The structure of simulation model in terms of program 'ARENA' is shown in fig.2.

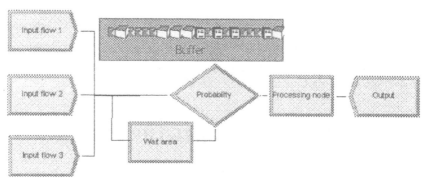

Fig. 2. Structure of single processing node simulation model

The results of conducted simulation experiments using the model in fig.1 are represented in Table 1 and in Fig.3.

The diagrams, shown in fig.3, indicate little spread of flow-times at different simulation experiments. Moreover, the values of flow times, obtained in simulation experiments, are very close to the values obtained on the base of analytical model (p.3.1). It shows a good adequacy of the proposed analytical model, that allows to use it for primary evaluation of decision making and for low bound at accurate methods of optimization.

The numerical results of another simulation experiment with the variable buffer capacity are represented in Table 2 and in fig.4

The second simulation model was constructed under the following conditions:
1. QN consists of one processing node as it is shown in Figure 2. It corresponds to the multi-channel queuing system with one kind of a server. All the servers operating in parallel have the same productivity and maintenance cost. The input buffer has limited capacity equal 20 jobs.
2. The observation period is *300 tu*. It ensures the truth of a simulation trial. Provided simulation experiments shown that simulation which lasts longer than *15tu* is stationary. The warm-up interval is *15 tu*.
3. The simulation experiment has 12 replications

4. Input flows are the Poisson ones with arrival rates $\lambda_1 = 20$, $\lambda_2 = 10$, $\lambda_3 = 40$, $\lambda_4 = 50$

5. Servers are exponential. with rates of servicing $\mu_1 = 0.1$, $\mu_2 = 0.07$, $\mu_3 = 0.04$, $\mu_4 = 0.05$

6. Repeating time $\tau_R = 2$

Utilization	Analytical	Exponential	Poisson	Constant
0.966	0.615	0.452	3.66	0.159
0.919	0.279	0.223	1.322	0.124
0.885	0.204	0.177	0.907	0.114
0.847	0.153	0.144	0.582	0.107
0.812	0.13	0.11	0.464	0.103
0.775	0.119	0.109	0.353	0.102
0.732	0.111	0.113	0.267	0.101
0.694	0.107	0.109	0.239	0.1
0.651	0.104	0.106	0.193	0.1
0.611	0.101	0.102	0.165	0.099
0.57	0.099	0.1	0.145	0.098
0.53	0.099	0.101	0.132	0.099
0.492	0.098	0.1	0.123	0.099

Tab. 1. The values of flow time in provided experiments for servers' utilization varying from 0.5 to 1

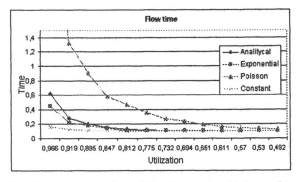

Fig. 3. Graphical representation of flow time in provided experiments for different servers utilization

The presented simulation examples proved an adequacy of the proposed analytical model. The conducted simulation experiments have shown that obtained by simulation results are the same or very close to the ones calculated with the analytical model.

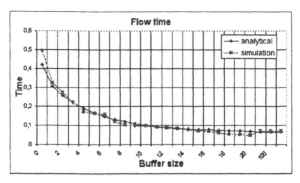

Fig. 4. Flow time obtained form analytical model and simulation experiments

Buffer size	Analytical	simulation
0	0.41804	0.494
1	0.30456	0.324
2	0.25463	0.273
3	0.21773	0.22
4	0.18858	0.173
5	0.16528	0.163
6	0.14655	0.157
7	0.13144	0.122
8	0.11922	0.102
9	0.1093	0.099
10	0.10124	0.097
15	0.07849	0.071
20	0.07017	0.048
50	0.06533	0.072
100	0.06532	0.072
200	0.06532	0.072

Tab. 2. The values of flow time in simulation experiments for buffer capacity.
Varying from 0 to 200

4. CONCLUSION

1. The model of multi-stream and multi-server queuing system with the limited capacity of the waiting queue is examined in the paper. Because of its generality such model can be the basic one for analysis of production, corporate and telecommunication networks with various structures and configurations.

2. In general case there is not analytical solution for definition of performance measures of this kind of QS. Nevertheless with some admissions about arrival and servicing time an analytical solution can be obtained for primary evaluation of a possible decision. The method of mean value analysis used by authors is based on the Kleinrock approximation and the Jackson theorem for open queuing network.

3. Verification and validation of the proposed analytical solution can be conducted at stochastic simulation experiment with using program Arena. Simulation experiments were conducted for different kinds of incoming streams. as well as for different numbers of servers and utilization. Comparisons of simulation and analytical results have shown a high adequacy of the proposed MVA method that allows to use obtained analytical results as primary evaluation for decision making and as a low bound in optimization algorithm.

5. REFERENCES

Buzacott J. and Shanthikumar J. - Modelling and analysis of manufacturing systems, Wiley & Sons. N.Y.. 1993.
Chee Hock Ng. - Queuing Modelling Fundamentals: John Wiley & Sons. New York. 1997.
Hall R.W. - Queuing methods for service and manufacturing. Prentice Hall. Englewood Cliffs. N. Y. 1991.
Kelton W.D. Sadowski R.P. and Sadowski D.A. - Simulation with Arena, McGraw-Hill. N. Y. 1997.
Kleirock L. –Performance evaluation of Distributed Computer- Communication Systems. Queuing theory and its applications. Amsterdam. North Holland. 1988

MEME*: An Adaptive Email-based Knowledge Sharing System for Educational Institutions

JACK BRZEZINSKI, MICHAEL DAIN

DePaul Univesity, School of Computer Science, Telecommunications and Information Systems
243 S. Wabash Ave., Chicago IL, 60604, [MDain, JBrzezinski]@cti.depaul.edu

Abstract: Messaging systems are essential for circulating information within an organization, yet currently the email-based exchange of information does not take advantage of technologies that could change several aspects of the way people share information and knowledge. In this paper we discuss basic functionality and technologies for an adaptive messaging system. Potentially, messaging systems could be utilized in a number of different modes. They help users to distribute information based on certain explicit or implicit criterions. They can help to find the recipient or a group of recipients for a message to be sent. Proactive information delivery based on information semantics and user profiles is another feature. In this paper we concentrate on just one component of the system – clustering of users based on their educational background.
              *Meme: Function: noun. An idea, behavior, style or usage that spreads from person to person within a culture. Source: New Dictionary Search, 2000, Merriam-Webster Incorporated

Key words: Knowledge sharing, machine learning, clustering, user profiling

1.   SYSTEM OVERVIEW

This paper presents an adaptive information sharing system called MEME. The system is not merely capable of sending information via email. It can evaluate information based on user profiles or explicit preferences. MEME adds a lot of value to information and turns it into knowledge about the content being exchanged. MEME also generates knowledge about the system users.

The system can assign relevance value to any piece of information and send it to a person, which might be interested in it.

Moreover, the system creates groups of users of similar profiles. In order to streamline information to the most appropriate user or a group of users the system can compare knowledge about groups of users with the knowledge about the content being distributed. However, if a user chooses to, all the information modelling procedures can be transparent.

The starting point of the analysis is an overview of the system architecture. Major components of the system can be roughly divided into system side and client side: The system side functionality consists of actions executed by the system without user involvement. The client side features are those that allow users to interact with the system and explicitly change and influence models generated by the system.

System side:
- Identification of groups of people based on the employee/user information
- Identification and fine-tuning of groups of people based on their interests and information needs
- Adaptation to changes in user interests and information needs based on explicit and implicit feedback about the content of messages circulating within the system.

Client side:
- Support for users that are willing to develop arbitrary groups, which other users can join if interested.
- Fostering information-sharing culture by allowing users to control their own groups in terms of message content and group membership.
- User specific clustering and classification of messages in order to make the system adapt to changing user preferences and interests.
- Acceptance of user explicit and implicit feedback about the relevance and classification of content.

Here is an example of an application for which MEME can be used. A project manager in a large company is looking for a Java programmer. For the sake of an example, let us assume that in the company there are two advanced Java programmers, but their records do not show that they received formal training in Java. This means that searching corporate white pages will not be helpful. However, let's make another assumption that those two employees worked on a number of Java projects and they exchanged lots of email messages about system development issues in this programming language. How can we take advantage of the information contained in those emails in order to make sure that another employee can direct his or her message to the relevant group of people? The answer is that the messaging system should be able to create a profile not only based on employee demographics, which is static and most likely outdated. It is important that the system takes advantage of the information semantics and based on that build individual profiles or group profiles. If the nature of information being exchanged by individuals or within a group changes, user profiles or group profiles will change as well. This is what we mean by adaptation. Naturally, users should have control over the system adaptation if he or she chooses to. However, if they are not willing to provide any explicit feedback, the messaging system will build user models and models of information being exchanged based on implicit feedback. The major sources of implicit feedback are messages that users write and distribute using the system and the demographic information.

2. CLUSTERING OF USERS BASED ON DEMOGRHAPHIC IFORMATION

In general a clustering algorithm allows for partitioning of a data set into groups (clusters) based on similarities between data points [1,7,8,9]. Those similarities can be given by a number of different metrics. One of the most common similarity metrics is Euclidean distance in a space. Each data point can be positioned in a n-dimensional space. By calculating distances between data points we can measure similarities or relevance between data points. If similarities are known, then we can distinguish groups with similar data points.

In the context of our adaptive messaging system, clustering is important because it allows the system to create groups of users without human intervention imposing semantic constraints on group membership. Clustering technologies may be very important in the initial stage of the system's life cycle when there us little or none feedback from users.

2.1 Data used for clustering

Right now we are testing MEME's components in an academic environment. As a result one of the primary users of the MEME system will be undergraduate and graduate students. Therefore for clustering experiments described in this research we used real data collected at DePaul Univesity. The data contains course history, course descriptions, names of instructors and student identification data. In Table 1 we display an example of the data set with user profiles that we processed in our experiments.

At this point we used a data set consisting of 1200 observations (rows) about 250 unique students. The data set has been converted into a vector space representation[15]. The preprocessing procedure involved removal of the so-called stop words using a database containing 400 words with no semantic bearing. The resulting feature vector, consisting of unique words, was 1337 words long. For clustering purposes all information about an individual student has been combined into one row. Each entry in the database consists of a word count in the collection for a given student. For example, if the first term in the feature vector is "abstract" then the term frequency in the entire database for Student 1 is $tf_{1,1}$ (term frequency). In Figure 1 we display the format of the Term/Student Matrix.

Tab. 1. Course history data sets used for clustering experiments

Last name	First name	Academic Advisor	Quarter/ year	Course Title	Course Title and description
Callahan*	Harry	Coppola	Fall/ 2000	PROGRAMMING IN JAVA (PREREQUISITE: CSC 311 OR CSC 336)	An introduction to programming in Java for students already having programming experience in an object-oriented language. Topics are: Java datatypes, expressions, objects, basic I/O, applications, applets, the Java event model. As time permits, additional advanced topics will be discussed such as JDBC, object serialization, and network programming. PREREQUISTE(S): CSC 310 or CSC 336.
Callahan	Harry	Coppola	Spring/ 2000	DATA ANALYSIS AND STATISTICAL SOFTWARE I (PREREQUISITE: MAT 130 OR BMS 125)	Computing with the statistical package SAS. Introduction to data analysis, elementary statistical inference. Regression and correlation. PREREQUISTE(S): CSC 110 or CSC 150, Mathematics 130 or BMS 125.
McQuinn	Steve	Verhoven	Winter/ 1999	ADVANCED DATABASE SYSTEMS (PREREQUISITE: CSC 449)	Physical data organization and database indexes. Query processing and optimization. Failure and recovery in database systems. Concurrency control and transaction management. Selected topics: intelligent databases, temporal databases, multimedia databases, spatial databases, fuzzy databases, etc. PREREQUISTE(S): CSC 449.
...	....	...	...	...	...

(*) Names of students have been changed. Any resemblance with real people is accidental.

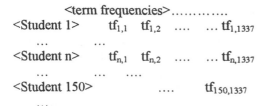

<term frequencies>............

<Student 1> $tf_{1,1}$ $tf_{1,2}$ .... $tf_{1,1337}$

...   ...

<Student n> $tf_{n,1}$ $tf_{n,2}$ .... $tf_{n,1337}$

...   ...

<Student 150>   .... $tf_{150,1337}$

...

Fig. 1. The Term/Student Matrix

The matrix that has been used for the clustering experiments described below had 1337 columns and 250 rows.

2.2 Clustering algorithms tested using course history data

For our initial experiments aimed at ascertaining the most appropriate settings for algorithms and gaining insight into quality of modeling, we used the SAS [16,17] statistical package. In terms of clustering SAS allows for several types of clustering:

– Disjoint clusters place each object in one and only one cluster.
– Hierarchical clusters are organized so that one cluster may be entirely contained within another cluster, but no other kind of overlap between clusters is allowed.
– Overlapping clusters can be constrained to limit the number of objects that belong simultaneously to two clusters, or they can be unconstrained, allowing any degree of overlap in cluster membership.
– Fuzzy clusters are defined by a probability or grade of membership of each object in each cluster. Fuzzy clusters can be disjoint, hierarchical, or overlapping[11].

In order to find the best clustering algorithm that fits our data sets we tested several clustering algorithms that are available in SAS. Here is the listing of algorithms that have been using in our experiments. The notation and formulas are based on the SAS documentation [17].

– Centroid method [Milligan 1980].
– k-Nearest Neighbour Method [19]
– Single linkage [6]
– Ward's minimum variance method [18].

2.3 Quality assessment of clusters

The critical problem in unsupervised learning is selection of the number of clusters. In the context of the MEME system, too few clusters would mean that we there might be different groups of people that belong to the same cluster. Too many clusters would mean that we divided good, homogenous clusters without (statistical) justification. Secondly, how do we ascertain that the clustering algorithm produces good clusters in the first place. Experiments described in the next section help us solve both problems. SAS generates several measures that help to assess the best number of clusters for the data at hand. In this research we were looking at the following statistics:

- Cubic Clustering Criterion (CCC). We are looking for local peaks in CCC values. The higher the value for a given number of clusters the better. Values of the cubic clustering criterion greater than 2 or 3 indicate good clusters; values between 0 and 2 indicate potential clusters, but they should be considered with caution; large negative values can indicate poor data partitioning and possible outliers.
- pseudo F (PSF). Relatively large values indicate a good split of data and therefore good clusters.
- t^2 (PST2). A general rule for interpreting the values of the pseudo t^2 statistic is to move down the column in which rows are determined by the number of clusters. If you find the first value markedly larger than the previous value and move back in the column in the direction of larger number of clusters, by one cluster [17].

2.4 Experimental comparison of different clustering algorithms

In Figures 2 - 5 we present evaluation of clusters generated by four clustering algorithms applied to the full data set. The horizontal axis denotes number of clusters. Starting, on the left hand side, the biggest number of clusters that we impose for all algorithms is 50. The smallest number is 1. Vertical axis denotes score for three statistics used to evaluate the goodness of clusters.

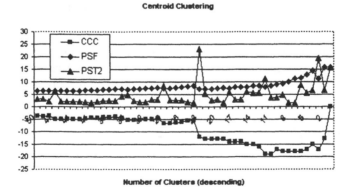

Fig. 2 Centroid clustering algorithm applied to the full data set

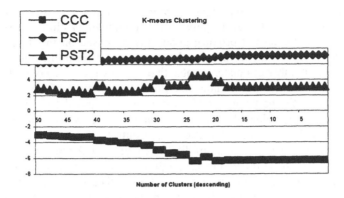

Fig. 3 K-means clustering algorithm applied to the full data set.

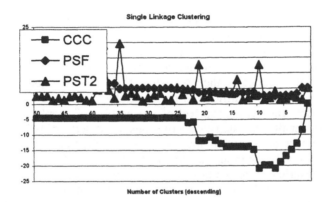

Fig. 4 Single linkage clustering algorithm applied to the full data set

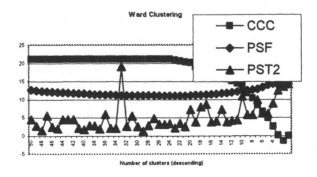

Fig. 5 Ward clustering algorithm applied to the full data set.

For centroid, k-means and single linkage algorithms the values for the cubic clustering criterions (CCC) are negative for any number of clusters, which means that those algorithms did not produce good clusters based on the data set at hand. Ward clustering algorithm, on the other hand worked well on this high dimensional data set. For the number of cluster greater than 2 the values for both CCC and PSF criterions are positive, which indicates good partitioning of data. In order to determine what is the best number of clusters we can use the t^2 (PST2) criterion. There is an outlying value of PST2 criterion for 32 clusters. This suggests that 33 clusters is the best number of clusters according to this criterion. However, for other numbers of clusters, values of PST2 go up and down quite often, so for example the spike around the 9th cluster might suggest that 10 clusters is also a good choice. On the other hand, for clusters 27-21 the PST2 statistics is relatively flat, which suggests that it is not advisable to divide our data into 27 – 21 clusters.

3.   CONCLUSIONS AND FUTURE RESEARCH

In this paper we discussed a few aspects of the MEME adaptive messaging system. There are several aspects of the system functioning that we omitted due to space limitations. For example, in this paper we discussed only the statistical aspect of evaluating the goodness of a clustering algorithm. There is another angle of this very problem which concerns the user perception of those "good" clusters. Our results show that it is very difficult to meaningfully label those clusters of system users so that users can get a good feel of the profiles of people grouped in those clust+ers. Additionally, the statistical criterions we described earlier may suggest that a large number of clusters is the way to go. While this might be statistically justifiable, large number of groups is difficult for users to utilize effectively.

Besides clustering, there is a large number of research problems that have to be addressed. First, it is likely that the system will accumulate large amount of data so dimensionality reduction and feature extraction will be necessary in order to speed up the modelling processes. Problems related to unsupervised learning center on effective cluster naming and cluster summarization procedures. Issues related to supervised learning center on accurate classification of semantically similar documents. It is important to finetune the explicit and implicit feedback procedures to maximize classification accuracy. We are planning on conducting studies that will evaluate user perception of system's performance changes due to explicit and implicit feedback. Also, usability studies will be conducted to assess the user interface.

The machine learning aspect of the system functionality involves also supervised learning for classification of messages into classes of documents being of different relevance to the user profile or user information needs [10,12,13]. Our current experiments have shown that using logistic regression algorithm [2,3,4,5], achieved over 95% of correct classifications of message relevance to user information needs using a five point scale of relevance. We achieved this accuracy based only on explicit user feedback. We are currently conducting experiments in which we try to develop classification models using demographic information on users only as well using both sources: explicit feedback and demographic information.

4. REFERENCES

[1] Baker D., L., McCallum A., K., "Distributional Clustering of Words for Text Classification", in B. Croft., A. Moffat, C. J. van Rijsbergen, R. Wilkinson, J. Zobel (eds.), Proceedings of the 21st Annual International ACM SIGIR Conference on Research and Development in Information Retrieval, ACM Press, 1998, pp.96-103

[2] Brzezinski J., R., Knafl G., J., "Logistic Regression Modeling for Context-Based Classification", in proceedings of the Internet Data Management Conference (IDM'99), Florence, Italy, 1999

[3] Brzezinski J., R., Knafl G., J., "Logistic Regression and Singular Value Decomposition Pre-processing for Classification of Documents" (co-author) in Proceedings of the Advanced Computer Systems Conference (ACS'99), Technical University of Szczecin Press, Szczecin, Poland, 1999

[4] Brzezinski J., R., Knafl G., J., "Data Mining Approach to Document Classification Using Logistic Regression", in Proceedings of the CTI Research Conferece, DePaul University, Chicago, 1999

[5] Brzezinski J., R., "Logistic regression for classification of text documents", Ph.D. dissertation, DePaul Univesity, School of Computer Science, Telecommunications and Information Systems, 2000.

[6] Florek, K., Lukaszewicz, J., Perkal, J., and Zubrzycki, S. (1951a), "Sur la Liaison et la Division des Points d'un Ensemble Fini," *Colloquium Mathematicae*, 2, 282 -285. Florek, K., Lukaszewicz, J., Perkal, J., and Zubrzycki, S. (1951b), "Taksonomia Wroclawska," *Przeglad Antropol.*, 17, 193 -211.

[7] Fraley C., Raftery A., E., "How many clusters? Which clustering method? – Answers via model-based cluster analysis", 1998, Department of Statistics, University of Washington: Technical Report no. 329.

[8] Fritzche M., "Automatic clustering techniques in information retrieval", Diplomarbeit, Institut fuer Informatik der Universitaet Stuttgart, 1973

[9] Kaufman L., Rousseeuw P., J., "Finding groups in data: An introduction to cluster analysis", NY, 1990, John Wiley and Sons, Inc.

[10] Loh W., Y., Shih Y., S., "Split selection methods for classification trees", Statistica Sinica analysis (with discussion), Journal of the American Statistical Association, 83:715-728, 1997

[11] Massart, D.L. and Kaufman, L. (1983), *The Interpretation of Analytical Chemical Data by the Use of Cluster Analysis*, New York: John Wiley & Sons, Inc.

[12] "Neural Computing. NeuralWoeks Professional II/PLUS and NeuralWorks Explorer", Neural Ware, Inc., Technical Publications Group, 1991

[13] Quinlan J., 1993, "C4.5 Programs for Machine Learning", San Mateo, CA: Morgan Kaufmann, 1993

[14] [Ramoni and Sebastiani, 1999] Ramoni M., Sebastiani P., "An Introduction to the Robust Bayesian Classifier", Tech Report Kmi-TR-79, Knowledge Media Institute, The Open Institute, Milton Keynes, UK, 1999

[15] Salton G., Automatic Text Processing. The transformation, Analysis and Retrieval of Information by Computer, Addison-Wesley Publishing Company, 1989

[16] SAS Institute Inc.

[17] SAS Institute Inc. Cary, NC, USA

[18] Ward, J.H. (1963), "Hierarchical Grouping to Optimize an Objective Function," *Journal of the American Statistical Association*, 58, 236 -244.

[19] Wong, M.A. and Lane, T. (1983), "A *k*th Nearest Neighbor Clustering Procedure," *Journal of the Royal Statistical Society*, Series B, 45, 362 -368.

Chapter 3

Distributed Production Networks and Modelling Complex Systems

Models and Methods of Optimal Planning of Sales Volume for Manufacture With Probability Character of Technological Process

EDUARD PESIKOV

Department of Information Management Systems, St. Petersburg Institute of Moscow State University of Print, 13, Dszambula st., St. Petersburg, 191180, Russia, ph: +7 (812) 1649518, e-mail: ed_pesikov@mail.ru

Abstract: The problems of optimization models construction and algorithms of strategic planning of production sales volumes for single-stage stochastic manufacturing systems are considered. The problems of practical application of the offered approach to the goods strategy development within the framework of the computer system of decision making support for want of strategic planning of marketing for manufacturing of electronic engineering are considered.

Key words: stochastic manufacturing systems, strategic marketing, sales volumes, optimization models and methods of decision making, stochastic and nonlinear programming, penalty functions method.

1. INTRODUCTION

In the researched class of manufacturing because of probability and multialternative character of a technological process the manufacturing and marketing costs depend both on a structure of demand and accepted intensities of the discrete technological conditions usage. The probability character of the technological process (PCTP) demonstrates that the choice of technological condition variant does not define univalently the value of parameters of a final product. Because of the large dimensionalities development of the marketing strategies which are taking into account PCTP, satisfying given need and restrictions on resources and possessing the most favourable from a point of view of marketing and manufacturing expenditures by structure basically can not be maid by manual methods, whereas the task of strategic planning of marketing is the "exterior" task concerning only volumes of primary and final products, the operation of an manufacturing system in a planned phase is considered as uniform operation on transformation of primary products in final. For the purposes of strategic marketing planning the probability model of manufacturing with PCTP describing an asymptotical distribution of output on modifications in an association with intensities of the discrete technological conditions use is offered. It is shown, that the vector of intensities of output has asymptotically normal distribution with parameters linearly depending on a vector of intensities of the discrete technological conditions use.

For the situation described by enough rarefied structure of demand and insignificant crossing of quality areas of final products, the variant of a model of stochastic programming (SP) intended for strategic planning of marketing (account of sales volumes of final product) is offered. Because of obtained probability association issue of final products with intensities of the conditions use of process engineering becomes a probable passage from a model of SP with line probability restrictions to an equivalent determined model. For the analysis of a stochastic model of a choice of sales volumes optimization of final products the procedure of the passage with the given risk levels to an equivalent determined model of intensities of start of primary products optimization based on application of the Charnes and Cooper method is offered. It is shown, that for want of high levels of probabilities of restrictions realization the determined equivalent of a stochastic model represents the task of nonlinear nonconvex programming. For the analysis of a determined equivalent the algorithm of global optimization based on combination of undirected casual exhaustive search of index points and peephole optimization by the method of penalty functions is developed.

The shortages of models with fixing of a risk level of restrictions omission are eliminated for want of statement of the task of SP without probability restrictions consisting in direct minimization of expectation of a sum of weighed quadrates of "discrepancies" of restrictions. It is shown, that for want of such statement of the task it is obviously possible to proceed to a determined equivalent concerning to class of convex programming models. The analysis of a determined equivalent will be maid by the method of penalty functions (the method of exterior point).

2. MATHEMATICAL MODEL OF SINGLE-STAGE STOCHASTIC MANUFACTURING SYSTEM

The construction of a probability model of a single-stage stochastic manufacturing system is reduced to the definition of the law of share distribution of intensities issue of products of required quality for want of probable parameters of the technological process and intensities of the discrete technological conditions use.

It is offered to formalize the process of handling of a batch of fixed bars volume on technological operation described by an individual and sequential condition of handling, model of sequential and independent trials. By trial we understand passing of one bar through a knot of transformation, and under an event (outcome) for want of realizations of a trial (issue of a product), which parameters values belong to some fixed area. In an outcome of each trial there can be with some probability one and only one event from the given set of probable incompatible events.

From organization both content of processes of handling and modification of parameters of a product there follows the legitimacy of assumption about independence of the trials entered by us, i.e. independence of outcome of one trial of outcomes probability in other trials. For want of practical accounts which are not requiring a high exactitude, the replacement of aleatory variables - probabilities of emerging of events, their expectations are admissible. Because of lack of such replacement a situation of realization of independent trials in stationary conditions is described by the same probability of emerging of each event in all trials.

The construction of manufacturing system model is based on application of the theory of probabilities outcomes for casual events of mass character.

Let for issue *"l"* of modifications "j" of an item "n" of conditions "i" be used. Let the researched manufacturing have a property of an autonomy of conditions. The operation of one condition does not depend on operations of the other conditions. An input of the module we shall present by $x = \{x_i\}(i = \overline{1,n})$ vector of intensities x_i of conditions "i". In the case of the use of only one condition "i" with intensity x_i an exit of the module we shall present by casual vector $a^{(i)} = \{a_{ij}\}(j = \overline{1,l})$ of intensities a_{ij} issue of items "j". In the case of use of "n" conditions with vector "x" of intensities x_i an output of the module we shall present by a vector $a = \{a_j\}(j = \overline{1,l})$ of intensities a_j issue of items "j".

Let the matrix $P = \|p_{ij}\|$ $(i = \overline{1,n}, j = \overline{1,l})$ of technological parameters p_{ij} be given probabilities issue of items "j" for want of single intensity of condition use "i" .

It is necessary to define an aspect and distribution parameters of the issue vector of final products a={a_j} (j∈J) for want of uses (fixed a vector) of discrete technological conditions x={x_j} (i∈I) and a matrix of technological parameters P={p_{ij}} (i∈I, j∈J).

Construction of a model we perform in two stages. At the first stage the law of distribution is an investigated issue of items for want of the use of only one technological condition. The task is formulated as follows : under given x_i and $p^{(i)} = \{p_{ij}\}(j = \overline{1,l})$ it is required to determine:

a) Law of distribution of a casual vector $a^{(i)}$;
b) Law of distribution of aleatory variable a_{ij};
c) Numerical performances $\{a_{ij}\}(j = \overline{1,l})$ systems from l of correlated aleatory

variables a_{ij}: expectations $ma_{ij}(x_i)$ of magnitudes a_{ij}; covariances $\lambda'_{jj'}(x_i)$ between aleatory variables a_{ij} and $a_{ij'}$. Let's give without the proof the following statements.

Statement 1. Let x_i and $p^{(i)} = \{p_{ij}\}(j = \overline{1,l})$, then the vector $a^{(i)}$ is disrtibuted on multynominal (polynomial) law with vector of expectations $\{ma_{ij}\}(j = \overline{1,l})$ and covariance matrix $\|\lambda'_{jj'}(x_i)\|$ $(j, j' = \overline{1,l})$ linearly depending on magnitude x_i:

$$m \quad a_{ij}(x_i) = x_i p_{ij},$$

$$\lambda'_{ij}(x_i) = x_i p_{ij}(\delta_{ij} - p_{ij}),$$

when $\delta_{jj'} = \begin{cases} 0, & j \neq j' \\ 1, & j = j' \end{cases}$;

The aleatory variable a_{ij} is disrtibuted as the binomial law with distribution parameters $m_{a_{ij}}(x_i)\, \lambda'_{jj'}(x_i)$.

Statement 2. For want of large "x" the vector $a^{(i)}$ has asymptotically normal l-dimension distribution with vector of expectations $\{m_{a_{ij}}(x_i)\}$ and covariance matrix $\|\lambda'_{j\,j'}(x_i)\|$; the magnitude a_{ij} has asymptotically normal distribution with expectation $m_{a_{ij}}(x_i)$ and $\lambda'_{jj}(x_i)$, i.e. for want of $x_i \to \infty$:

$$1) \quad a^{(i)} \in N\left(\left\{m_{a_{ij}}(x_i)\right\}, \quad \left\| \lambda'_{jj'}(x_i) \right\| \right);$$

$$2)\ a_{ij} \in N\ \left(m_{a_{ij}}(x_i),\quad \lambda'_{jj}(x_i)\right),$$

where $N\ \left(\left\{m_{a_{ij}}(x_i)\right\}, \quad \left\| \lambda'_{jj'}(x_i) \right\| \right)$ - label of normal distribution of casual

l-dimension vector $a^{(i)}$ with a denseness of probabilities

$$f\!\left(a^{(i)}\right) = \frac{1}{\sqrt{(2\pi)^l |\Lambda_{jj}|}}\ \exp\left[-\frac{1}{2}\sum_{j,j'}\Lambda_{jj'}\!\left(a_j - m_{a_j}(x)\right)\left(a_{j'} - m_{a_{j'}}(x)\right)\right];$$

$\left\|\Lambda_{jj'}\right\|$ - matrix inverse to covariance matrix $\left\|\lambda'_{jj'}(x_i)\right\|$;

$\left|\Lambda_{jj'}\right|$ - continuant of matrix $\left\|\Lambda_{jj'}\right\|$.

At the second stage the law of distribution is an investigated issue of items for want of use of "n" technological conditions.

Statement 3. Let given vector "x" and matrix "P" be given, then for want of $x_i \to \infty\, (i = \overline{1,\ n})$:

1) Vector a $\in N\left\{\left\{m_{a_j}(x)\right\}, \quad \left\| \lambda_{jj}(x) \right\| \right\}$, (1)

Where $m_{a_j}(x) = \sum_{i \in I} x_i p_{ij}$ - (2)

expectation of magnitude a_j;

$\lambda_{jj}(x) = \sum_{i \in I} x_i \left(p_{ij} \delta_{jj} - p_{ij} p_{ij} \right)$ - (3)

covariance between magnitudes a_j and a_j;

2) Magnitude $a_j \in N\left(m_{a_j}(x); \quad \lambda_{jj}(x) \right)$. (4)

3. OPTIMIZATION MODELS OF SALES VOLUMES PLANNING

3.1 Stochastic model of sales volumes planning concerning to class of stochastic programming models with probability restrictions

In a model of mathematical programming in which the task of planning of sales volumes is reduced, the goal function and functions in the left parts of restrictions because of casual issue of final products are random functions. It is known, that the analysis of planning model, in which the casual parameters are substituted in their expectations can reduce in a solution which does not satisfy conditions the tasks for want of various realizations of casual parameters. More effective is the application of a model of SP with probability restrictions [1, 2, 3].

If in the model of planning controlled variable accepts intensities issue of final products, the task of planning of sales volumes is formulated as follows: it is required so to arrange sales volumes of final products on modifications, that for want of fixed consumer demand for final manufacturing and manufacturing resources produce manufacturing for a planned phase with the least manufacturing expenditures.

The stochastic model of planning with line restrictions on probability looks like:

to find min $\quad m\left[\sum_{j \in J} S_j a_j \right]$ (5)

for want of conditions:

$P\left(\sum_{j \in J} a_j \geq D \right) \geq u_1$ (6)

$$P\left(\sum_{j\in J} g_j a_j \geq D'\right) \geq u_2 \tag{7}$$

$$P\left(\underline{a}_j \leq a_j\right) \geq u_k, k = \overline{3, \ n_J +} \tag{8}$$

$$P\left(\overline{a}_j \geq a_j\right) \geq u_k, k = \overline{n_J + 3, \ 2n_J +} \tag{9}$$

$$P\left(\sum_{j \in J} \beta_{if} a_j \leq M_f\right) \geq u_k,$$

$$k = \overline{2n_J + 3, \ 2n_J + 2 + n_F}, \tag{10}$$

where m - numeral of expectation;

$n_J, \ n_F$ - potency of set J of modifications "j" and set F of components "f";

D, D ' - target indexes on total sales volume of final products in planned phase (in natural and cost expression);

$\underline{a}_j, \ \overline{a}_j$ - lower and upper boundary of demand on final product "j";

g_j - value per unit of final product "j";

M_f - resources selected in the planned phase of component "f";

β_{jf} - expenditure of component "f" per unit of final product "j";

$\left(1 - u_k\right)$ - risk level of restriction "k" omission $(0 < u_k < \ )$;

s_j - manufacturing expenditures per unit of final product "j".

The optimum solution of the task (5) - (10) is meant as a casual vector of controlled variables $a^* = \left\{a^*_j\right\} (j \in J)$ ensuring realization of restriction "k" with unconditional probability P; not smaller then given magnitude u_k, and supplying minimum to expectation of the goal function. The task (5) - (10) is more compactly noted as follows:

$$\text{to find min } m\left[q\left(a_1,...,a_{n_J}\right)\right] \tag{11}$$

for want of conditions:

$$P\left(\sum_{j\in J} c_{kj} a_j \geq t_k\right) \geq u_k, k \in \ , \tag{12}$$

where K - set of numbers "k" of restrictions of the task (5) - (10);

t_k - fixed scalar, such, that for each "k":

$$t_k \geq 0 \text{ If } c_{kj} \geq 0, (j \in J) \tag{13}$$

$$t_k \geq 0 \text{ If } c_{kj} \leq 0, (j \in J). \tag{14}$$

Because of the obtained probability association issue of final products from intensities of the conditions use of a process engineering becomes a probable passage from the model of SP with the line probability restrictions to an equivalent determined model [4, 5]. Beforehand we give without a proof the following statements.

Statement 4. If $a = \{a_j\}$ $\left(j = \overline{1, n_J} \right)$ $-$ n_J - dimensional normal magnitude with a vector of expectations $\{m_{aj}(x)\}$ and covariance matrix $\left\| \lambda_{jj}(x) \right\|$, definiendum with the formulas (2), (3),the linear function

$$L = \sum_{j \in J} c_j a_j, \tag{15}$$

where $c_1,..., c_{n_J}$ - some constants not equal to zero simultaneously and such, that:

$$\text{all } c_j \geq 0, j \in J, \tag{16}$$

or

$$\text{all } c_j \leq 0, j \in J \tag{17}$$

is disrtibuted as the normal law with expectation

$$m_L = \sum_{j \in J} c_j m_{aj}(x) \tag{18}$$

and variance

$$\sigma_L^2 = \sum_{j, j' \in J} c_j c_{j'} \lambda_{jj'}(x) \tag{19}$$

Statement 5. Let $h_k = \sum_{j \in J} c_{kj} a_j$ and $0 < u_k < 1$. Then the conditions $P(h_k \geq t_k) \geq u_k$ and $P(h_k \leq t_k) \geq u_k$ are equivalent to appropriate determined inequalities:

$$\sum_{j \in J} c_{kj} m_{aj}(x) \;+\; \alpha_k \left(\sum_{j, j' \in J} c_{kj} c_{kj'} \lambda_{jj'}(x) \right)^{\frac{1}{2}} \geq t_k$$

and

$$- \sum_{j \in J} c_{kj} m_{aj}(x) \;+\; \alpha_k \left(\sum_{j, j' \in J} c_{kj} c_{kj'} \lambda_{jj'}(x) \right)^{\frac{1}{2}} \geq -t_k$$

where $\alpha_k - (1 - u_k)$ - quantile of normal normalized aleatory variable.

According to the Charnes and Cooper method [6] and because of statements 4, 5 stochastic models (11) - (14) of optimization of the choice of intensities issue of final products can be with the given risk levels shown on an equivalent determined model of optimization of intensities of primary products start:

$$\text{to find min } z(x) \;=\; \sum_{j \in J} s_j \, m_{a_j}(x), \tag{20}$$

for want of conditions:

$$q_k(x) = \sum_{j \in J} c_{kj} m_{aj}(x) + \alpha_k \left(\sum_{j, j' \in J} c_{kj} c_{kj'} \lambda_{jj'}(x) \right)^{\frac{1}{2}} \geq t_k \,,$$

$$k \in K, \tag{21}$$

$$x \in E_+^{n_I} = \left\{ x / \; x > 0, \; x_i \geq 0, \; i \in I \right\}. \tag{22}$$

The outcomes of research on convexity of a determined equivalent are formulated as the following statement.

Statement 6. The task (20) - (22) is the task of convex programming for want of $u_k \leq 0,5 \quad (k \in K)$.

After the definition of n_I-dimensional vector x^* - the solutions of the task (20) - (22) are easy to calculate distribution parameters of n_J-dimensional vector a^*. It is supposed as a plan issue of a final product "j" to use magnitude a^j* - α-quantile of normal distribution of an aleatory variable a_j^* i.e.

$$\frac{1}{\sqrt{2\pi \lambda_{jj}(x^*)}} \int_{-\infty}^{\hat{a}_j^*} \exp\left[- \frac{(a_j - m_{aj}(x^*))^2}{2\lambda_{jj}(x^*)} \right] da_j \;=\; \alpha$$

where α - the given order of quantile.

Basic shortages of the model of SP with the line probability restrictions (11) - (14) are connected with the following difficulties:

a) Analysis of nonconvex determined equivalent (20) - (22) of task (11) - (14), constructed in accordance with the Charnes and Cooper method for important in manufacturing practice case $u_k > 0,5$ $(k \in K)$;

b) Solution of a problem of the choice of vector $u = \{u_k\}$ of probabilities levels of restrictions realization.

It is worth noting, that any procedure of an information of the SP model to an equivalent determined model is effective only in that case, when the determined equivalent represents the task of linear or convex programming. In this sense the offered procedure of an information of a stochastic model (11) - (14) to a determined equivalent is ineffective.

The shortages of models with fixing of a risk level of omission of restrictions are eliminated for want of the statement of the SP task without probability restrictions.

3.2 Mathematical model without probability restrictions

The statement of the task consisting in direct minimization of expectation of a sum of weighed guadrates of "discrepancies" of restrictions is offered. It is possible to show, that for want of such statement of the task the procedure of an information to a determined equivalent is effective.

Statement 7. Let casual vector $a = \{aj\} \square$ such, that: $a \in N(\{m_{aj}(x)\}, \| \lambda_{jj'}(x)\|)$, the magnitudes $m_{aj}(x)$, $\lambda_{jj'}(x)$ be defined by the formulas (2), (3); then the task

$$\text{to find } \min_{a \in A} \{ m \ [\sum_{k \in K} w_k \varphi_k^2 (a)] \},$$

where m - numeral of expectation;

$w = \{w_k\}$ $(k \in K)$ is the given vector of penal factors w_k $(w_k \ 0)$;

K - set of numbers "k" of restrictions of the task (11) - (14);

A - set of vectors "a";

$\varphi_k (a) = \sum_{j \in J} c_{kj} a_j - t_k$ - "discrepancy" of restriction "k" of the task (11) - (14);

c_{kj}, t_k – the given scalar magnitudes possessing properties (11), (14);

is reduced to the equivalent task of convex programming:

to find

$$\min_{k \in K} \sum w_k \{ (\sum_{j \in J} c_{kj} m_{aj}(x) - t_k)^2 + \sum_{j,j' \in J} c_{kj} c_{kj'} \lambda_{jj'}(x) \tag{23}$$

$$x \in E_+^{n_i} = \left\{ x \ / \ x > 0, \ x_i \ \geq 0, \ i \in I \right\}$$

The analysis of the determined equivalent will be made by the method of penalty functions (method of exterior point) [7, 8].

4. ALGORITHM OF THE ANALYSIS OF DETERMINED EQUIVALENT OF THE STOCHASTIC TASK OF MANUFACTURING SALES VOLUMES PLANNING WITH LINE RESTRICTIONS ON PROBABILITY

The algorithm of the analysis of the determined equivalent of stochastic model with line restrictions on probability (5) - (10) is considered. The offered algorithm of global optimization for the task of nonconvex programming is based on combination of undirected casual exhaustive search of index points and local minimization by the method of penalty functions.

The determined equivalent of the task (5) - (10) in the expanded form:

$$\text{to find } \min_{x} z(x) = \sum_{j \in J} s_J m_{aj}(x) \tag{24}$$

for want of conditions:

$$\varphi_k(x) = m_c(x) - \alpha_k \sigma_c(x) - D^{(k)} \geq 0, \ k = \overline{1, e} \ ; \ e = 2 \tag{26}$$

$$\varphi_k(x) = \bar{a}_{k-n_j-e} - m_{a_{k-n_j-e}}(x) - \alpha_k \sigma_{a_{k-n_j-e}}(x) \geq 0, \ k = \overline{n_j + e + 1, 2n_j + e}, \tag{27}$$

$$\varphi_k(x) = M_{k-2n_j-e} - m_{w_{k-2n_j-e}}(x) - \alpha_k \sigma_{w_{k-2n_j-e}}(x) \geq 0$$

$$k = \overline{2n_j + e + 1, 2n_j + e + n_F}, \tag{28}$$

$$\varphi_k(x_{k-2n_j-e-n_F}) = \bar{x}_{k-2n_j-e-n_F} - x_{k-2n_j-e-n_F} \geq 0$$

$$k = \overline{2n_j + e + 1 + n_F, 2n_j + e + n_F + n_I}, \tag{29}$$

where $\bar{x}_i$ is much possible admissible of value x_i;

$$m_{aj}(x) = \sum_{i \in I} x_i p_{ij} \ ;$$

$$m_c(x) = \sum_{j \in J} g_j^{(k)} m_{aj}(x), \text{ where } g_j^{(k)} = \begin{cases} 1, \text{if } k=1 \\ g_j, \text{if } k=2 \end{cases} ;$$

$$\sigma_{aj}(x) = \sqrt{\sum_{i \in I} x_i p_{ij}(1 - p_{ij})} \ ;$$

$$\sigma_c(x) = \sqrt{\sum_{j,j' \in J} \sum_{i \in I} g_j^{(k)} g_{j'}^{(k)} p_{ij}(\delta_{jj'} - p_{ij'})} \ ; \ \delta_{jj'} = \begin{cases} 0, & j \neq j' \\ 1, & j = j' \end{cases}$$

$$m_{wf}(x) = \sum_{j \in J} \beta_{jf} m_{aj}(x) \; ;$$

$$\sigma_{wf}(x) = \sqrt{\sum_{j,j' \in J} \sum_{i \in I} \beta_{jf} \beta_{j'f} x_i p_{ij} (\delta_{jj'} - p_{ij'})} \; .$$

For the nonconvex task (24) - (29) (even one $\alpha_k < 0$) with continuously differentiable functions $z(x)$ and $\varphi_k(x)$, only convergence to one of local minimums takes place [7].

For searching the global minimum of the modified goal function

$$F_\mu(x) = z(x) + \sum_{k=1}^{1} P_k(\mu, \varphi_k(x)),$$
$$1 = 2n_J + e + n_F + n_I),$$

where μ - penalty factor ($\mu > 0$), and penalty function $P_k(\mu, \varphi_k(x))$ such

that $\lim_{\mu \to \infty} P_k(\mu, \varphi_k(x)) = \begin{cases} 0, & \text{if } \varphi_k(x) \ge 0 \\ +\infty, & \text{if } \varphi_k(x) < 0 \end{cases}$

It is offered to apply the combined method of searching constructed on combination of casual exhaustive search of points of local minimization with the quickest descent [9, 10].

Method of searching. Let $x^{(0)} \in [0, x_{max}]$ - arbitrary index point and $x^{(1)}$ be appropriate point of local minimum with value of function $F_\mu(x^{(1)})$. If all $\alpha_k \ge 0$, a global minimum of convex downwards functions $F_\mu(x)$ is reached at point $x^{(1)}$. If even one $\alpha_k < 0$, we take a casual initial point $x^{(2)}$ ($0 \le x^{(2)} \le x_{max}$), remote enough from a point $x^{(0)}$.

I.e. $\left\| x^{(0)} - x^{(2)} \right\| \ge \rho$, where ρ - minimum admissible distance between index points. From the point $x^{(2)}$ the quickest descent will be given and the new local minimum $F_\mu(x^{(3)})$ at point $x^{(3)}$ is discovered. In correspondence with the recommendations formulated in work [10], the search comes to an end if τ ($2 \le \tau \le 16$) of time fails to receive a value of function $F_\mu(x)$, smaller

$$\min_{\nu}\{F\mu\,(x^{(\nu)})\}\,,\text{ where } \nu = 1,3,5,\dots$$

The necessary amount of casual index points is limited below by requirement of reaching of the given exactitude of a solution, and above by the fixed resource of machine time.

Algorithm of local minimization

In a method of penalty functions (the method of an exterior point) solution of the task of nonlinear programming sounds:

to find $\min_{x}\{z(x)/\varphi(x)\geq 0; x \geq 0\}$,   (30)

where x={x_j} - n-dimensional vector of variables x_j;
$\varphi(x)$={$\varphi_i(x)$} - m-dimensional vector function with components $\varphi_i(x)$;
f(x), $\varphi_i(x)$ - convex functions;

It is reduced to solution of the task of sequential unconstrained minimization of the modified goal function

$$F_\mu(x) = z(x) + \sum_{k=1}^{1} p_k(\mu, \varphi_k(x)).$$

For want of realization of some natural conditions [7, 8] the solution x* of the initial task (30) can be obtained from a limiting relation $x^* = \lim_{\mu \to +\infty} x\,(\mu)$, where x($\mu$) - point of unconditional minimum of function $F_\mu(x)$ for want of fixed μ. For practical realization of algorithm of function $F_\mu(x)$ minimization we shall apply the construction of function $P_k(\mu,\ \varphi_k(x))$ as follows:

$$P_k(\mu,\ \varphi_k\,x(\mu)] = \mu(\min\{\varphi_k\,[x(\mu)],0\})^4.$$

For models researched in work, the analytical expressions for gradient of the modified goal function and its first partial derivative on a pitch of gradient method are obtained. It is worth noting, that the computing difficulties of application of penalty functions method consist in the large complexity of deriving and programming realization of obtained analytical expressions.

5.   COMPUTING EXPERIMENTS

By the example of quantity manufacturing of items of an electronic engineering (ceramic condensers and metal-taped resistors) posed, the task of SP with probability restrictions for a case of sales volumes planning of manufacturing with not intersected areas of quality is solved. The effectiveness of the offered method of searching for a local solution of the task of nonconvex programming with nonlinear restrictions is confirmed experimentally.

The association of an optimum solution of the task of SP with probability restrictions from variations of admissible levels of probabilities of restrictions realization is investigated experimentally. It's shown that the magnitude of intensity consists of two components. The first is determined by average values of casual parameters of planning model. The second component is for maintaining the lower "insurance" level ensuring the defined sufficient warranty for demand. It is established that with magnification of levels of probabilities the sum of increments to solutions (intensities of technological conditions use) obtained on a model "for average" will increase.

For realization of the offered stochastic models on PC and realization of the analysis of solutions sensitivity to variations of input data the use of the special software and program LINDO is offered.

6. REFERENCES

[1] Udin D.D. Mathematical methods of control in conditions of incomplete information. Moscow, Soviet Radio, 1974.

[2] Charnes A., Cooper W.W. Deterministic equivalents for optimizing and satisfying under chance constraints. Operation Research, 1963, Vol.11, No 1, pp.18-39.

[3] Kataoka S.A., Stochastic programming model, Econometrica, Vol.31, No 1-2, 1963.

[4] Pesikov E.B. About stochastic models of optimization of expenditures also issue in manufacturing with probability character of the technological process// Collection "Condition and perspectives of development of automated control systems". CNIITEI of instrument making, Moscow, 1977.

[5] Sovetov B.J., Zaikin O.A., Pesikov E.B. Complex of models for optimal planning of manufacturing with probability character of the technological process// Proceedings of IV All-Union symposium "Problems of systems engineering" (Jan. 24–27, 1978), Moscow, 1980, pp.259 - 262.

[6] Charnes A., Cooper W.W. Deterministic equivalents for optimizing and satisfying under chance constraints. Operation Research, 1963, Vol.11, No 1, pp.18-39.

[7] Zangwill U.N. Nonlinear programming, Uniform approach. Moscow, Soviet Radio, 1973.

[8] Fiacco A., McCormick G. Nonlinear programming. Methods of sequential unconstrained minimization. Moscow, World, 1972.

[9] Rastrigin L.A. Statistical methods of searching. Moscow, Science, 1968.

[10] Gurin L.S., Dimarsky J.S., Merkulov A.D. The tasks and methods of optimal resource allocation. Moscow, Soviet Radio, 1968.

Approximation-Decomposition Method for Modelling Thermal Systems

MICHAIL FEDOROV

Institute of Computer Science & Information Systems, Technical University of Szczecin,
49, Zolnierska st., 71-210 Szczecin, Poland, ph: +4891 4495568,
e-mail: mykhaylo.fedorov@wi.ps.pl

Abstract: System aspects of modelling thermal systems (TS) with compressible working fluids are considered (air-conditioning and ventilation systems). A mathematical model and algorithm of the approximation-decomposition method are proposed for flow rate distribution and thermal analysis of TS having recuperative heat exchangers of arbitrary flow arrangement and multistage turbomachines (TM).

Key words: network, heat exchanger, turbomachine, approximation, decomposition, analysis, algorithm

1. INTRODUCTION

In the given paper by TS is meant a piping network with recuperative heat exchangers of arbitrary flow arrangement and types of surfaces as well as multistage turbomachines whose passes and stages may belong to any TS edge. It is evident that such types of elements are basic for all classes of TSs.

In [1] the existing approaches are analyzed for modelling TS thermal modes; the Gauss convolution method is suggested and its mathematical interpretation is demonstrated for thermal analysis of heat exchanger systems. In [2] the method extends to model networks of heat exchangers and comparative theoretical evaluations of RAM required are shown when programming method using matrix or data set representation. The heat exchanger component of the TS mathematical model has the following form [1,2]

$$T_{q,x+1}^{(i+1)} = a_{q,x+1,1}^{(i)} \left(\widetilde{C}_{q,x}^{(i)}, \widetilde{C}_{s,y}^{(i)}, \widetilde{T}_{q,x}^{(i)} \right) \cdot T_{q,x}^{(i+1)} + a_{q,x+1,2}^{(i)} \left(\widetilde{C}_{q,x}^{(i)}, \widetilde{C}_{s,y}^{(i)}, \widetilde{T}_{s,y}^{(i)} \right) \cdot T_{s,y}^{(i+1)}, x =$$

$$= \overline{1, n_k}, q = \overline{1, |E|} \tag{1}$$

$$T_{k,1}^{(i+1)} = \frac{\sum\limits_{k \in E_i^-} \widetilde{C}_{k,n_k+1}^{(i)} T_{k,n_k+1}^{(i+1)} G_k}{\sum\limits_{k \in E_i^-} \widetilde{C}_{k,1}^{(i)} G_k}, \tag{2}$$

$$l = \overline{1, v_{in}}, \quad \forall k \in E_l^-$$

where i is an iteration number, $q,\, s$ is an edge number, $x,\, y$ are numbers of elements from the binary relation set $B = (x_q, y_s)$, defining thermal connections between elements being heat exchanger surfaces constituting a pass of heat exchanger and formed during its decomposition for the purpose of creating a calculation diagram of TS where each heat exchanger surface becomes the separate and hydraulically independent a TS element for both flow rate and thermal analysis, E_l^+, E_l^- are sets of edges which input to and exit from node l, v_{in} is a number of inner nodes of a TS graph, n_k is an element number in edge k, E is a set of edge numbers of the TS graph, T - temperature.

Decomposition of a TM model results in that that each TM stage becomes the independent TS element analogous to a heat exchanger. Further, the TM mathematical model is presented to be the TS element.

TM MATHEMATICAL MODEL

At present there does not exist adequate analytical mathematical models to simulate a TM stage, semi-empirical ones as a rule are used. More often the following model based on the adiabatic process is used

$$\overline{N} = c_p \overline{G} \cdot \Delta T \tag{3}$$

$$T_{out,t} = T_{in,t} \left[1 - \eta_t \left(1 - \pi_t^{-\frac{k-1}{k}} \right) \right] \tag{4}$$

$$T_{out,c} = T_{in,c} \left[1 + \frac{1}{\eta_c} \left(\pi_c^{\frac{k-1}{k}} - 1 \right) \right] \tag{5}$$

where $\overline{N}$ is a TM stage corrected power, c_p is a specific heat at constant pressure, $\overline{G}$ is a flow rate, ΔT is a stage temperature difference, $T_{in,t}$, $T_{out,t}$ ($T_{in,c}, T_{out,c}$) are input and output turbine (compressor) stage temperatures, respectively, η_t (η_c) is a turbine (compressor) stage efficiency, π_t (π_c) is a turbine (compressor) stage pressure ratios, k is a specific heat ratio.

The stage pressure ratios and efficiencies in (4)-(5) are complex empirical functions of the form

$$\pi = \pi(\overline{G}, \overline{n}), \tag{6}$$

$$\eta = \eta(\overline{G}, \overline{n}) \tag{7}$$

Two problems exist in modeling a TM represented by models of the form (3)-(7), they are

- its essential non-linearity. It means that the TM characteristics (6)-(7) are nonmonotonic, as a result the TS analysis solution may not be unique;
- the lack of the formulated network-like mathematical model of a TM.

Both problems are discussed in the paper. The TM mathematical model is formulated at first. To do so we linearize equation (6) - (7)

$$\Delta \pi = \frac{\partial \pi}{\partial \overline{G}} \Delta \overline{G} + \frac{\partial \pi}{\partial \overline{n}} \Delta \overline{n} \tag{8}$$

$$\Delta \eta = \frac{\partial \eta}{\partial \overline{G}} \Delta \overline{G} + \frac{\partial \eta}{\partial \overline{n}} \Delta \overline{n} \tag{9}$$

In a general form the stage temperature difference formula may be written down as follows

$$\Delta T = T_{in} K(\pi, \eta) \tag{10}$$

where $\overline{n}$ is a corrected rotation speed.

In turn, variable K for a turbine or compressor stage has the following form, respectively

$$K_t = \eta_t \left(1 - \pi_t^{-\frac{k-1}{k}}\right), \; K_c = \frac{1}{\eta_c}\left(\pi_c^{\frac{k-1}{k}} - 1\right).$$

Linearizing K gives

$$\Delta K = \frac{\partial K}{\partial \eta} \Delta \eta + \frac{\partial K}{\partial \pi} \Delta \pi \tag{11}$$

Further, we define derivatives of (11) for each stage type

$$\frac{\partial K_c}{\partial \eta_c} = -\frac{1}{\eta_c^2}\left(\pi_c^{\frac{k-1}{k}} - 1\right), \; \frac{\partial K_c}{\partial \pi_c} = \frac{k-1}{k}\frac{1}{\eta_c}\pi_c^{-\frac{1}{k}} \tag{12}$$

$$\frac{\partial K_t}{\partial \eta_t} = \pi_t^{-\frac{k-1}{k}} - 1, \; \frac{\partial K_t}{\partial \pi_t} = -\frac{k-1}{k}\eta_t \pi_t^{-\frac{2k-1}{k}} \tag{13}$$

It is evident that each stage introduces in the TM model a pair of unknowns $\delta\Delta T$ and ΔG followed from linearization of (3)

$$\Delta \overline{N} = \frac{\partial N}{\partial \overline{G}} \Delta \overline{G} + \frac{\partial N}{\partial \Delta T} \delta\Delta T \tag{15}$$

The stage temperature difference is fully defined by the value of input temperature. Hence, the temperature difference correction in (15) may be deduced from (10) as follows

$$\delta\Delta T = T_{in}\Delta K \tag{16}$$

Then, we substitute (11) into (16)

$$\delta\Delta T = T_{in}\left(\frac{\partial K}{\partial \eta}\Delta\eta + \frac{\partial K}{\partial \pi}\Delta\pi\right). \tag{17}$$

From (17) and (8)-(9) we get

$$\delta\Delta T = T_{in}\cdot\left[\frac{\partial K}{\partial \eta}\left(\frac{\partial \eta}{\partial \overline{G}}\Delta\overline{G} + \frac{\partial \eta}{\partial \overline{n}}\Delta\overline{n}\right) + \frac{\partial K}{\partial \pi}\left(\frac{\partial \pi}{\partial \overline{G}}\Delta\overline{G} + \frac{\partial \pi}{\partial \overline{n}}\Delta\overline{n}\right)\right] \tag{18}$$

Finally, the formula for calculation of corrections to the stage corrected power has the following form

$$\Delta\overline{N} = \left[\frac{\partial \overline{N}}{\partial \overline{G}} + T_{in}\left(\frac{\partial K}{\partial \eta}\frac{\partial \eta}{\partial \overline{G}} + \frac{\partial K}{\partial \pi}\frac{\partial \pi}{\partial \overline{G}}\right)\frac{\partial \overline{N}}{\partial \Delta T}\right]\Delta\overline{G} + T_{in}\left(\frac{\partial K}{\partial \eta}\frac{\partial \eta}{\partial \overline{n}} + \frac{\partial K}{\partial \pi}\frac{\partial \pi}{\partial \overline{n}}\right)\frac{\partial \overline{N}}{\partial \Delta T}\Delta\overline{n} \tag{19}$$

Further, we suppose that at the current step of TM calculation the TM characteristics may be approximated by parabolas for each of the independent variables, then

$$\begin{aligned}
\pi_c^G(\overline{G}) &= A_{c,\pi}^G\overline{G}^2 + B_{c,\pi}^G\overline{G} + C_{c,\pi}^G, & \overline{n} = const \\
\eta_c^G(\overline{G}) &= A_{c,\eta}^G\overline{G}^2 + B_{c,\eta}^G\overline{G} + C_{c,\eta}^G, & \overline{n} = const \\
\pi_c^n(\overline{n}) &= A_{c,\pi}^n\overline{n}^2 + B_{c,\pi}^n\overline{n} + C_{c,\pi}^n, & \overline{G} = const \\
\eta_c^n(\overline{n}) &= A_{c,\eta}^n\overline{n}^2 + B_{c,\eta}^n\overline{n} + C_{c,\eta}^n, & \overline{G} = const \\
\pi_t^G(\overline{G}) &= A_{t,\pi}^G\overline{G}^2 + B_{t,\pi}^G\overline{G} + C_{t,\pi}^G, & \overline{n} = const \\
\eta_t^G(\overline{G}) &= A_{t,\eta}^G\overline{G}^2 + B_{t,\eta}^G\overline{G} + C_{t,\eta}^G, & \overline{n} = const \\
\pi_t^n(\overline{n}) &= A_{t,\pi}^n\overline{n}^2 + B_{t,\pi}^n\overline{n} + C_{t,\pi}^n, & \overline{G} = const \\
\eta_t^n(\overline{n}) &= A_{t,\eta}^n\overline{n}^2 + B_{t,\eta}^n\overline{n} + C_{t,\eta}^n, & \overline{G} = const
\end{aligned} \tag{20}$$

From the above formulas, expressions for their derivatives are easy to be obtained

$$\frac{\partial \pi_c^G}{\partial \overline{G}} = 2A_{c,\pi}^G \overline{G} + B_{c,\pi}^G, \qquad \overline{n} = const$$

$$\frac{\partial \eta_c^G}{\partial \overline{G}} = 2A_{c,\eta}^G \overline{G} + B_{c,\eta}^G, \qquad \overline{n} = const$$

$$\frac{\partial \pi_c^n}{\partial \overline{n}} = 2A_{c,\pi}^n \overline{n} + B_{c,\pi}^n, \qquad \overline{G} = const$$

$$\frac{\partial \eta_c^n}{\partial \overline{n}} = 2A_{c,\eta}^n \overline{n} + B_{c,\eta}^n, \qquad \overline{G} = const$$

$$\frac{\partial \pi_t^G}{\partial \overline{G}} = 2A_{t,\pi}^G \overline{G} + B_{t,\pi}^G, \qquad \overline{n} = const \qquad (21)$$

$$\frac{\partial \eta_t^G}{\partial \overline{G}} = 2A_{t,\eta}^G \overline{G} + B_{t,\eta}^G, \qquad \overline{n} = const$$

$$\frac{\partial \pi_t^n}{\partial \overline{n}} = 2A_{t,\pi}^n \overline{n} + B_{t,\pi}^n, \qquad \overline{G} = const$$

$$\frac{\partial \eta_t^n}{\partial \overline{n}} = 2A_{t,\eta}^n \overline{n} + B_{t,\eta}^n, \qquad \overline{G} = const$$

It can be seen from the above that the stage equation has two unknowns. If a TM consists of stn stages, then the number of unknowns equals to $2stn + 1$, hence, to have the problem defined it is necessary to have $2stn$ equations, in addition. It is such an equation number the pairs of stage characteristics (8), (9) give. It is clear, that for the given number of TM tm and stages per each machine stn_i, the number of uknowns equals to $2\sum_{i=1}^{tm} stn_i + tm$ in tm equations of the power balance equation system. Then, it requires $2\sum_{i=1}^{tm} stn_i$ characteristic equations.

Let an elementary TM consist of one shaft (in the case of multiple-shaft TM it can be decomposed to some one-shaft ones interacting with each other along a gas channel, i.e. the gas channel connecting them becomes the TS element). Each TM (shaft) has a set of compressor or turbine stages STM_m, where $m = 1 \div tm$, and tm - the TM (shaft) number in a TS. The elements of these sets are the pairs

$$STM_m = \left\{ (q_1, x_1), (q_2, x_2), \dots, (q_r, x_r) \right\}_m$$

where (q_r, x_r) is a pair consisting of numbers of edges q_r and and an edge serial number of the element in edge x_r being the TM stage element. At the same time x_r serves as a section number of the given stage. Now, any stage may be indexed by $STM_{m,r}$. Then formula (19) may be used to describe a TM network as follows

$$\sum_{l=1}^{|STM_j|}\left\{\left[c_p\Delta T+c_p\overline{G}T_{in}\left(\frac{\partial}{\partial\eta}\frac{K}{\partial}\frac{\partial\eta}{\overline{G}}+\frac{\partial}{\partial\pi}\frac{K}{\partial}\frac{\partial\pi}{\overline{G}}\right)\right]_{STM_{j,l}}^{(i)}\Delta\overline{G}_{STM_{j,l}}^{(i)}\right\}+$$

$$+\sum_{l=1}^{|STM_j|}\left[c_p\overline{G}T_{in}\left(\frac{\partial}{\partial\eta}\frac{K}{\partial}\frac{\partial}{\partial\overline{n}}+\frac{\partial}{\partial\pi}\frac{K}{\partial\overline{n}}\frac{\partial\pi}{\partial\overline{n}}\right)\right]_{STM_{j,l}}^{(i)}\Delta\overline{n}_j^{(i)}=-\sum_{l=1}^{|STM_j|}\overline{N}_{STM_{j,l}}^{(i)}, \qquad (22)$$

$$j=1\div tm$$

$$\left(\frac{\partial\pi}{\partial\overline{G}}\right)_{STM_{j,l}}^{(i)}\Delta\overline{G}_{STM_{j,l}}^{(i)}+\left(\frac{\partial\pi}{\partial\overline{n}}\right)_{STM_{j,l}}^{(i)}\Delta\overline{n}_j^{(i)}=\pi_{TM_{j,l}}^{(i)}\quad l=1\div|STM_j|,\quad j=1\div tm \qquad (23)$$

$$\left(\frac{\partial\eta}{\partial\overline{G}}\right)_{STM_{j,l}}^{(i}\Delta\overline{G}_{STM_{j,l}}^{(i)}+\left(\frac{\partial\eta}{\partial\overline{n}}\right)_{STM_{j,l}}^{(i}\Delta\overline{n}_j^{(i)}=\eta_{STM_{j,l}}^{(i}\quad l=1\div|STM_j|,\quad j=1\div tm \qquad (24)$$

where

$$\left(\frac{\partial K}{\partial\eta}\frac{\partial\eta}{\partial\overline{G}}+\frac{\partial K}{\partial\pi}\frac{\partial\pi}{\partial\overline{G}}\right)=-\frac{1}{\eta_c^2}\left(\pi_c^{\frac{k-1}{k}}-1\right)\cdot\left(2A_{c,\eta}^G\overline{G}+B_{c,\eta}^G\right)+\frac{k-1}{k}\frac{1}{\eta_c}\pi_c^{-\frac{1}{k}}\left(2A_{c,\pi}^G\overline{G}+B_{c,\pi}^G\right)$$

$$\left(\frac{\partial K}{\partial\eta}\frac{\partial\eta}{\partial\overline{n}}+\frac{\partial K}{\partial\pi}\frac{\partial\pi}{\partial\overline{n}}\right)=-\frac{1}{\eta_c^2}\left(\pi_c^{\frac{k-1}{k}}-1\right)\cdot\left(2A_{c,\eta}^n\overline{n}+B_{c,\eta}^n\right)+\frac{k-1}{k}\frac{1}{\eta_c}\pi_c^{-\frac{1}{k}}\left(2A_{c,\pi}^n\overline{n}+B_{c,\pi}^n\right)$$

is for a compressor;

$$\left(\frac{\partial K}{\partial\eta}\frac{\partial\eta}{\partial\overline{G}}+\frac{\partial K}{\partial\pi}\frac{\partial\pi}{\partial\overline{G}}\right)=\left(\pi_t^{\frac{k-1}{k}}-1\right)\cdot\left(2A_{t,\eta}^G\overline{G}+B_{t,\eta}^G\right)-\frac{k-1}{k}\eta_t\pi_t^{-\frac{2k-1}{k}}\left(2A_{t,\varepsilon}^G\overline{G}+B_{t,\varepsilon}^G\right),$$

$$\left(\frac{\partial K}{\partial\eta}\frac{\partial\eta}{\partial\overline{n}}+\frac{\partial K}{\partial\pi}\frac{\partial\pi}{\partial\overline{n}}\right)=\left(\pi_t^{\frac{k-1}{k}}-1\right)\cdot\left(2A_{t,\eta}^n\overline{n}+B_{t,\eta}^n\right)-\frac{k-1}{k}\eta_t\pi_t^{-\frac{2k-1}{k}}\left(2A_{t,\pi}^n\overline{n}+B_{t,\pi}^n\right),$$

is for a turbine, i - an iteration step number.

TM DECOMPOSITION MODEL

The TS mathematical model may be solved as it is by the Newton method. However, there is a sense to analyze whether it is possible to decompose it. The fact that earlier calculations in engineering envisaged decomposition to decrease labour capacity of hand calculations. The method of representation of TM characteristics (6) - (7) is a result of it. It is worth noting that the characteristic of pressure ratio to flow rate is a TM hydraulic model and both these characteristics are mutually independent i.e. having a corrected rotation speed and flow rate given π_t, π_c and η_t, η_c are calculated independently. Why is any decomposition necessary ? The problem consists in building a model into a whole TS model. The method of doing so depends on the method chosen to solve the TS model, i.e. to perform simultaneously the mass, thermal and hydraulic loss balances. Using the Newton method for that purpose where every element is considered to be a separate equation is the most simple way. However, with this approach model data demensions and RAM required grow up proportionally to quadrat of TS elements. Therefore the decomposition methods are used more often at present.

In the class of flow rate distibution models the methods like loop for flow rates and node for presssures are designed for analysis of mass and hydraulic loss balances [3, 4]. The hydraulic loss equation is the basic element of flow distribution models. It has the following form

$$\Delta P = R \cdot G|G| \tag{25}$$

To apply one of the flow distribution methods it is necessary to approximate the TM hydraulic model by the model (25) at each step of its analysis. It requires, in turn, to decompose the TM model into hydraulic and thermal components. With such a decomposition the calculation of R is the task of the TM hydraulic model (20)-(24). Then the thermal model is defined by equations (4)-(5), and its solution is associated with making use of the average temperature method.

AVERAGE TEMPERATURE METHOD CONVERGENCE

In applying the Gauss convolution method [1-2] to the heat exchanger model (1)-(2) it was supposed that its coefficients remain constant. In this case it means the coefficients of TS element models are linearized. The answer to what extent the linearization is valid is known. It has been widely used in calculating working fluid state parameters and heat transfer coefficients in practice of hand engineering calculations of complex thermal systems. In other words, the truth of such linearization is being postulated.

Further, it is demonstrated that the convergence of simple thermal element models may be proved. It substantiates the convolution [1-2] for the class of elements considered in the paper. However to prove analytically the convergence for more complex models of elements will be of great difficulty. In this case the proof of convergence should be supported by a numerical experiment that demonstrates monotonicity of a model in the interval on which function is defined. The latter is a necessary and sufficient condition for convergence of the nonlinear model given.

Let's prove the convergence of the average temperature method by the example of the model for calculation of the straight channel output temperature. We assume the channel wall temperature is held constant. In the case of such a model the heat transfer rate to the working fluid has the form

$$q = c_p G \left(T_{out} - T_{in} \right) \tag{26}$$

The average heat transfer coefficient of the fluid in the channel is defined from

$$q = \overline{\alpha S} \overline{\left(T_s - T \right)}$$

Since wall temperature T_s is assumed to be constant, then the last equation may be rewritten as

$$q = \bar{\alpha}S\left(T_s - \bar{T}\right) \tag{27}$$

Equating the transfer rates in (26) to (27), we have

$$c_p G\left(T_{out} - T_{in}\right) = \bar{\alpha}S\left(T_s - \bar{T}\right)$$

Expressing heat transfer coefficient through the Nusselt number, we have

$$c_p G\left(T_{out} - T_{in}\right) = \frac{k}{D_h} Nu \cdot S\left(T_s - \bar{T}\right) \tag{28}$$

Coefficients of (28) in accordance with the average temperature method should be determined by a specific temperature

$$\bar{T} = \frac{T_s + \tilde{T}}{2}$$

where

$$\tilde{T} = \frac{T_{in} + T_{out}}{2}$$

is the average temperature. Then we substitute $\bar{T}$ in (28), and with account for temperature being constant, we have

$$c_p(\bar{T}) \cdot G\left(T_{out} - T_{in}\right) = \frac{k(\bar{T})}{D_h} Nu(\bar{T}) \cdot S\left(T_s - \frac{T_{out} + T_{in}}{2}\right) \tag{29}$$

c_p, k, Nu are empirical functions with respect to temperature with behavior being close to linear in the wide range of their definition domains (in particular, $Nu(Re)$ for the smooth tube, tube bundles, etc. [5]). Assuming that fluid properties and similarity criteria are monotonic functions with respect to temperature we approximate them by linear ones going through functions values at the boundaries of argument definition domain. Then (29) may be reformulated as

$$F(\tilde{T})\left(\frac{T_{out} + T_{in}}{2}\right) \cdot \left(T_{out} - T_{in}\right) = \frac{S}{2GD_h}\left(T_s - \frac{T_{out} + T_{in}}{2}\right)$$

where the function

$$F = a + \frac{b}{2}\left(T_{in} + T_{out}\right)$$

is supposed to be also a linear one of an averaged mass temperature, then performing some simple transformations we have

$$\frac{b}{2}T_{out}^2 + \left(a + \frac{S}{4G \cdot D_h}\right)T_{out} = \frac{b}{2}T_{in}^2 + \left(a - \frac{S}{4G \cdot D_h}\right)T_{in} + \frac{S}{2GD_h}T_s$$

Reducing the last equation to the form

$$T_{out} = \varphi\left(T_{out}\right)$$

we obtain

$$T_{out} = \frac{1}{B}\left(1 - \frac{A}{T_{out}}\right)$$

then the convergence condition of the iteration method may be formulated as

$$\varphi'\left(T_{out}\right) = \left|\frac{A}{B}\frac{1}{T_{out}^2}\right| < 1 \tag{30}$$

It follows from (30) that always there is some positive temperature, under the given constant coefficients A and B, the inequality holds true. This is in agreement with a physical point of view. Since the function F is monotonic, by definition, then application of such approximation at each step of solving the nonlinear thermal problem guarantees that the unique solution will be obtained. It is worth noting that the above may be extended to any thermal element.

Provided that element characteristics are nonmonotonic some additional preparation work is necessary to make a model valid for computations. It is specially actual for turbomachine characteristics. The preparation work consists in representing the initial nonmonotonic element characteristic as a set of monotonic ones in a way its domain definition range would be as wide as possible. In this case, the beneath algorithm of the approximation-decomposition method must be added by the loop implementing exhaustive search for all combinations of characteristics transformed from the set of monotonic ones.

METHOD ALGORITHM

The algorithm of the approximation-decomposition method for the TS analysis having exchangers and TMs is the following :

1. Assume initial values of heat exchanger efficiencies, fluid properties and π_t, π_c, η_t, η_c, $\bar{n}$ equal to design point ones which are always known for any TM designed.

2. Assign initial values to hydraulic losses for all the TS elements.
3. Solve a flow distribution problem based on the model (25).
4. Calculate pressures at each TS section.
5. Calculate pressures at TS element outputs under input pressures and flows known using hydraulic models for TS elements. The hydraulic model for a TM is adequate to pressure ratio-to-flow rate characteristics (6). One can find the pressure loss formulas for heat exchanger calculation in [6].
6. Calculate the hydraulic approximation model for each TS element, i.e. having calculated flows and pressure losses evaluate Rs with (25).
7. Repeat steps 3 - 7 until a relative error in the flow rate vector is satisfied.
8. Solve the thermal problem by the Gauss convolution method using models (1), (2), (4), (5) under known π_t , π_c , η_t , η_c , $\bar{n}$, exchanger efficiencies and fluid properties.
9. Repeat steps 3 - 8 until a relative error in the temperature vector is satisfied, thereby influence temperature on flow rate is accounted for (mainly it is meant for heat exchangers).
10. Having calculated the temperature, pressure and flow rate vectors, we evaluate efficiencies and pressure ratio factors of all the TS element models. In particular, the heat exchanger efficiencies may be recalculated according to the efficiency method [6].As for a TM is concerned the equations (22) - (24) are its model. Solving them we get flow rate and rotation speed vectors with which new π_t , π_c , η_t , η_c , $\bar{n}$ from (6)-(7) are obtained.
11. Repeat steps 3 - 10 until a relative error in the rotation speed vector is satisfied.
12. Calculate new average temperatures for each TS section and evaluate new fluid properties then.
13. Repeat steps 3 - 12 until a relative error in the fluid property vector is satisfied, otherwise it is the end of the algorithm.

The above algorithm of the approximation-decomposition method proposed in the article, permits performing both hydraulic and thermal analyses for TS systems having recuperative multipass heat exchangers and mutistage TMs whose characteristics occur nonmonotonic.

REFERENCES

[1] *Fedorov M.* Construction automation of mathematical model for thermal analysis of heat exchanger systems by the Gauss convolution method. Int. J. Engineering simulation, 2000, №6.
[2] *Fedorov M.* Modeling of heat exchanger net-works, Int. J. Engineering simulation, 2001.- №6.
[3] *Merenkov A., Khasilev V.* Teoria gidravlicheskich tsepei (Hydraulic circuit theory), Nauka Publisher, Moscow, 1985.
[4] *Nielsen H.B.* Methods for analyzing pipe networks. J.Hydr.Engrg., ASCE, 115(2), 1989, pp. 139-157.
[5] Heat exchanger design handbook. Heat exchanger theory, Hemisphere publishing corporation, 1983.
[6] Kays W., London A., Compact heat exchangers, McGraw Hill, New York, 1964

An analysis of performance of CAN (Controller Area Network) Fieldbus

MARIA ANABELA COELHO
Escola Superior Agrária, Quinta Sra de Mercoles,
6000-098 Castelo Branco, Portugal, e-mail: anabela@esa.ipcb.pt

Abstract: In this paper is presented a performance analysis of Controller Area Network (CAN) fieldbus on real-time systems using the Hartstone Uniprocessor Benchmark (HUB). Two nodes form the CAN platform of test: a PCI 712 card and a DIOC 711, digital input/output module. For each experience is presented the calculations of theorical results and the experimental results of bus occupation, when the breakdown point is reached. It is include some experiences extra benchmark that we consider necessary to that analysis and the respective results.

It is obtained results both on the test applicability and on fieldbus performance. The results of performance analysis demonstrated that CAN fieldbus works reasonably well with any kind of traffic: periodic messages with harmonic frequencies periodic messages with non-harmonic frequencies and messages with aperiodic processing.

Key words: benchmark, fieldbus, scheduling

1. INTRODUCTION

The limits of traditional arquitecture based on centralised communication systems have increasingly, led to their replacement by distributed systems. In this context the use of *fieldbus* has recently been increased. Nowadays the solution currently adopted in distributed systems, is to distribute the control functions over several processing nodes [3].

The use of a *fieldbus* that allows to tie all the sensors, actuators and equipment of control is a easier solution to install and more economically than the traditional point to point connections [2].

The industrial processes with real time characteristics, should be capable, to synchronise with external signs and produce correct results in right intervals of time.

Catastrophic consequences will result if the logical or timing constraints of the systems are not met [10], [2].

The main goal of real time systems is to guarantee that tasks with hard timing constraints will always meet their deadlines and provides fast average response times for tasks with soft deadlines [12].

Our goal is to analyze the adaptability in real-time of the *fieldbus* to control the industry processes that communicate among themselves through a group of cooperative applications and a physical bus.

There is a set of questions, which we'd like to contribute with elements, to help getting the answers. Some of these questions we present continuously:

Which the *fieldbus* that best satisfies the type of traffic of a generic system in function of the application type?

How the *fieldbus* is adapted to the different type of traffic?

Which are the *fieldbus* that have the best answer in our real time requisites?

We imagine that it is not possible to give an only and concise answer to these questions, even so it will be of hoping the characteristics of an or other *fieldbus* are more or less adapted to each one of the real application types.

However interests to define a methodology that indicate, the *fieldbus* more adapted in agreement to the real application. To choice a *fieldbus,* we must ask which is the tip of tasks that we have in our network:

- If our system that controls the industrial process is compost by periodic and harmonic tasks[1], which are the *fiedbus* that have best performance to transmit this tip of traffic? If the traffic are formed by periodic tasks but with non-harmonic[2] frequencies, which are the consequence of the performance of the network traffic?

- There exist industrial processes, with structured control, oriented to the event. For example the control of alarms generates, by nature, an aperiodic traffic. How and with what performance, could the *fieldbus* answer these requests?

- Frequently an application industrial in real time is complex and it is natural that the messages transmitted by the *fieldbus* are as varied as for instance:

– Information 0 or 1, corresponding to the logical state of a sensor.

– A chain of characters, for instance for the configuration of a variation of speed of alternating current motors, that typically can go even by tens of bits.

- This way, it is verified that although the traffic that circulates in the *fieldbus* is constituted typically by short messages, but also interests to ask: How the several types of *fieldbus* is adapt to the heterogeneity of the dimension of the messages that is transmitted in the *fieldbus*?

- But how to realise these tests? What tool type will be necessary to choose, to realise a performance analysis, so that the obtained results, be so close of the reality as possible?

---

[1] Periodic and harmonic tasks are tasks that their period are multiple between each other. For example: 2, 4, 8, 16, 32.

[2] Periodic and non harmonic tasks are tasks that their period are not multiple between each other. For example: 3, 5, 7, 17, 31.

The hypotheses that we analysed were: the mathematical models, the simulation and the performance tests (*Benchmarks*).

We could accomplish one mathematical model of all the process, but such task would be complex, slow and eventually unattainable. To be attainable it would be probably necessary to put restrictions, what would lead to the study of restricted cases, and would limit the analysis of performance of the *fieldbus*, not allowing a widespread analysis.

For example, the study of a single *fieldbus* using a mathematical model, in that case gave origin by itself to a phd thesis [Son 91] and nevertheless the analysis was only valid for restrictive cases. This study concluded that is not possible do a mathematical model of total net and only was possible to obtain resulted, just for the situations of very reduced traffic and very high traffic.

The simulation of the process, appealing statistical models would be an interesting alternative but unhappily, these lead to the following problems:

*   It is practically impossible to guarantee that all of the sceneries were tested and simulated.

*   Being systems industrial real time sometimes plenty complex, it is debatable if existed models (of wait lines for example) that describe the system faithfully.

*   Finally, the fact that the probabilistic methods present the results in a statistical way, have certainly more applications in several areas, but they are inadequate to study systems in real time, because it interest us to know if the variables in real time are transmitted, always respecting their time constraints and not the probability of that event.

On the other hand still exist the tests of performance designated for *benchmarks*, which consists of a group of very defined tasks, characteristics of the applications of real time. Associate to each group of tasks a group of procedures exists, representative of a great variety of application sceneries.

It seems us that the use of a *benchmark* is considered the "most honest" option, once are not us to define the tasks, neither the group of tests that composes each experience.

Using a *benchmark* it is possible compare a performance of real time systems, with the same base, avoiding tendentious analyses.

This paper is organised as follows: In the following section the Experimental Platform is presented. In section 3 the benchmark is presented as well as the realized experiences. In section 5 we show the experimental results and the respective analysis. Section 6 some experiencies extra benchmark is presented. In section 7 some conclusions are drawn.

2. EXPERIMENTAL PLATFORM

A huge number of *fieldbuses* exist on market, with different levels of standardisation (ASI, *Bitbus*, CAN, DIN-*Messbus*, *Interbus*-S, LON, P-Net, *Profibus*, *Sercos*, *WorldFip* etc.). To deal with the problem CERN developed a task force [1] which conclusions were that the major three fieldbus proposals were *Profibus*, *WorldFip* and CAN. We limited our analysis to a CAN *fieldbus* because they represent two opposite ways of dealing with message scheduling (Deterministic Access in *WorldFip* opposed to Random Access in CAN). This work presents mainly the tests made for the CAN protocol because the study for the *WorldFip* protocol is already presented in [7].

The network configuration adopted for the CAN test is a SELECTRON MAS system composed by a PCI 712 card, based on an 82C200 microcontroler and a DIOC 711 digital input/output module.

Fig. 1. Starter kit of *Selectron* adopted to realize the tests of *benchmark*.

The following figure presented a experimental platform, used for realize all the experiences of the *Hartstone Uniprocessor Benchmark*.

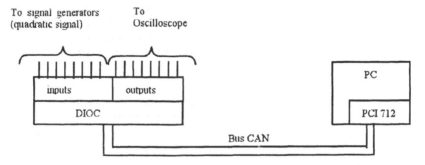

Fig. 2. Experimental platform

A PCI 712 card was installed in the computer, and with the bus is possible communicate with the module of input/output DIOC 711, therefore it was possible transmit tasks over the two nodes constituent of the network.

3.   APPLICABILITY TO FIELBUSES OF HARTSTONE UNIPROCESSOR BENCHMARK (HUB)

In real time systems it is very important the instant of time in that the results are produced. These systems are characterized by the serious consequences that can be happen if the produced results are late [Sta 88], [Ram 94]. The instant for besides which, a result, even if is correctly calculated, is considered late and therefore incorrect, is designated by deadline.

If the system is distributed, as the tasks as the messages, transmitted by the *fieldbuses* have deadlines. A common concern for the people that project the real time systems is to implement systems that guarantee the answer to the tasks with hard deadlines and minimize the time to satisfy the tasks with soft deadlines. This is a challenge that not always it is accomplished [12].

Naturally these different schedule strategies lead to different results consonant the applications the one that are destined. A certain strategy can be correct for one certain application type, but incorrect for other. The *fieldbus,* are inspired by several tcchniqucs, and is possible have some in that the scheduling is based in a static table (*Woldfip*) and others where is based in priorities (CAN).

It is not possible define if one strategy of scheduling is better or worse than the other, in the general case it interests to obtain a group of typical tasks of industrial applications, and realise a study based in these tasks. This set of typical tasks of industrial applications can be meet in the *benchmarks* existent in the literature, that although they can sometimes be debatable in terms of its representativeness to characterize industrial applications, they supply a set of tasks and procedures of test that allow to compare different strategies of schedule, starting from a same base.

There is a SAE benchmark [8], [11], describes a set of signals sent between seven different subsystems in a prototype electric car, but we opted by using the *Hartstone Uniprocessor Benchmark* (HUB), that is a well know benchmark and it permits to do a study more generic related with the type of traffic that is transmitted in the *fieldbus.*

We don't use a SAE benchmark because it only permits a study for a specific application and it was out of our goal.

We adapted the HUB, because is well know in *Journal of Real Time Systems* and is possible realise an analogy with *fieldbuses.*

The purpose of *Hartstone Uniprocessor benchmark* [12] is to measure the breakdown point of a real time system. The breakdown point is defined as the point at which, the computational and scheduling load causes a hard deadline to be missed. This *Benchmark* consists in a group of well-defined tasks, as well as, a group of procedures, representative of a wide variety of scenarios.

With the analogy that exists between the scheduling of tasks in a uniprocessador system and the scheduling of messages in a fieldbus [5], [2], [7], [4], is possible use this *benchmark,* to realise performance analysis for *fieldbus* networks.

3.1   Use of Hartstone Uniprocessor Benchmark

The *hartstone benchmark*[12], is composed by a set of periodic, aperiodic (sporadic) and synchronisation tasks.

Our purpose is to measure the breakdown point of the CAN network, using the HUB. The proceeding in each experience is to change one of the task parameters until a deadline is missed.

Experiences are divided in three series:

- PH series - periodic tasks, harmonic frequencies.
- PN series -periodic tasks, nonharmonic frequencies.
- AH series -periodic tasks with aperiodic processing.

The experience series are summarised in the following table:

	EXP 1	EXP 2	EXP 3	EXP 4	EXP 5	EXP 6
PH	T5 ↓	T1–T5↓	C1- C5↑	NT3 ↑	----	----
PN	T5 ↓	T1–T5↓	C1- C5↑	NT3 ↑	--	--
AH	IATsp↓	Csp ↑	C1- C5↑	NT3 ↑	IATap↓	Cap ↑

Tab. 1. Full set of HUB experiments.

The following legend helps to understand the experiences associated to each one of the three series, presented in the Table 1.

T5 ↓- - Decrease the period of P5 Task.

T1 - T5 ↓ - Decrease the period of P1 to P5 Tasks.

C1- C5 ↑ - Increase the execution time of P1 to P5 Tasks.

NT3 ↑ - Increase the number of P3 Tasks.

IATsp/ap ↓ - Decrease the medium of arrival time among tasks sporadic / aperiodics (IAT – *Inter arrival time*).

Csp/ap ↑ - Increase the execution time of the task sporadic / aperiodic).

The following table presents the set of experiences defined by the HUB, for the three series: PH series, PN series and AH series.

Tasks	PH			PN			AH		
	Freq (Hz)	Period (ms)	Work load (KW)	Freq (Hz)	Period (ms)	Work load (KW)	Freq (Hz)	Period (ms)	Work load (KW)
P1	2	500.00	32	3	333.33	21	2	500.00	32
P2	4	250.00	16	5	200.00	13	4	250.00	16
P3	8	125.00	8	7	142.86	9	8	125.00	8
P4	16	62.50	4	17	58.82	4	16	62.50	4
P5	32	31.25	2	31	32.26	2	32	31.25	2
S1	-	-	-	-	-	-	32	31.25	1
B1	-	-	-	-	-	-	2	500.00	16

Tab. 2. PH, PN and AH task set defined by HUB.

The workload of a task on an operating system may here be treated as the number of bits that a message requires to be broadcast through the *fieldbus*.

The set of experiences for aperiodic series (AH) includes the tasks defined for PH series and more two aperiodic tasks. The benchmark [12], defines one of them as background and another as sporadic.

The use of the *Hartstone Benchmark* to realize the performance analysis of CAN, have to be done considering some particularities of the messages, that circulate in the net.

The field of data of the messages that is transmitted in the CAN *fieldbus*, just could varied between 0 e 8 *bytes*, so it was possible to determine the performance of the network to messages of 1, 2, 4, 8 *bytes*.

For all of the experiences, it is presented the theoretical calculations of occupation of the *bus* and the results obtained experimentally.

3.1.1 Theoretical forecast

Liu e *Layland* in [6] they defines the factor of use of the processor as the fraction of the time of processor, used in the execution of a group of tasks. Since Ci/Ti, be the fraction of time that the processor spends to execute the task τ_i, this way for *n* tasks, the factor of occupation is:

$$\mu = \sum_{i=1}^{n} \frac{C_i}{T_i}$$

Equation 1 - Occupation of Bus.
n – Number of messages
Ti – Period of message
Ci – Number of bits of the message + number of bits of envelope of the message (used by protocol CAN) + number of bits between consecutive messages.

To accomplish the theoretical calculation of network occupation for each one of the presented experiences, was used the Equation 1, considering as Ti the period of the message and Ci the time that the message is in the bus, to be sent. The speed of transmission considered is 1Mb/s in all of the experiences.

3.2 Realized experiences

It was realized all the experiences of the *Hartstone Uniprocessor Benchmark*, the set of experiences are composed by the series: PH (periodic tasks with harmonic frequencies), PN (periodic tasks with non harmonic frequencies) and AH (periodic tasks with aperiodic processing).

3.2.1 PH Series – 1st experience

It consists of increasing the value of the frequency of the message P4 to the message P5, in each test until the deadlines of the messages is lost, the frequencies of the other messages are not altered. By this way the frequency of the message P5 is increased by 16hz, in each test.
To realise this experience, five frequency generators were used, in each one of these a square wave was generated with the frequencies presented in Table 2, the output of each frequency generators of functions it was connected to each one of the first five inputs of the module of inputs/outputs designated by *Dioc*.
The inputs (0, 1, 2, 3, 4) of the module of inputs/outputs (*Dioc*), they are activates in agreement with the square waves generated in each one of the generators of functions. When a input varies the module (*Dioc*) sent one message to the computer, and this sent this message to the digital output corresponding.
During the experience it is observed in the oscilloscopes the square wave of the input that is the wave of larger frequency (P5), and the wave of output. When in the oscilloscope the square wave P5 stops following the wave of input it is assumed that the net is saturated.

This way the following equation presents the network occupation calculations for this experience.

$$\mu = \sum_{i=1}^{5} \frac{C_i}{T_i} = \frac{C_1}{T_1} + \frac{C_2}{T_2} + \frac{C_3}{T_3} + \frac{C_4}{T_4} + \frac{C_5}{T_5}$$

Equation 2 - Application of Equation 1 to PH1 experience.

For example for task 5:

T5 – is varying as the *Hartstone Benchmark*.

C5 = Number of bits sent by the *Dioc* to the PC + Number of bits sent by the PC to the *Dioc*.

C5 = 8 + 46 + 10 + 8 + 46 + 10 = 128

It is foreseen that when the frequency of P5 reach values above 7808hz the network occupation reaches to the 100%.

3.2.2 2nd Experience

It consists of multiplying the frequencies of the messages successively by 1.1, 1.2, etc., is to be increase the value of the frequency of 10% in each test.

In this experience the output of the generator of functions is connected to the input of the module *DIOC*. The activation/deactivation of the input zero happened of agreement, with the frequency of the P5 square wave. When the input zero is active, the PC sends to the network the corresponding sequence of messages (P5P4P3P2P1, P5, P5P4, P5, P5P4P3, P5, P5P4, P5, P5P4P3P2, P5, P5P4, P5, P5P4P3, P5,P5P4, P5, P5P4P3P2P1).

For this experience the occupation of the network is presented in the following equation:

$$\mu = \frac{120*10^{-6}}{500*10^{-3}}*f + \frac{120*10^{-6}}{250*10^{-3}}*f + \frac{88*10^{-6}}{125*10^{-3}}*f + \frac{72*10^{-6}}{62.5*10^{-3}}*f + \frac{64*10^{-6}}{31.25*10^{-3}}*f$$

Equation 3 Application of Equation 1 to PH2 experience.

Initially the value of f (multiplicative factor) is equal to 1, this value is successively increased, in agreement with *Benchmark*, until the network enters in rupture.

It is foreseen that theoretically, for a multiplicative factor of 216, the net occupation reaches the 100%.

3.2.3 3nd Experience

This experience consist in increase the length of the messages until the breaking point of the network is reach. In this experience it was not possible to increase the dimension of the messages P1 e P2, so it is increased successively, the dimension of the messages P3, P4 e P5, until to the maximum supported by the CAN network.

The following equation shows the maxim occupancy of the network in this experience:

$$\mu = \frac{120^*10^6}{500^*10^3} + \frac{120^*10^6}{250^*10^3} + \frac{120^*10^6}{125^*10^3} + \frac{120^*10^6}{625^*10^3} + \frac{120^*10^6}{3125^*10^3}$$

Equation 4 - Application of Equation 1 to PH3 experience.

It is foreseen that the net occupation is always below 0.8% for this experience

3.2.4 4nd Experience

In this experience the number of messages P3 is increased successively. The following equation shows the calculation of the occupancy of the network to this experience:

$$\mu = \frac{120*10^{-6}}{500*10^{-3}} + \frac{120*10^{-6}}{250*10^{-3}} + \frac{(88*NumP3)*10^{-6}}{125*10^{-3}} + \frac{72*10^{-6}}{62.5*10^{-3}} + \frac{64*10^{-6}}{31.25*10^{-3}}$$

Equation 5 - Application of Equation 1 to PH3 experience.

In equation 5 the variable *NumP3*, presents the number of messages P3 that are transmitted in the network.

It is foreseen that theoretically the network just support about 1410 messages P3. Which corresponds of an occupation of bus of 100%.

After realize the tests that compose the PH series, it was realised the testes of the PN series and AH series. In the following section is presented all the results obtained.

4.   ANALYSIS OF RESULTS

The following table presents the results obtained for CAN network, for the experiences defined in the HUB.

	Série PH	Série PN	Série AH
	1060hz	1060hz	1060hz
1st experience	14%	14,10%	14,40%
2nd experience	1200hz	1060hz	☆
	17%	31%	
3rd experience	☆	☆	☆
4th experience	Obtido = 900	Obtido = 550	Obtido = 800
	64%	59%	57%
5th experience			1050hz
			17%
6th experience			☆

Tab. 3. Summary of the results obtained for benchmark experiences.

For first experience of PH, PN and AH series we obtained 14%, 14.1% and 14.4% respectively of bus occupation, when the breakdown point was reached. For second experience of PH and PN series we obtained 17% and 31% respectively. For fifth experience of AH series, we obtained 17%, when theoretically for all of these experiences it should be reached by 100%.

It seems that there exists a strange coincidence in all of these results, because the frequency of the breakdown point is always near 1khz. A detailed analysis of Selectron manual [9], revealed the existence of a filter in the inputs of Dioc module, limiting the frequency to 1Khz.

We felt that is necessary verify for other process that this was a really limitation, and to prove that the theoretical analysis was valid. In the attempt of proving that it was possible to obtain higher values of bus occupation, we decided to realise some experiences extra *benchmark*. These experiences will be introduced later on.

In all of experiences that increase the length of the messages, the messages never missed their deadlines, but the occupation rate was too far from 100%. This is because CAN messages are short by nature, each message may only have, up to eight bytes of data. This is a limitation of the protocol and this is why we did not achieve higher rates.

In experiences that increase the number of messages P3, we obtained for PH, PN and AH series respectively: 64%, 59% and 57% of bus occupation for breakdown point. We did not achieve the 100% bus occupancy but the capacities of the PC system were responsible for it. The CAN protocol allowed to go further by the PC performance wasn't enough to achieve higher rates.

In experiences with harmonic frequencies versus non harmonic frequencies, the results obtained for PH and PN series, shows that for CAN protocol is irrelevant the fact of the frequencies being harmonic or non harmonic, given the proximity of the results obtained in both series.

5. EXPERIENCES EXTRA BENCHMARK

For the experiences where it is necessary increased the frequency of the messages, it was not possible increased for values above 1200hz, that fact lead to obtain very low bus occupancy. To overcome this inconvenience it was decided to realize some experiences extra *Benchmark*, to prove that the theoretical calculation of bus occupancy are correct.

5.1   1st Experience

This experience has a purpose to create a lot of traffic in the network, without being necessary increase the frequency for values higher than 1 Khz.

The experience consisted on connect one generator of functions to one input of the module of input/output (*Dioc*), whenever the input zero was active, sent one message to the PC, and this sent multiple copies of the message to the network. The messages has the field of data of 8 bytes, because is the maximum supported by CAN *fieldbus*.

The idea was to start from a configuration achieving almost 100% and then increase the frequency of a task. The goal was to prove that the breaking point would be attained in 100% as previewed by the theoretical analysis.

The theoretical calculations values, were obtained in agreement with the equation presented continuously:

$$\mu = \frac{8*(120+64)*10^{-6}}{T*10^{-3}}$$

Equation 6 - Calculation of the network occupation for to 1st experience Extra Benchmark.

The value of the frequency P5 is progressively increased of the generator of functions connected to the input zero, until the point of rupture of the network is reached; the frequency value obtained was of 970hz, which corresponds to 99.3% of network occupation.

In this experience it was possible to obtain experimental results near of the 100% and they were in agreement with the theoretical calculations realized.

5.2   2nd Experience

This experience is based in the first experience of each one series, the frequencies adopted were the set of the 1st experience of PH series, however in this experience it was opted to send 10 messages of each one of the types, whenever one of the inputs of the *Dioc* was active. By this way it was possible to reach the 100% of bus occupancy, without the frequency of the messages reaches the value of 1 *khz*.

It is foreseen that for values of frequency near of 750 *hz* the network reaches the point of rupture, because theoretically the bus occupation was 100%. This value was calculated in agreement with the equation presented continuously:

$$\mu = 10*\frac{184*10^{-6}}{500*10^{-3}} + 10*\frac{184*10^{-6}}{250*10^{-3}} + 10*\frac{152*10^{-6}}{125*10^{-3}} + 10*\frac{136*10^{-6}}{62.5*10^{-3}} + 10*\frac{128*10^{-6}}{T5*10^{-3}}$$

Equation 7 - Calculation of the network occupation for to 2nd experience Extra Benchmark.

The value of *T5* is the period of the P5 messages, this value is 32.25ms initially and it is going decreasing successively as we increased the frequency of arrival of messages P5 to PC.

The frequency value obtained in the breaking point of the network was of 730hz, which corresponds to 98% of net occupation.

5.3   3rd Experience

This experience is based on 2nd experience of all the series, the set of frequencies adopted are of 2nd experience of the PH series. However in this experience 10 messages are sent of each one of the types, whenever one of the inputs of Dioc is active. By this way is possible reach 100% of the theoretical bus occupancy of the network, without the frequency of the messages reaches the value of 1 *khz*.

The network occupation for this experience was calculated in agreement with the following equation:

$$\mu = \frac{10^*120^*10^6}{500^*10^3} * f + \frac{10^*120^*10^6}{250^*10^3} * f + \frac{10^*88^*10^6}{125^*10^3} * f + \frac{10^*72^*10^6}{625^*10^3} * f + \frac{10^*64^*10^6}{3125^*10^3} * f$$

Equation 8 - Calculation of the network occupation for to 3rd experience Extra *Benchmark.*

The value of f in the previous equation represents the multiplicative factor, applied to the frequencies of the messages in each test. It is foreseen that the net supports frequency values to a multiplicative factor of 22, because theoretically the net occupation reaches the 100%. This value of net occupation corresponds to close frequency values of 700 *hz* to the P5 messages.

The point of rupture of the net, it was obtained for the value of frequency of 670hz for the messages P5, what corresponds to 97% of network occupation.

We can verify that in these three experiences realized extra *Benchmark*, was possible obtaining values of bus occupancy of network all of them near of the 100%.

This way we can conclude that the values of net occupation obtained for the experiences of the *Benchmark*, in that it was necessary to increase the frequency of one of the messages, they don't correspond to values of net saturation, but the a limitation in the entrances of the inputs/outputs module Dioc. This way it was possible to prove that:

1. The CAN network reaches values of bus occupancy by 99%, 98% and 97%, for the experiences realized extra *benchmark*, crossing the values of bus occupation obtained, for all of the experiences of the benchmark, demonstrating the existent limitation in the module of inputs/outputs (*Dioc*).
2. The theoretical calculations realized were correct, since in this set of experiences it was possible to obtain results in agreement with the theoretical calculations realized, demonstrating their truthfulness.

6.   CONCLUSIONS

The *Hartstone Uniprocessor Benchmark* has demonstrated that the fieldbus CAN reasonably support all the types of traffic analysed:

*   Traffic constituted by periodic and harmonic messages, for example of the signals transmitted by the sensors in that their periods are multiple amongst themselves.
*   Traffic constituted by periodic and non harmonic messages, it was possible conclude that the fact of the periodicity of the messages transmitted by the *fieldbus* CAN is or isn't harmonics between itself it is irrelevant for the CAN network.
*   Traffic aperiodic, for example signals transmitted by the alarms.

The comparative analysis of results for *WorldFip*[7] and CAN *fieldbus* for the same *fieldbus* has demonstrated, that there are significant differences in the results obtained for each one of the networks:

1. It exists a huge difference between the results obtained for CAN and *WorldFip* networks for traffic with non harmonic frequencies. The results obtained for CAN network concerning traffic with harmonic frequencies were similar to the results obtained for traffic with non harmonic frequencies. In the case of *WorldFip* network, It was not possible obtain results to traffic with non harmonic frequencies. This great difference reveals one of *WorldFip* disadvantages, because *WorldFip* is based on a bus referee table and it is easy that there would not be enough memory for building these tables.
2. For all the experiences of AH series, CAN results were similar to the results obtained for PH series. For *WorldFip* network, the same experiences lead to inconclusive results. This shows that the aperiodical traffic is better handled by the CAN protocol than by *WorldFip* protocol.

About the applicability of use the *Hartstone Uniprocessor Benchmark* for performance analysis of *fieldbuses*:

1. Is of great applicability the experiences that:
    ♦   Increase the frequency of one of the messages.
    ♦   Increase the frequency of the several messages.
    ♦   Increase the number of messages of a certain type.
2. We considered that do not have applicability for *fieldbuses* the experiences that increase the size of the messages in the network, because the size of messages in the *fieldbuses* are usually short.

7.   REFERENCES

[1] Baribaud, G., "Recommendations for the Use of *Fieldbuses* at CERN", in http://ecpcowww.cern.ch/fieldbus/report1.html, September 1996.
[2] Cardeira, C., Mammeri Z., "A Schedulability Analysis of Tasks and Network Traffic in Distributed Real-Time Systems", in *Measurement, The Journal of the International Measurement Confederation IMEKO,* n° 15, 1995, pp. 71-83.
[3] Cavalieri S., Stefano A. D., Mirabella O., "Impact of FieldBus Communication in Robotic Systems", in IEEE Transactions on Robotics and Automation, Vol.13, N. 1, pp. 30-48, February 1997.
[4] Coelho, A., "Using the Hartstone Uniprocessor Benchmark para análise de desempenho de redes de terreno", tese de Mestrado, Instituto Superior Técnico, Julho 1999.
[5] Kopetz, H., "Scheduling in Distributed Real Time Systems," Tech. Rep. Mars nr. 1/86, Austria, January 1986.
[6] Liu, C., Layland, J., "Scheduling algorithms for multiprogramming in a Hard Real-Time environment", in Journal of the Association Computing Machinery, Vol. 20, N.1, pp. 46-61, 1973.
[7] Pasadas, F., "Protocolos de Comunicação em Redes Locais para Ambientes Industriais: trafego aperiódico em redes de terreno", tese de Mestrado, Instituto Superior Técnico, Dezembro 1996.

[8] SAE, "Class C Application Requirement Considerations", SAE Technical Report J2056/1, June, 1991.

[9] Selectron, "SELECONTROL® MAS, System manual CANopen", September, 1997.

[10] Stankovic, J. A. "Misconceptions About Real -Time Computing: A serious Problem for Next-generation Systems", in IEEE Computer, vol. 21, n°10, pp. 10-19, October 1988.

[11] Tindell, K., Burns A., "Guaranteeing Message Latencies on Control Area Network (CAN)", available in the web via FTP from minster.york.ac.uk in the directory /pub/realtime/papers, 1999.

[12] Weiderman N. H., Kamenoff, N. I., "Hartstone Uniprocessor Benchmark: definitions and Experiments for Real -Time Systems", in a Journal of Real Time Systems, Vol. 4, pp. 353-382, 1992.

Effective Methods of Temporal Data Representation in Data Warehouse Systems

BOŻENA ŚMIAŁKOWSKA

Technical University of Szczecin, Faculty of Computer Science & Information System, 49 Żołnierska st., 71-210 Szczecin, Poland, tel:+4891 4495590, fax:+4891 4876439

Abstract: Some methods for extraction and transformation of data in warehouses with a time (temporary) representation will be shown in this paper. Those methods will be valued as a point of possible dynamic systems for computer aided management of enterprise.

Key words: Business information systems, data warehouse systems, temporal data representation

1.   THE ROLE OF DATA WAREHOUSES IN COMPUTER AIDED MANAGEMENT AND DECISION MAKING SYSTEMS

The assurance of an information readiness is a very important part of decision management processes (tactical and strategic decisions as well). It is also very important for enterprise management at any level, especially in fast alternating environment of the market economy. The database systems have played the meaningful role to obtain that goal. In the past the most popular approach was to construct the data bases and computer aided systems for decision making and management taking into account the enterprise purposes. There were dedicated systems for goods distribution, customer services, stock and finances management, finacial and accounting files management, etc. The common feature for those systems is simultaneous data processing of many individual operations (transactions, actions, services) but every operation (transaction, action, service) requires usually processing of small information (data) quantities. Such systems support the economical processes in the majority of industrial organisations and are called usually the enterprise information systems or the enterprise data base operating systems. The data storage in database operating systems does not constitute the value itself, even if it is very important in everyday activities. Performed investigations have indicated that in some operating systems not more than 30 % of reports from the whole are useful as tools in decision making and management activities. Therefore, only the proper usage of information collected in data base operating systems is able to ensure the satisfied level of an information readiness in an enterprise management process. The proper usage of information stored in databases forces the need of data integration, composition, aggregation and transformation (processing) of the data in accordance with decisions made. In Information Technology the neccessity of an integration at the level of system functionality or system data for computer aided decision management was indicated very early especially in the case of strategic and tactical ones. In the case of integration it is possible to obtain the complete integration through the implementation of an enterprise information system. Usually such an integration is achieved firstly due to the construction of an integrated vision and then due to the creation and implementation of subsequent „bricks" – information subsystems consistent with that vision. Even if the implementation of an integrated oriented system in an enterpise succedeed, it was visible after some time period of system exploitation that such a system is not able to perform the tasks predicted before the implementation – it simply does not support the decision management in proper manner. Many different reasons caused that very often the complete integrated system has not been constructed. In companies where the construction of an integrated system was the way for the integration usually only some database operating systems have been implemented. The need of the fast enterprise adaptation in the strong competitive environment on the market weakens also the theoretical vision of an indiviudal approach in an enterprise integrated system construction. Firstly - it is difficult to predict the future roles and the mission of computerized companies, secondly – it is nearly impossible to determine the roles for future IT systems.

If an integrated system for functionality integration has not been built in the enetrprise, then the integration performed at the data level for management and decision making purposes is difficult. Some of the reasons are:

- different software and hardware environments used for transactional (operating) IT systems creation,
- the usage of different data base management systems in operating data bases,
- an implementation of different data models in operating (domain oriented) data bases,
- usually data base operating systems are created in different phases of an enterprise activity,
- different technologies applied in operating systems, e.g.: some operating systems (transactional or domain oriented as human resources and wages systems, production accounting, stock management, capital assets management, etc.) have been made with the usage of older technologies, the other with the usage of newer ones (new generations of system tools and application generators).

However, the data integration could be achieved through:

- the creation and usage of the global data scheme; that model enables an access to heterogeneous database in real time,

- the creation of the integrated database based on operating (domain oriented) databases and additional information concerning eneterprise environment; this information forms so-called data warehouse and is used for data analysis, aggregation and decomposition (data processing with the usage of analytic tools for decision management purposes).

That second approach seems to be easier and less costly in realization because usually the reconstruction of operating (domain oriented) systems verified during exploitation is not recommended. In such cases usually the complete documentation of design and implementation processes do not exist or it is difficult to recover them. The means to achieve this goal are the systems called DATA WAREHOUSE (abbr.: DW).

Usually DW system is created on the base of operating systems (domain oriented, transactional, eg.: human resources and wages systems, order management, production support, etc.) and provides neccessary information for MIS (Management Information Systems), EIS (Execution Information Systems) and DSS (Decision Support Systems). The general concept for DW is shown on figure 1. There are distinguished n (any number) of data base operating systems (domain oriented) which are the fundamental information protection for DW system.

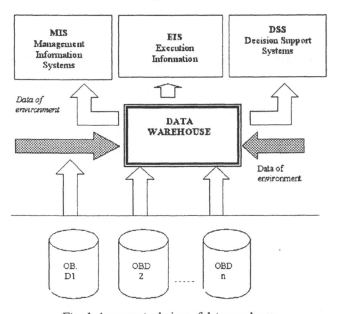

Fig. 1. A conceptual view of data warehouse

The monitoring of the most important indices and factors (from organization's point of view) is one of the basic tasks in management and decision making process. Those indices are time variable, changing their quality and quantity as well. Today, the set of those indices includes: profitability, risk, customer satisfaction level, customer rotation, production quality, service quality, customer behaviour index, etc. In the future some other factors and indices could become important. Moreover, some of them – important and essential nowadays – could become negligible in the future. DATA WAREHOUSES do not deal with tasks resulting from enterprise industrial processes and services. They also do not deal with tasks performed successfully at the database operating systems level.

The most essential criteria of DATA WAREHOUSES evaluation are:
- Credibility of provided data,
- Data adequacy for decision management processes,
- The choice of data structures applied in DATA WAREHOUSE – they should provide the possibilty of „just-in-time" methods usage (e.g: ordered reports) in DW data manipulation process for the purpose of multidimensional analysis of enterprise events,
- Data consistency,
- Information readiness.

The higher credibility and adequacy of the data provided from DW, the better selection of data structures and the higher information readiness of consistent data in DW – they are essential conditions to evaluate DATA WAREHOUSE as well implemented, i.e.: DATA WAREHOUSE could perform expected tasks more efficiently and support enterprise decision processes much better.

2. COMPONENTS OF DATA WAREHOUSE SYSTEM

The main components of every data warehouse system are:
- OBD_i – operating databases (where $i \in <1,n>$),
- SD_i – data scheme in the operating data base OBD_i ($i \in <1,n>$),
- $MONITOR_i$ – the module for detection of altered data in the source data set of OBD (operating databases),
- $CONVERTER_i$ – data transfer from operating data base format (source data) to DW,
- AGGREGATOR, INTEGRATOR and CLASSIFIER – integrates, classifies and updates DW data provided by MONITOR,
- SDW – data scheme in DATA WAREHOUSE,
- SMD – meta-data scheme (scheme for data concerning SD_i)
- DWMS – DATA WAREHOUSE management system,
- DATA WAREHOUSE - data store with determined SDW.

DATA WAREHOUSE, aided by those components and applying the tools and methods for analysis and decision management, provides the neccessary tactical and strategic information for the purpose of management and decision making. An access to DATA WAREHOUSE is performed according to the scheme shown in figure 2.

The following data are stored in DATA WAREHOUSE systems:

- Elementary data – including also time attribute – the copies of source data values provided from operating data bases; very often with unified representation,
- Materialized and aggregated data (so called „aggregates") – calculated in different projects, daily, monthly and yearly total amounts,
- Meta-data – the description of source data and/or DW data structures; meta-data includes also various dictionaries (translation form operating data to bussiness information) and data predefinitions.

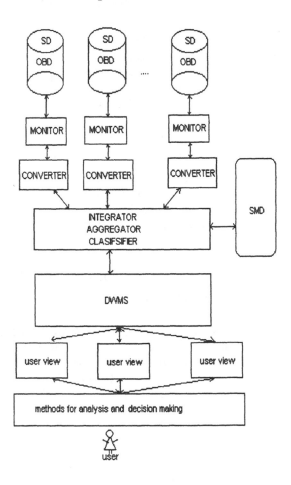

Fig. 2. Schema of use the data warehouse

DATA WAREHOUSE can be considered as an formalized enterprise mass memory. The facts stored in DATA WAREHOUSE are changing due to the various events (the changes of dimensions values and facts measures) and have their own history. There are also stored information concerning facts measures and other dimensions. Therefore DW provides time variable information about the facts form the past. An example of database with facts and dimensions is presented in figure 3.

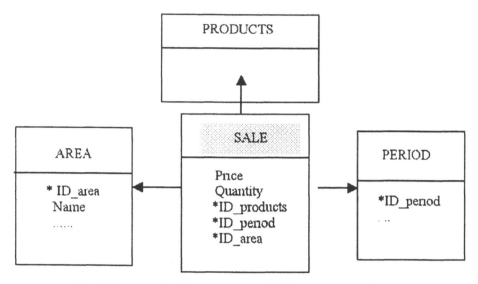

Fig. 3. An example of data structure model for the DataWarehouse.

In example above the facts are stored in SALE table. PRODUCTS, AREAS and PERIODS are the dimensions of facts stored in the SALE table. Those facts are additionally characterized by measures Price and Quantity. The measures and facts attributes marked with * are data indexing attributes.

3. THE ROLE OF TIME DIMENSION IN DATA WAREHOUSE

Time is the dimension in every DATA WAREHOUSE. The time model accepted and defined for the purposes of DATA WAREHOUSE is very substantial to enable DW meet the expected requirements and criteria for the time itself is the factor integrating the data in DATA WAREHOUSE. The proper selection of the time model should ensure that stated previously evaluation criteria for DATA WAREHOUSE obtain adequate indices suitable for current needs.

The time in DATA WAREHOUSE is the dimension neccessary for:

- the state of facts representation at any time – now and in any moment in the past (e.g.: 5 days ago, currently, etc.),
- the description of facts changes (states, processes, values of indices) and resources changes caused by execution and decision processes considered in any time perspective (trends investigation, anomalies analysis),
- the description and analysis of changes in relations between facts, the search of rules for relations existence and changes, e.g.: relations between sale and costs, etc.,
- the expression of correlation, integrity and dependency constraints for facts and measures, e.g.: investigations of relations between production and sale areas (territories).

Nowadays it is hard to state authoritatively that such a formalized mass memory of enterprise as DATA WAREHOUSE will be satisfied solution for the forecast of the future. There are many opinions that as long as the enterprise exists – the knowledge resources concerning the past are used in better or worse manner. There are various sources of so-called retrospective knowledge, eg.: responces for inquiries concerning the past, various reports and visualization of the data from the past. The another approach are the methods called knowledge discovery (Data Mining or Knowledge Discovery and DataBases – KDD), for they provide the models able to search and represent patterns hidden inside the data. They enable, for example, to receive the answer for questions „why something goes as it goes, what can happen, what will be results if something occurs ?". The traditional DATA WAREHOUSES are not able to provide the proper answers. Knowledge discovery systems have close relations with neural networks, genetic algorithms and fuzzy logic. They are especially important in decision management processes. Nevertheless very often DATA WAREHOUSES are used as the source of integrated information in those systems. It is some form of support in knowledge deduction process treated as services built over DATA WAREHOUSE.

4. MODELS FOR TEMPORAL DATA REPRESENTATION FOR THE PURPOSES OF DATA WAREHOUSES

There are the following data models in DATA WAREHOUSES:

- Conceptual model, so called view of economy data classification for the purposes of an analysis and modelling of events (also known as bussiness model or bussiness view) [2].
- Global logical data model for DATA WAREHOUSE,
- Physical data scheme for DATA WAREHOUSE.

The first and second model are realized on the basis of multidimensional modelling (the field of science), the third one is related with the requirement of the most effective performance of hardware and software logic scheme solutions in real commercial systems.

The data representation in DATA WAREHOUSE depends significantly on temporal data representation. Diagram shown in figure 4 illustrates schematically the standard calendar model and very often it is the only base for time modelling in commercial data warehouse systems.

Despite of the model presented in figure 4 some additional models of tree calendar structures are used in DATA WAREHOUSES (see: figure 5).

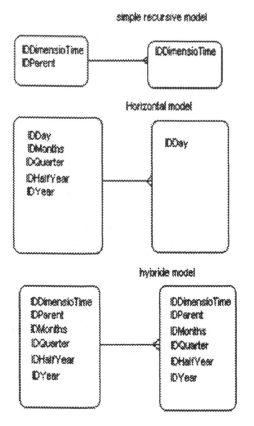

Fig. 4. Prymitive model for temporal data

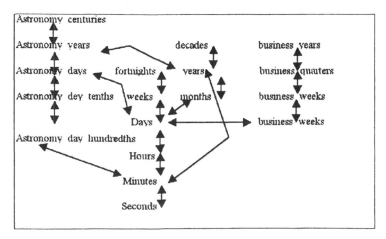

Fig. 5. A multicalendar granularity graph. ([1])

However, it seems the time representation model according to figures 4 and 5 is not satisfied for the purposes of the enterprise decision processes. It is especially in that case when decisions are related with management and decision making at the strategic and tactical level. The temporal model in DATA WAREHOUSE should be selected taking into account its accordance with:

- Decision needs (indices and the methods of their calculation) ,
- Possibilities of information provision form data base operating systems.

Due to the various data models implemented in data base operating systems and different attempts to time representation in these systems it is important to determine the global model for time dimension in DATA WAREHOUSE, even then if for any $i \in <1,n>$:

- OBD_i does not represent the time explicitly,
- OBD_i depends on the time and all OBD_i systems are based on the same temporal models with the same granulation,
- OBD_i depends on the time and all OBD_i systems are based on the same temporal models with different granulation,
- OBD_i depends on the time and all OBD_i systems are based on different temporal models with the same granulation,
- OBD_i depends on the time and all OBD_i systems are based on different temporal models with different granulation.

Additionally, in OBD_i systems service query languages based on standards SQL, OQL (object query language) or TQL (temporary query language) can be used. The classification of time representation (temporal) models for OBD_i systems (where $i \in <1,n>$) is shown on figure 6.

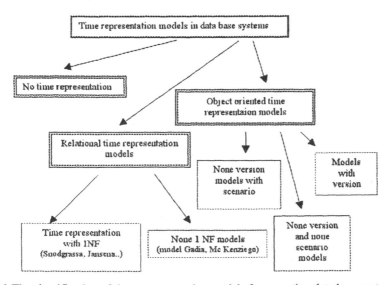

Fig. 6. The classification of time representation models for operating data base systems ([4])

Every OBD_i system (where $i \in <1,n>$) stores the data as various attributes with values adequate to real values. The set of OBD_i attributes creates so-called „data base scheme". Taking into account the temporal data representation point of view the following notation is selected for the set of attributes ASD_i related with database OBD_i:

$$ASD_i = <A^i_1, A^i_2, ..., A^i_p>$$

where A^i_q - attribute q in base OBD_i (for $q \in <1,p>$) different from time (temporal) attribute. To reflect the temporal changes of attribute values it is possible (in OBD_i systems) to determine for every $A^i_q \in ASD_i$ the function INFO such that:

$$INFO(A^1_q) = 0$$

when only the last values of attribute A^i_q are stored in ODB_i

$$INFO(A^1_q) = 1$$

when many values of attribute A^i_q are stored in ODB_i (for $q \in <1,p>$).

For every attribute $A^i_q \in ASD_i$ if $q \in <1,p>$, so it is possible to determine the time of the last storage of this attribute before time t in datebase OBD_i consisting of this attribute, namely:

$$RT(A^1_q, t) \le t$$

If for any $A^i_q \in ASD_i$ in ODB_i system the relation $INFO(A^i_q) = 0$ is true, then using the value $RT(A^i_q, t)$ one can determine the set of time points TA^i_q such that

$$TA^1_q = \{ t^i_{q1}, t^i_{q2}, ..., t^i_{qr} \}$$

and

$$t^1_{ql} = RT(A^i_q, t^i_{ql}), l \in <1, r_i>$$

It should be noticed that for any attribute A_l with $l \in <1, r_i>$, $i \in <1,n>$ and

$$A_l \in ASD_i$$

it is possible to determine the value of this attribute $val(A_l, T_{op})$ at any time T_{op}, with one of the following three formulas:
- if $INFO(A^i_q) = 1$ and $A^i_q \in ASD_i$ and $A^i_q = A_l$ then
  $val(A_l, T_{op}) = val(A^i_q)$
- if $INFO(A^i_q) = 0$, $A^1_q \in ASD_i$, $T_{op} \in TA^i_q$ and $A^i_q = A_l$, then
  $val(A_l, T_{op}) = val(A^i_q, T_{op})$
- if $INFO(A^i_q) = 0$, $A^i_q \in ASD_i$, $T_{op} \notin TA^i_q$ and $A^i_q = A_l$, then
  $val(A_l, T_{op}) = aprox(val(A^i_q, t^i_{q1}), val(A^i_q, t^i_{q2}), ..., val(A^i_q, t^i_{qr}))$

where aprox( ) means approximation function, regression or interpolation of unknown value val(A_1 , T_{op}), according to the needs adequate to reality representation.

The following components constitute the global data model for DATA WAREHOUSE:

- The set of facts $F = \{f_1, f_2, ..., f_f\}$
- The set of dimensions (in the case of DATA WAREHOUSE the time always belongs to this set) $\underline{W} = \{w_1, w_2, ..., w_w\}$
- The set of dimensions and facts $M = \{m_1, m_2, ..., m_m\}$

Because in DW time does not play the role of fact but always is only the one of dimensions, it is possible to distinguish in the set of dimensions $\underline{W}$ the time dimension denoted as T. Then, assuming W denotes the set of dimensions different from the time, the following realtions are fulfilled:

$$\underline{W} = T \cup W \text{ and } W = \underline{W} - T$$

Let us assume for further considerations that S is the set including the time, facts and dimensions, ie.:

$$S = F \cup W \cup T \text{ and } X = F \cup W$$

Facts and dimensions in DATA WAREHOUSE are bound and they constitute multidimensional structures in the form of stars, constellations, snow flakes, etc. (see: figure 7), generally: any hierarchical tree-shaped structures.

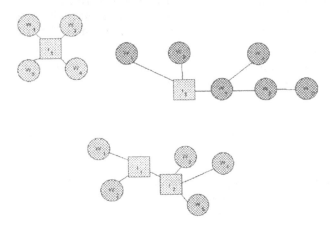

Fig. 7. An example relation between dimensions and facts in data warehouse.

The relation between dimensions and facts can be described using the relation R, such that:

R: F × S→ {0,1}

and the relation between dimensions, facts and measures using the relation RM, such that RM: X × M→ {0,1}

5. SELECTION OF GLOBAL LOGICAL MODEL WITH TIME REPRESENTATION FOR THE PURPOSES OF DATA WAREHOUSES, MANAGEMENT AND DECISION MAKING

The following problems concerning data representation should be solved in data modelling process for the purpose of DATA WAREHOUSES, decision making and management at all.:

- to determine the least time chronon (basic unit MT) for data recording in DATA WAREHOUSE,
- to determine the data representation for bussiness problems described in facts and dimensions tables: mean values (daily average production, mean value of customer service costs), actual values (precise sale time desribed with the chronon consisting of calendar date, hour, minute and second of sale) , maximal values (eg.: maximal stock of machine tools shutdown in minutes),
- to identify the rules for historical data correction, eg.: the value W_1 of attribute A related with fact f (an attribute is the measure or the dimension in DATA WAREHOUSE), was recorded at time t_1 in operating data base OBD_j , and transferred to DATA WAREHOUSE (in aggregated form or not) at time t_w , then it was replaced in OBD_j at time t_2 by the new (corrected) value W_2 , where $t_1 < t_w < t_2$; the the dilemma is which one of values should be stored in DATA WAREHOUSE: A_1 or A_2? In that case the correction can be related to other facts, predicted or not in DATA WAREHOUSE,
- to select the temporal data transfer methods for data recorded in accordance with different logical time models in OBD_i ($1 \in <1,n>$) into one accepted global data model SDW;
- to select data modelling methods for DATA WAREHOUSES (structural, object and operating methods), for the existing (obligatory) are not adequate for data modelling in DW.

As it was stated previously, the temporal model in DATA WAREHOUSE should be selected taking into account its accordance with:

- Decision needs (indices and the methods of their calculation),
- Possibilities of information provision form data base operating systems.

It was assumed, for the determination of rules valid to adopt the temporal model for the purposes of DATA WAREHOUSE, management and decision making, that for every enterprise (company) the measures suitable for enterprise state description are known. They result from company mission and at any time t they constitute the set of indices for company state evaluation – $S(t)$. It means that at any time t the indices ws_1, ws_2, ..., ws_k are valid, (k – number of decision indices), and moreover these indices define at time t the state $S(t)$ of an enterprise according to system approach, namely:

$$S(t) = < ws_1, ws_2, ..., ws_k ,t>$$

For the purposes of an enterprise decision management (especially tactical and strategic ones) it is required to know

$$S(T_1), S(T_2), ... , S(T_c)$$

where in special cases c can be finite value or the value of the power of the natural numbers set.

Let us assume for further considerations that T_{op} is one of the time moments essential for decision management process, i.e.:

$$T_{op} \in TP = \{ T_1, T_2,... , T_c\}$$

For every index ws_j , where $j \in <1,k>$, there exist in DW the measures $M^j = \{m_1^j, m_2^j, ..., m_q^j \}$ which at any time T_{op} unambigously determine that index ws_j . It means that for every index ws_j some method mws^j exists enabling the calculation of ws_j value denoted as $val(ws_{j,} T_{op})$ according to the following formula

$$val(ws_{j,} T_{op}) = mws^j(M^j \times T_{op})$$

The demand PD for all information required in decision making and management, i.e.: demand for measure values related with indices neccessary to determine $S(T_1)$, $S(T_2)$, ... , $S(T_c)$ for the purposes of planning, management and decision making, can be defined as follows:

$$PD =\{(m, T_{op}) : m \in M^j , T_{op} \in TP, j \in <1,k> , val(ws_{j,} T_{op}) = mws^j(M^j \times T_{op})\}$$

For any measure m_l and any time $T_r \in TP$ and $T_q \in TP$ such that

$$(m_l,T_r) \subset PD \wedge (m_l,T_q) \subset PD$$

it is possible to determine time distance $\mu(m_l, T_r, T_q)$
calculated according to unified reference scale (e.g.: in seconds) and so-called „measure chronon" m_l

$$chronon(m_l) = \inf_{Tc} (\Delta(m_l, Tc))$$

where

$$\Delta(m_l, Tc) = \min_{Tr \in TP \wedge Tq \in TP} (\mu(m_l,Tr,Tq))$$

and inf $_{Tc}$( ) denotes the lower limit of the set of values due to the time Tc. An example: for any measure $m_l \in M$ at time Tr and Tq the distance $\mu(m_l, T_r, T_q)$ can be determined on the basis of an absolute value

|Tr-Tq| calculated according to the unified reference scale (in fixed time units, e.g.: in seconds). Any measure $m_l \in M$ can be obtained from ODB_i (i $\in$ <1,n>) through the composition of the following operations: conversion (conv), monitoring (monit) and aggregation (agreg). Namely it could be done with the composition:

conv $\otimes$ agreg $\otimes$ monit

performed on the set of an operating base ODB_i attributes: $\{A_1^1, A_2^1, ..., A_p^1\}$, where

$$\forall_{m_l \in M} \exists_{(1 \leq p \leq pi \wedge 1 \leq i \leq n)} m_l = conv \otimes agreg \otimes monit(A_1^1, A_2^1, ..., A_p^1)$$

6.   SUMMARY

In the paper only some trial is undertaken to work out the methods of modelling for temporal data representation in DW. The two different points of view are presented. One of them deals with the problem of an accordance of a data representation model with the purposes of decision making and enterprise management, the other considers the verification of this model against the possibilities of enterprise operating databases. There are not practical results of investigations. Only the specific approach to modelling of time (temporal) dimension representation is reported. Practical researches and investigations are the subject of the author's current activity.

7.   BIBLIOGRAPHY

[1] Dyreson C.E., Evans W., Hong Lin, Snodgrass R.: Efficiently Supporting Temporal Granularities. A time Center Technical Report, 1998; september 3.
[2] Gorawski M., Frączek J.: Projekt i opis modelu hurtowni danych, Informatyka 2000; 5.
[3] Królikowska B., Marcinkiewicz J.: Czas jako atrybut zdarzenia w relacyjnych i obiektowych bazach danych. Informatyka 2000; 9.
[4] Majkowski A., Mazur Z.: Wybrane zagadnienia dotyczące systemów temporalnych baz danych. Informatyka 1998; 12.

Outsourcing it and Virtualization in E-Business Solutions (Selected Issues)

RYSZARD BUDZIŃSKI[1], TOMASZ ORDYSIŃSKI[2]
[1]Technical University of Szczecin
[2]University of Szczecin

Abstract: In the article there are presented different methods of e-business service, mainly IT outsourcing, as a possibility for small and middle class enterprises of joining e-economy. There are described advantages and disadvantages of this method and examples of putting IT outsourcing solutions into practice. Following part is devoted to different methods of e-business service: agents and virtual organizations. Final part is a summary of introduced information and includes future prognosis of outsourcing development.

Key words: e-economy, e-business, outsourcing, agents, virtual organization

1. INTRODUCTION

The XX century was technical revolution era, which results are the most significant in computer science. The observed changes concern human life both aspects: personal and professional. The most important transformation factor was the Internet – the largest worldwide computer network. It was established in 1969 as an experimental network of US Defense Department named ARPANET. Then it connected four computers. Currently it concentrates 8 millions of computers and the users number is valued at 35 millions. The users group can be divided into the two main types: private persons and enterprises. The first ones identify the Internet as an electronic mail and commercial or educational WEB pages. The second group is represented by business world. It considers the Internet as the fast and efficient communication media, which is necessary while dealing with business, and as a new instrument of reaching the customer [2]. The initial stage of presence in Internet, by WEB sites with information about products and services offered by the company, changes currently into attempt at placing whole company information system into this worldwide network. The result of this process is fast software and infrastructure development of the Internet. The eighties were characterized with enormous growth of IT departures in companies. They took care about enterprise control and supervision programs and applications. Later it became not efficient enough. Huge enterprises desired complex solution that could supervise all aspects of company work: from production management by distribution, accounts to, popular today, customer relationship management. These were the reasons of MRP, ERP systems origin. Unfortunately, only the biggest companies or international enterprises could afford these systems with all necessary computer equipment. In the nineties the situation changed. The way of using information systems transformed – now they are available to customers by electronic media (outsourcing). The customer does not have to invest in buying the solution – he can reap profit from the system simply by paying for using it. He can focus on placing, processing and drawing important data – system and infrastructure security is ensured by a solution provider. What is more, he can work being out of his company – access to his enterprise information system can be available from any computer connected to the Internet. This significant change in the way of access and payment for new IT systems enables software producers to reach new customers among small and middle class companies. They cannot afford buying MRP or ERP solutions but are able to rent it [1].

The aim of this article is presentation of different e-business service methods, with drawing special attention to the IT outsourcing. Paper assumption is that this new method is a perfect solution, which enables many companies to join e-economy, reduction of electronic data management costs (by commission it to professional firms) and improving work efficiency (by better flexibility and faster market adaptation). Information presented in this article is based mainly on the Internet resources.

2.   BASIC DEFINITIONS AND TERMS CONNECTED WITH E-BUSINESS

The most general term connected with e-business is an electronic market. This issue (according to prof. Oleński) can be considered in two definitions: in narrow and broad scope. The first one describes the electronic market as "IT or IT-telecommunications system or a complex of systems which is designed for execution of product purchase or sale transactions in specific trade" [3]. In a broad scope „electronic market is a segment of national or worldwide economy in which economic transactions are executed with IT-telecommunications systems. These systems form a complex of connected and cooperating information systems, which are the basis of molding demand, supply, prices, transaction conditions and all execution stages of transaction [3].

Electronic economy consists of three elementary elements: infrastructure, electronic business (e-business) and e-commerce transactions. Each part carries out a specific function and only their complete connection and cooperation can be defined as e-economy [4]. An E-business infrastructure is an element of an economic infrastructure, which is applied to operate e-business and execute e-commerce transactions. It consists of: electronic hardware (a computer, router etc.), software (operating systems and applications), telecommunication network (a cable, satellite links etc.), supporting services (WEB site development, electronic payment etc.) and human resources (mainly programmers) [4]. Electronic business is defined as each process, which takes place in an organization (working for profit or not) through a computer network. These processes can concern production, customers or management [5]. E-commerce transaction is described as each transaction executed through the computer network which cause property or ownership transfer of goods or services. The condition is at least one of the transaction devices must be computer controlled [6].

E-business is a completely new approach to trade of entities interested in trade exchange. It enables much faster information flow between market participants by transferring most of these operations on computer with an appropriate software. There are two basic advantages of this solution: decreasing costs of company operating and development of telecommunication infrastructure of enterprises and their surroundings [7]. There are distinguished two main e-business models: B2C (bussiness-to-consumer) and B2B (bussiness-to-bussiness). The best examples of the first kind are Internet markets (like Amazon.com or polish E-market), which offer products to the individual consumer. The second type is much more complex and consist in companies cooperation via the Internet. It can concern electronic data exchange about products, services, customers, current orders etc. but also consultations or real time designing of products.

3.   DIRECTIONS OF E-BUSINESS DEVELOPMENT

There are two main attitudes of enterprises towards the Internet usage. The first one treats this worldwide computer network as a traditional marketing supplement that enables to reach more customers and new way of product advertising. The perfect example of this attitude are company WEB sites with basic information about the firm, its products or services. However, this is a one-way communication: from a company to a customer. A further contact is established by traditional communication methods: by phone or personally. Currently, this type of "presence in the Internet" has become a standard among companies. The second attitude concerns totally a new form of business development, which takes an advantage of all the Internet possibilities: on-line communication and enormous information resources. Today this hind of e-business reduces mainly to e-commerce and popular home-banking. There are only a few enterprises that have managed to place their information system in the Internet enabling customers to get any relevant data from any computer connected to this network. Polish management personnel perceives the Internet potential. 91% of company representatives consider this network as an important instrument of doing business. 78% think that the Internet usage gives competitive advantage. 46% assume that companies, which do not appreciate Internet solutions, will lose customers in favor of those that appriciate [7].

The specialists from the GartnerGroup research the issue of e-business application development. According to their strategic planning assumptions by 2005, 70 percent of new application investments and 50 percent of new IT infrastructure investment will focus on e-business transformation. Through 2002, 60 percent of e-business initiatives remain tactical IT projects rather than strategic business mandates that demand business process transformation. Through 2003, 75 percent of enterprises will be under budget e-business transformation costs by 50 percent or more, especially when they are trading-partner-related. The situation is presented in the figure above (Fig. 1), which shows e-business development against the increasing business value and prices of e-business application background.

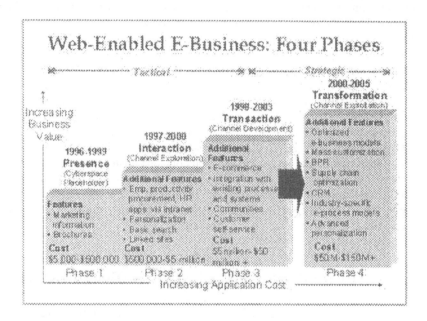

Fig. 1. GartnerGroup's four phases of e-business

4.   OUTSOURCING AS A METHOD OF E-BUSINESS SERVICE

Current market situation makes enterprises concentrate on these fields that they are the best in. Outsourcing (outside-resource-using) for a company usually means cost reduction by commission of some of the supporting internal services, which were done not efficiently enough by inner departments, to professional firms. The main advantage of this solution is cost reduction and better market flexibility of the company [16]. Outsourcing is defined as a conception of improving company function, which consist in services or semi-finished products usage offered by external providers. The aim is to reduce the cost of company products with simultaneous improving its quality. Outsourcing objects are those internal services that can be done cheaper by provider with the same or better quality. This phenomenon can be divided into internal and external types. The first one takes place inside one company by tasks delegation to lower grades. The external outsourcing uses services of outside providers [18]. This is a stage in company improving process, which assures quality and competition. Some enterprises have put this so much into practice that they just put their trademark on product, which is in 100% done by other companies (e.g. PUMA) [19]. In the eighties enterprises noticed that appropriate information system enabled to beat competitive companies, improve deliveries or win over customer trust. In present computer era information systems support both small (accounting, chambers etc.) and big enterprises (banks, travel agencies, post office etc.). At the same time the tendency of changing IS management from internal into commissioning it to professional firms is observed. This kind of commission is defined as IT outsourcing [17]. Classic researchers divide outsourcing into three types: complete, selective and that consisting of one or a few functions. The first type consists in complete provider responsibility for company information system: hardware, software, putting it into practice and management [20]. Selective outsourcing characterizes by commission of some company function to a provider (e.g. software management or hardware service). The third type has the narrowest range – one or a few IS functions are commissioned (e.g. assurance of communication links between departures). Providers usually offer very various contracts that enables companies to choose appropriate solution. The IT outsourcing is becoming very popular among different kinds of enterprises. This is a result of increasing maintenance costs that are determined by:

1. Enormous technology and software development. To be competitive a company must use the best organizational and technological solutions.
2. Lack of well qualified computer staff.
3. Necessity of following and choosing the strategically best solution from many new offered.

The maintenance cost of company information functions is increasing and still will be. However its strategic role is becoming essential. So the best and most efficient solution is outsourcing of these expensive but crucial for company processes [21].

5. ADVANTAGES AND DISADVANTAGES OF IT OUTSOURCING

The basic advantage of getting rid of internal support function is the cost reduction. However currently factors like better product quality, work specialization or access to professional knowledge are becoming important, too. Outsourcing enables company to focus workforce on elementary its functions. The enterprise achieves better results by increasing flexibility and time and human resources saving so its market value grows [27]. After taking a decision on IT outsourcing customer can reap different profits. Their type depends on the form and range of commissioned functions:

- lower cost because of personnel reduction,
- an entrusting part of a company to a group of professionals who are better qualified and experienced than the company staff,
- an improved service of commissioned functions because of independence from personnel illness, holiday etc.,
- a possibility of using knowledge and experience of professionals who would be extremely expensive to employ,

- more efficient work time – provider works till all the contract conditions are completed,
- an easy access to latest IT technology,
- a high quality service based on experience and specialization of provider,
- an investment in company IS reduction – customer pays for usage and does not have to invest in infrastructure,
- a provider must ensure up-to-date technology,
- a 24 hour help support in case of any problems [28].

From the list above follows that outsourcing has many advantages. However, growing popularity of this solution has showed some negative aspects. First of all, customers who decide on commission of some or all company IS functions must be aware of the risk. It is possible that the provider will not do his duty, his service will not be done in all aspects or he will not complete his tasks in time. What is more there is a chance that a provider will take advantage of a customer. If a provider's market is not competitive then he is not forced to minimize his costs, so the customer must accept his high prices [17]. The next of the basic disadvantages of outsourcing are improperly defined needs and expectations to the provider. This strategic cooperation requires accurate communication, exact planning and common vision of both sides [27]. What is more, cost reduction is done by personnel limitation that can cause disintegration of an employee society [28]. The extreme case is when provider starts to act as a competitor and tries to take over the company. He can also use his access to company data dishonestly and cooperate with another enterprise. The last disadvantage is difficulty and cost of giving outsourcing service up by customer. This close collaboration makes customer highly dependent [17].

6.   IT OUTSOURCING IN PRACTICE – EXAMPLES

The demand for IT outsourcing is increasing every year. According to the analysis done by consultants from The Corbett Group in the USA almost all researched companies postulated growth of expenses on external IT outsourcing. 97% stated that these expenditures could increase 25% annually. The most important conclusion was that over 60% managers were satisfied with this new approach to information system usage [23]. The most significant outsourcing contract has been reached between Electronic Data Systems (EDS) and MCI WorldCom valued at 12,4 billions of USD. According to this agreement EDS takes over most of MCI information system services. EDS hands over part of MCI network infrastructure. As the result 1000 of EDS employees start job in MCI and 1300 of MCI personnel start job in EDS [22].

Another contract has been reached between Canadian Nortel Network and Computer Sciences Corp. (CSC). The CSC takes over almost all functions carried out by the internal Nortel IT department. The agreement is valued at 3 billion USD and CSC will secure technical support and development of existing applications [25].

One of the most active firms which offer outsourcing service is IBM which only in 1999 reached 16 contracts with European companies valued at 100 millions of USD. They were e.g. Cazenove (Great Britain), Parion (Germany), Portugal Telecom, Winterthur (Switzerland), Geodis (France) [26].

Outsourcing is put into practice also in Poland, especially among financial institutions like banks or pension funds. One of the first centers of outsourcing service is built by Apcon in Tarnów Podgórny (near Poznań). Initially, it will be used for company named Reemtsma, which will rent system of enterprise resource planning (ERP) SAP R/3 and SMART – system of sales representatives service. Additionally there will be installed telecommunication devices to make possible modem communication and Internet connections. An investment plan anticipates also phone info line and help desk [23].

The first Polish bank that decided on IT outsourcing is Gospodarczy Bank Wielkopoplski S.A. (GBW S.A.). Information system of this regional bank, which associates 125 cooperative banks, is serviced by SOFTBANK S.A. The user interfaces have been installed in a few hundred departments so in each of them the bank customer can use every of a bank offer [24].

7.   ANOTHER METHODS OF E-BUSINESS IT SERVICE

The „e-" prefix in e-business term means that this kind of business is done by electronic media. They can be divided into two groups that complement one another: hardware and software. To the first one almost every electronic device is rated, which collects, sends, processes or stores data. There can be scanners, cables, all kind of computers, communication satellite or simply mobile phones etc. This group forms the basis but is useless without appropriate software for business. The proper program or application, which can process data, makes the complete usage of technical infrastructure possible. The communication media in e-business is the Internet. An enormous fascination of this new method created huge demand for „e-applications" which enables enterprises to open for international net-market and electronic cooperation. However, currently, some inconveniences of e-business have appeared. The main are: the rush of information in the Internet and the data security. These problems have resulted some new ideas of taking in this worldwide computer network for e-business purpose. The most significant of them, besides outsourcing described above, are presented below.

a)   AGENTS

A sudden Internet development has caused enormous increase in number of information, which this media makes available. This phenomenon has become crucial problem for quickly evolving e-business. Customers who are looking for specific product or cooperation partner by standard WEB browser gets many links. But only a few of them include significant information – the rest is useless. So the research process becomes time-consuming and in business time is money. Special programs named agents are the solution to this problem[8]. One of agent definition is: "An intelligent agent is software that assists people and acts on their behalf.

Intelligent agents work by allowing people to delegate work that they could have done, to the software agent. Agents can, just as assistants can, automate repetitive tasks, remember things you forgot, intelligently summarize complex data, learn from you, and even make recommendations to you [9]." Another definition describes agent as: "... semi-autonomous computer programs that intelligently assist the user with computer applications. Agents employ artificial intelligence techniques to assist users with daily computer tasks, such as reading electronic mail, maintaining a calendar, and filing information. Agents learn through example-based reasoning and are able to improve their performance over time" [10]. Quality of this software is measured by degree of three main features fulfilling: agency (autonomy), intelligence and mobility (Fig. 2). The degree of autonomy and authority vested in the agent is called its agency. It can be measured at least qualitatively by the nature of the interaction between the agent and other entities in the system in which it operates. At a minimum, an agent must run a-synchronously. The degree of agency is enhanced if an agent represents a user in some way. This is one of the key values of agents. A more advanced agent can interact with other entities such as data, applications, or services. Further advanced agents collaborate and negotiate with other agents. Next feature is intelligence. It is defined as the degree of reasoning and learned behavior: the agent's ability to accept the user's statement of goals and carry out the task delegated to it. At a minimum, there can be some statement of preferences, perhaps in the form of rules, with an inference engine or some other reasoning mechanism to act on these preferences. Higher levels of intelligence include a user model or some other form of understanding and reasoning about what a user wants to be done, and planning the means to achieve this goal. Further out on the intelligence scale are systems that learn and adapt to their environment, both in terms of the user's objectives, and in terms of the resources available to the agent. Such a system might, like a human assistant, discover new relationships, connections, or concepts independently from the human user, and exploit these in anticipating and satisfying user needs [8]. The last significant feature is mobility that is strongly connected to issue of data privacy and security. At the lowest level is a static agent, which operates and collects data only on user computer. The medium level mobile agent is programmed on a user computer and next sent to another one to fulfill the task. This process is repeated until the task is completed or an agent is stopped by a user. At this level the collected data are well secured.

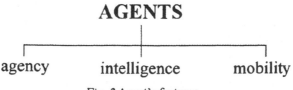

Fig. 2 Agent's features

At the highest level agent program wanders through Internet collecting data until all available network resources are checked. A program saves gathered data and carries it during searching. This fact enables agent to exchange data with another agents. However, security at this level is rather poor. To sum up, agents are programs, which enable user to save time and money spent on the Internet research. Distinct from standard WEB browsers, which offer a list of links to the document with a sought phrase, agents check all documents and collect data without any user action. The next advantage is an agent independence - user can just log on, define the task and log out. An agent will search network resources and all the results can be sent on the user e-mail address. He can just pick it up later – does not have to stay on-line during searching [8]. All these enumerated advantages together with user-friendly interfaces cause increase in popularity of agent in e-business solutions.

b) VIRTUAL ORGANIZATION

The XX century was the era of enormous development of big enterprises that succeeded because of ability of production and marketing integration. It enabled well-controlled management. However, each organization must adapt to changing environment conditions to survive. So agility has become the crucial issue. There are many ways to be agile in business: from big corporation, which do independently whole stages of production, to small but dynamic companies with an efficient net of partners and providers [11]. The second group is specially interested in possibilities of the Internet development and virtual organization. This new attitude to using worldwide computer network deals perfectly with constantly changing client's and co-worker's requirements. It becomes a standard in business solutions changing it into e-business [12]. The issue of virtual organization is casual relationships between different organizations in order to complete specific task. This causality is an advantage that enables connected organizations to be more flexible and react faster on market changes. The assumption of creating virtual organization is to maximize potential of each participant. According to *Business Week* a virtual organization consist of companies of providers, consumers or even recent competitors, whose aim is to share abilities, experience or costs to take advantage of market opportunities. The connection of all participants of virtual organization is established by a computer network – mainly the Internet. It is the reason of cost reduction but simultaneously requires trust and discipline from each related company. This virtual connection enables a whole organization to use the best abilities of each participant for common good. However, this flexible union has some relevant dangers. There are:

- lack of control over work of individual participant – he can make unintended or intended mistake,
- threat of revealing some secret information to unauthorized organizations,
- „tension" because of lack of trust between participants.

The management of virtual organization requires creating some new techniques and instruments of supervision. The advantages of distance work cause lack of control and the only determinant of work quality is a task accomplishment. The idea of virtual organization is mainly practicable among companies which business characterizes by a knowledge and information usage [13]. According to specific of trade or product this type of organization has different kinds. Three basic ones are distinguished (Fig. 3):

1. Dominant Organization, Networked Suppliers - one dominant player sets the ground rules and uses a network of small firms to meet its needs and those of its customers. This model is often used within large organizations to create the effect of small businesses working together. Any large organization that uses a

network of suppliers fits this model. The business need not own the whole value chain - the recent trend for large firms to outsource non-core activities has added significant momentum. Examples in this category range from conglomerates such as General Electric (their suppliers of physical goods are all networked via the Web into and outsourcing of non-core business services). Other examples are not hard to find – most major manufacturers and retailers already run a network of independent suppliers. Processes in this type of relationship are normally focused on the repetitive supply of a service or product. The terms of the relationship are (usually) well known in advance (with little opportunity for variation). Whilst an individual supplier may provide a given product or service, it may, in turn, rely on other suppliers to fulfill these needs.

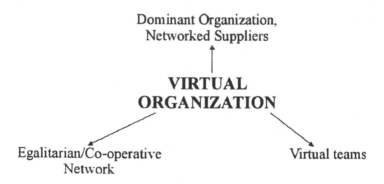

Fig. 3 Types of virtual organization

2. Egalitarian/Co-operative Network - this type of virtual enterprise involves networks of small businesses working together to support larger projects or services (which in turn may be supplied to larger or more dominant players). Typically such a network has 2 to 5 organizations collaborating on a project by project basis. Processes are project oriented and require a trusting relationship between the parties with a strong desire to co-operate. In such a network, there are usually broad outlines of agreement as to the division of responsibilities but formal contracts that cover all possibilities are impracticable. We see this as the area with the greatest potential for growth. At present, small organizations are badly served in terms of available technology (the level of skill required) and the services offered.

3. Virtual Teams - the trend in most large businesses is toward teams that are managed on a project by project basis (making for a more agile business structures). From this point it is just a short step to virtual organizational forms. In some businesses the concept of virtual teams has formalized – the Exploration & Production functions in the Oil and Gas business is a good example. Virtual teams normally co-ordinate their activities via informal mechanisms, relying on trust and co-operation among the parties. Companies such as Ford are using virtual global teams for designing the latest car models. In other cases, companies are operating on a 24-hour day in which the design of computer chips is communicated at the end of the work to another part of the world where the work continues uninterrupted [11].

4. Egalitarian/Co-operative Network - this type of virtual enterprise involves networks of small businesses working together to support larger projects or services (which in turn may be supplied to larger or more dominant players). Typically such a network has 2 to 5 organizations collaborating on a project by project basis. Processes are project oriented and require a trusting relationship between the parties with a strong desire to co-operate. In such a network, there are usually broad outlines of agreement as to the division of responsibilities but formal contracts that cover all possibilities are impracticable. We see this as the area with the greatest potential for growth. At present, small organizations are badly served in terms of available technology (the level of skill required) and the services offered.

5. Virtual Teams - the trend in most large businesses is toward teams that are managed on a project by project basis (making for a more agile business structures). From this point it is just a short step to virtual organizational forms. In some businesses the concept of virtual teams has formalized – the Exploration & Production functions in the Oil and Gas business is a good example. Virtual teams normally co-ordinate their activities via informal mechanisms, relying on trust and co-operation among the parties. Companies such as Ford are using virtual global teams for designing the latest car models. In other cases, companies are operating on a 24-hour day in which the design of computer chips is communicated at the end of the work to another part of the world where the work continues uninterrupted [11].

To sum up, the idea of virtual organization is a response of enterprises to constantly and faster changes of market. As the most relevant advantages of creating this type of organization can be listed:
1. common infrastructure, costs and risk of participants
2. association of complementary abilities of participants,
3. easier market access and winning over customer's trust,
4. migration from sale of the product to sale of the solution [15].

Currently the market competition is changing rapidly. Short-term business opportunities have become often phenomenon so companies try to meet customer's requirements by better understanding of their needs. If companies cooperate with each other as virtual organization they will be able to do it faster so they will become more competitive [14].

8. SUMMARY

To summarize all information presented above there are three basic methods distinguished of e-business IT services: agents, virtual organizations and IT outsourcing. Development of each of them is closely connected with increase in popularity of the Internet usage in companies business. The idea of agents has been introduced as the response to information chaos in this worldwide computer network. Agent program abilities enable user to save time and money spent on WEB searching. Virtual organization uses the Internet as communication media between associated companies or co-operating departments of one enterprise. It makes possible distance work, faster reaction on change of market conditions and union of abilities for realization of specific task. However, the most popular method is outsourcing. Current managers appreciate the role of this solution in present e-economy. After spreading from the United States, where this idea has arisen, all over the world it has created a value of its own. It has evaluated from a branch of management to the most profitable trade, which still develops. The meaning of this solution by its instruments, professional software, services and associations becomes more and more significant. According to research of FORTUNE magazine, leading companies use outsourcing solutions more eagerly to achieve better economic results.

This phenomenon can be clearly presented by numbers:

- American companies allocated more than 100 billions of USD on outsourcing in 1996,
- in 1997 the value of outsourcing services on European market came to 15 billions of USD - it is expected to come to 27 billion in 2001,
- over 90% of economic organizations use outsourcing solutions of at least one function
- according to estimations global outsourcing expenditures will come to 318 billions of USD in 2001 [30].

Information presented on figures (Fig. 4, Fig.5) shows expenditures on outsourcing on European and United States markets. It is clear that they are doubled every year.

The most conservative estimations assume triple increase of money spent on this solution during the next 5 years what is enormous growth, rare in any other economic trade. These prognoses present the great prospect of outsourcing services market. In spite of the fact that the value of European market is still much lower than American, its growth rate is 100% per year. To sum up, phenomenon of outsourcing has become important part of world market. Many Polish companies consider commission of their IT departures to professionals. It specially concerns those, which start to be e-business participants.

The crucial advantages of outsourcing services are:

1. concentration of company work and organizational abilities on elementary function (they do what they can do the best),
2. guaranty of high quality of outsourcing services,
3. internal cost reduction,
4. access to the latest technological and organizational solutions,
5. employment reduction [27].

These advantages of outsourcing, as the new method of e-business service, cause that this solution is profitable for both sides: a customer and provider. It becomes a standard of support during process of joining new electronic economy by more and more companies.

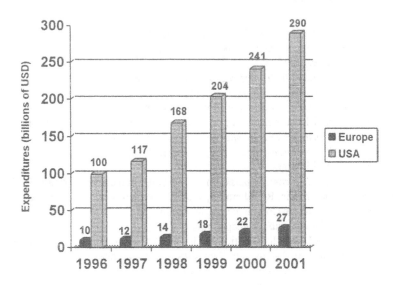

Fig. 4. Global expenditures on outsourcing solution in The United States
and Europe in 1996-2001

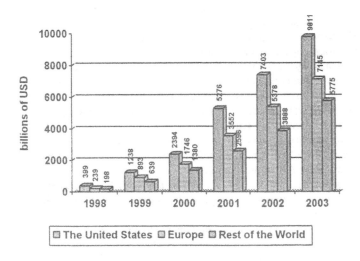

Fig. 5. Value of outsourcing market and estimated growth in 2000-2003

9.   REFERENCES

[1] Adamczyk Michał: *Następca ERP.* PCkurier 23/1999
[2] Rafa Jarosław: *Co biznes może uzyskać dzięki sieci.* Wystąpienie na konferencji Internet w
    Polsce, 21 września 1995
[3] Kulisiewicz Tomasz: *Elektroniczna gospodarka i informacja.*
    http://www.teleinfo.com.pl/ti/2000/26/t41.html
[4] Mesenbourg Thomas L.: Measuring Electronic Business: Definitions, Underlying
    Concepts, and Measurement Plans. http://www.census.gov/epcd/www/ebusines.htm
[5] Jones Frank: *E-business Transformation in the Manufacturing Industry.*
[6] *E-business vs E-commerce.* http://www.bretabennett.com/babrwc/e-
    business_definition.htm
[7] Karpiński Michał: *E-biznes po polsku.* http://www.teleinfo.com.pl/ti/2000/25/t05.html
[8] Do Orlantha, March Eric, Rich Jennifer, Wolff Tara: Intelligent Agents & The Internet:
    Effects On Electronic Commerce and Marketing.
    http://bold.coba.unr.edu/Tara/paper.html
[9] Zick Laura: The Work of Information Mediators: A Comparison of Librarians and
    Intelligent Software Agents. http://www.dochzi.com/ai/index.html
[10] Jansen James: Using an Intelligent Agent to Enhance Search Engine Performance.
    http://www.firstmonday.dk/issues/issue2_3/jansen/index.html
[11] Technology Futures for the World Wide Web. Business Needs Something Better !!
    http://www.enix.co.uk/webtech.htm
[12] Virtual Organization as Process: Integrating Cognitive and Social Structure Across Time
    and Space. http://www.msu.edu/~prestons/virtual.html
[13] Internetowa Skarbnica Wiedzy o Zarządzaniu: *Organizacja Wirtualna.*
    http://www.infomanager.free.ecig.pl/wirt.html
[14] Nowak Oktawian: *Organizacja wirtualna*
    http://chimera.ae.krakow.pl/intraed/zajecia/intern97/NowakO/DODATEK/org_wirt.htm
[15] Pańkowska Małgorzata: *Typologia organizacji wirtualnych*
    http://figaro.ae.katowice.pl/~pank/typol.htm
[16] Charakterystyka nowoczesnej koncepcji logistyki.
    http://boss.zie.pg.gda.pl/nkl/kierunki.htm
[17] Pańkowska Małgorzata: OUTSOURCING - alternatywa zarządzania systemem
    informatycznym przedsiębiorstwa. http://www.pol.pl/informatyka/1996_06/6f4.htm
[18] Outsourcing. http://www.bci.krakow.pl/TF/leksykon/l_outsourcing.html
[19] Skarżyński Rafał: Outsourcing. http://www.infomanager.free.ecig.pl/outsourcing.html
[20] Kniaź Anna: Wschodzący rynek.
    http://www.pckurier.pl/archiwum/artykuly/kniaz_anna/1999_24_38
[21] Outsorcing - idea Centrum Informatyki Medycznej dla Służby Zdrowia
    http://www.uhc.lublin.pl/centrum.html
[22] Obuchowicz Maciej: *EDS i MCI WorldCom podpisały kontrakt outsourcingowy.*
    http://www.computerworld.com.pl/wiadomosci/archiwum/1/4/1404.asp
[23] W ręce fachowców.
    www.rzeczpospolita.pl/Pliso/dodatki/komputer_990617/komputer_a_4.html
[24] Zwierzchowski Zbigniew: Informatyka bez (własnych) komputerów.
    http://www.rzeczpospolita.pl/Pliso/gazeta/wydanie_990225/nauka/nauka_a_5.html
[25] Łęgowski Wojciech: *Nortel przekazuje w outsourcing swój dział informatyki.*
    http://www.computerworld.com.pl/wiadomosci/archiwum/2/7/2799.asp
[26] IBM wchodzi w europejski outsourcing. http://www.teleinfo.com.pl/ti/2000/13/t08.html
[27] Cieślak-Grzegorczyk Małgorzata: *Outsourcing.* Modern Marketing, listopad 2000

[28] Outsourcing. http://www.webmedia.pl/bp2000/biznesplan/outsourcing,html

[29] Tarasiewicz Andrzej: *O tym co dziś, o tym co jutro.*
http://www.computerworld.com.pl/online/1999/13/numer/O_tym_co_dzis_o_tym_co_j
utro.asp

[30] Outsourcing na świecie. http://www.csf.com.pl/uslugi/outsourcing1.htm

[31] *GartnerGroup on the Future of E-Business.*
http://www.netron.com/transform/gg_four_phases.html

Algorithmic Models for Supervectoring Calculation in Solving Base DSP Problems

ALEXANDR P. TARIOV[1], TOMASZ MĄKA[1], EDUARD MELNIC[2]

Faculty of Computer Science & Information Systems, Technical university of Szczecin,
Zolnierska 49, 71-210 Szczecin, Poland, e-mails: acarev@wi.ps.pl, tmaka@wi.ps.pl
College of Foreign Language and International Business,
Moldova 2068, Kishinev, str. A. Ruso, 1, e-mail: melnic@inivers.net.md

Abstract: New hardware-oriented supervectorized algorithmic models for numerical sequences discrete Fourier transform, convolution and correlation computing are described. The models being fully parallelized give possibility to achieve minimal calculation time in comparison with known ones.

Key words: digital signal processing, discrete Fourier Transform, supervectoring calculations

1.   INTRODUCTION

The convolution along with correlation function and discrete Fourier transform (DFT) are basic operation of the majority of tasks of digital signal processing [1]. The necessity of fulfilling numerous time-consuming multiplication operations stimulated elaboration of economical "fast" algorithms aimed at minimization of total quantity of these operations [2,3]. The effectiveness of such algorithms manifests itself mainly by single-processor computing. At transition to parallel supertechnologies, increased complexity of organization of computing processes while realizing "fast" algorithms, and increase of data transfer operations share are transforming into complexity of inter-processor exchange procedures and increasing the total time of computation. This fact can bring to naught the advantage in speed obtained due to the reduction of quantity of arithmetic operations necessary for realization of fast DSP algorithms. The indicated circumstance forces to refuse too complicated but effective from the computing point of view algorithms of DSP problems realization and stimulates elaboration of new ones, specially oriented towards parallel processing.

Thus, for example parallel algorithms, had been elaborated based on systolic principle of paralleling of computations [4]. However, this approach requires organization of special regime of data supply to the inputs of systolic DSP-processor, but it can be not always easily realized.

Another approach to the synthesis of parallel algorithms of digital signal processing is shown in the papers [5,6]. Within this approach algorithmic models were obtained proposed in the present article.

The following denotes are used below [6,7]:

$\otimes$, $\displaystyle\bigotimes_{i=0}^{N-1}$ - tensor product sign of two and N matrices, respectively;

$\oplus$, $\displaystyle\bigoplus_{i=0}^{N-1}$ - tensor sum sign of two and N matrices, respectively;

$\displaystyle\frac{\blacksquare}{\blacksquare}$, $\displaystyle\frac{\blacksquare}{\blacksquare}_{i=0}^{N-1}$ - vertical concatenation sign of two and N matrices, respectively;

$\blacksquare|\blacksquare$, $\displaystyle\blacksquare|\blacksquare_{n=0}^{N-1}$ - horizontal concatenation sign of two and N matrices, respectively;

$\mathbf{I}_N$- is here and further on a unitary matrix whose order is defined by the lower index;

$\mathbf{1}_{N\times 1}$- is a column-matrix all the elements of which are equal to 1 while its dimension is defined by the lower index;

$\mathbf{0}_{M\times N}$- is a zero matrix of the dimensionality indicated.

2.   DFT – SUPERVECTORIZATION MODELS

Let $\mathbf{X}_N = [x_0, x_1, ... x_{N-1}]^T$, $\mathbf{C}_N = [c_0, c_1, ..., c_{N-1}]^T$, are   dimension $N \times 1$ vectors ($N = r^m$, m-integer positive number) describing signal samples in time and frequency domains, respectively.

A DFT is defined as follows:

$$c_n = \sum_{n=0}^{N-1} x_n \cdot e^{-j\frac{2\pi nk}{N}} \; ; \; n, k = \overline{0, N-1} \tag{1}$$

where $e^{-j\frac{2\pi nk}{N}}$ is a discrete exponential function (DEF) [7].

The expression obtained completely defines the list of mathematical operations, which are to be used in order to implement a DFT coefficient computation. Though, the peculiarities of data processing organization are not quite evident, the investigation of these problems is of interest in order to find out some efficient methods of parallel computation for solving this problem.

Further, parallel algorithms are considered to aim at fast computation of coefficients of discrete Fourier transform which use fast methods for computation. In these algorithms a computation redundancy is minimized at the expense of periodicity and multiplicativity properties of discrete exponential functions and of symmetry of a transformation matrix.

Organization of calculations is based on the general approach for various bases which envisages splitting an initial data sequence of coefficients being calculated into groups taken $M = r^q$, $M \ll N$, at a time in each one, where r, q - integer positive numbers. In this case DFT coefficients in each data group can be calculated with the help of the "reduced" fast DFT algorithms, independently. As it takes place, the last (first) q iterations of FFT algorithms are to be performed depending on the type of decimation of initial data.

The algorithmic models for these calculations are described by the following generalized vector-matrix procedure:

$$C_{r^m} = A_{r^m \times r^{2m-q}} \cdot C_{r^{2m-q}} \tag{2}$$

where $A_{r^m \times r^{2m-q}}$ denotes a summation matrix of column matrix $C_{r^{2m-q}}$ elements which is fully definite for each concrete model . These vector elements in their turn are calculated with the help of one of the following formula:

$$C_{r^{2m-q}} = F_{r^{2m-q}} \cdot (I_{r^{m-q}} \otimes \Xi) \cdot P_{r^{2m-q} \times r^m} \cdot X_{r^m}$$

for FFT with decimation in time,

$$C_{r^{2m-q}} = (I_{r^{m-q}} \otimes \Psi) \cdot F_{r^{2m-q}} \cdot P_{r^{2m-q} \times r^m} \cdot X_{r^m}$$

for FFT with decimation in frequency,

where Ξ and Ψ denote matrix formulae which represent the last(first) q iterations of the concrete modifications of FFT algorithms with decimation in time (frequency), respectively;

$P_{r^{2m-q} \times r^m}$ are supervectoring matrices of initial data vector X for decimation in time (frequency), respectively;

$F_{r^{2m-q}}$ is a phase shift diagonal matrix which elements and structure are defined by the level of data processing parallelism and basis where transformation is performed.

The algorithmic models proposed allow to minimize calculation redundancy and processor operating resource of discrete orthogonal transform at the expense of fast algorithms. In this case, in contrast to FFT models, data are processed in groups taken $M = r^q$ elements in each at a time that allows to use the reduced fast FFT algorithms in data processing. From the point of view of calculation organization, the approach generalizes already known algorithms. Besides, it permits a totality of new algorithms for DFT calculation to be synthesized. Adjusting parameter correspondingly, one may design DSP special processors with parallel calculation organization, efficient in performance on the basis of speed required of DFT realization internal performance and number of processor modules which are at hand a designer.

Let's consider the algorithms suggested in details.

The matrices in formula (2) for basis DEF decimation in time method are formed in the following way:

$$\mathbf{C}_{{}_r 2m-q} = \mathbf{F}_{{}_r 2m-q} \cdot \mathbf{W}^{(m)}_{{}_r 2m-q} \cdot \mathbf{D}^{(m)}_{{}_r 2m-q} \cdots$$
$$\cdot \mathbf{W}^{(m-q+1)}_{{}_r 2m-q} \cdot \mathbf{D}^{(m-q+1)}_{{}_r 2m-q} \mathbf{P}_{{}_r 2m-q \,_{x\,r} m} \cdot \mathbf{X}_{{}_r m}$$

where

$$\mathbf{P}_{{}_r 2m-q \,_{x\,r} m} = (\mathbf{I}_{{}_r m-q} \otimes \mathbf{I}_{{}_r q} \otimes \mathbf{1}_{{}_r 2m-q \times 1}) \cdot$$
$$\cdot (\mathbf{I}_{{}_r m-q} \otimes \mathbf{S}_{{}_r q});$$

$$\mathbf{F}_{{}_r 2m-q} = diag[\mathbf{I}_{{}_r m}, \mathbf{\Phi}^{(M\to)}_{{}_r m}, \mathbf{\Phi}^{(2M\to)}_{{}_r m}, \ldots,$$
$$\mathbf{\Phi}^{(\alpha M\to)}_{{}_r m}, \ldots, \mathbf{\Phi}^{((\frac{N}{M}-1)M\to)}_{{}_r m}];$$

$$\mathbf{W}^{(i)}_{{}_r 2m-q} = \mathbf{I}_{{}_r m-q} \otimes \mathbf{W}^{(i)}_{{}_r m};$$

$$\mathbf{D}^{(i)}_{{}_r 2m-q} = \mathbf{I}_{{}_r m-q} \otimes \mathbf{D}^{(i)}_{{}_r m};$$

$$\mathbf{W}^{(i)}_{{}_r m} = \mathbf{I}_{{}_r m-i} \otimes \mathbf{E}_r \otimes \mathbf{I}_{{}_r i-1}, \quad i = \overline{1, m}$$

$$\mathbf{D}^{(i)}_{{}_r m} = \mathbf{I}_{{}_r m-i} \otimes \mathbf{D}_{{}_r i}$$
$$\mathbf{D}_{{}_r i} = diag(\mathbf{D}^{(0)}_R, \mathbf{D}^{(1)}_R, \ldots, \mathbf{D}^{(r-1)}_R),$$
$$\mathbf{D}^{(k)}_R = diag(w^0, w^1, w^2, \ldots, w^{(r-1)})^{(k)},$$
$$w = \exp(-j\frac{2\pi}{r^{(i)}}), \quad R = r^{i-1},$$

$\mathbf{E}_r$ - DEF-matrix of r order;

$\mathbf{\Phi}^{(\alpha M\to)}_{{}_r m} = diag(\omega^0, \omega^{\alpha M}, \omega^{2\alpha M}, \ldots, \omega^{(N-1)\alpha M})$ is a phase coefficient matrix [7];

$\mathbf{S}_{{}_r m}$ - r -radix digit inversion monomial matrix [7].

$$\mathbf{A}_{{}_r m \times_r 2m-q} = \mathbf{1}^T_{{}_r m-q \times 1} \otimes \mathbf{I}_{{}_r m}$$

Data processing using the method considered can be carried out simultaneously over N/M channels irrespective of the data input speed to the input of the device which implements this procedure.

For the decimation in frequency method the respective vectors and matrices will be formed as follows:

$$\mathbf{C}_{r^{2m-q}} = (\mathbf{D}_{r^{2m-q}}^{(m-q+1)} \cdot \mathbf{W}_{r^{2m-q}}^{(m-q+1)} \cdot \ldots$$

$$\cdot \mathbf{D}_{r^{2m-q}}^{(m)} \mathbf{W}_{r^{2m-q}}^{(m)} \mathbf{F}_{r^{2m-q}} \mathbf{X}_{r^{2m-q}});$$

where

$$\mathbf{A}_{r^m \times r^{2m-q}} = \mathbf{I}_{r^{m-q}} \otimes \mathbf{I}_{r^q} \otimes \mathbf{1}_{r^{m-q} \times 1}^{\mathsf{T}};$$

$$\mathbf{X}_{r^{2m-q}} = \mathbf{P}_{r^{2m-q} \times r^m} \cdot \mathbf{X}_{r^m};$$

$$\mathbf{P}_{r^{2m-q} \times r^q} = \mathbf{1}_{r^{m-q} \times 1} \otimes \mathbf{I}_{r^m};$$

and matrices $\mathbf{D}_{r^{2m-q}}^{(m)}$; $\mathbf{W}_{r^{2m-q}}^{(m)}$; $\mathbf{F}_{r^{2m-q}}$ are above determined.

At maximum computation paralleling when the simultaneously processed data vector dimension is equal to N^2/M, i.e., is maximal, both methods are equivalent from the point of view of a computation delay. Such implementation requires considerable hardware expenditure of $N^2 q / r^{q+1}$ "butterfly" units and N (N/M)-input adders. A time delay for a DFT implementing is minimal $\tau = q\tau_* + \tau_+$, where τ_*, τ_+ are the duration of "butterfly" and (N/M)-input addition operations.

It is obvious that the application of maximum computation paralleling is permitted either when the total data input time to the device inputs is extremely short (compared to the processing time in each channel) or when all the data are coming simultaneously and minimum delay time of the result readiness is required. In practical work such fast acting is not, as a rule, required. In some cases it is enough to implement just parallel- serial processing. Within the methods described there exist several variants of a parallel-serial data processing. In case the designers have at their disposal no more than Nq/r "butterfly" units and only M (N/M)-input adder, it would be advisable to use the parallel-successive implementation of the second method, and the time required for data processing will be defined by the value of $\tau = (q\tau_* + \tau_+) N/M$.

In still another case, when the data are coming to the device input with some delay, it is possible to syntheses the efficient implementation of the first method which permits to rationally combine the data input and processing. In this case, due to some complication of computation process control (when additional multiplexing is introduced) both time and hardware expenditures are optimized. For this example, when there are Nq/r "butterfly" units and the N of accumulating adders, it would be more convenient to make use of the parallel-successive implementation of the first method. This time the calculation result delay will be defined as follows:

$\tau = (q\tau_* + \tau_\Sigma)$, where τ_Σ is an accumulating type summarizer processing time.

Thus, proceeding from the requirements of a particular problem to data processing time, from the peculiarities of this problem, from the number and the nomenclature of standard units the designer has at his disposal, also from weight and overall dimension restrictions, the algorithms designed enable to select one or another variant of implementing one of the above described computation paralleling methods and to find a reasonable compromise between the device fast acting required and the hardware expenditure. It is quite natural that in the article it is impossible to consider all the varieties of parallelism implementation variants within the conceptions listed above, as well as the peculiarities of hardware solutions. However, the principal aspects of computation process paralleling of DFT coefficient computing which permit evaluating the possibilities of raising the efficiency of devices for implementing the given operation have been reflected on. As for the problems of these devices practical implementation they deserve a special discussion and do not enter into the scope of the present work.

3. CONVOLUTION SUPERVECTORIZATION MODELS

Let $\mathbf{X} = [x_0, x_1, ... x_{N-1}]^T$ be a dimension $N \times 1$ vector and $\mathbf{H} = [h_0, h_1, ... h_{M-1}]^T$ be a dimension $M \times 1$ vector $M < N$;

Aperiodical convolution elements of this vectors are defined as follows:

$$y_l = \sum_{n=0}^{l} h_{l-n} \cdot x_n, \quad l = 0, ..., N + M - 2, \tag{3.1}$$

and dimension of output data vector $\mathbf{Y} = [y_0, y_1, ..., y_{N+M-2}]^T$ is equal to $(N + M - 1) \times 1$. It is admitted that $h_{l-n} = 0$ under $l - n < 0$.

Evidently the data processing in (1) may be performed in different ways. Let's consider there the models which are simple and efficient enough at the same time for supervectoring calculation of aperiodic convolution.

A generalized computational procedure describing the vectorized computational process that implements a convolution computing may be presented as follows:

$$\mathbf{Y}^{(j)} = \mathbf{A}^{(j)}_{(N+M-1)\times NM} \cdot \mathbf{H}^{(j)}_{NM} \cdot \mathbf{P}^{(j)}_{NM \times N} \cdot \mathbf{X}, \tag{3.2}$$

where

$\mathbf{P}^{(j)}_{NM \times N}$ is a initial data vector supervectorization matrix, which structure and formation methods depend on the particular model modification;

$\mathbf{H}^{(j)}_{NM}$ is a "weight factors" diagonal matrix which formed from elements of vector $\mathbf{H}$;

$\mathbf{A}^{(j)}_{(N+M-1)\times NM}$ is a summation matrix, which form, structure and its formation methods depend on the particular model modification.

$j = \overline{1,3}$ is an index of model modification.

One of the most natural models for vectoring computation these matrices are formed in the following way:

$$\mathbf{P}^{(1)}_{NM \times N} = \overset{N-1}{\underset{\alpha=0}{\oplus}} \mathbf{1}^{(\alpha)}_M; \quad \mathbf{H}^{(1)}_{NM} = \mathbf{I}_N \otimes \mathbf{H}_M,$$

where $\mathbf{H}_M = diag(h_0, h_1, \ldots, h_{M-1})$

$$\mathbf{A}^{(1)}_{(N+M-1)\times NM} = \overset{N-1}{\underset{i=0}{\blacksquare|\blacksquare}} \mathbf{A}^{(i)}_{(N+M-1)\times M},$$

where

$$\mathbf{A}^{(i)}_{(N+M-1)\times M} = \mathbf{I}^{(i\rightarrow)}_{N+M-1} \cdot \mathbf{V}_{(N+M-1)\times M},$$

$$\text{and } \mathbf{V}_{(N+M-1)\times M} = \mathbf{I}_M \frac{\blacksquare}{\blacksquare} \cdot \mathbf{0}_{(N-1)\times M}$$

If initial data vector supervectorization is carried out in another way we obtain some different element arrangement of the "weight factors" diagonal matrix and another element summation principle of the resulting vector. Thus we obtain the next model for parallel convolution calculation. According to this model the above matrices are formed as follows:

$$\mathbf{P}^{(2)}_{NM \times M} = (\overset{M-1}{\underset{m=1}{\frac{\blacksquare}{\blacksquare}}} \mathbf{V}^{(m)}_{m\times N}) \frac{\blacksquare}{\blacksquare} (\overset{N-M}{\underset{\alpha=0}{\frac{\blacksquare}{\blacksquare}}} \mathbf{W}^{(\alpha)}_{M\times N}) (\overset{M-1}{\underset{m=1}{\frac{\blacksquare}{\blacksquare}}} \mathbf{\Lambda}_{(M-m)\times N}),$$

where

$$\mathbf{V}_{m \times N}^{(m)} = \mathbf{I}_m \ \blacksquare|\blacksquare \ \mathbf{0}_{m \times (N-m)};$$

$$\mathbf{W}_{M \times N}^{(\alpha)} = \mathbf{W}_{M \times N} \cdot \mathbf{I}_N^{(\alpha \to)};$$

$$\mathbf{W}_{M \times N} = \mathbf{I}_M \ \blacksquare|\blacksquare \ \mathbf{0}_{M \times (N-M)};$$

$$\mathbf{\Lambda}_{(M-1) \times N}^{(m)} = \mathbf{0}_{(M-m) \times (N-m)} \ \blacksquare|\blacksquare \ \mathbf{I}_{M-m};$$

$$\mathbf{A}_{(N+M-1) \times NM}^{(2)} = (\bigoplus_{m=1}^{M-1} \mathbf{1}_m^{\mathrm{T}}) \oplus (\mathbf{I}_{N-M+1} \otimes \mathbf{1}_M^{\mathrm{T}})$$

$$\oplus (\bigoplus_{m=1}^{M-1} \mathbf{1}_{M-m}^{\mathrm{T}});$$

$$\mathbf{H}_{NM}^{(2)} = (\bigoplus_{m=1}^{M-1} \mathbf{D}^{(m)}) \oplus (\mathbf{I}_{N-M+1} \otimes (\bigoplus_{k=1}^{M} h_{M-k})) \oplus$$

$$\oplus (\bigoplus_{m=1}^{M-1} \mathbf{B}^{(m)}),$$

where $\mathbf{D}^{(m)} = \bigoplus_{\alpha=1}^{m} h_{m-\alpha}$, $\mathbf{B}^{(m)} = \bigoplus_{\alpha=1}^{M-m} h_{M-\alpha}$.

Finally, one can synthesize one more model defining the third method for paralleling calculations of data linear convolution. Matrices corresponding to the model take the following form:

$$\mathbf{P}_{NM \times N}^{(3)} = \mathbf{1}_M \otimes \mathbf{I}_N;$$

$$\mathbf{H}_{NM}^{(3)} = diag((\mathbf{I}_N \cdot h_0), (\mathbf{I}_N \cdot h_1), ..., (\mathbf{I}_N \cdot h_{M-1}));$$

$$\mathbf{A}_{(N+M-1) \times NM}^{(3)} = \blacksquare|\blacksquare \ \bigg|_{\alpha=0}^{M-1} \mathbf{A}_{(N+M-1) \times N}^{(\alpha)};$$

$$\mathbf{A}_{(N+M-1) \times N}^{(\alpha)} = \mathbf{I}_{N+M-1}^{(\alpha \to)} \cdot \mathbf{V}_{(N+M-1) \times N};$$

$$\mathbf{V}_{(N+M-1) \times N} = \mathbf{I}_N \ \frac{\blacksquare}{\blacksquare} \ \mathbf{0}_{(M-1) \times N}$$

All the three above models are of equal value as to hardware expenditures. They provide the minimal data delay of final result. This delay is determined by the value:

$$\tau = \tau_{mx} + \tau_{\times} + \tau_{+}^{(M)},$$

where

τ_{mx} is a data multiplexing delay;

$\tau_{\times}$ is a duration of two operands multiplication;

$\tau_{+}^{(M)}$ is a duration of M - input addition operation.

Under the total paralleling calculations such implementation requires the commutative environment which performs multiplication and simultaneously initial data supervectorization; $N \cdot M$ multipliers and $N + M - 3$ adders with different number of inputs which vary from two to M. Obviously, this implementation requires essential increase in operational resource of convolution processor. But it allows to get the most maximal speed of data processing which can't be obtained in systolic structures.

In cases, when data processing speed, provided by fully parallel implementation is not required, the above mentioned models can be effectively implemented in a parallel-sequential manner.

4. CORRELATION FUNCTION SUPERVECTORIZATION MODELS

Let $\mathbf{X} = [x_0, x_1, ... x_{N-1}]^T$ be a dimension $N \times 1$ vector and $\mathbf{H} = [h_0, h_1, ... h_{M-1}]^T$ be a dimension $M \times 1$ vector $M < N$;

A correlation function is defined as follow:

$$y_l = \sum_{m=0}^{M-1} h_{l+m} \cdot x_m; \quad l = \overline{0, N - M} \qquad (4.1)$$

The generalized computational procedure describing the vectorized computational process that implements a correlation function computing may be presented as follows:

$$\mathbf{Y} = \mathbf{A}_{(N-M+1) \times M(N-M+1)}^{(j)} \cdot \mathbf{H}_{M(N-M+1)}^{(j)} \cdot$$
$$\cdot \mathbf{P}_{M(N-M+1) \times N}^{(j)} \cdot \mathbf{X}, \qquad (4.2)$$

where

$\mathbf{H}_{M(N-M+1)}^{(j)}$ is a diagonal matrix of the $M(N-M+1)$ order formed out of elements of vector $\mathbf{H}$;

$\mathbf{A}_{(N-M+1) \times M(N-M+1)}^{(j)}$ is a summation matrix, whose dimension is defined by the lower index;

$\mathbf{P}_{M(N-M+1) \times N}^{(j)}$ - is an input data multiplexing matrix;

j - is an index of model modification.

$\mathbf{Y} = [y_0, y_1, ..., y_n]^T$ is a $(N - M + 1) \times 1$ dimension vector describing the result of the given operation implementation.

One of the most natural methods for vectoring of computation these matrices are formed in the following way:

$$\mathbf{P}_{M(N-M+1)\times N}^{(1)} = \overset{N-M}{\underset{l=0}{\blacksquare}} \mathbf{P}_{M\times N}^{(l)} \, ;$$

$$\mathbf{P}_{M\times N}^{(l)} = \mathbf{V}_{M\times N} \cdot \mathbf{I}_{N}^{(l\to)} \, ;$$

$$\mathbf{V}_{M\times N} = \mathbf{I}_{M} \,\blacksquare|\blacksquare\, \mathbf{0}_{M\times(N-M)} \, ,$$

where $\mathbf{I}$ is here and further on a unitary matrix whose order is defined by the lower index whereas the upper index (if there is one) shows the number of positions to which the columns of this matrix are to be shifted in the direction of the arrow [7].

$$\mathbf{H}_{M(N-M+1)}^{(1)} = \mathbf{I}_{N-M+1} \otimes \mathbf{H}_{M} \, ,$$

where

$$\mathbf{H}_{M} = diag(h_0, h_1, \dots, h_{M-1}) \, ;$$
$$\mathbf{A}_{(N-M+1)\times M(N-M+1)}^{(1)} = \mathbf{I}_{N-M+1} \otimes \mathbf{1}_{M\times 1}^{\mathrm{T}}$$

As seen from the figure, data processing using the method considered can be carried out simultaneously over $N-M+1$ channels, irrespective of the data input speed to the input of the device which implements this procedure.

For the second method the respective matrices will be formed as follows:

$$\mathbf{P}_{M(N-M+1)\times N}^{(2)} = \overset{M-1}{\underset{\alpha=1}{\blacksquare}} \mathbf{P}_{(N-M+1)\times N}^{(\alpha)} \, ,$$

$$\mathbf{P}_{(N-M+1)\times N}^{(\alpha)} = \mathbf{V}_{(N-M+1)\times N} \cdot \mathbf{I}_{N}^{(\alpha\to)} \, ;$$

$$\mathbf{V}_{(N-M+1)\times N} = \mathbf{I}_{N-M+1} \,\blacksquare|\blacksquare\, \mathbf{0}_{(N-M+1)\times(M-1)} \, ;$$

$$\mathbf{H}_{M(N-M+1)} = \overset{M-1}{\underset{\alpha=0}{\oplus}} \mathbf{H}_{N-M+1}^{(\alpha)} \, ;$$

$$\mathbf{H}_{N-M+1}^{(\alpha)} = \mathbf{I}_{N-M+1} \cdot h_\alpha \, ;$$

$$\mathbf{A}_{(N-M+1)\times M(N-M+1)}^{(2)} = \mathbf{1}_{M\times 1}^{\mathrm{T}} \otimes \mathbf{I}_{N-M+1}$$

This method is different from the previous one in that it supposes that there are M parallel operating channels in the device which implements the procedure, $N-M+1$ elements of the initial data vector being to be processed in each channel.

The third method of a correlation function computing paralleling presupposes data processing in N channels at a time, and the respective matrices can be formed as follows:

$$\mathbf{P}^{(3)}_{M(N+M-1)\times N} = (\bigoplus_{m=1}^{M-1} \mathbf{1}_{m\times1}) \oplus (\mathbf{I}_M \otimes \mathbf{1}_{M\times1}) \oplus$$

$$\oplus (\bigoplus_{m=1}^{M-1} \mathbf{1}_{(M-m)\times1});$$

$$\mathbf{H}^{(3)}_{M(N-M+1)} = (\bigoplus_{m=1}^{M-1} \mathbf{D}^{(m)}) \oplus (\mathbf{I}_M \otimes (\bigoplus_{k=1}^{M} h_{M-k})) \oplus (\bigoplus_{m=1}^{M-1} \mathbf{B}^{(m)}),$$

where $\mathbf{D}^{(m)} = \bigoplus\limits_{\alpha=1}^{m} h_{m-\alpha}$ and $\mathbf{B}^{(m)} = \bigoplus\limits_{\alpha=1}^{M-m} h_{M-\alpha}$ are diagonal matrices formed out of vector $\mathbf{H}$ elements;

$$\mathbf{A}^{(3)}_{(N-M+1)\times M(N-M+1)} = (\blacksquare|\blacksquare \bigvee_{m=1}^{M-1} \mathbf{V}^{(m)}_{(N-M+1)\times m})\blacksquare|\blacksquare$$

$$(\blacksquare|\blacksquare \bigvee_{l=0}^{N-M} \mathbf{W}^{(l)}_{(N-M+1)\times M})\blacksquare|\blacksquare(\blacksquare|\blacksquare \bigvee_{m=1}^{M-1} \mathbf{\Lambda}_{(N-M+1)\times(M-m)}),$$

$$\mathbf{V}^{(m)}_{(N-M+1)\times m} = \mathbf{I}_m \, \frac{\blacksquare}{\blacksquare} \, \mathbf{0}_{((N-M+1)-m)\times m};$$

$$\mathbf{W}^{(l)}_{(N-M+1)\times M} = \mathbf{I}^{(l\rightarrow)}_{N-M+1} \cdot \mathbf{W}_{(N-M+1)\times M};$$

$$\mathbf{W}_{(N-M+1)\times M} = \mathbf{I}_M \, \frac{\blacksquare}{\blacksquare} \, \mathbf{0}_{M\times(N-M)};$$

$$\mathbf{\Lambda}_{(N-M+1)\times(M-m)} = \mathbf{0}_{((N-M+1)-(M-m))\times(M-m)} \, \frac{\blacksquare}{\blacksquare}$$

$$\frac{\blacksquare}{\blacksquare} \, \mathbf{I}_{M-m};$$

At maximum computation paralleling when the simultaneously processed data vector dimension is equal to $M(N-M+1)\times1$, i.e., is maximal, all the three methods are equivalent from the point of view of computation delay. Such implementation requires considerable hardware expenditure of $M(N-M+1)$ multipliers and $N-M+1$ M-input adders. The time delay for a correlation function implementing is minimal $\tau = \tau_x + \tau_+^{(M)}$, where $\tau_x, \tau_+^{(M)}$ are the duration of multiplication and M-input addition operations. It is obvious that the application of maximum computation paralleling is permitted either when the total data input time to the device inputs is extremely short (compared to the processing time in each channel) or when all the data are coming simultaneously and minimum delay time of the result readiness is required. In practical work such fast acting is not, as a rule, required. In some cases it is enough to implement just parallel-successive processing. Within the methods described there exist several variants of parallel-successive data processing. In case the designers have at their disposal no more than M multipliers and only one M-input adder, it would be advisable to use the parallel-successive implementation of the first method, and the time required for

data processing will be defined by the value of $\tau = (\tau_x + \tau_+^{(M)}) \times (N - M + 1)$.
In another case, when there are $N - M + 1$ multipliers and the same number of accumulating adders, it would be more convenient to make use of the parallel-successive implementation of the second method. This time the calculation result delay will be defined as follows:

$$\tau = (\tau_x + \tau_+)M,$$

where τ_+ is an accumulating type summarizer processing time.

In still another case, when the data are coming to the device input with some delay, it is possible to synthesize the efficient implementation of the third method which permits to rationally combine the data input and processing. In this case due to some complication of computation process control (when additional multiplexing is introduced) both time and hardware expenditures are optimized. For instance, if the input data are coming to the input of the device which implements the operation under consideration after a $\Delta t \geq \tau_+^{(M)} + \tau_x$ time interval, it is sufficient to have no more than M multipliers and M accumulating adders whose inputs are to be multiplexed. In this case the data at the device output will appear after at $\tau_M \approx (\tau_+^{(M)} + \tau_x) \cdot M$ time interval, whereas the last result value y_{N-M+1} will appear a $\tau_N \approx (\tau_+^{(M)} + \tau_x) \cdot N$.

Thus, proceeding from the requirements of a particular problem to data processing time, from the peculiarities of this problem, from the number and the nomenclature of standard units the designer has at his disposal, also from weight and overall dimensions restrictions, the algorithmic models designed enable to select one or another variant of implementing one of the above described computation paralleling methods and to find a reasonable compromise between the device fast acting required and the hardware expenditure. It is quite natural that in the article it is impossible to consider all the varieties of parallelism implementation variants within the conceptions listed above as well as the peculiarities of hardware solutions. However, the principal aspects of computation process paralleling of DSP computation problems which permit evaluating the possibilities of raising the efficiency of devices for implementing the given operation have been reflected on. As or the problems of these devices practical implementation they deserve a special discussion and are going to be considered in the next publication.

5.   REFERENCES

[1] S.Y. Kung, H.J. Whitehouse, T. Kailath. VLSI and Modern Signal processing. Prentice-Hall, Inc., Englewood Cliffs, N.J., 1985 .

[2] L.R. Rabiner and B. Gold. Theory and application of digital signal processing. Prentice-Hall, Inc., Englewood Cliffs, N.J., 1975

[3] A. V. Openheim, R. V. Shafer. Digital signal processing. Prentice-Hall, Inc., Englewood Cliffs, N.J., 1988.

[4] S.Y. Kung. VLSI array processors. Prentice-Hall, Inc., Englewood Cliffs,N.J., 1975

[5] A. P. Tsaryov. Parallel algorithm adaptation for accelerated Fourier Discrete Transformation computation to be realized on vector computers. Proceedings of Higher Schools of the USSR, Series: Radioelectronics, 1985, №11, p. 98-100.

[6] A. P. Tsaryov. Algorithmic principles of vectorizing computations over digital date arrays. Acta ACademia, International Informatization Academi, Chişinău. Evrica, 1997, pp.67-99.

[7] E. E. Dagman and G. A. Kukharev. Fast discrete orthogonal transforms. Novosibirsk, Nauka, 1983.

Chapter 4

Computer Graphics and Pattern Recognition

Perception-Driven Global Illumination and Rendering Computation

KAROL MYSZKOWSKI
Max-Planck-Institut für Informatik 66123 Saarbrücken, Germany,
email myszkowski@mpi-sb.mpg.de

Abstract: We investigate applications of the Visible Difference Predictor (VDP) to steer global illumination computation. We use the VDP to monitor the progression of computation as a function of time for major global illumination algorithms. Based on the results obtained, we propose a novel global illumination algorithm which is a hybrid of stochastic (density estimation) and deterministic (adaptive mesh refinement) techniques used in an optimized sequence to reduce the differences between the intermediate and final images as predicted by the VDP. Also, the VDP is applied to decide upon stopping conditions for global illumination simulation, when further continuation of computation does not contribute to perceivable changes in the quality of the resulting

Key words: Human Visual System, image qualitymetrics, radiosity, density estimation, Monte Carlo methods.

1. INTRODUCTION

The basic goal of realistic rendering is to create images which are perceptually indistinguishable from real scenes. Since the fidelity and quality of the resulting images are judged by the human observer, the perceivable differences between the appearance of a virtual world (reconstructed on a computer) and its real world counterpart should be minimized. Thus, perception issues are clearly involved in realistic rendering, and should be considered at various stages of computation such as global illumination computation, rendering, and image display.

In this paper we focus on embedding the characteristics of the Human Visual System (HVS) directly into global illumination and rendering algorithms to improve their efficiency. This research direction has recently gained much attention within the computer graphics community [13, 2, 27, 32]. Since global illumination solutions are costly in terms of computation, significant efficiency improvements can be made by focusing computation on those scene features which can be readily perceived by the human observer under given viewing conditions. This means that those features that are below perceptual visibility thresholds, can be simply omitted from the computation without causing any perceivable difference in the final image appearance.

Current global illumination algorithms usually rely on energy-based metrics of solution errors which do not necessarily correspond to the visible improvements of the image quality [18]. Ideally, one may advocate the development of perceptually-based error metrics which can control the accuracy of every light interaction between surfaces. This can be done by predicting the visual impact those errors may have on the perceived fidelity of the rendered images. In practice, there is a trade-off between the robustness of such low-level error metrics and their computational costs. In Section 2 we give some examples of such low-level metrics applied in the context of hierarchical radiosity and adaptive meshing computations.

Another approach is to develop a perceptual metric which operates directly on the rendered images. If the goal of rendering is just a still frame, then the image-based error metric is adequate. In practice, instead of measuring the image quality in absolute terms, it is much easier to derive a relative metric which predicts the perceived differences between a pair of images [33]. (It is well-known that the common mean-squared error metric usually fails in such a task [7, 36, 33, 11].) A single numeric value might be adequate for some applications; however, for more specific guiding of computation, a local metric operating at the pixel level is required.In Section 3 we give a brief overview of the application of such local metrics to guide the global illumination and rendering solutions. Such metrics usually involve advanced HVS models which may incur non-negligible computation costs. An important issue becomes whether the savings in computation that are obtained through the usage of such metrics can compensate these costs.

A representative exampleof such an advanced image fidelity metric is the Visible Differences Predictor (VDP) developed by Daly [7]. The main advantage of the VDP is a prediction of local differences between images (on the pixel level). Since the VDP is a general purpose image fidelity metric, we validate its performance in these tasks. In Section 4.1 we report the results of comparisons of the VDP predictions when the model incorporates a variety of contrast definitions, spatial and orientation channel decomposition methods, and Contrast Sensitivity Functions (CSFs) derived from different psychophysical experiments. The goal of these experiments was to test the VDP integrity and sensitivity to differing models of visual mechanisms, which were derived by different authors and for different tasks than those which have been originally used by Daly. Also, we conducted psychophysical experiments with human subjects to validate the VDP performance in typical global illumination tasks (Section 4.2).

When our rigorous validation procedure of the VDP performance was successfully completed, we could then apply the metric to our actual global illumination applications. We used the VDP to monitor the progression of computation as a function of time for hierarchical radiosity and Monte Carlo solutions (Section 5.1). Based on the results obtained, we propose a novel global illumination algorithm which is a hybrid of stochastic (density estimation) and deterministic (adaptive mesh refinement) techniques used in an optimized sequence to reduce the differences between the intermediate and final images as perceived by the human observer in the course of lighting computation (Section 5.2). The VDP responses are used to support selection of the best component algorithms from a pool of global illumination solutions, and to enhance the selected algorithms for even better progressive refinement of the image quality. The VDP is used to determine the optimal sequential order of component-algorithm execution, and to choose the points at which switchover between algorithms should take place. Also, we used the VDP to decide upon stopping conditions for global illuminationsimulation, when further continuation of computation does not contribute to perceivable changes in the quality of the resulting images (Section 5.3).

2.   LOW-LEVEL PERCEPTION-BASED ERROR METRICS

One of the research directions towards perception-driven improvement of global illumination computation performance relies on direct embedding of some simple error metrics to find the adequate level of light interactions between surfaces.Gibson and Hubbold [12] proposed a perception-driven hierarchical algorithm in which a TMO and the perceptually uniform color space CIE $L*u*v$ are used to decide when to stop the hierarchy refinement. Links between patches are not further refined once the difference between successive levels of elements becomes unlikely to be detected perceptually. Gibson and Hubbold applied a similar error metric to measure the perceptual impact of the energy transfer between two interacting patches, and to decide upon the number of shadow rays that should be used in a visibility test for these patches. A similar strategy was assumed by Martin *et al.* [25], whose oracle of patch refinement operates directly in the image space and tries to improve the radiosity-based image quality for a given view. More detailed analysis of these and other similar techniques can be found in [31].

Perceptually-informed error metrics were also successfully introduced to control adaptive mesh subdivision [30, 12, 14] and mesh simplification [41] in order to minimize the number of mesh elements used to reconstruct the lighting function without introducing visible shading artifacts. The quality of lighting reconstruction is judged by the human observer, so it is not a surprise that purely energy-based criteria used in the discontinuity meshing [20, 9] and adaptive mesh subdivision [4, 39, 19] methods are far from optimal. These methods drive meshing refinement based on the measures of lighting differences between sample points, which are expressed as radiometric or photometric quantities. However, the same absolute values of such differences might have a different impact on the final image appearance, depending on the scene illumination and observation conditions (which determine the eye sensitivity). To make things even more complicated, a TMO must also be taken into account because it determines the mapping of simulated radiometric or photometric values into the corresponding values of the display device.

Myszkowski *et al.* [30] were the first to notice that mesh refinement can be driven by some metrics which measure quantitatively visual sensation such as brightness instead of commonly used radiometric or photometric quantities. Myszkowski et al. transformed the stimulus luminance values to predicted perceived brightness using Stevens' power law [37] and a decision on the edge splitting was made based on the local differences in brightness. The threshold differences of brightness, which triggered such subdivision, corresponded to the Just Noticeable Difference (JND) values that were selected experimentally and had different values depending on the local illumination level. For darker regions of the displayed image the eye is more sensitive and smaller values of the thresholds are chosen. Conversely,for bright regions that are close to the image saturation the threshold values are significantly larger. For the optimal threshold selection the global illumination should be known. However, in the radiosity technique [28] only direct illumination is known at the stage of mesh refinement, which might result in an overly conservative threshold selection.In such conditions, some lighting discontinuities predicted as perceivable could be washed out in the regions of significant indirect lighting. Obviously, this could lead to excessive mesh refinement, which is a drawback of the technique presented in [30].

Gibson and Hubbold [12] showed that the meshing performance can be improved even if some crude approximation of global illumination such as the ambient correction term [5] is used. Also, Gibson and Hubbold improved the method from [30] further by introducing color considerations into their mesh subdivision criteria.

Further improvement of meshing performance was reported in [40] by using a lighting simulation algorithm (discussed in more detail in Section 5.2) which provides local estimates of global illumination quickly. These estimates are available at the mesh refinement stage, which makes a more reliable evaluation of the contrast at lighting discontinuities possible. Thus, the prediction of discontinuity perceivability also becomes more robust and excessive mesh subdivision can be avoided. In the example given in [40], the uniform mesh built of 30,200 triangles was subdivided into 121,000, 97,000, and 86,000 elements using techniques proposed in [30], [12], and [40] respectively, without any noticeable difference in the resulting image quality. Perception-based criteria have also been used to remove superfluous mesh elements in the discontinuity meshing approach [14]. Also, a similar perception-driven mesh simplification was performed as a post-process to a density estimation solution applying a dense, uniform mesh [41].

All techniques discussed so far used perceptual error metrics on the atomic level (e.g., every light interaction between patches, every mesh element subdivision), causing a significant overhead on procedures that are repeated thousands of times in the course of the radiosity solution. This imposes severe limitations on the complexity of human spatial vision models, which in practice are restricted to models of brightness and contrast perception. Recently, more complete (and costly) vision models have been used in rendering to develop higher level perceptual error metrics which operate on the complete images. In the following section we briefly overview applications of such metrics to global illumination and rendering solutions.

3. ADVANCED PERCEPTION-BASED ERROR METRICS

Embedding advanced HVS models into global illumination and rendering algorithms is very attractive scenario, which enables computation to be perception-driven specifically for a given scene. Bolin and Meyer [2] have developed an efficient approximation of the Sarnoff Visual Discrimination Model (VDM) [22], which made it possible to use this model to guide the placement of samples in a rendered image. Because samples were only taken in areas where there were visible artifacts, some savings in rendering time compared to the traditional uniform or adaptive sampling were reported. Myszkowski [27] has shown some applications of the VDP to drive adaptive mesh subdivision taking into account visual masking of the mesh-reconstructed lighting function by textures. Ramasubramanian *et al.* [32] have developed their own image quality metric, which they applied to predict the sensitivity of the human observer to noise in the indirect lighting component. This made a more efficient distribution of indirect lighting samples possible by reducing their number for pixels with higher spatial masking (in areas of images with high frequency texture patterns, geometric details, and direct lighting variations). All computations were performed within the framework of the costly path tracing algorithm [16] and a significant speedup of computation was reported compared to the sample distribution based on purely stochastic error measures.

A practical problem arises due to the fact that the computational costs incurred by the HVS models introduce an overhead to the actual lighting computation, which may become more significant the more rapid the lighting computation becomes. The potential gains of such perception-driven computation can be easily canceled out by this overhead, depending on many factors such as scene complexity, performance of a given lighting simulation algorithm for a given type of scene, image resolution, and so on. The HVS models can be simplified to reduce the overhead, e.g., Ramasubramanian *et al.* [32] ignore spatial orientation channels in their visual masking model, but then underestimation of visible image artifacts becomes more likely. To prevent such problems and to compensate for ignored perceptual mechanisms, more conservative (sensitive) settings of the HVS models should be applied, which may also reduce gains in the lighting computation driven by such models.

It seems that keeping the HVS models at some high level of sophistication and embedding them into rendering algorithms, which are supposed to provide a meaningful response rapidly, e.g., in tens of seconds or single minutes, may be a difficult task. For example, full processing of the difference map between a pair of images at a resolution of **256 x 256** pixels using the VDP model [7] takes about 20 seconds on a R10000, 195 MHz processor and such processing should be repeated a number of times to get reasonable monitoring of progress in image quality. In this work we explore two different approaches, in which the advanced HVS models are used off-line or on-line. In the former case, the VDP is used only at the design stage of the global illumination algorithms and the tuning of their parameters. Thus, the resulting algorithms can spend 100% of their computation time in lighting simulation, and the costs of HVS processing (which is performed off-line) are of secondary importance (Section 5.2). In the latter case, the VDP processing is performed along with the time-consuming global illumination computation to decide upon its stopping condition. However, in this application the VDP computation is performed exclusively at later stages of computation, and involves only a small fraction of the overall computation costs (Section 5.3).

In the following section we briefly describe the VDP as a representative example of an advanced image fidelity metric that is strongly backed by findings in physiology and psychophysics.

4.   VISIBLE DIFFERENCES PREDICTOR

Although substantial progress in the study of physiology and psychophysics has been made in recent years, the HVS as a whole and the higher order cognitive mechanisms in particular, are not yet fully understood. Only the early stages of the visual pathway beginning with the retina and ending with the visual cortex are considered as mostly explored [8]. It is believed that the internal representation of an image by cells in the visual cortex is based on spatial frequency and orientation channels [23, 42, 44]. The channel model explains well such visual characteristics as:
- the overall behavioral Contrast Sensitivity Function (CSF) visual system sensitivity is a function of the spatial frequency and orientation content of the stimulus pattern;
- spatial masking - detectability of a particular pattern is reduced by the presence of a second pattern of similar frequency content;
- sub-threshold summation - adding two patterns of sub-threshold contrast together can improve detectability within a common channel;
- contrast adaptation - sensitivity to selected spatial frequencies is temporarily lost after observing high contrast patterns of the same frequencies; and,
- the spatial frequency after-effects - as result of the eye's adaptation to a certain grating pattern, other nearby spatial frequencies appear to be shifted.

Because of these favorable characteristics, the channel model provides the core of the most recent HVS models that attempt to describe spatial vision. Our application of the HVS model is concerned with how to predict whether a visible difference will be observed between two images.   Therefore, we were most interested in the HVS models developed for similar tasks [46, 21, 26, 7, 36, 6, 43, 10, 11, 35] which arise from studying lossy image compression, evaluating dithering algorithms, designing CRT and flat-panel displays, and generating computer graphics. Let us now describe briefly the Visible Differences Predictor (VDP) developed by Daly [7] as a representative example, which was selected by us for our experiments on global illumination algorithms.

The VDP is considered one of the leading computational models for predicting the differences between images that can be perceived by the human observer [17]. The VDP receives as input a pair of images, and as output it generates a map of probability values, which characterize perceivability of the differences. The input target and mask images undergo identical initial processing (Figure 1). At first, the original pixel intensities are converted to physical luminance values in the display device. If the exact range of luminance values is not known for a given CRT display it is usually assumed that the maximum luminance value is about 100cd/m². Weber's law-like behavior is applied to derive brightness sensation for every pixel based on the corresponding luminance values. The non-linear response of retinal neurons and their adaptation characteristics are taken into account. For the sake of simplicity it is assumed that the HVS adapts separately to each pixel. Then the resulting image is converted into the frequency domain and processing of the CSF is performed. The resulting data is decomposed into the spatial frequency and orientation channels using the Cortex transform, which is a pyramid-style, invertible, and computationally efficient image representation. After decomposing the input image into six frequency bands, each of these bands (except the lowest-frequency baseband) undergoes identical orientational selectivity processing. Then the individual channels are transformed back to the spatial domain, in which visual masking is processed.

As the result of CSF computation the contrast values in all channels are normalized by the corresponding values of detection thresholds. Due to visual masking characteristics of the HVS those threshold values can be further elevated with increases in the contrast of image (mask) pattern. For every channel and for every pixel, the elevation of the detection threshold is calculated based on the mask contrast for that channel and that pixel. It is usually assumed that the threshold elevation is computed for the mask image. Also, more conservative approach can be chosen in which mutual masking is considered by taking the minimal threshold elevation value for the corresponding channels and pixels of the two input images. The resulting threshold elevation maps are then used to normalize the contrast differences between target and mask images. The normalized differences are input to the psychometric function which estimates the probability of detecting the differences for a given channel. This estimated probability value is summed across all channels for every pixel. Finally, the probability values are used to visualize visible differences between the target and mask images. It is assumed that the difference can be perceived for a given pixel when the probability value is greater than 0.75, which is the standard threshold value for discrimination tasks [44]. When a single numeric value is needed to characterize the differences between images, the percentage of pixels with probability greater than this threshold value is reported. The former measure is suitable to estimate the differences locally, while the latter measure provides global information on the differences for the whole image.

The main advantage of the VDP is a prediction of local differences between images (on the pixel level). The Daly model also takes into account the visual characteristics that we think are extremely important in our application: a Weber's law-like amplitude compression, advanced CSF model, and visual masking function.

The original Daly model also has some disadvantages, for example, it does not process chromatic channels in input images. However, in global illumination applications many important effects such as the solution convergence or the quality of shadow reconstruction can be relatively well captured by the achromatic mechanism, which is far more sensitive than its chromatic counterparts.

The VDP seems to be one of the best existing choices for our applications involving prediction of image quality for various settings of global illumination solutions. This claim is supported by our extensive VDP integrity checking, and validation in psychophysical experiments that we briefly summarize in the following two sections. More extensive documentation of these tests is provided on the VDP project Web pages [1].

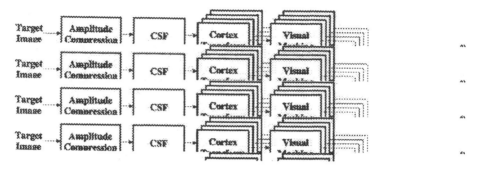

Fig. 1. Block diagram of the Visible Differences Predictor (multiple arrows indicate parallel processing of the spatial frequency and orientation channels).

4.1   VDP Integrity

The VDP model predicts many characteristics of human perception. However, the computational models of these characteristics were often derived from the results of various unrelated experiments, which were conducted using completely different tasks. As pointed out by Taylor *et al.* [35] this is a potential threat for the VDP integrity. The approach promoted in [35, 45] was to execute psychophysical experiments that directly determined the model parameters. However, such experiments usually cover significantly less visual mechanisms, for example, the model proposed by Taylor et al. does not support visual masking. In this respect, the strategy taken by Daly results in a more complete model, although, perhaps at the expense of its integrity.

We decided to examine the integrity of Daly's model to understand how critical are its major components in maintaining a reasonable output. We replaced some model components by functionally similar components, which we obtained from well-established research results published in the literature. We investigated how the VDP responses will be affected by such replacements.

We experimented with three types of CSF used in the following HVS models: [7], [26, 10], and [11]. The response of the VDP was very similar in the former two cases, while for the latter one discrepancies were more significant. A possible reason for such discrepancies is that the CSF used in [11] does not take into account luminance adaptation for our test, which could differ from the conditions under which the CSF was originally measured.

Also, we experimented with different spatial and orientation channel decomposition methods. We compared the Cortex transform [7] with 6 spatial and 6 orientation channels (a typical output of every channel for our standard test image is shown on the VDP project Web pages [1]) and the band-pass (Laplacian) pyramid proposed by Burt [3] with 6 spatial frequency channels, and extended to include 4 orientation channels. While the quantitative results are different, the distribution of probabilities of detection differences between images corresponds quite well. The quantitative differences can be reduced by an appropriate scaling of the VDP responses.

Daly's original VDP model used an average image mean to compute the global contrast for every channel of the Cortex transform. We experimented with the local contrast using a lowpass filter on the input image to provide an estimate of luminance adaptation for every pixel. This made the VDP more sensitive to differences in dark image regions, and we found that in many cases the VDP responses better matched our subjective impressions.

In experiments we performed, we found that the VDP prediction was quite robust across the tasks we examined and variations in the configuration of VDP modules. While the quantitative results we obtained were different in many cases (i.e., the probability values for perceiving a difference which are reported for every pixel), the distribution of predicted perceivable differences over the image surface usually matched quite well. A comparison of the VDP output for all experiments discussed in this section is provided on the VDP project Web pages [1].

In [27] we report representative results of more specialized VDP experiments, which were focused on prediction of the perceived shadow quality as a function of the visual masking by a texture, the CRT device observation distance, and the global illumination solution convergence. In all cases tested we obtained predictions that matched well our subjective judgments. On the VDP project Web pages [1] we provide input images along with the VDP predictions for the full set of experiments we performed. We disseminate this material on the Internet so that it can be used for testing other metrics of differences between images.

4.2 Psychophysical Validation of the VDP

Since the VDP is a general purpose predictor of the differences between images, it can be used to evaluate sets of images from a wide range of applications. In our experiments we chose to test its performance in global illumination tasks, which correspond to our intended use of the VDP. In this work we discuss one selected experiment in which we compared VDP responses with those obtained from human subjects for a series of image pairs resulting from successive refinement in a progressive hierarchical radiosity solution. We chose this experiment because it validates the VDP role in the development of our novel global illumination algorithm described in Section 5.2. The description of our other psychophysical experiments with subjects concerning visual masking of shadows by textures, and image fidelity following JPEG compression can be found in [24]. As postulated in [13] the experiments were performed in cooperation with an experimental psychologist.

In the experiment reported here, subjective judgments from 11 human observers were collected for pairs of images presented on a high-quality CRT display under controlled viewing conditions. The experimental subjects were requested to rank on a scale from 1 to 9 the perceived global difference between each of a pair of images. In every pair, the final image for the fully converged radiosity solution was presented side-by-side with an image generated at an intermediate stage of radiosity computation. In total ten intermediate images taken at different stages of computation were considered, and presented to subjects in a random order. We used the HTML forms to present stimuli, and the subjects could freely scroll the display and adjust their ranking (we include examples of our HTML forms on the VDP project Web pages [1]). The prediction of differences for the same pairs of images was computed using the VDP, and compared against the subjects' judgments. Figure 2 summarizes the results obtained. A good agreement was observed between VDP results and subjective ratings. This means that as the progressive radiosity solution converged, close agreement between the VDP predictions and the subjective judgments was maintained.

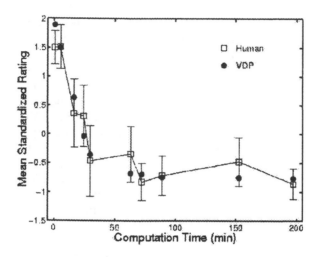

Fig. 2. The standardized mean ratings (squares) at each of 10 cumulative computation times are shown along with corresponding VDP predictions (filled circles).

The results of our psychophysical experiment suggest that the VDP can be used to estimate what might be termed "perceptual" convergence in image quality rather than "physical" convergence. Such an image quality measure can be used to compare the performance of various rendering techniques as a function of the computation time, and to decide when the computation can be finished because further improvement of the image quality cannot be perceived by the human observer [27].

Encouraged by the positive results of VDP validation in psychophysical experiments and integrity tests, we used the VDP in actual applications where the main goal was to improve the performance of global illumination computation. In the following section we discuss a number of examples of such applications.

5.   VDP APPLICATIONS IN GLOBAL ILLUMINATION COMPUTAION

A common measure of the physical convergence of a global illumination solution is the Root Mean Square (RMS) error computed for differences between pixel values of the intermediate and final images. Myszkowski [27] has shown that the RMS error is not suitable to monitor the progress of computation because it poorly predicts the differences as perceived by the human observer (a similar conclusion on this metric, although reached for different applications was reported in [7, 36, 33, 11]). In Section 4.2 a new metric of the perceptual convergence in image quality was discussed, and we used this metric to compare the performance of selected global illumination techniques (Section 5.1). As the result of such a comparison, a hybrid global illumination solution has been proposed in which the technique that performs best in terms of the perceptual convergence is selected at every stage of computation [40]. We discuss this hybrid technique in Section 5.2.

As can be seen in Figure 2 the ranking for the final stages of the radiosity solution (70 – 200 minutes) was considerably more difficult because the corresponding images were very similar. This suggests a novel application of the VDP (and other similar metrics) to decide upon the computation stopping conditions, when further computation will not result in noticeable changes in the image quality as perceived by the human observer. We discuss this topic more in detail in Section 5.3.

5.1   Evaluating Progression of Global Illumination Computation

In many practical applications it is important to obtain the intermediate images which correspond well to the final image at possibly early stages of solution. A practical problem arises how to measure the solution progression, which could lead to the selection of an optimal global illumination technique for a given task. Clearly, since the human observer ultimately judges the image quality, basic characteristics of the HVS must be involved in such a measure of the solution progression. We used the VDP to provide the quantitative measures of the perceptual convergence by predicting the perceivable differences between the intermediate and final images [27].

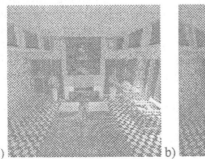

Fig. 3. Test scene POINT:
a) full global illumination solution,
b) indirect lighting only.

We investigated the perceptual convergence of the following view-independent algorithms:
–   Deterministic Direct Lighting (DDL) computation with perceptually-based adaptive mesh subdivision [29].

- Shooting iteration Hierarchical (link-less and cluster-based) Radiosity (SHR) [29] for indirect lighting computation. By default, a pre-calculated fixed mesh is used to store the resulting lighting.
- Density Estimation Photon Tracing (DEPT) from light sources with photons bucketed into a non-adaptive mesh [40]. By Direct DEPT (DDEPT) we denote buckets with photons coming directly from light sources, and by Indirect DEPT (IDEPT) we denote a different set of buckets with photons coming via at least one reflection.

The DDL and SHR techniques are deterministic, while the DEPT algorithm is stochastic. Obviously direct (DDL and DDEPT) and indirect (SHR and IDEPT) lighting computation techniques are complementary, but in practice the following combinations of these basic algorithms are used: DDL+SHR, DDL+IDEPT, and DDEPT+IDEPT (DEPT for short).

We measured the performance of these basic techniques in terms of perceived differences between the intermediate and final images using the VDP responses. The VDP response provides the probability of difference detection between a pair of images, which is estimated for every pixel [7]. We measured the difference between images as the percentage of pixels for which the probability of difference detection is over 0.75, which is the standard threshold value for discrimination tasks [44]. In all tests performed, we used images of resolution 512×512. The diagonal of the images displayed on our CRT device was 0.2 meters, and we assumed that images were observed from the distance of 0.5 meters.

We assumed that the final images used for the VDP computation are based on the DDL+SHR and DDL+IDEPT global illumination solutions, which converge within some negligible error tolerance. The final images obtained using these methods are usually only slightly different. Minor discrepancies can be explained by various approximations assumed by each of these completely different algorithms, e.g., different handling of the visibility problem, the lighting function discretization during computation used by the SHR technique. To eliminate the influence of these differences on the VDP response, for a given method we considered the final image generated using this particular method. The only exception is the DDEPT+IDEPT method, for which we use the final image generated using the DDL+IDEPT technique because it provides more accurate direct lighting reconstruction for a given mesh/bucket density.

In this work we report results obtained for a scene, which we will refer to as the POINT (in [40] we consider three different scenes of various complexity of geometry and lighting). Both direct and indirect lighting play a significant role in the illumination of the {\sc point} scene. The scene is built of about 5,000 polygons, and the original scene geometry was tessellated into 30, 200 mesh elements using the DDL technique.

The graphs in Figure 4 show that the perceptual convergence of the indirect lighting solution for the SHR technique is slower than the IDEPT approach (direct lighting is computed using the same DDL method). In our experience, the difference in performance between the IDEPT over SHR methods is far more significant for complex scenes. The SHR technique shows better performance for simple scenes only. Based on these results, we use the DDL+SHR technique for scenes built of fewer than 500 polygons. For scenes of more practical complexity, we consider the

DDL, DDEPT and IDEPT techniques to optimize the progressive refinement of image quality.

The graphs in Figure 4 show that at the initial stages of computation the DEPT technique provides the best performance, and rapidly gives meaningful feedback to the user. At later stages, the DDL+IDEPT hybrid shows faster perceptual convergence to the final image. In both cases, we used the same fixed mesh to bucket photons. Due to the basic mesh-element granularity, many subtle details of direct lighting distribution could not be captured well using the DDEPT technique. For example, small and/or narrow lighting patterns may be completely washed out. Also, when shadows are somehow reconstructed, they can be distorted and shifted with respect to their original appearance, and their boundaries can be excessively smooth. The problem of excessive discretization error, which is inherent in our DDEPT method, is reduced by the adaptive mesh subdivision used by the DDL technique.

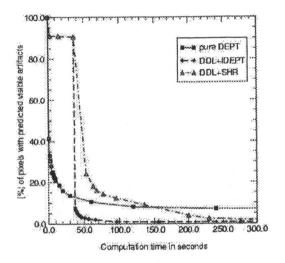

Fig. 4. Plots of the VDP results (predicted global differences between the intermediate and final images) measuring the performance of the DEPT, DDL+IDEPT, and DDL+SHR algorithms for the POINT scene.

The graphs in Figure 4 show that the algorithms examined have different performance at different stages of computation. This makes possible the development of a hybrid (composite) algorithm which uses the best candidate algorithm at a given stage of computation. This idea is further investigated in the following section.

5.2 Optimizing Progression of Global Illumination Computation

Based on the results of experiments measuring the perceptual convergence which were presented in the previous section for the POINT scene, and similar results obtained for different scenes we investigated (e.g., refer to [40]), a new hybrid technique that uses DDEPT, IDEPT and DDL can be proposed:

1. First, stochastic computations of direct and indirect lighting should be performed.
2. Second, the stochastically computed direct component should be gradually replaced by its deterministically computed counterpart to reconstruct the fine details of the lighting function.
3. Finally, stochastic indirect computation should be continued until some stopping criterion is reached, e.g., a criterion that is energy-based in terms of the solution variance (some engineering applications may require precise illumination values), or perception-based in terms of perceivable differences between the intermediate and final images [27].

All algorithms discussed use mesh vertices to store the results of direct and indirect lighting computations separately, so switching between them can easily be performed. The mesh is adaptively refined to fit the lighting distribution better in the case of the DDL technique only, but then indirect lighting computed using the IDEPT can be interpolated at the new vertices.

While the obtained ordering of the basic algorithms was the same across all tested scenes (refer also to [40]), the optimal selection of switchover points between the sequentially executed algorithms depended on the given scene characteristics. Ideally, the switchover points should be selected automatically based on the performance of component algorithms for a given scene, which could be measured by the on-line VDP computation. However, performing the VDP computation at the runtime of the composite algorithm computation is not acceptable because of the high costs of the VDP processing [27].

To overcome this problem we decided to elaborate a robust heuristic of the switchover points selection which provides good progression of the image quality for a wide range of indoor scenes. For this purpose, we designed another experiment involving the VDP off-line, and our experimental setting is shown in Figure 5. Within this framework we applied the VDP to get quantitative measures of the image quality progression as a function of time points T_i at which switching between our basic algorithms DEPT (DDEPT+IDEPT), DDL, and IDEPT was performed.

The results of our experiments for the POINT test scene are summarized in Figure 6a. The thick line between two switchover points T_1 and T_2 depicts possible performance gains if DEPT is replaced by DDL at T_1, and then DDL is replaced by IDEPT at T_2. Also, we tried a different switching strategy, in which after switching from DEPT to DDL at T_1, we performed switching back and forth between the DDL and IDEPT algorithms. We refer to this strategy as $T_1, ..., T_N$, where N stands for the number of switchover points. We investigated various choices of T_i ($i > 1$), which controlled switching between the DDL and IDEPT algorithms. For example, we performed the switching after completion of every single iteration of the DDL computation, or every two such iterations and so on. Also, we changed T_1, which effectively controls the initial DEPT computation time. The thin line in Figure 6a shows an envelope of all graphs depicting our composite algorithm performance for all combinations of switchover points investigated by us. This envelope approximates the best expected performance of our composite technique assuming an "optimal" switching strategy between the DDL and IDEPT algorithms with multiple switchover points T_1, ..., T_N. As can be seen, gains in performance achieved using the T_1, ..., T_N strategy were negligible compared to the strategy based on well-chosen switchover points T_1 and T_2. This observation was confirmed for other tests we performed [40].

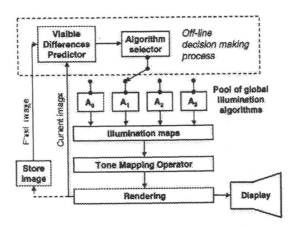

Fig. 5. Experimental setting for evaluation of the image quality progression and selection of the switchover points between global illumination algorithms (the human-assisted selection is based on minimizing the perceptual distance between the intermediate and final images).

For the sake of simplicity of our composite algorithm, we decided to use just two switchover points T_1 and T_2. We investigated various choices of T_1, which measures the duration of the initial DEPT computation. We assumed that T_2 is decided automatically when the DDL computation is completed. The composite algorithm performance for various T_1 is shown in Figure 6b. As can be seen our composite algorithm performs much better than the standalone DDL+IDEPT or DEPT methods for all choices of T_1 which are considered in Figure 6b. In [40] we show that the choice of T_1 is not extremely critical in terms of the image quality progressive refinement. However, a too short T_1 may result in a poor quality of indirect lighting, which cannot be improved during the DDL computation. On the other hand, a too long T_1 may result in an undesirable delay in reconstruction of shadows and other shading details. Because of this, the upper bound for T_1 should be comparable to the computation time of the first iteration T_{i0} in the DDL processing, after which the first rendering of a complete direct lighting distribution becomes possible. We can estimate T_{i0} well by measuring the timings of pilot photons tracing and by knowing the number of initial mesh vertices, the number of light sources, and estimating the average number of shadow feelers (i.e., rays traced to obtain visibility information) for area and linear light sources.

Our heuristic for the T_1 selection proceeds as follows. At first, we run the DEPT computation for time $T_\alpha = \alpha \, T_{i0}$ (where $\alpha=0.1$, and $T_\alpha \geq 0.5$ seconds, since in our implementation we assumed that 0.5 seconds is the minimal interval for sampling DEPT solution errors). We then estimate the *RMS* error $\square$ of the indirect lighting simulation. Based on the results of DEPT computation for multiple scenes, we assume that a reasonable approximation of indirect lighting can usually be obtained for the **RMS** error threshold value $E_{thr} \approx 15\%$. Taking into account the basic properties of stochastic solution convergence [34], we estimate the required computation time T_{thr} to reach the accuracy level E_{thr} as

$$T_{thr} = T_a \frac{\tilde{E}^2}{E_{thr}^2}$$

and finally, we set T_1 as $T_1 = \min(T_{thr}, T_{i0})$.

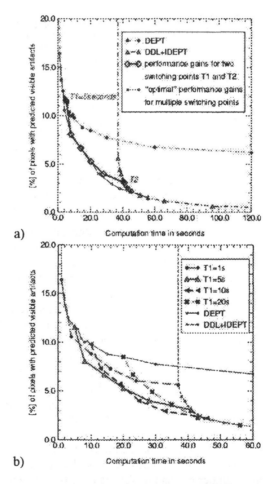

a)

b)

Fig. 6. Plots of the VDP results (magnified from Figure 4) measuring the performance of DEPT and DDL+DEPT algorithms for the POINT test. a) The thick line between two switchover points T_1 and T_2 depicts possible performance gains if the DEPT is replaced by the DDL at T_1, and then the IDEPT is activated at T_2. The thin line depicts an "optimal" switching strategy between the DDL and IDEPT algorithms with multiple switchover points $T_1, ..., T_N$. b) Performance gains for various choices of switching time T_1

For simplicity, our heuristic relies on the energy-based criterion of indirect lighting accuracy. Obviously, in the perceptual sense this criterion does not guarantee the optimal T_1 switchover point selection. However, we found that this heuristic provided stable progressive refinement of rendered image quality for all tests performed with multiple scenes. The robust behavior of our heuristic can be explained by the relative insensivity of our composite algorithm to the selection of T_1 [40], and the strong lowpass filtering properties of our lighting reconstruction method at the initial stages of computation.

Figure 7 shows an example of fastperceptual convergence of the intermediate solutions in terms of the perceived quality of the corresponding images. The THEATER scene is built of 17,300 polygons (tessellated into 22,300 mesh elements) and is illuminated by 581 light sources. Figure 7a depicts filtered illumination maps obtained after 30 seconds of the DEPT computation. Figure 7a closely resembles the corresponding image in Figure 7b, which represents the final antialiased image rendered using ray tracing (the computation took 234 minutes). In the ray tracing computation, direct lighting was recomputed for every image sample. This solution is typical for multipass approaches, e.g., [15]. The indirect lighting was interpolated based on the results of the IDEPT computation, which are stored at mesh vertices. Since all surfaces of the scene in Figure 7 exhibit the Lambertian properties of light reflection, the illumination maps (Figure 7a) are of similar quality to that obtained using the ray tracing computation (Figure 7b). Obviously, once calculated, illumination maps make possible walkthroughs of adequate image quality almost immediately, while the ray tracing approach requires many hours of computation if the viewing parameters are changed. This example shows the advantages of high quality view-independent solutions for rendering environments with prevailing Lambertian properties.

It was impractical to use the VDP on-line (because of its computational costs) in algorithms that produce some intermediate results (images) rapidly, which was the case of our composite global illumination solution. However, for applications which require substantial computation time, embedding advanced HVS models might be profitable. In the following section we discuss an example of using the VDP on-line to decide upon the stopping conditions for global illumination computation which often requires many hours to be completed.

5.3 Stopping Conditions for Global Illumination Computation

Global illumination computation may be performed just to generate realistic images, or for some more demanding engineering applications. In both cases, quite different criteria to stop computation proved to be useful [27]. In the former case, computation should be stopped immediately when the image quality becomes indistinguishable from that of the fully converged solution for the human observer. A practical problem here is that the final solution is not known, because it is actually the goal of the computation. In the latter case, stopping conditions usually involve estimates of the simulation error in terms of energy, which is provided by the lighting simulation algorithm, and compared against a threshold value imposed by the user. For some algorithms such as radiosity it might be difficult to obtain a reliable estimate of simulation accuracy, while it is a relatively easy task for Monte Carlo techniques [38, 41].

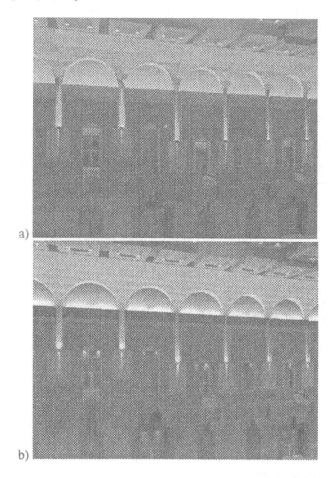

Fig. 7. Comparison of various renderings for the THEATER scene:
a) photon tracing with filtering (30 seconds) and
b) ray traced image (234 minutes).

A common practice is to use energy-based error metrics to stop computation in realistic rendering applications. In our observation, such error metrics are usually too conservative, and lead to excessive computation times. For example, significant differences of radiance between the intermediate and final stages of solution which may appear in some scene regions, can lead to negligible differences in the resulting images due to the compressive power of the TMO used to convert radiance to displayable RGB. Occasionally, energy-based metrics prove to be unreliable and visible image artifacts may appear even though the error threshold value is set very low. Since the error is measured globally, it may achieve a low value for the whole scene but locally it can be still very high.

Clearly, some perception-informed metrics, which capture well local errors are needed to stop global illumination computation without affecting the final image quality. We decided to use the VDP for this purpose, encouraged by positive results of psychophysical experiments in similar tasks [27]. We assume that computation can be stopped if the VDP does not report significant differences between intermediate images. A practical problem is to select an appropriate intermediate image which should be compared against the current image to get robust stopping conditions.

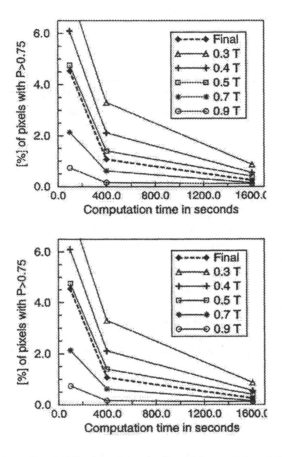

Fig. 8. The VDP predicted differences between $\Im_C$ and $\Im_T$, and $\Im_T$ and $\Im_{\alpha T}$ images.

We attempt to find a heuristic solution for this problem through experiments with the DDL+IDEPT technique which we described in Section 5.1. In this work we discuss the results obtained for the POINT test scene shown in Figure 3. However, we achieved similar results for other scenes we tested.

Let us assume that the current image $\Im_T$ is obtained after the computation time T, and let us denote by $VDP(\Im_T, \Im_{\alpha T})$ the VDP response for a pair of images $\Im_T$ and $\Im_{\alpha T}$ where $0 < \alpha < 1$. We should find an α to get a reasonable match between $VDP(\Im_T, \Im_{\alpha T})$ and $VDP(\Im_C, \Im_T)$, where $\Im_C$ is an image for the fully converged solution. Figure 3 shows the numerical values of $VDP(\Im_C, \Im_T)$ and $VDP(\Im_T, \Im_{\alpha T})$ for $T=\{100,400,1600\}$ seconds and various α, for scene shown in Figure 3. While the numerical values of $VDP(\mathfrak{I}_T, \mathfrak{I}_{0.5T})$ provide the upper bound for $VDP(\mathfrak{I}_C, \mathfrak{I}_T)$ over all investigated T, it is even more important that the image regions with the perceivable differences are similar in both cases (refer to the VDP project Web pages [1] for color images with $VDP(\mathfrak{I}_C, \mathfrak{I}_T)$ and $VDP(\mathfrak{I}_T, \mathfrak{I}_{0.5T})$). This means that for certain regions of $\mathfrak{I}_{0.5T}$ and $\mathfrak{I}_T$ the variance of the luminance estimate is very small (below the perceived level), and it is likely that it will be so for $\mathfrak{I}_C$. For other regions such variance is high, and it is likely that luminance estimates for $\mathfrak{I}_{0.5T}$ and $\mathfrak{I}_T$ which fluctuate around the converged values for $\mathfrak{I}_C$ will be different, and can be captured by the VDP. Thus, the choice of α is a trade-off. The α should be small enough to capture such perceivable fluctuations. However, it should not be too small because $\mathfrak{I}_{\alpha T}$ may exhibit high variance in the regions in which the solution for $\mathfrak{I}_T$ converged to that of $\mathfrak{I}_C$ with luminance differences below the noticeable level. In our experiments with stopping conditions for the DEPT technique for various scenes we found that $\alpha=0.5$ (50% of photons are the same for $\mathfrak{I}_T$ and $\mathfrak{I}_{0.5T}$) is such a reasonable trade-off.

6.   CONCLUSIONS

In this paper, we have proposed a novel composite global illumination technique which was designed specifically for reducing the perceptual distance between the intermediate and final images as a function of the computation time. The technique exploits the particular strengths of different lighting simulation algorithms in terms of the progressive refinement of image quality as perceived by the human observer. To select the most effective component algorithm at every stage of computations, and to decide upon the switch-over points between the component algorithms, important characteristics of the HVS captured in the VDP were taken into account. The resulting mixture of sequentially executed algorithms provides intermediate images of high quality rapidly, usually within minutes or even seconds, for complex scenes.

7.   REFERENCES

[1] http://www.mpi-sb.mpg.de/vdp - the Web page with documentation of the VDP validation experiments.
[2] M.R. Bolin and G.W. Meyer. A Perceptually Based Adaptive Sampling Algorithm. In Proc.of Siggraph'98, 299--310, 1998
[3] P.K. Burt. Fast filter transforms for image processing. Computer Vision, Graphics and Image Processing, 21:368-382, 1981.
[4] M.F, Cohen, D.P. Greenberg, D.S. Immel, and P.J. Brock. An efficient radiosity approach for realistic image synthesis. IEEE Computer Graphics and Applications, 6(3):26-35, March 1986.
[5] M.F. Cohen, S.E. Chen, J.R. Wallace, and D.P. Greenberg. A progressive refinement approach to fast radiosity image generation. In Proc. of Siggraph'88, pages 75-84, 1988.

[6] S. Comes, O. Bruyndonckx, and B. Macq. Image quality criterion based on the cancellation of the masked noise. In Proc. of IEEE Int'l Conference on Acoustics, Speech and Signal Processing, pages 2635-2638, 1995.

[7] S. Daly. The Visible Differences Predictor: An algorithm for the assessment of image fidelity. In A.B. Watson, editor, Digital Image and Human Vision, pages 179-206. Cambridge, Ma: MIT Press, 1993.

[8] R.L. De Valois and De Valois K.K. Spatial vision. Oxforf University Press, Oxford, 1990.

[9] G. Drettakis and F.X. Sillion. Accurate visibility and meshing calculations for hierarchical radiosity. In X. Pueyo and P. Schroder, editors, Rendering Techniques '96, pages 269-278. Springer, June 1996.

[10] J.A. Ferwerda, S. Pattanaik, P. Shirley, and D.P. Greenberg. A model of visual masking for computer graphics. In Proc. of Siggraph'97, pages 143-152, 1997.

[11] A. Gaddipatti, R. Machiraju, and R. Yagel. Steering image generation with wavelet based perceptual metric. Computer Graphics Forum (Eurographics '97), 16(3):241-251, September 1997.

[12] S. Gibson and R.J. Hubbold. Perceptuallydriven radiosity. Computer Graphics Forum, 16(2):129-141, 1997.

[13] D.P. Greenberg, K.E. Torrance, P. Shirley, J. Arvo, K.A. Ferwerda, S.N. Pattanaik, E.P.F. Lafortune, B. Walter, S.C. Foo, and B. Trumbore. A framework for realistic image synthesis. In Proc. of Siggraph'97, pages 477-494, 1997.

[14] D. Hedley and A. Worrall and D. Paddon. Selective Culling of Discontinuity Lines. In Dorsey, J. and Slusallek P., editors, Rendering Techniques '97, pages 69-80. Springer, 1997.

[15] H. W. Jensen. Global Illumination Using Photon Maps. In X. Pueyo and P. Schroder, editors, Rendering Techniques '96, pages 21-30. Springer, 1996.

[16] J.T. Kajiya. The rendering equation. In Proc. of Siggraph'86, pages 143-150, 1986.

[17] B. Li, G.W. Meyer, and R.V. Klassen. A comparison of two images quality models. In Human Vision and Electronic Imageing III, pages 98-109. SPIE Vol. 3299, 1998.

[18] D. Lischinski, B. Smits, and D.P. Greenberg. Bounds and error estimates for radiosity. In Proc. of Siggraph '94, pages 67-74, 1994.

[19] D. Lischinski, F. Tampieri, and D.P. Greenberg. Discontinuity meshing for accurate radiosity. IEEE Computer Graphics and Applications, 12(6):25-39, November 1992.

[20] D. Lischiski, F. Tampieri, and D.P. Greenberg. Combinin hierachical radiosity and discontinuity meshing. In Proc. of Siggraph'93, pages 199-208, 1993.

[21] C. Lloyd and R.J. Beaton. Design of spatialchromatic human vision model for evaluating full.color display systems. In Human Vision and Electronic Imaging: Models, Methodes, and Appl., pages 23-37. SPIE Vol. 1249, 1990.

[22] J. Lubin. A visual discrimination model for imaging system design and development. In Peli. E., editor, Vision models for target detection and recognition, pages 245-283. World Scientific, 1995.

[23] S. Marcelja. Mathematical desscription of the responses of simple cortical cells. Journal of the Optical Society of America, 70:1297-1300, 1980.

[24] W.L. Martens and K. Myszkowski. Psychophysical validation of the Visible Differences Predictor for global illumination applications. In IEEE Visualization '98 (Late Breaking Hot Topics), pages 49-52, 1998.

[25] I. Martin, X. Pueyo, and D. Tost. An imagespace refinement criterion for linear hierarchical radiosity. In Graphics Interface '97, pages 26-36, 1997.

[26] R.A. Martin, A.J. Ahumada, and J.O. Larimer. Color matrix display sim,ulation based upon luminace and chrominace contrast sensitivity of early vision. In Human Vision, Visual Processing, and Digital Display III, pages 336-342. SPIE Vol. 1666, 1992.

[27] K. Myszkowski. The Visible Differences Predictor: Applications to global illumination problems. In G. Drettakis and N. Max, editors, Rendering Techniques '98, pages 223-236. Springer, 1998.

[28] K. Myszkowski and T.L. Kunii. An efficient cluster-based hierarchical progressive radiosity algorithm. In ICSC '95, volume 1024 of Lecture Notes in Computer Science, pages 292-303. Springer-Verlag, 1995.

[29] K. Myszkowski anf T.L. Kunii. A case study towards validation of global illumination algorithms: progressive hierarchical radiosity with clustering. The Visual Computer, 16(5):271-288, 2000.

[30] K. Myszkowski, A. Wojdala, and K. Wicynski. Non-uniform adaptive meshing for global illumination. Machine Graphics and Vision, 3(4):601-610, 1994.

[31] J. Prikryl and W. Purgathofer. State of the art in perceptually driven radiosity. In State of the Art Reports. Eurographics, 1998.

[32] M. Ramasubramanian, S.N. Pattanaik, and D.P. Greenberg. A perceptually based physical error metric for realistic image synthesis. In Proc. of Siggraph '99, pages 73-82, 1999.

[33] H. Rushmeier, G. Ward, C. Piatko, P. Sanders, and B. Rust. Comparing real and synthetic images: some ideas about metrics. In P. Hanrahan W. Purgathofer, editors, Rendering Techninques ,95, pages 82-91. Springer, 1995.

[34] F.X. Sillion and C. Puech. Radiosity and Global Illumination. Morgan Kaufmann, San Francisco, 1994.

[35] C.C. Taylor, Y. Pizlo, J.P. Allebach, and C.A. Bouman. Image quality assessment with a Gabor pyramid model of the Human Visual System. In Human Vision and Electronic Imaging, pages 58-69. SPIE Vol. 3016, 1997.

[36] P.C. Teo and D:J: Heeger. Perceptual iamge distortion. Pages 127-141. SPIE Vol. 2179, 1994.

[37] J. Tumblin and H.E. Rushmeier. Tone reproduction for realistic images. IEEE Computer Graphics and Applications, 13(6):42-48, November 1993.

[38] E. Veach. Robust Monte Carlo methods for lighting simulation. Ph.D. thesis, Stanford University, 1997.

[39] C. Vedel and C. Puech. A testbed for adaptive subdividion in progressive radiosity. In P. Brunet and F.W. Jansen, editors, Photorealistic Rendering in Computer Graphics, 1991.

[40] V.Volevich, K. Myszkowski, A. Khodulev, and Kopylov E.A. Using the Visible Differences Predictor to improve performance of Progressive global illumination computations. ACM Transactions on Graphics, 19(2):122-161, 2000.

[41] B.J. Walter, P.M. Hubbard, P. Shirley, and D.P. Greenberg. Global illumination using local linear density estimation. ACM Transactions on Graphics, 16(3):217-259, 1997.

[42] A.B. Watson. The Cortex transform: rapid computation of simulated neural images. Comp. Vision Graphics ans Image Processing, 39:311-327, 1987.

[43] S.J.P. Westen, R.L. Lagensijk, and J.Biemond. Perceptual image quality based on a multiple channel HVS model. In Proc. of IEEE Int'l Conference on Acoustics, Speech and Signal Processing, pages 2351-2354, 1995.

[44] H.R. Wilson. Psychophysical models of spatial vision and hyperacuity. In D. Regan, editor, Spatial vision, Vol. 10, Vision and Visual Disfunction, pages 179-206. Cambridge, MA: MIT Press, 1991.

[45] H.R. Wilson and D.J. Gelb. Modified lineelemnt theory for spatial-frequency and width discrimination. Journal of the Optical Society od America, 1(1):124-131, 1984.

[46] C. Zetzsche and Hauske G. Multiple channel model for the prediction od subjective image quality. In Human Vision, Visual Processing, and Digital Display, pages 209-216. SPIE Vol. 1077, 1989.

Real-Time Shadow Casting in Virtual Studio

ANDRZEJ WOJDAŁA, MAREK GRUSZEWSKI, RYSZARD OLECH
Accom Poland, Szczecin, Poland

Abstract: Combining real and computer-generated imagery, Virtual Studio imposes the requirement for these two worlds to interact properly in the composite image. In particular, it is expected that shadows will be correctly cast between the virtual and real environments. This paper describes real-time algorithms, that allow actors and real objects to cast shadows on virtual elements of the scene and vice versa.

1.   INTRODUCTION

Virtual Studio is a technology, which allows to combine real-time computer graphics with the video produced by the TV camera. The idea is based on the blue-box technique, in which actors are filmed in front of the uniformly blue screen. The camera signal (foreground) is mixed using the chroma key with another video signal (background), generated by the graphic computer in the correct perspective, calculated based on the information delivered by the camera tracking system [Wojdała, 1996]. The challenge of the Virtual Studio technology is to generate the background that looks and behaves realistically enough to create a convincing illusion that actors and real objects are immersed in a computer-generated scene [Wojdała, 1998]. One of the key elements to achieve that goal is proper shadowing.

Shadows were always recognized as an important element responsible for proper understanding of computer-generated images. Generation of shadows is an integral part of realistic image synthesis methods, but it was always more difficult in real-time rendering algorithms. Application in Virtual Studio makes it even more difficult, because it imposes the requirement of sustained display rate equal to the video frame rate (50Hz in PAL, 59.94Hz in NTSC).

Shadows are equally important in the blue screen technique, and particularly in the Virtual Studio. Without them, actors and props would appear to levitate over the virtual floor, with no apparent way to tell where they are located in respect to the computer-generated scenery.

This paper is an attempt to bring computer graphics and chroma key worlds together on the issue of shadowing. In Virtual Studio, four types of the shadow interaction can be distinguished:

- virtual-to-virtual (casting shadows of virtual elements on virtual elements),
- real-to-real
- real-to-virtual
- virtual-to-real

Shadow-related issues in the graphics and blue screen are not new; Virtual Studio simply imposes more demand on the performance and the quality of existing techniques. Therefore, it is necessary to review them from these points of view. But the biggest challenge is to address the problem created by and specific to Virtual Studio: casting shadows of real elements on virtual ones and vice versa. In the next sections, we propose algorithms that allow to do that; we will also try to answer the question, how all shadowing interactions work together.

2.   VIRTUAL–TO-VIRTUAL SHADOW CASTING

Virtual-to-virtual shadow casting is purely computer graphics related issue. To allow dynamic lighting and animated objects, it is necessary to employ hardware-assisted shadowing techniques [Blythe et al., 1999]. Also, commercially available graphics hardware used by all existing Virtual Studio systems must be able to run these algorithms, which can be categorized into several methods.

In *Shadow textures* algorithm, for each partially shadowed polygon of the scene textures representing its lighting are created [Heckbert et al., 1996]. Graphics hardware is used to determine visibility and calculate shading. The method is primarily designed to generate soft shadows by sampling area light sources and averaging the results. When limited to hard shadows, the performance increases, but in dynamic environments still remains interactive rather than real-time in the sense of Virtual Studio.

Shadow volume algorithms construct pyramidal objects from rays cast from the light source through vertices of shadowing object and continued further into the scene [Crow, 1977] [Bergeron, 1986] [Heidmann, 1991] [Kilgard, 1997]. The scene is displayed twice, with shadow volumes drawn between the passes in order to set the stencil buffer, which is used to mark these parts of scene objects that remain in the shadow and should not be re-drawn in the second pass. The method can be extended to multiple light sources, requiring one additional scene and shadow volumes drawing pass per light. The advantage is that there is no requirement for the shadowed objects to be planar, as in some other methods described below. The drawback is that for complex shadowing objects it can be very difficult to compute shadow volume. Also, the cost of the method is quite significant, which makes it less practical for Virtual Studio.

Shadow z-buffer algorithms [Williams, 1978] [Reeves et al., 1987] consist of two stages. In the first stage, the light source is used as a view point. The stored depth (the distances of objects from the light source) is used in the second stage to determine, whether drawn pixels are in the shadow. Without any additional hardware support, the transformation and comparison of depth values make this algorithm non-real time. Segal [Segal et. al., 1992] proposed an algorithm, that uses texture mapping hardware for all transformations and comparisons. Also needed is an OpenGL hardware extension, SGIX_shadow, currently available only on the SGI's high-end graphics InfiniteReality. The biggest advantage of this method is that both shadowing and shadowed objects can be of any complexity and shape. The disadvantage is that aliasing effects become the problem. However, the biggest issue is performance. Shadowing from a single light source requires three display passes plus reading the frame buffer and writing it to the texture memory. The situation is even worse with multiple light sources, which require additional passes. Since the only way to maintain real time is to reduce the scene complexity accordingly, in many cases this method is simply impractical for Virtual Studio.

In *projection shadow* algorithms (called also *fake shadows*), after drawing the scene shadow-casting objects are drawn once again with a perspective projection matrix calculated based on parameters of the light source and the plane on which the shadow is to be projected [Blinn, 1988] [Tessman, 1989]. The primary drawback of this method is that it is designed for flat surfaces. Casting shadows on multi-faceted surfaces requires additional operations, primarily clipping, and significantly affects the performance because of multiple drawing. Only shadows on the floor or such simple cases as room's corners can be handled easily and efficiently. On the other hand, such limitations in the Virtual Studio are frequently acceptable. Projection shadows can be extended to multiple light sources, although in such case it is difficult to control the color of umbrae.

Similar approach, frequently used in Virtual Studio and computer games is to create flat *shadow objects* (usually textured with pre-computed black and white texture with alpha channel), associated with the shadow casters in such a way, that their size, position and shear depends on the location of the light source and the location and size of the object casting shadow. The advantage is that shadow objects potentially consist of less polygons than projected shadows. The shadow of the globe visible on the photo 1 was created and animated as one rectangle textured with the image obtained earlier by viewing the globe from the top. The performance cost of the shadow created this way was negligible. It is also easier to extend this method to multiple light sources. The drawback of the method is that it has even more limitations, especially on the shape of shadowing objects.

It is possible to modify the above method in such a way, that no shadow objects are actually drawn. Instead, only the mapping of the pre-computed texture on shadowed objects is changed according to the parameters of the light source and the shadow caster. This solution is better, because it gives more flexibility when shadowed objects are non-planar. To be useful however, it requires the hardware to be capable of double texturing. Ironically, no graphics workstation powerful enough to run Virtual Studio can do that – at present, only some of PC graphics boards designed for games support such feature.

A simple and efficient way of creating and using shadow textures was described in [Tchou, 1999] as *Texture projection* method. Objects textured with shadow texture are drawn one by one, in the order of the distance from the light source. After each object, the shadow texture is updated by drawing this object in black color from the light source point of view. The performance of the algorithm is quite good, because each polygon is drawn exactly twice. It could be further increased by applying culling. The problem is that to be practical, this method requires double textures, because in virtual sets most objects are usually already textured.

Summarizing, it must be said that in practical cases only *projection shadow* and *shadow object* methods, being the most efficient, can be used in Virtual Studio. Otherwise, multiple display passes would degrade the performance and the scene complexity would have to be reduced several times to maintain the real-time requirement. The good thing about these methods is that they can naturally benefit from hardware antialiasing, which is very important quality factor in our application. Unfortunately, they also have limitations, primarily the shape of shadowed objects. Therefore, if the virtual lighting of the scene does not change, and there are no animated objects, then the texture rendering technique can be used to preprocess shadows (which remain static) and incorporate them into textures [Wojdała et al., 1994] [Myszkowski et al., 1994] [Goslin, 1995]. This allows shadows to be soft and subtle, like those cast by columns on the photo 6. In many cases, texture rendering actually allows for performance increase, so it does not in any way interfere with the Virtual Studio performance requirements. In some cases, even dynamic shadows can be handled this way, by rendering textures for several lighting situations and dissolving between them.

3.   REAL–TO-REAL SHADOW CASTING

Real elements of the scene cast shadows on each other according to the stage lighting. If the shadowed object is non-blue, then the shadow simply darkens its color. It is shadows cast on blue areas that need special treatment.

Virtual Studio utilizes the compositing process, in which all the blue in the foreground video is replaced by the corresponding fragments of the background. Blue color is most frequently used, because it is complementary to the flesh tone. Green is sometimes favored, especially when it is difficult to avoid blue in the foreground (for example, programs with children wearing jeans). Rarely, red is used for special purposes.

In the video industry, the process that leads to the creation of the composite image is called *chroma keying*. Modern chroma keyers use both chrominance and luminance values of the video input, allowing to specify hue, saturation and luminance ranges to control the creation of matte – a grayscale signal, which is used to combine foreground and background images together. *Ultimatte* is a more sophisticated process using the color difference method. Detailed discussion of the blue screen compositing and related issues can be found in [Smith and Blinn, 1996]. Here it is enough to say, that hardware Ultimatte and good chroma keyers are able to create matte, that allows to extract shadows from the foreground (photo 3) and retain them in the composite image (photo 4) in real time.

Shadows produced this way usually work well for the floor but frequently create problems when cast on blue-box walls. This will be discussed in more detail in the next section. Another problem is that the intensity of shadows can be normally tuned using the keyer controls such as Ultimatte's cleanup, but if they are cast on both blue and the real props, then it is necessary to match the intensity level of extracted shadow with that on the prop.

4. REAL–TO-VIRTUAL SHADOW CASTING

The problem with shadows extracted by the keyer is that their shape depends on what they are cast on. This is usually floor, so the shadow is flat and horizontal. But, depending on what lies in the shadowed area in a virtual scene, such flat shape can be incorrect. On the photo 2 the shadow is visible in the hole in the floor, while of course it should not be there. Shadowing error would also happen, if any vertical virtual object was there. Another manifestation of the same problem are shadows extended from the blue-box floor to its walls, if in the virtual set there are no walls there. Shadows are then unnaturally bent on the surface, on which they should be flat (photos 3, 4). Generalizing, whenever the shape of the blue-box does not match the shape of the virtual set, there is a potential problem with the shadow distortion.

The immediate conclusion is that to assure proper shadow behavior, blue-painted objects can be built with shapes and locations corresponding to virtual objects. Indeed, this is sometimes done, but such method has many drawbacks. Firstly, it severely limits the freedom of virtual set creation. Secondly, matching real and virtual worlds becomes more difficult: very precise calibration and sometimes even simulation of lens distortion is necessary [Wojdała, 1998]. And finally, why build objects and paint them with blue, if they can be painted to match the virtual set coloring, thus eliminating the whole shadowing issue altogether (which, by the way, is frequently done). In practice, using blue objects is primarily limited to situations when they are fixed elements of the scene, big and simple and it is necessary for actors to physically interact with them (e.g., leaning or stepping on them). In such cases it frequently happens, that these objects do not match virtual shapes and even their sizes, because only fragments that require interaction or shadowing are build. In effect, although some shadowing problems are cured, new unwanted shadows are created in wrong places because of these mismatches.

So far, occlusion and shadowing between real and virtual elements of the scene were in the scope of interest of computer vision rather than computer graphics. As was pointed out by Klinker in her review of Augmented Reality [Klinker, 1999], to properly model such interaction it is necessary to have the geometrical model of the real environment; photometric model is also desired (ref. also to the Proceedings of the First International Symposium on Mixed Reality, Yokohama, March 1999).

Our solution starts with the observation, that if we narrow the problem to real-to-virtual shadowing, then instead of the 3D model of the real objects we could use their 2D projection from the light source viewpoint and refer to virtual-to-virtual shadowing methods. Because actors are part of the shadow-casting reality, the projection must be updated in real time. The most natural way to obtain it is to use the video camera located in the assumed position of the light, as was demonstrated in some virtual studio systems, most notably in Larus by RT Set.

The idea is then to use the video signal of such "shadow camera" as a shadow texture, changing it in every video field. In order to do that, the graphics workstation used for background generation must have the capability to efficiently input the video signal. Indeed, computers used for virtual studio have the hardware support for reading serial digital video and converting it to RGB memory images. But, for the camera the entire image is "real", while we are interested only in the projection of non-blue elements, because it is their shadow that we need. We also need the texture to be black-and-white, with white color assigned to blue areas and black to everything else. In other words, we are not really interested in the video itself, but in its matte. One possibility is to use dedicated chroma keyer to perform the job (it must have the matte output). But, since the purpose of the matte is to get silhouettes of real things, such issues as blue-spill elimination are not critical. In fact, good-quality hardware is not needed, because it is necessary anyway to clean up shadows extracted by the keyer or "shadow of the shadow" will occur. Since virtual studio typically uses more than single-processor computers and it is rather graphically than computationally intensive application, using CPU for matte generation is a viable option (ref. to fig. 1 below).

	Pentium II 233MHz	Pentium III 450MHz	MIPS R4400 250MHz	MIPS R10000 195 MHz
PAL	10.7	6.7	12.7	5.3
NTSC	8.6	5.6	11.1	4.4

Fig 1. Timings of lookup-table matte generation (msec).

Black-and-white matte – the "shadow image" - is used as a projected texture [Segal et al., 1992]. In the first display pass the scene is rendered normally from the view camera. In the next passes (one per each shadow camera), the following actions are performed:
– the shadow image is loaded to texture memory,
– the texture matrix is calculated based on the position of the shadow camera and the view camera,
– the shadow texture is assigned to all polygons with texture coordinates generated linearly,
– all materials of all polygons are set to full white, ambient-only,
– alpha blending function is set to multiply the contents of the frame buffer by the drawn pixels,
– the scene is rendered again from the view camera; z-buffer is not cleared after the first pass, but the depth function is changed to "equal".

As a result, non-shadowed areas of the scene retain the color from the first rendering pass, and all shadowed pixels become black. It is possible to control the darkness of the shadow by applying bias during the operation of loading image to the texture memory (photos 5, 6). If the matte is generated using the CPU, then another way to achieve the same effect is to generate gray rather than black color for non-blue areas. Changing the gray level towards the top of the matte image allows to make the shadow darker where the real object meets the floor and brighter elsewhere. To make the shadow soft-edged, the shadow camera should be defocused so that the chroma key can generate grayscale matte on edges, or - if the matte is generated by the CPU – the matte image should be blurred.

It should be noted, that unlike in pure virtual-to-virtual shadowing algorithms, the depth information is not available for the shadow texture. Thus, the technique with using OpenGL's SGIX_shadow extension [Segal et al., 1992] cannot be used to avoid shadowing of virtual objects located between the light source (shadow camera) and the real elements of the scene. Finding positions of real objects in the scene is another subject of computer vision research [Klinker, 1999]. In Virtual

Studio, not very sophisticated distance-key technique is used for positioning virtual objects in front of the real ones [Wojdała, 1998]. The same method can be used to determine, which objects should be excluded from shadowing.

The most critical issue of the algorithm is to precisely determine the projected texture matrix, so that the shadow is properly attached to the real scene elements standing on the floor, for example – to actor's feet (photo 6). The texture matrix is calculated as follows:

$$T = P \cdot M_s^{-1} \cdot M_c$$

where:
P – projection matrix,
M_s, M_c – matrices for shadow and view camera, respectively.

$$
P = \begin{bmatrix}
0.5 \cdot \text{ctg}(v/2)/aspect & 0 & -0.5 & 0 \\
0 & 0.5 \cdot \text{ctg}(v/2) & -0.5 & 0 \\
0 & 0 & (far+near)/(near-far) & 2 \cdot far \cdot near/(near-far) \\
0 & 0 & -1 & 0
\end{bmatrix}
$$

where:
v – vertical field of view of the shadow camera,
aspect – aspect ratio of the shadow camera,
far, near – clipping planes.

$$
M_s, M_c = \begin{bmatrix}
\cos p \cdot \cos r & -\sin t \cdot \sin p \cdot \cos r + \cos t \cdot \sin r & \cos t \cdot \sin p \cdot \cos r + \sin t \cdot \sin r & x \\
\cos p \cdot \sin r & -\sin t \cdot \sin p \cdot \sin r + \cos t \cdot \cos r & \cos t \cdot \sin p \cdot \sin r + \sin t \cdot \cos r & y \\
-\sin p & -\sin t \cdot \cos p & \cos t \cdot \cos p & z \\
0 & 0 & 0 & 1
\end{bmatrix}
$$

where:
p, t, r – pan, tilt, roll angles of the shadow and view camera, respectively,
x, y, z – position of the shadow and view camera, respectively.

Finding parameters of the shadow camera defining matrices P and M_s, is a well-known inter-camera blocking issue of virtual studio [Wojdała, 1998], except that errors in positioning would be more visible here. Since the shadow camera is usually stationary, determining its parameters should be done only once and does not have to be a real-time process. Camera calibration, or finding its extrinsic and intrinsic parameters, has been the subject of computer vision research for several years now [Tuceryan et al., 1995]. All parameters can be derived from the image the camera "sees", by placing the construction of the known shape and sizes in the known location on the stage and then analyzing the image of the shadow camera. The minimum of five points (with no four of them coplanar) is sufficient to unambiguously find all camera parameters [Bogart, 1991]. On the other hand, if the system with the common reference is used for tracking cameras, then another way of approaching the problem is to track the shadow camera as well (ref. to pattern recognition tracking from Orad [Tamir, 1996], Free•D from Radamec/BBC [Thomas et al., 1997], Constellation from InterSense [Foxlin et al., 1998], Walkfinder from Thoma Filmtechnik or X-pecto from Xync). Of all mentioned systems Orad is perhaps best to efficiently perform this task because it retrieves all camera parameters directly from the video signal. All these systems will typically have problems with tracking if the camera is located too high, but the benefit is that the shadow camera can move, emulating dynamic light source (of course, after one-time calibration even sensor-based system can be used to track moving shadow camera).

Performance is another concern when using the proposed shadowing algorithm for real-time display in virtual studio. At the first glance, if one shadow camera is used, it reduces the performance of the drawing by more than half, because the matte image must be loaded to texture memory in each field and there are two display passes. In fact however, typically it is not so. Loading the texture takes constant, non-negligible time, indeed: about 2.5 msec on SGI Onyx2/InfiniteReality with Digital Video Option (DIVO) and 2 msec on SGI Visual Workstation 540 with Digital Video Option. On the other hand, usually not all objects need to be drawn in the second pass. Culling can be used to eliminate objects not "seen" by the shadow camera and some objects can be purposefully excluded from being shadowed (especially, those marked by the distance key as being in front of the real ones). If the matte is generated using CPU, then it is also possible to detect the boundaries of non-blue areas to further narrow the culled frustum. Also, no hardware lights are used and the texture mapped on all objects is an 8-bit image, which is less "expensive" in drawing than 32-bit textures that are used in the first pass. Obviously, adding more cameras to generate multiple shadows increases the performance cost; in most practical scenes only one shadow camera can be handled in real time.

Finally, we should address the issue of video delays in Virtual Studio, resulting from the real-to-virtual shadowing. The goal is to have the proper alignment (in the time domain) between projected shadow, foreground and background. Fig. 2 shows how this should be done in the general case:

5.   VIRTUAL-TO-REAL SHADOW CASTING

A simple solution allowing to cast shadows of virtual objects on real elements of the scene is to cover the studio lights with masks of the desired shapes. Props and actors passing below the mask-covered lights will exhibit the lighting gradation according to the shape of the mask, while on the blue areas lighting will be extracted by the chroma keyer (photos 7, 8). This method is mainly limited to static lights and scenes; any dynamic virtual objects appearing in front of the light source will not influence the shadow. For such cases, our proposal is to use the video projector located in the position of the light source.

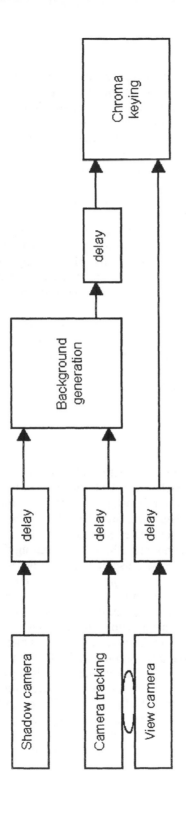

Fig. 2. Delays resulting from the real-to-virtual shadowing

The video signal delivered to the projector (shadow mask) should come from the computer, displaying only these objects of the scene that are supposed to cast shadows, viewed from the light source viewpoint and drawn in black on the white background. As in the case of real-to-virtual shadowing, the distance key technique can be used to determine, which objects should be excluded from drawing. In theory, alpha channel of the background video could be used to carry the shadow mask. In practice however, alpha is already used for distance keying and the virtual blue-box [Wojdała, 1998], so it is necessary to use either additional video output, or the second computer. In typical case, the drawn subset of the scene is simple enough to justify the use of the low-end graphics computers.

It should be noted, that the projector is really projecting a light, not shadow. Although sometimes it might be desired, generally it is necessary first to make the projector with all-white video signal a part of the blue-box lighting. The same applies to masks covering studio lights. The video delay matching can be addressed in a similar way as in the real-to-virtual shadow casting. Calibration is a different issue because – unlike the shadow camera – the projector does not "see" the stage. However, since the field of view is arbitrarily assumed, only the position and orientation have to be found. This can be done by projecting the known shape first on the floor and then on the blue surface parallel to it, and picking its characteristic points on the composite image plane (since all parameters of the view camera are known, 3D positions of picked points can be calculated; fig.3).

6. FUTURE WORKS

It is natural to expect, that shadow interaction mechanisms described in the previous sections will complement each other. Unfortunately, it is quite opposite. Shadows extracted by the chroma keyer interfere with real-to-virtual shadowing, because they have potentially bad shape and are cast from different light source position than the shadow camera location. The temptation is then to get rid of real-to-real shadowing completely. This is not easy, however. Washing the shadows out with crude settings of the chroma keyer will also eliminate all desired detail (of the hair, for example) and transparencies. Setting flat and very bright lighting for the whole stage, including actors and foreground objects precludes the possibility of dramatic lighting, which – contrary to the popular belief – can be achieved in a blue screen, especially when replacing the paint with retro-reflective material (HoloSet from Play, Inc., developed by BBC and formerly known as Truematte). Besides, real-to-virtual shadows do not have the same subtlety and softness as those extracted by the good keyer. Virtual-to-real shadows cast on blue and extracted by the chroma keyer interfere with virtual-to-virtual ones. Problems also occur when textures are rendered to create subtle virtual-to-virtual shadows. The difference between lighting used for rendering (frequently, multiple area light sources processed with radiosity or similar algorithm) and simple spot lights used for real-to-virtual shadowing makes shadows of the real elements go through virtual objects on which they are cast.

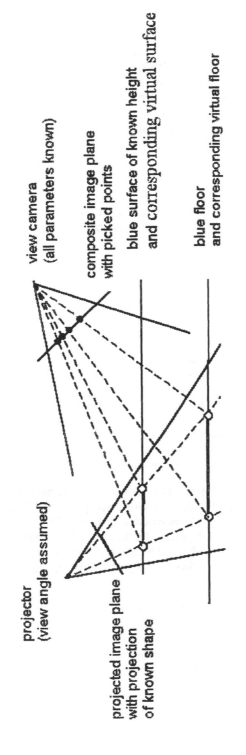

view camera
(all parameters known)

composite image plane
with picked points

blue surface of known height
and corresponding virtual surface

blue floor
and corresponding virtual floor

projector
(view angle assumed)

projected image plane
with projection
of known shape

Fig. 3. Finding position and orientation of the projector

Thus, the most challenging task is the unification of all shadow interactions. One of the key issues to address is lack of depth in the algorithm for real-to-virtual shadowing. The solution became possible in April 1999, when the Israeli company 3DV Systems introduced Zcam – the first camera with z-buffer [Kirk et al., 1999]. Eventually, it might be necessary to extend the functionality of the chroma keyer, since this is the component of the Virtual Studio that combines real and virtual images

Acknowledgements

Algorithms proposed in this paper were tested in ELSET - the Virtual Studio system by Accom. All presented photos were generated using ELSET Live and ELSET Live NT.

7.   REFERENCES

[1] Bergeron P (1986): A general version of Crow's shadow volumes, IEEE Computer Graphics and Applications, 6(9), 1986, 17-28
[2] Blinn J. (1988): Me and my (fake) shadow. IEEE Computer Graphics and Applications, 8(1), Jan. 1988, 82-86 (reprinted in the book: „Jim Blinn's Corner: A trip down the graphics pipeline", 1996)
[3] Blythe D, McReynolds T (1999): Advanced graphics programming techniques using OpenGL, Siggraph '99 Course Notes.
[4] Bogart, R.G (1991), View Correlation, Graphics Gems II, James (Ed.), Academic Press, 1991, 181-190
[5] Crow F (1977): Shadow algorithms for computer graphics, ACM Computer Graphics, 11(3), 1977, 242-248.
[6] Foxlin E, Harrington M, Pfeifer G (1998): Constellation™: a wide-range wireless motion tracking system for Augmented Reality and Virtual Set applications, Computer Graphics Proceedings, Annual Conference Series, 1998, 371-378
[7] Goslin M (1995): Illumination as texture maps for faster rendering, Technical Report 95-042, Dept. Of Computer Science, Univ. Of North Carolina, Chapel Hill, 1995.
[8] Heckbert P, Herf M (1996): Fast Soft Shadows, Visual Proceedings, Siggraph '96, Aug. 1996, p.145
[9] Heidmann T (1991): Real shadows, real time, Iris Universe, vol.18, 1991, 28-31
[10] Kilgard M (1997): OpenGL-based Real-Time Shadows, http://reality.sgi.com/opengl/tips/, Jun. '97 update
[11] May/June 1999; see also the web site www.3dvsystems.com
[12] Klinker G (1999): Augmented Reality: A problem in need of many computer vision – based solutions, Proceedings of Advanced Research Workshop on Confluence of Computer Vision and Computer Graphics, August 1999, Ljubljana, Slovenia (to be published by Kluwer).
[13] Myszkowski K., Kunii T.L. (1994): Texture mapping as an alternative for meshing during walkthrough animation, Proceedings of 5th Eurographics Workshop on Rendering, Darmstadt, Germany, 1994
[14] Reeves W, Salesin D, Cook R (1987): Rendering antialiased shadows with depth maps, ACM Computer Graphics, 21(4), 1987, 283-291.

[15] Segal M, Korobkin C (1992): Fast shadows and lighting effects using texture mapping, ACM Comput Graph, 26(2), 1992, 249-252

[16] Smith AR, Blinn J (1996): Blue screen matting, Computer Graphics Proceedings, Annual Conference Series, 1996, 259-268

[17] Tamir M. (1996): The Orad Virtual Set, Broadcast Origination, March 1996, 16-18

[18] Tchou C (1999): Realtime shadows and lighting project, Poster presentation, http://www/watson.org/~tesla, Feb. '99 update

[19] Tessman T. (1989): Casting shadows on flat surfaces. Iris Universe, Winter, 1989, 16-19

[20] Thomas G.A., Jin J., Niblett T., Urquhart C. (1997): A versatile camera position measurement system for virtual reality TV production, International Broadcasting Convention '97 Proceedings, 284-289, IEE Conference Publication.

[21] Tuceryan M, Greer D, Whitaker R, Breen D, Crampton C, Rose E, Ahlers K (1995): Calibration Requirements and Procedures for a Monitor-Based Augmented Reality System, IEEE Transactions on Visualization and Computer Graphics, vol. 1, no. 3, pp. 255-273, September 1995

[22] Williams, L. (1978): Casting curved shadows on curved surfaces, ACM Computer Graphics, 12(3), 1978, 270-274

[23] Wojdała A., Gruszewski M., Dudkiewicz K. (1994): Using hardware texture mapping for efficient image synthesis and walkthrough with specular effects, Machine Graphics & Vision, vol. no.1/2, 1994, 139-151

[24] Wojdała A (1996): Virtual Set: the State of the Art, Proceedings of International Broadcasting Convention, Amsterdam, Sept. 1996, 143-154

[25] Wojdała A. (1998): Challenges of Virtual Set technology, IEEE Multimedia, Jan-Mar 1998, vol.5, no.1, 50-57

JaTrac – an exercise in designing educational raytracer

MIŁOSŁAW SMYK, MAGDALENA SZABER, RADOSŁAW MANTIUK
Computer Science & Information Systems Faculty, Technical University of Szczecin

Abstract: The main goal of the paper is to propose the architecture of a highly realistic system of image synthesis based on a ray tracing method that could be useful in educational applications. Architectural designs and teaching-oriented features are discussed based on real-world implementation.

Key words: image synthesis, computer graphics, ray tracing, education

1. INTRODUCTION

The main goal of the paper is to propose the architecture of a highly realistic system of image synthesis based on a ray tracing method. The structure of the system is guided by the usage in teaching applications. The main emphasis was put on legibility of the implementation of ray tracing algorithms and on supporting the process of teaching students. JaTrac software was created in the Computer Science Faculty of the Technical University of Szczecin.

JaTrac was written in Java language with full object oriented architecture. It employs open input and output data formats (a 3D scene is saved in XML-based format). This approach assures easy development of the software, straight addition of new ray tracing algorithms and optimization of existing ones. JaTrac implementation takes into consideration such teaching mechanisms like visualization of ray distribution, parametrization of ray tracing function results or testing of various ray tracing optimization methods.

In the paper classification and description of teaching methods helpful in image synthesis workshops was done. The architecture of the software system supporting teaching process was proposed. We present implementation of the system and the examples of JaTrac usage. Future works associated with this topic are discussed.

2.   TEACHING RAY TRACING

Ray tracing is an image synthesis method characterized by highly realistic images it delivers. It attempts to simulate physical process of seeing or taking a picture by tracing virtual paths of photons that, first emitted by light (photon) sources, bounce around the environment "gathering" information about surfaces present in the scene, to finally reach eye retina or film/CCD in a camera. Because only a fraction of all photons in the scene environment contributes to perceived image and taking all of them into account is still computationally infeasible, classical ray tracing algorithm reverses the process and only calculates the paths of photons that reached the defined image plane, thus tracing the rays backward from the observation point (Fig. 1). While this simplification does not allow for a proper simulation of all light transport modes (e.g. specular to diffuse and diffuse to diffuse), in many cases the results obtained are still not far from photographic quality.

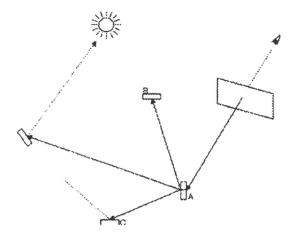

Fig. 1. An example ray tree in classical ray tracing

Although ray tracing in the basic form is conceptually simple process (and thus lends itself well to educational purposes) the same can not be said about its actual implementations. The amount of ray-object intersection tests as well as complex calculations involved in some surface shading algorithms make ray tracing one of the more computationally intensive image synthesis methods [3]. Consequently, practical implementations of it are most often heavily optimized to increase the execution speed, forsaking the clarity and structure of a code, and thus lowering its educational value due to:

*   making find parallelisms between textbook descriptions and real-world implementations more difficult,

*   obscuring the details of implementation with low-level optimization tricks,

*   increasing (sometimes prohibitively) the amount of time necessary to get sufficient expertise to introduce meaningful modifications and enhancements to the code

However, the internal workings of a ray tracer is not the only area that we set out to make easier to comprehend for our students. There are many concepts in ray tracing - mostly, but not solely related to optimization - that are explained during the course with help of pictures: uniform and non-uniform grids, bounding volumes, ray tree, light buffers etc. Unfortunately, students rarely have the opportunity to observe them in real-world ray tracer by means other than indirect, i.e. by segments of a code that implement them, or by reduced time of computation. We found that supplementing synthesized images with graphical representations of these concepts is a powerful visual aid in both understanding how they work, as well as in tweaking their behavior.

Thus, the design goals of JaTrac were twosome:

- to make overall architecture, structure of the source code and the code low-level details comprehensible, readable and extensible, even at cost of reduced performance,
- to allow for visualisation of data structures oft-used in ray tracing software.

Next two sections describe how they were actually implemented.

3. JATRAC'S CAPABILITIES

3.1 Ray tracing engine

JaTrac ray tracing engine is fairly standard. Here is a brief description of its major features:

- Scene structure: hierarchical. JaTrac scene can be constructed of multiple levels of hierarchy that can be used to group related model elements or for advanced material handling (see section 3.3).
- Camera: two models built-in - observer, target, up vector and angular spreads on both axes or observer and projection screen.
- Primitives: spheres, planes, rectangles, cylinders and triangles. These are basic building blocks that can be used to create a scene.
- Lighting: point, linear and area lights with definable colors (see section 3.2) and intensity. Linear and area lights are casting soft shadows that are computed with stochastic ray tracing using jittered samples.
- Material properties: diffuse and specular reflections, Phong highlights, transparency. Also, each object's properties can be modified to disable casting and/or receiving shadows and to make it invisible for reflected and transmitted rays.
- Texturing: procedural and image-based color- and bump-textures. Procedural handlers demonstrating gradient and random colormaps are included.
- Mapping: spherical, cylindrical and planar. Type of mapping used for applying texture data to object is separated from object's type (see section 3.3).

- Antialiasing: adaptive supersampling with adjustable threshold value of allowed color difference.
- Optimization: uniform grid and hierarchical bounding volumes for reducing number of ray-object intersection tests.

Some of these features, like soft shadows, procedural textures and recursive reflections are demonstrated with help of two example scenes (Fig. 2).

3.2 Color model

In a bid to decouple color calculations from limitations of RGB space as well as to get rid of thrice-repeated lines of code dealing with successive color components that make reading the sources more difficult, we decided to abstract all color related operations. This way the door is open for future enhancements in this area that could implement more complicated models of color spectrum as well as those of interactions between light and surface colors.

An example class that demonstrates handling of RGB space is included.

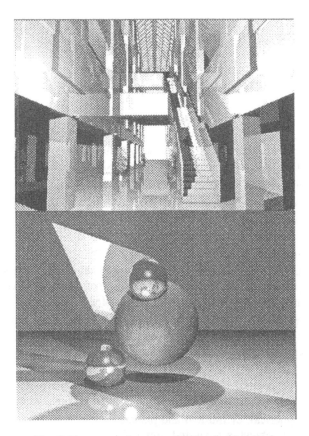

Fig. 2. Two example scenes: "atrium" and "balls"

3.3   Scene object hierarchy and material handling

JaTrac departs from typical relationship between primitives and their materials employed by majority of ray tracing software. Instead of defining a list of materials and then assigning them on one-to-one basis to primitives, JaTrac uses scene hierarchy to decide about material assignment and inheritance. A graph for a simple scene is depicted in Fig. 3.

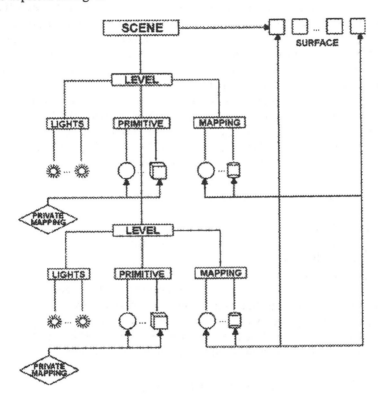

Fig. 3. Hierarchy graph for a simple scene

Starting from the top, **SCENE** is a root node that holds references to all entities comprising given scene. Among these entities is a list of **SURFACE**s, which in turn store information about properties like reflectance coefficient, refraction index, texture map etc. This is more or less equivalent to other implementations.

Below **SCENE** there is a node called **LEVEL**, which is used for grouping various entities appearing in the scene. Each **LEVEL** can have three types of children nodes: **LIGHT**s, **PRIMITIVE**s and **MAPPING**s. **LIGHT**s are simply a set of light sources associated with the given level of the hierarchy. This association is purely positional, i.e. the lights are always affecting all the objects in the scene, but their position may be influenced by the movements of **LEVEL** that contains them.

PRIMITIVEs define basic primitives present at the given level. Again, the association is only positional. Additionally, among **PRIMITIVE**s further **LEVEL**s of the hierarchy may be found (as it is actually the case with our example). There is no fundamental limit to the depth of this hierarchy except for the size of available memory.

The most interesting part of a **LEVEL** are **MAPPING**s, that define which **SURFACE**s and in what way should be assigned to current level primitives and recursively to **all** of the level descendants. A single **MAPPING** defines what type of projection should be used (e.g. planar, spherical or cylindrical) and which **SURFACE** should be applied. If multiple **MAPPING**s are affecting a primitive object - as it is the case in situation where there are two or more **MAPPING**s on a single level or when primitive "inherits" **MAPPING**s from ancestor node(s) - then resulting surface appearance is a product of all **MAPPING**s that contributed to it. Each **MAPPING**s' influence is adjustable in percentage points. It should be noted that **MAPPING**s behave like normal objects and can be, for example, independently moved to achieve all kinds of special effects.

Finally, to ease importing models created in software packages that use "one object - one material" paradigm, a notion of **PRIVATE MAPPING**s is introduced. They only influence objects that they are assigned to (thus can't be inherited) and at the same time they disable inheritance of normal **MAPPING**s by these objects, thus becoming their exclusive source of **SURFACE** information.

3.3.1 Ray tree storage and visualisation

In a normal mode of operation JaTrac only preserves information about final color of a primary (eye) ray, and even this only for a time required by particular antialiasing algorithm (two rasterlines in default case). It can, however, be ordered to store complete ray data which actually involves whole ray tree that contributes to the particular pixel color. This information may be then used to generate images that show exact paths of photons that ended their way in given pixel. This data is also useful for debugging purposes and in the future we hope it will be able to use it to quickly rerender scenes with a few parameteres modified (like object texture or reflection coefficient) without the need to recompute intersections.

3.4 Bounding volume visualisation

Another mode of work makes JaTrac construct objects based on bounding volumes it created to reduce the number of ray-object intersection tests.

These objects have the exact shape of bounding volumes [2] and are inserted into scene hierarchy just before rendering commences. Surface properties of these objects are set in a way that makes them appear translucent. Additionally, they do not cast nor receive shadows and are invisible for secondary rays, which means they are not reflected by specular (mirrorlike) surfaces. Fig. 4 demonstrates a scene where two different approaches (here called "lazy" and "complex") to bounding volume construction were tested. Contribution of this type of visualisation to aiding debugging and facilitating understanding of the particular algorithm weaknesses is obvious.

Fig. 4. Comparison of bounding volumes generated with lazy and complex evaluation

4. RELEVANT IMPLEMENTATION DETAILS

4.1 Language

When deciding on programming language that would be used to implement JaTrac, we considered factors like portability (we did not want to limit the users of our software to a single platform), strong support for object-oriented paradigm (a ray tracer is an excellent candidate for an OO implementation), clarity (obvious necessity for an educational tool), popularity, quick development process and speed.

Rather quickly we settled on Java [1], as it complied with all our requirements, with arguable exception of speed. However, the notion that "Java is slow" turned out to be at least partially false, because in purely computational tasks new JVM (Java Virtual Machine) implementations from Sun and IBM are on par with natively compiled C/C++. In practice, we did not encounter any serious performance-related obstacles, although some time-proven optimization techniques that worked well in ray tracers programmed in C behaved in far-from-optimal way when reimplemented in Java and had to be replaced.

4.2   Object-oriented programming

Basically everything in JaTrac is an object: primitives, mappings, textures, pixels, rays are all parts of well-defined hierarchy of objects. While this may seem to be an overkill (and in some parts actually is, if we consider performance), we found that it lets us put different parts of code into separate compartments that can be easily studied, enhanced or even replaced.

4.3   XML-based scene description file format

For some time we've considered using some off-the-shelf 3D model file specification format, but they all had their drawbacks and did not map well to in-memory structure of objects JaTrac uses.

XML (The Extensible Markup Language), as a popular, ASCII-based, easy to parse and to comprehend standard was thus a natural choice for constructing our own file description format. Coupled with the object-oriented structure of JaTrac, XML made it possible to create a file format that at the same time defines both structure of the scene and structure of the ray tracer itself, by letting a user specify names of the modules that (by implementing required interfaces) can insert themselves into the class structure of JaTrac.

In practical terms it means that for example classes that implement the "IntersectionTester" interface can replace a simple and naive tester that is built into our software. This is how "UniformGrid" does it by means of the following snipped of XML code in scene description file:

```
<UniformGrid>
<size>50 50 50</size>
</UniformGrid>
```

The same is true for almost all parts of JaTrac and, for instance, plugins generating complex objects on the fly (i.e. during loading) as well as plugins importing data from other 3D formats are also implemented this way.

4.4   Availability

JaTrac is available as Open Source software under GNU General Public License and can be downloaded from http://ibr.edu.pl/jatrac/.

5.   FUTURE WORK

In its present state JaTrac is by no means finished. The work is currently ongoing to enhance intersection routines with ability to handle CSG (Constructive Solid Geometry) involving basic primitives and groups of them.

While it is already possible to generate animated sequences with JaTrac with help of external scripting, major addition planned for next version is a capability to efficiently handle animation by introducing the concept of time flow into the ray tracing engine: we are working on design modifications that should let all objects (as opposed to just camera) move freely. We feel that it's going to be a good opportunity to tackle still-difficult problem of temporal aliasing, which is especially hard in animations that are more than just walk-throughs.

Another interesting lead is departing from "pure ray tracing" path and implementing other image syntesis algorithms in JaTrac. Especially worthy of investigation would be the IBR (Image Based Rendering) method, which could be used to accelerate rendering of in-between frames in animation.

6. REFERENCES

[1] Sun Microsystems. http://java.sun.com/.
[2] S. Rubin and T. Whitted. A three-dimensional representation for fast rendering of complex scenes. *Computer Graphics*, 14(3):110–116, 1980.
[3] T. Whitted. An improved illumination model for shaded display. *Comm. ACM*, 8(23), 1980.

A Few Approaches To Face Detection
In Face Recognition Systems

GEORGI KOUKHAREV[1], TOMASZ PONIKOWSKI[1], LIMING CHEN[2]
[1]Computer Science and Information Systems Department, Technical University of Szczecin,
ul. Żołnierska 49, 71-210 Szczecin, e-mail: gkoukharev@wi.ps.pl, tponikowski@wi.ps.pl
[2]Departement MI, Ecole Centrale de Lyon, laboratoire ICTT,
BP 163, 36 avenue Guy de Collongue, 69131 Ecully Cedex, France,
e-mail: liming.chen@ec-lyon.fr

Abstract: Accuracy of face detection process is the most important task for efficient face
              recognition systems. In this paper a few methods for face detection are
              presented, which we use in our face recognition systems. Comparing and
              examining the methods presented may be useful for improving these systems.
              The methods presented in this paper are based on different, but simple ideas,
              i.e.: skin color analysis, image gradient analysis or template matching. Their
              simplicity is an advantage, which allows us to implement them in real time
              face recognition systems.

Key words: face detection, face region, template, color analysis, gradient analysis,

1.   INTRODUCTION

The ideas presented in this article are very useful for face identification systems.

A personal identification system based on face recognition can be divided into two functional modules (fig. 1).

One of these modules is designed for data acquisition (an enrollment module) and building an example database. It is a very important phase for properly functioning of the personal identification system. In the second module of the system identification of a person is performed. Personal identification systems based on face recognition have been presented in [1,8].

In this article we focus on finding face-like regions in complex images, and face detection in these regions (the first stage of the face recognition system is presented in fig. 1). If the face detection system works properly, we have a strong base for solving further tasks (feature extraction & matching). It is very important, that these results should be given with high accuracy (different faces extracted from different image should have similar sizes, be located at the same place – without shifts, have the similar orientation – connected with face image normalization). Very often face detection is integrated with normalization.

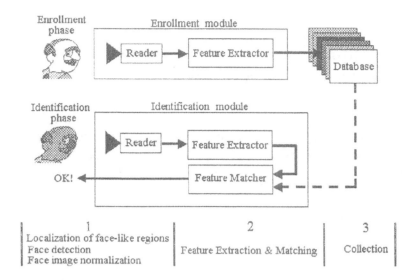

Fig. 1. Functional modules of the personal identification system based on face recognition.

We have presented a few simple approaches. The presented methods are based on locating objects with the similar face shapes and colors by simple single template matching, image gradient analysis or colors analysis in different color models (fig. 2). The result of such methods can be improved by additional solutions, described later in the article.

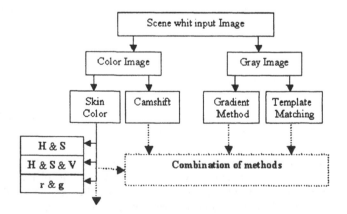

Fig. 2. Approaches to face detection.

We are also interested in searching for some face characteristic features, like: face oval shape, forehead shape, symmetry, chin arc, cheek arcs, ears, eyes, mouth etc. We can measure some characteristics distances or proportions between these elements in face image for using them in the face detection or recognition systems (fig.3).

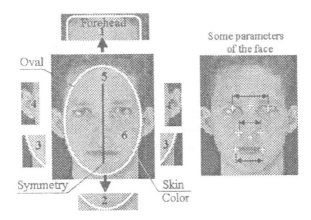

Fig. 3. Examples of face characteristic features.

2. SIMPLE AND VERY FAST FACE DETECTION BASED ON TEMPLATE MATCHING

This method was implemented for the first time in the systems presented in [1] and [8]. We didn't describe it precisely in that publication. The method is based on template face image presented below (fig. 4) This template is an average face the calculated from large face database (ORL Face Database).

Calculating a minimum distance between template and the examined portion of an image (standard deviation) is a main idea of this face detection method. Pixels of the examined image are scanned in one of the few possible ways (pixel by pixel; spiral; with or without pixel scanning step).

*Fig. 4.*Template face image (average face from ORL Database).

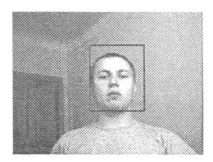

Fig. 5. Result of the face detection method based on the standard deviation in typical situation (one face, quite uniform background).

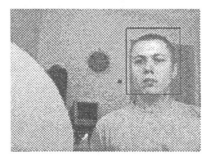

Fig. 6. Result of the face detection method based on the standard deviation for an image with additional non-face objects.

This method is very useful for detecting parts of a face (i.e mouth-nose-eyes region), or for determining face orientation. Implementing of this method to such tasks is very simple and consists in changing a face template to a template of the interesting region (fig. 7).

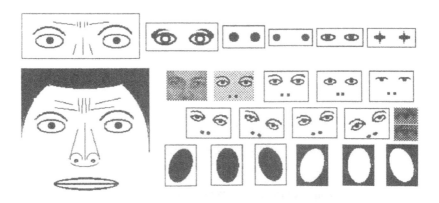

Fig. 7. Different templates (real and synthesized) for different searching tasks.

3.   GRADIENT BASED FACE DETECTION METHOD

This method was described in [2]. It is a modification of the method proposed by Dario Maio and Davide Maltoni in [3]. In the modified method, we are not searching for ellipses but circles. For this simplification, source images should be scaled to the size in which a face has circular proportions. Method is based on searching for circular gradient distribution on the head boundary (after changing proportions).

Fig. 8. Image with changed proportions and its gradient form.

In fig. 9 the original image with two persons and corresponding images with estimated face positions calculated by the gradient detection method (two blackened blobs on face positions) are presented.

Fig. 9. Original image, and estimated face positions in it (two blackened blobs in circles)

Characteristic feature of this method is finding more then one face in the image (shown in [2]).

4.   CAMSHIFT FACE DETECTION METHOD

This simple method based on moment finding was described in [4]. The examined pictures should be converted from RGB color space to the HSV model. The main operation in this method is to calculate the zero, first, and second moments values of an image.

Aside from face coordinates, the CAMSHIFT method gives us a possibility of calculating frame dimensions containing the face and head orientation (precisely described in [4]).

Fig. 10. CAMSHIFT result for typical situation (one face, quite uniform background).

The CAMSHIFT method is quite good for face detection of images containing only one face without additional elements. The center of a face located by moments has a tendency to migrate to non-face elements direction (fig.11). The CAMSHIFT is unreliable if a processed region contains more then one face.

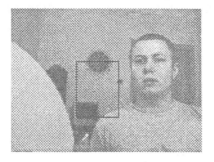

Fig. 11. CAMSHIFT result for image with additional non-face objects (migration into non-face elements direction).

5. APPROACHES BASED ON COLOR ANALYSIS

In many publications the face detection problem is solved by the image color analysis. The results described in these publications demonstrate us pixel color to skin color similarity measures. Such measures we can find in [5], [6], [7]. These methods give us very confident results in selecting face-like colored regions (fig. 12).

In fig. 12 an arrow indicates a small face-like colored region. It is a side-view of a distant man's head. This example shows, that skin-color detection methods based on different color models are very sensitive. Size and shape of selected regions allows us to decide about face localization in the examined image.

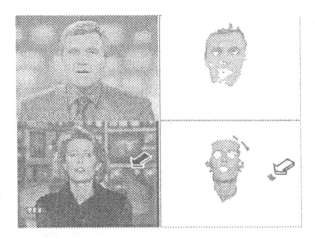

Fig. 12. Face-like colored regions detected by color analysis.

Results given by color analysis depend on image acquisition conditions and the type of analysis (fig. 13, top image – the HSV color model, bottom image – normalized RG color model).

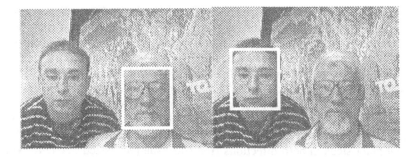

Fig. 13. Results given by two different color analysis methods by the same example.

The methods based on color analysis could not properly works in case of examples with face-like colored elements (in the selected color model) (fig. 14).

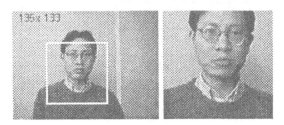

Fig. 14. Face localisation error in the HSV color model.

Effectiveness of color analysis methods could be improved by additional implementing of face detection methods based on templates or gradient images.

Combining color and template/gradient methods can be done in two different ways:

1. first step – color analysis, second step – result verification by template matching/gradient analysis,
2. first step – template matching/gradient analysis, second step – color verification of the detected object.

Fig. 15. The face detected in the example from fig. 14 by additional use of the template method (different scaled faces selected from the given example).

Combining the methods based on templates or gradient images with color analysis is the most efficient solution for fast and reliable face detection.

6.   SPEEDING UP OF FACE DETECTION METHODS

The original methods described above were performed for every pixel in an image, starting from the top-left corner, ending in the bottom-right one. In modifications of these methods processing is performed for every few pixels (1, 2, 3 or more) in both directions (standard deviation, gradient analysis).

All the tests were performed on Intel Celeron 400 MHz with 128 MB of RAM with Matlab 5.2 environment.

The first method (based on the calculating standard deviation) is very resistant for such an improvement. It could be performed for every sixteenth pixel without significant loss of effectiveness. In the table in fig. 16 results of this method for different pixel steps in both directions (for 100 examples, sized 320x240 with one face) are presented.

x/y step	avg. time	Effectiveness
2/2	18.8715 s	100 %
6/6	2.0995 s	100 %
8/8	1.2483 s	100 %
12/12	0.5418 s	100 %
16/16	0.3130 s	100 %

Fig. 16. Improving of the template based face detection method.

In the typical situations face detection algorithm could be performed correctly for pixel step at 16.

The gradient searching method is more sensitive to changing the pixel step. In fig. 17 the results of the improving gradient method are presented at different pixel steps.

x/y step	avg. time.	Effectiveness
2/2	**2.3159 s**	100 %
4/4	**1.2331 s**	100 %
6/6	**1.0242 s**	96 %

Fig. 17. Improving of the gradient-based face detection method.

Another kind of speeding up of the face detection methods (especially the color analysis methods) could be a reduction in image resolution (fig. 18). Such a modification could improve the speed of the face detection method significantly (two times decreased resolution in both dimensions – about four times shorter duration of the detection algorithm).

128 × 96

Fig. 18. The color analysis method performed on the image with decreased resolution (at the right the image detected face region is presented).

The next method for improving performance of the described face detection methods is searching for a face by spiral trajectory, starting from the center of an image. It is probable, that a face is located near the center of an image, but it depends on the kind of a face recognition system (i.e. in a visitor identification system a face could be located in the different places). This method is effective only if a face is centered in the image. For faces not located near the center it could be slower than normal performing of the algorithm (column by column, row by row).

7. CONCLUSIONS

The solution of the face detection problem is very important for face recognition systems. It can be done by many methods connected with different aspects of object finding. The presented approaches are based on searching for face like colored and shaped regions in complex images. Face detection can be solved by use of methods connected with neural networks or with other classification tools (i.e. PCA face detection). Simplification of the ideas used in face detection algorithms is very useful in the case of the real time personal identification system based on face recognition procedures. Fast and properly working face detection algorithms give us strong base for further identification researches. Our future investigations connected with face detection will be focused on improving accuracy and speed of detection. In our opinion combining different approaches and speeding up solutions is a good way for taking efficient face detection algorithms.

8. ACKOWNLEDGEMENTS

The authors would like to thank Tomasz Brylka for the rights to present his examination results.

9. REFERENCES

[1] Georgii Koukharev, Paweł Forczmański, Paweł Kraszewski, Tomasz Bryłka, Tomasz Ponikowski: *Realtime - Face recognition System for Personal Identification* – Proceedings of Advanced Computer Systems 1999, Technical University of Szczecin, Poland

[2] Tomasz Bryłka, Tomasz Ponikowski: *Image Preprocessing For Face Identification System* – Proceedings of Advanced Computer Systems 1999, Technical University of Szczecin, Poland.

[3] Dario Maio and Davide Maltoni: *Fast Face Location in Complex Backgrounds* – Nato Asi Conference on Faces, Stirling (UK), Jun 1997

[4] Gary R. Bradski: *Computer Vision Face Tracking For Use in a Perceptual User Interface* – Proc. IEEE Workshop on Applications of Computer Vision, Princeton, 1998.

[5] K. Sobottka, I. Pitas. *Looking for Faces and Facial Features in Color Images* – Advances in Mathematical Theory and Applications, Russian Academy of Sciences, 1996.

[6] Nikolaidis, Pitas: *Robust Watermarking of Facial Images Based on Salient Geometric Pattern Matching.* – IEEE Transactions on Multimedia, vol. 2, no. 3, september 2000, pp. 172 – 184

[7] C. Garcia, G. Tziritas: *Face detection using Quantized Skin Color Regions Merging and Wavelet Packet Analysis* – IEEE Transactions on Multimedia, vol. 1, no. 3, september 1999, pp. 264 – 277

[8] Georgii Koukharev, Andrzej Tujaka: *Real-time face recognition system for visitor identification* - Proceedings of Advanced Computer Systems 2000, Technical University of Szczecin, Poland

Chapter 5

Computer Security and Safety

Software support for collaborative risk management

JAKUB MILER, JANUSZ GÓRSKI
Department of Applied Informatics, Technical University of Gdańsk, Gdańsk, Poland

Abstract: The paper recognises the increasing role of risk management in present software projects and aims at providing more support in this area. First we overview the objectives and processes of risk management with the particular stress on the need for effective and continuous communication. Then we develop a generic collaboration model that shows the roles and communication paths among the project members to support risk management activities as well as a data model showing the abstract data objects supporting the collaboration. Further, we propose a software architecture that supports the collaborative risk management in a project course. And finally we present a pilot implementation of a tool that facilitates collaborative risk management over the Internet and the first results of its use.

Key words: software development, project risk management, collaboration, the Internet

1.   INTRODUCTION

The increasing competition in the market and the challenging expectations of the clients force software developers to reduce the overall development time and cost and to strive for increased product quality. At the same time the systems are getting larger and more complex and consequently the development processes tend to involve more people, often of different organisations, representing different competencies and working from distance locations. Effective management of such diverse groups of people requires great skill of project managers as well as the application of various supporting techniques and tools.

Despite of the progress in technology, the software engineering project management still faces similar problems as before [1]. The requirements are not defined precisely enough, change management is poor, the project scope and objectives are drifting and the turn over of the workforce is high. The result is that many (too many) projects are still overrunning their budgets, are delivering poor quality products and are delayed or, in extreme cases, even cancelled.

The real challenge in the present software development is effective risk management that would improve the success-to-failure ratio of software projects. This would require a deep change in the attitude of the project participants towards the way the project is conducted. The scope has to be broadened to account for alternative ways of the project development and to analyse various factors that could affect the future events. The project members would have to develop a deeper understanding of project objectives to be able to recognise risks before they start to adversely influence the project course. All this calls for more intensive and more thorough communication within the project and outside the project boundaries. The need for more efficient communication is even higher if we recognise that present projects often involve multiple and diverse groups that have to co-operate from geographically separated locations using Internet as the primary communication medium.

The aim of this paper is to present a Web-based environment that supports risk management within a software development project. The tool supports effective information exchange about risks and covers risk identification, risk analysis and risk mitigation activities.

In the next section we give an overview of the risk management domain. Then we present simple communication and data models of risk management. Next two sections present the design and implementation of those models in the form of a Web-based co-operative workspace. The last section presents preliminary results of applying this tool to support a number of student projects.

2.   OVERVIEW OF RISK MANAGEMENT

In general terms risk is defined as the possibility of loss, injury, damage or disadvantage. This definition describes two important features of risk [2, 11, 13]:
1.   risk brings about negative consequences,
2.   there is a degree of probability that these negative consequences come true.

Risk is formulated in the context of an undertaking, activity or opportunity (e.g. an investment or a project), because risks threaten the success of the undertaking meant by reaching the specified goals [2, 3, 13]. A project takes an opportunity to achieve success and create new value for the client, so it is automatically exposed to the risk of failure. No project is free of risk. A project without risk management recognises that there was a risk after the risk materialises as a real problem (e.g. it becomes obvious that the project overruns the budget or misses the deadline). Then the project team usually reacts and strives to minimise the negative consequences of the problem. As the rule, it is expensive and time-consuming. This price could have been much less if the risk were coped with before it converted to the problem. The lack of open communication, forward-looking attitude, team involvement in the management and the knowledge of typical problems, expose the project to a great risk of failure [4].

The essential factors of the project success are the quality, the time and the budget [13]. In the essential project aspects, the lack of risk management results in:
−   schedule slippage,
−   budget overrun,

- unsatisfactory quality of the product,
- failure to accomplish business goals of the project,
- disappointment of the employees and breakdown of their careers.

All of these failures refer to the primary project objectives, so they are unacceptable under ordinary circumstances. In some conditions, they may even be critical.

The only way to avoid serious consequences of a risk when it materialises is to catch the risk as early as possible and minimise its impact on the project. Though this advice sounds simple, it may be only realised through a defined set of activities focused on risk resolution. Altogether, it calls for a definition and elaboration of a systematic and explicit approach to risk management [9].

Software Engineering Institute (SEI) has elaborated a risk management approach that can be tailored to the specific environment of a software engineering project [4, 5, 11, 12, 13]. The generic risk management methodology is enhanced and transformed into five recurring phases. The subsequent phases cover the risk management aspects:

- Risk assessment: identification, analysis.
- Risk mitigation: planning, tracking, controlling.
- Communication

The process starts with the identification of existing risks. Once the risks are identified, they are evaluated and prioritised and then appropriate corrective actions are planed and executed. To reach the acceptable level of success guarantee, the introduced actions must be controlled and the risks in mitigation must be continuously tracked for their status. This process continues all through the whole project schedule and across all the phases of development. Although the process is recurring, it may implement pipeline processing, when different phases of the risk management are executed in particular project areas. The SEI process model is shown in Fig. 1.

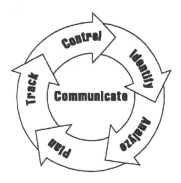

Fig. 1. The SEI risk management paradigm

The risk management paradigm defines a set of continually performed activities that are based on communication among the participants. The cost and effort of these activities must be smaller than the estimated profit from the successful risk mitigation. To increase the 'rate of return', the risk management efficiency may be increased by means of computer-based tools.

3.   COMMUNICATION MODEL OF RISK MANAGEMENT

The risk management process is a team activity involving all the project members, the customer representatives and the upper management of both the developer and the customer's organisation. To be both effective and profitable, this collective effort must be well organised, the roles must be defined and delegated, the means of communication established and the reporting standards set up. From the process point of view, the following roles can be distinguished:

a) Risk manager: he/she is responsible for facilitation of the risk management process. Analyses risk information, prioritises risks, prepares plans, receives tracking information and makes control decisions.

b) Information supplier: project members as well as the people involved from outside are acting as the information suppliers when they report the identified risks and the tracking information on the risks and the mitigation progress.

c) Information recipient: project members are acting as the information recipients when they receive the management plans and decisions.

d) Process sponsor: this is the project management role. It is responsible for assigning the other roles, establishing the communication and documentation infrastructure and encouraging the effort.

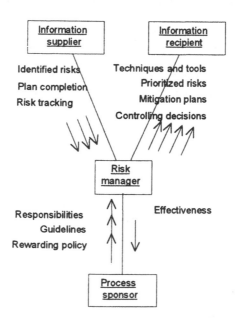

Fig. 2. Communication model of risk management

Normally, a project member plays both, the supplier and recipient roles. Often, e.g. in case of technical-level risks, a person who identifies a risk can effectively mitigate it as well. In the general case, however, the information about risk has to be *communicated* if the risk is to be dealt with properly and in due time.

The resulting communication model is presented on Fig. 2.

4. DATA MODEL OF RISK MANAGEMENT

The data model of risk management underpins the activities of the risk management paradigm of Fig.1. Because of the space limitations we present here only a part of the model, that relates to the risk identification phase. It is shown in Fig. 3.

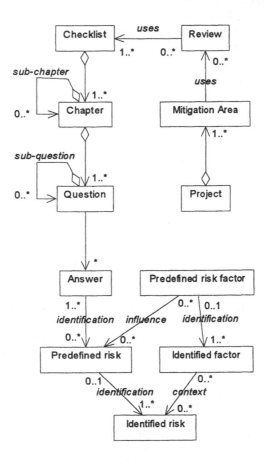

Fig. 3. Risk identification data model

The model comprises the following elements:
- Project – General project description (process, methodology, organization, size, initiation date).
- Mitigation area – Area of a project that is exposed to a common type of risks (e.g. requirement specification, personnel management etc.)

–   Review – This is the root object of the identification phase. Opening a new review starts risk identification activities whereas closing the review ends the risk information acquisition

–   Checklist – Checklists are used to collect information that helps to identify risks. A checklist includes its name, description, authors identification and its components.

–   Chapter – is a component of a checklist. It can be hierarchically decomposed into more fine structuring elements as shown in Fig. 3.

–   Question – this is the lowest structuring level of a checklist (nevertheless it may include some sub-questions).

–   answer – represents the answer to a checklist question (it may be of different type: yes/no, range etc).

–   Predefined risk – Risk that is stored in the risk knowledge base. It may be *selected* by one or more answers to the questions.

–   Predefined risk factor – Risk factor providing the context for a risk stored in the risk knowledge base.

–   Identified risk – Detailed risk description (from the risk knowledge base) in the context of a particular project. It is extracted from the knowledge base using the selection of predefined risks resulting from the answers to the checklist questions.

–   Identified factor – Context of the identified risk extracted from the risk knowledge base.

Similar data structures were developed for the other phases of the risk management paradigm. The details can be found in [8]

5.   SYSTEM ARCHITECTURE

The system architecture employs the client-server model with one central server and the user stations connected by a network. The hardware architecture is presented in Fig. 4.

The software architecture is formed upon the three-tier distributed application concept. The application is built in three levels: database, server components and interface. This concept is very useful in effective implementation of the applications accessed via the Internet. The resulting application is well scalable, robust and portable. The general concept of the three-tier application is presented in Fig. 5.

The three tiers are highly independent. The system code modules are written individually for each tier. They communicate through program interfaces – function calls. As all the server applications for the tiers (SQL-Server, MTS, IIS, MSIE) are developed by the same vendor, no compatibility problems arise. The code was written using different programming languages, but nearly all data types were compatible and the values were automatically converted by the servers.

The advanced Internet technology used in the construction of our collaborative risk management tool led to the following features of the system:

–   encapsulation of data processing,

–   minimal software requirements for client workstations,

–   multi-access,

–   effective communication in distributed project teams,

- easy system maintenance,
- open user interface,
- short time of system development.

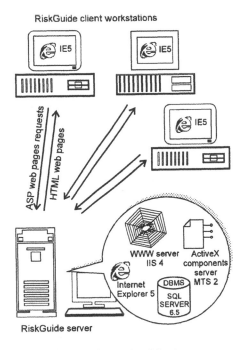

Fig. 4. System architecture

6. THE PILOT IMPLEMENTATION

A pilot implementation of the collaborative risk management tool called Risk-Guide has been accomplished to provide for some experiments. Risk-Guide supports the risk identification and analysis phases using checklists together with qualitative risk evaluation. The system offers a knowledge base of structured checklists and lists of common risks. It is designed to support multiple projects at a time with independent risk identification and analysis. Nevertheless, the knowledge base is shared by all those projects.

The checklists are accessed on-line and can be interactively answered by project members. To build the project risk repository the Risk Manager opens a review of the project and instructs the project members to browse the checklists and to provide answers to the questions. Risk-Guide automatically searches the knowledge base and selects the risks that are implied by the answers. When the Risk Manager closes the current review, the system provides him/her with a list of risks that were identified during the review. The risks can then be individually assessed in three dimensions: possibility, severity and timeframe. For each dimension Risk-Guide offers a qualitative evaluation scale. After the individual assessment of risks is done, Risk-Guide calculates a list of risks ordered by priorities. The priorities are calculated from individual assessments using the risk evaluation matrix. Such a list can then be used to select the most dangerous risks for further mitigation.

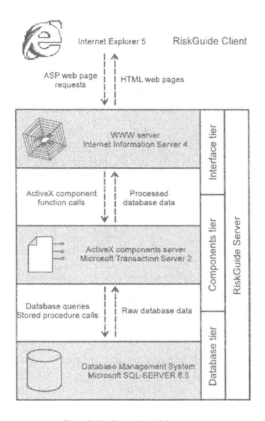

Fig. 5. Software architecture

As for now, the Risk-Guide knowledge base includes as the checklist the SEI Taxonomy-Based Questionnaire [12] and the Steve McConnell's Complete List of Schedule Risks [6, 7] as the list of risks. Nevertheless, due to the flexible data structures, it is easy to modify/extend the checklists and lists of risks as well as to modify their relationships. The present version of Risk-Guide is accessible on-line at [10].

7.   THE EXPERIMENT

In the academic year 2000/2001, Risk-Guide was used by some 38 student groups as a supporting tool during the Software Engineering Project Management course at the Technical University of Gdansk. Each group comprised 3-4 members. The task of a group was to practice selected project management activities such as effort estimation and project planning. The size of the projects taken under consideration ranged from 3 man-months to 40 man-years. Risk-Guide was used by a group to support risk identification in relation to the preliminary project planning phase. The risks were then taken under consideration while building the detailed project plan and developing risk mitigation plans.

The details of this experiment are summarised in Table 1.

No of projects	38
Experiment duration	10 weeks
Team size	3÷4 students
Project size	3 mm (3 persons / 1 month) ÷ 40.5 my (27 persons / 1.5 years) (22 projects – 10 ÷ 40 mm, 10 projects – 100 ÷ 250 mm, 6 other projects)
Phases	Planning, Design
Tasks	Prepare project strategy plan, identify project risks (answer TBQ questions, evaluate risks, select top 5 risks, describe top 5 risks, prepare mitigation and contingency plans for top 5 risks), elaborate detailed project plan
Products	Preliminary project plan, Risk management plan (list of identified risks (generated by Risk-Guide), risk evaluation, detailed description of top 5 risks, mitigation and contingency plans for top 5 risks), Detailed project plan

Tab. 1. Experiment constraints

The experiment was then evaluated using a questionnaire that was distributed among the students to gather their opinions. The questions aimed at evaluation of the ease of use of Risk-Guide and assessing the effectiveness of its support. According to the collected answers (25 groups out of 38) and the opinions collected directly by the teaching staff, the experiment resulted in:

– better understanding of vulnerable project areas,
– bringing to the surface many potential problems that otherwise would have been omitted,
– increasing students' interest in risk management (increased awareness),
– elaboration of more realistic detailed plans,
– effective collaboration and parallel working
– "common memory" of potential problems that can affect the future of the project.

In addition to the above many users stressed that the user interface of Risk-Guide was intuitive and user-friendly.

8. CONCLUSION

In the paper, we have argued that risk management is an important activity area in software development projects and that, because it is a team-oriented activity, it can benefit from tools that support communication and collaboration. As Internet is providing global interconnectivity and its use in businesses is rapidly increasing, such a tool should be Internet based and offered to a software development team disregarding the actual geographic dislocation of team members.

The paper introduced the idea of collaborative risk management and presented a tool that supports this concept. The tool has its pilot implementation that includes software project risk questionnaires and checklists that are publicly available. It has been applied during a number of student projects at our university. The preliminary results of those experiments are encouraging.

The further plans include:

– research in new ways of risk identification and representation including cause-effect chains (risk scenarios),
– research in new ways of overall project risk assessment from the assessments of individual risks,
– carrying out more case studies on real projects,
– further development of Risk-Guide towards a matured tool for collaborative risk management.

9. REFERENCES

[1] Brooks F. P., Jr., The Mythical Man-Month, Essays on Software Engineering, Anniversary Edition, Addison Wesley Longman Inc., 1995.
[2] Galagher B. P., Software Acquisition Risk Management Key Process Area (KPA) – A Guidebook Version 1.02, SEI report CMU/SEI-99-HB-001, Carnegie Mellon University, Pittsburgh PA, October 1999.
[3] Górski J., Risk Management, In: Project oriented software engineering, edited by J. Górski, Mikom, 2nd edition, 2000 (in Polish).
[4] Higuera R. P., Gluch D. P., Dorofee A. J., Murphy R. L., Walker J. A., Williams R. C., An Introduction to Team Risk Management, SEI report CMU/SEI--94-SR-01, Carnegie Mellon University, Pittsburgh PA, May 1994.
[5] Higuera R. P., Haimes Y. Y., Software Risk Management, SEI report CMU/SEI--96-TR-012, Carnegie Mellon University, Pittsburgh PA, June 1996.
[6] McConnell S., Code Complete, Microsoft Press, 1993.
[7] McConnell S., Rapid Development, Microsoft Press, 1996.
[8] Miler J., Computer system for supporting risk management in a software engineering project, Master's dissertation, Technical University of Gdańsk, Poland, 2000.
[9] Ould M. A., Strategies for Software Engineering, The management of risk and quality, John Wiley & Sons, Chichester, England, 1990.
[10] http://knot241.eti.pg.gda.pl/riskguide
[11] Rosenberg, L. H., Dr., Hammer T., Gallo A., Continuous Risk Management at NASA, presented at the Applied Software Measurement / Software Management Conference, San Jose, CA, February 1999.
[12] Sisti F. J., Joseph S., Software Risk Evaluation Method, SEI report CMU/SEI-94-TR-19, Carnegie Mellon University, Pittsburgh PA, December 1994.
[13] Van Scoy R. L., Software Development Risk: Opportunity, Not Problem, SEI report CMU/SEI-92-TR-30, Carnegie Mellon University, Pittsburgh PA, September 1992.

New Experimental Results in Differential – Linear Cryptanalysis of Reduced Variants of DES[1]

ANNA GÓRSKA[1], KAROL GÓRSKI[1], ZBIGNIEW KOTULSKI[2],
ANDRZEJ PASZKIEWICZ[3], JANUSZ SZCZEPAŃSKI[2]

[1]ENIGMA Information Security Systems Sp. z o.o., Cryptography Dept.
ul. Cietrzewia 8, 02-492 Warsaw, POLAND, e-mail: {ania,karol}@enigma.com.pl
[2]Institute of Fundamental Technological Research, Polish Academy of Sciences,
ul. Świętokrzyska 21, 00-049 Warsaw, POLAND, e-mail: {zkotulsk,jszczepa}@ippt.gov.pl
[3]Institute of Telecommunications, Warsaw University of Technology,
ul. Nowowiejska 15/19, 00-665 Warsaw, POLAND, e-mail: anpa@tele.pw.edu.pl

Abstract: At the beginning of the paper we give an overview of the linear and differential cryptanalysis of block ciphers. We describe two extensions of linear cryptanalysis (analysis with multiple expressions [7] and differential-linear cryptanalysis [10] which form the basis of the conducted experiments. Then we describe the functioning of truncated differentials [1,8] and the usage of differential structures [1,2,3].

In the second part of the article we present experimental results of implementation of the differential-linear cryptanalysis with multiple expressions applied to reduced DES variants. In an attack on DES reduced to 8 rounds we obtained a significant reduction in the number of needed chosen pairs of texts – reduction by a factor greater than 4.

Key words: cryptology, linear cryptanalysis, differential cryptanalysis, multiple expressions, differential structures

1. INTRODUCTION

Symmetric block ciphers are one of the fundamental tools in modern cryptography. Their popularity requires a high level of trust in their security. Unfortunately there are neither known constructions of block ciphers, which offer unconditional security nor practical constructions, which offer provable

This work has been supported by grant No 8 T11D 020 19 of the Polish Scientific Research Committee.

computational security. So in practice evaluations of the security of these ciphers are heuristic. The effectiveness of an attack is measured by a comparison of its complexity (time and memory) with the exhaustive search attack. During this evaluation only those attacks are taken into account, which are known at the time. One of the most important attacks considered is the linear cryptanalysis. In 1993 it was successfully used by Matsui to analyse DES [11]. It needed 2^{43} known plaintext/ciphertext pairs to derive 26 bits of the key.

Since 1993 several extensions of the linear cryptanalysis appeared (from the use of multiple expressions [7], through non-linear approximations in outer rounds[9], probabilistic counting [15] and Shimoyama's extension [16] to differential-linear cryptanalysis [10]). In our previous paper [20] we have suggested that the complete evaluation of the resistance of a block cipher to the linear cryptanalysis should consider combining the extensions mentioned above.

The purpose of this paper is to describe recent experimental results of combining the extensions of linear cryptanalysis. We have added multiple expressions to the differential-linear analysis, which results in a decrease of the amount of analysed texts in an attack on DES reduced to 8 rounds by a factor greater than 4.

1.1   NOTATION AND DEFINITIONS

Throughout this paper we use Matsui's numbering of DES bits. The input bits, key bits and output bits of F-functions, S-boxes, etc. are numbered from right to left starting from 0. We also use Matsui's notation in which $A[i]$ denotes i-th bit of vector A, while $A[i_1, i_2, \ldots i_n]$ denotes exclusive or the bits of vector A located in positions $i_1, i_2, \ldots i_n$. We also use the notation of Harpes [6] in which $A \bullet \Gamma\!A$ denotes scalar multiplication of two binary vectors over GF(2), which is equivalent to an exclusive or of the bits of A chosen by binary vector $\Gamma\!A$ (e.g. $A = 1011$, $\Gamma\!A = 0001$, then $A \bullet \Gamma\!A = 0 \oplus 0 \oplus 0 \oplus 1 = A[i_4]$).

Let P, C, K denote plaintext, ciphertext and key. We assume that plaintexts, ciphertexts and keys are uniformly distributed in appropriate spaces. We also assume that round keys are independent.

By r we denote the number of rounds, while by C_i we denote the ciphertext after round i, which means that $P = C_0$ and $C = C_r$. N denotes the number of analysed pairs of texts.

A linear approximation is a linear dependence between bits of the round input block, bits of the round output block and bits of the round subkey. A linear expression is a linear dependence between bits of the cipher input, cipher output and bits of all the subkeys. An effective linear expression is an expression which holds with probability different from 1/2.

The probability of the linear approximation (p) is defined in the probabilistic space with:

- a set of elementary events Ω, which is a Cartesian product of the set of all input blocks to the round and all subkey blocks,
- σ - field which is the set of all subsets of Ω,
- probability distribution among the elementary events assigning to each of them equal probability.

There is a random variable defined in this space, which assigns to each elementary event the value 0 or 1, dependent on whether the approximation holds or not. Event X is defined as a sum of the elementary events for which the random variable is equal to 0. The probability of the linear approximation is equal to the probability of event X in this probabilistic space.

1.2 LINEAR CRYPTANALYSIS

The basic idea of the linear cryptanalysis is to find an effective linear expression for an analysed block cipher, s.t.:

$$(P \bullet \Gamma P) \oplus (C \bullet \Gamma C) = \Sigma_z (K_z \bullet \Gamma K_z). \tag{1}$$

with a certain probability p, measured over all choices of plaintext P and key K.

In the case of iterative block ciphers, finding the linear expression has 2 steps. At first we linearise one round, looking for effective approximations of non-linear elements, then we combine them to derive the round approximation of the following form

$$(C_{i-1} \bullet \Gamma C_{i-1}) \oplus (C_i \bullet \Gamma C_i) = K_i \bullet \Gamma K_i \tag{2}$$

where C_{i-1} is the input vector to round i, C_i is the output vector from round i and K_i is the key used in round i. A linear expression is obtained by combining linear approximations in such a way, that only bits of plaintext, ciphertext and subkeys appear in the final expression. For a few rounds of a cipher and for ciphers with a simple structure (e.g. RC5) this process can be done manually, but in most cases it is easier to use a computer. The algorithms for finding linear expressions for DES can be found in [13,14,17], the comparison of their effectiveness can be found in [17] and the discussion of the potential mistakes can be found in [4].

With the effective linear expression we can start a so-called 0R attack (algorithm 1), based on the maximum likelihood method. This attack determines with the required probability whether the right side of equation 1 is equal to 0 or 1. The success rate of the attack increases with the number of analysed texts and with the bias $|p - 1/2|$.

Algorithm 1 (attack 0R) [11]
Input:
    N the known pairs of a plaintext and ciphertext,
    the effective linear expression with probability p
Step 1:
    For each pair count the value of left side of equation 1. Let N_0 be the number of
    the pairs for which the left side of the equation is equal to 0.
Step 2:
    If $N_0 > N/2$ then
        set $\Sigma_z(K_z \bullet \Gamma K_z) = 0$, if $p>1/2$ and 1 if $p<1/2$,
    else
        set $\Sigma_z(K_z \bullet \Gamma K_z) = 1$, if $p>1/2$ and 0 if $p<1/2$.
Output:
    the value of $\Sigma_z(K_z \bullet \Gamma K_z)$ (correct with probability dependent on N and $|p - 1/2|$).

In practical attacks with similar complexity we can obtain more subkey bits. For this purpose attacks with round reduction are used (1R and 2R). The first uses an effective linear expression for r-1 rounds and computes the inverse of the last round of the cipher for each candidate for the last round subkey. For each candidate we count the difference between the number of times when the left side of the linear expression is equal to 0 and when it is equal to 1. For the correct subkey the difference between this value and $N/2$ (relative to N) will be close to the expected bias for the expression in use. For incorrect keys it will be close to 0. In this way we can determine with the required probability the subkey bits in the last round and the value of the modulo 2 sum of the subkey bits appearing in the linear expression. The idea of this attack is based on a hypothesis described by Harpes [6] that the choice of an incorrect key in the last round is equivalent to adding an additional round to the cipher, which decreases the effectiveness of the linear expression in use. In practice checking all the possible values of the subkey in the last round is too complex (requires too much memory). The solution is to check only a subset of the bits of the last round subkey.

In a similar way the 1R attack can be used for the reduction of the first round of the cipher.

Algorithm 2 (attack 1R) [11]
    Input:
    N the known pairs of a plaintext and ciphertext,
    the effective subset of the last round subkey bits being searched
    the effective linear expression for r-1 rounds with probability p, which uses only
    these bits of C_{r-1} which can be computed from the effective subset of subkey bits
Step 1:
    For value of K', effective bits of subkey K_r, let N_0^i denote the number of pairs of
    texts for which the left side of the $(r-1)$ - round linear expression is equal to 0.
Step 2:
    Let $N_{0max} = \max_i (N_0^i)$ and $N_{0min} = \min_i (N_0^i)$.
Step 3:
    If $|N_{0max} - N/2| > | N_{0min} - N/2 |$ then
        set the value of effective subkey bits K'_r corresponding to N_{0max},
        set $\Sigma_z(K_z \bullet \Gamma K_z) = 0$, if $p>1/2$ and 1 if $p<1/2$,
    If $|N_{0max} - N/2| < | N_{0min} - N/2 |$ then
        set the value of effective subkey bits K'_r corresponding to N_{0min},
        set $\Sigma_z(K_z \bullet \Gamma K_z) = 1$, if $p>1/2$ and 0 if $p<1/2$,
Output:
    effective subkey bits in the last round,
    the value of $\Sigma_z(K_z \bullet \Gamma K_z)$ for rounds 1 to r-1,
    both results returned with the probability dependent on N and $|p-1/2|$.

The 2R attack allows further increase of the effectiveness of the analysis. The idea is similar to the 1R attack: we use an expression for r-2 rounds of the cipher and invert the first and the last round.

2. PROBABILISTIC FUNDAMENTALS OF LINEAR CRYPTANALYSIS

In this section we sketch the probabilistic tools which form the basis of the linear cryptanalysis. Among these tools we should list first the piling-up lemma (used to calculate the linear expression probability from probabilities of linear approximations and to calculate the success rate), the Moivre-Laplace theorem and the formula for total probability (which are fundamental for the construction of the algorithms for 0R, 1R and 2R attacks).

Lemma 1 (Piling-Up) [11]

Let $Appr_i$ $(1 \leq i \leq r)$ be independent, random variables, which are equal to 0 with probability p_i and are equal to 1 with probability $1 - p_i$. Then the probability that

$$Appr_1 \oplus Appr_2 \oplus ... \oplus Appr_r = 0 \qquad (3)$$

is equal to:

$$1/2 + 2^{r-1} \prod_{i=1}^{r} (p_i - 1/2). \qquad (4)$$

Theorem 1 (Moivre-Laplace) [5]

Let random variable $Appr$ realise some event (called success) with probability p, and opposite event with probability $q = 1 - p$. By S_N we denote a random variable which represents the number of successes in N independent trials of variable $Appr$. We define a standardised random variable S_N':

$$S_N' = \frac{\dfrac{S_N}{N} - p}{\sqrt{\dfrac{pq}{N}}} \qquad (5)$$

Then, if $0 < p < 1$:

$$\lim_{N \to \infty} \Pr(\{a < S_N' < b\}) = \frac{1}{\sqrt{2\pi}} \int_a^b e^{-t^2/2} dt, \qquad (6)$$

where $a, b \in \mathbb{R}$.

According to this theorem, for large enough N, the distribution of S_N' converges to the standardised normal distribution ($N(0;1)$).

2.1   Probabilistic fundamentals of the OR attack

From the probabilistic point of view a (random) choice of N plaintext blocks and evaluation of the left side of equation (1) can be treated as N independent trials, where by success we mean obtaining zero (with probability p), and by failure obtaining one (with probability $q = 1 - p$).

Let $p > 1/2$. The probability of correct decision is equal to the probability that the number of successes N_0 in the Bernoulli scheme is greater than $N/2$. In this case N_0 describes the random variable S_N in theorem 1 formulated above. We get a sequence of equivalences:

$$N_0 > N/2 \Leftrightarrow S_N > N/2 \Leftrightarrow S_N/N > 1/2 \Leftrightarrow$$

$$\Leftrightarrow \frac{S_N}{N} - p > \frac{1}{2} - p \Leftrightarrow \frac{\dfrac{S_N}{N} - p}{\sqrt{\dfrac{pq}{N}}} > \frac{\dfrac{1}{2} - p}{\sqrt{\dfrac{pq}{N}}}. \tag{7}$$

Therefore:

$$Pr(N_0 > N/2) = Pr(S_N > N/2) = Pr(S_N/N > 1/2) =$$

$$= Pr(\frac{\dfrac{S_N}{N} - p}{\sqrt{\dfrac{pq}{N}}} > (\frac{\dfrac{1}{2} - p}{\sqrt{\dfrac{pq}{N}}}) = Pr(S_N > \frac{\dfrac{1}{2} - p}{\sqrt{\dfrac{pq}{N}}}). \tag{8}$$

In practical ciphers probability p (and also q) should be close to 1/2, so we obtain that $\sqrt{pq} \approx 1/2$ and, in consequence, an approximation of (8):

$$Pr(N_0 > N/2) = Pr(S_N > -2\sqrt{N}\ (p-1/2)). \tag{9}$$

For large enough N from theorem 1 we obtain:

$$Pr(N_0 > N/2) = \frac{1}{\sqrt{2\pi}} \int\limits_{-2\sqrt{N}(p-1/2)}^{\infty} e^{-t^2/2} dt. \tag{10}$$

This equation describes the success rate (Table 1) for some probability p of a linear expression. This probability increases when the number of analysed texts increases and when bias $|p-1/2|$ increases.

N	$1/4|p-1/2|^{-2}$	$1/2|p-1/2|^{-2}$	$|p-1/2|^{-2}$	$2|p-1/2|^{-2}$
SR	84,1%	92,1%	97,7%	99,8%

Tab. 1. Success rate of OR attack

2.2 Probabilistic fundamentals of 1R attack

We assume that the following equations hold with probability q_i:

$$F_r(C_r, k_r) \bullet \Gamma C_{r-1} = F_r(C_r, K'_r) \bullet \Gamma C_{r-1}, \tag{11}$$

where C_r are randomly chosen, k_r is the real value of the last round subkey, K'_r are the candidates for the subkey value. F_r is the last round function with one of the arguments reduced to the length of effective subkey bits. The F_r value for each candidate K'_r is substituted in place of C_{r-1} used in the linear expression for r-1 rounds.

Assume for simplicity $|N_{0max} - N/2| > |N_{0min} - N/2|$. Then the probability of the correct choice of subkey bits is:

$$\Pr(K^i_{r\,max} = k_r) = \frac{1}{\sqrt{2\pi}} \int_{-2\sqrt{N}(p-1/2)}^{\infty} t e^{-x^2/2} dx,$$

where

$$t = \prod_{K'_i \neq k_r} \int_{-x-4\sqrt{N}(p-1/2)q^i}^{x+4\sqrt{N}(p-1/2)(1-q^i)} \frac{1}{\sqrt{2\pi}} e^{-y^2/2} dy$$

The above equation describes the success rate (Table 2) of the 1R attack.

N	$2\|p-1/2\|^{-2}$	$4\|p-1/2\|^{-2}$	$8\|p-1/2\|^{-2}$	$16\|p-1/2\|^{-2}$
SR	48,6%	78,5%	96,7%	99,9%

Tab. 2. Success rate of 1R attack

3. DIFFERENTIAL CRYPTANALYSIS

Differential cryptanalysis is a method which analyses the effect of the differences of plaintext pairs on differences of ciphertext pairs. These differences are used to assign probabilities to keys and to determine the most probable key. In the case of DES the used difference is a modulo 2 sum (XOR) of a pair of plaintexts. The XOR operation of two texts is invariant for most of the DES elements (expansion E, permutation P, xor with subkey and xor with the left half of the text). Only in the case of S boxes knowledge of the input XOR does not guarantee the knowledge of the output XOR, but the input XOR of an S box suggests a probabilistic distribution of output XORs (table containing probabilities for all possible input XORs and all possible output XORs is called the differential profile of an S box). There are entries in the differential profile table which have 0 or near 0 probability, and there are entries which have high probability e.g. 16/64. This property can be used to identify key bits. If we have the output XOR of the

F function in the last round and we know the pair of resultant ciphertexts, we can calculate the input XOR to the F function in the last round, and then input and output XOR to each S box in the last round. So it is possible to check in the differential profile table how many input pairs can lead to the entry determined by the input and output XOR of an S box. If there are k input pairs, which lead to the entry, exactly k values of the corresponding six bit key are possible. Most subkey values are suggested by only a few pairs, but the real value is suggested by all the pairs and this makes it possible to recognise it.

Let us give an example [3], XOR of two plaintexts, denoted by P* = 00808200 60000000$_x$ results in the same difference of ciphertexts after three rounds of DES C* = 00808200 60000000$_x$ with probability $p = (14/64)^2 \approx 0.05$. Above 3-round characteristic can be used to analyse 6-round DES (in so-called attack with round reduction) by deciphering a part of ciphertexts to determine when the characteristic occurs, in which case it is possible to derive some bits of the subkey. The attack is possible, because the partial deciphering of ciphertexts after round 6, which tells us when the characteristic occurs depends on a small subset of subkey bits, possible to search exhaustively. Further details of the differential attack can be found in [3].

In [8] Knudsen introduced the concept of the truncated differential, which is used in the differential-linear cryptanalysis. Just to sketch the concept, the truncated differential is a set of differential characteristics, which have a defined input XOR, and which have a defined output XOR truncated to some bits (the rest of the output XOR bits remains unknown).

The differential attack usually requires a large amount of chosen texts. To reduce the number of texts needed to be analysed Biham and Shamir [3,1] proposed the use of differential structures (these structures are of interest to us, because they also let us reduce the number of analysed texts in the differential-linear analysis [10]. The basic idea is the following: whenever it is possible to use a set of characteristics we can analyse a structure of plaintexts instead of only one pair, and this allows to get more pairs with particular differential from the same amount of plaintexts. Let us assume, that we need in an attack pairs of texts, which have all possible differences on the two youngest bits of the first byte of the plaintext. The construction is as follows: for a randomly chosen plaintext P we construct 4-tuple of plaintexts: P, P $\oplus$ 0100000000000000$_x$, P $\oplus$ 0200000000000000$_x$, P $\oplus$ 0300000000000000$_x$ and denote them by P, P$_1$, P$_2$ and P$_3$. Using them we can obtain two pairs of plaintexts of characteristic with input difference 0100000000000000$_x$ (P $\oplus$ P$_1$, P$_2$ $\oplus$ P$_3$), two pairs of plaintexts of the characteristic with input difference 0200000000000000$_x$ (P $\oplus$ P$_2$, P$_1$ $\oplus$ P$_3$), and two pairs of plaintexts of characteristic with input difference 0300000000000000$_x$ (P $\oplus$ P$_3$, P$_1$ $\oplus$ P$_2$). So after encryption of only four texts we receive six pairs of plaintexts, satisfying the input difference.

4.   EXTENSIONS OF LINEAR CRYPTANALYSIS

Several extensions to linear cryptanalysis were proposed, which improve the effectiveness of the attack, e.g. use of non-linear approximations in outer rounds reduces the number of analysed texts by a factor of $1/\sqrt{2}$.

Differential-linear cryptanalysis is a very powerful attack on DES with a reduced number of rounds. In comparison to linear cryptanalysis of DES reduced to 8 rounds which needs to analyse 500,000 of known plaintexts and to differential cryptanalysis which needs to analyse 5,000 chosen plaintexts, a differential-linear attack uses only 512 chosen plaintexts to obtain the same success probability.

Multiple expression[1] attack reduces the number of analysed texts by a factor of

$$\frac{p - 1/2}{\sqrt{\sum_i (p_i - 1/2)^2}},$$

where p is the probability of the best linear expression in use, and p_i are the probabilities of each of the expressions.

The latest extension proposed by Shimoyama reduces the number of plaintexts by the factor 25/34.

The extension proposed by Sakurai and Furuya [15], which uses probabilistic counting in reduction of rounds was originally applied to LOKI. The major advantage of this extension was the increase of the flexibility of an attack, by allowing to determine in the reduced rounds a number of bits, which is not a multiple of the number of S-box inputs. The use of this extension in an attack on DES can be found in [21].

In this section we sketch the use of multiple expression and differential-linear attack.

4.1 Differential-linear cryptanalysis

The differential-linear cryptanalysis was proposed by Langford and Hellman [10]. They noticed that three round differential characteristics [2,3], which hold with probability 1 can be effectively used in linear cryptanalysis.

The main idea of the attack is the observation that complementing two bits (which after expansion are the middle bits of an input to an S-box) in one of the analysed texts leaves many bits of C_3 unchanged.

Among these bits are input bits to Matsui's best 3-round linear expression (bits number 57, 46, 40, 35 and 17). Because the parity of these bits never changes, the parity of output bits from the linear expression is unchanged with probability $p' = p^2 \oplus (1-p)^2 = 0.576$, where $p = 0.695$ is the probability of Matsui's linear expression. (This result comes directly from the Piling-Up Lemma.)

To attack DES the cryptanalyst for each pair of plaintexts inverts the first round and is looking for a key (denote by i) which toggles bits 2 and/or 3 in the input to the second round and for each pair of ciphertexts inverts the last round, computes the parity for both inverted ciphertexts and, if the parity is equal increases N_0^{ij} where j is the index of the analysed candidate for the last round subkey. The largest N_0^{ij} indicates the correct subkeys with a probability depending on the probability of the linear expression in use and the number of analysed pairs.

---

[1] called multiple approximation in the original paper [7].

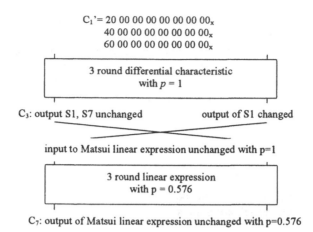

$C_1' = 20\ 00\ 00\ 00\ 00\ 00\ 00\ 00_x$
$40\ 00\ 00\ 00\ 00\ 00\ 00\ 00_x$
$60\ 00\ 00\ 00\ 00\ 00\ 00\ 00_x$

3 round differential characteristic
with $p = 1$

C_3: output S1, S7 unchanged   output of S1 changed

input to Matsui linear expression unchanged with p=1

3 round linear expression
with p = 0.576

C_7: output of Matsui linear expression unchanged with p=0.576

Fig. 1. Differential-linear attack on DES reduced to 8 rounds

Further improvement of this attack can be achieved by using differential structures mentioned above, proposed by [1,3] for packing the analysed plaintexts.

4.2   Multiple expressions

The extension proposed by Kaliski and Robshaw [7] was based on the observation that during the attack, the cryptanalyst differentiates between the distribution with an expected value equal to p and variance p^2 and the distribution with an expected value equal to $1-p$ and variance p^2. Use of multiple expressions decreases the variance of the distributions.

Modified equation 1 assumes the following form:

$$(P \bullet \mathit{\Gamma P}^j) \oplus (C \bullet \mathit{\Gamma C}^j) = \Sigma_z (K_z \bullet \mathit{\Gamma K_z}), \tag{12}$$

where $\mathit{\Gamma P}^j$, $\mathit{\Gamma C}^j$ denote binary masking vectors of a plaintext and ciphertext used in linear expression number j ($1 \leq j \leq J$).

Instead of N_0 in algorithm 1, Kaliski proposed to use the statistic of the following form:

$$U = \sum_{j=1}^{J} a_j N_0^j \tag{13}$$

where a_1, a_2, ..., a_J, are positive and s.t.

$$\sum_{j=1}^{J} a_j = 1.$$

For simplicity we assume that $p_j - 1/2 > 0$.

Algorithm 3 (attack 0R with multiple expressions) [7]
Input:
    N the known pairs of texts,
    the effective linear expressions with probability p_j.
Step 1:
    For each linear expression let N_0^j be the number of pairs for which the left side
    of equation 12 was equal to 0.
Step 2:

    Count the value $U = \sum_{j=1}^{J} a_j N_0^j$.

Step 3:
    If $U > N/2$ then
        set $\Sigma_z(K_z \bullet \Gamma K_z) = 0$, if $p > 1/2$ and 1 if $p < 1/2$,
    else
        set $\Sigma_z(K_z \bullet \Gamma K_z) = 1$, if $p > 1/2$ and 0 if $p < 1/2$.
Output:
    the value of $\Sigma_z(K_z \bullet \Gamma K_z)$ (correct with the probability dependent on N and $|p - 1/2|$ and weights a_j.)

Kaliski noticed that the distribution of statistic U can be modelled using a normal distribution. He calculated the expected values and the variance. He also indicated that when the weights a_j are proportional to the biases $(p_j-1/2)$ of linear expressions, the distance between $N/2$ and $E[U]$ is maximised. He calculated the success rate of the modified algorithm, which is equal to:

$$\Phi(2\sqrt{N} \sqrt{\frac{\sum_{j=1}^{n}(p_j - 1/2)^2}{1 - 4\sum_{j=1}^{n}(p_j - 1/2)^2}}) , \tag{14}$$

where $\Phi(.)$ denotes the normal cumulative distribution function. When $\sum_{j=1}^{J}(p_j - 1/2)$ is small, the success rate can be approximated as $\Phi(2\sqrt{N}\sqrt{\sum_{j=1}^{n}(p_j - 1/2)^2})$, while the success rate of Matsui's algorithm is equal to $\Phi(2\sqrt{N}(p - 1/2))$.

Algorithm 3 can be easily extended to 1R and 2R attacks.

5.   EXPERIMENTS

We have extended our work already presented in [20]. We propose the differential-linear cryptanalysis with multiple expressions and list decoding [12] as a tool, which enables further decrease in the number of texts in an attack on DES. We improved the result obtained by Langford [10] for analysis of 8 round DES (they achieved probability of success 80% after analysing 512 chosen plaintexts), getting the success rate improved by a factor larger than 4.

We obtained the best results by using differential 3=round characteristic proposed by Langford (ch_L) which holds with probability 1 (presented above) and the following linear expressions: Matsui's best 3-round linear expression (e_M) and:

$C_4[39,50,56,15] \oplus C_7[39,50,56,15] = 0$,
denoted by e_1, which holds with probability $p_1 = 1/2 + 0.78 / 16$,
$C_4[37,43,49,59,1] \oplus C_7[37,43,49,59,1] = 0$,
denoted by e_2, which holds with probability $p_2 = 1/2 + 0.76 / 8$,
$C_4[34,40,48,58,23] \oplus C_7[34,40,48,58,23] = 0$,
denoted by e_3, which holds with probability $p_3 = 1/2 + 0.56 / 8$, and
$C_4[34,40,58,23] \oplus C_7[34,40,58,23] = 0$,
denoted by e_4, which holds with probability $p_4 = 1/2 + 0.78 / 16$.

We have obtained the following success rate function for the basic differential-linear attack:

N	192	384	512	704
SR	0,33	0,67	0,81	0,92

Tab. 3. Success rate of differential linear cryptanalysis (linear expression e_M, differential characteristic ch_L)

and the following success rate function for the proposed differential linear attack with multiple expressions and list decoding (which basically means checking the candidates for the last round subkey, ordered by decreasing number of counts instead of checking only the best candidate). A list of candidates in our experiments has a length of 100.

N	128	192	384	512
SR	0,86	0,97	1	1

Table 4. Success rate of differential linear cryptanalysis with multiple expressions and list decoding(linear expressions e_M, e_0, e_2, e_3, e_4, differential characteristic ch_L).

6.   CONCLUSIONS AND FURTHER RESEARCH

We have presented the experimental results of the differential-linear cryptanalysis with multiple linear expressions and the list decoding method. We have achieved an improvement over previous results by decreasing the number of chosen texts by a factor greater than 4. So, the first conclusion is that to evaluate the real security of a cipher, the combinations of extensions of the basic attack have to be taken into account.

The presented attack can be effectively extended up to 11 DES rounds which is a slight improvement in comparison to previous experiments [20], but it still cannot be extended further. So, we conclude that the differential-linear cryptanalysis even extended, still remains only a theoretical attack for DES.

Our further research will concentrate on combining extensions of the linear cryptanalysis with higher order differentials [8] and impossible differentials [3,1]. Also our attention will be concentrated on combining the extensions of the linear cryptanalysis with Shimoyama's attack.

7. REFERENCES

[1] E. Biham, "Differential Cryptanalysis and its Extensions", Proceedings of V National Conference on Applications of Cryptography ENIGMA'2001, ISBN 83-911317-7-7.

[2] E. Biham, A. Shamir, "Differential Cryptanalysis of DES-like cryptosystems", Journal of Cryptology, 4(1):3-72, 1991.

[3] E. Biham, A. Shamir, "Differential Cryptanalysis of Data Encryption Standard", Springer Verlag, 1993.

[4] U. Blöcher, M. Dichtl, „Problems with the Linear Cryptanalysis of DES Using more than one Active S-Box per Round", Fast Software Encryption, Springer Verlag 1994, ISBN 3-540-60590-8.

[5] W. Feller, „Introduction to the probability theory", PWN 1977.

[6] C. Harpes, G.G. Kramer, J. L. Massey, „A Generalization of Linear Cryptanalysis and Applicability of Matsui's piling-up Lemma", Advances in Cryptology Eurocrypt'95, Springer Verlag 1995, ISBN 3-540-59409-4.

[7] B. S. Kaliski Jr., M.J.B Robshaw, „Linear Cryptanalysis Using Multiple Approximations", Advances in Cryptology Crypto'94, Springer Verlag 1994, ISBN 3-540-58333-5.

[8] L.R. Knudsen, "Truncated and Higher Order Differentials", Second International Workshop on Fast Software Encryption, Lueven, Belgium, 1994, pp. 196-211.

[9] L.R. Knudsen, M.J.B. Robshaw, „Non-Linear Approximations in Linear Cryptanalysis, Advances in Cryptology Eurocrypt'96, Springer Verlag 1996, ISBN 3-540-61186-X.

[10] S. Langford, M.E. Hellman, „Differential-linear Cryptanalysis", Advances in Cryptology Crypto'94, Springer Verlag 1994, ISBN 3-540-58333-5.

[11] M. Matsui, „Linear Cryptanalysis Method for DES Cipher", Advances in Cryptology Eurocrypt'93.

[12] M. Matsui, „On Correlation Between the Order of S-boxes and the Strength of DES", Advances in Cryptology Eurocrypt'94, Springer Verlag 1994, ISBN 3-540-60176-7.

[13] M. Matsui, „The First Experimental cryptanalysis of Data Encryption Standard", Advances in Cryptology Crypto'94, Springer Verlag 1994, ISBN 3-540-58333-5.

[14] K. Ohta, S. Morai, K. Aoki, „Improving the Search Algorithm for Best Linear Expression", Advances in Cryptology Crypto'95, Springer Verlag 1995, ISBN 3-540-60221-6.

[15] K. Sakurai, S. Furuya, "Improving linear cryptanalysis of LOKI91 by probabilistic counting method", Fast Software Encryption Workshop (FSE4), Haifa, Israel, 1997.

[16] T. Shimoyama, T. Kaneko, "Quadratic Relation of S-Box and Its Application to the Linear Attack of Full Round DES", Advances in Cryptology, Crypto'98. ISBN 3-540-64892-5.

[17] A. Zugaj, "The linear expression search algorithms", Proceedings of IV National Conference on Applications of Cryptography ENIGMA'2000, ISBN 83-911317-3-4.

[18] A. Zugaj, K. Górski, Z. Kotulski, A. Paszkiewicz, J. Szczepański, S. Trznadel, "Linear cryptanalysis of DES algorithm", (in Polish), seminar notes Institute of Telecommunications, Warsaw University of Technology, April 1998.

[19] A. Zugaj, K. Górski, Z. Kotulski, A. Paszkiewicz, J. Szczepański, S. Trznadel, „Linear cryptanalysis", (in Polish) PWT, December 1998.

[20] A.Zugaj, K. Górski, Z. Kotulski, J. Szczepański, A. Paszkiewicz, "Extending linear cryptanalysis – theory and experiments", Regional Conference on Military Communication and Information Systems, RCMCIS'99, October 6-8, 1999.

[21] A.Zugaj, K. Górski, Z. Kotulski, A. Paszkiewicz, J. Szczepański, "New constructions in linear cryptanalysis of block ciphers", ACS'2000, October 2000.

A Complete Logic of Authentication

MIROSŁAW KURKOWSKI
Institute of Mathematics & Computer Science, Pedagogical University
of Częstochowa, al.Armii Krajowej 13/15, 42-200 Częstochowa, Poland,
e-mail: m.kurkowski@wsp.czest.pl

Abstract: This paper is devoted to one of the hot topics these days: open computer networks security. It relies on the use of secure protocols called *authentication cryptographic protocols*. In the recent several years a lot of attention has been paid to analyze these protocols. One of the methods of their analysis is that of formal methods. Burrows, Abadi, Needham and others have proposed a few logics for verification of the authentication protocols properties (called *BAN-logic*). These are specialized versions of modal belief logic with special constructs for expressing some of the central concepts used in authentication processes. These logics have revealed many subtleties and serious flaws in published and widely applied authentication protocols. Unfortunately, they have also created some confusion. For example, they are not complete. In the present paper we propose a new version of authentication logic. We introduce a convenient formal language for specifying and reasoning about ryptographic protocols properties. We also provide an axiomatic inference system, a model of computation, and semantics. We prove completeness and some other important properties of this logic and discuss its expressive power.

Key words: authentication, security protocols, verification.

1. INTRODUCTION

One way of verification of cryptographic protocols is by deduction methods. They are based on constructing special dedicated logical systems with a language that allows the description of events taking place in real open computer networks and expression of the properties of the cryptographic protocols. The deduction systems are intended to enable verification of correctness of the protocols.

In the last decade a number of such logics have been proposed, first by Burrows, Abadi and Needham in [3]. Other systems named after the pioneers *BAN-logic* were published in [4], [5], [6], [7], [8], [11]. The language of this logics allows mimiching the scheme of a given protocol as a logical formula. A well done deduction can answer the question whether a protocol has a given property or not. The most important property has always been the protocol correctness formulated in a different way for various classes of protocols.

The above mentioned systems are different when it comes to their logical structure. What also differentiates them is the expressive power of their languages. Application of those systems has allowed finding numerous flaws in known and used in practice protocols. Other verification methods, however, model checking as a prominent example, have given evidence that even the protocols positively verified by logical methods may not be free of flaws and are susceptible of attacks by an intruder.

It seems there are at least two reasons for this state of things:

- the power of expression of events in real open computer networks was too weak,
- the formulas used for verification promoted the protocol from the known methods of attack no logical system, however, was able to construct the method of a new kind attack on the protocol.

We think that G. Lowe seems to be right stating that even the best BAN type logics cannot be the ideal tool for verification (see [9]). They do, however, allow us to omit many mistakes and flaws in the first stage of verification of the constructed protocol.

What should also be said that the logical system that had been presented has not many important properties relevant to a logical point of view. That means that none of them had been complete and decidable.

A logic presented in this paper is a new type of authentication logic. It's language allows precisely description of many situations taking place while the protocols are executed in real open computer networks.

This paper consists of eight sections. In the first section we introduce the language of our logic, the construction of messages and formulas, the inference rule and the axioms, as well as the basic syntactic concepts. In the second section we build a computation structure. The third section is devoted to basic semantic concepts of the system. In the fourth section we give few lemmas and theorems and sketch their proofs. The fifth section concerns computational complexity of our logic. The sixth one concerns possible application of our logic, especially about it's expressing power with respects to the correctness properties of protocols. Some conclusion can be found in the final section.

2.   SYNTAX

Let $\Sigma = \Sigma_A \cup \Sigma_P \cup \Sigma_G \cup \Sigma_S$ be a set of primitive terms, where:

$\Sigma_A = \{\varepsilon, a_1, \ldots, a_n\}$ is any finite alphabet with ε distinguished as the empty string;

$\Sigma_P = \{P_1, \ldots, P_n\}$ is a set of constants representing the participants;

$\Sigma_K = \{K_T, K_{P_1}, \ldots, K_{P_n}, K_{P_1}^{-1}, \ldots, K_{P_n}^{-1}\}$ is a set of constans representing public and private keys of the participants, with K_T distinguished as a key representing the identity encryption;

$\Sigma_G = \Sigma_K \cup \{K_1, \ldots, K_k\}$, where K_i ($i = 1, \ldots, k$) are constants representing the keys to possibly be generated;

$\Sigma_S = \{N_1, ..., N_m\}$ is a set of constants representing the secrets to possibly be generated (like *nonces*).

We extend the set Σ by induction to the set Λ of *messages*. We also define by induction the sets of formulas Φ_a, Φ_p, Φ, Φ_{n_Σ} as subsets of Λ.

Basic logical connectives:

$\neg, \wedge, \vee, \Rightarrow, \equiv, \triangleright, \triangleleft, \rightarrow, \mapsto, \angle.$

Auxiliary logical connectives:

$\succ, \prec, \#.$

The set Λ of messages is defined as follows:
1. If $m_1, m_2, .., m_\sigma \in \Sigma$ and $\sigma < n_\Sigma$, then $(m_1, m_2, .., m_\sigma) \in \Lambda$, $((m_1, m_2, .., m_\sigma)$ denotes concatenation of $m_1, m_2, .., m_\sigma$, we assume that a number n_Σ is large enough to bound the length of all possible messages).
2. If $L \in \Lambda$ and $K \in \Sigma_K$, then $\{L\}_K \in \Lambda$, $(\{L\}_K$ denotes a ciphertext consisting of a message L and encrypted under a key K).
3. If $\alpha \in \Phi_{n_\Sigma}$, then $\alpha \in \Lambda$, where Φ_{n_Σ} is a special subset of Φ which are defined as follows.

There will be defined four kinds of sets of formulas.
We first define Φ_a as a set of special formulas called *action* formulas.
Let Φ_a be a smallest set such that:
1. If $P \in \Sigma_P$ and $K \in \Sigma_G$, then $\rightarrow^K P \in \Phi_a$, ($\rightarrow^K P$ that P has an encryption key K)
2. If $L \in \Lambda$ and $P \in \Sigma_P$, then $P \triangleright L$, $P \triangleleft L \in \Phi_a$, ($P \triangleright L$ that P received a message L; $P \triangleleft L$ – P has sent a message L).
3. If $P \in \Sigma_P$ and $N \in \Sigma_S$, then $P \mapsto N \in \Phi_a$, ($P \mapsto N$ that P has generated a secret N).

Now, we define a set Φ_p of so called auxiliary formulas.
4. If $\{K_1, .., K_n\} \subseteq \Sigma_G$ and $M, L \in \Lambda$, then $M \angle_{\{K_1, .., K_n\}} L \in \Phi_p$, ($M \angle_{\{K_1, .., K_n\}} L$ that a message M is a part of message L encrypted under keys $K_1, .., K_n$; for example $M \angle_{\{K\}} L_1, \{M\}_K, L_2)$.
5. If $M \in \Lambda$ and $L \in \Lambda$, then $M \angle L \in \Phi_p$, ($M \angle L$ that M is an arbitrary part of message L)
6. If $L \in \Lambda$, then $\#L \in \Phi_p$, ($\#L$ that a message L is "fresh")
7. If $L \in \Lambda$ and $P \in \Sigma_P$, then $P \succ L$, $P \prec L \in \Phi_p$, ($P \succ L$ that P see a message L; $P \prec L$ P say a message L).

Finally we define Φ the set of all formulas.
Let Φ be a smallest set such that:
8. $\Phi_a \cup \Phi_p \subseteq \Phi$,
9. If $\alpha, \beta \in \Phi$, then $\neg\alpha, \alpha \wedge \beta, \alpha \vee \beta, \alpha \Rightarrow \beta, \alpha \equiv \beta \in \Phi$.

Let **At** be a set of all formulas of the form: $\to^K P$, $P \triangleright L$, $P \triangleleft L$, $P \mapsto N$, $M \angle_{\{K_1,..,K_n\}} L$, $M \angle L$.

Let **Lit** be a smallest set of all formulas such that:

1   **At** $\subseteq$ **Lit**,
2.   If $\alpha \in$ **At**, then $\neg\alpha \in$ **Lit**.

We define also usefull abbreviations:

$$\#L \text{ iff } \bigvee_{\lambda\in\Lambda} \bigvee_{P\in\Sigma_P} (\lambda \angle L \wedge P \mapsto \lambda),$$

$$P \prec L \text{ iff } \bigvee_{\lambda\in\Lambda} (P \triangleleft \lambda \wedge L \angle \lambda),$$

$$P \succ L \text{ iff } \bigvee_{\lambda\in\Lambda} (P \triangleright \lambda \wedge (L \angle_{\{K_1,..,K_n\}} \lambda \Rightarrow \wedge_{i=1,..,n} \to^{K_i} P)).$$

Let $l : \Phi \to N$ (**N** denotes the set of natural number) be a function such that:

1.   If $\alpha \in \Phi_a \cup \Phi_p$ then $l(\alpha) = 1$,
2.   If $l(\alpha) = k$ then $l(\neg\alpha) = k + 1$,
3.   If $l(\alpha) = k$ and $l(\beta) = m$ then $l(\alpha \bullet \beta) = k + m$, (for $\bullet \in \{\wedge, \vee, \Rightarrow, \equiv\}$).

Last $\Phi_{n_\Sigma} = \{\alpha \in \Phi : l(\alpha) < n_\Sigma\}$.

Observe that Λ is a finite set.

In our system we have modus ponens as the only inference rule.

$$r_o \subseteq (\Phi \times \Phi) \times \Phi, \quad (r_o): \frac{\alpha,\ \alpha \Rightarrow \beta}{\beta}.$$

We take as axioms all substitutions of classical tautologies (we denote the set of those substitutions by A_0).

Here are the other axioms:

1. $P \mapsto N \Rightarrow \#N$,
2. $\#L \Rightarrow (L \angle M \Rightarrow \#M)$,
3. $M \angle_{\{K_T\}} M,L$,
4. $M \angle_{\{K_T\}} L,M$,
5. $L,M \angle \{L\}_K$,
6. $P \triangleright L \Rightarrow \bigvee_{Q\in\Sigma_P-\{P\}} Q \triangleleft L$.

Let $A = A_0 \cup \{A\ 1, \ldots, A\ 6\}$ be a set of all axioms. We denote our deduction system by $\Theta = (r_0, A)$.

If a formula α has a proof in Θ from a set of formulas $X \subseteq \Phi$, then we say α is *a consequence* of X.

The set of all consequences of X is denoted by $Cn(X)$.

By *a theory* we mean a set X of formulas such that $X = Cn(X)$.

Proposition 1. The following formulas are consequences of $\varnothing$.
1. $P \rhd L \implies P \succ L$,
2. $P \succ M,L \implies P \succ M \land P \succ L$,
3. $P \succ \{L\}_K \implies (\to^K P \implies P \succ L)$,
4. $P \lhd L \implies P \prec L$,
5. $P \prec M,L \implies P \prec M \land P \prec L$,
6. $P \prec \{L\}_K \implies P \prec L$.

3. COMPUTATION STRUCTURE

Let $P_1, \dots, P_n$ denote the participants (users, agents, principals) cooperating in an open computer network.

Let P_e be the *environment,* representing all the others users having access to the net (P_e also stands for an intruder).

Each user of the network can perform the following *actions*

β 1. (P_m *send* L) – P_m sent out a message L,

β 2. (P_m *rec* L) – P_m received a message L,

β 3. (P_m *gen* L) – P_m generated a new secret L,

β 4. (P_m) – the empty action.

By the *local history* of user P_m ($m \in \{e, 1, .., n\}$) we mean the named sequence of actions $(\alpha_1, \dots, \alpha_k)$ executed by this user. Number k indicates the time instance by which P_m has performed actions $\alpha_1, \dots, \alpha_k$. The local history of P_m in time k we denote by h_m^k.

We distinguish the time instance $k = 0$, in which all local user histories are empty sequences.

A sequence of local histories ($h_e^k, h_1^k, .., h_n^k$) is called *a global history* in time k (denoted by h^k).

Every user P_m in any instant k has:

a set of encryption keys (denoted by K_m^k), which P_m knows how to use in the given moment. In the time $k = 0$ this set can be arbitrary but it includes P_m's private key and all the users' public keys. The sequence of sets $K_m^0, \dots, K_m^k$ satisfies $K_m^i \subseteq K_m^{i+1}$ (for all $i = 1, \dots, k-1$). Each of the sets K_m^{i+1} can be larger than its predecessor K_m^i by containing the key generated by P_m (the effect of action (P_m *gen* K) or obtained by P_m as part of a message; for example as a result of executing action (P_m *rec* A,K,B));

a set of messages sent by P_m up to the moment k (denoted by $Send_m^k$), enlarged gradually in time after executing action of type (P_m *send* L);

a set of messages received by P_m up to the moment k (denoted by Rec_m^k);

a set of messages generated by P_m up to moment k (denoted by Gen_m^k),

On top of it user P_e has a *buffer* m – a set of messages sent to other users but not received by them (effect of action $(P \text{ } send \text{ } L)$), yet . After executing action $(P \text{ } rec \text{ } L)$ a message L is removed from the set m.

The local state of user P_i ($i = 1, .., n$) in moment k consists of:

1. the local history h_i^k,

2. the set K_i^k of encryption keys,

3. the set $Send_i^k$ of messages sent,

4. the set Rec_i^k of messages received,

5. the set Gen_i^k of messages generated.

We denote by s_i^k the local state of user P_i in moment k.

The local state of user P_e in moment k consists of:

1. the local history h_e^k,

2. the set K_e^k of encryption keys,

3. the set $Send_e^k$ of messages sent,

4. the set Rec_e^k of messages received,

5. the set c_e^k of messages generated.

6. the buffer m^k.

We denote by s_e^k the local state of environment P_e in moment k.

By *a global state* in moment k (denote by s^k) we mean a sequence $(s_e^k, s_1^k, ..., s_n^k)$ of local states.

By *a run r* we mean a sequence of global states:
$r = (s^0, s^1, ...)$ such that any element s^{k+1} is obtained from s^k by adding one of the actions β1, β2 or β3 to a local history of single user while the other local histories get the empty action (β4).

By *a system* ℜ we mean the set of all possible runs satisfying the following condition: if $(P \text{ } rec \text{ } L)$ is the last member of h_P^k, then $(Q \text{ } send \text{ } L)$ occurs in h_Q^{k-1}, for some $Q \neq P$.

By *a point of the system* ℜ we mean a pair *(r,k)*, where r denotes a run from system ℜ and k is natural number.

4. SEMANTICS

The truth of a formula α ($\alpha \in \Phi$) at a point *(r,k)* of the system ℜ is defined by induction on the structure of α:

$(r,k) \ \square \ P \rhd L$	iff	$L \in Rec_m^k$,	
$(r,k) \ \square \ P \lhd L$	iff	$L \in Send_m^k$,	
$(r,k) \ \square \ P \mapsto N$	iff	$N \in Gen_m^k$,	
$(r,k) \ \square \ \to^K P$	iff	$K \in K_m^k$,	

$(r,k) \ \square \ M \angle_{\{K_1,..,K_n\}} L$ iff   L is of the following form

$$A_0, \{A_1, .. \{A_n, L, B_n\}, .., B_1\}, B_0,$$

for some $n \in N$ and $A_i, B_i \in \Lambda$ ($i = 1, .., n$),

$(r,k) \ \square \ \neg\alpha$	iff	non $((r,k) \ \square \ \alpha)$,
$(r,k) \ \square \ \alpha \wedge \beta$	iff	$(r,k) \ \square \ \alpha$ and $(r,k) \ \square \ \beta$,
$(r,k) \ \square \ \alpha \vee \beta$	iff	$(r,k) \ \square \ \alpha$ or $(r,k) \ \square \ \beta$.

A formula α is *a tautology* if for any point *(r,k)* of the system $\Re$ *(r,k)*$\square \ \alpha$.

A formula α is called *a semantical consequence of set* X (denoted X$\square \ \alpha$) iff for any point *(r,k)* of the system $\Re$ and for any formula $\beta \in X$ if *(r,k)*$\square \ \beta$, then *(r,k)*$\square \ \alpha$.

A point *(r,k)* of the system $\Re$ is called *a* model for a set X iff all formulas of X hold in *(r,k)*.

5. COMPLETENESS

In this section we give our main result showing the basic properties of our logic. We prove the completeness following the main ideas due to Tarski and Lindenbaum [1]. *TL(X)* in following lemmas denotes what is often called the Tarski-Lindenbaum extension of X.

Lemma 1. For any consistent theory X (i.e., X $\neq$ Φ, X = Cn(X)) there exists a theory *TL(X)* such that:
1. $X \subseteq TL(X)$,
2. $TL(X) \neq \Phi$,
3. $TL(X) = Cn(TL(X))$
4. $\forall_{\alpha \in \Phi} (\alpha \in TL(X) \vee \neg\alpha \in TL(X))$.

Proof (sketch). We order the formulas belonging to sets Φ_a, Φ in sequences $\Phi_a = \{\varphi_1, ..., \varphi_k\}$ and $\Phi = \{\psi_1, ..., \psi_m, ...\}$.

Now, let us define sequences $(X_n)_{n=1,..,k}$, $(Z_n)_{n \in N}$ of sets of formulas in the following way:

$$X_0 = X,$$

$$X_{n+1} = \begin{cases} Cn(X_n \cup \{\varphi_{n+1}\}), & \text{if} \quad \varphi_{n+1} \in Cn(X_n) \\ Cn(X_n \cup \{\neg\varphi_{n+1}\}), & \text{otherwise.} \end{cases}$$

$$Z_0 = X_k,$$

$$Z_{n+1} = \begin{cases} Cn(Z_n \cup \{\psi_{n+1}\}), & \text{if} \quad \psi_{n+1} \in Cn(Z_n) \\ Cn(Z_n \cup \{\neg\psi_{n+1}\}), & \text{otherwise} \end{cases}$$

Finally we define $TL(X) = \bigcup_{n \in N} Z_n$.

$\square$

Lemma 2. Every consistent theory has a model.

Proof (sketch). Let X be a consistent set of formulas such that $X = Cn(X)$. We construct a model $TL(X)$. To this end we order the formulas belonging to $TL(X) \cap \Phi_a$ in the following sequence:

$$TL(X) \cap \Phi_a = \{ \alpha_1,..,\alpha_{n_1}, \beta_1,..,\beta_{n_2}, \gamma_1,..,\gamma_{n_3} \},$$

where formulas α are of type $P \mapsto L$, β of type $P \triangleleft L$ and γ of type $P \triangleright L$.

Now we construct a run r in the computation structure introduced in section 2. We start off with all empty local histories. The local histories develop by adequately inserting the users actions representing the formulas from $TL(X) \cap \Phi_a$. Let $k = n_1 + n_2 + n_3$.

At a point (r,k) constructed this way all the formulas $\alpha \in TL(X) \cap \Phi_a$ hold.

Now, we prove by induction on α that:

$$\alpha \in TL(X) \text{ iff } (r,k) \square \ \alpha.$$

for all formulas $\alpha \in \Phi$.

It is obvious for all $\alpha \in \Phi_a$ (by construction of (r,k)).

Assuming that the above property holds for formulas α and β we show that this property holds for $\neg\alpha$ and $\alpha \wedge \beta$, too.

($\neg\alpha$) Since $\neg\alpha \in TL(X)$ is equal to $\alpha \notin TL(X)$ and by induction hypothesis we have $\text{non}((r,k) \square \ \alpha)$. Hence $(r,k) \ \neg\alpha$.

($\alpha \wedge \beta$) Since $\alpha \wedge \beta \in TL(X)$ is equal to $\alpha \in TL(X)$ and $\beta \in TL(X)$ and by induction hypothesis we have $(r,k) \square \ \alpha$ and $(r,k) \square \ \beta$. Hence $(r,k) \square \ \alpha \wedge \beta$.

Since $X \subseteq TL(X)$ the point (r,k) constructed above models X too.

$\square$

The Completeness Theorem. For any set of formulas X, $\alpha \in Cn(X)$ iff $X \square \ \alpha$.
Proof (sketch). $\rightarrow$ We can show that the axioms are tautologies and the derivations preserve truth.

← (A contrario) We assume $\alpha \notin Cn(X)$. By Lemma 1, there exists a set $TL(X)$ such that $\neg\alpha \in TL(X)$. By Lemmas 1 and 2 $TL(X \cup \{\neg\alpha\})$ has a model. I.e., $(r,k)\square \neg\alpha$, for some (r,k). Since $X \subseteq TL(X \cup \{\neg\alpha\})$, (r,k) models X as well. Thus α is not a semantical consequence of X.

$\square$

6. COMPUTATIONAL COMPLEXITY

One of the most important properties of deduction (logical) systems is their decidability a possibility of automatic verification whether a given formula is a tautology or not. In this section we show a decidability procedure for our logic.

1. **Satisfiability.** Let α be a formula of our language. We can convert α into the disjunctive normal form $\alpha \equiv \alpha_1 \vee \alpha_2 \vee \ldots \vee \alpha_n$, where formulas α_i ($i = 1,..,n$) are conjunctions of formulas from the set **Lit**: $\alpha_i \equiv \alpha_i^1 \wedge \alpha_i^2 \wedge \ldots \wedge \alpha_i^{n_i}$ (where $\alpha_i^1, \alpha_i^2, \ldots, \alpha_i^{n_i} \in$ **Lit**). Consider all these conjunctions for $i = 1,\ldots,n$. If the set $Cn(\alpha_i^1 \wedge \alpha_i^2 \wedge \ldots \wedge \alpha_i^{n_i})$ is consistent, then there exists a point (r,k) in the computation structure such that: $(r,k)\square (\alpha_i^1 \wedge \alpha_i^2 \wedge \ldots \wedge \alpha_i^{n_i})$. We have $(r,k)\square \alpha_1 \vee \alpha_2 \vee \ldots \vee \alpha_n$, so $(r,k)\square \alpha$.

2. **Tautologies.** It is obvious that a formula α is a tautology iff formula $\neg\alpha$ is not satisfable. To check if a formula α is a tautology we verify satisfability of $\neg\alpha$. If all of sets $Cn(\alpha_i^1 \wedge \alpha_i^2 \wedge \ldots \wedge \alpha_i^{n_i})$, ($i = 1,\ldots,n$) are inconsistent, then α is a tautology.

Presented algorithms have complexity $O(n!2^n)$ in the number of atomic formulas occurring in α. But it is important to note that the formulas to be considered for verification of cryptographic protocol properties are very short.

7. APPLICATIONS TO VERIFICATION OF PROTOCOLS

As we are mentioned in the introduction we think that G. Lowe seems to be right stating that even the best BAN type logics cannot be the ideal tool for verification. However applying these logics allow us to omit many mistakes and flaws in the first stage of verification of the constructed protocol.

To express the basic properties of the cryptographic protocols, like their correctness, researchers use some construction containing *the belief connective* $\models$, bringing it into the language of the deduction systems as one of the basic connectives. We think that this is one of main reasons of the positive verification of the protocols using this approach, even through some of them are susceptible to an intruder's attack.

In our logic we propose the language without the belief connective as a basic one. However it is definable in our language.

Also this allows modifications of the definition of the believe connective when a new type of attack is revealed.

We propose the following definition (by induction) of the belief connective:
For formulas of Φ_a.

1. $P \models P \rhd L \equiv P \rhd L,$
2. $P \models P \lhd L \equiv P \lhd L,$
3. $P \models P \mapsto L \equiv P \mapsto L,$
4. $P \models \to^K P \equiv \to^K P,$

5. $P \models (Q \lhd L) \equiv P \rhd L \wedge \bigvee_{\lambda_1, \lambda_2 \in \Lambda}$

   $[P \mapsto \lambda_1 \wedge \lambda_1 \angle L \wedge P \prec \{\lambda_2\}_{K_Q} \wedge P \angle \lambda_2 \wedge \lambda_1 \angle \lambda_2],$

6. $P \models (Q \rhd L) \equiv P \lhd L \wedge \bigvee_{\lambda_1, \lambda_2 \in \Lambda}$

   $[P \mapsto \lambda_1 \wedge \lambda_1 \angle L \wedge P \succ \{\lambda_2\}_{K_P} \wedge Q \angle \lambda_2 \wedge \lambda_1 \angle \lambda_2],$

For the other formulas.

7. $P \models (P \models \alpha) \equiv P \models \alpha,$
8. $P \models (Q \models P \lhd L) \equiv P \models (Q \rhd L),$

9. $P \models (Q \models P \rhd L) \equiv P \rhd L \wedge \bigvee_{\lambda_1, \lambda_2, \lambda_3 \in \Lambda}$

   $[\lambda_1 \angle L \wedge \lambda_1 \angle \lambda_2 \wedge \{\lambda_2\}_{K_Q} \angle \lambda_3 \ P \models Q \rhd \lambda_3),$

10. $P \models \neg \alpha \equiv \neg P \models \alpha$
11. $P \models \alpha \wedge \beta \equiv P \models \alpha \wedge P \models \beta,$
12. $P \models \alpha \vee \beta \equiv P \models \alpha \vee P \models \beta.$

We think that in such an extended language many properties of cryptographic protocols, for example the correctness property, can be expressed.

8.   CONCLUSION

In this paper we have proposed a new type of authentication logic. Its language allows the description of events taking place in real open computer networks and the expression of the properties of the cryptographic protocols. Our logic has important structural properties: completeness and decidability.

This paper is a part of the authors doctoral dissertation to be submitted to The Institute of Computer Science, Polish Academy of Sciences under the supervision of Professor Marian Srebrny.

We would like to thank Marian Srebrny and Andrzej Zbrzezny for usefull discusions and Anna Berezowska for help at work with the text.

9. REFERENCES

[1] **Tarski A., Mostowski A., Robinson R.**, *Undecidable theories*, North Holland 1953.

[2] **Needham R., Schroeder M.**, *Using encryption for authentication in large networks of computers*, Communications of the ACM, 21(12), (1978) pp. 993-999.

[3] **Burrows M., Abadi M.** and **Needham R.**, *A logic of authentication*, Research Report 39, Digital Systems Research Center, February 1989.

[4] **Gong L., Needham R., Yahalom R.**, *Reasoning about belief in cryptographic protocols*, In Proceedings of the 1990 IEEE Symposium on Security and Privacy, (1990) pp. 234-248, IEEE Computer Society Press.

[5] **Abadi M., Tuttle M.**, *A semantics for a logic of authentication*, In Proceedings of the tenth ACM Symposium on Principles of Distributed Computing, pp. 201 - 216, ACM Press, August 1991.

[6] **Syverson P.**, *The use of logic in the analysis of cryptographic protocols*, In Proceedings of the 1991 IEEE Computer Security Symposium on Security and Privacy, (1991) pp. 156-170, IEEE Computer Society Press.

[7] **Syverson P., Meadows C.**, *A logical language for specifying cryptographic protocol requirements*, In Proceedings of the 1993 IEEE Computer Security Symposium on Security and Privacy, (1993) pp. 165-177, IEEE Computer Society Press.

[8] **Syverson P., van Oorschot P.C.**, *On unifying some cryptographic protocol logics*, In Proceedings of the 1994 IEEE Computer Security Foundations Workshop VII, (1994) pp. 14-29, IEEE Computer Society Press.

[9] **Lowe G.**, *An attack on the Needham- Schroeder public-key authentication protocol*,. Information Processing Letters, 56, (1995) pp. 131-133.

[10] **Lowe G.**, *Breaking and Fixing the Needham-Schroeder Public-Key Protocol Using FDR*, In Proceedings of TACAS, (1996) 147-166, Springer Verlag.

[1] **Bleeker A., Meertens L.**, *A semantics for BAN logic*, In Proceedings of DIMACS'97, (1997) New Brunswick NJ.

Generating Bent Functions

ANNA GROCHOLEWSKA-CZURYLO, JANUSZ STOKLOSA
Poznań University of Technology, pl. Skłodowskiej-Curie 5, 60-965 Poznań, Poland

Abstract: In the paper a method of efficient generation of random bent functions is presented. Obtaining a random bent function is not a straight forward process, since the introduction of bent functions in the most of published works studied their construction and gave algorithms for their generation. Drawing such functions at random from a set of all the Boolean functions is not feasible for n-argument functions for n higher than 4. On the other hand, all the known algorithms for constructing bent functions have deterministic dependencies which introduce certain low complexity problems and significantly narrow the range of bent functions that can be generated with each algorithm (bent function class). We describe a new method of obtaining random bent functions without constraints described above. The algorithm for generating bent functions operates in the Algebraic Normal Form domain. This approach allows for generation of bent functions of arbitrary order and even some special nonlinear requirements as homogeneity.

Key words: Cryptography, S-boxes, Boolean functions, random generation of bent functions.

1.   INTRODUCTION

S-box theory emerged quite recently from the field of cryptography. It deals with the basic design criteria of secure cryptographic systems based on the so-called substitution-permutation networks. Many modern cryptographic algorithms built upon the foundations laid by C. E. Shannon in 1976 [2] are implemented as a series of iterations: substitutions (realized by substitution boxes (so called S-boxes) and permutations (realized by permutation boxes, or P-boxes). S-boxes provide confusion, as they are controlled by an unknown cryptographic key. P-boxes, which have no key, provide diffusion.

Such ciphers are relatively easy to implement. If both P-boxes and S-boxes are selected at random, there is a good chance that the cipher would be secure, assuming that the algorithm runs a sufficiently large number of iterations and also that S-boxes themselves are sufficiently large. Before being applied, S-boxes generated at the random are verified against a collection of the S-box criteria. This approach was analysed by O'Connor [1].

However, because of time constrains (like real time enciphering) the real challenge in S-box theory is to minimize the number of iterations required for achieving the required level of security. The systematic design of S-boxes is a major and growing area of cryptography [3,4].

The Boolean functions, whose properties have been extensively studied, are a universal tool used to construct S-boxes. The quality of a single, cryptographically strong Boolean function, is measured by its cryptographic properties. The criteria against which a function quality is measured are mainly nonlinearity, balanced, avalanche and propagation criteria.

These criteria (with the exception of balanced) are best fulfilled by a special class of the Boolean functions, namely bent functions (or perfect nonlinear functions). Cryptographically strong, bent functions have been under the scrutiny of international cryptographic community since their introduction in 1976 by Rothaus [5]. A lot of work has been devoted to the generation of bent functions [6,7,8,9] and S-box construction using bent functions [3,10,11,12,13,14]. The main subject of this paper is the efficient generation of random bent functions with specific nonlinear properties.

2. PRELIMINARIES

Let $GF(2) = <\Sigma, \oplus, \cdot>$ be two-element Galois field, where $\Sigma = \{0, 1\}$, $\oplus$ and $\bullet$ denotes the sum and multiplication mod 2, respectively. A function $f: \Sigma^n \rightarrow \Sigma$ is an n-argument Boolean function. Let $z = x_1 \cdot 2^{n-1} + x_2 \cdot 2^{n-2} + \ldots + x_n \cdot 2^0$ be the decimal representation of arguments $(x_1, x_2, \ldots, x_n)$ of the function f. Let us denote $f(x_1, x_2, \ldots, x_n)$ as y_z. Then $[y_0, y_1, \ldots, y_{2^n-1}]$ is called a truth table of the function f.

The n-argument Boolean function f is linear if it can be represented in the following form: $f(x_1, x_2, \ldots, x_n) = a_1 x_1 \oplus a_2 x_2 \oplus \ldots \oplus a_n x_n$. Let L_n be a set of all the n-argument linear Boolean functions. Let $M_n = \{g: \Sigma^n \rightarrow \Sigma \mid g(x_1, x_2, \ldots, x_n) = 1 \oplus f(x_1, x_2, \ldots, x_n)$ and $f \in L_n\}$. A set $A_n = L_n \cup M_n$ is called a set of n-argument affine Boolean functions. The Boolean function $f: \Sigma^n \rightarrow \Sigma$ that is not affine is called a nonlinear Boolean function.

Let $N_0[y_0, y_1, \ldots, y_{2^n-1}]$ be a number of zeros (0's) in the truth table $[y_0, y_1, \ldots, y_{2^n-1}]$ of function f, and $N_1[y_0, y_1, \ldots, y_{2^n-1}]$ be number of ones (1's). A Boolean function is balanced if $N_0[y_0, y_1, \ldots, y_{2^n-1}]$ = $N_1[y_0, y_1, \ldots, y_{2^n-1}]$.

A Boolean function can also be represented as a maximum of 2^n coefficients of the Algebraic Normal Form. These coefficients provide a formula for the evaluation of the function for any given input $x = (x_1, x_2, \ldots, x_n)$:

where $\sum$, $\oplus$ denote the modulo 2 summation.

The order of nonlinearity of the Boolean function $f(x)$ is a maximum number of variables in a product term with non-zero coefficient a_J, where J is a subset of {1, 2,

3, ..., n}. In the case where J is an empty set the coefficient is denoted as a_0 and is called a zero order coefficient. Coefficients of order 1 are a_1, a_2, ..., a_n, coefficients of order 2 are a_{12}, a_{13},..., $a_{(n-1)n}$,..., coefficient of order n is $a_{12...n}$. The number of all ANF coefficients equals to 2^n.

Let us denote the number of all (zero and non-zero) coefficients of order i of function f as $\sigma_i(f)$. For n-argument function f there are as many coefficients of a given order as there are i-element combinations in n-element set, i.e. $\sigma_i(f) = \binom{n}{i}$.

The Hamming weight of a binary vector $x \in \Sigma^n$, denoted as $hwt(x)$, is the number of ones in that vector.

The Hamming distance between the two Boolean functions f, g: $\Sigma^n \rightarrow \Sigma$ is denoted by $d(f, g)$ and is defined as follows:

$$d(f,g) = \sum_{x \in \Sigma^n} f(x) \oplus g(x)$$

i.e. it is equal to the number of arguments at which the values of functions f and g differ.

The distance of the Boolean function f from a set of n-argument Boolean functions X_n is defined as follows:

$$\delta(f) = \min_{g \in X_n} d(f, g)$$

where $d(f, g)$ is the Hamming distance between functions f and g. The distance of a function f from a set of affine functions A_n is the distance of function f from the nearest function $g \in A_n$.

The distance of function f from a set of all affine functions is called the nonlinearity of function f and is denoted by N_f.

3. CRYPTOGRAPHIC CRITERIA AND BENT FUNCTIONS

Strict avalanche criterion was first defined by Webster and Tavares [14]. A Boolean function f: $\Sigma^n \rightarrow \Sigma$ is said to satisfy the strict avalanche criterion (SAC) if and only if $f(x) \oplus f(x \oplus \alpha)$ is balanced for any $\alpha \in \Sigma^n$ such that $hwt(\alpha) = 1$.

For a Boolean function satisfying the SAC, any 1-bit change of inputs causes the change of the output with probability 1/2.

The SAC was generalized by Forré [15]. Forré defines that a function f satisfies the SAC of order k if a partial function obtained by keeping any k input bits to f constant still satisfies the SAC.

The Boolean function f: $\Sigma^n \rightarrow \Sigma$ is perfectly nonlinear if and only if $f(x) \oplus f(x \oplus \alpha)$ is balanced for any $\alpha \in \Sigma^n$ such that $1 \square hwt(\alpha) \square n$.

For a perfectly nonlinear Boolean function, any change of inputs causes the change of the output with probability of 1/2.

Meier and Staffelbach [16] proved that the set of perfectly nonlinear Boolean functions is the same as the set of Boolean bent functions defined by Rothaus [5].

Another generalization of the SAC, introduced by Adams and Tavares [8] and independently by Preneel *et al.* [6], is now called the propagation criterion. It extends the notion of perfect nonlinearity.

The Booleam function $f: \Sigma^n \to \Sigma$ is said to satisfy the propagation criterion (PC) of degree k if and only if $f(x) \oplus f(x \oplus \alpha)$ is balanced for any $\alpha \in \Sigma^n$ such that $1 \square hwt(\alpha) \square k$.

Let $PC_n(k)$ denote the set of the Boolean functions with n variables satisfying the propagation criterion of degree k. $PC_n(n)$ is the set of the perfect nonlinear Boolean functions with n variables.

Perfectly nonlinear functions (or bent functions) have the same, and the maximum possible distance to all affine functions. So their correlation to any affine function is consistently bad (minimal). Linear cryptanalysis works if it is possible to find a good linear approximation of the S-box

Bent functions are not balanced. This property prohibits their direct application in S-box construction, however there exist numerous methods for modifying bent function in such a way so that the resulting function is balanced and still maintains the good cryptographic properties of a bent function [16]. Hamming weight of a bent function equals $2^{n-1} \pm 2^{n/2-1}$.

Differential analysis [18] can be seen as an extension of the ideas of attacks based on the presence of linear structures [3]. As the perfect nonlinear Boolean function has maximum distance to the class of linear structures (equal to 2^{n-2}), they are a useful class of functions for constructing mappings that are resistant to differential attacks.

Bent functions exist only for even n. The nonlinear order of bent functions is bounded from above by $n/2$ for $n > 2$. The number of Boolean bent function for $n > 6$ remains an open problem.

4. GENERATING BENT FUNCTIONS

As mentioned earlier, there exist a number of algorithms for bent functions construction. The most known ones are enumerated in [20]: the two Rothaus constructions[5], the eigenvectors of Walsh-Hadamard matrices [19],], constructions based on the Kronecker algebra, concatenation, dyadic shifts and linear transformations of variables. The generalization of the Rothaus construction by Maiorana and McFarland is discussed in [21].

For Boolean functions with $n \square 6$ all bent functions are known. Homogenous Boolean bent functions of order 2 and 3 are known for Boolean functions with $n = 8$. Homogenous bent functions of order $n/2$ do not exist for $n \square 8$.

As an example of a method for bent functions construction let us consider the following [8,22]:

Let B_n denote a set of bent functions $f: \Sigma^n \to \Sigma$ with n even.

Given a set of bent functions B_6, bent functions in B_8 can be constructed using the following method:

Let $a, b \in B_6$. Then the function $f: \Sigma^8 \to \Sigma$ defined by:

$$f(x_0...x_7) = \begin{cases} a(x_0...x_5), & x_6 = 0, x_7 = 0 \\ a(x_0...x_5), & x_6 = 0, x_7 = 1 \\ b(x_0...x_5), & x_6 = 0, x_7 = 0 \\ b(x_0...x_5) \oplus 1, & x_6 = 0, x_7 = 0 \end{cases}$$

is bent [8]. Rearrangements of the 64 blocks in the expression above also result in bent functions.

Most of the known bent function constructions take bent functions of n arguments as their input and generate bent functions of $n+2$ arguments.

One major drawback of these methods is the fact that they are deterministic. Only short bent functions ($n = 4$ or 6) are selected at random and the resulting function is obtained using the same, deterministic formula every time. Even if there is some "random" element in such generation (like adding a linear term to the resulting bent function) it does not bring any new quality to the generated function.

It is infeasible to draw bent functions at random already for $n \geq 6$. For $n = 6$ the probability of a bent function generated at random equals to *ca.* $1.38*10^{-17}$.

The main idea presented in this paper is to generate bent functions randomly in algebraic normal form instead of generating random Boolean function as truth tables.

Operating ANF representation gives a great control over the nonlinear characteristics of generated functions. The basic properties of a bent function can then be used to tremendously narrow search space which makes generation of bent functions feasible for $n \geq 8$ even on a standard PC machine.

The algorithm for the generating bent functions in the ANF domain takes as its input the minimum and maximum number of ANF coefficients of every order that the resulting functions are allowed to have. Since the nonlinear order of bent functions is less or equal to $n/2$, clearly in ANF of a bent function can not be any ANF coefficient of order higher then $n/2$. This restriction is the major reason for random generation feasibility, since it considerably reduces the possible search space.

The number of ANF coefficients of orders less or equal to $n/2$ can be fixed or randomly selected within allowed range (i.e. between 0 and $\sigma_i(f) = \binom{n}{i}$). If the number of coefficients for a given order i is fixed then all generated functions will have the same number of coefficients of that order, but the coefficients themselves will be different in each generated function. If the number of coefficients for a given order i is randomly selected then all generated functions will not only have different coefficients but also the number of coefficients of order i will vary from function to function.

It is of course possible to fix the number of coefficients for some orders and have the varied number of coefficients for other orders.

One important consequence of this approach is the possibility of prohibiting the generation of bent functions which are merely a linear transformations of other bent functions. This is easily achieved by setting the number of coefficients of order 0 and 1 to 0. So in the ANF of the resulting functions there will be no linear part.

Bent functions of any order can be generated with this method, simply by setting any higher order coefficients to 0.

Homogenous bent functions can also be generated easily.

One drawback of the method is the fact that it does not guarantee the generation of bent functions without repetitions, although the chance of generating two identical bent functions is minimal with any reasonably selected ranges of number of ANF coefficients. However, if avoiding repetitions is an absolute requirement, the set of generated bent functions must be checked for duplicates.

The limitations of this approach are twofold. First there is a feasibility limit. Number of possible functions grows with the number of coefficients of higher orders ($i > 2$) and generating a bent function quickly becomes infeasible. So the algorithm works best with the low number of higher order coefficients (e.g. < 6 for $n = 8$ and order $i = 3$ and 4).

Due to the above limitation, this method does not generate all possible bent functions with equal probability. In principle, it would be possible but is not feasible for the reason described above. One has to limit the number of higher order coefficients and at the same time prohibit the generation of some bent functions.

5.   RESULTS

A number of bent functions have been generated with different parameters of their ANF representation. In this section we present the results of comparing a set of bent functions obtained with the use of random ANF generation and a set of bent functions obtained by using the construction method described in the previous section.

First, we present some statistical properties of bent functions generated using our method. This results will be used to streamline the algorithm's parameters for faster bent function generation.

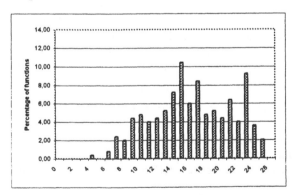

Fig. 1. 2nd order coefficients with $\sigma_3(f)=0$

Figures 1–4 show the distribution of a number of the generated bent functions with all possible numbers of the 2nd order ANF coefficients. For every experiment the number of the 3rd order coefficients is fixed and equals 0 for experiment 1, it equals 1 for experiment 2 and so on. The number of the 4th order coefficients is set to 0 for all the experiments.

It can be easily seen that for the certain numbers of the 2nd order coefficients there are no bent functions or they are very seldom. The most of the bent functions (except for experiment 1 with the homogenous bent functions of order 2) have from 7 to 17 coefficients of the 2nd order. This tendency is even more apparent when ANF of a function includes also coefficients of order 4, as in experiment 5 depicted in Figure 5.

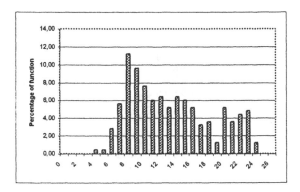

Fig. 2. 2nd order coefficients with $\sigma_3(f)=1$

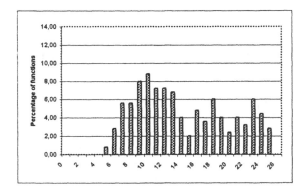

Fig. 3. 2nd order coefficients with $\sigma_3(f)=2$

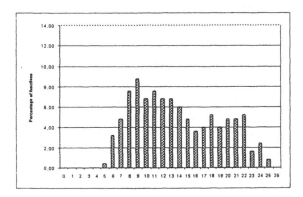

Fig. 4. 2nd order coefficients with $\sigma_3(f)=3$

Based on these results we have restricted the number of the 2nd order coefficients to fall between 7 and 14. This allows faster bent function generation, as only potentially "fruitful" combinations of the 2nd order coefficients are used. At the same time, we run experiments with all the feasible 2nd order coefficients enabled and we do not notice a significant difference in bent functions qualities.

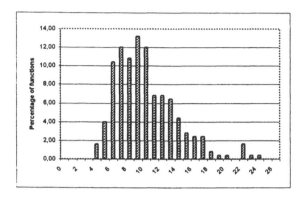

Fig. 5. 2nd order coefficients with σ3(f)=2, σ4(f)=2

Now we present a comparison study of bent functions sets. One set of bent functions has been generated using the construction method described in section 4 and in [22]. For random and distinct i, j the nonlinearity of $f_i \oplus f_j$ was calculated. Figure 6 shows the resulting nonlinearity distribution (in percentage).

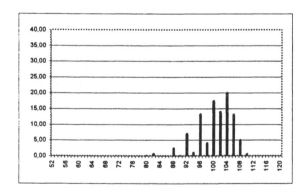

Fig. 6. Nonlinearity distribution of pairs of constructed bent functions

In Figure 7 the nonlinearity of pairs of randomly generated bent functions is depicted. There is a clear difference in the distribution. For randomly generated functions the distribution is shifted towards higher values (i.e. pairs have better nonlinearity) and is also much more narrow – more appropriate pairs can be found in this set of functions.

The random bent functions were generated with the following parameters: a number of the 2nd order coefficients was from 7 to 14, a number of the 3rd order a coefficients was fixed at 2, and a number of the 4th order ANF coefficients was also fixed at 2. There were no coefficients of order 0 and 1 to prevent the occurrences of the bent functions that would be just linear transformations of one another.

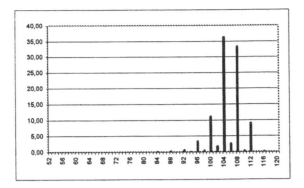

Fig. 7. Nonlinearity distribution for pairs of randomly generated bent functions

The results obtained in our experiments are also better then those presented in [22] for the special subsets of bent functions i.e. for the Maiorana functions and Maiorana functions with permuted inputs. That last set of functions shows the best nonlinearity distribution for pairs of functions constructed using standard methods. It is shown on figure 8.

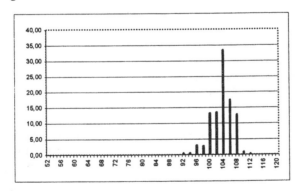

Fig. 8. Nonlinearity distribution for pairs of Maiorana functions with permuted inputs

It is an interesting fact that there are relatively small number of pairs with nonlinearity non divisible by 4 in the sets of randomly generated bent functions (in comparison to the sets of constructed bent functions).

6. CONCLUSIONS AND FURTHER RESEARCH

We are certain that random bent function generation is an interesting alternative to bent function construction based on deterministic formulas. Bent functions randomly generated in ANF seem to have better properties then functions obtained using some of the well-known constructions. However, more detailed experiments are necessary to precisely assess the cryptographic qualities of these functions.

Perhaps a combined method of ANF generation of relatively short bent functions (i.e. $n \square 10$) and then supplying them as an input for deterministic construction can yield some interesting results.

7.   REFERENCES

[1] O'Connor L.J. An analysis of a class of algorithms for S-box construction. *Journal of Cryptology*, 7(3):133-152, 1994.

[2] Shannon C.E. Communication Theory of Secrecy Systems. *Bell Systems Technical Journal*, 28:656-715, 1949.

[3] Nyberg K. Perfect nonlinear S-boxes. *Advances of Cryptology – EUROCRYPT'91, LNCS*, 547:378-386, 1991.

[4] Seberry J., Zhang X.M., Zheng Y. Systematic generation of cryptographically robust S-boxes. *Proceedings of the 1st ACM Conference on Computer and Communication Security*, 1993.

[5] Rothaus O.S. On bent functions. *Journal of Combinatorial Theory*, 20:300-305, 1976.

[6] Preneel B, Van Leekwijck W, Van Linden L, Govaerts R, Vandewalle J. Propagation characteristics of Boolean functions. *Advances in Cryptology – EUROCRYPT'90, LNCS*, 473:161-173, 1991.

[7] Dillon J.F. A Survey of Bent Functions, *NSA Technical Journal, Special Issue*, 191-215, 1972.

[8] Adams C.M., Tavares S.E. Generating and Counting Binary Bent Sequences, *IEEE Transactions on Information Theory*, IT-36:1170-1173, 1990.

[9] Maiorana J.A. A Class of Bent Functions, *R41 Technical Paper*, 1971.

[10] Adams C.M. A Formal and Practical Design Procedure for Substitution Permutation Network Cryptosystems, *Ph.D. Thesis, Department of Electrical Engineering*, Queen's University, 1990.

[11] Dawson M., Tavares S. E. An Expanded Set of S-Box Design Criteria Based on Information Theory and its Relation to Differential-Like Attacks, *Advances in Cryptology. Proc. of EUROCRYPT'91*, 352-367, 1991.

[12] Kam J.B., Davida G. Structured Design of Substitution-Permutation Encryption Networks, *IEEE Transactions on Computers*, C-28:747-753, 1979.

[13] O'Connor L. An Analysis of Product Ciphers Based on the Properties of Boolean Functions, *Ph.D. Thesis, Dept. of Computer Science*, University of Waterloo, 1992.

[14] Webster A.F., Tavares S.E. On the Design of S-Boxes, *Advances in Cryptology: Proc. of CRYPTO'85*, 523-534, 1986.

[15] Forré R. The strict avalanche criterion: spectral properties of Boolean functions with high nonlinearity. *Advances in Cryptology – CRYPTO'88*, Springer-Verlag, 1990.

[16] Meier W., Staffelbach O. Nonlinearity criteria for cryptographic functions. *Advances in Cryptology - EUROCRYPT '89, LNCS*, 434:549-562, 1990.

[17] Biham E., Shamir A. Differential Cryptanalysis of the Data Encryption Standard. Springer-Verlag, 1993.

[18] Matsui M. Linear cryptanalysis method for DES cipher. *Abstracts of EUROCRYPT'93*, 1993.

[19] Yarlagadda R., Hershey J.E. A note on the eigenvectors of Hadamard matrices of order 2^n, *Linear Algebra & Appl.*, 45:43-53, 1982.

[20] Yarlagadda R., Hershey J.E. Analysis and synthesis of bent sequences, *Proc. IEE*, 136:112-123, 1989.

[21] Nyberg K. Constructions of bent functions and difference sets, *Advances in Cryptology – EUROCRYPT'90, LNCS*, 473, 1991.

[22] Mister S., Adams C. Practical S-Box Design, *Workshop on Selected Areas in Cryptography (SAC '96) Workshop Record*, Queens University, pp. 61-76, 1996.

Multilevel Lattice-Based Authorization in Distributed Supervisory and Control Systems

JERZY PEJAŚ

Faculty of Computer Science & Information Systems,
Department of Software Engineering & Information Security, Technical University of Szczecin,
49, Żołnierska st., 71-210 Szczecin, Poland, phone:(+48 91) 4495662, fax: +4891 4876439,
e-mail: jerzy.pejas@wi.ps.pl

Abstract: The paper presents a new approach to building the access control systems, which allows eliminating the access matrix control (ACL) and defining the local, decentralized access policy. This approach leads to the decentralization of the access control system both in case of DAC and MAC access policies. However there is a need to introduce: (1) new data structures such as attribute certificates AC (privileges certificates), use-condition certificates UCC instead of centralized rules of the access policy, capability certificates (CC), which secure state of the access control system is dependent on, and (2) the partition of the supervisory and control system into separated protection domains. Considering the distribution of the certificates, related to the access control system, they ought to be delivered to the reference monitor in a proper way, and applied to the subject request authorization. The protection domain structure is also specified. This structure models the trust relations between users (subjects) of the system and protected domains. The security theorem, which is formulated in the paper, specifies the necessary conditions for a distributed supervisory and control system to be secure.

Key words: access control, security models, Biba and LaPadula model, public key certificate, attribute certificate, public key infrastructure

1.   INTRODUCTION

The modern supervisory and control systems are complex and distributed computer systems, which components are able to communicate each other. Such components can be treated as physical pieces of hardware, the group of hardware, logical devices or as combinations of all these elements. Objects (devices) are created, activated and then form a process named a device server. Each device server understands the previously defined set of commands, which are specific for a class of objects of the device server. The objects of the device server can be exported and then accessed via a network interface.

The main problem of supervisory and control systems is the open access to devices from any network point and by all network users. It allows the unauthorized subject to modify system parameters (e.g. controller settings) and input (steering or command) signals as well. Such accesses can be restricted by the standard system administration means. However, it is rather obvious, that classical solutions, e.g. direct access control to sensors, actuators, links and terminals are not applicable because of distributed nature and accessibility of particular system components from many, even remote places.

It is not possible to protect sensitive actions on devices because, for once rendered accessible device, all commands could be executed. Also, there is no ability to block a device in kind of single user mode to do some actions, which are required exclusively for a user (e.g. tuning or calibration of hardware).

Furthermore, data sets of different device servers are integrated. It means, that these sets belong not only to one user, but also to more ones (shared data bases, shared information resources located in different control and supervisory subsystems), of whom everybody can be interested in some part of data that can overlap.

The access to shared information from different places by using different applications (software) can create many new problems, which threaten efficiency and assurance of supervisory and control systems. These threats arise mainly in cases when there is a necessity to decentralize, in some rational manner, the access to information and delegate the obligation, privileges and responsibility to the proper subject. Such decentralization requires the access control system that allows giving to subject the properly selected set of access permissions to particular objects and then to control the information flowing between these objects.

To guarantee the security of a distributed supervisory and control system many concerns need to be addressed. Among others authorization is the most important. The problem of authorization can be divided into two related subproblems: representations and evaluation. Representation refers to the specification of authorization requirements, while evaluation refers to the actual determination of the authorities of subjects, which the authorization requirements are given.

It is obvious, that each distributed supervisory and control system should contain an information protection subsystem, which must be based on precisely defined mathematical models for controlling access to this information. In the paper we consider a new information protection model (security model) derived form two commonly used models: a discretionary security model and a mandatory security model (see S. Castano, et.al. [9]). The proposed model aims at achieving both information secrecy and integrity. The model defines a set of privileges, requests and properties. All specified properties have to be satisfied for the system to be secure. Each required operation is controlled and its execution is allowed if and only if a new system state still remains secure, i.e. it satisfies all properties of the model.

If we assume, that resources are assigned to physically different domains (device servers) and managed by different administrators or owners and co-owners of these resources, then within each domain must exist mechanism, which enforces the realisation of particular access policy to resources of this domain. Furthermore, each subject must be willing to trust that these mechanisms will enforce access control, but the owners and co-owners should be able to flexibly specify access requirements for their resources.

Assuming the separation of the protection domains, subjects and objects the paper deals with the model of a secure and decentralized access control system, which protects the resources of the supervisory and control (steering) system and does not allow for unauthorized leakage both privileges and information. The current system state is controlled by the distributed reference monitor, which is related to each protection domain. The distributed reference monitor stores the data, which allows it to make decision if privileges (more generally, evidences) submitted by some subject meet simultaneously the predefined conditions and allows for the required access. The evidences are based on digitally signed documents, called certificates, that convey identity (a public key certificate, PKC), use conditions (a use-conditions certificate, UCC), attributes (an attribute certificate, AC) and authorization (a capability certificate, CC).

2. RELATION TO OTHER WORK

The paper touches three essential problems. The first problem concerns the proposal of the modified security model, which allows to control both all accesses to objects and undesirable flows between them. The new security model is built on the ground of Bell-LaPadula model (Bell D.E., L.J.LaPadula [1, 2, 3, 4]), Biba model (K.J.Biba [5]) and their modifications adapted to the needs of supervisory and control systems, presented in works of J.Pejaś and W.Chocianowicz [16, 17]. A new security model does not contain classical access matrix. Instead of this, the access rights and other subject privileges are inserted into the attribute certificate (S. Farrell, R. Housley [11]), issued by attribute authority.

The second problem is related to the first problem and refers to the proposal of removing the access matrix (an access control list, ACL) from the security model and substituting it for the attribute certificate. Using the attribute certificate in this role is not a new idea. Probably, Ellison (C.Ellison, et.al. [10]) has formulated it firstly and then Johnston and Mudumbai applied it in the system Akenti (W.Johnston, S. Mudumbai [12]). These works state, that attribute certificates contain a set of attributes, which are digitally signed (certified) by an appropriate attribute authority (AA). The owner of the attribute certificate is eventually able to delegate some subset (may be entire) of possessed privileges (in the form of a delegation certificate - DC) to an entity that is permitted to act also as an attribute authority and further delegate the privileges (until to an end-entity, that can not further delegate that privileges). Our solution states that the attribute certificate can be issued by end entity that are the owners or co-owners of some objects as well as by domain administrators (however, it is only allowed when the administrator is in the possession of the attribute certificate validating this right).

The third proposal is integrally related to the security model and allows defining and realization of the different security policies within the particular protection domains. The security policy can be formulated by any subjects and particularly by owners or co-owners of resources which are members of these domains. Each subject can create and digitally sign use-condition certificates (W. Johnston, S. Mudumbai [12]) that define conditions (in the form of rules, axioms, etc.) that must be satisfied by user before being given access to resources. The active system of access policy management that is described in the paper can be compared with existing proposals and solutions, for example with the trust management systems for widely distributed resources *PolicyMaker* (M. Blaze, et. al. [7]), *KeyNote* (M. Blaze, et. al. [8]) and *Akenti* (W. Johnston, et. al. [12]). However these systems are only prepared to enforce the discretionary access policy (DAC).

3. CENTRALIZED SECURITY MODEL

Assume the existence of a set of objects O (devices), which can be intuitively viewed as consisting of information receptacles, and a set of subjects S, which can be intuitively viewed as consisting of agents (clients) who can operate on objects in various ways. The security of the supervisory and control system can be informally defined as appropriately governing subjects access to objects.

The proposed security model is modelled as an automaton with inputs, an internal state and output. The inputs correspond to the commands users give to the system. The internal state of the automaton corresponds to the information stored in the device servers. Output from the automation consists of command responses – the things that users view or obtain in response to particular requests.

In this section we define what it is to be a system state and what it is for a system state to be secure. We assume the existence of the following basic sets: O – a set of objects (devices), $S{\subset}O$ – a set of subjects, L – a set of security levels, where $\geq$ is a partial order on L such that $(L, \geq)$ is a lattice, $F=L^S{\times}L^O$ – a set of all possible ordered pairs of functions $f=\{f_S, f_O\}$ such that f_S gives the security level (clearance) associated with each subject, f_O – gives the security level (classification) associated with each object, A – a set of standard and non-standard access attributes (i.e, read, write, append, etc.), UC – a set of use condition attributes, RA – a set of request components (i.e. get, give, change security level, create an attribute certificate, etc.) and T – a set of indices (i.e., elements of a time set, identification of discrete moments).

Additionally, we define the complementary sets, which allow us to assign a public key certificate (PKC), an attribute certificate (AC) and a use condition certificate (UCC)to each subject and object. They are as follows: $K = \{K_{PR}, K_{PUB}\}$ – a set of asymmetric key pairs (a private and a public, respectively) such, that for each private key $k_{PR}{\in}K_{PR}$ exists exactly one public key $k_{PUB}{\in}K_{PUB}$, $F_K=K^S$ – a set of all functions f_K, which associates the key pair with each subject, $C = P(K)^S{\times} P((A{\cup}\phi){\cup}(RA{\cup}\phi))^S{\times} P(S)^O$ – a set of all functions $\{c_{CA}, c_{AA}, c_{PA}\}$ such, that c_{CA} – the total function from S to $P(K)^2$, c_{AA} – the total function from S to $P((A{\cup}\phi){\cup}(RA{\cup}\phi))$ and c_{PA} - total functions from O to $P(S)$. Intuitively, $c_{PA}(x)$ is the set of subjects which can create an use condition certificate for an object x while two other sets $c_{CA}(m)$ and $c_{AA}(n)$ mean the asymmetric key set that can be certificated by

---

[1] The symbol ϕ denotes null element of a set.

[2] P(α) denotes all subset of a set α.

subject m and the set of standard and non-standard access attributes and request components, that are allowed to be placed into attribute certificate by a subject n.

The designed protection system is divided distinctly into two parts. The first part is directly related to the Bell-LaPadula security model and describes a finite set of subjects, a finite set of objects and the security level associated with each subject and object. The security levels can be only changed by an authorized set of subjects. The second part of the designed system concerns the creation of certificates. The certificates are issued by subjects which have the special permissions and belong to the pre-selected set of authorized subjects. The proper certificates should be attached to each request submitted by the requestor to the protected system. In particular, the sets of various certificate types and their general structures are as follows:

- a set of public key certificates *CertPKC* is defined by function f_{pkc}, which has the form f_{pkc}: $S \times S \times K_{PR} \times K_{PUB} \times T \times T \rightarrow CertPKC$, where $S \times S$ means who issues the certificate and whom the certificate is issued by while the $T \times T$ defines the certificate validity period,

- a set of attribute certificates *CertAttr* is formed by a function f_{ac}: $S \times S \times K_{PR} \times CertPKC \times CertPKC \times (O \cup \phi) \times (A \cup \phi) \times (RA \cup \phi) \times T \times T \rightarrow CertAC$, where ϕ means null element of the set **A** or **RA**,

- a set of use condition certificates *CertUCC* is formed by a function f_{ucc}: $S \times (O \cup \phi) \times K_{PR} \times CertPKC \times CertPKC \times UC \times T \times T \rightarrow CertUCC$; in case, when use condition is defined for the null element of set, then it means the general use condition certificate; the general use condition is applied by default to all objects.

Conceptually, the rights of subjects to access objects can be stored in an access matrix with rows corresponding to subjects, columns corresponding to objects, and subjects, and matrix entries indicating various access rights. The access matrix is usually stored by rows (access rights form the capability lists) or by column (access control lists). The set of attribute certificates presented above allows to remove the necessity of using the access matrix and to solve new problems in the specification of authorization requirements, which result from the distributed systems nature and the prevalent client-server style of computing (see T.Y.C. Woo, S.S. Lam [18]).

A system is a state machine such that each state $v=(b, f, certAttr, certUCC)$ is an element of $V=(B \times F \times CertAttr \times CertUCC)$, where $B=P(S \times O \times A)$ is the set of all possible current access sets such that a subject $s \in S$ has access $a \in A$ to an object $o \in O$ if and only if $(s, o, a) \in b$ (see Bell D.E., L.J.LaPadula [1]). The state transition function T_R: $R \times Cred \times V \rightarrow V$, where R is a particular set of requests as a function of set S, O, F, A and RA, $Cred=P(CertPKC) \times P(CertAttr) \times K_{PR}$, moves the system from one state to another.

A system $\Sigma(T_R, V, v_0) \subset R^T \times V^T \times CertCAP^T$ is the finite state machine consisting of states V, transition function T_R, and initial state $v_0 \in V$. *CertCAP* is a capability certificate, which is created by reference monitor (see section 3) in response to each request submitted by a subject concerning the access to some object.

Definition 1 *(Bell and LaPadula [1]):* State $v=(b, f, certAttr, certUCC) \in V$ is *simple secure* relative to functon f if and only if for each $certAttr \in CertAttr$,

$certUCC \in CertUCC$ and $(s,o,\underline{x}) \in b$ $(s \in S,\ o \in O,\ \underline{x} \in A)$ such that $\underline{x} = read$ or $\underline{x} = write$ the clearance of the subject s dominates the classification of the object o, i.e. $f_S(s) \geq f_O(o)$.

We assume that access attributes *read*, *write* and *append* with respect to some object allow a subject to have, respectively, a read-only, read and write, and write-only capability with respect to that object.

Definition 2 *(Bell and LaPadula [1])*: Let's consider a set $\Theta(s:\underline{x},\underline{y},...,\underline{z}) = \{o:o \in O \wedge [(s,o,\underline{x}) \in b \vee (s,o,\underline{y}) \in b \vee ... \vee (s,o,\underline{z}) \in b]\}$. We say, that the state $v=(b,\ f,\ certAttr,\ certUCC) \in V$ is **-secure* if and only if for each $s \in S$ and a set $[\Theta(s:write,\ append) \neq \phi \wedge \Theta(s:read,write) \neq \phi]$ the relation $f_O(o_1) \geq f_O(o_2)$ is true for each $o_1 \in \Theta(s: write,\ append)$ and $o_2 \in \Theta(s:read,\ write)$.

Definition 3: A state is state secure if and only if it is *simple secure* and **-secure*.

Not all public key certificates, attribute certificates, use condition certificates and capability certificates that belong to sets *CertAttr*, *CertUCC*, *CertPKC* and *CertCAP*, respectively, are properly defined. Intuitively, the correctness means the certificate which has been created by an authorized subject using the suitable private key being in his or her own possession. The conditions of certificates correctness are given in the definition presented below.

Definition 4: For the given public key $k_{PUB} \in K_{PUB}$ a public key certificate $f_{pkc}(s_i,\ s_s,\ k'_{PR},\ k^*_{PUB},\ t_{nb},\ t_{na}) \in CertPKC$, where $s_i \in S$ - a certificate issuer, $s_s \in S$ – a certificate subject, $k'_{PR} \in K_{PR},\ k^*_{PUB} \in K_{PUB},\ f_K(s_i)=(k'_{PR},\ k'_{PUB}),\ f_K(s_s)=(k^*_{PR},\ k^*_{PUB}),$ $t_{nb} \in T$ and $t_{na} \in T$, is properly defined certificate if and only if $s_i \in c_{CA}(k_{PUB})$.

Definition 5: For the given attribute or request $a \in P((A \cup \phi) \cup (RA \cup \phi))$ an attribute certificate $f_{ac}(s_i,\ s_s,\ k_{PR},\ certPKC_i,\ certPKC_s,\ a,\ t_{nb},\ t_{na}) \in CertAC$, where $s_i \in S$ - a certificate issuer, $s_s \in S$ – a certificate subject, $k_{PR} \in K_{PR},\ f_K(s_i)=(k_{PR},\ k_{PUB}),$ $certPKC_i=f_{pkc}(..,\ s_i,\ ..,\ k_{PUB},\ ..,\ ..)$ and $certPKC_i=f_{pkc}(..,\ s_s,\ ...)$ – a properly defined public key certificates, $t_{nb} \in T$ and $t_{na} \in T$, is properly defined attribute certificate if and only if $s_i \in c_{AA}(a)$.

Definition 6: For the given use condition attribute $uc \in UC$ use condition certificate $f_{ucc}(s_i,\ o_s,\ k_{PR},\ certPKC_i,\ uc,\ t_{nb},\ t_{na}) \in CertUCC$, where $s_i \in S$ - a certificate issuer, $o_s \in O \cup \phi$ – an object (may be none), $k_{PR} \in K_{PR},\ f_K(s_i)=(k_{PR},\ k_{PUB}),$ $certPKC_i=f_{pkc}(..,\ s_i,\ ..,\ k_{PUB},\ ..,\ ..)$ – the properly defined public key certificate, $t_{nb} \in T$ and $t_{na} \in T$, is properly defined attribute certificate if and only if $s_i \in c_{PA}(o_s)$.

The definitions formulated above allow to introducing the definition of the state transition function and give the necessary conditions for system $\Sigma(T_R,\ V,\ v_0)$ in order to be secure.

Definition 7: The state transition function T_R is secure if and only if each transition $T_R(c,\ v)=v^*$, where $v=(b,\ f,\ certAttr,\ certUCC)$ and $v^*=(b^*,\ f^*,\ certAttr^*,$

certUCC*), implies that each time when $v \neq v^*$, then credentials $c \in Cred$ submitted by the subject s fulfil the use condition of the object o (conditions are placed into use condition certificates), and public key certificates, attribute certificates and use condition certificates are properly defined.

Definition 8 (J.McLean [15]): A system $\Sigma(T_R, V, v_0)$ is secure only if (1) initial state $v_0 \in V$ is both *simple secure* and **-secure* state, (2) its transition function T_R is *transition secure* and (2) all states reachable from v_0 by a finite sequence of one or more requests from R are *simple secure* and **-secure*.

4. DISTRIBUTED SECURITY MODEL

The widely distributed resources are the most important feature of the supervisory and control systems. Therefore each supervisory and control system should enforce the use of mechanisms which enable the secure information to exchange with the subject and the object. It should be related to subjects and objects which belong to the same as well to different protection domains.

Assume, that the supervisory and control system consist of r protection domains. Let $\Sigma(T_{Ri}, V_i, v_{i0})$ mean the protection system related to the i-th protection domain $(i=1,...,r)$, where the set of states $V_i=(\underline{B}_i \times F \times CertAttr \times CertUCC)$ is a set of ordered 4-tuple $(\underline{b}_i,f,certAttr,certUCC)$ such that $\underline{b}_i=(b_i,b^i) \in B_i=(B_i,B^i)$ while $b_i \in B_i=P((S-S_i) \times O_i \times A)$ and $b^i \in B^i=P(S_i \times O \times A)$, $f=\{f_s,f_o\} \in F=L^S \times L^O$, $certAttr \in CertAttr$, $certUCC \in CertUCC$, and the state transition function has the form $T_{Ri}:R \times Cred \times V_i \rightarrow V_i$. The distributed protection system is described then as the relation of the form $\Sigma(T_R, V, v_0)$, where $V = V_1 \cup V_2 \cup ... \cup V_r$ and $T_R = V_1^{R \times Cred \times V1} \times V_2^{R \times Cred \times V2} \times ... \times V_r^{R \times Cred \times Vr} = \{T_{R1}, T_{R2}, ..., T_{Rr}\}$ for the set of subjects $S = S_1 \cup S_2 \cup ... \cup S_r$ (we assume, that a condition $S_i \cap S_j = \phi$ is fulfilled for each pair (i, j); it means, that each subject has a strictly assigned entry point to the system) and objects $O = O_1 \cup O_2 \cup ... O_r$ (now we assume that a condition $O_i \cap O_j = \phi$ is fulfilled for each pair (i, j). i.e. there is no object which belongs to different protection domains).

The partition of the whole system into protection domains allows to connect the single reference monitor with each domain[1], that keeps track of the status of system state (see Fig.1). The reference monitor can be treated as a subject, which has permissions to control the authorization process and to validate the privileges of another subjects. The set of reference monitors is defined by any function $c_{ref} \in C_{ref} = P(S)^D$ such that c_{ref} – the total function from D to $P(S)$ and where D = $\{1, 2, ..., r\}$ is a set of protection domain indexes.

Note, that the given subject $s_i \in S_i$ which belongs to the i-th protection domain (called his or her domestic domain) can possess attribute certificates issued by any authorized subject being in particular a member of another domain than a subject s_i. The similar remark concerns the use condition certificate: for the given object $o_i \in O_i$ only authorized subject can be involved in issuing this type of certificates. The

---

[1] The set of all reference monitors forms a distributed reference monitor.

reference monitor of each protection domain should know the list of authorized subjects in both cases.

Reference monitor inspects the process of giving a subject *s* the access rights to the object *o*. If the authorization is finished successfully then the reference monitor of the subject domestic domain creates the capability certificate, which validates the rights of the subject *s* to the object *o*. Additionally, if the protection domains of the subject and object are different, then the capability certificate is also simultaneously created both by the object and subject domestic domains. In result each domestic domain contains two validated lists of capability certificates. The first one, called validated capability list (VCL), describes all current rights of subjects, which are the members of domestic domain. The second one is the validated access list (VAL) of the objects and contains the set of all authorized accesses to these objects, which are allowed for subjects not being a member of objects domestic domain.

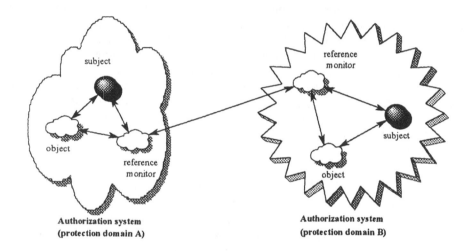

Fig. 1. Two protection domains

The procedure of the subject request confirmation is organized as follows:

- When the subject logs into the system the reference monitor of the domestic domain (assume, that this is the *i-th* protection domain) creates new session number $id_{ses} \in \mathbf{ID_{ses}}$. This number is the argument of each subject requests and each capability certificates issued by the reference certificate.

- The subject prepares the request R which involves the transition function T_i, signs it, attaches the public key certificate, attribute certificates and sends all as the package to his or her domestic domain.

- The reference monitor of i-th protection domain validates the request authenticity. If the request sent by the subject concerns the object which belongs to the subject domestic domain, then the reference monitor based on the validated capability list (VCL) and object use condition certificate is (or is not) able to confirm the subject rights to the object. The reference monitor decision has the form of the capability certificate which is added to the validated capability list.

- If the request doesn't concern the object of i-th protection domain (suppose it is the j-th domain), then the reference monitor completes the request by adding the entire subject validated capability list, signs and sends the package to the reference monitor of the j-th domain. If submitted evidences can be correctly verified, then the reference monitor of the j-th domain issues the capability certificate. This certificate is added to the object validated access list (VAL) of the j-th domain and then sent (together with use-condition certificate) to the reference monitor of the i-th domain. The monitor of i-th domain verifies the correctness and validity of the received certificate and then adds it to the validated capability list (VCL) if the verification process returns the positive results.

- When the subject of the i-th protection domain shut down the session, then the reference monitor broadcasts this fact to all reference monitors, which are founded on the subject validated capability list (VCL).

There are two advantages of issuing the complementary capability certificates. First, both protection domains are in possession of the mechanism which allows them to control the freshness of the subject privileges. The second one, at any moment each side may remove the previously issued capability certificate sending the properly specified message to all reference monitors which previously have accepted these certificates and have added them to the appropriate validated access list (VAL).

It is obvious, that the capability certificate plays the essential role in the presented procedure of the subject request confirmation. A set of capability certificates *CertCAP* is defined by function f_{cab} which has the form: f_{cab}: $S \times K_{PR} \times S \times O \times A \times D \times ID_{ses} \times T \rightarrow CertCAP$, where S means the D protection domain reference monitor which issues the certificate signed using the private key K_{PR}, ID_{ses} – the unique session identifier, while T defines the time when the certificate has been created.

Using the definition of the simple secure and *-secure state (see Definition 1 and 2) it is possible to formulate the following Lemma:

Lemma 1: State $v=(b, f, certAttr, certUCC) \in V$ of distributed authorization system, where $v = v_1 \cup v_2 \cup ... \cup v_r$, $v \in V$, $v_2 \in V_1$, $v_2 \in V_2$, ..., $v_r \in V_r$, $V = V_1 \cup V_2 \cup ... \cup V_r$, ($r$ – the number of the protection domains) is *simple secure* relative to function f if and only if for each existing protection domain $i \in D$ the state $v_i=(b_i, f, certAttr, certUCC) \in V_i$ is *simple secure* relative to function f; it means that for each v_i which depends on $(s,o,\underline{x}) \in b_i$ ($s \in S$, $o \in O_i$, $\underline{x} \in A$) such that $\underline{x} = read$ or $\underline{x} = write$ the clearance of the subject s dominates the classification of the object o, i.e. $f_S(s) \geq f_O(o)$, And vice versa, if $\underline{x} = read$ or $\underline{x} = write$ and $f_S(s) \geq f_O(o)$ for given subject s and object o, then the state v_i is *simple secure*.

Proof: The proof is immediate and results from the assumption about strict separation of the objects being the members of different domains and the definition of the whole system state in the form $V = V_1 \cup V_2 \cup ... \cup V_r$.

The special way of the capability certificate creation which is used by the request confirmation procedure, also allows describing the necessary and sufficient conditions for the system state to be *-secure.

Lemma 2: Let the set $\Theta_i(s:\underline{x},\underline{y},...,\underline{z};\underline{b}_i,O_i) = \{o:o\in O_i \wedge [(s,o,\underline{x})\in\underline{b}_i \vee (s,o,\underline{y})\in\underline{b}_i \vee ... \vee (s,o,\underline{z})\in\underline{b}_i]\}$. We say, that the state $v=(b,\ f,\ certAttr,\ certUCC)\in V$ of the distributed authorization system, where $v= v_1\cup v_2\cup...\cup v_r$, $v\in V$, $v_2\in V_1$, $v_2\in V_2$, ..., $v_r\in V_r$, $V = V_1\cup V_2\cup \ ... \ \cup V_r$ is **-secure* if and only if for each existing protection domain $i\in D$ the state $v_i=(\underline{b}_i,\ f,\ certAttr,\ certUCC)\in V_i$ is **-secure* relative to function f, it means that for the given state $v_i\in V_i$ (i=1, 2, ..., r) and for each $s\in S$ the nonempty set $[\bigcup_{i=1}^r\Theta_i(s:write,append;\underline{b}_i,O_i)\neq\phi\wedge\bigcup_{i=1}^r\Theta_i(s:read,write;\underline{b}_i,O_i)\neq\phi]$ implies the inequality $f_O(o_1)\geq f_O(o_2)$ for all $o_1\in\bigcup_{i=1}^r\Theta_i(s:write,append;\underline{b}_i,O_i)$ and $o_2\in\bigcup_{i=1}^r\Theta_i(s:read,write;\underline{b}_i,O_i)$.

Proof: It is obvious, that $O_{w,a} = \bigcup_{i=1}^r\Theta_i(s:write,append;\underline{b}_i,O_i)$ is the set of all objects of the distributed system $\Sigma(T_R,V,v_0)$ which are accessible for given subject $s\in S_i$ (for each $i\in D$) with the right *write* or *append*. Next, the $O_{r,w} = \bigcup_{i=1}^r\Theta_i(s:read,write;\underline{b}_i,O_i)$ is the set of all objects, which are accessible by the same subject with the right *read* or *write*. Thus, if $f_O(o_1)\geq f_O(o_2)$ holds for all $o_1\in O_{w,a}$ and $o_2\in O_{r,w}$, then $v_i=(\underline{b}_i,\ f,\ certAttr,\ certUCC)\in V_i$ is **-secure* and from relation $v_i\in v$ results, that the state v is also **-secure*.

Going the other direction, if $v=(b,\ f,\ certAttr,\ certUCC)\in V$ is **-secure*, then for each $s\in S$ such the nonempty set $[\Theta(s:write,append)\neq\phi \wedge \Theta(s:read,write) \neq\phi]]$ implies $f_O(o_1)\geq f_O(o_2)$ for all $o_1\in\Theta(s:write,\ append)$ and $o_2\in\Theta(s:read,\ write)$. By assumption $\Theta(s:write,append) = \bigcup_{i=1}^r\Theta_i(s:write,append;\underline{b}_i,\ O_i)$ and $\Theta(s:read,\ write) = \bigcup_{i=1}^r\Theta_i(s:read,write;\ \underline{b}_i,O_i)$. Hence the inequality $f_O(o_1)\geq f_O(o_2)$ is satisfied for any $o_1\in\bigcup_{i=1}^r\Theta_i(s:write,append;\ \underline{b}_i,O_i)$ and $o_2\in\bigcup_{i=1}^r\Theta_i(s:read,write;\ \underline{b}_i,O_i)$. It means, that the state $v_i=(\underline{b}_i,\ f,\ certAttr,\ certUCC)$ is **-secure*, too. The proof of the Lemma is complete.

5.   SECURITY THEOREM FOR SUPERVISORY AND CONTROL SYSTEM

It is possible, by the Definition 4 and Lemmas 1 and 2, to define the necessary and sufficient conditions for a system starting in a secure state to never reach a nonsecure state.

Security Theorem: A distributed system $\Sigma(T_R,\ V,\ v_0)$, where $v_0= v_{01}\cup v_{02}\cup...\cup v_{0r}$, $v_0\in V$, $v_{01}\in V_1$, $v_{02}\in V_2$, ..., $v_{0r}\in V_r$, $V = V_1\cup V_2\cup \ ... \ \cup V_r$ and $T_R=\{T_{R1},\ T_{R2},\ ...,\ T_{Rr}\}$ is secure only if for each protection domain $i\in D$: (1) initial state v_{0i}, where $v_i\in V$ is both simple secure and **-secure* state, (2) state transition function T_{Ri} is *transition secure* and (3) if $T_{Ri}(c,\ v_i)=v_i{}^*$ where $c\in Cred$, $v_i=(\underline{b}_i,\ f,\ certAttr,\ certUCC)$ and $v_i{}^*=(\underline{b}_i{}^*,\ f^*,\ certAttr^*,\ certUCC^*)$, then new state $v_i{}^*$ is *simple secure* and **-secure* relative to functon f.

Proof (sketch): Under conditions (1) and (2) the initial state v_0 of the system $\Sigma(T_R,\ V,\ v_0)$ is *simple secure* and **-secure*, whereas the state transition function T_{Ri} is *transition secure*. Furthermore, if the condition (3) is fulfilled for each domain, then by Lemma 1 and 2 we have that new state $v^*= v_1{}^*\cup v_2{}^*\cup...\cup v_r{}^*$ is *simple* *secure* and *∗–secure*. Since all three conditions of Definition 8 are satisfied, we have shown that the system $\Sigma(T_R, V, v_0)$ is secure.

The theorem states that a total system is secure only if all its subsystems (protection domain) are secure. It means, that different administrators can manage protection domains, but also that the subject's domestic reference monitor must negotiate all subject requests with reference monitors of other domains and verify if the acceptance of the request allows proving that the resulting system is still secure.

Note that Security Theorem gives necessary, but not sufficient conditions for a system to be secure. Hence, the system can be secured also in case of construction a new security models from old ones. More generally, there is possibility to define security model for implementing user-defined security policies in distributed multi-policy environments (W. E. Kuhnhauser [14]). This approach is valuable because several security policies address a wide variety of system security aspects such as access control, information flow control, authentication, availability and auditing. As a consequence, the integration of application dependent security policies into a distributed multipolicy computer system has become a major challenge for computer security.

6. CONCLUSION

The implementation of the security models based on MAC mechanisms requires the centralized protection system with main security server, which stores all information needed to keep the system in secure state.

In the paper we proposed the partition of the supervisory and control system into the separated protection domains. Next all subjects are obligated to be in the possession of the public key certificate and the attribute (the privilege) certificate. Additionally, the authorizations of the access policy definition are delegated to the owners or co-owners of the protected resources. Such solutions enable us to decentralize the realization of MAC security policy and to support it by the distributed reference monitor. Each reference monitor is a part of the distributed reference monitor and is only responsible for the security of domain which is connected with.

The decentralized access policy requires the specification of the abstract syntax of the use condition certificate. The works concerning such abstract syntax are conducted and based among other things on the experiences of creators of PolicyMaker (M. Blaze, et. al. [7]), KeyNote (M. Blaze, et. al. [8]), and Akenti (W.Johnston, et. al. [12]) systems.

The Security Theorem formulated in the paper specifies the necessary condition for the supervisory and control system to be remaining in secure state. The theorem allows drawing rather pessimistic conclusion: there does not exist only one security model, which keeps the system in the secure state. The reason seems to be rather obvious: there does not exist only one universal security policy of the system. The great number of such policies leads to the hypothesis, that the security model is rather the complex set of various models enforcing the different but not contradictory security policies. Such hypothesis seems to be confirmed by the works of W. E. Kuhnhauser [13] and W. E. Kuhnhauser, M. Von Kopp Ostrowski [14],

7.   REFERENCES

[1] Bell D.E., L.J.LaPadula *Secure computer systems: mathematical foundations*, ESD-TR-73-278, vol.1-2, ESD/AFSC, Hanscom AFB, Bedford, MA, November 1973 (MTR-2547, vol.1-2, MITRE Corp., Bedford, MA)

[2] Bell D.E., L.J.LaPadula *Secure computer systems: a refinement of the mathematical model*, Technical Report ESD-TR-73-278, vol.3, ESD/AFSC, Hanscom AFB, Bedford, MA, April 1974 (MTR-2547, vol.3, MITRE Corp., Bedford, MA)

[3] Bell D.E., L.J.LaPadula *Secure computer systems: mathematical foundations and model*, Technical Report M74-244, The MITRE Corp., Bedford, MA, 1974

[4] Bell D.E., L.J.LaPadula *Secure computer systems: unified exposition and Multics interpretation*, The MITRE Corp., Bedford, MA, 1975

[5] E. Bertino, E. Ferrari, F. Buccafurri, P. Rullo *A Logical Framework for Reasoning on Data Access Control Policies*, Proceeding of the 12th IEEE Computer Security Workshop, IEEE Computer Society Press, July 1999

[6] K.J.Biba *Integrity considerations for secure computer systems*, ESD-TR-76-372, ESD/AFSC, Hanscom AFB, Bedford, MA, April 1977 (MTR-3153, MITRE Corp., Bedford, MA)

[7] M. Blaze, J. Feigenbaum, J. Lacy *Decetralized Trust Management*, in Proc.1996 IEEE Synposium on Security and Privacy, pp.164-173, Oakland, CA, May 1996, IEEE Computer Society Press

[8] M. Blaze, J. Feigenbaum, J. Ioannidis,, A.D. Keromytis *The Role of Trust Management in Distributed Systems Security*, in *Secure Internet Pogramming: Security Issues for Mobile and Distributed Objects*, ed. Jan Vitek and Ch. Jensen, *Springer-Verlag Inc, New York*

[9] S. Castano, M.G. Fugini, G. Martella, P. Samarati *Database security*, Addison-Wesley Publishing Company, New York 1994.

[10] C.Ellison, B.Frantz, B.Lampson,, R.Rivest, B.M.Thomas, T.Ylonen *SPKI Certificate Theory*, Network Working Group, RFC 2693, September 1993

[11] S. Farrell, R. Housley - *Internet X.509 Public Key Infrastructure – An Internet Attribute Certificate Profile for Authorization*, PKIX Working Group, Internet Draft, May 2000, <*http://www.ietf.org/internet-drafts/draft-ietf-pkix-ac509prof-06.txt*>

[12] W.Johnston, S. Mudumbai, M. Thompson *Authorization and Attribute Certificates for Widely Distributed Access Control*, IEEE 7th International Workshops on Enabling Technologies: Infrastructure for Collaborative Enterprises, WETICE '98

[13] W. E. Kuhnhauser *Paradigm for User-Defined security Policies*, Proceedings of 14th IEEE Symposium on Reliable Distributed Systems, 1995, IEEE Press

[14] W. E. Kuhnhauser, M. Von Kopp Ostrowski *A Formal Framework to Support Multiple Security Policies*, Proceedings of 7th Canadian Computer Security Symposium, Ottawa, Canada, May 1995

[15] J.McLean *Security models*, in *Encyclopedia of Software Engineering*, ed.J.Marciniak, Weley Press, 1994

[16] J.Pejaś, W.Chocianowicz *Model of Multilevel Infromation Security for Distributed Supervisory and Control Systems*, Third National Scientifically-Technical Conference on *Diagnostics of Industrial Processes*, September 7-10, 1998 r, Jurata k/Gdańska

[17] J.Pejaś, W.Chocianowicz *The Role of the Trusted Third Party in Management of Cryptographic Keys Containers for Distributed Supervisory and Control Systems* (in polish), Fourth Third National Scientifically-Technical Conference on *Diagnostics of Industrial Processes*, September 13-16, 1999, Kazimierz Dolny

[18] T.Y.C. Woo, S.S. Lam *Authorization in Distributed Systems: A New Approach*, Journal of Computer Security, 2, pp.107-136, 1993

Specification of timed authentication protocols with colored Petri nets

GIZELA JAKUBOWSKA[1], MARIAN SREBRNY[2]
[1] *Faculty of Computer Science & Information Systems, Department of Software Engineering & Information Security, Technical University of Szczecin,*
Zolnierska 49, 71-210 Szczecin, Poland, e-mail: gjakubowska@wi.ps.pl
[2] *Institute of Computer Science, Polish Academy of Sciences,*
Ordona 21, 01-237 Warszawa, Poland, e-mail: marians@ipipan.waw.pl

Abstract: In this paper we present a colored Petri net model of a cryptographic challenge-response entity authentication protocol with time stamping features. Its correctness/security requirements are expressed as formulas of some version of the temporal Computation Tree Logic - ASKCTL. The reachability state space graph is analyzed. Some experimental results are reported, using the Aarhus Design/CPN tool.

Key words: authentication, cryptography, verification, Petri nets.

1. INTRODUCTION

Entity authentication is a technique of providing evidence that the identity of a party is as declared. One party verifies the identity of another one, typically, in real time. Basically, this does not involve any document message. The idea is that one party sends a challenge to another party which is the only one that can respond to it correctly; e.g., by demonstrating knowledge of a shared key. The challenge-response protocols often include time-variant parameters. Countless design flaws in authentication protocols have been documented in the literature. See [7], section 12.9.1.

Formal verification methods have received a lot of attention over the last decade followed by many successful attacks on the authentication protocols. See Moore [9], [10], Meadows [8]. The time parameters bring an extra challenge. We pursue a colored Petri net (CPN) framework for formal analysis and verification of the challenge-response entity authentication protocols with time parameters. As a case study we focus one such protocol introduced in [10], called KSL. We show one more security flaw of it. We restrict attention to two-party protocols, although the definitions and models may be generalized. up to our knowledge, cryptographic protocols with time parameters have not been modeled as the colored Petri nets so far.

We formulate correctness and security requirements of such a protocol in a temporal logic called ASKCTL. (Compare with [2]). The language of ASKCTL has two sets of formulas: state and transition formulas, in which path quantifiers are combined with the until operator. Interpreted over the state and transition paths, respectively, they can express temporal properties. One can express an undesirable interleaving chain of states and transitions mimicing a known attack on a protocol. Negation of such a formula could then be entered as (a part of) the protocol specification.

The paper is organized as follows. A brief introduction to the area of cryptographic entity authentication schemes is given in the next section. In section 3 we recall the notion of the colored Petri nets. In section 4 we present our model of the KSL protocol as a hierarchical colored Petri net. Its state space is built in section 5. The main ideas of the methods of formal specification of the considered protocol are presented and discussed in section 6. Some future work is outlined in the last section.

2.   TIMED ENTITY AUTHENTICATION

The cryptographic keys may not be fixed for all time but updated according to special lifetime requirements, providing enhanced protection. Typically, a third party server establishes and affixes a trusted date and exact time to a fresh key, its life period, activates and certifies the key life cycle. The KSL protocol is more flexible. The participants do not need synchronized clocks because checking all the time-dependent values (inside a generalized timestamp) is a concern of the agent who creates the component containing it. The role of the server is only to generate a session key for authorized participants. The initial KSL protocol to establish a shared key and a ticket can be presented as follows:

Message 1. A → B :   Na, A
Message 2. B → S : Na, A, Nb, B
Message 3. S → B : {Nb, A, Kab}Kbs, {Na, B, Kab}Kas
Message 4. B → A :   {Na, B, Kab}Kas, {Tb,A,Kab}Kbb, Nb', {Na}Kab
Message 5. A → B :   {Nb'}Kab

The KSL protocol for repeated authentication involves three steps:
Message 1'.   A → B :   Na', {Tb, A, Kab}Kbb
Message 2'.   B → A :   Nb", {Na'}Kab
Message 3'.   A → B :   {Nb"}Kab

The KSL protocol for repeated authentication involves three steps:

3. COLORED PETRI NETS

The colored Petri nets are special kind of the well-known Place/Transition nets in which tokens carry some typed data. Here we give only a formal definition of CPN; see [6]. A sample subroutine CPN is shown in Figure 5 below.

Definition 1: A **CP-net** is a tuple $CPN = (\Sigma, P, T, A, N, C, G, E, I)$ where:
(i) Σ is a finite set of nonempty types, also called *colour sets*.
(ii) P is a finite set of *places*.
(iii) T is a finite set of *transitions*.
(iv) A is a finite set of *arcs* such that: $P \cap T = P \cap A = T \cap A = \varnothing$.
(v) N is a *node* function; $N: A \rightarrow P \times T \cup T \times P$.
(vi) C is a *colour* function; $C: P \rightarrow \Sigma$.
(vii) G is a *guard* function;
        $G: \forall t \in T: [\text{Type}(G(t)) = \text{Bool} \wedge \text{Type}(\text{Var}(G(t))) \subseteq \Sigma]$.
(viii) E is an *arc expression* function;
        $E: \forall a \in A: [\text{Type}(E(a)) = C(p(a))_{MS} \wedge \text{Type}(\text{Var}(E(a))) \subseteq \Sigma]$,
        where p is the place of $N(a)$.
(ix) I is an *initialisation* function;
        $I: \forall p \in P: [\text{Type}(I(p)) = C(p)_{MS} \wedge \text{Var}(I(p)) = \varnothing]$.
(x)   A *token element* is a pair (p,c) where $p \in P$ and $c \in C(p)$.

By a *path* starting at M_0 we mean a finite or infinite sequence $(M_0 t_1 M_1 t_2 M_2 t_3 M_3...)$ of markings and transitions such that $M_i[t_{i+1} > M_{i+1}$, for each i. The latter can be read as: t_{i+1} is feasible at M_i and whenever fired t_{i+1} gives marking M_{i+1}.

4. MODELING THE AUTHENTICATION PROTOCOLS

This section contains a description of the KSL protocol as a hierarchical CPN. The KSL protocol has important time–dependent features, such as time–outs and lifetime of certain objects (tickets). We present it with a simplified model. A global clock representing a discrete time flow has been built in to model the intended behavior of the program. We gave up using the timed version of the Design/CPN tool for the sake of simplicity.

Figure 1 provides an overview of the model. HS stands for hierarchical subpage (subprogram).

The model of KSL is given in three main parts: Sender, Receiver and Server. Sender part is contained in four subpages representing sender actions during a protocol run. Receiver part is contained in five subpages.

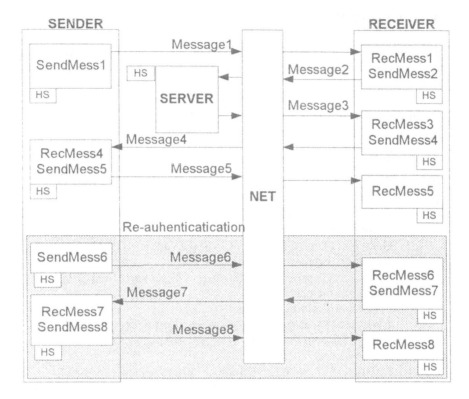

Fig. 1. A model of KSL protocol

4.1 Characteristic of the model

Participants. The model describes the protocol for two participants A and B. Each of them can act as a sender and also as a receiver and take part in other session (or sessions) simultaneously.

Server. Server is a kind of trusted party which is responsible for issuing session keys for the participants.

Keys. We have three sets of keys: session keys generated by the server, private (symmetric) keys: *KeyAA, KeyBB* known only to the participants they belong to, and secure keys: *KeySA, KeySB* used for communication between the server and the other participants, respectively.

Nonces. Nonces are (pseudo)random numbers used once during the authentication process.

Tickets and timestamps. Ticket is a part of a message used to re-establish the session key. The main component of the ticket is its timestamp containing the value of the time at which the key was created and a lifetime of the ticket. Checking timestamp is a duty of the agent who issued it.

Cryptography. We do not enter any details of encryption algorithms, since their strength is not of our concern in this paper.

The storage requirements. We use fusion places (*FG*) to represent global data (such as values of the global clock) and also to keep local data for Sender and Receiver necessary to complete properly all runs of the protocol.

A local state of each participant contains some stored data:

– this agent's session keys, full list of users the keys are shared with, and the received tickets. Upon completion of a run of the protocol the used nonces are deleted.

– the set of nonces recently generated and used by this agent;

Local data can only be modified by the subnet of the participant they belong to.

In order to simplify our analysis of the protocol we use the following assumption: the lifetime of all the tickets is a constant value preset and fixed for all possible runs of the protocol.

4.2 Data declaration in the KSL CP-net

We follow the usual notation for CP-nets. (See [1]) The main set of colors includes a description of basic types of data used in the KSL protocol. Some of them are usual types, such as int, some other are more complex; e.g., a color named *FieldMsg3* whose set of values is declared as the Cartesian product of the four previously declared colorsets. Most important colorsets are presented in Figure 2.

```
color CLK = int;
color User = with A | B | S;
color Nonce = int;
color Key = int;
color EncNonce = product Key * Nonce;
color SetKey = with KeySA | KeySB | KeyAA | KeyBB;
color SesInfo = product User * Nonce;
color Ses = product User * User;
color USERxKey = product User * Key;
color Check = with ERROR | OK.;
color FieldMsg3 = product SetKey * Nonce * User * Key;
color Timestamp = int;
color Ticket = product SetKey * Timestamp * User * Key;
```

Fig. 2. The main colorsets

Every message is built as a product of some other colorsets with regard to the syntax of this message specified by the protocol (see Figure 3). A color named *Ses* represents the direction of the flow of the message.

A variable is an identifier whose value can be changed during an execution of the program and it bounds to a variety of different values from its colorset. Some variables are shown in Figure 4.

```
color Msg1 = product Ses * Nonce * User;
color Msg2 = product Ses * Nonce * User * Nonce *User;
color Msg3 = product Ses * FieldMsg3 * FieldMsg3;
color Msg4 = product Ses * FieldMsg3 * Ticket * Nonce *
                                                EncNonce;
color Msg5 = product Ses * EncNonce;
color Msg6 = product Ses * Nonce * Ticket;
color Msg7 = product Ses * Nonce * EncNonce;
color Msg8 = product Ses * EncNonce;
```

Fig. 3. Colorsets of messages

Figure 5 presents a sample fragment of the *RecMess6SendMess7* subpage (subprogram). At this point one verifies whether the ticket is valid or not.

```
var X1,Y1, ..., X8,Y8 : User;
var SendID,RecID : User;
var Nonce1, ..., Nonce5 : Nonce;
var tm, tickTime : CLK;
var SecEncNonce : EncNonce;
var SesKey, SesKey2, RmSesKey : Key;
var PKey : SetKey;
var Message1 : Msg1;
....
val valid = 20;
```

Fig. 4. Global variables

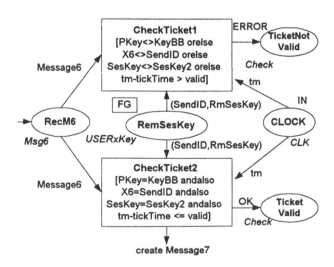

Fig. 5. Checking the ticket

Transition *CheckTicket2* is feasible whenever there is a marking satisfying the guard on the transition. The guard is true if *Pkey* is bound to *KeyBB* and also the sender's identifier *X6* of this message is bound to the same value as *SendID* stored inside the ticket. Also session keys: one from the ticket and the other one stored by the agent should have the same value. At the end we check the time saved as a timestamp and compare it to the actual time with regard to the lifetime of the timestamp kept by variable *valid*.When *CheckTicket2* fires it separates the components, creates a *Message7* with the session key and generates *Nonce5* and creates a *Check* token whose value is given by the arc inscription and puts it in the *TicketValid* place.

Transition *CheckTicket1* behaves in the same way as *CheckTicket2* except for the guard conditions.

5. THE STATE SPACE

In this section we deal with the reachable state space graph (also called occurrence graph, *OG*) for the KSL protocol. Figure 6 illustrates a fragment of the finite state space generated by the Design/CPN, exhibiting a new security flaw. The whole *OG* has 1143 nodes and 1989 arcs. Each node represents a marking and each edge represents a transition step. Due to the space limitations in this paper in our picture we label each node with the number of its state (with no description of the corresponding marking of the net). In Table 1, for some edges we give the corresponding transition a source node and destination node: $v_1 \rightarrow v_2$. Sample numbers are supplied as nonces.

Edges	Transition and binding
23→27	*RecM6*: {X6=A, Y6=B, Ticket=(KeyBB, 291, A, 384), Nonce4=5267}
27→32	*CheckTicket2*: {X6=A, Y6=B, SesKey2=384, SesKey=384, Key=KeyBB, SendID=A, Nonce5=5268, Nonce4=5267, tm=293, tickTime=291}
32→39	*SendM7*: {X7=B, Y7=A, SecEncNonce=(384, 5267), Nonce5=5268}
39→49	*Return*: {X7=B, Y7=A, SecEncNonce=(384, 5267), Nonce5=5268, counter=2}
49→61	*SendM6*: {X6=A,Y6=B, Ticket=(KeyBB, 291, A, 384), Nonce4=5268}
61→72	*RecM6*: {X6=A, Y6=B, Ticket=(KeyBB, 291, A, 384), Nonce4=5268}
72→81	*CheckTicket2*: {X6=A, Y6=B, Key=KeyBB, SesKey2=384, SesKey=384, tm=295, tickTime=291}
81→88	*SendM7*: {X7=B, Y7=A, SecEncNonce=(384, 5268), Nonce5=5269}
88→94	*RecM7*: {X7=B, Y7=A, SecEncNonce=(384, 5268), Nonce5=5269}
94→102	*NoSesKey*: {X7=B, Y7=A, SecEncNonce=(384, 5268), Nonce5=5269}
102→110	*SendM8*: Message8=(A,B,(384, 5268))}
110→116	*RecM8*: {X8=A, Y8=B, SecEncNonce=(384, 5268)}
116→120	*CheckM8*: {X8=A, Y8=B, SesKey2=384, SesKey=384, SentLaz=5268, SendID=A, Nonce5=5268}

Tab. 1. The edges of sample reauthentication protocol session

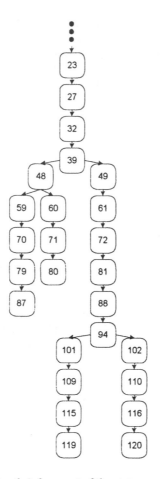

Fig. 6. A fragment of the state space

6.   CORRECTNESS AND SECURITY REQUIREMENTS

In this section we show how correctness and security requirements of the entity authentication protocols can be expressed formally. This is essential for ultimate automatic, or half-automatic, verification of those properties. We express all the requirements in the certain logic syntax appropriate for use as queries in the Design/CPN model checking verification tool. This logic is called ASKCTL. It is a version of CTL introduced in [3]. CTL was originally motivated and tailored for model checking techniques. ASKCTL has an extra, very practical advantage that it is expressive enough to demonstrate the occurrence of certain transitions on paths, in addition to the states, as in CTL itself. This is the main motivation that in our approach we use ASKCTL, the Design/CPN, and the colored Petri nets. When interpreted over the state space of a colored Petri net model of a protocol, those formulas can express properties of the edges of the state space graph, in addition to the properties of its nodes.

For a given fixed colored Petri net N, we introduce the ASKCTL deduction system, in a slightly different way than that in [2]. There is a denumerable number of *state variables* in the language of ASKCTL. Their subscripts are arranged in such a way that each place of the underlying net N has at least one state variable associated with it. The state variables are typed (colored). The intended *Boolean valuations* of the state variables reflect the presence or absence of a token of a given type at a given place of N. The *state* and *transition formulas* of the language of ASKCTL are defined by simultaneous recursion as the least sets such that: logical constant *tt* and each of the denumerable state variables is a state formula, if α, $\alpha 1$ and $\alpha 2$ are state formulas and β is a transition formula then $\neg\alpha$, $\alpha 1 \vee \alpha 2$, $<\beta>$, $EU(\alpha 1, \alpha 2)$ and $AU(\alpha 1, \alpha 2)$ are state formulas too; similarly, for each transition t of the net, the Boolean *transition constant ct* is a transition formula, if β, $\beta 1$ and $\beta 2$ are transition formulas and α is a state formula then $\neg\beta$, $\beta 1 \vee \beta 2$, $<\alpha>$, $EU(\beta 1, \beta 2)$ and $AU(\beta 1, \beta 2)$ are transition formulas too. The path *quantifier-until operators EU* and *AU* cannot be nested.

The semantics can be viewed as follows. By a *valuation* of the state variables we mean a two-valued Boolean function from the set of all the state variables. Such functions can be identified with the markings of the net. Similarly, the transition constants get Boolean values *0* or *1*. A formal definition of this semantics shall be given in the full version of this paper. Here we only indicate its main points. The logic is interpreted over the state space graph. We define two binary satisfaction relations: $M\square_{st}\alpha$ and $e\square_{tr}\beta$, where M is a marking, e is an edge triple (M,t,M') of the state space graph with a transition t leading from a marking M to a new marking M', α and β are any state and transition formulas, respectively. The meaning of *tt*, $\neg$, and $\vee$ is classical.

The state path-existential-until formula is intended to mean at M: there exists a path from M on which α_1 holds always until certain node (state) is reached at which α_2 holds. Similarly, the state path-general-until means at M: α_1 until α_2 on every path from M. The intended meaning of the operator $<\beta>$ at M is: there is an immediate successor M' of M such that β holds at the edge between M and M'.

The interpretation of the two transition quantifier-until operators is informally defined as follows. $e\square_{tr}EU(\beta 1, \beta 2)$ iff for some path with e as its first edge, $\beta 1$ holds at every edge until the edge at which $\beta 2$ holds; and $e\square_{tr}AU(\beta 1, \beta 2)$ iff on every path from e, $\beta 1$ until $\beta 2$. Finally, the intended meaning of the operator $<\alpha>$ at $e=(M,t,M')$ is: $M'\square_{st}\alpha$.

Now, ASKCTL is expressive enough to allow a formal definition in the ASKCTL logic of an undesired path of an attack on the KSL protocol of section 4, figure 6: there exists a path on which a sequence of states and transitions defined in table 1 occurs.

7. CONCLUSION

We have presented a way to model the cryptographic challenge-response entity authentication protocols with timestamps features as colored Petri nets and we have proposed the idea of analysis and verification of their correctness and security properties in the Design/CPN environment. A new security flaw of the KSL protocol was shown in section 2. It seems necessary to alleviate the state space explosion by adequately invariant reduction procedures. Different correctness and security requirements should be investigated especially these, expressing the successful attacks on KSL which have been uncovered so far. Other entity authentication protocols with the time-variant features are of great interest here. First of all, the Kerberos protocol is a challenging example. Mostly, because it is actually widely applied around the world these days.

8. REFERENCES

[1] Jensen K., An introduction to the theoretical aspects of coloured Petri nets, in: J.W. de Bakker, W.-P. de Roever, G. Rozenberg (eds.), *A decade of concurrency*, LNCS 803, Springer-Verlag, 1994, 230-272.

[2] Cheng A., Christensen S., and Mortensen H.H., Model checking coloured Petri nets exploiting strongly connected components, Technical Report DAIMI PB -- 519, University of Aarhus, Computer Science, Department, March 1997. ISSN 0105-8517

[3] Clarke E.M., Emerson E.A. and Sistla A.P., Automatic verification of finite state concurrent systems using temporal logic, *ACM Transactions on Programming Languages and Systems*, 8(2)(1986), 244-263.

[4] *Design/CPN*, http://www.daimi.aau.dk/designCPN/

[5] Jakubowska G., Using rewriting logic for specification and analysis of authentication protocols, Proc of the 7-th International Conference on Advanced Computer Systems *ACS'2000*, Szczecin, 2000.

[6] Jensen K. Coloured Petri nets – basic concepts, analysis methods and practical use, Volume 1, Basic concepts, EATCS Monographs, Springer-Verlag, 1992

[7] Menezes A.J., van Oorschot P.C. and Vanstone S.A., *Handbook of Applied Cryptography*, CRC Press, 1997; http://www.cacr.math.uwaterloo.ca/hac/, 5th printing, August 2001,

[8] Meadows C.A., Formal verification of cryptographic protocols: a survey, *Advances in cryptology – ASIACRYPT'94*, LNCS 917, Springer-Verlag, 1995, 133-150.

[9] Moore J.H, Protocol failures in cryptosystems, in: Simmons J., (ed.), *Contemporary cryptology: the science of information integrity*, IEEE Press, 1992, 541-558.

[10] Kehne A., Schönwälder J., Langendörfer H., A nonce-based protocol for multiple authentications. *Operating Systems Review*. Vol. (27), No. 4, pp. 84-89, Oct. 1992.

A Combinatorial Algorithm for Sharing a Key

ZBIGNIEW LONC[1], MARIAN SREBRNY[2]
*[1] Faculty of Mathematics and Information Science, Warsaw University of Technology
pl. Politechniki 1, 01-661 Warszawa, Poland, e-mail: zblonc@alpha.mini.pw.edu.pl
[2] Institute of Computer Science, Polish Academy of Sciences,
Ordona 21, 01-237 Warszawa, Poland, e-mail: marians@ipipan.waw.pl*

Abstract: We propose a novel algorithm for sharing a key. This algorithm is similar to
              that proposed by Benaloh and Leichter, but does not require to store (or
              compute online) the minimal authorized subsets. The algorithm uses the
              representation of the access structure (that is the collection of authorized sets)
              by means of transversals of the set of maximal elements of the ideal dual to the
              access structure.

1.   INTRODUCTION

In this paper we present a combinatorial algorithm for sharing a secret key
between several parties, persons or computers. Its cryptographic strength is based on
the intractability of the integer factorization.

The basic idea of secret sharing was introduced by Shamir [14]. The problem
can be formalized as follows. Let $k \geq 2$ be a natural number. Assume that we want to
split a sensitive secret key K between n participants/users $P_1, ..., P_n$ in such a way
that for any coalition $Z \subseteq \{1, ..., n\}$, $|Z| \square k-1$, the participants $\{P_j: j \in Z\}$ cannot recover
the secret key K, but for any set $Z \subseteq \{1, ..., n\}$, $|Z| \geq k$, the participants $\{P_j: j \in Z\}$ can
compute K from the information they jointly hold. Instead of physically chopping K,
we extract certain pieces (*shares, shadows*) of information about K and distribute
them to each participant.

One can think of a number of practical applications. For example, the nuclear
button, a bank safe, voting procedures, countersigning bills by the president and the
prime minister in variuos countries, signing company checks by three highest
excecutives, *et cetera*. Any cryptosystem private key or just an access passphrase
could be provided with enhanced protection by distributing its shares between a
number of computers and thus avoiding storing them in single pieces on a single
computer. An elegant application in the area of management of sensitive private
encryption/decryption keys was given in [16].

A few schemes of sharing secrets have been known. Shamir's original proposal [14] uses the properties of polynomials over finite fields. Another well known scheme of secret sharing, introduced by Mignotte [9,6], uses the Chinese Remainder Theorem to provide the unique solution of a system of k linear congruences while less than k of the congruences have many possible solutions. Mignotte's scheme is based on the existence of sets of prime numbers with appropriate distribution.

In contrast, our reduction of this problem to a combinatorial property is based on the following easy observation. Let $p_1,...,p_n$ be distinct prime numbers, and let h be their product $p_1 \cdot ... \cdot p_n$. Then the family of all divisors of h partially ordered by the divisibility relation is isomorphic to the Boolean algebra $\wp(\{1,...,n\})$ of all subsets of $\{1,...,n\}$ ordered by inclusion. See Section 2 for details.

Simple cardinality constraints, or a cardinality threshold, are just one example of applications of sharing a secret key. Other variants can significantly contribute to enhance the level of security in practical situations. As a motivating example take the highly sensitive master–keys at the Certification Authority in various implementations of the Public Key Infracture systems such as VeriSing, Visa, system "Płatnik" of Poland's Social Security, national interbanking clearance chambers, *et cetera*. In one of such systems we are aware of, the highest security requirements are met by splitting the master–key into 11 shares. 8 of them are being stored on 8 highly guarded computers. The other 3 – on three diskettes which are in charge of especially certified high level ranked officers. In order to run a procedure with the master–key, e.g., in order to issue a new key certificate for a new user–client, the system requires that at least 5 out of the 8 computers provide their shares as well as at least one of the 3 ranked officers comes in and inserts her diskette. Clearly, this is not a simple cardinality threshold.

A similar situation arises in practice when a voting procedure is to be executed with the numbers of legal votes associated to various groups of shareholders with distinct weigth. For example, consider a meeting of the Executive Board of a big bank consisting of a number of representatives of several financial groups, including possibly representatives of the state government, executing public ownership.

In general, by a *quorum constraint* or a (positive) *constraint* over a set X we mean a pair $\langle Y,k \rangle$ where $Y \subseteq X$, and $|Y| \geq k$. Such constraint expresses the requirement on a quorum necessary for some decision. For instance, the original Shamir scheme is expressed as a single constraint $\langle X,k \rangle$ (where X is a set over which we partition the key, and k is the threshold), while in the example given above, we have a set X of 11 elements, with two disjoint subsets X_1, X_2, $|X_1|=8$, and $|X_2|=3$ and the constraints $\langle X_1,5 \rangle$, and $\langle X_2,1 \rangle$. The family of subsets of X satisfying a given set of constraints is called *an access structure*, or the family of *authorized sets*.

We give an algorithm for sharing a secret key for any given set of positive constraints. It takes a large prime number K representing a secret key, a number m of users to share the key and a set of constraints Q. It returns a sequence of shares h_i, for $i=1,...,m$.

Our approach is similar to that proposed by Benaloh and Leichter [2], see Stinson [15], Section 11.3 for details. However, unlike in their scheme, in our approach the users do not have to have any knowledge about the access structure to compute the secret key. We get a sizable speed up due to the fact that we need only a single pass (when we construct the shares h_i) through the structure of all subsets of the set of participants. In the scheme of Benaloh and Leichter such a time consuming pass is required each time one recovers the secret key. In our method we do not need to do it. This results in a much more effective processing and is the main advantage of our approach. The practical limitations of our approach are discussed in the last section.

Other types of constraints will be considered in a forthcoming paper. It is an intriguing open question whether one can construct a good scheme of sharing a secret key for richer types of constraints, for instance for sets of constraints that, in addition to the quorum constraints considered in this paper, allow negations of such constraints. Access structures with respect to such generalized constraints are not closed under the superset operation. Consequently, the known techniques do not appear to work in such a case.

One of basic ideas of this paper is to represent a secret key as a large prime and its shares as products of this prime with other large primes. This idea has been studied in [4][1]. We take advantage of the fact that computing the greatest common divisor is efficient ([1], p.70), while factorization of products of prime numbers is not. The shares produced by our algorithm are products of more than two primes.

The current status of the integer factorization problem is that there is no computer capable of efficiently finding the prime factors of large integers. As for now, no one knows a polynomial time factoring algorithm [13,10,5]. Public key cryptosystems based on the conjectured intractability of factorization [12,11,8] are in common use. It is believed that for the next 20 to 30 years the systems of data protection based on the difficulty of factoring will be secure. Today's best known integer factorization algorithms are described in [3] and [8].

The paper is organized as follows. In the next section we introduce the concept of constraints and sets of thereof. We discuss the basic properties of the sets satisfying such sets of constraints. The algorithm for sharing a secret is presented in Section 3. Conclusions and future work are outlined in Section 4.

2. QUORUM CONSTRAINTS

A group of individuals forms a board of a corporation. During a meeting some members of the board are present. At the end of the meeting when decision is taken, the group wants to send an enciphered message that describes the decision made by that group, and attesting that the meeting was valid. The board consists of seven individuals. Four of these are representatives of the shareholders (x_1, x_2, x_3, x_4) and the remaining three represent the employees (x_5, x_6, x_7). The meeting is valid if at least four members of the board are present, of these at least two representatives of the employees.

In order to solve this problem we will assign to each member of the board a very large number which is the product of large different primes. We will not discuss here the criteria for selecting the primes that are used in the products, however we will assume that any of the products (even of two of these primes) is difficult to factor.

[1] Our attention to this idea was called by Mateusz Srebrny.

We will select 17 different prime numbers, $p_1,...,p_{16}$ and p. The number p will be a key used to encode the message. We will construct the following 7 numbers:

$$h_1=p_1{\cdot}p_2{\cdot}p_3{\cdot}p_4{\cdot}p_5{\cdot}p_6{\cdot}p$$
$$h_2=p_1{\cdot}p_2{\cdot}p_3{\cdot}p_7{\cdot}p_8{\cdot}p_9{\cdot}p$$
$$h_3=p_1{\cdot}p_2{\cdot}p_3{\cdot}p_{10}{\cdot}p_{11}{\cdot}p_{12}{\cdot}p$$
$$h_4=p_1{\cdot}p_2{\cdot}p_3{\cdot}p_{13}{\cdot}p_{14}{\cdot}p_{15}{\cdot}p$$
$$h_5=p_1{\cdot}p_4{\cdot}p_5{\cdot}p_7{\cdot}p_8{\cdot}p_{10}{\cdot}p_{11}{\cdot}p_{13}{\cdot}p_{14}{\cdot}p_{16}{\cdot}p$$
$$h_6=p_2{\cdot}p_4{\cdot}p_6{\cdot}p_7{\cdot}p_9{\cdot}p_{10}{\cdot}p_{12}{\cdot}p_{13}{\cdot}p_{15}{\cdot}p_{16}{\cdot}p$$
$$h_7=p_3{\cdot}p_5{\cdot}p_6{\cdot}p_8{\cdot}p_9{\cdot}p_{11}{\cdot}p_{12}{\cdot}p_{14}{\cdot}p_{15}{\cdot}p_{16}{\cdot}p$$

We provide the representatives of the shareholders x_1,x_2,x_3,x_4 with numbers h_1,h_2,h_3,h_4, respectively. Similarly, the representatives of the employees: x_5,x_6,x_7 receive h_5,h_6,h_7, respectively.

Now, the following is true (and is left to the reader to check). Whenever a group of present board members satisfies the constraints (i.e., at least four present, and of these at least two employees) then the greatest common divisor of the numbers assigned to the present board members is p. But for any nonempty set of board members *not* satisfying our conditions, the greatest common divisor of the numbers assigned to those present is greater than p (and, of course, divisible by p). Since our assumption is that it is infeasible to factor any of the products (while certainly the computation of the greatest common divisor of any of these collections of numbers is feasible), the secret key $k=p$ is protected.

We will characterize the sets of constraints for which the above scheme of protecting secrets works.

Generalizing from the above example we define a *quorum constraint* as a pair $\langle F,k \rangle$, where $|F| \geq k$. Intuitively, a quorum constraint is a constraint on a putative set I requiring that out of the elements of F, at least k elements belong to I. In our example 2.1 we had two constraints:

1. $\langle \{x_1,x_2,x_3,x_4,x_5,x_6,x_7\},4 \rangle$ expressing the constraint that at least four board members are present, and

2. $\langle \{x_5,x_6,x_7\},2 \rangle$ expressing the constraint that at least two representatives of the employees are present.

Formally, we will say that a·set I is an *authorized set with respect to a quorum constraint* $q=\langle F,k \rangle$ if $|I \cap F| \geq k$. We denote this by $I \square q$. When Q is a set of quorum constraints, then we say that I is an authorized set with respect to Q (in symbols $I \square Q$) if $I \square q$ for every quorum constraint $q \in Q$.

Throughout the paper we denote the set $\{1,2,...m\}$ by $[m]$. We call a subfamily $I \subseteq \wp([m])$ an *ideal* if for all $X \in I$, and for all Y, if $Y \subseteq X$ then $Y \in I$. Similarly, we call a subfamily $F \subseteq \wp([m])$ a *filter* if for all $X \in F$, and for all Y, if $X \subseteq Y$ then $Y \in F$. If I is an authorized set with respect to some positive quorum constraint q and $I \subseteq J$ then J is also an authorized set with respect to q. Thus the same holds for sets Q of quorum constraints. Hence, whenever Q is a set of quorum constraints, then the collection of authorized sets with respect to Q forms a filter. We will denote this filter by $F_Q = \{I \subseteq [m]: I \sqcap Q\}$. Consequently, the collection $I_Q = \wp([m]) \backslash F_Q$ of sets which are not authorized with respect to Q is an ideal called the *dual* to F_Q. It turns out that the connection between quorum constraints and filters is very close. Specifically, we have the following.

Proposition 2.1 A set $F \subseteq \wp([m])$ is a filter if and only if there is a set of quorum constraints Q so that $F = F_Q$.

Proof: Suppose F is a filter. Let M_i be a list of all the sets that are maximal elements of the ideal dual to F. Then, $I \notin F$ iff $I \subseteq M_i$, for some i. Hence, $I \in F$ iff $I \not\subseteq M_i$, for all i. The latter means that $I \cap ([m] \backslash M_i) \neq \varnothing$, for all i. Taking $F_i = [m] \backslash M_i$ one gets a list Q of quorum constraints $\langle F_i, 1 \rangle$ such that $F = F_Q$. The converse implication is immediate. $\square$

It is instructive to compare Proposition 2.1 with the approach of Benaloh and Leichter (as presented in Stinson, [15]). This approach is based on the following observation. Assign to each element $i \in [m]$ a propositional variable P_i. A set $X \subseteq [m]$ *satisfies* P_i if $i \in X$. The definition of satisfaction is extended to all propositional formulas based on the set of atoms $\{P_i : i \in [m]\}$. A formula is *positive* if it does not use the negation symbol. Given a positive formula φ, the set of all subsets $X \subseteq [m]$ that satisfy φ forms a filter. Clearly, every filter is definable by a positive formula. Now, it is quite clear what the constraints considered in our paper are. Specifically, the constraint $\langle Y, k \rangle$ is, in the language of Benaloh and Leichter,

$$\bigvee_{\substack{Z \subseteq Y \\ |Z| = k}} \bigwedge_{i \in Z} P_i. \tag{1}$$

Proposition 2.1 implies that the formulas that are conjunctions of formulas of the form (1) are sufficient to express all positive formulas. Of course, Shamir's constraint is expressible as a formula of the form (1).

While the conjunctions of formulas of the form (1) are sufficient to describe all filters, it should be noticed that such formula descriptions can be very long. In [7] it is shown that, although some descriptions can be drastically simplified by admitting more complex formulas, in general there are access structures (that is filters) without simple descriptions at all.

Consider a sequence of distinct prime numbers $p_1, p_2, ..., p_t$ and let a prime number p, $p \neq p_i$, $i = 1, ..., t$, represent a secret. Let $G = \{G_1, ..., G_m\}$ be a family of subsets of some set $X = \{a_1, ..., a_t\}$. One can think of $a_1, ..., a_t$ as auxiliary integers representing $p_1, ..., p_t$, so that we avoid carrying, storing and manipulating the large primes until necessary. Define a sequence of integers $h_i = (\prod\{p_j : a_j \in G_i\}) \cdot p$, $i = 1, ..., m$. Observe that the following is true.

Proposition 2.2 For any $I \subseteq [m.]$, the greatest common divisor of the integers h_i, $i \in I$, is equal to p if and only if $\square\{G_i: i \in I\} = \varnothing$. $\square$

It follows from the above proposition that in order to generalize the idea described in Example 2.1, we need, for a given set of quorum constraints Q, to find a family of sets $G_Q = \{G_1,...,G_t\}$ such that for every $I \subseteq [m]$, $\square\{G_i: i \in I\} = \varnothing$ if and only if $I \square Q$. It turns out that the following construction does precisely that.

Let $\{A_1,...,A_t\}$ be the set of all maximal elements of I_Q. Notice the one-to-one correspondence between these sets and the auxiliary integers $a_1,...,a_t$, as well as the primes $p_1,...,p_t$. Define

$$G_i = \{a_j \in X : i \in A_j\}, i=1,...,m. \tag{2}$$

Theorem 2.3 Let Q be a set of quorum constraints on $[m]$. Then for every $I \subseteq [m]$, $\square\{G_i: i \in I\} = \varnothing$ if and only if $I \square Q$.

Proof: ($\rightarrow$) Assume $I \notin F_Q$. Then $I \subseteq A_j$, for some $j=1,...,t$. This gives $a_j \in G_i$, for each $i \in I$, since $G_i = \{a_j: i \in A_j\}$. Hence, $\square\{G_i: i \in I\} \neq \varnothing$, as required.

($\leftarrow$) Assume $\cap\{G_i : i \in I\} \neq \varnothing$. Then for some j, $a_j \in G_i$, for each $i \in I$. That is, $i \in A_j$, for each $i \in I$. Hence $I \subseteq A_j$; and $I \notin F_Q$, as required. $\square$

Notice that Theorem 2.3 allows us to reduce the problem of verification if a set I is an authorized set to testing if the intersection of some sets is empty.

To give an algorithm of constructing the family G_Q we need to be able to find the collection of maximal elements in I_Q in an efficient way.

A quorum constraint $\langle X,k \rangle$ is *unitary* if $k=1$.

Recall that an *antichain* is a family of sets A with all elements incomparable under inclusion.

Theorem 2.4 For every set of quorum constraints Q there exists a set of unitary quorum constraints Q', where the family $\{X \in P([m]): \langle X,1 \rangle \in Q'\}$ forms an antichain, such that for every $I \subseteq [m]$, $I \square Q$ if and only if $I \square Q'$.

Proof: Consider $Q' = \{\langle X,1 \rangle: [m] \backslash X$ is maximal in $I_Q\}$. The sets maximal in any ideal form an antichain, and so do their complements. Moreover, Q' and Q generate the same filter. $\square$

By the above theorem, we get $I_Q = \{I \subseteq [m]: non(I \square Q)\} = \{I \subseteq [m]: non(I \square Q')\} = I_{Q'}$.

It turns out that finding the set of maximal elements in $I_{Q'}$ is easy, provided that Q' is given. The following proposition allows us to do it.

Proposition 2.5 If Q' is a set of unitary quorum constraints such that the family $\{X \in P([m]): \langle X,1 \rangle \in Q'\}$ forms an antichain then the sets $Y = [m] \backslash X$, where $\langle X,1 \rangle \in Q'$, are precisely the maximal elements of $I_{Q'}$.

Proof: Assume Q' is a set of unitary quorum constraints for a filter F such that the family $C = \{X \in P([m]): \langle X,1 \rangle \in Q'\}$ forms an antichain. First, note that $[m] \backslash X \in I_{Q'}$ whenever $X \in C$; i.e., that $[m] \backslash X \notin F_{Q'}$. Otherwise, i.e., if $[m] \backslash X \in F_{Q'}$, we would get for each $X' \in C$, $X' \cap ([m] \backslash X) \neq \varnothing$. In particular, for $X' = X$, a contradiction. Second, we show that for each $X \in C$, $[m] \backslash X$ is maximal in $I_{Q'}$. Suppose otherwise. Then there is a

$Y \in I_Q$, such that $[m]\backslash X \subseteq Y$ and $[m]\backslash X \neq Y$, for some $X \in C$. Hence, $Y \cap X' = \emptyset$, for some $X' \in C$. Thus also $([m]\backslash X) \cap X' = \emptyset$, and $X' \subseteq X$, contradicting to the assumption that C is an antichain.

It remains to show that if M is maximal in $I_{Q'}$ then $M = ([m]\backslash X')$, for some X' such that $\langle X',1\rangle \in Q'$. But $M \cap X = \emptyset$, for some X such that $\langle X,1\rangle \in Q'$, since $M \in I_{Q'}$. Thus $M \subseteq [m]\backslash X$. Suppose $M \neq [m]\backslash X$, i.e., there is an $x \in ([m]\backslash X)\backslash M$. Hence, $(M \cup \{x\}) \cap X = \emptyset$, and so $M \cup \{x\} \in I_{Q'}$. This contradicts the maximality of M. □

By a *transversal* of a family of sets B we mean any set intersecting each member of B. Observe that the access structure defined by a set of unitary quorum constraints Q' is just the family of transversals of the family $B = \{X \in \wp([m]): \langle X,1\rangle \in Q'\}$. Therefore it follows from Proposition 2.1, Theorem 2.4 and Proposition 2.5 that every access structure F is the family of transversals of the family of complements of maximal elements in the ideal $I = \wp([m])\backslash F$. Various representations of the filters in finite Boolean lattices are investigated in [7].

It remains to be explained how to find, for a given set of quorum constraints, the required set of unitary quorum constraints Q' equivalent to Q. The main idea is given in the next proposition.

Proposition 2.6 Let $q = \langle X,k\rangle$, $k \geq 2$, be a quorum constraint. Then $I \square q$ if and only if for every $x \in X$, $I \square \langle X\backslash\{x\}, k-1\rangle$.

Proof: Assume that $I \cap X$ has at least k members. Deleting any one of the elements of X, so possibly also of $I \cap X$, we are still left with at least $k-1$ members in this intersection.

For the other way round, suppose $I \cap (X\backslash\{x\})$ has at least $k-1$ members, for each $x \in X$. Suppose *a contrario* that $|I \cap X| < k$. Then for some $x \in I \cap X$, we would have $|(I \cap X)\backslash\{x\}| < k-1$, a contradiction. □

Observe that by an iterated application of the above proposition we are able to replace any set of quorum constraints with an equivalent set of unitary quorum constraints.

We shall also use the following easy to verify property of quorum constraints.

Proposition 2.7 If $X_1 \subseteq X_2$ and $n_2 \leq n_1$, then $\langle X_1,n_1\rangle$ implies $\langle X_2,n_2\rangle$. □

3. ALGORITHM

Let us now describe the algorithm for constructing, for a given input set of quorum constraints Q on $[m]$, a sequence of positive integers $h_1,...,h_m$ such that for every $I \subseteq [m]$, the greatest common divisor of the integers h_i, $i \in I$ is equal to p if and only if $I \square Q$.

Denote $Q = \{\langle A_i,k_i\rangle : i=1,...,w\}$. Since, by Proposition 2.7, $\langle A,n_1\rangle$ implies $\langle A,n_2\rangle$, for $n_2 \leq n_1$, we can assume without loss of generality, that $A_i \neq A_j$, for $i \neq j$. Define, for every $A \in P([m])$,

$$q_A = \begin{cases} k & \text{if } \langle A, k \rangle = \langle A_i, k_i \rangle \in Q \\ 0 & \text{otherwise.} \end{cases}$$

In the algorithm we represent the input set of quorum constraints Q by the set $\{q_A\colon A \in \wp([m])\}$. An input prime number p is a secret we want to share. Let $\{a_B\colon B \in \wp([m])\}$ be a set of auxiliary integers (markers) which will contain all constructed sets $G_1,...,G_m$ in G_Q. The algorithm returns a sequence of positive integers $h_1,...,h_m$ such that for every $I \subseteq [m]$, the greatest common divisor of the integers h_i, with $i \in I$, is equal to p if and only if $I \square Q$.

Algorithm 1
1   **for** $i=m, m-1,...,1$ **do**
2   { **for all** subsets $A \subseteq [m]$ such that $|A|=i$ **do**
3   { **if** $q_A > 1$ **then**
4   { **for every** $a \in A$ **do** $q_{A-\{a\}}:=max(q_{A-\{a\}}, q_A-1)$;
5                $q_A:=0$ } } } ;
6    $A:=\varnothing$,
7    $M:= \varnothing$,
8   **for** $i=1,2,...,m$ **do**
9   { **for all** subsets $A \subseteq [m]$ such that $|A|=i$ **do**
10   { **if** $A \in \mathcal{A}$ **then**
11   **for every** $a \in [m]-A$ **do** $\mathcal{A}:=\mathcal{A} \cup \{A \cup \{a\}\}$;
12   { **if** ($A \notin \mathcal{A}$ **and** $q_A=1$) **then**
13                $M:=M \cup \{[m]-A\}$;
14   **for every** $a \in [m]-A$ **do** { $\mathcal{A}:=\mathcal{A} \cup \{A \cup \{a\}\}$ } } } };
15    $G_1,...,G_m:=\varnothing$;
16   **for every** $B = \{i_1,...,i_{s_B}\} \in M$ **do**
17   { **for** $j=1,...,s_B$ **do** { $G_{i_j} := G_{i_j} \cup \{a_B\}$ } };
18   { **for all** $a_s \in \bigcup_{j=1}^{m} G_j$ **do**
19   { generate pairwise distinct primes $p_B \neq p$ } };
20   **for** $i=1,...,m$ **do**
21   **return** $h_i:=(p \cdot \prod\{p_B\colon a_B \in G_i\})$;

The algorithm consists of four main parts. In the first part (lines 1-5) we construct a unitary set of quorum constraints (let us call it Q') equivalent to the input set Q. In the second part (lines 6-14) we find the minimum set of unitary quorum constraints (say Q'') which is equivalent to Q' (thus also to Q). In the third part of the algorithm (lines 15-18) we construct the family of sets G_Q. Finally, in the last part (lines 19-22) we find the output integers $h_1,...,h_m$.

Let us consider in more detail the four parts of the algorithm. In lines 1-7 we scan all sets $A \subseteq [m]$ in the order from the largest to the smallest and find those for which the parameter $q_A>1$. For such sets we make use of Proposition 2.6. We replace each quorum constraint $\langle A,k \rangle$, $k \geq 2$, by $|A|$ quorum constraints $\langle A-\{x\},k-1 \rangle$, for every $x \in A$. It may happen that for some $x \in A$ we already have a quorum constraint $\langle A-\{x\},l \rangle$ (which is either in the input set Q or was earlier obtained by a similar replacement). In this case we apply Proposition 2.7 and eliminate (lines 4-5) one of the quorum constraints keeping $\langle A-\{x\},\max(k-1,l) \rangle$. The final result of lines 1-5 is a set Q' of unitary quorum constraints (defined by the sets A for which $q_A=1$) which is equivalent to the original set of quorum constraints Q.

In lines 6-14 we choose the minimal (with respect to inclusion) sets A in the family $A=\{A \in \wp([m]): \langle A,1 \rangle \in Q'\}$. It follows from Proposition 2.7 that the family A' of these sets defines a set of quorum constraints Q'' which is equivalent to Q. Clearly A' is an antichain so, by Proposition 2.5, the set of complements of the sets in A' (denoted by M in the algorithm) is precisely the set of maximal elements in the ideal I_Q.

In lines 15-17 we use the set M of maximal elements in the ideal I_Q to implement the construction of the desired family G_Q described in (2).

Finally, in lines 18-21 we find the output integers $h_1,...,h_m$. It follows from Proposition 2.2 and Theorem 2.3 that for every $I \subseteq [m]$, the greatest common divisor of the integers h_i, $i \in I$, is equal to p if and only if $I \square Q$.

Let us estimate time complexity of the combinatorial part (lines 1-17) of the above algorithm. The operations in the remaining lines can be done on specialized devices and we are not going to discuss the running time of them here. Let us count the number of executions of the most embedded loops in lines 1-17. It is easy to see that the loop in line 4 is executed not more than $\sum_{i=1}^{m} i \binom{m}{i} \leq m 2^m$ times. Similarly, the number of passes of the loop in line 12 is not larger than $\sum_{i=1}^{m} (m-i) \binom{m}{i} \leq m 2^m$.

Finally, the loop in line 17 is executed $\sum_{B \in M} s_B \leq m |M| \leq m 2^m$ times. Hence the running time of lines 1-17 of our algorithm is $O(m 2^m)$.

Let us now pass on to an estimate of a lower bound on the time complexity of any algorithm finding a family G_Q such that for every $I \subseteq [m]$, $\bigcap \{G_i : \in I\} = \varnothing$ if and only if $I \square Q$.

To this end we need the following lemma. A family of sets G is a *k-threshold* family if the intersection of every $k-1$ sets from G is nonempty, but the intersection of any k distinct sets from G is empty.

Lemma 3.1 Let $m \geq 2$ and $2 \leq k \leq m$. If $G=\{G_1,G_2,...,G_m\}$ is a k-threshold family then $|G_i| \geq \binom{m-1}{k-2}$, for every $i=1,...,m$.

Proof: Since G is a k-threshold family, for every choice $1 \leq i_1 < ... < i_{k-1} \leq m$ of indices, there must be $x_{i_1,...,i_{k-1}}$ so that $x_{i_1,...,i_{k-1}} \in G_{i_1} \cap ... \cap G_{i_{k-1}}$. Moreover, for different increasing sequences $\langle i_l < ... < i_{k-l} \rangle \neq \langle j_l < ... < j_{k-l} \rangle$ it must be the case that $x_{i_1,...,i_{k-1}} \neq x_{j_1,...,j_{k-1}}$, for under our assumption of the sequences being different, $|\{i_1,...,i_{k-1}\} \cup \{j_1,...,j_{k-1}\}| \geq k$ and $x_{i_1,...,i_{k-1}} \in G_{i_1} \cap ... G_{i_{k-1}} \cap G_{j_1} \cap ... G_{j_{k-1}}$, contradicting to the fact that G is a k-threshold family.

Now, each $i \in \{1,...,m\}$ belongs to exactly $\binom{m-1}{k-2}$ $(k-1)$-element subsets of $\{1,...,m\}$ (because we need to choose the remaining k–2 elements of such set). Therefore, every G_i contains $\binom{m-1}{k-2}$ elements among those of the form $x_{i_1,...,i_{k-1}}$, namely those which have i in its set of indices. Thus $|G_i| \geq \binom{m-1}{k-2}$. $\square$

It follows from the above lemma that any algorithm solving our problem of constructing a family G_Q has the worst case time performance $O(m^{1/2} 2^m)$. Indeed, consider the problem of finding a family G_Q, for $Q = \{\langle [m] \lfloor \frac{m}{2} \rfloor \rangle\}$. For this particular quorum constraint Q, $G_Q = \{F_1,...,F_m\}$ is such a family of sets that $\cap \{F_i : i \in I\} \neq \emptyset$ if and only if $|I| \leq \lfloor \frac{m}{2} \rfloor - 1$. It follows from Lemma 3.1 that for every $G_i \in G_Q$, $|G_i| \geq \binom{m-1}{\lfloor \frac{m}{2} \rfloor - 2}$. Hence to print the family G_Q alone we need $m \binom{m-1}{\lfloor \frac{m}{2} \rfloor - 2}$ time. By Stirling formula we have $\binom{m-1}{\lfloor \frac{m}{2} \rfloor - 2} = \Omega(\sqrt{\frac{1}{m}} 2^m)$ so, indeed, the worst case running time of any algorithm solving our problem is $\Omega(\sqrt{m} 2^m)$.

We contrast now our approach with that of Benaloh and Leichter [2]. In their scheme, the formula describing the filter (access structure) is public knowledge. Here is how the secret is shared. For each minimal set X in the filter the secret key K is decomposed into a sequence $\langle X_j : j \in X \rangle$ so that $\Sigma \{X_j : j \in X\} = K$. Then, each participant j receives the sequence of X_j for all minimal sets X such that $j \in X$. Clearly, once the set A of participants is present, it is enough to compute any minimal set Z in the access structure so that $Z \subseteq A$. Only the information held by the elements of Z is considered. The sum of corresponding shares of Z allows the reconstruction of K as a sum of the shares.

Observe that in this scheme, either the set of all minimal elements of the filter is stored (and must be searched each time a group of participants wants to recover the secret key), or even worse, a minimal authorized subset included in A must be found 'on line'. By contrast, in our approach, the shares are computed *once*, and all that needs to be computed subsequently (when a group of participants wishes to recover the key) is the greatest common divisor of strings of digits that are assigned to participants.

It is worth mentioning that this property of our method has nothing to do with the way we represent the access structures (i.e., by means of conjunctions of quorum constraints). If an access structure F is defined in any other way then we need to modify lines 1-14 of our algorithm where we find the set M of complements of maximal sets in the ideal $\wp([m])\backslash F$ (used later to construct the shares h_i). The way we find these maximal sets depends on the way the input access structure is represented. The point of our method is that no matter how we find these maximal sets, we have to do it only once, when constructing the shares. We do not have to do it while recovering the secret key. We refer the reader to [7] for more information on filters and their representations.

The strings (of bits or of digits) representing the numbers that constitute shares may be very long. One needs to realize that the operations on strings that correspond to multiplication and the Euclidean algorithm are fast, see [1] p. 70. In contrast, the security of the key is based on the same assumption as the public key cryptosystem, namely of the hardness of the factorization in the product of primes.

We return to the example provided at the beginning of the paper and show how the Algorithm 1 is used to construct the desired family of sets.

Example 3.1 Denoting by B the entire Board, and by E the set of employee board members, the constraints described above are expressed by two quorum constraints: $\langle B,4 \rangle$ and $\langle E,2 \rangle$. Let Q be the set consisting of these two quorum constraints.

Using Algorithm 1 we see that the following sets are maximal in I_Q:

$A_1=\{x_1,x_2,x_3,x_4,x_5\}$, $A_2=\{x_1,x_2,x_3,x_4,x_6\}$, $A_3=\{x_1,x_2,x_3,x_4,x_7\}$, $A_4=\{x_1,x_5,x_6\}$,

$A_5=\{x_1,x_5,x_7\}$, $A_6=\{x_1,x_6,x_7\}$, $A_7=\{x_2,x_5,x_6\}$, $A_8=\{x_2,x_5,x_7\}$, $A_9=\{x_2,x_6,x_7\}$

$A_{10}=\{x_3,x_5,x_6\}$, $A_{11}=\{x_3,x_5,x_7\}$, $A_{12}=\{x_3,x_6,x_7\}$, $A_{13}=\{x_4,x_5,x_6\}$, $A_{14}=\{x_4,x_5,x_7\}$

$A_{15}=\{x_4,x_6,x_7\}$, $A_{16}=\{x_5,x_6,x_7\}$.

Assign to the shareholders representatives x_1,x_2,x_3,x_4 the sets G_1,G_2,G_3,G_4, respectively, and to the representatives of employees x_5,x_6,x_7 the sets G_5,G_6,G_7, respectively. Thus we construct the family G_Q of 7 sets $G_1,G_2,G_3,G_4,G_5,G_6,G_7$ as follows:

$G_1=\{a_1,a_2,a_3,a_4,a_5,a_6\}$, $G_2=\{a_1,a_2,a_3,a_7,a_8,a_9\}$, $G_3=\{a_1,a_2,a_3,a_{10},a_{11},a_{12}\}$,

$G_4=\{a_1,a_2,a_3,a_{13},a_{14},a_{15}\}$, $G_5=\{a_1,a_4,a_5,a_7,a_8,a_{10},a_{11},a_{13},a_{14},a_{16}\}$,

$G_6=\{a_2,a_4,a_6,a_7,a_9,a_{10},a_{12},a_{13},a_{15},a_{16}\}$, $G_7=\{a_3,a_5,a_6,a_8,a_9,a_{11},a_{12},a_{14},a_{15},a_{16}\}$.

This is the desired family G_Q. That is, the intersection of a subfamily of G_Q is empty if and only if the index set of this subfamily is an authorized set with respect to Q.

Now, recall our construction of the integers $h_1,...,h_7$. We selected 17 distinct prime numbers (one more than the number of indices of the sets maximal in I_Q), $p_1,...,p_{16}$ and p. Of those 16 numbers $p_1,...,p_{16}$ are used to hide the secret. The secret itself is the 17th number, p. Let h_i, $i=1,...,7$, be constructed as in the Example 2.1, that is $h_i = \prod\{p_j : a_j \in G_i\} \cdot p$.

Given a set $\{h_{i_1}, \ldots, h_{i_k}\}$ where $1 \leq i_1, \ldots, i_k \leq 7$, the greatest common divisor of $\{h_{i_1}, \ldots, h_{i_k}\}$ is either p (if $\{i_1, \ldots, i_k\}$ satisfies the constraints Q) or otherwise a larger number that cannot be efficiently factored. Indeed, the greatest common divisor of $\{h_{i_1}, \ldots, h_{i_k}\}$ is equal to: $\prod \{p_j : j \in \bigcap_{r=1}^{k} G_{i_r}\} \cdot p$.

The intersection $\bigcap_{r=1}^{k} G_{i_r}$ is empty precisely when the quorum constraints are satisfied. Thus exactly in such case the computed greatest common divisor is p. Consequently, precisely in the presence of an authorized set with respect to the set of constraints Q the secret can be reconstructed.

4.   DISCUSSION AND CONCLUSIONS

In this paper we proposed an algorithm for sharing a secret cryptographic key or for a voting procedure with the constraints requiring 'numerical participation'. These constraints generalize the ones proposed by Shamir in [14]. That is, instead of just one cardinality constraint requiring the presence of at least k members from some set we admit several such constraints. The price we pay is the complexity of the algorithm proposed in our paper.

Although our scheme, as well as the scheme of Benaloh and Leichter, has an exponential time complexity in the worst case, there are many cases when it works in polynomial time. It is so, for example, when the ideal being the complement of an access structure consists of the sets of cardinality not exceeding a certain fixed value. In particular, for a fixed k, Shamir's filter has this property. Other examples can easily be constructed.

The authors are fully aware that the proposed scheme has several practical limitations. Its security is conditional, based on the presumed intractability of the integer factorization. Computational overhead is high - the shares are large. The numbers involved in the implementation of our scheme need to be very large. Even for a moderately complex access structure, the shares are likely to be of order of thousands of decimal digits. For larger groups of shareholders computing the shares considered in our scheme gets excessively time-consuming. The generation of a set of suitable primes, line 25 in our algorithm, needs a lot of time since already the set-up time for the RSA system where only two primes in that order of magnitude are needed takes significant time. Furthermore, the shares get very long with the number of people involved. Although the complexity of computation of gcd's is comparably low, for such large numbers it will rend the key-recovery slow as well.

As often in more theoretical investigations, only future will show if the proposed scheme can be successfully applied in real-life environment. In this context, it would be interesting to replace the multiplication of large numbers by a more practical operation with similar properties. We have no idea how to do it, but may be there is a solution to this problem.

On the other hand, an advantage of the proposed scheme is that the users do not need to be aware of the access structure while they try to extract the secret. The access structure does not need to be public knowledge and does not need to be stored at all. For changing the key one does not need to set up the whole system again, the quorum constraints need to be known only by the key-distributor, verifying whether a set is authorized can be done by computing the intersection of certain sets, and the key can be recovered by computing the greatest common divisor of the shares.

In our scheme to verify whether a set of users is authorized, we compute the gcd of certain set of integers. This can be time-consuming, when the numbers are very large. In the Benaloh-Leichter scheme the corresponding step is not too fast either since one computes certain sums there while there might be exponentially many of those sums.

The constraints considered in this paper determine a filter. Such filter can be presented in a variety of ways - quorum constraints is just one possible representation (see [7]). It follows from Proposition 2.1 that, for any of these representations, the technique expressed in Theorem 2.3 can be used.

It should be noted that the constraints considered here are not the only ones that are natural in applications. For instance, we could consider the constraints of the form $\langle Z, k \rangle$, requiring that less than k are present out of the elements of set a Z. These constraints are related to ideals in $\wp([m])$ in a manner analogous to the relationship of the constraints considered here and filters. The mixed sets of constraints are related to segments in $\wp([m])$.

Yet other constraints may be reasonable in some applications. For instance, the ones requiring that the putative set I contains more elements of some set Y than of some other set Z. Those constraints do not generate segments and are difficult to handle.

Notice that the structure computed by the lines 1-24 of our algorithm is *reusable*. That is, as long as the access structure is not changed we can use it with the different assignments of the numbers p_j. That is, the underlying combinatorial structure can be reused.

Shamir's construction can be used for multiple quorum constraints, by assigning to each constraint the collection of shares that are given to participants. In principle, this requires the access structure to be public knowledge. This is not the case in our construction. The access structure itself may be secret in our case.

Finally, notice that the secret and the shares do not have to be prime numbers nor their products. Elements of any ring with the unique factorization will do. This could be a ring of polynomials, for instance, or even some algebra of formal series.

5. ACKNOWLEDGEMENTS

This paper has been written while the first author was visiting the Department of Computer Science of the University of Kentucky.

The authors would like to thank Professor Victor W. Marek for his inspiring role in the course of writing this paper.

Remarks of dr Andrzej Borzyszkowski to the first draft of this paper are gratefully acknowlegded. Mr. Robert Osowiecki of Warsaw University helped to improve the presentation of the algorithm.

6.   BIBLIOGRAPHY

[1] E. Bach and J. Shallit, *Algorithmic Number Theory*, MIT Press, 1996.
[2] J. Benaloh and J. Leichter, Generalized secret sharing and monotone functions, in: *Advances in cryptology - CRYPTO '88*, Lecture Notes in Computer Science, vol. 403, Springer–Verlag, 1990, pp. 27-35.
[3] H. Cohen, *A Course in Computational Algebraic Number Theory*, Springer–Verlag, 1995. (Second editon)
[4] W. Dobrzański, A. Soroczuk, M. Srebrny and M.A. Srebrny Jr, *Distributed password*, Technical Report, Institute of Computer Science, Polish Academy of Sciences, Warsaw, Poland, December 1999; also in this volume.
[5] N. Koblitz, *Algebraic Aspects of Cryptography*, Springer–Verlag, 1998.
[6] E. Kranakis, *Primality and Cryptography*, Wiley, 1986.
[7] Z. Lonc, V.W. Marek, Filters in Boolean Lattices with Applications, submitted..
[8] A. Menezes, P.V. Oorschot and S. Vanstone, *Handbook of Applied Cryptography*, CRC Press, 1997.
[9] M. Mignotte, How to share a secret, in: *Cryptography*, Lecture Notes in Computer Science, vol. 149, Springer–Verlag, 1983, pp. 371–375.
[10] Ch.H. Papadimitriou, *Computational complexity*, Addison Wesley, 1994.
[11] R.L. Rivest, Cryptography, In: *Handbook of Theoretical Computer Science*, vol. A, pp. 717–755.
[12] R.L. Rivest, A. Shamir and L.M. Adleman, A method for obtaining digital signatures and public-key cryptosystems, *Communications of the ACM* 20(1978), pp. 120–126.
[13] B. Schneider, *Applied Cryptography*, Wiley, 1996.
[14] A. Shamir, How to share a secret, *Communications of the ACM*, 22(1979), p. 612–613.
[15] D. R. Stinson, *Cryptography, Theory and Practice*, CRC Press 1995.
[16] D.R. Stinson, On some methods for unconditionally secure key distribution and broadcast encryption, *Designs, codes and cryptography* 12(1997)3, pp. 215–243.

Distributed Password

WOJCIECH DOBRZAŃSKI[(1)], ARTUR SOROCZUK[(2)],
MARIAN SREBRNY[1(3)], MATEUSZ SREBRNY[(4)]

[1] *Institute of Mathematics and Computer Science, Technical University of Częstochowa, Poland; e-mail: wojtekd@matinf.pcz.czest.pl*
[2] *Institute of Mathematics and Computer Science, Pedagogical University, Częstochowa, Poland; e-mail: a.soroczuk@wsp.czest.pl*
[3] *Institute of Computer Science, Polish Academy of Sciences, Warsaw, Poland; e-mail: marians@ipipan.waw.pl*
[4] *Department of Mathematics, Informatics and Mechanics, University of Warsaw, Poland; e-mail: m.srebrny@students.mimuw.edu.pl*

Abstract: A new scheme of password/key distribution, or secret sharing, is presented. Its cryptographic strength is based on the integer factorization problem. It realizes the idea of a threshold scheme in which distributed trust or shared control is ensured by gating a critical action on cooperation by t of n users, with $1<t<n$. A secret passphrase or a private key is divided into pieces, called 'shares', which are distributed and stored between n users or n networked computers in such a way that pooling shares of at least t users enables reconstruction of the original password/key. We provide an elementary introduction illustrated with one of the simplest known protocols based on modular arithmetic, the Chinese Remainder Theorem and Euclid's Algorithm computing the greatest common divisor.

Key words: access control, security models, Biba and LaPadula model, public key certificate, attribute certificate, public key infrastructure

1. INTRODUCTION

Splitting personal access passwords and cryptographic private keys between a number of pieces (shares, shadows) and distributing them between distinct networked computers has got a lot of attention recently and has been distinguished as an important and challenging area of modern cryptology, called secret sharing.

---

[1] This author gratefully acknowledges calling his attention to the problem of password distribution by Antoni Mazurkiewicz

Usually, secret keys and passphrases in computer systems are stored on a single computer (server), where their verification is done as well. This involves comparison of the key input by a user of the system with its master counterpart recorded in the system .

To minimize the risk associated with open storage of access passphrases or secret keys, these are first encoded using a known ciphering or digesting algorithm (e.g., DES, MD5, SHA-1), and their encoded versions are then memorized by the system. The verification process, on the other hand, is preceded by encoding (using the same coding algorithm) of the password input by the system's user, and only then checking of conformance of the encoded password as given by the user with its encoded counterpart recorded in the system follows.

An idea of enhanced access protection by secret sharing is useful in various real life situations. For example, bank strong-rooms which, to be opened, require the use of several different keys being in possession of authorized persons. Another example, the nuclear push-button whose triggering involves the use of several different keys that form its activating combination. A situation can be thought of, in which the consent of both spouses is required; for example, to issue a passport for their child. Instead of requiring from both parents to appear in front of an appropriate clerk in person, in the electronic society of the future the spouses will be able to express their approval electronically using a system of distributing a password into two shares with a threshold of two. Each of the spouses will have his/her respective share of the (conjugal) password and they will be able to confirm their consent by providing those shares.

Personal identification numbers provide entity authentication and open user's capability to communicate with the computer systems in banks, electronic shops, telecommunication networks, *et cetera*, operating even in huge computer network environments. Encoding and decoding keys play a similar role in cryptographic systems.

Breaking a protected system requires primarily recovering its secret password/key. The rule is adopted that the coding mechanism (algorithm) is publicly known to all interested parties. The passwords and keys must be strictly protected in secret. The longer a cryptosystem is exposed to attacks by independent circles analyzing its power and no one has found out the system-breaking algorithm, the more reliable that system is.

Splitting a secret key into a number of shares and storing each of the shares separately on different computers, in different locations, strengthens the system against interference by unauthorized persons, organizations, agencies, etc.

In this paper we introduce a new procedure of sharing secret passwords/keys. This involves splitting a password or a secret key K (an arbitrary large number being kept secret), into a finite number of component pieces, called shares, with the threshold t. For example, into five pieces (shares) with a threshold of three (Fig. 1). This means that, in order to reconstruct K, it is necessary to collect and process at least three of the five distributed key's shares.

To minimize the risk associated with open storage of access passphrases or secret keys, these are first encoded using a known ciphering or digesting algorithm (e.g., DES, MD5, SHA-1), and their encoded versions are then memorized by the system. The verification process, on the other hand, is preceded by encoding (using the same coding algorithm) of the password input by the system's user, and only then checking of conformance of the encoded password as given by the user with its encoded counterpart recorded in the system follows (Fig. 2).

An idea of enhanced access protection by secret sharing is useful in various real life situations. For example, bank strong-rooms which, to be opened, require the use of several different keys being in possession of authorized persons. Another example, the nuclear push-button whose triggering involves the use of several different keys that form its activating combination. A situation can be thought of, in which the consent of both spouses is required; for example, to issue a passport for their child. Instead of requiring from both parents to appear in front of an appropriate clerk in person, in the electronic society of the future the spouses will be able to express their approval electronically using a system of distributing a password into two shares with a threshold of two. Each of the spouses will have his/her respective share of the (conjugal) password and they will be able to confirm their consent by providing those shares.

Personal identification numbers provide entity authentication and open user's capability to communicate with the computer systems in banks, electronic shops, telecommunication networks, *et cetera*, operating even in huge computer network environments. Encoding and decoding keys play a similar role in cryptographic systems.

Breaking a protected system requires primarily recovering its secret password/key. The rule is adopted that the coding mechanism (algorithm) is publicly known to all interested parties. The passwords and keys must be strictly protected in secret. The longer a cryptosystem is exposed to attacks by independent circles analyzing its power and no one has found out the system-breaking algorithm, the more reliable that system is.

Splitting a secret key into a number of shares and storing each of the shares separately on different computers, in different locations, strengthens the system against interference by unauthorized persons, organizations, agencies, etc.

In this paper we introduce a new procedure sharing secret passwords/keys. This involves splitting a password or a secret key K (an arbitrary large number being kept secret), into a finite number of component pieces, called shares, with the threshold t. For example, into five pieces (shares) with a threshold of three (Fig. 3). This means that, in order to reconstruct K, it is necessary to collect and process at least three of the five distributed key's shares.

If those shares are stored on different computers in a network then breaking in to at least three of the five computers would be necessary for an intruder to reproduce the secret key K.

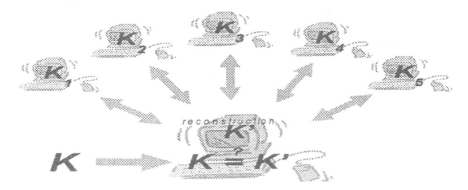

Figure 3

An elementary material is provided in the next section which consists of our seminar notes on a well known secret sharing scheme based on elementary properties of the integer congruence relation and the Chinese Remainder Theorem. In section 3 we introduce and discuss a new scheme of secret password/key sharing based on the computational hardness of the integer factorization.

2.   NOTATION AND SURVEY

2.1   The modular arithmetic distribution

First, let us recall some basic terminology and notation. Two integers, x and y, are called *congruent modulo m*, $x \equiv y$ *(mod m)*, iff $r(x,m) = r(y,m)$, where $r(a,b)$ stands for *the remainder of the division of a by b*. Given a modulus m, this is an *equivalence relation*. For a prime m, each of the *equivalence classes* has exactly one representative among the numbers from 0 through $m-1$. Any set of the representatives of all the classes of remainders modulo m is called *the full set of remainders modulo m*. If $a \equiv b$ *(mod m)* and $c \equiv d$ *(mod m)*, then $a \pm b \equiv b \pm d$ *(mod m)* and $ab \equiv bd$ *(mod m)*. The set of equivalence classes, with the natural arithmetic operations of modular addition and multiplication on representatives forms *a commutative ring*.

The following easy properties will be useful in what follows:

If $a \equiv b$ *(mod m)* then $a \equiv b$ *(mod d)* for any divisor $d \mid m$.

If $a \equiv b$ *(mod m)*, $a \equiv b$ *(mod n)* and m and n are relatively prime, then $a \equiv b$ *(mod mn)*.

If $m \mid a$, $n \mid a$ and $GCD(m,n)=1$ then $mn \mid a$.

Euclid's algorithm provides a procedure for computing the $GCD(a,b)$, even when the prime factorization of these numbers is not known. To compute $GCD(a, b)$, where $a > b$, we first divide a by b and write down the quotient q_1 and the remainder r_1 : $a = q_1 b + r_1$. Then we perform another division, in which b acts as a and r_1 as b: $b = q_2 r_1 + r_2$. Then we divide r_1 by r_2 : $r_1 = q_3 r_2 + r_3$. We continue these procedure of division operations until we get a remainder which divides the previous one; i.e., $r_{n-2} = q_n r_{n-1} + r_n$ *where* $r_n = 0$. This means that $r_{n-1} = GCD(a, b)$.

The Extended Euclid's Algorithm says that there exist $u, v \in Z$ such that $d = ua + vb$, whenever $d = GCD(a,b)$ and $a > b$. This is used for computing the modular multiplication inverse; i.e., such an integer x that $ax \equiv 1 \bmod n$. Furthermore, if $n > 1$ and $GCD(a, n) = 1$, then the equation $ax \equiv 1 \bmod n$ has exactly one solution.

The Chinese Remainder Theorem. *Consider a system of congruencies with different moduli*

$x \equiv a_1$ *(mod m_1)*,
$x \equiv a_2$ *(mod m_2)*,
. . . .
$x \equiv a_r$ *(mod m_r)*.

Assume that any two of the above modules are relatively prime: $GCD(m_i, n_j) = 1$
for $i \neq j$. *Then there is a common solution x for all those congruencies, and any two
solutions are congruent to each other modulo* $M = m_1 m_2 ... m_r$.

Distribution of secret key *K* into five shares with threshold three.

Suppose a secret key K (any large number), is given. To distribute K into five shares
with a threshold of three, we generate five random prime numbers p_i such that:

$$< p_i < \sqrt{K} \quad \text{for each} \quad i = 1, 2, ..., 5. \tag{1}$$

Then, we calculate:

$$a_i = r(K, p_i) \tag{2}$$

The obtained pairs of numbers (p_i, a_i) represent the distribution of the secret key
K. Now, we demonstrate that pooling at least three pairs (p_i, a_i), the secret key K can
be reproduced. Let us consider the following system of linear congruences:

$$x \equiv a_i \ (mod \ p_i)$$
$$x \equiv a_j \ (mod \ p_j)$$
$$x \equiv a_k \ (mod \ p_k)$$

where $i \neq j \neq k$ and $i, j, k = 1, ..., 5$. By the Chinese Remainder Theorem such a
solution x exists and each two solutions are congruent to each other modulo $P = p_i$
$p_j p_k$.

Lemma: $a \equiv r(a, m) \ (mod \ m)$.
In addition, it can be seen from (2) and the above lemma that one of the solutions to the
system must be K. Hence we have: $x = n \cdot P + K$, for $n \in N$. By (1) we also find out that:
$K < p$. Hence, we can uniquely determine the secret key searched for, as: $K = r(x, P)$.

Easy to see that we have: $K \neq r(x, P)$, in the case when $P = p_i p_j$; $i \neq j$; $i, j = 1 ... 5$
(i.e., we know two pairs (p_i, a_i) out of five), since $K > P$ (following (1)). This means
that if one or even two of the distributed secret key shares are disclosed, there will
be no possibility of reproducing (and thus compromising) K based on those
elements. We assume that the parameters are large enough, so that a brute force
attack would be computationally infeasible.

2.2 Other schemes

In addition to the above mechanism several other schemes of password
distribution have been known. See [5]. The best known ones include Shamir's
scheme [8] employing Lagrange's polynomial interpolation theorem. A secret key is
represented by a polynomial of degree k with integer coefficients, that is a sequence
of the integer coefficients of that polynomial. The values of this polynomial for
several inputs can be considered as shares. The well known Lagrange's interpolation
theorem provides an algorithm of reproducing the polynomial (coefficients), if k+1 of its
values are known. Thus, the system's administrator can assign one polynomial value to
each of the arbitrary number of users. To reconstruct the password, pooling k of them is
sufficient. This is a password distribution mechanism with a threshold of k+1.

Another mechanism of password distribution is provided by the fact known from elementary geometry that any two points determine a straight line. Based on this, a method of secret key distribution with a threshold of two can be developed. The distributed shares will be the coordinates of points in the space lying on a fixed straight line, whereas the secret key will be the angle of intersection of that line with a certain fixed plane. For example, ane can take the angle of inclination of the line relative to the X-axis in the plane as the password (key). The system's administrator assigns one point lying on that line to each of the users. To reproduce the password (inclination angle), the consent of at least two users is necessary and sufficient, which is expressed by pooling the point coordinates that can be regarded as "shares" of the password being in the possession of individual users. Thus we obtain a system of password distribution into any finite number of shares with a threshold of two. Similarly, any three points determine a plane in the three-dimensional space. This way a system of password distribution with a threshold of three can be designed. This idea can be continued to higher dimensions. In general, in the n-dimensional space, k+1 points determine a k-dimensional hyperplane. We assume k<n, and obtain a mechanism of password distribution with a threshold of k+1.

In [2] the authors gave an interesting application of a key distribution mechanism to an algorithm of collective generation of the DSS standard electronic signature.

3. FACTORIZATION DISTRIBUTION

In this section we present a new scheme of password/key distribution based on the computational hardness of the integer factorization.

3.1. In this subsection the idea of factorization distribution is illustrated with the following example of splitting a given password/key between $n=5$ shares with a threshold of $t=3$. The password to be distributed is a large prime number, say p. The scheme starts off by generating ten auxiliary large primes: q_1, q_2, q_3, q_4, q_5, q_6, q_7, q_8, q_9, q_{10}. The shares to be distributed between five parties (computers) will be denoted by a_i, for $i=1, 2, ... ,5$, and computed as follows:

$$a_1 = p \cdot q_1 \cdot q_2 \cdot q_3 \cdot q_4$$
$$a_2 = p \cdot q_1 \cdot q_5 \cdot q_6 \cdot q_7$$
$$a_3 = p \cdot q_2 \cdot q_5 \cdot q_8 \cdot q_9$$
$$a_4 = p \cdot q_3 \cdot q_6 \cdot q_8 \cdot q_{10}$$
$$a_5 = p \cdot q_4 \cdot q_7 \cdot q_9 \cdot q_{10}$$

Note that knowing three shares one can easily compute p by finding their GCD running Euclid's algorithm. The GCD of two shares is the product value $p \cdot q_i$, for $i \in \{1, 2, ... ,10\}$. To get p from the product one would need to factorize the product. There is no algorithm known performing it in polynomial time.

3.2. In this subsection the idea of factorization distribution is described in full generality. We are to split a given password/key between n shares with a threshold of t, $1<t \leq n$. The password to be distributed is a large prime number, say p. The basic idea is that each share will be the product of p and some auxiliary large primes, so that each $t-1$ shares will have a common divisor of the form $p \cdot q$, where

q is one of the auxiliary primes, and each t shares will have just one common divisor p. We need $l=\binom{n}{t-1}$ auxiliary large primes: $q_1, q_2,...,q_l$, because this is the number of $(t-1)$-element subsets of a set of cardinality n. The scheme starts off by generating l (pseudo)random primes: $q_1, q_2,...,q_l$. The shares to be distributed between n parties will be denoted by a_i, for $i=1, 2, ... , l$, and computed as follows.

l - *the number of $(t-1)$-element subsets of $\{1,...,n\}$*
$\{c_j\}_{1 \leqslant j \leqslant l}$ - *all those subsets*
$\{q_j\}_{1 \leqslant j \leqslant l}$ - *q_j a prime number associated to set c_j*

> *for* $i := 1$ *to* n *do*
>   *product* $:= p$;
>   *for* $j := 1$ *to* l *do*
>   *if* $i \in c_j$ *then*
>   *product* $:= product \cdot q_j$
>   *fi*
>   *od*;
> $a_i := product$
> *od*;

In other words, $a_i = p \cdot \Pi\{q_A : A \subset \{1,...,n\}, |A|=t-1, i \in A\}$ where q_A is a prime associated to set A.

This procedure returns each share a_i as the product of p and $k=\binom{n-1}{t-2}$ different large primes, since this is the number of possible extensions of singleton $\{i\}$ to a set of $(t-1)$ elements using the members of $\{1,...,n\}\backslash\{i\}$. Note that the GCD of t shares is p, while the GCD of $t-1$ shares is the product of p and a large prime. Recovering p is not feasible.

3.3. We analyse the worst-case running time of generating the shares as a function of the size of n, t and p. The number $k=\binom{n-1}{t-2}$ of the auxiliary primes in each share is decisive. The maximum value of $\binom{n-1}{t-2}$ is achieved when $t \approx n/2$ and it is exponential in n. Similarly, the worst-case running time of the verification procedure is a function of the size of n, t, and p, since each share a_i is the product of p and $k=\binom{n-1}{t-2}$ auxiliary primes each of the same size as p. The overall running time of the verification procedure is $O(GCD(a_1, a_2, ..., a_l))$ which is $O(t+|max_i \; a_i|)$ divisions; see [1, section 33.2-8]. Again, this is dominated by $k=\binom{n-1}{t-2}$ and is less than or equal to $|t| \cdot |p| \cdot 2^n$.

Thus, we see that for t roughly around the half of n both the generation and verification procedures become infeasible. However, when t is either very small or close to n both have polynomial (in n) execution time.

3.4. Security requirements

The computational factorization distribution problem as introduced above can be formulated as searching for p, given one or two shares, in the case of distribution between n parties with a threshold of 3. This problem is contained in the integer factorization problem; i.e., if one can solve the factorization problem in polynomial time, then one can recover the secret password p. Here is a list of the currently best known algorithms factoring efficiently in certain special cases: „Monte Carlo" method (see [4, pages 172-177], [5, pages 91-92], [10]), Las Vegas algorithm ([10, page 141]), Fermat method and factor bases ([4, pages 178-191]), [5, pages 94-95], the continued fraction factoring algorithm ([4, pages 191- 198]), the quadratic sieve method ([4, 199-205], [5, 95-97]), Pollard's p-1 algorithm ([4, page 206], [5, page 94]), the number field sieve ([4, page 205]), the elliptic curve factoring algorithm ([5, §3.2.4]).

In order to prevent all of the above powerful factoring algorithms and those types of attack the following recommendations should be applied.

The primes p and $q_1, q_2,...,q_l$ should be selected so that factoring $p \cdot q_i$ is computationally infeasible. A 512-bit product $p \cdot q_i$ provides only a marginal security. A product $p \cdot q_i$ of 768 bits is recommended. For long-term security, 1024-bit or larger product should be used. Moreover, p and q should be about the same bit length, and sufficiently large. For example, if a 1024-bit product $p \cdot q_i$ is to be used, then each of p and q_i should be about 512 bits in length. When concerning a 1024-bit product of four primes, each of them should be about 256-bit prime.

In addition to these restrictions, many authors' recommendations amount to p and q_i's being strong primes. A prime p is a *strong prime* if the following three conditions hold:

(a) $p-1$ has a large prime factor, denoted r;

(b) $p+1$ has a large prime factor; and

(c) $r-1$ has a large prime factor.

According to [5], strong primes offer a little protection beyond that offered by random primes. Given the current state of knowledge of factoring algorithms, there is no compelling reason for requiring the use of strong primes. On the other hand, they are no less secure than random primes, and require only minimal additional running time to compute, thus there is a little real additional cost in using them.

3.6. One can relax slightly the requirement that p and q_i's are primes, when security is not the primary goal. It suffices to have them pairwise relatively prime; i.e., such that $GCD(p,q_i)=1$ and $GCD(q_i,q_j)=1$, for each $1 \leq i, j \leq 10$. Moreover, all those products can be taken from a Gaussian ring instead of the integers. Let us recall, a ring is *Gaussian* if it has the unique factorization property. The indecomposable elements play the role of primes. The rings of polynomials are Gaussian, for example. Some Gaussian rings are very convenient for implementation. Their operations are easy to implement and fast.

3.7. Consider a distributed computation system consisting of n computers communicating freely by identical broadcast channels. On each computer there is one sequential program executed. These programs cooperate according to a protocol and perform a common distributed task.

A password distribution task can be implemented as an application in the *PVM (Parallel Virtual Machine)* [11] environment, which makes it possible to write one distributed protocol program (application, task) which runs on a number of physically distributed computers. A task performs execution and communication between its subtasks. The *MPI (Message Passing Interface)* [12] environment can be used as well instead of *PVM*.

4. CONCLUSION AND PERSPECTIVES

Password distribution, by the method presented in this paper, or the other methods mentioned above, provides enhanced protection of secret passwords and keys against unauthorized access. Designing new distribution mechanisms seems to be an intriguing theoretical problem with important practical significance. From a mathematician's point of view, the problem is concerned with methods for reconstructing certain object using only some partial information about it. In the aspect of cryptographic power, it is necessary to assure that the number of possible "candidates" for the password is very large. It should be large enough so that it would not be computationally feasible to check out all of them one by one (brute force attack). In the mechanism presented in this paper, this is taken care of by the size of the distributed password. It is assumed in selecting a sufficiently large K for this purpose in section 2 and p in section 3 above. The complexity bounds give serious practical limitations on our scheme.

5. REFERENCES

[1] Cormen T.H., Leiserson C.E., Rivest R.L.: *Introduction to algorithms*, The MIT Press, 1990.
[2] Gennaro R., Jarecki S., Krawczyk H., Rabin T.: *Robust Threshold DSS signatures*, http://theory.lcs.mit.edu/~cis/pubs/stasio/dss-full.ps.gz.
[3] Grzegorczyk A.: *Zarys arytmetyki teoretycznej*, Biblioteka Matematyczna, tom 39, WNT, Warszawa 1971.
[4] Koblitz N.: *A course in number theory and cryptography*, Springer-Verlag, 1994.
[5] Menezes A.J., van Oorschot P.C., Vanstone S.A.: *Handbook of applied cryptography*, CRC Press, 1996; http://www.cacr.math.uwaterloo.ca/hac/, 5th printing, August 2001.
[6] Narkiewicz W.: *Teoria liczb*, Biblioteka Matematyczna, tom 50, PWN, Warszawa 1977.
[7] Denning D.E.R.: *Cryptography and data security*, Addison Wesley, 1983.
[8] Shamir A.: How to share a secret, *Communications of the ACM* 22(1979), pp. 612-613.
[9] Sierpiński W.: *Arytmetyka teoretyczna*, PWN, 1959.
[10] Stinson D.R.: *Cryptography: theory and practice*, CRC Press, 1995.
[11] Geist A., Beguelin A., Dongarra J., Jiang W., Manchek R. and Sunderam V.: *PVM - Parallel Virtual Machine*, MIT Press, 1994.
[12] MPI Forum: MPI - A message passing interface standard, *Int. Journal Supercomputer Application* 8(3/4)(1994), pp. 165-416.

Chapter 6

Logic Synthesis and Simulation

Utilizing High-Level Information for Formal Hardware Verification

PEER JOHANNSEN, ROLF DRECHSLER
Siemens AG, Corporate Technology, Design Automation,
CT--SE—4,81730 Munich, Germany, e-mail:
peer.johannsen@mchp.siemens.de
rolf.drechsler@mchp.siemens.de

Abstract: Today's digital circuit designs frequently contain up to several million transistors and designs need to be checked to ensure that manufactured chips operate correctly. Formal methods for verification are becoming increasingly attractive since they confirm design behavior without exhaustively simulating a design. Reducing runtimes and the amount of memory needed for computations is one requirement in order to match ever increasing design sizes in hardware verification. Designs are usually given as Register-Trbansfer-Level (RTL) specifications, but most industrial hardware verification tools are based on bit-level methods.

However, designs, like for example ALUs or bus interfaces, often have very regular structures that can be described easily on a higher level of abstraction. This information is lost on bit-level and thus cannot be utilized by verification tools, if verification procedures operate on the basis of bit-level descriptions. Recently, several approaches to formal circuit verification have been proposed, which are based on word-level descriptions and which make use of such regularities. We introduce the main concepts of formal verification on the RTL and give an overview of existing techniques. Recent developments are outlined, and based on industrial examples the advantages and disadvantages are discussed.

Key words: Formal hardware verification, RTL, abstraction.

1.   INTRODUCTION

Formal verification has become one of the most important steps in digital circuit design. Since nowadays circuits frequently contain up to several million transistors and since design sizes are ever increasing, verification of such large designs becomes more and more difficult. Circuit designs need to be checked to ensure that manufactured chips operate correctly. Pure simulation cannot guarantee the correct behavior and exhaustive simulation is often impossible.

The average time-to-market for custom chip designs today is about 18 months, and approximately between 60--70% of project costs result from error detection and correction. Fabricating the hardware of prototype chips is timeconsuming and expensive, and production of faulty circuits requires redesigns and enlarges the number of design cycles. Effient testing for correct behavior thus becomes more and more important and a major economical issue. It is desirable to detect design faults before manufacturing and thus to keep the number of design cycles and redesign costs as small as possible. Formal methods for verification are becoming increasingly attractive since they prove correct design behavior before manufacturing and without exhaustively simulating a design. Bounded Model Checking (see e.g. [1]) and Bounded Property Checking have gained significance in Electronic Design Automation as recently surveyed in [16]. The majority of today's industrial hardware verification tools employ bit-level techniques, like SAT-procedures or ATPG and BDD methods (see e.g. [3, 4, 15]), for circuit verification. The task of verifying a specific property of a digital design is turned into an instance of propositional SAT and solved within the Boolean domain, using the above mentioned techniques.

While design sizes are persistently growing, verification itself becomes more complex, and verification tasks often fail due to resource limitations of today's computing machinery. Industrial digital circuit designs are usually specified in Hardware Description Languages (HDLs), like VHDL or Verilog. HDL specifications of digital circuits contain explicite structural information which is lost when they are transformed into bit-level representations while synthesis. On bit-level, all signals are of one-bit width, and all available functional units are Boolean connectives. In contrast to that, in HDLs, the control flow and data flow of a circuit are specified on the RTL, allowing single bits to be grouped into word-level signals (e.g. bitvectors and busses). High-level operators (e.g. adders, multipliers, and shifters) are available, and structural regularities of circuit designs can easily be described on this level of abstraction. Thus, RTL specifications o#er additional high-level information which is not used by plain bit-level verification techniques. Several approaches to formal circuit verification have been proposed which make use of such high-level information, see e.g. [2, 7, 8,12, 17].

In the following sections, we survey several examples of how highlevel information contained in RTL specifications can be used to aid in digital hardware verification. We outline the respective verification techniques and discuss their advantages and disadvantages. The main focus is laid on automated abstraction techniques, which are a promising approach to enhance capabilities of formal verification tools and of existing verification techniques. As an example, we present in detail a new word-level abstraction technique, which has recently been developed and successfully been applied in industrial circuit verification.

2. BOUNDED PROPERTY CHECKING OF DIGITAL CIRCUITS

The problem of verifying that digital circuit behavior is in accordance with the intention of the circuit designer, is a problem of checking whether design behavior meets specific properties.

In bounded model checking of digital hardware, a specification D of a circuit design and a property specification P are transformed into an instance φ (D, P) of propositional SAT, i.e. a Boolean formula. Design specifications are usually given as VHDL or Verilog source code. Properties are specified in a linear time logic used in symbolic trajectory evaluation and describe the intended behavior of the design within a finite bounded interval of time.

In property checking of digital circuits, a check for faulty behavior is performed. Of interest is whether there exists a situation, i.e. values for all circuit signals of D, which contradicts P . The Boolean formula φ (D, P) is satisfiable if and only if the property P does not hold for the given design D, i.e. we have:

$$\begin{array}{c} \varphi(D,P) \ is \\ satisfiable \end{array} \iff \begin{array}{c} Property\ P \\ does\ not\ hold \\ for\ design\ D, \end{array}$$

in other words:

$$\begin{array}{c} Design\ D \\ has\ property\ P \end{array} \iff \begin{array}{c} \varphi(D,P)\ is \\ unsatisfiable. \end{array}$$

Satisfiability of φ (D, P) is to be determined. If φ (D, P) is satisfiable, this is an indication that the circuit does not function in the way intended by the designer. Property P is not valid for D, and a satisfying solution of φ (D, P) yields a counterexample. Counterexamples are given in terms of assignments of values to the circuit inputs, such that a violation of the desired behavior, which is described by the property, can be observed.

The SAT problem is known to be NP-complete and a variety of decision procedures has been proposed and has been well investigated (see e.g. [15]). SAT procedures have shown to be particularly useful in bounded model checking. The majority of today's industrial hardware verification tools for property checking of digital designs relies on multiengine concepts of such decision procedures.

However, all these procedures operate on bit-level. The problem whether a specific property holds for a circuit design, is solved in the Boolean domain. This means that all variables occurring in φ (D, P), are Boolean variables.

Each variable corresponds to a 1-bit signal of D. Yet, circuit designs are usually given in terms of RTL specifications. An RTL specification of a digital design D contains explicit structural high-level information, which is not contained in φ (D, P) anymore and thus cannot be used by a SAT solver that only inspects φ (D, P).

In the following section, several examples are given, which illustrate that RTL and Boolean domain contain diffrent levels of structural information. We discuss diffrent techniques and illustrate how the additional wordlevel information, which is available on RTL, can be used in order to simplify and to speed up property checking tasks for digital hardware.

3.   UTILIZING RTL INFORMATION FOR VERIFICATION

A lot of circuit designs, e.g. ALUs, have very regular structures that can be described easily on a high level of abstraction. On RTL, as in HDLs for example, word-level data structures (e.g. multi-bit signals, arrays, memories) as well as high-level operators can be used to describe a circuit's functionality. As an illustration, consider addition of two 2-bit signals $x_{[2]} =< x_1, x_0 >$, $y_{[2]} =< y_1, y_0 >$ and a 1-bit carry-in $c_{[1]} =< c_0 >$. Sample bit-level equations, describing the data-path dependencies for the result signal $z_{[2]} =< z_1, z_0 >$ are:

$$
\begin{aligned}
z_0 &= ((x_0\overline{y_0} \vee \overline{x_0}y_0) \wedge \overline{c_0}) \vee \\
&\quad ((x_0 y_0 \vee \overline{x_0 y_0}) \wedge c_0) \\
c_1 &= x_0 y_0 \vee y_0 c_0 \vee c_0 x_0 \\
z_1 &= ((x_1\overline{y_1} \vee \overline{x_1}y_1) \wedge \overline{c_1}) \vee \\
&\quad ((x_1 y_1 \vee \overline{x_0 y_1}) \wedge c_1) \\
c_2 &= x_1 y_1 \vee y_1 c_1 \vee c_1 x_1
\end{aligned}
$$

$$(1)$$

The connotation that, for example, x_1 and x_0 resemble a 2-bit signal $< x_1, x_0 >$, is not visible on bit-level, and thus is not visible to a SAT solver. On RTL, such word-level addition can easily be described by the following bitvector equation

$$
z_{[2]} = x_{[2]} + y_{[2]} + c_{[1]} ,
$$

$$(2)$$

which allows special high-level decision procedures (here e.g. for high-level arithmetics) to be evoked by a verification tool. Several approaches to formal circuit verification are known, which are based on word-level formalisms. All these approaches make use of RTL design information, and a selection of the most important ones is surveyed in the following sections.

3.1   Integer Linear Programming

One approach to RTL based verification is to treat arithmetic units by Integer Linear Programming (ILP) methods. Word-level arithmetic is transformed into a linear program, i.e. a collection of arithmetic equations and inequalities over integer valued variables.

Linear programs are solved in the integer domain by ILP solvers. Equation (2), for example, can be transformed into the following linear program (note that solutions of ILP (3) and solutions of Equation (2) have a one-to-one correspondence):

$$E = x + y + c$$
$$E = 4 \cdot d + z$$
$$0 \leq x < 4$$
$$0 \leq y < 4$$
$$0 \leq c < 2$$
$$0 \leq z < 4$$
$$0 \leq d$$
$$0 \leq E$$

(3)

Integer Linear Programming is suitable for data-path verification of arithmetic circuits but lacks adequate modeling of the control path. Another drawback is that efficient ILP solvers often restrict integers and thus data-path signals to be words of fixed, machinedependent width, e.g. 32 bits. Furthermore, bit-level addition and multiplication of n-bit signals corresponds to modulo-arithmetic in the ring Z n and requires caution when generating the ILP (cf. [17]). In Example (3), the second equation and all the inequalities are used only to model moduloarithmetic on 2-bit bitvectors.

3.2 Rewriting

Term-rewriting techniques (cf. [10] for an overview) can be used to simplify verification tasks. RTL rewriting can utilize high-level information on operators, which is not present on bit-level. Let $x_{[2]}, y_{[2]}$ and $z_{[2]}$ be 2-bit signals and consider checking if

$$(x_{[2]} + y_{[2]}) + z_{[2]} =$$
$$y_{[2]} + (z_{[2]} + x_{[2]})$$

(4)

is satisfiable. Due to associativity and symmetry of addition, the left and right side of Equation (4) can be rewritten to

$$x_{[2]} + y_{[2]} + z_{[2]}$$
$$x_{[2]} + y_{[2]} + z_{[2]}$$

(5)

and easily be recognized as a tautology. However, a sample bit-level representation of (4) is shown below,

$$
\begin{aligned}
a_0 &= (x_0 \overline{y_0} \vee \overline{x_0} y_0) \\
c_{00} &= x_0 y_0 \\
a_1 &= ((x_1 \overline{y_1} \vee \overline{x_1} y_1) \wedge \overline{c_{00}}) \vee \\
&\quad ((x_1 y_1 \vee \overline{x_1 y_1}) \wedge c_{00}) \\
c_{01} &= x_1 y_1 \vee y_1 c_{00} \vee c_{00} x_0 \\
b_0 &= ((z_0 \overline{a_0} \vee \overline{z_0} a_0) \wedge \overline{c_{01}}) \vee \\
&\quad ((z_0 a_0 \vee \overline{z_0 a_0}) \wedge c_{01}) \\
c_{10} &= z_0 a_0 \vee a_0 c_{01} \vee c_{01} z_0 \\
b_1 &= ((z_1 \overline{a_1} \vee \overline{z_1} a_1) \wedge \overline{c_{10}}) \vee \\
&\quad ((z_1 a_1 \vee \overline{z_1 a_1}) \wedge c_{10}) \\
d_0 &= (z_0 \overline{x_0} \vee \overline{z_0} x_0) \\
e_{00} &= z_0 x_0 \\
d_1 &= ((z_1 \overline{x_1} \vee \overline{z_1} x_1) \wedge \overline{e_{00}}) \vee \\
&\quad ((z_1 x_1 \vee \overline{z_1 x_1}) \wedge e_{00}) \\
e_{01} &= z_1 x_1 \vee x_1 e_{00} \vee e_{00} z_0 \\
f_0 &= ((y_0 \overline{d_0} \vee \overline{y_0} d_0) \wedge \overline{e_{01}}) \vee \\
&\quad ((y_0 d_0 \vee \overline{y_0 d_0}) \wedge e_{01}) \\
e_{10} &= y_0 d_0 \vee d_0 e_{01} \vee e_{01} y_0 \\
f_1 &= ((y_1 \overline{d_1} \vee \overline{y_1} d_1) \wedge \overline{e_{10}}) \vee \\
&\quad ((y_1 d_1 \vee \overline{y_1 d_1}) \wedge e_{10}) \\
b_0 &= f_0 \\
b_1 &= f_1
\end{aligned}
$$

$$\tag{6}$$

introducing auxiliary variables for carry bits and for temporary results of the additions. Syntactically deducing equality of $< b_1, b_0 >$ and $< f_1, f_0 >$ from (6) is far from being easy. Term rewriting techniques, for example, are applied in proof systems which automatically deduce equality of terms, and in preprocessors which simplify highlevel expressions before other verification techniques are applied.

3.3 Symmetry Reductions

Another approach to exploit regular structures of high-level operators is to restrict the sizes of signal domains by symmetry reduction (cf. [5, 11]). Symmetries occur, for example, when operator arguments are commutable. Consider addition of 16-bit signals:

$$
x_{[16]} + y_{[16]} = z_{[16]}
$$

Both signals $x_{[16]}$ and $y_{[17]}$ are used symmetrically with respect to addition. Here, without loss of generality, it is possible to assume $x_{[16]} \leq y_{[16]}$, because a satisfying solution of Equation (7) exists if and only if a satisfying solution exists which additionally satisfies $x_{[16]} \leq y_{[16]}$.

Such additional constraint on $x_{[16]}$ and $y_{[16]}$ can help to decrease the size of search spaces in guidedsearch algorithms (cf. [15]) as employed in most SAT procedures. Obviously, it is impossible to automatically deduce such a constraint from a bit-level representation like the one shown in (6).

3.4 Uniform Data-Flow Reductions

A different type of symmetries of high-level operators are uniform data dependencies. Certain operators have a very regular dataflow structure with respect to the individual bits of their input and output signals. One simple example are bitwise Boolean connectives. Assume, we want to check if the bitwise Boolean conjunction of two 8-bit word-level signals $x_{[8]}$ and $y_{[8]}$ can evaluate to the 8-bit zero vector. On RTL, this is described by the equation

$$x_{[8]} \text{ and } y_{[8]} = 00000000 .$$
(8)

In bounded model checking, the word-level equation (8) is translated into the Boolean domain, yielding the following SAT instance

$$(x_0 \text{ and } y_0 = 0) \wedge$$
$$(x_1 \text{ and } y_1 = 0) \wedge$$
$$\dots \wedge$$
$$(x_7 \text{ and } y_7 = 0),$$
(9)

which involves 16 1-bit variables and 8 equations. Obviously it is not necessary to solve all 8 equations separately, as a conventional SAT solver would do, because bit positions 0-7 are treated uniformly. Instead it would be suffcient so solve the following SAT instance, which is significantly smaller, only once:

$$x \text{ and } y = 0 .$$
(10)

In order to determine a satisfying solution for (8), the values for x and y of a satisfying solution of (10) are copied into all bits of the corresponding high-level signals of (8). Uniform data-flow reductions for property checking of digital designs are investigated in [14].

3.5 Word-Level Decision Diagrams

For representation and manipulation of Boolean functions Binary Decision Diagrams (BDDs) have been proposed and are used successfully in many industrial verification tools. Several extensions of BDDs to the word-level have been suggested. These approaches are based on Word-Level Decision Diagrams (WLDDs), which are graphbased representations of functions that allow for the representation of functions with a Boolean range and an integer domain. For an overview see [9].

WLDDs have received a lot of attention, since based on these data structures for the first time large arithmetic circuits, including multipliers, have been formally verified. But, in contrast to BDDs, the manipulation algorithms can be more expensive and often have exponential worst-case behavior.

3.6 Abstraction

Abstraction techniques (see e.g. [6]) in general implement the following approach. Instead of directly solving a given verification problem φ, a smaller or simpler instance φ' is computed, which is then solved by conventional methods. Depending on the degree of reduction between φ and φ', solving φ' can be done faster and might require significantly less resources than solving φ.

Abstraction techniques have to ensure that the computation of φ' preserves certain satisfiability criteria. An abstraction is one-to-one if the smaller problem is solvable if and only if the original problem is solvable.

$$\varphi' \text{ satisfiable} \iff \varphi \text{ satisfiable}$$

For example, Equation (10) is a one-to-one abstraction of Equation (8). Additionally, abstractions usually provide a transformation τ which computes solutions of the original problem from solutions found on the abstract problem instance, i.e. if s is a solution of φ', then τ (s) is a solution of φ. Thus, solving the original problem can be completely replaced by solving the smaller problem instance, provided that the total of computing the smaller problem instance and then solving it is still faster than solving the original problem.

If an abstraction is not one-to-one, then for each solution s found for φ', an additional consistency check has to be performed, which inspects, if τ (s) indeed is a solution of φ, or not (false-negative). Such an abstraction still might be of interested if establishing a one-to-one abstraction is not possible, but finding solutions s of φ' and doing the consistency check for τ (s) is fast. In such a case abstraction is usually combined with guidedsearch techniques on φ'. After a solution has been found, a consistency check is performed, and the search is continued if this check fails. The amount of reduction of the problem size achieved by the abstraction must justify the additional costs for validating solutions found for the abstract problem instance.

One-to-one abstractions are highly attractive in digital hardware verification because reduced or simplified problem instances can significantly increase the performance of existing verification tools. If the abstract problem instance is specified in the same formalism which is used for the original problem, then one-to-one abstractions can easily be embedded in verification flows without having to modify the underlying verification techniques. Thereby, abstractions which operate on RTL, can incorporate and utilize all high-level information which is available in the problem specification.

In the following section, we will give an example of a word-level abstraction technique, which exploits RTL information to speed up property checking of digital circuit designs by using uniform data-flow reductions.

4. RTL ABSTRACTION BY SIGNAL WIDTH REDUCTION

We consider the property checking flow, which is shown left in Fig. 1, and which is a typical flow used by existing industrial property checking tools.

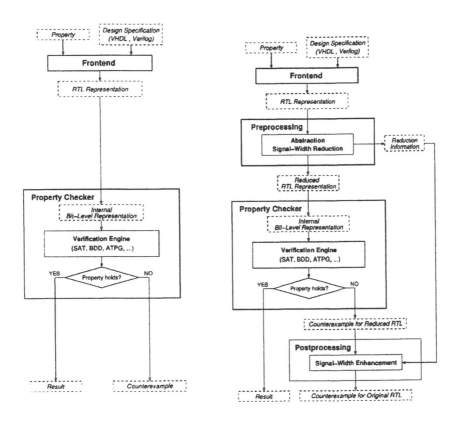

Fig. 1. Property Checking Flow without and with RTL Abstraction

Design specifications are given as HDL source code, and properties are specified in a linear time logic over finite bounded intervals of time. A frontend reads design and property specification and generates an intermediate RTL representation. A property checker, which reads such RTL representations of design and property as input, computes an internal bit-level representation (i.e. an instance of propositional SAT), which is satisfiable if and only of the property does not hold for the given design. The bit-level representation is passed on to a verification multiengine, which uses SAT, BDD and ATPG methods to either prove unsatisfiability or to compute a satisfying solution. If a solution is found, then the property does not hold and a counterexample is generated.

The abstraction technique, which we consider here, is embedded within such a flow as illustrated on the right in Fig. 1, indicated by the grey-shaded areas. The presented method is a new word-level abstraction technique described in [13], which can readily be integrated into existing property checking flows.

In a preprocessing step prior to the property checker, the RTL representation is taken, and a scaled down RTL model of the design is computed, in which each wordlevel signal x is replaced by a corresponding shrunken signal of width $m_x \leq n$, where n is the original width of x. The abstraction technique guarantees that the property holds for the reduced RTL if and only if it holds for the original RTL. Design and abstract model differ from each other only as far as signal widths are concerned. The general control-flow and data-flow aspects are preserved. The reduced RTL is handed to the property checker instead of the original RTL. Since the size of the internal bit-level representation depends on the number of bits occurring in the RTL and thus on the widths of the RTL signals, the internal bit-level representation computed from the reduced RTL can contain significantly less variables than the one computed when using the non-reduced RTL, depending on the degree of reduction achieved by the abstraction. The satisfiability test is executed using the same verification engine as before.

If the property does not hold, the counterexample returned by the property checker is taken, which is a counterexample relating to the signals of the reduced RTL. A corresponding counterexample for the original RTL is computed by enhancing signal values to their original width.

For modeling RTL representations of digital hardware, we a formal theory of fixed-size bitvectors based on [14] is used, which is an extension of the core theory of bitvectors presented in [8]. The theory features high-level operators, like bitwise Boolean operations, arithmetics and an if-then-else operator, which allows dynamic data dependencies to be specified. Complete HDL designs can be modeled within this theory. The RTL representation of design and property consists of a system E of bitvector equations, which is satisfiable within the mentioned bitvector theory if and only if the property does not hold for the design. A satisfying solution of E corresponds to a counterexample for the design and the property.

Word-level signals of the design correspond to bitvector variables in E. Each bitvector variable $x_{[n]}$ has a fixed width $n \in N_+$ and takes bitvectors of respective length as values. Thus the high-level information, which individual bits are comprised in a specific word-level signal, is available in E and can be exploited for computing the reduced RTL model. For each bitvector variable occurring in E, the smallest possible number of bits is computed, such that a second system E' of bitvector equations, which differs from E solely in the manner that variable widths are shrunken to these computed numbers, is satisfiable if and only if E is satisfiable, see Fig. 2.

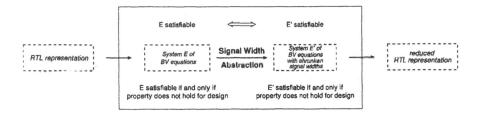

Fig. 2. Reduced Model Generation

E' is generated using these minimum signal widths and represents a scaled down version of the original RTL. The process of scaling down signal widths is separated into two subsequent phases. The high-level operators occurring in the equations of E impose structural and functional dependencies on the bitvector variables. Thereby, variables typically have non-uniform data dependencies, i.e. di#erent dependencies exist for different chunks of a signal. The presented method analyzes such dependencies and, for each variable, determines contiguous parts in which all bits are treated uniformly in the exact same manner with respect to data dependencies (cf. Sect. 3.4 on uniform data-flow reductions). For each such chunk of a signal, the necessary minimum width is computed, as required by dynamical data dependencies. According to these computed minimum chunk widths, the reduced width for the corresponding shrunken signal is reassembled, as shown in Fig. 3.

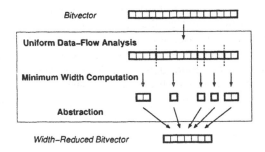

Fig. 3. Basic Abstraction Technique

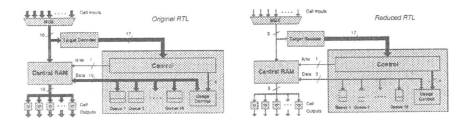

Fig. 4. RTL Block Diagrams before and after Preprocessing

The proposed abstraction technique has been implemented in C_{++} in the BooStER tool (Boolean String Length Reduction ([13]), and was tested in several case studies at the EDA department of Siemens Corporation in Munich and at the Computer Network Peripherals department of Infineon Technologies in San Jose, CA. In Fig. 4 an example of two RTL block diagrams of an address management unit of an ATM switching element is shown. The design is illustrated before and after signalwidth scaling.

The design consists of roughly 3.000 lines of Verilog code, the netlist synthesis has approximately 24.000 gates and 35.000 RAM cells. The RTL incorporates 16 FIFO queue buffers and complex control logic. Data packages are fed on 33 input channels to the management unit, stored in the FIFOs and upon request output on one of 17 output channels again, while the cell sequence has to be preserved and no package must be dropped from the management unit. In the example illustrated in Fig. 4 the width of data path signals could be reduced from 10 bits to 3 bits. The size of the bit-level model, which was generated from the abstraction, was about 30% of the size of the original bit-level model, and a tremendous drop of the runtimes of the property checkers up to only 5% of the former runtimes was encountered. Further details on the experiments can be found in [13].

5.   CONCLUSION

Constantly growing design sizes of digital circuits require ever improving verification methods. We have presented several existing RTL-based approaches to circuit verification which suggest the use of word-level techniques and the exploitation of high-level information in property checking of digital hardware. These techniques are promising candidates for speeding up and enhancing the capabilities of existing verification tools. As a detailed example, we have presented an RTL abstraction technique which e#ciently analyzes word-level data-flow and scales down design sizes before property checking. The method can easily be integrated into existing flows, and experiments on large industrial circuits have demonstrated its applicability and effciency.

6.   REFERENCES

[1] A. Biere, A. Cimatti, E.M. Clarke, M. Fujita, Y. Zhu. Symbolic Model Checking Using SAT Procedures instead of BDDs. DAC'99, pp 317- 320. 1999.
[2] C.W. Barrett, D.L. Dill, J.R. Levitt. A Decision Procedure for Bit- Vector Arithmetic. DAC'98, pp 522-527. 1998.
[3] R.E. Bryant. Symbolic Boolean Manipulation with Ordered Binary- Decision Diagrams. ACM Computing Surveys 24(3), pp 293-318. 1992.
[4] R.E. Bryant. Binary Decision Diagrams and Beyond: Enabeling Techniques for Formal Verification. ICCAD'95, pp 236-243. 1995.
[5] E.M. Clarke, E.A. Emerson, S. Jha, A.P. Sistla. Symmetry Reductions in Model Checking. CAV'98, pp 147-158. 1998.

[6] E.M. Clarke, O. Grumberg, D.E. Long. Model Checking and Abstraction. POPL'92, pp 342-354. 1992.

[7] C.Y. Huang, K.T. Cheng. Assertion checking by combined word-level ATPG and modular arithmetic constraint-solving techniques. DAC'00, pp 118-123. 2000.

[8] D. Cyrluk, M.O. M¨oller, H. Ruess. An E#cient Decision Procedure for the Theory of Fixed-Sized Bit-Vectors. CAV'97, pp 60-71. 1997.

[9] R. Drechsler. Formal Verification of Circuits. Kluwer Academic Publishers. 2000.

[10] N. Dershowitz, J.P. Jouannaud. Rewrite Systems. Handbook of Theoretical Computer Science, Formal Model and Semantics. Ed. J.v. Leeuwen, Elsevier, pp 243-320. 1990.

[11] E.A. Emerson, R.J. Trefler. From Asymmetry to Full Symmetry: New Techniques for Symmetry Reduction in Model Checking. CHARME'99, pp 142-156. 1999.

[12] S. Höoreth, R. Drechsler. Formal Verification of Word-Level Specifications. DATE'99, pp 52-58. 1999.

[13] P. Johannsen. BooStER : Speeding Up RTL Property Checking of Digital Designs by Word-Level Abstraction. CAV'01. 2001.

[14] P. Johannsen. Scaling Down Design Sizes in Hardware Verification. PhD Dissertation at the University of Kiel, to appear in 2001.

[15] J.P. Marques da Silva. Search Algorithms for Satisfiability Problems in Combinational Switching Circuits. Ph.D. Dissertation, University of Michigan. 1995.

[16] J.P. Marques da Silva, K.A. Sakallah. Boolean satisfiability in electronic design automation. DAC'00, pp 675-680. 2000.

[17] Z. Zeng, P. Kalla, M. Ciesielski. LPSAT: A Unified Approach to RTL Satisfiability. DATE'01. 2001.

Tabular Techniques for MV Logic

DRAGAN JANKOVIĆ[1], RADOMIR S. STANKOVIĆ[1],
ROLF DRECHSLER[2]
[1] *University of Niš, Faculty of Electronics, 18 000 Niš, Yugoslavia*
[2] *Albert-Ludwigs-University, Institute of Computer Science,*
79110 Freiburg im Breisgau, Germany

Abstract: Similar as in the binary case, the optimization of polynomial representations of multilevalued (MV) logic functions is possible by using different polarities for variables which leads to the fixed polarity polynomial expressions. There is few methods for calculation of coefficients in these expressions. In this paper, we define a tabular technique (TT) for calculation of fixed-polarity polynomial expressions for MV functions as a generalization of the corresponding methods for Fixed-polarity Reed-Muller (FPRM) expressions for switching functions. All useful features of tabular techniques for FPRMs, as for example, simplicity of involved opera- tions and high possibilities for parallelization of the calculation procedure, are preserved. The proposed method can be applied for Kronecker polynomial representation of MV functions.

The method permits to calculate the polynomial expression for a given function and specified polarity by starting from the expression for an arbitrary polarity. Moreover, it can be used for fixed-polarity expressions where an extended set of complements is allowed, as for example, in Reed-Muller-Fourier expressions.

1.   INTRODUCTION

Fixed-Polarity Reed-Muller (FPRM) expressions are a way for optimization of Positive polarity Reed-Muller (PPRM) expressions derived by allowing to freely choose the negative $\overline{x}_i$ or the positive x_i literal, but not both, for each variable in a given switching function $f(x_1, ..., x_n)$. The assignment of literals to variables is uniquely specified by the polarity $p = (p_1, ..., p_n)$, $p_i \in \{0,1\}$, where $p_i = 1$ and $p_i = 0$ determine the assignment of negative and positive literals to the i-th variable, respectively. Complexity of FPRMs is usually estimated through the number of non-zero coefficients, and the FPRM with the minimum number of coefficients is considered as the optimum FPRM for f.

There are several methods for generation of FPRMs for a given f and the required polarity p. These methods can be classified as matrix methods [?], FFT-like methods [?], and tabular techniques (TT) [1, 2, 13, 14].

TT-methods exploit linearity of Reed-Muller expressions, which permits to determine the value of a coefficient c_i in FPRM for f as EXOR sum of the contributions of each true minterm in f to c_i. Although described in terms of minterms, these methods may be extended to operate over disjoint cubes [5, 6]. The advantages of the TT methods can be summarized as follows.

1. In TTs, FPRM coefficients are calculated through 1-minterms. Contribution of each minterm to the FPRM-spectrum for f can be determined separately and independently of the contribution of other minterms. Thus, TTs possess an inherent possibility for efficient parallelization of the calculation procedure [13]

2. The processing of each minterm is very simple, since there are no arithmetic operations. Instead, processing of a minterm reduces to transferring of the minterm into another minterm by using some relatively simple processing rules.

Therefore, parallelism and simple processing are features giving advantages to tabular techniques compared to other methods [13, 8, 4].

In this paper, the method in [13] is generalized to MV functions with some improvements in particular steps of related algorithms proposed. These improvements reduce the computational complexity in determination of required fixed-polarity expressions for MV functions. At the same time, the good features of TT methods for switching functions are preserved also in the MV case. We discuss the implementation of this method by an algorithm using either an index table or a hash table, depending on possible limitations on the time and space resources, respectively. Then, we briefly discuss extensions of the proposed method to determination of Kronecker Galois field (GF) expressions for MV functions [10], and further extensions to the expressions permitting the use of an extended set of complements for MV variables, as for example Reed-Muller-Fourier (RMF) expressions [?].

We also provide a modification of the proposed method enabling to determine a fixed polarity polynomial expression for a given f and the fixed polarity p_i directly from the corresponding expression for f for an arbitrary polarity p_j, without returning necessarily to the positive-polarity expression or to some other representation of f.

For simplicity of notation, our method will be given by the example of polynomial representation of MV function defined on Galois field GF(4). Extension to arbitrary Kronecker product based polynomial expressions on arbitrary GF(p), and other related polynomial expressions are straightforward.

2. GALOIS FIELD EXPRESSIONS

In this section we consider GF-expressions over GF(4).

Denote by E(4) the set of four elements. For convenience, we will identify the elements of E(4) with the non-negative integers 0,1,2,3.

Definition 1 E(4) *expresses the structure of the Galois field modulo 4, GF(4), under the addition and the multiplication defined as in Table 1 and Table 2, respectively.*

+	0	1	2	3
0	0	1	2	3
1	1	0	3	2
2	2	3	0	1
3	3	2	1	0

Tab. 1. Additions in GF(4)

·	0	1	2	3
0	0	0	0	0
1	0	1	2	3
2	2	3	0	1
3	3	2	1	0

Tab. 2. Multiplication in GF(4)

The set of elementary functions $1, x, x^2, x^3$ is a basis in the space of one-variable functions over GF(4). Therefore, each function f given by the truth-vector $F = [f(0), ..., f(3)]^T$ can be represented by GF-expression given in the matrix form as

$$f(x_1, \ldots, x_n) = [\, 1 \quad x_i \quad x_i^2 \quad x_i^3 \,] \cdot (\mathbf{G}_4(1) \cdot \mathbf{F}),$$

where

$$\mathbf{G}_4(1) = \begin{bmatrix} 1 & 0 & 0 & 0 \\ 0 & 1 & 3 & 2 \\ 0 & 1 & 2 & 3 \\ 1 & 1 & 1 & 1 \end{bmatrix},$$

and all calculations are carried out in GF(4).

In this notation the basic functions $1, x, x^2, x^3$ can be considered as columns of the matrix $G_4^{-1}(1)$, inverse to $G_4(1)$, given by

$$\mathbf{G_4^{-1}(1)} = \begin{bmatrix} 1 & 0 & 0 & 0 \\ 1 & 1 & 1 & 1 \\ 1 & 2 & 3 & 1 \\ 1 & 3 & 2 & 1 \end{bmatrix}.$$

The extension of GF-expression to an n-variable functions defined on GF(4) is straightforward through the Kronecker product.

Definition 2 *A GF-expressions for an n-variable four-valued function f given by its truth-vector $F = [f(0),...,f(4^n - 1)]^T$ is*

$$f(x_1,...,x_n) =$$

$$= (\bigotimes_{i=1}^{n}[1 x_i x_i^2 x_i^3]) \cdot ((\bigotimes_{i=1}^{n} G_4(1)) \cdot F)'$$

where $\otimes$ denotes the Kronecker product and all calculations are carried out in GF(4).

Optimization of polynomial representation of MV functions is possible by using different variable complements [7]. For functions defined on GF(4) there are 3 complements denoted as $\overset{i}{x}$, $i = 1; 2; 3$ and defined as $\overset{i}{x} = x \otimes i, i = 1; 2; 3$. The use of complements for a variable, requires permutation of columns in the corresponding basic GF-matrix. Table Tab. 3 shows complements for variables over GF(4) and the corresponding basic transform matrices.

Definition 3 *An arbitrary n-variable function f defined on GF(4) for polarity $p = (p_1,..., p_n)$ can be represented by the following expression*

$$f(x_1,...,x_n) =$$

$$= (\bigotimes_{i=1}^{n}([1 \overset{p_i-}{x}_i (\overset{p_i-}{x}_i)^2 (\overset{p_i-}{x}_i)^3])^{-1}) \cdot ((\bigotimes_{i=1}^{n} G_4^{<p_i>}) \cdot F) \tag{1}$$

where $G_4^{<p_i>}$ is GF(4) transform matrix for the polarity p.

$$x = \begin{bmatrix} 0 \\ 1 \\ 2 \\ 3 \end{bmatrix} \quad G_4 = \begin{bmatrix} 1 & 0 & 0 & 0 \\ 0 & 1 & 3 & 2 \\ 0 & 1 & 2 & 3 \\ 1 & 1 & 1 & 1 \end{bmatrix} \quad (G_4)^{-1} = \begin{bmatrix} 1 & 0 & 0 & 0 \\ 1 & 1 & 1 & 1 \\ 1 & 2 & 3 & 1 \\ 1 & 3 & 2 & 1 \end{bmatrix}$$

$$^1\bar{x} = \begin{bmatrix} 1 \\ 0 \\ 3 \\ 2 \end{bmatrix} \quad G_4^{<1>} = \begin{bmatrix} 0 & 1 & 0 & 0 \\ 1 & 0 & 2 & 3 \\ 1 & 0 & 3 & 2 \\ 1 & 1 & 1 & 1 \end{bmatrix} \quad (G_4^{<1>})^{-1} = \begin{bmatrix} 1 & 1 & 1 & 1 \\ 1 & 0 & 0 & 0 \\ 1 & 3 & 2 & 1 \\ 1 & 2 & 3 & 1 \end{bmatrix}$$

$$^2\bar{x} = \begin{bmatrix} 2 \\ 3 \\ 0 \\ 1 \end{bmatrix} \quad G_4^{<2>} = \begin{bmatrix} 0 & 0 & 1 & 0 \\ 3 & 2 & 0 & 1 \\ 2 & 3 & 0 & 1 \\ 1 & 1 & 1 & 1 \end{bmatrix} \quad (G_4^{<2>})^{-1} = \begin{bmatrix} 1 & 2 & 3 & 1 \\ 1 & 3 & 2 & 1 \\ 1 & 0 & 0 & 0 \\ 1 & 1 & 1 & 1 \end{bmatrix}$$

$$^3\bar{x} = \begin{bmatrix} 3 \\ 2 \\ 1 \\ 0 \end{bmatrix} \quad G_4^{<3>} = \begin{bmatrix} 0 & 0 & 0 & 1 \\ 2 & 3 & 1 & 0 \\ 3 & 2 & 1 & 0 \\ 1 & 1 & 1 & 1 \end{bmatrix} \quad (G_4^{<3>})^{-1} = \begin{bmatrix} 1 & 3 & 2 & 1 \\ 1 & 2 & 3 & 1 \\ 1 & 1 & 1 & 1 \\ 1 & 0 & 0 & 0 \end{bmatrix}$$

Tab. 3. GF(4) complements and transform matrices

3. TABULAR TECHNIQUE FOR GF-EXPRESSIONS

In this section, we introduce a tabular technique for calculation of coefficients in fixed polarity GF-expressions for functions defined on GF(4).

The tabular technique for calculation of FPRM-expressions proposed in [13] is an improvement of tabular techniques in [2, 1, 14]. This TT starts from a table of minterms for a given switching function f. The terms in FPRMs for f are generated by performing a set of simple rules over each minterm. The equal product terms that have been already generated from previously processed minterms are deleted by a cancelation procedure. The method processes each minterm separately. Thus, it can be applied to functions of an arbitrary number of variables.

The method consists of three important steps

1. Generation of new product terms from minterm by using some appropriately defined processing rules.
2. Canceling of equal terms.
3. EXOR of all uncancelled terms with the polarity p.

Tabular technique for MV functions (MVTT) proposed in what follows performs the same steps generalized to MV minterms. However, since the procedure of cancellation of previously generated product terms proposed in [13] is rather time consuming, we proposed some modifications permitting to improve the efficiency of MVTT.

3.1   Generation of new terms

The rule for generation of new terms from a MV minterm is derived by using the folowing properties of GF-expressions.

From linearity of GF-expressions, for arbitrary functions f and g defined on GF(4),

$$GF(f \oplus g) = GF(f) \oplus GF(g).$$

From properties of the Kronecker product,

$$GF^{<p>}(f \oplus g) = GF^{<p>}(f) \oplus GF^{<p>}(g). \tag{2}$$

Let an n-variable four-valued function f is given by the truth-vector $F = [f(0), f(1), ..., f(4^n - 1)]^T$. Then, f can be represented as a sum of truth-vectors for MV minterms

$$\mathbf{F} = \mathbf{F}_0 \oplus \mathbf{F}_1 \oplus \ldots \oplus \mathbf{F}_{4^n - 1},$$

where

$$
\begin{aligned}
\mathbf{F}_0 \quad &= [f(0), 0, \ldots, 0]^T, \\
\vdots \quad &\quad \vdots \\
\mathbf{F}_i \quad &= [0, 0, \ldots, 0, f(i), 0, \ldots, 0]^T, \\
\vdots \quad &\quad \vdots \\
\mathbf{F}_{4^n - 1} \quad &= [0, 0, \ldots, 0, f(4^n - 1)]^T.
\end{aligned}
$$

From (2),

$$GF^{<p>}(\mathbf{F}) = GF^{<p>}(\mathbf{F}_0) \oplus \ldots \oplus GF^{<p>}(\mathbf{F}_{4^n - 1}).$$

New terms generated from a MV minterm m represented by F_M, where M is the decimal index for m, are determined by $GF^{<p>}(F_M)$.

Since in each F_i, $i = 0, ..., 4^n - 1$, there is a single non-zero element $f(i)$, while $f(j) = 0$ for $j \neq i$, then $GF^{<p>}(F_i) = f(i)g_i$, where g_i is the i-th column of $G^{<p>}(n)$. Each value in $GF^{<p>}(F_i)$ can be considered as a contribution of minterms to the corresponding coefficients in $C^{<p>} = [c_0^{<p>}, ..., c_{4^n-1}^{<p>}]^T$. These contributions can be calculated as

$$c_u^{<p>} = \bigotimes_{v=0}^{4^n-1} (G^{<p>}[u,v] \cdot f_v) =$$

$$= \bigotimes_{v=0}^{4^n-1} (\prod_{z=1}^n G_4^{<p_z>}[u_z, v_z]) \cdot f(v)$$

(3)

where $u = 0, ..., 4^n - 1, u = (u_1, ..., u_n), v = (v_1, ..., v_n)$.

Example 1 *Consider the calculation of coefficients in GF-expression of a two-variable function f for the polarity $p = (2, 1)$.*

$$\mathbf{C}^{<p>} = (\mathbf{G}_4^{<2>} \otimes \mathbf{G}_4^{<1>}) \cdot \mathbf{F},$$

$$= \left(\begin{bmatrix} 0 & 0 & 1 & 0 \\ 3 & 2 & 0 & 1 \\ 2 & 3 & 0 & 1 \\ 1 & 1 & 1 & 1 \end{bmatrix} \otimes \begin{bmatrix} 0 & 1 & 0 & 0 \\ 1 & 0 & 2 & 3 \\ 1 & 0 & 3 & 2 \\ 1 & 1 & 1 & 1 \end{bmatrix} \right) \cdot \mathbf{F}.$$

(4)

Contribution of the function value f_3, i.e., the contribution of the minterm $m = 03) = x_1 \cdot \overset{3}{\overline{x_2}}$ to the coefficient c_6 is equal to $f_3 \cdot G^{<(21)>}[6,3] = f_3 \cdot 1$. This contribution can be calculated by using (3) as

$$f_3 \cdot \mathbf{G}_4^{<2>}[1,0] \cdot \mathbf{G}_4^{<1>}[2,3] = f_3 \cdot 3 \cdot 2 = f_3 \cdot 1,$$

where $G_1^{<p>}[i,j]$ denotes the element in the i-th row and the j-th column in $G_1^{<p>}$.

Contribution of the minterm $m = (03) = x_1 \cdot \overset{3}{\overline{x_2}}$ to all coefficients in the GF-expression for f is given by

$$GF^{<p>}(F_3) = G_4^{<2>} \otimes G_4^{<1>}) \cdot F_3$$

$$(G_4^{<2>} \otimes G_4^{<1>}) \cdot [00f_3 0000000000000]^T$$

$$[00000000 f_3 f_3 f_3 f_3 0000]^T$$

By using (3) we derive a rule for generation of new terms $\pi = (\pi_1, \pi_2, ..., \pi_n)$ and to determine the contribution $v(\pi)$ of a minterm m as

$$\pi_i \in \{j | \mathbf{G}_4^{<p_i>}[j, m_i] \neq 0\},$$

$$(5)$$

$$v(\pi) = (v_1 \cdot v_2 \cdot .... \cdot v_n) \cdot v(m),$$

$$(6)$$

where $v_i = G_4^{<p_i>}[\pi_i, m_i], i = 1, ... n$.

The number of newly generated terms from the minterm m depends on the number of mutually equal bits in the minterm m and the polarity p. If the number of equal bits is k, the number of new terms is $4^k - 1$.

3.2 Cancelling of terms

In TT for calculation of FPRM expressions, each two equal generated terms are deleted because contribution of each new term is equal 1 and $1 \otimes 1 = 0$. Therefore, in existing TT this process is called "cancelling of equal pairs". There are a two approaches to cancelling equal pairs, by using a hash table [2] or an index table with 2 n entries for an n variable function [13]. In hash table are stored only uncacelled terms. For each new generated terms we try to find it in hash table. If term exists in hash table it is deleted while in oposite it is inserted in hash table. This approach can be applied for an arbitrary number of variables, but it requires some considerable execution time.

The second approach requires considerably fewer time for term manipulation [13], but the size of the index table exponentially grows with the number of variables. However, the usage of the index table provides possibilities for parallelization of the related procedures.

In MV case, we process each minterm in a given function by using (5) to generate new terms and (6) to determine their contributions to the coefficients in a fixed-polarity GF-expression for f. The contribution of a term take values in E(4), therefore, we can not delete equal terms if they have different contributions, which means if they correspond to different function values. However, the total contribution of a subset of terms can be equal to zero, which means that we can delete these terms.

Example 2 *For a function* f, *assume that from a subset of minterms corresponding to non-zero values for* f, *we generated three new terms* $t_1 = t_2 = t_3$ *whose contributions to the coefficients in a fixed-polarity GF-expression for f are 2, 3, 1, respectively. The sum of these contributions is 2+3+1=0, and thus the terms* t_1, t_2, *and* t_3 *can be deleted.*

3.3 EXOR of uncancelatted terms with the polarity

In [13], the last step in TT performs EXOR of uncancelled terms with the given polarity p. However, the rule (5) for the generation of new terms from a minterm incorporate this step. Thus, this step does not exist in the algorithm to implement MVTT, which improves efficiency of the algorithm in terms of time. Therefore, MVTT consists of the following steps

1. Given a function f by the set of minterms corresponding to non-zero values in f and a polarity $p = (p_1, ..., p_n)$. Generate new terms by using the relation (5), and determine their contributions to the coefficients in the GF-expression for the polarity p by using the relation (6).

2. Cancel the terms when the sum of their contributions to the GF-coefficients for the polarity p is equal to zero, and store the other minterms.

Similar as in the binary case, the MVTT can be implemented by using either a hash table or an index table, and the choice depends on the available resources of implementation restrictions with respect to space and time. In what follows, we derive an algorithm to perform MVTT by using the index table. However, the same algorithm can be performed by using the hash table.

3.4 MVTT algorithm

Let I be the index table with 4^n entries $I = (I_0, ..., I_{4^n - 1}) = (I_{0,0,...,0)}, ..., I_{(4^n - 1, 4^n - 1, ..., 4^n - 1)})$.

The algorithm to perform MVTT for calculation of fixed polarity GF-expressions consists of the following steps.

1. Given a polarity $p = (p_1, p_2, ..., p_n)$.

2. Generate the fixed-polarity GF-transform matrix for each p_i in p, $G_4^{<p_i>}$, $p_i \in \{p_1, p_2, ..., p_n\}$ (see Table 3).

3. Express a minterm m as a four-valued n-tuple $m = (m_1, m_2, ..., m_n)$. Value of m is $f(m)$.

4. For minterm m generate new terms π_i and its contributions $v(\pi)$, by using the rule given by the relations (5) and (6), respectively.

5. For each generated term π, add the value $v(\pi)$ to the index table entry $I_{(\pi_1, ..., \pi_n)}$.

6. Repeat the steps 3, 4, and 5 for all the minterms.
   This algorithm to implement MVTT will be explained by the following example.

Example 3 *Consider the calculation of a GF-expression for a two variable function f f given by the truth vector* $F = [0,0,0,0,2,2,2,2,0,0,0,0,1,0,0,0]^T$, *for the polarity* $p = (2,1)$.

By definition, the vector of coefficients in the required GF-expression is

$$
\begin{aligned}
\mathbf{C}^{<p>} &= (\mathbf{G}_4^{<2>} \otimes \mathbf{G}_4^{<1>}) \cdot \mathbf{F} \\
&= \left(\begin{bmatrix} 0 & 0 & 1 & 0 \\ 3 & 2 & 0 & 1 \\ 2 & 3 & 0 & 1 \\ 1 & 1 & 1 & 1 \end{bmatrix} \otimes \begin{bmatrix} 0 & 1 & 0 & 0 \\ 1 & 0 & 2 & 3 \\ 1 & 0 & 3 & 2 \\ 1 & 1 & 1 & 1 \end{bmatrix} \right) \cdot \mathbf{F} \\
&= \begin{bmatrix} 0 & 0 & 0 & 0 & 3 & 1 & 1 & 1 & 1 & 1 & 1 & 1 & 2 & 1 & 1 & 1 \end{bmatrix}^T .
\end{aligned}
\tag{7}
$$

We calculate these coefficients by using MVTT as follows. From the non-zero values in the truth-vector F, *the function* f *is given by the set of minterms*

$$f(x_1, x_2) = 1 \quad for \quad (x_1 x_2) \in \{(30)\} \quad and \quad f(x_1, x_2) = 2 \quad for$$

$(x_1 x_2) \in \{(10), (11), (12), (13)\}$.

Contribution of the minterms to the coefficients vector $C^{<2,1>}$ *as well as the value of Index table are given in Table 4.*

i-th value in columns denoted as cont. is the contributions of minterms to the i-th coefficient in $C^{<2,1>}$. *These contributions are added to current value of Index table and the new values of the Index table are given in columns denoted by IT. The last calculated value of Index table includes the contributions of all minterms and is equal to coefficient vector.*

Contribution of each minterm given in the form of new generated terms are shown in Table 5

c.	(10)-2		(11)-2		(12)-2		(13)-2		(30)-1	
coef	cont.	IT	cont.	IT	cont.	IT	cont.	IT	cont.	IT
c_0	0	0	0	0	0	0	0	0	0	0
c_1	0	0	0	0	0	0	0	0	0	0
c_2	0	0	0	0	0	0	0	0	0	0
c_3	0	0	0	0	0	0	0	0	0	0
c_4	0	0	3	3	0	3	0	3	0	3
c_5	3	3	0	3	1	2	2	0	1	1
c_6	3	3	0	3	1	2	2	0	1	1
c_7	3	3	3	0	3	3	3	0	1	1
c_8	0	0	1	1	0	1	0	1	0	1
c_9	1	1	0	1	2	3	3	0	1	1
c_{10}	1	1	0	1	3	2	2	0	1	1
c_{11}	1	1	1	0	1	1	1	0	1	1
c_{12}	0	0	2	2	0	2	0	2	0	2
c_{13}	2	2	0	2	3	1	1	0	1	1
c_{14}	2	2	0	2	1	3	3	0	1	1
c_{15}	2	2	2	0	2	2	2	0	1	1

Tab. 4. Contributions and Index Table for minterms of function in example 3

minterm	generated minterms
(10)-2	(11)-2; (12)-2; (13)-2; (21)-1; (22)-1; (23)-1; (31)-2; (32)-2; (33)-2
(11)-2	(10)-3; (13)-3; (20)-1; (22)-1; (30)-2; (33)-2
(12)-2	(11)-1; (12)-2; (13)-3; (21)-2; (22)-3; (23)-1; (31)-3; (32)-1; (33)-2
(13)-2	(11)-2; (12)-1; (13)-3; (21)-3; (22)-2; (23)-1; (31)-1; (32)-3; (33)-2
(30)-1	(11)-1; (12)-1; (13)-1; (21)-1; (22)-1; (23)-1; (31)-1; (32)-1; (33)-1

Tab. 5. New minterms generated from function minterms minterm generated minterms

4. EXTENSIONS

Our TT method is explained on the example of calculation of FPGFRM expressions by using Index table and starting of function represented by minterms. But this method can be applied for the calculation some others fixed polarity polynomial expansions of MV functions. In this section we consider a some expressions of given method which make possible of these applications.

4.1 Calculation of Kronecker product based expansions

TT method given for GF(4) expressions can be extended to other MV expressions whose transform matrices $T(n)$ have a Kronecker product based structure. Consider Kronecker GF expressions of an n-variable 4-valued functions.

Definition 4 *An arbitrary n-variable function* f *defined on GF(4), given by its truth vector* F, *can be represented by the following Kronecker GF expressions*

$$f(x_1, \ldots, x_n) = \bigotimes_{i=1}^{n} \mathbf{X}_i \cdot \bigotimes_{i=1}^{n} \mathbf{K}_i \cdot \mathbf{F},$$

where

$$\mathbf{X}_i \in \left\{ \begin{bmatrix} 1 & \dot{x}_i & \dot{x}_i^2 & \dot{x}_i^3 \end{bmatrix}^T, \begin{bmatrix} J_0(x_i) & J_1(x_i) & J_2(x_i) & J_3(x_i) \end{bmatrix} \right\},$$

and

$$\mathbf{K}_i \in \left\{ \mathbf{G}_4^{<i>}, \mathbf{I}_4 \right\}$$

x_i *presents the corresponding complement of variable* x_i, *i.e.* $^i\overline{x_i}$ *while*
$J_j(x_i), j = 0,1,2,3$ *are the characteristic functions defined by*

$$J_j(x_i) = \begin{cases} 1, & if\, x_j = i, \\ 0, & otherwise. \end{cases}$$

Example 4 *Kronecker GF expression for the function* f *given in example 3 is calculated as*

$$C = \left(\begin{bmatrix} 0010 \\ 3201 \\ 2301 \\ 1111 \end{bmatrix} \otimes \begin{bmatrix} 1000 \\ 0100 \\ 0010 \\ 0001 \end{bmatrix} \right).$$

$$\cdot [0000222200001000] = [0000100001113222]$$

Expansion used for variable x_1 *is 2-Davio GF(4) expansion while Shannon expansion is used for the variable* x_2.

For generation of TT for calculation of fixed polarity Kronecker expression of MV functions defined in GF(4) the changes in given algorithm are minimal i.e. only rule for the generation of new terms (5), (6) should be changed. Concretely, instead matrix G in equation (5) it should be included the corresponding transform matrix K_t.

4.2   TT method starting from fixed polarity expressions

Proposed algorithm calculates FPGFRM coefficients starting from the function given by its minterms. It is important to note that the proposed algorithm can be used for the calculation of FPGFRM expression for polarity (p') starting from FPGFRM expression from an arbitrary polarity (p) by changing the rule for the generation of new terms. Matrix $G^{<p_i>}$ in equation (5) should be replaced by the matrix $T^{<p_i>} \cdot (T^{<p_i>})^{-1}$ for the case that function is given as fixed polarity expression for polarity p and fixed polarity expression for polarity p' is calculated.

This modification is obvious since new terms are considered as contribution of minterms to calculated coefficient vector, and the following equation

$$C^{<p'>} = T^{<p'>}(n) \cdot F = T^{<p'>}(n) \cdot (T^{<p>}(n))^{-1} \cdot C^{<p>}. \tag{8}$$

4.3 MVTT method for calculation of FPRM expression for extended set of polarities

As noted in Section 2, polarity of variables can be considered as permutation of values in variable vector. For GF(4), we use only 4 of 4! possible permutations because only these permutations can reduce the number of non-vanishing expression coefficients. But, there are the MV expressions where all the permutations of values for variables reduce the number of non-zero coefficients, as for example Reed-Muller-Fourier (RMF) expressions. For details about RMF transform see [11, 12].

The proposed method applies also to those expressions. For such expressions the transform matrix corresponding to the required permutation complement should be inserted in equation (5) instead of the matrix $G^{<p_i>}$.

Example 5 *Reed-Muller-Fourier (RMF) transform matrix for 4-valued function is given by*

$$R(1) = \begin{bmatrix} 1 & 0 & 0 & 0 \\ 1 & 3 & 0 & 0 \\ 1 & 2 & 1 & 0 \\ 1 & 1 & 3 & 3 \end{bmatrix}.$$

RMF transform matrix which corresponds to the 10-th complement of variable x, $\overset{10}{\overline{x}}$, is given by

$$R^{<10>}(1) = \begin{bmatrix} 0 & 0 & 1 & 0 \\ 3 & 0 & 1 & 0 \\ 2 & 0 & 1 & 1 \\ 1 & 3 & 1 & 3 \end{bmatrix},$$

and lexicographic order of permutation is used i.e. (0123, 0132, 0213, 0231, 0312, 0321, 1023, 1032, 1203, 1230, 1302, 1320, 2013, 2031, 2103, 2130, 2301, 2310, 3012, 3021, 3102, 3120, 3201, 3210).

4.4 Hash table or Index table based realisation

Proposed MVTT method is explained by using index table for cancelling of terms. Our method can works also by using a hash table for cancelling terms. The choice betwen these approaches depends on a concrete application.

Index table consists of 2^n entries, each entry for one minterm. Consumed memory depends exponentially on the number of variables, n. This is a disadvantage of using index table, but access to the desired entry is very fast.

In a hash table the generated terms are stored. Due to that the hash table consumes less memory than the index table. Access to the desired entry in hash table is on the average slower than access in index table.

Therefore, if the execute time is important, then the index table is used, and if the memory is critical than the hash table is used.

We use the term "cancelling of terms" by the analogue to the existing TT methods. However, in our method, this term has the following meaning. As is explained above, in our method we perform adding of minterm contribution to current value of calculated coefficients. This addition for the case of GF(2) is equall to the canceling, since $1 \oplus 1 = 0$. In our method, coefficient entry is deleted if its value is 0.

4.5 Minterms or disjoint cubes

Used approach in definition of rule for the new term generation from the minterm permits possibilities for relative simple deriving of MVTT methods which will start from a function represented by disjoint cubes [5, 6]. Cubes representing function f are disjoint if each function minterm m, $f(m) \neq 0$, is covered by only one cube. This function f is given by

$$\mathbf{F} = \mathbf{U}_1 \oplus \ldots \oplus \mathbf{U}_t,$$

where

$$\mathbf{U}_i = \mathbf{F}_{i_1} \oplus \ldots \oplus \mathbf{F}_{i_{2^r}}$$

t is the number of disjoint cubes and r is the order of the cube.

MVTT method starting from a function given by disjoint cubes is interesting because usually the number of disjoint cubes representing functions is less than the number of minterms. The rule for the generation of new terms from disjoint cubes is relatively simple as the rule for minterms. This means that MVTT methods for functions represented by cubes are more efficient than minterm based MVTT methods.

5. CONCLUDING REMARKS

We present a tabular technique for fixed polarity function expressions calculation for function defined in GF(4). Similar approach can be used to derive tabular techniques for other MV fixed polarity function expressions. With a simple modification the proposed algorithm can be applied to the calculation of fixed polarity expressions starting of expression from the expression for an arbitrary polarity. It is important to note that method can be applied also in the case when the complements of variables are considered as the arbitrary permutation in variable value vector. All useful features of TT used for calculation of fixed-polarity Reed-Muller expressions for Boolean functions, as simplicity of involved operations and high possibilities for parallelization, are preserved.

6. REFERENCES

[1] Almaini, A.E.A., McKenzie, L., "Tabular techniques for generating Kronecker expansion"', *IEE Proc.Comput. Digit. Tech.*, Vol. 143, No. 4, July 1996, 205-212.

[2] Almaini, A.E.A., Thompson, P., Hanson, D., "Tabular techniques for Reed-Muller logic", Int. J. Electron., Vol 70,No.1, 1991,23-34.

[3] Drechsler, R., Hengster, H., Schäfer, H., Hartman, J., Becker, B., "Testability of 2-Level AND/EXOR Circuits", *in Journal of Electronic Testing, Theory and Application (JETTA)*, Vol.14, No. 3, June 1999, 173-192.

[4] Drechsler, R., Becker, B., *Binary Decision Diagrams - Theory and Implementation*, Kluwer Academic Publishers, 1998.

[5] Falkowski, B.J., Schäfer, Perkowski, M.A.,"A fast computer methods for the calculation of disjoint cubes for completely and incompletely specified Boolean functions", in *Proc. 33rd Midwest Symp. on circuits and Systems*, Calgary, Canada, 1990, 1119-1122.

[6] Falkowski, B.J., Perkowski, M.A., "An algorithm for the generation of disjoint cubes for completely and incompletely specified Boolean functions", *Int. J. Electronics*, 1991, 70(3), 533-538.

[7] Harking, B., Moraga, C., "Efficient derivation of Reed-Muller expansions in multiple-valued logic systems", *Proc. 22nd Int. Symp. on Multiple-valued Logic*, 192, 436-441.

[8] Sarabi, A., Perkowski, M.A., "Fast exact and quasi-minimal minimization of highly testable fixed polarity AND/XOR canonical networks", *Proc. Design Automation Conference*, June 1992, 30-35.

[9] Sasao, T., Besslich, P., "On the complexity of mod-2 sum PLAs", *IEEE Transactions on Computers*, Vol. 21, 1990, 1183-1188.

[10] Stanković, R.S., Drechsler, Rolf, "Circuit design from Kronecker Galois field decision diagrams for multiple-valued functions", *Int. Symp. on Multiple-valued Logic Antigonish, Nova Scotia*, 1997.

[11] Stanković, R.S., Moraga, C., "Reed-Muller-Fourier representations of multiple-valued functions", in *Recent Developments in Abstract Harmonic Analysis with Applications in Signal Processing*, Nauka, Belgrade, 1996, 205-216.

[12] Stanković, R.S.,Janković, D., Moraga, C., "Reed-Muller-Fourier representations versus Galois field representations for four-valued logic functions", *Proc. 3rd Int. Workshop on Applications of the Reed-Muller Expansion in Circuit Design*, September 19-20, 1997, Oxford, UK, pp. 269-278.

[13] Tan, E.C., Yang, H., "Fast tabular technique for fixed-polarity Reed-Muller logic with inherent parallel processes", Int. J. Electronics, Vol. 85, No.85, 1998, 511-520.

[14] Tran, A., "Graphical method for the conversion of minterms to Reed-Muller coefficients and the minimization of EX-OR switching functions", *IEE Proc. Comput. Digit. Tech.*, Vol. 134, 1987, 93-99.

A Method of Analysis of Operational Petri Nets

ARKADIJ ZAKREVSKIJ[2], ANDREI KARATKEVICH[1],
MARIAN ADAMSKI[1]

[2]*Institute of Engineering Cybernetics, Surganov Str. 6, 220012 Minsk, Belarus*
[1]*Technical University of Zielona Gora, ul. Podgórna 50; 65-246 Zielona Gora, Poland*

Abstract: Petri nets, a popular discrete automaton model, are convenient for describing some parallel operations. A net used for such purpose cannot be a closed system but has to contain input and output places. Such a model is defined here as an operational Petri net.
              Analysis of Petri nets is a difficult task. In the paper the method of analysis is suggested, based on the original approach to decomposition and oriented for the considered class of nets. Applying the approach to the cyclic nets is also considered. Some experimental results are presented.

Key words: Petri nets, decomposition, analysis.

1.   INTRODUCTION

Petri nets [1] are widely used in computer science as a formal model for description of parallel processes and systems, such as parallel algorithms, communication protocols or asynchronous circuits. Analysis of such nets is an important and non-trivial task because even a simple net may have a huge number of possible states (markings).

A perspective approach to analysis of Petri nets and, generally, of parallel discrete systems, is based on the idea of decomposition [2,3]. In this paper the idea is used for analysis of operational Petri nets (OPN) – a special but wide sub-class of Petri nets [4,5]. The task of net analysis is reduced to the task of analysis of the blocks of its decomposition which may be considerably smaller than the net itself. That can simplify analysis of the big nets. The approach is also expanded onto reversible Petri nets [6].

Some results are recalled published before in Russian [7]. New results are added.

Two tasks of analysis are solved here: checking for correctness of an initial marking and, if it is correct, finding the set of terminal markings reachable from it. Also, the task of reversibility check for general Petri nets is reduced to the task of checking the initial markings of OPNs.

2.   NECESSARY DEFINITIONS

A *Petri net* is a triple Σ = (P, T, F), where P is a set of *places*, T – a set of *transitions*; P∩T=∅; F⊆(P×T)∪(T×P). For t∈T, $^{\bullet}$t denotes {p∈P|(p, t)∈F}; t$^{\bullet}$ denotes {p∈P|(t, p)∈F}; $^{\bullet}$t and t$^{\bullet}$ are the *sets of input* and *output places*, respectively. A Petri net can also be considered as an oriented bipartite graph. A *marking* of a net is defined as a function M: P→{0, 1, 2,...}. It can be considered as a number of *tokens* situated in the net places.

A transition t is *feasible* and can *fire* if all its input places contain tokens. Transition firing removes one token from each input place and adds one token to each output place changing the current marking in such a way. A marking that can be reached from M by a firing sequence is called *reachable* from M; the set of reachable markings is denoted as [M⟩. A transition is *live* if there is a reachable marking in which it is enabled; otherwise it is *dead*. The whole net is *live* if in all the reachable markings all the transitions of the net are live. The net is *safe* if in any reachable marking no place contains more than 1 token. As far as we are going to deal only with safe nets here, the markings will be specified by the sets of places containing tokens. A net is *reversible* if it can return to the initial marking from any reachable marking.

Let's define the next notions:

$$L = \bigcup_{i=1}^{n} {}^{\bullet}t_i; \; N = \bigcup_{i=1}^{n} t_i^{\bullet} , \tag{1}$$

where n is the number of transitions in the net. Let I=L\N be the *input* of the net, and elements of this set are the *input nodes*. Let O=N\L be the *output* of the net, and elements of this set are the *output nodes*. Let P=L∪N, and let the elements of the set L∩N be the *internal nodes* of the net.

Suppose that in any initial marking only the input nodes may contain tokens. Let an initial marking M_0 be *correct* if the next conditions are satisfied.

The net is safe for this initial marking.

From any marking M reachable from M_0, a *dead* marking is reachable (where all the transitions are dead).

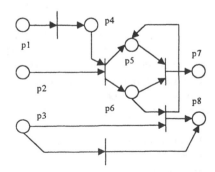

Fig. 1. An example of operational Petri net

All the reachable dead markings are *terminal* (only the output nodes contain tokens).

Such net is called an *operational Petri net*, or *OPN*.

An example of OPN is shown in Fig. 1. Here the correct initial markings are $\{1,2\}$ and $\{3\}$.

3. RELATION IMPLEMENTED BY OPN

Let's denote the set of all correct initial markings of an OPN by C, and the set of all the reachable terminal markings by E. The transformation R of C to E implemented by the OPN is its important characteristic. As far as several elements of E may correspond to a single element of C, the transformation is not functional; it is a binary relation $R \subseteq C \times E$. Some binary relations, however, cannot be implemented by an OPN.

Let's say that the OPN T recognizes the set C, if a set E exists such that T implements the relation $R \subseteq C \times E$. Set C is *recognizable* if an OPN exists recognizing it.

Several affirmations are given below. No proofs are given because of the lack of space.

Affirmation 1. If the initial markings x_i and x_j (specified as the sets of places containing tokens) are correct and $x_i \subset x_j$, then the initial marking $x_j \backslash x_i$ is correct.

Let's define the correct initial markings x_i and x_j as *compatible* if there exists a correct initial marking x_k such that $x_i \subseteq x_k$ and $x_j \subseteq x_k$.

Affirmation 2. If the correct initial markings x_i and x_j are compatible and orthogonal ($x_i \cap x_j = \varnothing$), then the initial marking $x_j \cup x_i$ is correct.

Affirmation 3. The correct orthogonal initial markings x_i and x_j are compatible if and only if $x_k \cap x_l = \varnothing$ for any states x_k and x_l such that $x_k \in [x_i\rangle$ and $x_l \in [x_j\rangle$.

Let us denote the set of terminal markings reachable from the correct initial marking x_i by D_i: $D_i = \{y_j/(x_i,y_j) \in R\}$. And let's denote the set of all the output nodes which can obtain tokens in the terminal markings reachable from x_i by $U[D_i]$.

Affirmation 4. If the correct initial markings x_i and x_j are compatible and orthogonal, then $U[D_i] \cap U[D_j] = \varnothing$.

Affirmation 5. If the initial markings x_i and x_j are correct, $x_i \subset x_j$ and $x_k = x_j \backslash x_i \neq \varnothing$, then $U[D_k] \cap U[D_i] = \varnothing$.

Let's call a correct initial marking x_i *minimum* if there is no correct initial marking x_j such that $x_j \subset x_i$. Let's denote the set of all the minimum correct initial markings as C_{min}.

Affirmation 6. The minimum possible number of output nodes of an OPN is equal to the chromatic number of the compatibility graph of the elements of C_{min}.

Consequence. If an OPN has only one output node, no correct initial markings include one another.

Affirmation 7. Any correct initial marking x_i is a unification of several (at least one) minimum and orthogonal to each other correct initial markings $x_{i1}, x_{i2}, ..., x_{iq}$, and

$$D_I = \{\{d_1, d_2, ..., d_q\} / d_1 \in D_{i1}, d_2 \in D_{i2}, ..., d_q \in D_{iq}\}. \tag{2}$$

The opposite statement is not true.

Affirmation 8. Any relation $R \subseteq C \times E$ satisfying the conditions of Affirmations 1 and 4 can be implemented by an OPN.

Affirmation 9. Any set of initial markings satisfying the conditions of Affirmation 1 can be recognized by an OPN.

4.   DECOMPOSITION OF OPN

An OPN T is a *unification* of the OPNs T_1 and T_2 if the set of transitions of T is a unification of the sets of transitions of T_1 and T_2. In such case $L = L_1 \cup L_2$, $N = N_1 \cup N_2$. The operation of unification can be generalized for any number of OPNs.

Unification of the nets T_1 and T_2 such that $L_1 \cap L_2 = \varnothing$ and $N = N_1 \cap N_2$ will be called their *composition*. It is easy to see that for such nets only those places can be common, which are the input nodes for one net and the output nodes for the other.

In Fig. 2 the different variants of composition of two OPNs are shown. The arrows specify orientation of the nets – from the input to output nodes. The common nodes of the nets are the internal nodes for their composition. If OPN T is a composition of OPNs T_1 and T_2, then

$$I = (I_1 \cup I_2) \backslash (O_1 \cup O_2), \; O = (O_1 \cup O_2) \backslash (I_1 \cup I_2). \tag{3}$$

The operation of composition can also be easily generalized for multiple nets.

Affirmation 10. A unification T of the operational Petri nets T_1 T_2, ..., T_r is their composition if and only if the next condition is satisfied: no place belongs to more than two nets of the set $\{T_1, T_2, ..., T_r\}$.

Now let us formulate the task of decomposition of a given OPN. The sub-nets T_1 T_2, ..., T_r which composition constitutes the net T will be called *blocks* in T.

Affirmation 11. A sub-net T_j of an operational Petri net T is a block, if and only if for every transition $t \in T \backslash T_j$: $t^{\bullet} \cap P_j \subseteq I_j$, $^{\bullet}t \cap P_j \subseteq O_j$.

Affirmation 12. If a sub-net T_j of the operational Petri net T is a block, then $T \backslash T_j$ is a block.

We will say that two transitions are in the relation of *alternative joint* if their input or output sets of places intersect.

Affirmation 13. Transitive closure of the relation of alternative joint of the set of transitions of an OPN specifies its decomposition into minimum blocks.

Note that there are nets, which cannot be decomposed into blocks, and there are nets, for which each transition is a block.

Affirmation 14. A unification of the blocks is a block.

5. ANALYSIS OF TWO-BLOCK COMPOSITIONS

Let the OPN T be a partial sequential composition of the blocks T_1, T_2 (Fig. 2c). The set of its input nodes $I=I_1\cup(I_2\backslash O_1)$, the set of its output nodes $O=O_2\cup(O_1\backslash I_2)$. The set $O_1\cup I_2$ we denote as Q. Let's consider now the task of behavior analysis of such composition. Below M_0 is an initial state of T.

Affirmation 15. Any marking M reachable from M_0 such that only output nodes of T_1 (and any places of T_2) may contain tokens, is also reachable from a marking M' such that only output nodes of T_1 and input nodes of T_2 may contain tokens.

That means that for analysis of the net behavior there is no need to consider the markings in which internal poles of both blocks contain tokens. The relation R implemented by the two-block composition can be calculated if the relations R_1 and R_2 implemented by the blocks are known.

Affirmation 16. Relation R implemented by the complete sequential composition of the blocks T_1 and T_2 is constituted of all the pairs (x,y) which satisfy the following conditions:

$$x\in C_1;$$
$$\exists z:(z\in R_1(x))\wedge(y\in R_2(z)); \qquad (4)$$
$$R_1(x)\subseteq C_2.$$

For the partial sequential composition the elements of relation R will be denoted as follows:

$$x = x' \cup x'', \text{ where } x' \subseteq I_1 \text{ and } x'' \subseteq I_2\backslash O_1;$$
$$y = y' \cup y'', \text{ where } y' \subseteq O_2 \text{ and } y'' \subseteq O_1\backslash I_2. \qquad (5)$$

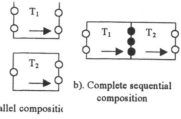

b). Complete sequential
composition

a). Parallel compositic

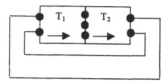

c). Partial sequential
composition

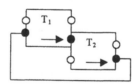

d). Complete cyclic composition

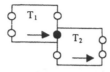

e). Partial cyclic composition

Fig. 2. Variants of composition of two OPNs

Affirmation 17. Relation R implemented by the partial sequential composition of the blocks T_1 and T_2 is constituted of all the pairs (x,y), which satisfy the following conditions:

a)$x' \in C_1$;
b)$\exists z:(z \in R_1(x')) \wedge (y' \in R_2(z \cap I_2 \cup x'')) \wedge (y''=z \backslash I_2)$;   (6)
c) $\forall z \in R_1(x'): (z \cap I_2 \cup x'') \in C_2$

Affirmation 18. Relation R implemented by the partial cyclic composition of the blocks T_1 and T_2 cannot be obtained from the relations implemented by these blocks.

6. DECOMPOSITION METHOD OF OPN ANALYSIS

The results of the previous section can be easily generalized for multi-block compositions. The next follows from Affirmations 16-18.

Affirmation 19. Analysis of an acyclic composition of several blocks can be reduced to analysis of blocks.

For the analysis of any OPN it should be decomposed into minimum blocks, and then each cyclic composition (not only of two blocks) must be united into single block. It can be performed by finding the transitive closure of the relation V of partial order, where two blocks T_1 and T_2 are in that relation if they have a common node – output for T_1 and input for T_2.

This relation specifies the order of the net analysis: a block T can be analyzed only when all the blocks, with which it shares its input nodes, have been analyzed.

So the following algorithm of OPN analysis is proposed.

Algorithm 1

The OPN T and initial marking M_0 are given.
1. Decompose the net T into minimum blocks.
2. Unite all the cycles composed by blocks.
3. $D := \{M_0\}$.
4. While D contains markings in which some tokens are situated at the non-output nodes of T, do:
    4.1. Find a block T_i such that there is no block T_j not analyzed yet for which $(T_j, T_i) \in V$.
    4.2. For each marking M belonging to D such that there are tokens in the input nodes of T_i, find the terminal markings of T_i reachable from it and replace M in D by those markings (tokens not belonging to the places of T_i don't change their positions).
    4.3. If at least one of the initial markings for T_i is found to be incorrect, go to 6.
5. The initial marking M_0 is correct, and D contains all the terminal markings reachable from it in T. The end.
6. The initial marking is incorrect. The end.

7. APPLYING THE APPROACH FOR REVERSIBLE NETS ANALYSIS

In [7] the notion of *quasi-liveness* is defined: a net is quasi-live if from any marking reachable from the initial one, a terminal marking is reachable. It is easy to see that adding to a quasi-live OPN a transition for each terminal marking, which firing changes the terminal marking for an initial one, transforms it into a live Petri net.

Analogously, a Petri net satisfying some conditions can be "unfolded" into an OPN. It can be easily done if its initial marking contains a single token. The condition can be generalized if for all the transitions such that their input sets of places intersect with the initial marking their input sets of places are the same, the net can be transformed into OPN. The same, if the similar statement is true for the *output* sets of places. It is easy to see that if and only if the original net is live and safe, the resulting OPN will be quasi-live, will have no dead transitions and will have only one correct initial marking and one terminal marking.

So, if a Petri net is supposed to be reversible, and if it satisfies the condition formulated above, then it can be transformed into OPN and analyzed by the described method. It would allow checking liveness and safeness of the original net. Also, if the net is not live or not safe, it would allow to obtain a non-safe marking or marking from which the net cannot return to the initial one together with firing sequence leading to such marking; or the list of dead transitions.

It follows that the next algorithm can be used for liveness and safeness analysis of a net, such that all the tokens from the places containing them in the initial marking can be removed (or put there) only by a single transition firing. For any non-LS net the algorithm will get a transition firing sequence leading to a "wrong" marking or the list of dead transitions.

Algorithm 2

The Petri net T and initial marking M_0 are given.
1. Add a place for each place having a token in M_0. Now all the edges in the net graph leading to the place having a token in M_0 are replaced with the edges leading to the new places (see Fig. 3). An OPN is obtained. Now the places having tokens in M_0 are its input nodes, and the new places are its output nodes.
2. Check the initial marking M_0 for this net using Algorithm 1.
3. If the initial marking is found incorrect:
   3.1. if from some reachable marking no terminal marking is reachable:
      3.1.1.   if such marking is reachable that all the output nodes are marked together with some internal – the net is not safe;
      3.1.2.   else it is not live;
   3.2. if an unsafe place is found – the original net is not safe.
4. If the initial marking is found correct:
   4.1. if a terminal marking is found such that not all the output nodes are marked or if some transitions have not fired during simulation – the original net is not live.
   4.2. else it is live and safe.
5. The end.

8. EXAMPLE OF ANALYSIS

Let's consider the nets in Fig. 3; one of them is operational (b), and another (b) can be transformed into OPN, as it is described in Algorithm 2. At Fig. 4 block decomposition of the net is shown.

In Fig.5 the reduced reachability graph (RRG) is shown which is constructed by the algorithm. The complete reachability graph for this net has 14 nodes and 32 edges.

In Fig. 6, 7 the analysis process is shown for the net similar to the net shown in Fig. 3 but with a dead but non-terminal marking reachable

It is interesting to compare this method with the method suggested in [8], where also a sub-graph of the reachability graph is constructed and where a similar object is analyzed. Comparative analysis of the methods and studying the effects of their combination is the topic of [10].

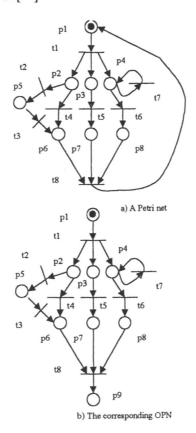

a) A Petri net

b) The corresponding OPN

Fig. 3. A Petri net and the corresponding OPN (p9 is an output node)

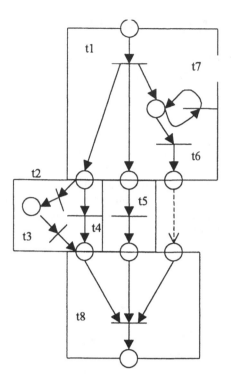

Fig. 4. Decomposition of the net shown at Fig. 3 b)

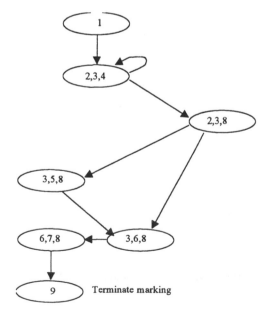

Fig. 5. RRG for the net shown at Fig. 3 b)

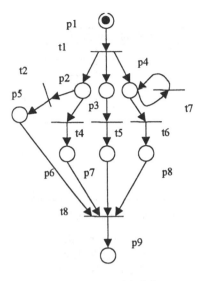

Fig. 6. A net with defect

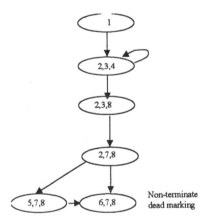

Fig. 7. RRG for the net shown at Fig. 6.

9. EXPERIMENTAL RESULTS

For the experiments (PC K6 II 266 MHz) the random net generator [9] and the program implementing the described method were used. For the biggest nets investigated – with 65 transitions and 120 places – the maximum time of analysis was 3 ms. As far as it is supposed that the blocks are analysed by constructing the complete reachability graphs for them, the most critical parameter of net decomposition is size of the biggest block. The size of a block means here the number of transitions in it. The average results obtained in series of experiments are shown in Table 1

Number of places	Number of transitions		
	20	40	60
20	16	35	
40	18	7	21
60	18	10	6
80	18	17	7
100	19	21	5
120			6
Average values in columns	18	18	9

Tab. 1. Average number of transitions in maximal blocks after the net decomposition

The next conclusion follows from those results: with the net growth, the relation between its size and the size of its biggest block grows. That means that the method is efficient for big nets. It is less efficient for the nets with $|P|<<|T|$; it is intuitively clear that the structure of such nets makes block decomposition less possible.

10. REFERENCES

[1] Peterson J.L. Petri net theory and the modeling of systems. - Prentice-Hall, Inc., Englewood Cliffs, 1981.
[2] Notomi M., Murata T. Hierarchical Reachability Graph of Bounded Petri Nets for Concurrent-Software Analysis. IEEE Transactions on software engineering, Vol. 20, No 5, May 1994.- pp. 325-336.
[3] Banaszak Z., Kus J., Adamski M. Sieci Petriego. Modelowanie, Sterowanie i Sinteza Systemów Dyskretnych.- Wydawnictwo WSInż, Zielona Góra, 1993.
[4] Zakrevskij A.D. Analysis of the operational Petri nets.- Minsk, 1987.- (Preprint – Institute of Engineering Cybernetics of the Academy of Sc. of BSSR, № 44) (in Russian).
[5] Zakrevskij A.D. Decomposition approach to analysis of parallel logical control algorithms.- Formal models of parallel computation.- Novosibirsk: Siberian section of the Academy of Sc. of USSR, 1988.- pp. 127-135 (in Russian).
[6] Murata T. Petri Nets: Properties, Analysis and Applications. Proceedings of the IEEE, Vol. 77, No. 4, 1989, pp. 541-580.
[7] Zakrevskij A.D.Parallel algorithms for logical control.- Inst. of Engineering Cybernetics of NAS of Belarus, Minsk, 1999 (in Russian).
[8] Karatkevich A.G. Correctness analysis of α-nets. – Logical design, Vol. 1, Inst. of Engineering Cybernetics of Academy of Sciences of Belarus, Minsk, 1996, pp. 86-96 (in Russian).
[9] Pottosin Yu.V. Generating parallel automata. Methods and algorithms of logical design. - Inst. of Engineering Cybernetics of Academy of Sciences of Belarus, Minsk, 1995, pp. 132-142 (in Russian).
[10] Karatkevich A. Optimal Simulation of α-Nets. - Proceedings of the Polish-German Symposium on SRE'2000, Zielona Góra, 2000.- P. 217-222.

Method and Validation for VHDL Case Statement Optimization

V. BELETSKYY[1], K. KRASKA[2]
Faculty of Computer Science & Information Systems, Technical University of Szczecin,
49, Zolnierska st., 71-210 Szczecin, Poland,
[1]e-mail: bielecki@man.szczecin.pl
[2]e-mail: krzysztof.kraska@wi.tuniv.szczecin.pl

Abstract: The number of events that occur during the simulation directly affects the performance and efficiency of VHDL event-driven simulations. To accelerate the simulation, there is a need to eliminate its unnecessary parts. In this paper we report on a method for the optimization of behavioral VHDL sources. Our method specifically targeted towards a sequential case statement eliminates ineffective VHDL events without modifications of existing VHDL design entities simulators. To prove the soundness of our optimization technique we take advantage of the Dynamic Model.

Key words: VHDL, event-driven simulation, optimization, method, validation.

1.   INTRODUCTION

VHDL is a hardware description language used to describe the behavior and structure of digital systems. VHDL can be used to describe and simulate an operation of wide variety of digital systems, ranging in complexity from a few gates to an interconnection of many complex integrated circuits. The VHDL language has become an IEEE standard and it is widely used in industry.

The event-driven simulation is well-known simulation technique that is currently used in building VHDL simulators. In the event-driven simulation an event appearance leads to the simulation. An event is a change in a current value of a signal, which occurs when the signal is updated with its effective value obtainable by evaluating a reference to the signal within a VHDL expression. Thus, the performance and efficiency of the event-driven simulations directly depend on the number of events that occur during the simulation time.

As the complexity of FPGA and ASIC grows the time of the simulations increases. To accelerate the VHDL simulation there is a need to eliminate its unnecessary parts. The inefficiencies are often introduced by the simulations, which do not change output signals and variables. Hence, all the events can be divided into two classes: effective and ineffective ones. The effective events cause the simulation that changes output signals and variables. The ineffective ones do not change output signals and variables. The effective events can be found by analyzing VHDL sources. The replacement of the sensitivity list with conditional *wait* statements according to the effective events leads to the optimization of VHDL sources.

The simulation inefficiencies were also considered in [7]. But a different approach from our one was taken to define the optimization methods. Constraints and validations were missing as well.

The other optimization methods of the VHDL simulation as the event suppression technique [1] only tries to suppress the events in synchronous circuits and the clock suppression technique [2] suppresses the clock events that do not affect output signals. But the implementation of this technique leads to greatly modification of a logical simulator.

In this paper we offer a new optimization method for the sequential *case* statement that eliminate the unnecessary simulation activity caused by the ineffective events without disadvantages mentioned earlier. The proposed method conducts to eliminate the ineffective events thereby reducing the number of iterations in the simulation, which in turn speeds up the simulation. The results have indicated a significant time improvement after the optimization.

To prove the soundness of our optimization technique we take advantage of the dynamic semantic model referred to as the Dynamic Model [8]. The optimization method is proved by showing the equivalence of the VHDL descriptions before and after the transformation. For the sake of brevity the explanation of the Dynamic Model is not provided herein. We have described some rudiments in [10].

2.   RULES OF A SEQUENTIAL CASE STATEMENT OPTMIZATION METHOD

According to [8] we find that: *two VHDL programs are equivalent if the waveforms of the signals of the two programs are identical.*

A waveform W for a signal s is a set given by:

$$W = \{< v_1, t_1 >, < v_2, t_2 >, < v_3, t_3 >, ... \},$$

where v_1 is the value of s in time interval t_1, v_2 is the value of s in time interval t_2, and so on. The evaluation of a *signal assignment* statement results in transaction containing value and delay information being posted on the corresponding driver. This transaction set contains time intervals that are used to determine the waveform of the signal. If the value projected by the former transaction is the same as that projected by the latter transaction and there does not exist a transaction that projects a different value at a time-stamp in between the earlier two time-stamps, then the event does not occur. It means that:

$$\neg event(s, \delta_i(j)) \Leftrightarrow \exists \hat{t} \bullet meets(\hat{t}, \delta_i(j)) \wedge$$

$$(F_{eff\text{-}val}(s, \delta_i(j)) = F_{eff\text{-}val}(s, \hat{t})) \text{ ,}$$

where s is a destination signal and $F_{eff\text{-}val}$ is a function which returns the effective value of the signal s in a given time interval. Thus, if the former and the latter transactions are posted by the same *signal assignment* statement, for example:

$$s \Leftarrow a \text{ ,}$$

and the event does not occur on the signal a in the meanwhile, then a value of related signal s does not change. It means that the event does not occur on s. For this reason, our optimization method assumes that for all of the events that occur during the simulation time causing the *process* statements evaluation, the state of output signals is not always changed. In such case, the simulation is not needed. It follows that the waveform W for the signal s shown below:

$$W = \{< v_1, t_1 >, < v_2, t_2 >, < v_3, t_3 >, ...\} \text{ ,}$$

where $<v_1, t_1>$ and $<v_2, t_2>$ arisen by evaluation of the same *signal assignment* statement and $v_1 = v_2$ as well, is equal to the waveform W' shown below:

$$W' = \{< v_1, t_{12} >, < v_3, t_3 >, ...\} \text{ ,}$$

where the element $<v_2, t_2>$ was deleted by means of the elimination of the simulation and therefore $t_{12} = t_1 + t_2$. It is important that for the ineffective events elimination to be valid, the behavior of the VHDL description should not be dependent on the activity of s.

A sequential *case* statement represents a lot of possible traces of the *process* statement simulation. A sensitivity list of such process describes static sensitivity rules where the simulation is needed. The sensitivity rules we named 'static' since they are the same for all traces of the simulation. According to [4], if the sensitivity list appears following the reserved word process then the *process* statement is assumed to contain an implicit *wait* statement of the form *wait on sensitivity_list* as the last statement of the *process* statement part. Therefore sensitivity list gives the set of signals common to all process traces. It follows that events on some part of sensitivity list signals may not lead to changing the state of output signals for some traces of the simulation to which the events do not have importance. We name these events as ineffective ones.

The syntax rule for the VHDL *case* statement is given by [4]:

```
case_statement ::=
   [ case_label : ]
      case expression is
         when choices =>
            { sequential_statement }
         { when choices =>
```

> *{ sequential_statement } }*
> *end case [case_label] ;*

where:

> *choices ::=*
> *simple_expression | discrete_range |*
> *element_simple_name | others ;*

are branches of the *case* statement. The sequential *case* statement selects for executing one of a number of alternative sequences of statements, depending on the value of the expression. The *case* statement choices are exhaustive and mutually exclusive. It follows that the transition between branches depends on a state of the signals that affect the expression or any of the choices. In consequence, the transition almost firmly leads to changing a behavior of a VHDL description.

To show the simulation inefficiencies, consider the behavior of a design entity representing 4 to 1 multiplexer described in the following way.

```
-- 4 to 1 multiplexer design with case construct
--  SEL: in STD_LOGIC_VECTOR(0 to 1);
--  A, B, C, D: in STD_LOGIC;
--  MUX_OUT: out STD_LOGIC;
process(SEL, A, B, C, D)
begin
    case SEL is
        when "00" => MUX_OUT <= A;
        when "01" => MUX_OUT <= B;
        when "10" => MUX_OUT <= C;
        when "11" => MUX_OUT <= D;
        when others => MUX_OUT <= 'X';
    end case;
end process;
```

The timing diagrams on Fig. 1 depict hypothetical stimulating input signals in the simulator. For assumed ones the simulation trace of the *process* statements always goes through the first branch of the *case* statement because the expression SEL yields the value "00" during the entire time of the simulation. Only events on the signal SEL (because they affect on the current value of the expression) and the signal A (because they change the current value of the output signal MUX_OUT) attach importance to this simulation trace. Events on the other signals do not attach importance and they cause the ineffective simulations. Therefore we may classify events on the signals B, C and D for the first simulation trace of the *process* statement as the ineffective ones.

The idea of our optimization method is to convert static sensitivity input rules of the *process* statement, determined by the form of its sensitivity list, into dynamic sensitivity input rules, determined by the explicit form of succeeding *wait* statements with a sensitivity set of signals to which a given simulation trace of the *process* statement attaches importance. In general, to deploy our method, there is a need to perform two optimization stages: (A) a *process* statement transformation, and (B) an elimination of the ineffective simulations.

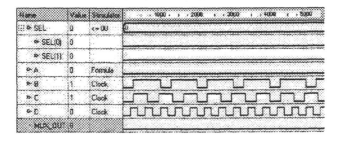

Fig. 1. Timing diagrams of stimulating input signals

An optimization method of the *case* statement within a *process* is as follows:

Stage One – the *process* statement transformation:

all the statements that follow the optimized *case* statement move to the end of each branch of this *case* one.

Stage Two – the elimination of the ineffective simulations:

delete the sensitivity list of the *process* statement,

to indicate the effective events and eliminate the ineffective ones in the end of each branch of the new *case* statement insert the *wait* statement of the form *wait on signal_list*, where the *signal_list* includes all the signals that occur on the sensitivity list of the process and simultaneously:

> (3a) occur as the waveform element on the right-hand side of the *signal assignment* statements,
>
> (3b) occur within any expression containing signal names (according to [4] an expression is also a function call),
>
> (3c) are passed as parameters to the procedure call statements,
>
> for the given simulation trace of the optimized *case* statement, i.e. on the path from the beginning of the process to the beginning of the optimized *case* statement, further for all choices and then likewise inside from the beginning to the end of the considered branch. These signals directly reflect the effective events,

for a nested *case* statement the optimization should be done at the most deepest level of the nesting,

Some constraints of using our method arise as a result of the elimination of the simulations. We classify the constraints into four categories below. For a considered trace of the simulation the optimization is not permitted if:

Because some signals indirectly reflect the effective events:

there is a signal specified in the points (3a), (3b) or (3c) above but it is not contained in the sensitivity list,

Because some values depend on the simulation time progress:

there is an expression contained an impure function call – the impure functions may return a different value each time they are called, even when multiple calls have the same actual parameter values [4]. The pure function calls are only allowed,

there is an expression contained a signal attribute that checks some appearances for the given units of time (i.e.: S'STABLE[(T)], S'QUIET[(T)]) or measures the time passage from the last appearance (i.e.: S'LAST_EVENT, S'LAST_ACTIVE),
Because the optimization leads to the elimination of the transactions:

there is more than one associated driver that drives the waveform of a target signal,

elsewhere in the VHDL description exists an expression contained a signal attribute that checks acquiring a new value by a target signal, regardless whether the new value is different from the previous one (i.e.: S'TRANSACTION, S'ACTIVE, S'QUIET[(T)], S'LAST_ACTIVE),
Because an influence of the variables on a behavior of the VHDL description must not be omitted:

there is a *variable assignment* statement – a value of a variable modified by the *variable assignment* statement has to be reflected immediately,

there is a reference to a shared variable – a value of a shared variable may be modified unforeseeable by several processes in the every point of the simulation time.

The explanation of the optimization constraints goes beyond the scope of this paper.

To exemplify the application of the method we provide the optimized source code of the 4 to 1 multiplexer described earlier.

```
process(SEL, A, B, C, D)
begin
    case SEL is
        when "00" => MUX_OUT <= A;
                     wait on SEL, A;
        when "01" => MUX_OUT <= B;
                     wait on SEL, B;
        when "10" => MUX_OUT <= C;
                     wait on SEL, C;
        when "11" => MUX_OUT <= D;
                     wait on SEL, D;
        when others => MUX_OUT <= 'X';
                     wait on SEL;
    end case;
end process;
```

3.   PROCESS STATEMENT TRANSFORMATION

In the remainder of the paper, transformations are proved by showing the equivalence of the VHDL descriptions before and after the transformations with respect to all signals common to the descriptions. On the basis of [8]: *if S is a set of signals common the two VHDL descriptions V_1 and V_2, then V_1 is equivalent to V_2 with respect to S if for every signal $s \in S$, the set of drivers for s in V_1 are similar to the set of drivers for s in V_2.*

To simplify our treatment we lean on the equivalence defined in [4]. According to this work the *process* statement P1 with sensitivity list has the same behavior as the *process* statement P2 with no sensitivity list and an added *wait* statement sensitive to the same signals as the former *process* statement.

The definition of evaluation ε for the *case* statement is given by:

$$\varepsilon(cs, t) \Rightarrow [\exists i, t_1, t_2 \bullet t_1 + t_2 = t \wedge \Delta(t_1) \wedge VAL(E, t_1) = A_i \wedge$$
$$\wedge (\forall j \in N : j \neq i \bullet VAL(E, t_1) \neq A_i) \wedge \varepsilon(OS_i, t_2) \wedge \quad ,$$
$$\wedge \sigma(cs, t) = \{< E, t_1 >\} \cup \sigma(OS_i, t_2)]$$

where E refers to cs.expression, A_i refers to (cs.alternative)$_i$.choices, OS_i refers to (cs.alternative)$_i$.ordered_statements and VAL(E, t) returns the value of expression E in time interval t.

For the sake of conformity, our optimization method orders to move all the statements that follow the optimized *case* statement to the end of each branch of this *case* statement. To prove the soundness of this transformation, consider the *process* statement P1 shown below. This *process* statement can be transformed into the equivalent process P2.

Notice that the method constraints do not apply to this stage of the optimization.

Proof: To validate the *case* statement transformation, it is necessary to show that the driver of each signal in the given VHDL description before transformation is

P1: process (sensitivity_list)
begin
  Seq1: \<sequence of statements>
  C1:case *expression* is
    when *choice1* =>
      OS2: \<ordered statements>
    when *choice2* =>
      OS3: \<ordered statements>
    end case;
  Seq4: \<sequence of statements>
end process;

P2: process
begin
  Seq1: \<sequence of statements>
  C1: case *expression* is
    when *choice1* =>
      OS2: \<ordered statements>
      Seq4: \<sequence of statements>
      W1: wait on sensitivity_list;
    when *choice2* =>
      OS3: \<ordered statements>
      Seq4: \<sequence of statements>
      W1: wait on sensitivity_list;
    end case;
end process;

similar to the driver after the transformation. This ensures that the waveforms of all signals in the given description are preserved after the transformation.

It is clear from the rules of the transformation that no sequential statement is deleted from the VHDL source code as a result of the transformation. Additionally in [8] there was shown if any sequence of statements does not contain a *wait* statement and their order is maintained, the entire sequence is constrained to be evaluated within a delta interval. For this reason it is sufficient to show that the evaluation order of the sequence of statements within the *process* is maintained after the transformation.

Lemma 3.1: If the sequence of statements is evaluated in the given order and delta interval $\delta_i(j)$ before the transformation, then it is evaluated in the same order and delta interval $\delta_i(j)$ after the transformation.

Proof: The trace set EV(P1) of the *process* statement P1 is shown below.

$$EV(P1) = \sigma(Seq1, t_1) \cup \sigma(C1, t_2) \cup \sigma(Seq4, t_3) \cup \sigma(wa, t_4) \cup \sigma(Seq1, t_5) \cup \cdots \cup$$

$$\cup \sigma(wa, t_n) = \sigma(Seq1, t_1) \cup \{< E, t_{21} >\} \cup \sigma(OS_i, t_{22}) \cup \sigma(Seq4, t_3) \cup \ ,$$

$$\cup \{< wa, t_4 >\} \cup \sigma(Seq1, t_5) \cup \cdots \cup \{< wa, t_n >\}$$

where $t_2 = t_{21} + t_{22}$ and "wa" means implicit *wait* statement with the same *sensitivity_set* field as the *sensitivity_list* of P1. It also follows that the following relation holds:

$$meets(t_1, t_{21}) \wedge meets(t_{21}, t_{22}) \wedge meets(t_{22}, t_3) \wedge$$
$$meets(t_3, t_4) \wedge meets(t_4, t_5) \wedge \cdots \wedge meets(t_{n-1}, t_n) \ .$$

However, the trace set EV(P2) of the *process* statement P2 is shown below:

$$EV(P2) = \sigma(Seq1, t_1) \cup \sigma(C1, t_2) \cup \sigma(Seq1, t3) \cup \cdots \cup \sigma(C1, t_n) = \sigma(Seq1, t_1) \cup$$

$$\cup \{< C_i, t_{21} >\} \sigma\sigma(O_i, t_{22}) \cup \sigma(Seq4, t_{23}) \cup \sigma(W1, t_{24}) \cup \sigma(Seq1, t_3) \cup$$

$$\cup \cdots \cup \sigma(W1, t_{n4}) = \sigma(Seq1, t_1) \cup \{< C_i, t_{21} >\} \cup \sigma(OS_i, t_{22}) \cup$$

$$\cup \sigma(Seq4, t_{23}) \cup \{< W1, t_{24} >\} \cup \sigma(Seq1, t_3) \cup \cdots \cup \{< W1, t_{n4} >\}$$

where $t_2 = t_{21} + t_{22} + t_{23} + t_{24}$ and the following relation holds:

$$meets(t_1, t_{21}) \wedge meets(t_{21}, t_{22}) \wedge meets(t_{22}, t_{23}) \wedge$$
$$meets(t_{23}, t_{24}) \wedge meets(t_{24}, t_3) \wedge \cdots \wedge meets(t_{n3}, t_{n4}) \ .$$

It is clear from the rules of the transformation that the *sensitivity_set* of the implicit *wait* statement in P1 is equal to the *sensitivity_set* of explicit W1 in P2. For this reason, the event on any signal s, where $s \in$ *sensitivity_set*, triggers the implicit *wait* statement wa in P1, it also triggers explicit W1 in P2. It follows that for $\varepsilon(wa, t_1)$ in P1, where overlaps($\delta_i(j), t_1$)∧overlaps($t_1, \delta_k(l)$), and $\varepsilon(W1, t_2)$ in P2, where overlaps($\delta_i(j), t_2$)∧overlaps($t_2, \delta_m(n)$), holds $(k = m) \wedge (l = n)$. It means that equals(t_1, t_2) hold. Thus, the trace set of P1 and P2 is as follows.

$$EV(P1) = \sigma(Seq1, t_1) \cup \{< E, t_{21} >\} \cup \sigma(OS_i, t_{22}) \cup \sigma(Seq4, t_3) \cup$$

$$\cup \{< wa, t_4 >\} \cup \sigma(Seq1, t_5) \cup \cdots \cup \{< wa, t_n >\} = \sigma(Seq1, t_1)$$

$$\cup \{< E, t_{21} >\} \cup \sigma(OS_i, t_{22}) \cup \sigma(Seq4, t_3) \cup \{< W1, t_4 >\} \cup \ ,$$

$$\cup \sigma(Seq1, t_5) \cup \cdots \cup \{< W1, t_n >\} = EV(P2)$$

and the corresponding statements of P1 and P2 are evaluated in the same delta intervals.

Corollary 3.1: Since the order of sequences of statements within the processes is maintained and they are evaluated in the same delta intervals, then for any signal s that is the destination for any assignment in P1 and P2, the sets ALL_TR(s,P1) and ALL_TR(s,P2) are similar.

Proof: From Lemma 3.1, it follows that if a transaction is posted on ALL_TR(s,P1) by a signal assignment with destination s in the interval $\delta_i(j)$, a corresponding transaction is posted on ALL_TR(s,P2) by the same assignment statement in the same delta interval. The two transactions are similar because they are posted in the same delta interval and have the same delay. Hence ALL_TR(s,P1) is similar to ALL_TR(s,P2).

Lemma 3.2: If a transaction $<v, t_d, t_r>$ in ALL_TR(s,P1) gets preempted, then the corresponding transaction $<v1, t1_d, t1_r>$ in ALL_TR(s,P2) will also get preempted.

Proof: The formal proof of corresponding transaction preemption within *process* statements, providing that the order of the sequential statement evaluation is maintained and every statement is evaluated in the same delta interval, is available in work [8]. From this result, it follows that the drivers of any signal s in P1 and P2 are similar.

Corollary 3.2: For a signal s, Driver(s,P1) is similar to Driver(s,P2).

4. ELIMINATION OF INEFFECTIVE SIMULATIONS

In a parallel VHDL simulator, *process* statements are executed as parallel threads, which communicate with one another and some information flows throughout the entire environment. To prove our optimization method for any given VHDL description it is necessary to take into consideration input and output data for every node (i.e. the *process* statement) of the entire environment. In that depiction, a *process* statement selected for the optimization can be perceived as an isolated element within an *architecture* body. The whole forms the net effect of autonomous processes evaluation with their interdependence where the simulation of every *process* statement obviously occurs under pressure from some input data exerted by other processes and results in some output data designed for the other ones (see Fig.2). The sensitivity to some of all inputs determines the dependence of every *process* statement simulation. Hence, for the elimination of the ineffective events to be valid, the information flow throughout the entire environment has to be maintained after our optimization method to a given VHDL description is applied.

Our approach to ineffective events elimination derives from the Dynamic Model and is greatly different from that presented in [7]. Therein, the simulation of a VHDL source was modeled by means of the extension to the Finite State Machine concept [11]. Some constraints and method validations were also missed. Instead, we perceive the simulation as the net effect of evaluating the VHDL programs. Additionally, taking advantage of the Dynamic Model we validate the optimization method.

To prove the soundness of ineffective events elimination in our depiction, consider the given VHDL description shown below.

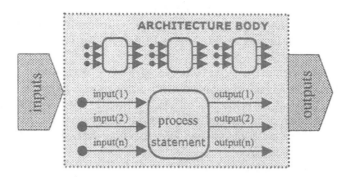

Fig. 2. An autonomous process statement within VHDL-world

In the example, the simulation of the *process* statement P2 is stimulated by the external input data. During the simulation time, P2 produces some data designed for the *process* statement P1. Input data are processed in P1 and result in output data designed for P3. Finally, P3 produces external output data of the TEST1 entity. Such situation occurs frequently in common VHDL descriptions especially those that use a dataflow style for describing hardware.

The example respects all constraints of the method applicability in detail specified in Section 2:

in P1 no signal indirectly reflects the events on the other one,

in P1 no value depends on the simulation time progress,

the behavior of the entire VHDL description is not dependent on the transactions on the target signals of P1,

the behavior of the entire VHDL description is not dependent on the modifications of the values of the variables (the shared variables as well),

Proof: The proof is presented under the following assumptions:
$X_1 > 0$, $X_2 > 0$, $X_3 > 0$, $X_4 > 0$.

The functions f_1, f_2, f_3, f_4, f_5 are bijective.

There is at most one event in any TK(i). This assumption is made only to simplify the proof presented here. It turns out that the results of the proof are the same without the assumption.

Let W_{Di1} be an arbitrary waveform for Di1 (isRealWF(W_{Di1}, s) holds), where:

$$W_{Di1} = \{\langle V_{initial}^{Di1}, \hat{\tau} \rangle,$$
$$\langle V_{initial}^{Di1}, \delta_0(0) \rangle, \langle v_0^1, \delta_0(1) \rangle, ...,$$
$$\langle v_1^0, \delta_1(0) \rangle, \langle v_1^1, \delta_1(1) \rangle, ...,$$
$$\vdots$$
$$\langle v_k^0, \delta_k(0) \rangle, ...,$$
$$\vdots \qquad\qquad \}$$

Before optimization: | After optimization:

```
entity TEST1 is
  port (SEL, Di1: in Bit; Do2: out Bit);
end TEST1;
architecture Behavior of TEST1 is
  signal A, B, C: Bit;
begin
  P1: process (SEL, A, B)
  begin
  C1: case expression(SEL) is
    when '0' =>
      S1: C <= transport f₁(A) after X₁ units;
    when '1' =>
      S2: C <= transport f₂(B) after X₂ units;
  end case;
  end process P1;

  P2: process (Di1)
  begin
  ...
  S3: A<=transport f₃(Di1) after X₃ units;
  ...
  S4: B<=transport f₄(Di1) after X₄ units;
  ...
  end process P2;
  P3: process (C)
  begin
  ...
  S5: Do2 <= f₅(C);
  ...
  end process P3;
end Behavior;
```

```
entity TEST1 is
  port (SEL, Di1: in Bit; Do2: out Bit);
end TEST1;
architecture Behavior of TEST1 is
  signal A, B, C: Bit;
begin
  P4: process
  begin
  C1: case expression(SEL) is
    when '0' =>
      S1: C <= transport f₁(A) after X₁ units;
      W1: wait on SEL, A;
    when '1' =>
      S2: C <= transport f₂(B) after X₂ units;
      W2: wait on SEL, B;
  end case;
  end process P4;
  P2: process (Di1)
  begin
  ...
  S3: A <= transport f₃(Di1) after X₃ units;
  ...
  S4: B <= transport f₄(Di1) after X₄ units;
  ...
  end process P2;
  P3: process (C)
  begin
  ...
  S5: Do2 <= f₅(C);
  ...
  end process P3;
end Behavior;
```

The above equation asserts that the value of Di1 in $\hat{\tau}$ and $\delta_0(0)$ is $V_{initial}^{Di1}$ (where $V_{initial}^{Di1}$ stands for Di1.initial_value), in $\delta_0(1)$ is v_0^1 and in general, the value of Di1 in $\delta_p(q)$ is v_p^q. We define a set εv_{Di1} to be the set of all delta intervals in which the event occurs on Di1. Let:

$$\varepsilon v_{Di1} = \{\delta_{m_1}(n_1), \delta_{m_2}(n_2), ..., \delta_{m_k}(n_k)\}.$$

It follows that $V_{initial}^{Di1} \neq v_{m_1}^{n_1}$, $v_{m_1}^{n_1} \neq v_{m_2}^{n_2}, ..., v_{m_{k-1}}^{n_{k-1}} \neq v_{m_k}^{n_k}$. Further, from Assumption 3, it follows that $m_1 \neq m_2 \neq ... \neq m_k$. Hence, every element of the set εv_{Di1} stimulates P2 simulation. Assume for the time being that S3 and S4 are evaluated exclusively. Then every P2 simulation causes the S3 or S4 evaluation and in result at most one transaction is posted to signal A or B in any TK(i). Therefore it can be determined, using the methods presented in [8], that no transaction in ALL_TR(A, P2) and ALL_TR(B, P2) will be preempted. Since f_3 and f_4 are bijective then every transaction causes the event on the signal A or B respectively. Let the sets εv_A and εv_B are given by:

$$\varepsilon v_A = \{\delta_{i_1} + X_1{}^{(0)}, \delta_{i_2} + X_1{}^{(0)}, \ldots, \delta_{i_k} + X_1{}^{(0)}\},$$

$$\varepsilon v_B = \{\delta_{j_1} + X_2{}^{(0)}, \delta_{j_2} + X_2{}^{(0)}, \ldots, \delta_{j_k} + X_2{}^{(0)}\},$$

where:

$$\forall i_k + X_1, j_k + X_2 \bullet TK(i_k + X_1) \neq TK(j_k + X_2).$$

In result P2 produces the waveforms of A and B where the sets εv_A and εv_B determine delta intervals in which P1 statement is simulated.

Simultaneously the simulation of P1 is stimulated by external input signal SEL where the set εv_{SEL} is given by:

$$\varepsilon v_{SEL} = \{\delta_{r_1}(s_1), \delta_{r_2}(s_2), \ldots, \delta_{r_k}(s_k)\}.$$

From Assumption 3 it follows that:

$$\forall i_k + X_1, j_k + X_2, r_k \bullet TK(i_k + X_1) \neq TK(j_k + X_2) \neq TK(r_k).$$

The combination of all delta intervals in which P1 is simulated gives the following set:

$$\varepsilon v_{P1} = \varepsilon v_A \cup \varepsilon v_B \cup \varepsilon v_{SEL},$$

where the subset εv_{SEL} determine the trace of P1 simulation. The completely unrestricted order of delta intervals succession in the set εv_{P1} enables the generalization of our proof.

Before optimization: Every delta interval of the set εv_{P1} stimulates the *process* statement P1 simulation. The sequential *case* statement C1 determines possibilities (traces) of P1 simulation.

Assume that the simulation trace of the *process* statement P1 always goes through the first branch of *case* statement C1. Since the *process* statement P1 is sensitive to SEL, A and B, statement S1 will be evaluated in every delta interval of the set εv_{P1}. Let εv_{P1} be an arbitrary set of all delta intervals:

$$\varepsilon v_{P1} = \{\delta_0(0), \delta_{j_1}(n_1), \delta_{i_1}(m_1), \delta_{r_1}(s_1), \delta_{i_2}(m_2),$$
$$\delta_{j_2}(n_2), \delta_{r_2}(s_2), \delta_{i_3}(m_3), \ldots \quad \},$$

where:

$\delta_{i_k}(m_k)$ — denotes delta intervals in which the event occurs on the signal A;

$\delta_{j_k}(n_k)$ — denotes delta intervals in which the event occurs on the signal B;

$\delta_{r_k}(s_k)$ — denotes delta intervals in which the event occurs on the signal SEL.

Then each evaluation of the *signal assignment* statement S1 corresponds to a transaction element in ALL_TR(C, P1). Thus:

$$ALL\_TR(C,P1) = \{\left\langle V_{initial}^C, \varnothing, \tau \right\rangle, \left\langle f_1(V_{initial}^A), \varnothing, T \right\rangle, \left\langle f_1(v_{j_1}^{n_1}), \varnothing, t_1 \right\rangle,$$

$$\left\langle f_1(v_{i_1}^{m_1}), \varnothing, t_2 \right\rangle, \left\langle f_1(v_{r_1}^{s_1}), \varnothing, t_3 \right\rangle, \left\langle f_1(v_{i_2}^{m_2}), \varnothing, t_4 \right\rangle, \left\langle f_1(v_{j_2}^{n_2}), \varnothing, t_5 \right\rangle,$$

$$\left\langle f_1(v_{r_2}^{s_2}), \varnothing, t_6 \right\rangle, \left\langle f_1(v_{i_3}^{m_3}), \varnothing, t_7 \right\rangle, \ldots \qquad \}$$

where the relations:

$$meets(\tau, TK(0)), meets(T, \delta_{X_1}(0)), meets(t_1, \delta_{j_1 + X_1}(0)),$$

$$meets(t_2, \delta_{i_1 + X_1}(0)), meets(t_3, \delta_{r_1 + X_1}(0)), meets(t_4, \delta_{i_2 + X_1}(0)),$$

$$meets(t_5, \delta_{j_2 + X_1}(0)), meets(t_6, \delta_{r_2 + X_1}(0)), meets(t_7, \delta_{i_3 + X_1}(0))$$

hold. The first element $\left\langle V_{initial}^C, \varnothing, \tau \right\rangle$ is a default element present in all pre-marking set of signals that ensures that the initial value of the signal is assigned to the signal in time interval $\hat{\tau}$. The element $\left\langle f_1(V_{initial}^A), \varnothing, T \right\rangle$ is the transaction posted by the evaluation of S1 in $\delta_0(0)$. The remaining elements are transactions posted by the evaluations of S1 in succeeding intervals of the set εv_{P1}.

Since, there is at most one event in any TK(i) then no transaction in ALL_TR(C, P1) will be preempted. Therefore, it follows that ALL_TR(C, P1) = Driver(C, P1). Hence, the waveform of C that can be determined directly by examining ALL_TR(C, P1), is given by:

$$W_C = \{\left\langle V_{initial}^C, \hat{\tau} \right\rangle, \left\langle V_{initial}^C, \delta_0(0) \right\rangle, \left\langle f_1(V_{initial}^A), \delta_{X_1}(0) \right\rangle,$$

$$\left\langle f_1(v_{j_1}^{n_1}), \delta_{j_1 + X_1}(0) \right\rangle, \left\langle f_1(v_{i_1}^{m_1}), \delta_{i_1 + X_1}(0) \right\rangle, \left\langle f_1(v_{r_1}^{s_1}), \delta_{r_1 + X_1}(0) \right\rangle,$$

$$\left\langle f_1(v_{i_2}^{m_2}), \delta_{i_2 + X_1}(0) \right\rangle, \left\langle f_1(v_{j_2}^{n_2}), \delta_{j_2 + X_1}(0) \right\rangle, \left\langle f_1(v_{r_2}^{s_2}), \delta_{r_2 + X_1}(0) \right\rangle,$$

$$\left\langle f_1(v_{i_3}^{m_3}), \delta_{i_3 + X_1}(0) \right\rangle, \ldots\}$$

Since f_1 is bijective and $V_{initial}^A \neq v_{i_1}^{m_1}$, $v_{i_1}^{m_1} \neq v_{i_2}^{m_2}$, $v_{i_2}^{m_2} \neq v_{i_3}^{m_3}$, it follows that

$f_1(V_{initial}^A) \neq f_1(v_{i_1}^{m_1})$, $f_1(v_{i_1}^{m_1}) \neq f_1(v_{i_2}^{m_2})$, $f_1(v_{i_2}^{m_2}) \neq f_1(v_{i_3}^{m_3})$. Assume for the time

being that $V_{initial}^C \neq f_1(V_{initial}^A)$. It's obvious that $f_1(V_{initial}^A) = f_1(v_{j_1}^{n_1})$,

$f_1(v_{i_1}^{m_1}) = f_1(v_{r_1}^{s_1})$, $f_1(v_{i_2}^{m_2}) = f_1(v_{j_2}^{n_2}) = f_1(v_{r_2}^{s_2})$ since $V_{initial}^A = v_{j_1}^{n_1}$, $v_{i_1}^{m_1} = v_{r_1}^{s_1}$,

$v_{i_2}^{m_2} = v_{j_2}^{n_2} = v_{r_2}^{s_2}$. Then the set εv_C is given by:

$$\varepsilon v_C = \{\delta_{X_1}{}^{(0)}, \delta_{i_1} + X_1{}^{(0)}, \delta_{i_2} + X_1{}^{(0)}, \delta_{i_3} + X_1{}^{(0),...}\} .$$

Let's make the inverse assumption that the simulation trace of the *process* statement P1 always goes through the second branch of the *case* statement C1. The second branch of the unoptimized source is sensitive to the same set of signals as the first branch of C1. Consistently, let εv_{P1} be the same set of all delta intervals where events occur on the signal SEL, A and B, respectively:

$$\varepsilon v_{P1} = \{\delta_0(0), \delta_{j_1}(n_1), \delta_{i_1}(m_1), \delta_{r_1}(s_1), \delta_{i_2}(m_2),$$
$$\delta_{j_2}(n_2), \delta_{r_2}(s_2), \delta_{i_3}(m_3), ... \qquad \} .$$

Then each delta interval of εv_{P1} causes the evaluation of the *signal assignment* statement S2 and each evaluation of S2 corresponds to a transaction element in ALL_TR(C, P1). Thus:

$$\text{ALL\_TR(C, P1)} = \{\left\langle V_{initial}^C, \varnothing, \tau \right\rangle, \left\langle f_2(V_{initial}^B), \varnothing, T \right\rangle, \left\langle f_2(v_{j_1}^{n_1}), \varnothing, t_1 \right\rangle,$$

$$\left\langle f_2(v_{i_1}^{m_1}), \varnothing, t_2 \right\rangle, \left\langle f_2(v_{r_1}^{s_1}), \varnothing, t_3 \right\rangle, \left\langle f_2(v_{i_2}^{m_2}), \varnothing, t_4 \right\rangle,$$

$$\left\langle f_2(v_{j_2}^{n_2}), \varnothing, t_5 \right\rangle, \left\langle f_2(v_{r_2}^{s_2}), \varnothing, t_6 \right\rangle, \left\langle f_2(v_{i_3}^{m_3}), \varnothing, t_7 \right\rangle, ... \qquad \}$$

where the relations:

$$\text{meets}(\tau, \text{TK}(0)), \text{meets}(T, \delta_{X_2}(0)), \text{meets}(t_1, \delta_{j_1} + X_2{}^{(0)}),$$

$$\text{meets}(t_2, \delta_{i_1} + X_2{}^{(0)}), \text{meets}(t_3, \delta_{r_1} + X_2{}^{(0)}), \text{meets}(t_4, \delta_{i_2} + X_2{}^{(0)}),$$

$$\text{meets}(t_5, \delta_{j_2} + X_2{}^{(0)}), \text{meets}(t_6, \delta_{r_2} + X_2{}^{(0)}), \text{meets}(t_7, \delta_{i_3} + X_2{}^{(0)})$$

hold. Since, according to Assumption 3, there is at most one event in any TK(i) then no transaction in ALL_TR(C, P1) will be preempted. Therefore, it follows that ALL_TR(C, P1) = Driver(C, P1) and the waveform of C, which can be determined directly by examining ALL_TR(C, P1), is given by:

$$W_C = \{\langle V_{initial}^C, \hat{\tau}\rangle, \langle V_{initial}^C, \delta_0(0)\rangle, \langle f_2(V_{initial}^B), \delta_{X_2}(0)\rangle,$$

$$\langle f_2(v_{j_1}^{n_1}), \delta_{j_1 + X_2}(0)\rangle, \langle f_2(v_{i_1}^{m_1}), \delta_{i_1 + X_2}(0)\rangle,$$

$$\langle f_2(v_{r_1}^{s_1}), \delta_{r_1 + X_2}(0)\rangle, \langle f_2(v_{i_2}^{m_2}), \delta_{i_2 + X_2}(0)\rangle, \quad \cdot$$

$$\langle f_2(v_{j_2}^{n_2}), \delta_{j_2 + X_2}(0)\rangle, \langle f_2(v_{r_2}^{s_2}), \delta_{r_2 + X_2}(0)\rangle,$$

$$\langle f_2(v_{i_3}^{m_3}), \delta_{i_3 + X_2}(0)\rangle, ...\}$$

Since f_2 is bijective and $V_{initial}^B \neq v_{j_1}^{n_1}$, $v_{j_1}^{n_1} \neq v_{j_2}^{n_2}$, it follows that $f_2(V_{initial}^B) \neq f_2(v_{j_1}^{n_1})$, $f_2(v_{j_1}^{n_1}) \neq f_2(v_{j_2}^{n_2})$. Assume for the time being that $V_{initial}^C \neq f_2(V_{initial}^B)$. It's obvious that $f_2(v_{j_1}^{n_1}) = f_2(v_{i_1}^{m_1}) = f_2(v_{r_1}^{s_1}) = f_2(v_{i_2}^{m_2})$, $f_2(v_{j_2}^{n_2}) = f_2(v_{r_2}^{s_2}) = f_2(v_{i_3}^{m_3})$ since $v_{j_1}^{n_1} = v_{i_1}^{m_1} = v_{r_1}^{s_1} = v_{i_2}^{m_2}$, $v_{j_2}^{n_2} = v_{r_2}^{s_2} = v_{i_3}^{m_3}$. Then the set εv_C is given by:

$$\varepsilon v_C = \{\delta_{X_2}(0), \delta_{j_1 + X_2}(0), \delta_{j_2 + X_2}(0), ...\} .$$

The sequential *case* statement selects for executing exclusively one of a number of alternative choices, depending on the value of the expression. The definition of evaluation ε for the *case* statement was provided in Section 3. Selecting for simulation the sequence of statements enclosed in the first branch of C1 depends on the evaluation of *expression*(SEL) to value '0'. Further, the value of *expression*(SEL) depends on the signal SEL. In this connection every event on SEL may (but don't need) change the current value of the *expression*(SEL). It follows that the simulation of the first branch of C1 statement in every delta interval $\delta_{r_k}(s_k)$ may lead to changing a possibility of P1 simulation. Hence, ALL_TR(C, P1) contains transactions posted by the evaluation of S1 in every $\delta_{r_k}(s_k)$. However, selecting for simulation the sequence of statements enclosed in the second choice of C1 statement depends on the evaluation *expression*(SEL) to value '1'. Since events on SEL may (but don't need) change the current value of *expression*(SEL) to the other one then the second choice simulation in every delta interval $\delta_{r_k}(s_k)$ may lead to changing a possibility of P1 simulation. Therefore, ALL_TR(C, P1) for the second choice of C1 statement contains transactions posted by the evaluation of S2 in every $\delta_{r_k}(s_k)$.

After optimization: According to the proposed method only certain delta intervals (where effective events hold) stimulate the optimized *process* statement P4 simulation.

The sensitivity of the first branch of the optimized *case* statement C1 is limited to signals SEL and A. However, the sensitivity to signal B was eliminated from the original source. It means that S1 is evaluated in delta intervals determined by the set εv_{P4}:

$$\varepsilon v_{P4} = \varepsilon v_A \cup \varepsilon v_{Di1} .$$

Each evaluation of the statement S1 corresponds to a transaction element in ALL_TR(C, P4). P4 simulation is not stimulated in every delta interval of the entire set εv_B where events occur on the signal B. Hence ALL_TR(C, P4) is determined by the elimination of every delta interval $\delta_{j_k}(n_k)$:

$$ALL\_TR(C,P4) = \{ \left\langle V_{initial}^C, \varnothing, \tau \right\rangle, \left\langle f_1(V_{initial}^A), \varnothing, T \right\rangle, \left\langle f_1(v_{i_1}^{m_1}), \varnothing, t_1 \right\rangle , $$

$$\left\langle f_1(v_{r_1}^{s_1}), \varnothing, t_2 \right\rangle, \left\langle f_1(v_{i_2}^{m_2}), \varnothing, t_3 \right\rangle, \left\langle f_1(v_{r_2}^{s_2}), \varnothing, t_4 \right\rangle, \left\langle f_1(v_{i_3}^{m_3}), \varnothing, t_5 \right\rangle, ... \}$$

and the following relations:

$$meets(\tau, TK(0)), meets(T, \delta_{X_1}(0)), meets(t_1, \delta_{i_1 + X_1}(0)),$$

$$meets(t_2, \delta_{r_1 + X_1}(0)), meets(t_3, \delta_{i_2 + X_1}(0)), \qquad ,$$

$$meets(t_4, \delta_{r_2 + X_1}(0)), meets(t_5, \delta_{i_3 + X_1}(0))$$

hold. Similar to an unoptimized source, there is at most one event in any TK(i) and no transaction in ALL_TR(C, P4) will be preempted. Therefore, it follows that ALL_TR(C, P4) = Driver(C, P4) and the waveform of C, which can be determined directly by examining ALL_TR(C, P4), is given by:

$$W_C = \{ \left\langle V_{initial}^C, \hat{\tau} \right\rangle, \left\langle V_{initial}^C, \delta_0(0) \right\rangle, \left\langle f_1(V_{initial}^A), \delta_{X_1}(0) \right\rangle,$$

$$\left\langle f_1(v_{i_1}^{m_1}), \delta_{i_1 + X_1}(0) \right\rangle, \left\langle f_1(v_{r_1}^{s_1}), \delta_{r_1 + X_1}(0) \right\rangle,$$

$$\left\langle f_1(v_{i_2}^{m_2}), \delta_{i_2 + X_1}(0) \right\rangle, \left\langle f_1(v_{r_2}^{s_2}), \delta_{r_2 + X_1}(0) \right\rangle,$$

$$\left\langle f_1(v_{i_3}^{m_3}), \delta_{i_3 + X_1}(0) \right\rangle, ... \}$$

Notice that ALL_TR(C, P4) contains transactions posted by the evaluation of S1 in every delta interval $\delta_{r_k}(s_k)$ of the entire set εv_{SEL} where events occur on the signal SEL. Since the simulations in δ_{r_k} (s_k) are not eliminated then possibilities of the trace simulation changing are maintained.

Since f_1 is bijective and $V_{initial}^A \neq v_{i_1}^{m_1}$, $v_{i_1}^{m_1} \neq v_{i_2}^{m_2}$, $v_{i_2}^{m_2} \neq v_{i_3}^{m_3}$, it follows that $f_1(V_{initial}^A) \neq f_1(v_{i_1}^{m_1})$, $f_1(v_{i_1}^{m_1}) \neq f_1(v_{i_2}^{m_2})$, $f_1(v_{i_2}^{m_2}) \neq f_1(v_{i_3}^{m_3})$. Assume for the time being that $V_{initial}^C \neq f_1(V_{initial}^A)$. It's obvious that $f_1(v_{i_1}^{m_1}) = f_1(v_{r_1}^{s_1})$, $f_1(v_{i_2}^{m_2}) = f_1(v_{r_2}^{s_2})$ since $v_{i_1}^{m_1} = v_{r_1}^{s_1}$, $v_{i_2}^{m_2} = v_{r_2}^{s_2}$. Then the set εv_C is given by:

$$\varepsilon v_C = \{\delta_{X_1}(0), \delta_{i_1} + X_1(0), \delta_{i_2} + X_1(0), \delta_{i_3} + X_1(0),...\},$$

and the equivalence to εv_C before the optimization is established.

Making the inverse assumption that the simulation trace of the *process* statement P4 always goes through the second branch of the optimized *case* statement C1, the sensitivity is limited to signals SEL and B. However, the sensitivity to the signal A was eliminated from the original source. It means that S2 is evaluated in delta intervals determined by the set εv_{P4}:

$$\varepsilon v_{P4} = \varepsilon v_B \cup \varepsilon v_{Di1}.$$

Each evaluation of the statement S2 corresponds to a transaction element in ALL_TR(C, P4). P4 simulation is not stimulated in every delta interval of the entire set εv_A where events occur on the signal A. Hence ALL_TR(C, P4) is determined by elimination of every delta interval $\delta_{i_k}(m_k)$:

$$ALL\_TR(C,P4) = \{ \left\langle V_{initial}^C, \varnothing, \tau \right\rangle, \left\langle f_2(V_{initial}^B), \varnothing, T \right\rangle, \left\langle f_2(v_{j_1}^{n_1}), \varnothing, t_1 \right\rangle,$$
$$\left\langle f_2(v_{r_1}^{s_1}), \varnothing, t_3 \right\rangle, \left\langle f_2(v_{j_2}^{n_2}), \varnothing, t_5 \right\rangle, \left\langle f_2(v_{r_2}^{s_2}), \varnothing, t_6 \right\rangle,... \}$$

and the following relations:

$$meets(\tau, TK(0)), meets(T, \delta_{X_2}(0)), meets(t_1, \delta_{j_1} + X_2(0)),$$
$$meets(t_2, \delta_{r_1} + X_2(0)), meets(t_3, \delta_{j_2} + X_2(0)), meets(t_4, \delta_{r_2} + X_2(0)),....$$

hold. Similar to an unoptimized source, there is at most one event in any TK(i) and no transaction in ALL_TR(C, P4) will be preempted. Therefore, it follows that ALL_TR(C, P4) = Driver(C, P4) and the waveform of C, which can be determined directly by examining ALL_TR(C, P4), is given by:

$$W_C = \{ \left\langle V_{initial}^C, \hat{\tau} \right\rangle, \left\langle V_{initial}^C, \delta_0(0) \right\rangle, \left\langle f_2(V_{initial}^B), \delta_{X_2}(0) \right\rangle,$$

$$\left\langle f_2(v_{j_1}^{n_1}), \delta_{j_1 + X_2}(0) \right\rangle, \left\langle f_2(v_{r_1}^{s_1}), \delta_{r_1 + X_2}(0) \right\rangle,$$

$$\left\langle f_2(v_{j_2}^{n_2}), \delta_{j_2 + X_2}(0) \right\rangle, \left\langle f_2(v_{r_2}^{s_2}), \delta_{r_2 + X_2}(0) \right\rangle, \dots \}$$

Since transactions posted by the evaluation of S2 in $\delta_{r_k}(s_k)$ are not eliminated then possibilities of the trace simulation changing are also maintained.

Further, since f_2 is bijective and $V_{initial}^B \ne v_{j_1}^{n_1}$, $v_{j_1}^{n_1} \ne v_{j_2}^{n_2}$, it follows that $f_2(V_{initial}^B) \ne f_2(v_{j_1}^{n_1})$, $f_2(v_{j_1}^{n_1}) \ne f_2(v_{j_2}^{n_2})$. Assume for the time being that $V_{initial}^C \ne f_2(V_{initial}^B)$. It's obvious that $f_2(v_{j_1}^{n_1}) = f_2(v_{r_1}^{s_1})$, $f_2(v_{j_2}^{n_2}) = f_2(v_{r_2}^{s_2})$ since $v_{j_1}^{n_1} = v_{r_1}^{s_1}$, $v_{j_2}^{n_2} = v_{r_2}^{s_2}$. Then the set εv_C is given by:

$$\varepsilon v_C = \{ \delta_{X_2}(0), \delta_{j_1 + X_2}(0), \delta_{j_2 + X_2}(0), \dots \},$$

and the equivalence to εv_C before the optimization is established.

The equivalence of the sets εv_C before and after the optimization results in the simulation of P3 in the same delta intervals. Since the form of P3 and the predicate isRealWF(W, C) of the source signal C for Di3 are maintained then it may be asserted that the Driver(Di3, C) is similar in both VHDL descriptions.

Consider the set εv_C produced by the evaluation of the first branch of C1. Since P3 is simulated within delta intervals given by:

$$\varepsilon v_C = \{ \delta_{X_1}(0), \delta_{i_1 + X_1}(0), \delta_{i_2 + X_1}(0), \delta_{i_3 + X_1}(0), \dots \},$$

before and after the optimization then each delta interval of εv_C causes evaluation of the *signal assignment* statement S5. Each evaluation of S5 corresponds to a transaction element in ALL_TR(Do2, P3). Since the predicate isRealWF(W, C) is similar in both VHDL descriptions and C is a source for Do2 then ALL_TR(Do2, P3) are similar before and after the optimization. From Assumption 3 it follows that no transaction in ALL_TR(Do2, P3) will be preempted. Therefore the Driver(Do2, P3) is similar in both VHDL descriptions.

The proof is similar for the set εv_C produced by the evaluation of the second branch of C1. Since the *signal assignment* statement S5 is evaluated in the same delta intervals determined by εv_C and the predicate isRealWF(W, C) of the source signal C for Do2 holds, then ALL_TR(Do2, P3) are similar in both VHDL descriptions. It follows that Driver(Do2, P3) is similar before and after the optimization.

5. CONCLUSION

The offer of a new method to optimize VHDL sources targeted towards the sequential *case* statement has been presented in the paper. Using the Dynamic Model, we have provided the proof of the soundness of our VHDL behavioral sources optimization technique. In general, our optimization technique eliminates ineffective VHDL events without modifications of existing VHDL design entities simulators. The method can be implemented as an additional tool or build-in automatic optimizer for existing VHDL simulators to decrease the time of the simulation. Some experiments carried out to evaluate the effectiveness of the proposed method indicated positive and negative speedups of optimized sources. For a lot of sources from Synopsis and Aldec libraries being optimized and simulated at various stimuli generated by means of the Active-VHDL tool, speedups have varied from -1.7 to 2.5. Therefore, there is a need to determine the conditions that will permit to answer the question when the optimization method gives positive speedup, i.e. when the time of the simulation of an optimized source is less than that of an original one. Presently authors are carrying out research to get such conditions and intend to create an analyzer predicting the speedup of an optimized VHDL source according to the suggested optimization method.

6. REFERENCES

[1] S. Devadas, S. Malik, K. Keutzer, A. Wang, „Event Suppression: Improving the Efficiency of timing simulation for synchronous digital circuits", *IEEE Trans. Computer Aided Design*, vol. 13, pp. 814-822, June 1994.

[2] R. Razdan, G. P. Bishoff, E. G. Ulrich, „Clock suppression techniques for synchronous circuits", *IEEE Trans. Computer Aided Design*, vol. 12, pp. 1457-1556, October 1993.

[3] V. Beletskyy and K. Kraska, "A package for optimization of behavioral VHDL programs", in *Proceedings of the IASTED International Conference, Applied Informatics*, Innsbruck, Austria, February 14-17, 2000, pp. 170-173.

[4] *IEEE standard VHDL Language Reference Manual. IEEE std.1076-1993*, The Institute of Electrical and Electronic Engineers, Inc., 1994.

[5] P.J. Ashenden, "The Designer's Guide to VHDL", Morgan Kaufmann Publishing, San Francisco, 1996.

[6] J. F. Allen, "Maintaining knowledge about temporal intervals", *Communications of the ACM*, vol. 26, pp. 832-843, November 1983.

[7] K. I. Park and K. H. Park, "Event Suppression by Optimizing VHDL Programs", *IEEE Transactions on Computer-Aided Design of Integrated Circuits and Systems*, vol. 17, no. 8, 1998.

[8] S. L. Pandey, K. Umamageswaran and P. A. Wilsey, "VHDL Semantics and Validating Transformations", *IEEE Transactions on Computer-Aided Design of Integrated Circuits and Systems*, vol. XX, no. Y, 1999.

[9] "VHDL for the ASIC Synthesizer User Guide", COMPASS Design Automation, January 1994.

[10] V. Beletskyy and K. Kraska, "Validating VHDL behavioral programs optimization methods", in *Proceedings of the ACS'2000 International Conference*, Szczecin, Poland, 2000, pp. 171-179.

[11] J. Hartmanis and R. E. Stearns, *Algebraic Structure Theory of Sequential Machines*, Englewood Cliffs, NJ:Prentice-Hall, 1966.

Algorithms of Generation Boolean Equations for a Multiplication Operation

TOMASZ WIERCINSKI
Faculty of Computer Science & Information Systems, Technical University of Szczecin,
49, Zolnierska st., 71-210 Szczecin, Poland

Abstract: The article presents a critical analysis of existing methods for multiplication operations. It shows a development necessary for them to be used in a programmable integrated circuit. This extension mainly ranges a method for the generation of a result in an easy way to optimize set of Boolean equations. Finally there are two methods described of generation of logical equations for the multiplication instruction destined for integrated circuits synthesis. Both of them deal with integer type arguments, but there are two variables in the case of the first algorithm and a variable with a constant value in the case of the second one. The result of those processes is a product represented by a set of Boolean equations that describes a designed logical unit. Every bit of the result is represented by a logical equation. There are also temporary variables created during compilation to store partial equations. The paper also describes problems that appear during the optimization the algorithms presented. It estimates the number of generated equations and compilation time.

Key words: VHDL language, Boolean equations.

1. INTRODUCTION

The algorithms described in this paper are dedicated to a VHDL compiler created at the Faculty of Computer Science & Information Systems of the Technical University of Szczecin. The compiler generates the set of Boolean equations that describes a synthesisable logical unit. There are two main reasons for using that method:

- Boolean equations may be optimized in an easy way (it allows to decrease a number of elements of a unit),
- Boolean equations may be simply converted to logical gates that integrated circuits are made of.

Arguments of both algorithms are integer type but the difference between them is that one of them deals with variables of an unknown value and the second one works with a variable and a constant value. There are temporary variables created during compilation to store partial equations. Every bit of the result is represented by Boolean equations composed of bits of arguments and temporary variables. The maximal number of bits for storing an integer variable is 32.

There are several methods for the binary multiplication operation but they can not be directly used to build algorithms that are going to be considered. The above methods must be modified to operate on symbolic variables and mainly to generate Boolean equations.

2.   MULTIPLICATION OF BINARY NUMBERS

A multiplication is mostly realized as a cycle of additions and shifts that the number and order depend on the value of a multiplier. A basic method for the multiplication is a sequential algorithm based on computing sequential partial products $x_i A$ where $A = \{a_0,...,a_m\}$ is a left shifted multiplicand and x_i is an i-th number of a multiplier $X = \{x_0,...,x_m\}$ and finally adding them up [1] (Figure 1). The shift of the multiplicand is equal to the weight of an i-th multiplier number x_i.

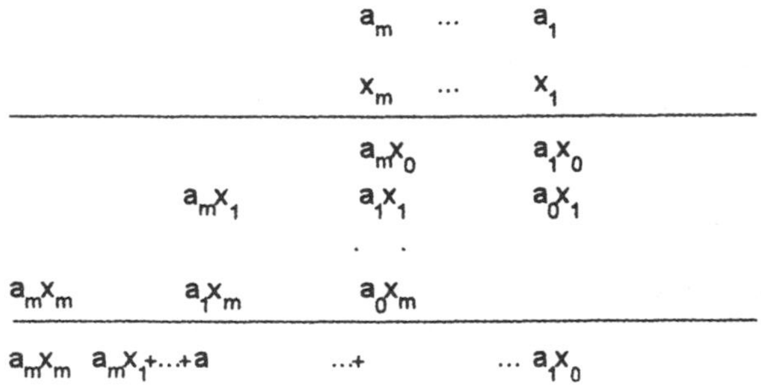

$$
\begin{array}{cccccc}
 & & & a_m & \cdots & a_1 \\
 & & & x_m & \cdots & x_1 \\
\hline
 & & & a_m x_0 & & a_1 x_0 \\
 & & a_m x_1 & a_1 x_1 & & a_0 x_1 \\
 & & & \cdot \quad \cdot & & \\
a_m x_m & a_1 x_m & & a_0 x_m & & \\
\hline
a_m x_m & a_m x_1 + ... + a & & ... + & & ... a_1 x_0 \\
\end{array}
$$

Fig. 1. Sequential method for a multiplication

A modification of the above method is an add-and-shift algorithm that based on an addition of the product Ax_i to a partial sum S_i at each step to compute the next sum S_{i+1} [2] (Figure 2). According to the above, the partial sum has the following form:

$$ S_{i+1} = S_i + x_i \beta^i A, \qquad i = 0,1,...,m-1, \qquad S_1 = 0. $$

2.1   Multiplication of signed numbers

It is necessary to modify the sequential algorithm of the binary multiplication for multiplying signed numbers represented in the second complement code. The first modification is to expand a partial sum on the left side using the sign bit of a multiplicand before adding it to a shifted multiplicand at each step. The second modification concerns the case of a negative multiplier. It needs to subtract a shifted multiplicand instead of adding it to the previous partial sum in the last step of computing [2]. Generally we have to consider the following four cases [3]:

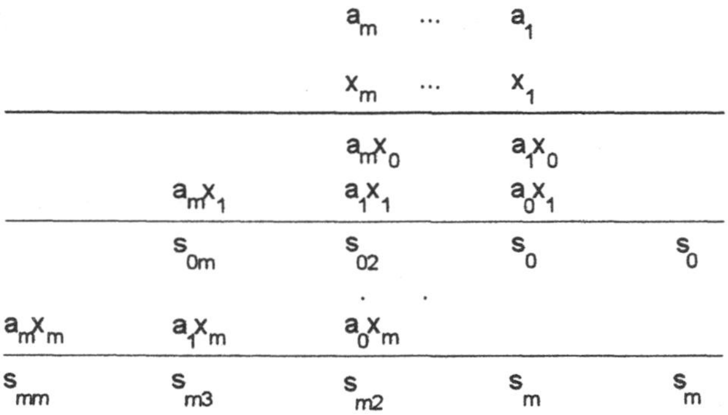

$$
\begin{array}{ccccc}
 & & a_m & \cdots & a_1 \\
 & & x_m & \cdots & x_1 \\
\hline
 & & a_m x_0 & & a_1 x_0 \quad a_1 x_0 \\
 & a_m x_1 & a_1 x_1 & & a_0 x_1 \\
\hline
 & s_{0m} & s_{02} & & s_0 \qquad s_0 \\
a_m x_m & a_1 x_m & a_0 x_m & & \\
s_{mm} & s_{m3} & s_{m2} & s_m & s_m
\end{array}
$$

Fig. 2. Modified algorithm of a multiplication

1. both arguments are positive, the sequential algorithm does not undergo changes,
2. a multiplicand is negative and a multiplier is positive we have to fill every partial sum up with a sign bit of the multiplicand,
3. a multiplicand is positive and a multiplier is negative, we have to subtract a left shifted multiplicand instead of adding it to a partial sum at the last step of computing,
4. both arguments are negative, we have to perform steps 2,3 both sequentially.

3. ALGORITHMS DESCRIPTION

There are two algorithms built for the multiplication operation which are extensions of the sequential method dedicated to the second complement numbers. Arguments of the first of them (Algorithm 1) are a variable or signal of an unknown value and a constant value.

The second algorithm (Algorithm 2) deals with arguments that both are variables or signals. In case of the first method there is a possibility to optimize a result that depends on a reduction of a number of equations and a time of compilation. If we know the value of a multiplier we can generate less number of equations and finally built a simpler logical unit. An advantage of using this method is exposed when a constant multiplier has some parts that consist of bits equal to 0. In this case we may save a number of shifts instead of generating equations for partial sums equal to 0 and equations for shifting these sums to the right. The stored shifts are realized (there are equations generated for them) just before computing a sum for the next bit of the multiplier equal to '1'. The above method does not change a value of a result.

In case of the second algorithm we do not know values of arguments so we can not skip needless computations and reduce a number of equations.

When the number of bits of a partial sum exceeds a range (32 bits) it is cut off to a maximal value and a multiplicand is decreased by one bit as well.

ALGORITHM 1.
1.   Change the order of arguments for a multiplier to be a constant value.
2.   If the multiplier value is equal to zero, assign zero to the result
     result = 0
3.   If the multiplier value is equal to 1, assign a multiplicand value *op1* to the result
     result = op1
4.   If the multiplier value is equal to −1 assign negative multiplicand value to the result
     result = !op1 + 1
5.   In other cases
     5.1. The number of multiplicand bits is equal to *op1BitsNr*
     5.2. The number of multiplier bits is equal to *op2BitsNr*
     5.3. Assign zero to shifts of a partial sum *shrNr*
          shrNr = 0
     5.4. Initial cut of a multiplicand *op1Shl* is equal to *op1BitsNr-1*
          op1Shl = op1BitsNr-1
     5.5. Generate equations for *i*-th bit of a multiplier *op2BitsNr-1 >= i > 0*
          5.5.1. If the value of i-th multiplier bit is equal to zero, increase the number of shifts *shrN*
          5.5.2. In another case if *i*-th bit of a multiplier is equal to 1
                  5.5.2.1. If this is the first occurrence of '1'
                           5.5.2.1.1. If there are not other shifts (*shrN=0*), a partial sum is equal to multiplicand value
                           5.5.2.1.2. Else
                           a) If *op1BitsNr+shrN* is less, then 32 assign *shrNr* left shifted and filled in '0' bits multiplicand to a partial sum
                           -   The number of a partial sum value is equal to
                               outBitsNr = op1BitsNr + shrNr
                           b) Else if op1BitsNr+shrNr > 32
                           -   Reduce a multiplicand to *(op1BitsNr+shrNr)-32* most significant bits and expand it by *shrNr* at the right side
                           -   Assign the above value to a partial sum
                           -   The value of shift *op1Shl* is
                               op1Shl = 32 – shrNr
                           -   The number of partial sum bits is equal to
                               outBitsNr = 32
                           5.5.2.1.3. Increase *shrNr*
                  5.5.2.2. In another case
                           5.5.2.2.1. If *shrNr <> 0*
                           a) If *outBitsNr+shrNr* is more then 32
                           -   Shift a partial sum by *(outBitsNr+shrNr)-32*
                           -   Decrease a cut *op1Shl* according to formula:
                               op1Shl = op1Shl – (shrNr + outBitsNr– 32)
                           -   The number of partial sum bits is 32

b) Else
- Shift a partial sum by *shrNr*
- The number of partial sum bits is equal to
  $outBitsNr = outBitsNr + shrNr$
  5.5.2.2.2. Add a cutting multiplicand to a partial sum
  $tmpRes = tmpRes + op1[0, op1Shl]$
  5.5.2.2.3. The number of shifts *shrNr* is equale to 1
5.6. If *shrNr* <> 0 shift a partial sum and expand it by multiplicand sign bit
  5.6.1. If *outBitsNr + shrNr > 32*
    5.6.1.1. *shrNr = outBitsNr + shrNr – 32*
    5.6.1.2. A cut *op1Shl = op1Shl - (shrNr + outBitsNr - 32)*
5.7. If a multiplier is negative
  5.7.1. Compute the negative value of a multiplicand including a cut *op1Shl*
  $unOp1 = !op1[0, op1Shl] + 1$
  5.7.2. Add *unOp1* to a partial sum
  $tmpRes = tmpRes + unOp1$
5.8. The result is equal to *tmpRes*
  $result = tmpRes$

ALGORITHM 2.
1. The number of multiplicand *op1* bits is equal to *op1BitsNr*
2. The number of multiplier *op2* bits is equal to *op2BitsNr*
3. If the number of multiplicand bits is less, then 32
    3.1. The initial value of a partial sum is equal to a multiplicand value expanded by the sign bit of a multiplicand and multiplied by the less significant bit of a multiplier
    $tmpRes = (op1Sign\_op1) \& op2(0)$
    3.2. The number of partial sum bits is
    $outBitsNr = op1BitsNr + 1$
    3.3. The cut of multiplicand *op1Shl=op1BitsNr-1*
4. In other cases
    4.1. The value of partial sum is equal to a multiplicand multiplied by the less significant bit of a multiplier
    $tmpRes = op1 \& op2(0)$
    4.2. The number of partial sum bits is
    $outBitsNr = op1BitsNr$
    4.3. The cut of a multiplicand
    $op1Shl=op1BitsNr–2$
5. Generate equations for *i*-th bit of a multiplier *1<= i < op2BitsNr-1*
    5.1. If the number of result bits is less, then 32 decrease the number of multiplicand bits
    5.2. If *op1Shl > 0*
      5.2.1. Multiply a multiplicand by *i*-th bit of a multiplier
      $mulOp1 = op1[0, op1Shl] \& op2(i)$
      5.2.2. Add a product to a partial sum
      $tmpRes = tmpRes + mulOp1$

5.2.3.   Else break the loop

5.2.4.   If the number of partial sum bits is less then 32 expand the sum by multiplicand sign bit multiplied by the logical sum of multiplier bits from *0* to *i*

tmpRes=(op1Sign&(op2(0)|...|op2(i)))_tmpRes

6.   If the number of a sum is less then 32 cut multiplicand bits off
op1Shl--

7.   If *op1Shl > 0*

7.1.   Compute the negative value of a multiplicand in range *[0, op1Shl]*
unOp1 = !op1[0, op1Shl]+1

7.2.   Multiply *unOp1* by the sign bit of a multiplier
mulUnOp1 = unOp1 & op2(op2BitsNr-1)

7.3.   Add *mulUnOp1* to a partial sum
tmpRes = tmpRes + mulUnOp1

8.   Check if a multiplier is not equal to zero

9.   *notEqu = op2(0)|...|op2(op2BitsNr-1)*

10.   The result is
result = notEqu & tmpRes

4.   TESTS AND ANALYSIS OF THE ALGORITHMS IMPLEMENTATION RESULTS

For the compiler, two criterions have the greatest importance: the number of generated equations and the time of their generation.

4.1   Estimation of equations number depending on an amount of arguments bits

In case of the algorithm 2 the number of generated equations depends on the amount of bits of arguments in logarithmic way ($O(log_2 n)$) when the number of result bits is more then 32 and it is necessary to cut them off at each computation step. A difference between the amount of equations at the current and the next step decreases step by step because we do not need to generate equations for bits we cut off. It can be described by the below formula:

$$R_0 = P$$
$$R_1 = R_0 + \Delta_1$$
$$R_2 = R_1 + \Delta_2, \text{ where } \Delta_2 = \Delta_1 - S$$
$$R_3 = R_2 + \Delta_3, \text{ where } \Delta_3 = \Delta_2 - S = \Delta_1 - 2S$$
$$\ldots$$
$$R_n = R_{n-1} + \Delta_n, \text{ where } \Delta_n = \Delta_{n-1} - S = \Delta_1 - (n-1)S$$

R_i – the amount of equations for the i-th bits number,

P- the amount of equations for the minimal bits number,
Δ_i – a difference between bits number in *i*-th and *i-1*-th steps,
S – the number of reduction difference Δ at each step.

If result bits number is less then 32, an amount of generated equations increase in exponential way $(O(2^n))$ in case of modification of the multiplier range:

$$R_0 = P$$
$$R_1 = R_0 + \Delta_1$$
$$R_2 = R_1 + \Delta_2, \text{where } \Delta_2 = \Delta_1 + S$$
$$R_3 = R_2 + \Delta_3, \text{where } \Delta_3 = \Delta_2 + S = \Delta_1 + 2S$$
$$\dots$$
$$R_n = R_{n-1} + \Delta_n, \text{where } \Delta_n = \Delta_{n-1} + S = \Delta_1 + (n-1)S$$

and linear $(O(n))$ in the case of modification of the multiplicand range:

$$R_0 = P$$
$$R_1 = R_0 + \Delta_1$$
$$R_2 = R_1 + \Delta_1$$
$$R_3 = R_2 + \Delta_1$$
$$\dots$$
$$R_n = R_{n-1} + \Delta_1$$

In the event of the algorithm 1 the number of equations do not depend on the bits of arguments but on the value of the multiplier and to be more exact on the number of multiplier bits equal to '0'. For example, in the case of multiplication of 4-bits argument by 17-bits value –65535 (10000000000000001) which has only two '1' bits a size of the result file amounts to about 4 kB. If we replace the value of the multiplier with variable composed of the same number of bits and we use the algorithm 2, an amount of the generated equations will rise to about 40 kB that is 10 times. The result file of the multiplication of 4-bits variable by 17-bits value –65533 (10000000000000011) consisted of three '1' bits has about 5 kB size.

4.2 Time of compilation

The time of a multiplication operation of 4-bits variable by 17-bits variable according to algorithm 2 require about 20% of a whole compilation time. It speeds up about 10 times to multiply 4-bits variable by 17-bits value –65535 (10000000000000001) using algorithm 1. If we replace previous value with 65535 (01111111111111111) the generation time of equations rises to about 20 % like in algorithm 2. It means that there is no acceleration in the last example according to the assumption described above.

5.   CONCLUSION

In the article the algorithms of multiplication for the VHDL compiler has been described that generate a result in a set of Boolean equations used to simulate and synthesise programmable FPGA integrated circuits. It was also specified by the reason that the processing algorithms must be specified on the arguments type. The solution as it turned out was correct and justifiable because it allows to reduce considerably a number of generated equations and to speed up the multiplication operation when a multiplier is a constant value.

6.   REFERENCES

[1] Boleslaw Pochopien: Arytmetyka Systemow Cyfrowych, Wydawnictwo Politechniki Sląskiej, Gliwice 1997
[2] Janusz Biernat: Arytmetyka Komputerow, Wydawnictwo Naukowe PWN, Warszawa 1996
[3] Charles H. Roth, Jr.: Digital Systems Design Using VHDL, PWS Publishing Company 1998
[4] IEEE standard VHDL Language Reference Manual, IEE std 1076-1993, The Institute (Electrical and Electronic Engineers Inc., 1994

Consideration of Task's Deadline for Scheduling Method with Used Processors Limitation

KOICHI KASHIWAGI, SHIN-YA KOBAYASHI
Department of Computer Science, Faculty of Engineering, Ehime University

Abstract: Task scheduling is one of the distinguishing features of parallel programming versus sequential one. Scheduling technique is essential to high performance computing. Scheduling to the processors is crucial for optimizing performance. The objective of scheduling is to minimize the overall completion time or schedule the length of the parallel program. For example, in CP/MISF, when there are available tasks and idle processors, these tasks are allocated to the idle processors even if this allocation shortens processing time a little. On the other hand, this allocation decreases processors operating ratio unfortunately. For improvement of processors operating ratio, there is the limitation method of used processors, which we have proposed. In this method, we calculate a limitation from the size of task, the critical path, the earliest starting time, and the latest completion time. Available processors are limited to the limitation. As a result, processors operating ratio has been improved with limiting the number of processors which can be used. On the other hand, processing time increases a little. Its reason is that some of tasks have not been allocated even if they reach the deadline. The deadline of each task is defined as the latest starting time. In this paper, we propose new method that achieves shorter processing time than the original limitation method. This method always allocated tasks at once even if the number of used processors is equal to or more than the limitation when they reach the deadline. By this method, the improvement of processors operating ratio is possible without the increase in processing time. For example, we achieve processors operating ratio about 2 times more for random generated sets of tasks. It indicates that our method brings the significant improvement of processors operating ratio for a multi-processor system.

Key words: Task Scheduling, Operating Ratio, Processing Time

1.   INTRODUCTION

First, we explain the target of multi-processor system. Job that is enterd by a user is divided into several tasks. The scheduling algorithm allocates these tasks to processors. The number of processors that are necessary for executing tasks is determined by the scheduling algorithm. All the processors that are allocated for tasks are exclusively reserved during the tasks are being executed.

In general, the more processors are, the less processing time is. On the other hand, the increment of the used processors decreases the operating ratio of processors.

For example, in CP/MISF [1], if there are ready tasks and idle processors, these tasks are allocated to the idle processors even if this allocation shortens processing time a little. On the other hand, some processors work only for a few time intervals during tasks are being executed. This situation brings unfortunately decrement of the operating ratio of processors. The additional processor does not improve the processing time but only reduces the operating ratio of processors.

There is the limitation method [2,3,4] that we have proposed to solve the problem. In this method, the limitation is applied to the number of available processors and some scheduling method is performed. By using this method for pseudo tasks, the operating ratio has been improved in several times. But in 1 % of cases the processing time was increased.

So, we propose the new deadline method. The latest starting time, explained in Section 2.3, of each task of tasks set is defined as a deadline of its allocation. Even if each task becomes the latest starting time, when it is not assigned, it is exceptionally allocated to the processor, which can not be used by the limitation. Consequently, the processing time becomes the shortest one. That is, when the job as which it is required mostly required for processing is completed by the critical path (*CP*) [5] is processed, the deadline method is effective.

2.   DEADLINE ALGORITHM

2.1   Property of tasks set

Let $T = \{T_1, T_2, \cdots, T_N$ denote a set of tasks T_i into which job is divided, where N is a number of tasks. All tasks have one or more predecessors and successors except for start tasks and end tasks. Let s_i be a task size of T_i, i.e., it is an amount of computation needed by T_i.

The set of tasks is conveniently represented as a directed acyclic graph called a task graph[1]. An arc (i, j) between two tasks T_i and T_j specifies that T_i must be

[1] Albert Y. Zomaya, PARALLERL & DISTRIBUTED COMPUTING HANDBOOK, New York: McGraw-Hill, 1996.

completed before T_j begins. Then, T_i is one of the predecessors of T_j and T_j is one of successors of T_i. Now pl_i denotes the longest path among paths from T_i to the end task in the task graph. The critical path (*CP*) of set of tasks is the longest path among pl_i in the task graph, i.e., it is the maximum of pl_i.

The task can be processed only after all predecessors of the task have been done, and then each task cannot start before certain time. The lower bound of this time when available processors are enough is called the 'earliest starting time (*EST*)'. We refer est_i as the earliest starting time of T_i. On the other hand, task must be done before certain time in order to achieve the shortest processing time of set of tasks. In other words, if task has not finished by the certain time, it takes longer time than CP to complete execution of all tasks. We call the time the 'latest completion time (*LCT*)' and lct_i is referred to as the latest completion time of T_i.

2.2 Limitation of available processors

Now we define an 'execution probability' of each task as a probability if the task is processed or not at any instant. Anyway, if the execution probability of T_i is 1 at some point, T_i must be processed in order to achieve the shortest processing time of set of tasks.

Its *EST* and *LCT* can determine the execution probability of task. We let $f_i(t)$ be the task execution probability of T_i at time t.

The $f_i(t)$ is equal to zero before the est_i or after the lct_i, and the $f_i(t)$ is not equal to zero between the est_i and the lct_i. Next, in case of $lct_i - est_i \leq 2s_i$, the $f_i(t)$ is determined by the following formula (see Figure 1).

$$f_i(t) \equiv \begin{cases} 0 & : \ t < est_i, lct_i \leq t \\ \dfrac{t - est_i}{lct_i - est_i - s_i} & : \ est_i \leq t < lct_i - s_i \\ 1 & : \ lct_i - s_i \leq t < est_i + s_i \\ \dfrac{lct_i - t}{lct_i - est_i - s_i} & : \ est_i + s_i \leq t < lct_i \end{cases}$$

Similarly, in case of $lct_i - est_i > 2s_i$, the $f_i(t)$ becomes the following (see Figure 2).

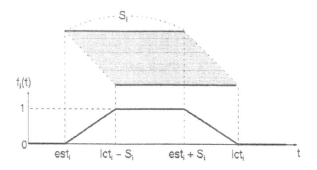

$$\text{Fig. 1. } [t \text{ vs. } f_i(t) \ (lct_i - est_i \leq 2s_i)]$$

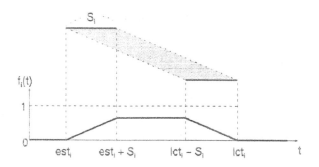

$$\text{Fig. 2. } [t \text{ vs. } f_i(t) \ (lct_i - est_i > 2s_i)]$$

$$
f_i(t) \equiv
\begin{cases}
0 & : \ t < est_i, \, lct_i \leq t \\[2mm]
\dfrac{t - est_i}{lct_i - est_i - s_i} & : \ est_i \leq t < est_i + s_i \\[2mm]
\dfrac{s_i}{lct_i - est_i - s_i} & : \ est_i + s_i \leq t < lct_i - s_i \\[2mm]
\dfrac{lct_i - t}{lct_i - est_i - s_i} & : \ lct_i - s_i \leq t < lct_i
\end{cases}
$$

So, we can consider the summation of the $f_i(t)$ from $i = 1$ to N, i.e.,

$$\sum_{i=1}^{N} f_i(t)$$

as expectation of required number of processors at time t in order to complete set of tasks for the shortest time. $F(t)$ is referred to as

$$\sum_{i=1}^{N} f_i(t).$$

In other words, at time t, the number of tasks that are processed is expected to be $F(t)$. And we make the maximum of $F(t)$ from time 0 to time CP by the limitation of available processors.

2.3 Release of the limitation

First, we define the time that subtracts task size from LCT as the 'latest starting time (LST)' and $lct_i - s_i$ is referred to as lst_i. All tasks $\{T_1, T_2, \cdots, T_N\}$ are allocated at each lst_i at the latest when processors exist infinitely and communication time is zero, then the processing time should be CP. In the limitation method, some tasks may not be allocated to available processors at each lst_i by the limitation. When such tasks exist, processing time increases from CP.

So, to task T_i which was not allocated at lst_i, the limitation is cancelled temporarily and it is allocated to the processor which could not be used by the limitation, at lst_i. In this way, since all tasks are allocated by LST at the latest, the processing time becomes CP. This is the fundamental part of the deadline method.

Next, we consider the following two methods for the use of processors outside the limitation.

The first method enables to use of these processors, only while processing the task allocated to them. We call this method A. Another one adds these processors to available processors. That is, it means that the increase in the limitation after performing allocation by the deadline method takes place. We call this method B.

3. EVALUATION

3.1 Evaluation value

We apply our deadline method to some actual tasks and pseudo tasks that are generated with random series in order to evaluate our method. We use CP/MISF as the scheduling algorithm. We evaluate the operating ratio of processors of the method A and B. In the deadline method, operating ratio is determined by the limitation and number of using processors outside the limitation. Operating ratio is concretely calculated by the following formula,

$$operating\ ratio = \frac{\sum s_i}{CP \times (Lim + Out)},$$

where Lim is the limitation and Out is the number of processors used outside the limitation.

3.2   About actual tasks

We apply our deadline method to actual three jobs: FFT [7], Runge-Kutta methods for solving ordinary differential equations (ODE), and Inverse Kinematics Equation (IKE) [8]. We show those properties of them in Table 1.

	FFT	Runge-Kutta	IKE
$\sum S_i$	2419.386	5765.283	778.500
CP	183.881	2316.485	314.1
Lim	30	5	5

Tab. 1. Property of actual tasks

3.3   About pseudo tasks

We apply our deadline method to pseudo tasks that are generated with random series in order to evaluate our method. We use CP/MISF as the scheduling algorithm and five types of sets of pseudo tasks for evaluation. We create the set of pseudo tasks with the following algorithm.

First of all, we create set of fundamental tasks. This set of tasks is prescribed by four parameters, *Num, bp, ep* and *prob. Num* is a number of tasks. Task T_i might depend on task T_j $(i + bp \le j < i + bp + ep)$ at probability *prob.* Anyway, task T_i has $(ep - 1) \times (prob)$ successors expectantly.

Secondly, duplicates are made using two parameters *dupRatio* and *dupNum*. $Num \times dupRatio$ tasks are chosen and those averages of *dupNum* duplicates are made. The duplicated tasks has the same predecessors and successors that the original task has. This duplication means a loop iteration.

However, this tasks generation algorithm has an unacceptable problem. The problem is that tasks are divided into some groups that are independent of each other; moreover there might be a task that has no predecessor and successor.

In order to avoid this problem, we impose 2 types restrictions on the tasks generation algorithm. The first one is that each task is forced to have one successor at least except for the end task, only. The second one is that each task is forced to have one predecessor or successor at least.

The first restriction (named restriction A) can avoid the problem completely, but the second restriction (named restriction B) can avoid only a solo task problem. In other words, even if the second restriction is applied, there are several independent sets of tasks, but it rarely occurs.

We consider the following five cases.
−   Case 1
  ♦ $bp \in \{1, 10, 50\}$
  ♦ $ep \in \{10, 50, 100\}$

- $prob \in \{0.1, 0.3, 0.5\}$
- Restriction A is used.
- Case 2
  - $bp \in \{1, 10, 50\}$
  - $bp \in \{1, 10, 50\}$
  - $prob \in \{0.1, 0.3, 0.5\}$
  - Restriction B is used.
- Case 3
  - $bp = 1$
  - $prob \in \{0.1, 0.3, 0.5\}$
  - ep takes an integer from 1 to $Num - i$ at random for each task T_i.
  - Restriction B is used.
- Case 4
  - $bp = 1$
  - ep is $Num - i$ for each task T_i.
  - $prob$ takes a number from 0.1 to 0.5 at random for each task T_i.
  - Restriction B is used.
- Case 5
  - $bp = 1$
  - ep takes an integer from 1 to $Num - i$ for task T_i.
  - $prob$ takes a number from 0.1 to 0.5 at random for task T_i.
  - Restriction B is used.

The following three parameters are common to all cases.

- $Num = \{200, 400, 600\}$
- $dupRatio \in \{0.0, 0.1, 0.3\}$
- $dupNum \in \{5, 10\}$

In addition, ten different pseudo tasks sets are generated for each pseudo tasks set generated with the chosen parameters.

3.4 Result of actual tasks

We show the operating ratio of actual tasks in method A and B in Table 2. In FFT and IKE, the operating ratio is the same for methods A and B. On the other hand, in the Runge-Kutta case, the operating ratio for method B is higher than for A. And then, the operating ratio is improved for the CP method, in any case.

	FFT	Runge-Kutta	IKE
Out (Method A)	7	1	0
Out (Method B)	7	9	0
Operating ratio (Method A)	0.3575	0.4148	0.4957
Operating ratio (Method B)	0.3575	0.1778	0.4957
Operating ratio (CP/MISF)	0.0696	0.0097	0.4131

Tab. 2. Operating ratio of actual tasks in method A and B

3.5   Result of pseudo tasks

Table 3 shows averages of the operating ratio for every case of pseudo tasks. Only in the case of the Case 3, in method B, the operating ratio is high. In other cases, for method A operating ratios are high.

And then, from Table 4, the operating ratio is improved from the CP/MISF method, in any case.

Table 5 shows the rate of tasks whose operating ratio is high, when we compare method A with method B. According to the results from pseudo tasks performed the method A is more effective than method B.

	Average of operating ratio (Method A)	Average of operating ratio (Method B)
Case 1	0.47913	0.47842
Case 2	0.50109	0.49983
Case 3	0.31323	0.31329
Case 4	0.26766	0.26766
Case 5	0.26749	0.26745

Tab. 3. Average of operating ratio of pseudo tasks for method A and B

	Average of operating ratio
Case 1	0.26102
Case 2	0.26902
Case 3	0.23787
Case 4	0.21142
Case 5	0.20751

Tab. 4. Average of operating ratio of pseudo tasks for CP/MISF

	Method A > B	Method A < B
Case 1	2.47 %	0.21 %
Case 2	2.80 %	0.19 %
Case 3	1.30 %	0.37 %
Case 4	0.00 %	0.00 %
Case 5	0.56 %	1.11 %

Tab. 5. The rate of tasks whose operating ratio is high

4. CONCLUSION

We proposed the limitation method for the improvement of the operating ratio, and we obtained the high operating ratio. However, by the limitation method, there was a problem where processing time took a bit more time. So, we proposed the deadline method according to which processing time became the shortest.

In this paper, we considered and evaluated two methods as the deadline method. In these methods the term using processors outside the limitation is different. Method A enables to use these processors only while processing the task allocated to them. Method B enables to use these processors, until processing of all tasks finishes.

We applied our methods to actual tasks and pseudo tasks to evaluate our methods. In the case of actual tasks, the operating ratio for method A was higher than it for method B. In the case of pseudo tasks, the operating ratio in method A was almost higher than it in method B. And then, the operating ratio is improved by the CP method both actual tasks and pseudo tasks.

Table 6 shows the rate that does not use processors outside the limitation. That is, even if it does not use the deadline method, it is the rate from which the shortest processing time was obtained. This shows that the limitation is a sufficient value to obtain the shortest processing time. So, the operating ratio may be more improved by applying the deadline method to value being smaller than the limitation. It is a future subject.

	Rate
Case 1	78.5 %
Case 2	79.0 %
Case 3	74.4 %
Case 4	79.4 %
Case 5	77.8 %

Tab. 6. The rate that does not use processors outside the limitation

5. REFERENCES

[1] H. Kasahara and S. Narita,
Practical Multiprocessor Scheduling Algorithms for Efficient Parallel Processing,
IEEE Trans. Computers, 33(11), 1984, 1,023-1,029
[2] S. Kobayashi,
How to Limit the Number of Used Processors for Task Scheduling (In Japanese),
IEICE Trans. D-I, J81(3), 1998, 353-355.
[3] K. Kashiwagi, M. Mori, and S. Kobayashi,
Improvement of Operating Ratio of Processors by Limitation Used Processors for Scheduling (In Japanese),
the 61st National Convention of IPSJ, Vol.1, 2000, 89-90.
[4] K. Kashiwagi and S. Kobayashi
4Limitation of Used Processor for Task Scheduling,

IASTED International Conference Applied Informatics, ISBN:0-88986-320-2, 2001, 122-126.

[5] THOMAS H. CORMEN, CHARLES E. LEISERSON, RONALD L.RIVEST,
INTRODUCTION TO ALGORITHMS,
Massachusetts: The MIT Press, 1994.

[6] Albert Y. Zomaya,
PARALLERL & DISTRIBUTED COMPUTING HANDBOOK,
New York: McGraw-Hill, 1996.

[7] S. Kobayashi,
Proposal and Evaluation of Task Allocation Method for Limited Connected
Multiprocessor System (In Japanese),
IEICE Trans. D-I, J79(2), 1996, 69-78.

[8] H. Kitagawa, F. Matsuda, Y. Uchikawa, and S. Hattori,
Task Scheduling Algorithm with Corrected Critical Path Length (In Japanese),
IEICE Trans. D-I, J73(10), 1990, 812-817.

Author Index

Lightning Source UK Ltd.
Milton Keynes UK
UKOW06f0015230216

268892UK00006B/36/P